THE REFORMED DUTCH CHURCH

NEW HACKENSACK, DUTCHESS COUNTY, NEW YORK

Erected in 1834, the present church building occupies the site on which an earlier church stood from 1766 to 1834. Uncrowded by other buildings and with open fields adjoining it, it presents an unspoiled record of a rural church of a century ago in the setting of that time. In front of it is the highway that leads from New Hackensack to Poughkeepsie. The double row of locust trees (the arched branches suggesting a cathedral nave) is a planting typical of Dutchess County in the eighteenth century.

THE
Records of the Reformed Dutch Church

OF

NEW HACKENSACK
DUTCHESS COUNTY
NEW YORK

Edited by

MARIA BOCKÉE CARPENTER TOWER

Comprising

Baptismal register, 1757—1906
Marriage register, 1765—1906
List of members and communicants
Register of church officers
Names of early pew holders
Financial accounts of trustees
Minutes of Consistory

COLLECTIONS
of
THE DUTCHESS COUNTY HISTORICAL SOCIETY
VOLUME V

CLEARFIELD

Originally published
Poughkeepsie, New York, 1932

Reprinted for
Clearfield Company, Inc. by
Genealogical Publishing Co., Inc.
Baltimore, Maryland
2002

International Standard Book Number: 0-8063-5170-5

Made in the United States of America

Dedicated to the Memory of
MY MOTHER
SARAH ELIZABETH THORN
of the fifth and last generation of
the Thorn family living at
New Hackensack, Dutchess County, New York,
THE WIFE OF JACOB BOCKÉE CARPENTER

THE REFORMED DUTCH CHURCH
NEW HACKENSACK, DUTCHESS COUNTY, NEW YORK
1932

Pastor
THE REVEREND CHESTER E. MCCAHAN

Elders

RICHARD L. DENNEY LEE JACKSON
JOSEPH J. DIDDELL STEPHEN BULMER

Deacons

FREEMAN DENNEY FRED G. PAASCH
LEONARD DENNEY CHARLES TEN BROECK
EDGAR M. JONES ABRAM VAN VLIET

FOREWORD

When the plan for this book was first taken under consideration application was made to the Consistory of the Reformed Church of New Hackensack for permission to copy the register of the church, and the editor desires to acknowledge the courtesy of the Consistory in granting that request.

The portion of the register written in Dutch was translated into English by Mr. A. J. F. van Laer, Archivist of the State of New York, a native of Holland and a specialist in Dutch as spoken in the eighteenth century. The remainder of the register, written in English, was copied by Mrs. Amy Pearce Ver Nooy of Poughkeepsie, New York, who also prepared the Index and supervised the press work on the manuscript. The sincere thanks of the editor are extended to Mr. van Laer and Mrs. Ver Nooy, whose careful work has made the following text accurate.

The editor is grateful for the cooperation of her friend, Miss Helen Wilkinson Reynolds, who outlined the plan of this work and carried it through to completion.

MARIA BOCKÉE CARPENTER TOWER.

INTRODUCTION

IN THE town of Wappinger, Dutchess County, New York, there is a place where three roads converge and form a triangle. Near the triangle are grouped a few dwellings and stores, while to the north on the highway to Poughkeepsie stands a church, surrounded by soil that is sacred as the resting-place of many former members of the congregation. This community, widely spread out and hardly numerous enough in population to be termed a village, is called New Hackensack.

The land now occupied by New Hackensack was sold by the Indians in 1683 to certain men in New York City, who bought it for its potential value in the fur-trade. It was a small part of a large purchase, which as a whole comprised eighty-five thousand acres at the southern end of Dutchess County, and title to the great tract was acquired under what became known as the Rombout Patent (Francis Rombout having been one of the original purchasers).

In 1708 the land covered by the patent, having been held as a unit from 1683, was divided into specific portions and assigned in lots to the representatives of the three rights that originally were held in it. By that partition the site of New Hackensack fell to the widow and children of Stephanus Van Cortlandt of New York City. Stephanus Van Cortlandt had died in 1700 and his heirs held the land in common until 1733, when, by a family settlement, title to it became vested in his daughter, Cornelia, wife of John Schuyler, Jr., of Albany. The next year (1734) Mrs. Schuyler sold it to Teunis Van Benschoten and Abraham Swartwout, who were residents of Dutchess County.

Teunis Van Benschoten and Abraham Swartwout bought in partnership in 1734 from Mrs. Schuyler eleven hundred and ninety-six acres and in 1736 they divided the land, which was then probably in a natural state, uncleared. Soon after 1736 Teunis Van Benschoten removed from Poughkeepsie, where he had been living, to his new property and created for himself a homestead-farm to the south and west of the spot where the roads have since made a triangular junction. His house, which stood a little distance west of the present triangle, has been torn down but a barn and a smokehouse of his day still remain. On a stream south of the triangle he built a mill, which became an important factor in the development of a new neighborhood but which is not now standing.

When Abraham Swartwout and Teunis Van Benschoten partitioned their joint holding in 1736 Abraham Swartwout took title to five hundred and fifty-six acres but nothing has been found to show that he ever occupied any of his purchase himself. Instead, he laid out the land in three portions and ultimately sold the same. One portion, consisting of two hundred and ten acres, he sold in 1751 to Samuel Thorn of Westchester County, who moved up to Dutchess and developed the property. Samuel Thorn's son, Dr. Stephen Thorn, built in 1772 on the farm that had been his father's the large brick house that is still standing north of the church at New Hackensack.

The land that lies immediately north and east of the modern road-junction at New Hackensack was sold by Abraham Swartwout as woodland and ownership of it changed several times. Part of it was apparently purchased for occupation in 1754, when it was acquired by Joseph Horton, for Joseph Horton is believed to have been the builder of a small house that is standing today east of the road-junction and which became known in the nineteenth century as *Old Hundred*.

In the general vicinity of the homesteads of Teunis Van Benschoten, Samuel Thorn and Joseph Horton many other farms were taken up at about the same time by men who moved in on the land as first settlers and who were of diverse origins. They came from other parts of Dutchess County, from Westchester County, from Long Island, New Jersey, Harlem and Esopus and included in their number representatives of families which, several generations earlier, had come to America from the Netherlands, the Walloon district, the Palatinate on the upper Rhine and from the British Isles. The Low Dutch from the Netherlands predominated in language and religion and (probably) in numbers and, due to their influence, a church-congregation was gathered and organized in union with the Reformed Church of Holland. Pastoral ministrations began as early as 1757; formal organization followed and on November 18, 1765, Joris Brinckerhoff and his wife, Ida Monfort, presented the congregation with land for a church and a burial ground. The church that was built soon after 1765 stood until replaced in 1834 by the building now in use.

As the new neighborhood grew it began to be called New Hackensack. Some of the first settlers were from Hackensack, New Jersey, and the name was undoubtedly given by them, either out of sentiment for their former home or because they thought the physical features of the two places were somewhat similar. There is a low lying stream at Hackensack, New Jersey, and also at New Hackensack, New York. Each stream is bordered by flats, above which rises higher ground. At Hackensack, however, the walls of the valley rise in hillsides, which are rather steep in slope, while at New Hackensack there is a plateau or open plain at a height not greatly above that of the stream. The plateau offered an advantageous location for farms and so it came about that on this wide, open expanse the beginnings of New Hackensack were made.

Very lovely are the natural features which form the setting for the church and the little community! The lush meadows close to the Wappinger and, above them, the arable flats were well known to the Indians, who called them *winni acki* or good land. And good land they proved for the white man. Those first settlers of the middle of the eighteenth century developed the locality into a productive region, which became prosperous and where a high standard in rural living was maintained. Industrialism has never come within the confines of this neighborhood, there has been but slight infiltration of alien immigration among the residents and New Hackensack stands out in 1932 as a surviving example of an eighteenth century agricultural community and one which still retains some of its original characteristics.

This volume (the fifth in the series of occasional *Collections* that have appeared under the auspices of the Dutchess County Historical Society) presents a verbatim transcript of the register of the Reformed Church at New Hackensack, the entries covering a period of one hundred and fifty years (1757-1906). It is hardly necessary to add that descendants of the early members of the church who are citizens of Dutchess today and also those who, in large numbers, are scattered far and wide beyond the borders of the county, will find in these pages much that is interesting about their forbears, while for students of the general history of Dutchess County the book provides informing material regarding the life and customs of another day. The Dutchess County Historical Society would express to Mrs. Joseph T. Tower of Millbrook, New York, a member and officer of the society, who has personally sponsored the preparation of this volume, its thanks for the valuable contribution she has made to the archives of the county and its appreciation of the honor she has conferred upon the society in allowing the book to be published under its auspices.

HELEN WILKINSON REYNOLDS.

Poughkeepsie
New York
1932

CONTENTS

	Page
The Beginning of the Church	1
Baptismal Register	5
Marriage Register	97
List of Members and Communicants	123
Register of Officers and Minutes of the Consistory	149
Index of Pews	241
Gifts from Peter and Jacob Van Bunschoten	267
Sundry Accounts	283
Index to Baptismal and Marriage Registers	297

THE BEGINNING OF THE CHURCH

Last part of the contract for the building of the Church, October 31, 1765, with the amounts pledged for the building.

These papers form, apparently, part of the "loose papers" mentioned in the Church records under "Acts and Resolves of the Elders and Deacons." A. D. 1765.

"any other minister than those hereinbefore mentioned." This means any other minister than those belonging to the Conferentie party, to which Rev. Isaac Rysdyk belonged. See E. T. Corwin's *Manual of the Reformed Church in America*, 4th ed., p. 102-117, 694-695.

See also James H. Smith, *History of Dutchess County*, p. 517; T. Van Wyck Brinckerhoff, *Historical Sketch of the Town of Fishkill*, p. 66-67; and Wm. Bancroft Hill, "The Church in Dutchess County," in *Tercentenary Studies 1928, Reformed Church in America. A Record of Beginnings*, compiled by the Tercentenary Committee on Research and Publication. Published by the Church, 1928. p. 307-723.

AGREEMENT TO BUILD A CHURCH[1]

[in] general and every one of us in particular, that we shall forfeit our right to this church as soon as we shall come to the conclusion that any other minister than those hereinbefore mentioned has the right to officiate in this church, or as soon as we shall wish to impose upon the congregation such a Reformed minister who has not been ordained with the foreknowledge and consent of the Classis of Amsterdam, and we solemnly promise that in such case we shall not seek to maintain our supposed right by legal proceedings or any other means; so that no one shall have any right to this church, be he a member of the Consistory or not, unless he be united with the body of the Holland Nether-Dutch Church, established in this country by the King's Charter[2] and subordinate to the Classis of Amsterdam, even though finally there should be but one church left and all the others should secede to the opposite party.

Article V. The church shall be built here in New Hakkingsak, on the site where now the schoolhouse stands, near the house of Joris Brinckerhoff.

---

[1] The first part of this agreement, which is written on separate sheets, is missing.

[2] Apparently referring to the charter granted by William III on May 11, 1696, printed in *Ecclesiastical Records of the State of New York*, 2: 1136-1165. This was the Charter of the Dutch Church in the City of New York, and not a charter of all Dutch churches in the province collectively.

The Reformed Dutch Church of New Hackensack

Article VI. We, the undersigned, each one according to the money which he subscribes or causes to be subscribed, shall be entitled to sittings in the aforesaid church, but shall have no right to force in another minister than as hereinbefore stated; and Joris Brinckerhoff, in return for his having ceded the land on which the church is to be built, shall have the right of preference in regard to 2 seats, for himself and his wife and their heirs, in addition to his being entitled to seats like others according to the amount of his subscription.

Article VII. When any one happens to die, or sells his seat or seats, it shall be the duty of the Church-masters to notify the purchasers or the heirs to have those seats transferred, and for every seat which shall be transferred, 3 shillings shall be paid.

Article VIII. We, the undersigned, promise that we shall pay to the builders chosen by us one-half of the money subscribed by us when they begin to build, which is to be on   , to defray the cost of the materials, and the other half when the church is finished or completed.

And of this agreement four authentic copies shall be made and delivered to the respective builders.

Hereto help us the Almighty, to whose glory this house shall be built, to the end that it be His dwelling place, of which it may be said: "The Lord dwelleth here."

That all that is above written is our sincere intent, we, the undersigned, without craft or deceit, witness by these our signatures hereunto affixed.

Actum in N. Hakkingsak, the 31st of October 1700 and sixty-five.

Izaäk Rysdyk, for 2 seats	£3— 0—0	John Heermans	1—10—0
Pieter Oudwater	23— 0—0	Nicolas de Mareast	1— 0—0
Cornelis Luyster	10— 0—0	Johs. Ferdon	1— 0—0
Wilhelmus Heermans	1— 0—0	Zachariah ferdon	1—10—0
Andr. Breested	1— 0—0	John Furdon	2— 0—0
Andries Heermans, yunier	4— 0—0	Carel Hoffman	1—10—0
Stephen Bates	0— 8—0	*Henry Heermans	4— 0—0
Johannis Boekhoud	1— 0—0	John Monfoort	0—10—0
Cornelius Polhemels "was the first to pay"	*2— 0—0	*Joris Brinckerhoff	10— 0—0
		*Samuel Hicks	0—10—0
Daniel Polhemels	1— 0—0	Abraham Lent	5— 0—0
Thomas van Bremen	1— 0—0	Reuben Bedel	0— 6—0
Samuel Quackenbos	0—15—0	Matthew Col	0— 5—0
Cornelis Brouwer	0— 8—0	Peter Noortstrant	0— 8—0
Nicolaes Brouwer	8— 0—0	*Daniel Bedell*	0— 4—0
Jacob Brouwer	1— 0—0	Jan Barint	0— 6—0
Ysack Brouwer	0—12—0	*hendrick grauberger*	0— 6—0
Nathaniel Brooks	1— 1(?)0	Elisabeth Palen	0— 6—0
William Way	0—10—0	Gysbert Palen	0— 6—0
Peter Dauison	0—10—0	myndert Viele	0—10—0
*Thys Luyster	8— 0—0	*Aerrie Kool*	0— 8—0

The Reformed Dutch Church of New Hackensack

Jurre hofman	0— 6—0	*Sweres van Clek*	3— 0—
*Willim Edwort	1— 0—0	*William Jacockes*	1— 0—
*tierk van kuere	0—16—0'	*Thomas Burnett	0— 6—0
Constin Golneck	5— 0—0	*Peter Harris*	1—10—0
Jacob Golneck	1— 0—0	Peter Js. Lawson	1— 0—0
Micel Golneck	0—10—0	Yohanes fermilier	0— 6—0
James Hicks	5— 0—0	Isaac Downing	0— 4—0
Jhon Willum	0—10—0	*Gysbert Schenck	5— 0—0
Dirck Brinckerhoff	10— 0—0	*Isaac Brinckerhoff	5— 0—0
Nichol. Emd. Gaberill	— 8—	Jacobus Swartwout	1—10—0
Simon Bloom	1—10—	*Michiel hofman*	0—16—0
*Phebe Bloom	1— 0—0	John Palen	1— 0—0
*Peter haff	1— 0—0	*Henry v. D. Burgh	0—16—0
Jems Comton	0—16—0	*Gideon Dubois*	1— 0—0
*Aert Middagh	*2— 0—0	*Cors. F. Dubois*	1—10—0
*Joris Middagh	*1— 0—0	*Mattheus J. dubois	1—00—0
*Jacobus Middagh	*1— 0—0	Kaspares westervelt	2— 0—0
francis Delavigne	0— 8—0	*Nelle Siffer*	0—10—0
Johannis Joost Snyder	1— 0—0	Johannis Hoogtyling	1—00—0
Johannes Berrerhert	0—10—0	John Rosekrans	2— 0—0
Johannis Schurri	15— 0—0	Thomas Allin	0— 4—0
Dolf Swartwout	4— 0—0	*Johannis Medler	0—16—0
John Church Chill	10— 0—0	*Joel Dubois	0— 4—0
Elias newkirck	0—15—0	Baltes van Clek	2— 0—0
Petrus Ostrander	1— 0—0	James Willse	1— 0—0
David Dean	0—10—0	Pieter Deeds	1—10—0
Hendrick Bell	3— 0—0	*Rodolves Swartwout	2— 0—0
*Jan orsstrom	2— 0—0	Muller	1— 0—0
Lawrence Concklin	3— 0—0	Pieter (?) H. monfoort	2— 0—0
Isaac Willse	1— 0—0	Isaac van noortstrant	1— 0—0

BAPTISMAL REGISTER

of the

newly organized church

of

New Hakkensak
on the Wappans Kill

Beginning with the 4th of May 1757
and continued from September 1764

by

IZAAK RYSDYK, V.D.M.

Pastor of the 4 united and to the Rev. Classis of Amsterdam and the Synod of North Holland subordinated Reformed Nether-Dutch churches of Poghkeepsie, Viskil, N. Hakkensak and Hoopwel; first minister in the last-named two places; installed at Poghkeepsie by Dom. J. C. Freyenmoed, V.D.M. in the Manor of Livingston, etc., the 22d of September 1765.

Symb. *Concordia res parvae Crescunt*, i. e. *Eendragt maakt magt* (Through concord little things grow—In unity there is strength).

Baptismal Register

Anno 1757. Copied to the 15th of September 1765 when I preached here for the first time from the notes of Rev. E. F. van Hoevenberg and the clerk.

Date of Baptism	Parents	Name of Child and Date of Birth	Witnesses
1757			
May 4	Moses Verweelen Hester de Graaff	Johanna May 18, 1756	Johannes Schurrig Annatje Oudwater, mar.
	Johannes Jorksen Engeltje Treves	Catharina	Willem Jorksen Catharina See
	Gerrit Noordstrant Arriaantje Luister	Johannes Feb. 28	
June 10	Gelein Akkerman Annatje Westerveld	Antje June 2	David Banta Antje Akkerman, mar.
	Dirk van Texel Marytje	Maria May 16	Johannes Jurrigsen Engeltje Travers, mar.
Aug. 27	Johannes Meyer Mercy Row	Cornelia July 4	Marytje Brincherhof
	Johannes Zwartwoud Neela van den Bogaard	Cornelis July 12	Cornelis van den Bogaard Elizabeth Zwartwoud, mar.
	Izaac Louis Marytje Dio	Richard July 24	Richard Green Jannetje Freer, mar.
	Cornelis van Keuren Elizabeth Westerveld	Aaltje July 22	Casparus Westerveld Aaltje Bogaard, mar.
	Abraham Verveelen Elizabeth Allin	Petrus July 2	Meindert Cool Pietje van Schurrvan, mar.
	Abraham Lent Catharina Brinkerhof	Izaac May 28	Izaac Lent Sara Luister
	John Brinkerhoff Maria ter Bosch	Rachel Aug. 15	
Oct. 4	Laurens Conchling Annatje Schurrig	Susanna Sep. 14	Abraham Conchling Susanna Conchling
	Pieter Montfoort Susanna Martense	Antje Sep. 18	
	Thomas Allin Hester Wiltse	Hanna	John Allin Hanna Allin
	Johannes v. Stambergen Sara van Cleek	Michiel v. Cleek	Barent van Cleek Elizabeth La Roy
1758			
Jan. 8	Leendert van Cleek Sara ten Broek	Jacoba Nov. 4	Pieter van Cleek Tryntje van Cleek
Apr. 16	Michel Hoffman Marytje Louis	Daniel Mar. 22	Daniel Diderik Cornelia Baker
	Teunis Wiltzee Cornelia Bortley	Catharina Mar. 15	Izaac Wiltzee Catharina Zwartwoud
	Izaäc Wiltzee Catharina Zwartwoud	Izaäc Mar. 18	Cornelis van den Bogaard Betje Zwartwoud, mar.
	Jacobus Steenbergen Mally Schouten	Annatje Dec. 14	Nicolaas Brouwer and his wife
	Thomas van Bremen Jannetje Oudwater	Thomas Jan. 10	Laurens Conchlin Annatje Schurrig
	Daniel Los Magdalene Los	Bastiaan Dec. 18	Bastiaan Keizerryk and his wife
	Jonathan Striklin Francyntje Krankheid	Fransyntje Dec. 10, 1757	Philip Heermans Claratje Heermans
Sep. 23	Simon Schouten Annatje Duitser	Annatje Aug. 27	Wilhelmus Duitser Elizabeth Brevoort, mar.

The Reformed Dutch Church of New Hackensack

Date of Baptism	Parents	Name of Child and Date of Birth	Witnesses
Sep. 24	Pieter Palmentier Catharina van de Bogard	Jacobus Aug. 4	Jacobus van den Bogaard Margrietje Dumon
	Richard Davids Francis Louis	Jhon Aug. 7	Nicolaas Hofman Mary Ludlow
	Johannes de Wit Sophia Masten	Endero Aug. 20	Henrik Masten Sara Masten
	Jurriaan ter Wilgen Mary van Cleek	Ahasuerus Aug. 22	Ahasuerus van Cleek Jannetje Freer
1759 Apr. 5	Frans la Roy Geertje Middag	Sara June 9	Jacobus Gonzales Sara la Roy
Jan. 25	Michel la Roy Johanna Kidney	Simeon	Blandina Freer Simeon la Roy
Feb. 16	Wilhelmus Heermans Antje, his wife	Henricus	Henricus Heermans Hannatje Heermans
Feb. 24	Jeremia de Boys Rachel Viele	Sara	Joel de Boys Rachel de Boys
	Joris Adriaanse Feben van Wyk	Catalina	Abraham Adriaanse Sara van Wyk
June 19	David Duitser Egje Freer	Jacomyntje	Johannes Knickebakker Jacomyntje Kick
July 3	Hendrik Bel Catrina Simson	Anna	
Aug. 19	Johannes van Steenbergen Sara van Cleek	Johannes May 4	Johan Schurrig and his wife
	Cornelis Westerveld Wyntje Berrit	Dirk	Roelof Westerveld Ariaantje Romein
	Dirk Brinkerhof Geertje Wykhof	Antje Aug. 6	
	Thomas Allin Hester Wiltsee	Maria	Francis Jacobs and his wife
	Gerrit Noordstrant Ariaantje Luister	Cornelies Apr. 22	Cornelis Luister Susanna Brinkerh, mar.
Sep. 16	Jonathan Taren Catharina Libston	Jacobus	Jacobus Libston Judith Libston
Sep. 24	Roelof Barbara	Sara	Elias de Boys Jenneke de Boys
	Johnes Brinkerhof Elizabeth Brinkerhof	F* Apr. 15	Femmetje Brinkerhof
	Jacob van Bunschoten Maria	Catharina Apr. 24	
	Rouger Sara Vermiljer	Willem May 24	John Juwel Engeltje Juwel
	Lewis Susanna van de Burg	Thomas	Derk van Keuren Maria van Keuren
	Gelein Akkerman Annatje Westerveld	Jacobus Jan. 21	Cornelis van Keuren Elizabeth van Keuren
	Johannes de Boys Elizabeth Lengden	Jacob May 13	Jacob de Boys Antje van Bommel
	Jan Oostrum Lena Westerveld	Johannes Nov. 5	Burger van Yveren Femmetje Westerveld
	Johannes Martha Row	Susanna Jan. 2	

*Thus in original. Probably meant for Femmetje.

Baptismal Register

Date of Baptism	Parents	Name of Child and Date of Birth	Witnesses
	Jesajas Reinders Elizabeth Westerveld	Andries Jan. 11	Jan Oostrum Lena Westerveld
	Elias van Bunschoten Jacomyn	Catharina Mar. 29	Simson Freer Catharina van Bunschoten
	Jacobus van Steenberg Blandina van Cleek	Grietje June 8	Johannes van Steenberg Sara van Cleek
Dec. 14	Willem Freelich Tanneke du Boys	Hiskia du Boys	Petrus van Vliet Clara du Boys
1760 Jan. 20	Pieter Deets Catharina Lent	Johannes Dec. 30, 1759	Johannes Lent Engeltje Hoogland, mar.
	Jeremias Jones Elizabeth Schurrig	Thomas Oct. 30, 1759	Johannes Schurrig Annatje Oudwater, mar.
	Jacobus Steenberg Maria Schouten	Jacobus Dec. 3	Jacobus Steenberg Margriet Duitser
June 19	Johannes Vermiljer Jacomyntje Kosse	Benjamin Aug. 13	Sara Vermiljer
1761 Mar. 5	Joseph Gonzales Margrietje Duitser	Emanúel	Jacobus Gonzales Sara Westbroek
Mar. 15	Jones Schoonhoven Engeltje van de Water	Leena	Lavinus van de Water Jannetje Losee
	Wilhelmus Heermans Antje Sniffens	Israël	Israel Sniffens Hester Oodel
	Berger van Yveren Femmetje Westerveld	Willem and Maria	Willem Hogeland Aaltje Brinkerhoff Nicolaas Brouwer Maria Duitser
May 2	Jonathan Taren Catharina Libston	Johannes Rutsen	Johannes Rutsen Cornelia Rutsen
May 20	Henrik Bel Catrina Simson	Hermannus	
June 16	Jan Bogardus Marytje du Boys	Sara	Izaac Teller Sara du Boys
July 4	Frans la Roy Geertje Middag	Aart Middag	Jacobus Middag Lena Viele, mar.
Oct. 25	Thomas van Bremen Jannetje Oudwater	Catharina Nov. 2, 1760	Johannes Schurrig Annatje Oudwater, mar.
1762 Jan. 11	Johannes du Boys Elizabeth Lengden	Thomas	Thomas Lengden Nelly Lengden
	Laurens Conchlin Annatje Schurrig	Mattheus	Mattheus Conchlin Catrina Schurrig
Feb. 20 Feb. 29		Rachel Femmetje	
Aug. 15	Johannes Conchlin Maria Schurrig	Johannes	Johannes Schurrig Annatje Oudwater
1763 Jan. 3	Pieter Deeds Catrina Lent	Elizabeth Jan. 20, 1762	Cornelis Luister Elizabeth Lent
Feb. 5	Izaak Wiltse Catharina Zwartwoud	Johannes Apr. 12, 1762	Johannes Hoogteeling Gertruid Ploeg
Feb. 20 1762	Johannes Hoogteeling Geertruid Ploeg	Rachel	Jeremias du Boys Rachel Viele

The Reformed Dutch Church of New Hackensack

Date of Baptism	Parents	Name of Child and Date of Birth	Witnesses
Feb. 29 1762	Jan Oostrum Lena Westerveld	Femmetje Apr. 12	Meindert van Yvere Sara van Yvere
Mar. 23	Elias Steenberg Rebecca Micki	Johannes May 17, 1762	Johannes Steenberg Sara van Cleek
May 2	Johannes Pouwels Graaf Margaretha Boomman	Johannes Apr. 3	Pieter Grauberger Dorétje Kigerer
	Jacobus Steenberg Blandina van Cleek	Blandina Oct. 9	Simon la Roy Blandina Freer
	Baltus Schneider Elizabeth Steenberg	Magdelena May 18	Jacob Schneider Elizabeth Schneider
	Thomas Oudwater Ezebia Morris	Francis Sep. 31	Pieter Oudwater and his wife
	Timotheus Hikkes Rachel Schurrig	Johannes	
May 13	Teunis Wiltsee Cornelia Bertele	Hester June 29	
May 22	Johannes Louw Aaltje Hoogland	Willem June 29	Willem Hoogland Aaltje Brinkerhoff
July 29	Tobias Steenberg Maria Asse	Antje Aug. 22, 1762	Matth. Asse Alida Asse
July 30	Jacob Brouwer Elsje Hiskok	Jacob	Willem Hiskok Antje van de Ryp
Aug. 1	Johannes Wiltsee Neeltje Stokholm	Elizabeth	
Aug. 6	Johannes van Steenberg Sara van Cleek	Sara	Willem Hikbi Cathrina van Wyke
Aug. 12	Izak Conchlin Catelyntje van Binneschuiten	Antje Sep. 20	Teunis van Binneschuiten Antje Slecht
Oct. 31	Tomas Ellen Hester Wiltsee	Rachel Aug. 27	Pieter Deeds Catrina Lent
Nov. 2	Elias Nieuwkerk Sara Lounsberri	Sara	
Nov. 17	Johannes Krymer Catrina Vlegelaar	Lena	Pieter Dop Geertruy Krymer
Nov. 7	Izak Wiltsee Catrina Zwartwoud	Catrina	Bernardus Tryntje Reinders
Dec. 1	Reinders Elizabeth Westerveld	Johannes	Jan la Roy Elizabeth van Cleek
Dec. 2	Willem Palmentier Mally van Tyn	Johannes	Dama Palmentier Elizabeth Bertele
Dec. 7	Steven van Voorhees Catrina Lek	Izak	
Dec. 16	Moses Rouger Mary	Philippus	Johannes Rouger Elizabeth la Roy
1764			
Jan. 14	Pieter Montfoort Nancy Taren	Hendrik	Jannetje Noordstrant
Mar. 8	Johannes Hoogteling Geertruid Ploeg	Wilhelmus	
July 13	Pieter Harris Sara du Boys	Sara	Gideon du Boys Neeltje Luister
July 24	Timotheus Rachel Schurrig	Gilbert	

Baptismal Register

Date of Baptism	Parents	Name of Child and Date of Birth	Witnesses
Dec. 25	Izak Donnly Jannetje Vermiljer	Sara	
	William Elizabeth Dop	Willem	Paulus Peele Sara Oosterhoud
1765	Johannes Conchlin Maria Schurrig	Sara Oct. 13, 1764	
	Joel du Boys Maria Hoogteeling	Jeremia Oct. 4	Jeremia du Boys Rachel du Boys
	Teunis Tappan Hester Conchlin	Elizabeth	
	Izak Brouwer Jacomyntje Kwakkenbosch	Izak Dec. 13, 1764	
	Michel Hofman Maria Lewis	Johannes Jan. 27, 1765	
	William Bel Rachel van Every	Petrus Jan. 17	Burger van Every Femmetje van Every
	Gideon Tietsoort Margaretha Bel	Catharina and Sara Sep. 10, 1764	Pieter Oudwater Beleltje Oudwater
Sep. 15	The following were baptized by Ds. Iz. Rysdyk, pastor at New Hakkingsak, installed at Pakeepsie the 22 Sept. 1765.		
	Izak Wiltsee Catharina Zwartwoud	Henricus Sep. 5, 1765	Ezechiel Pinkney Nelletje Wiltsee
	Jacobus Steenberg Blandina van Cleek	Elias May 5, 1765	Elias Steenberg Heyltje Borhans
	Johannes Montfoort Annatje Heermans	Claratje* Sep. 10, 1765	Henricus Heermans Claratje Heermans
	Jeremia du Boys Sara Hoogteeling	Geertruid Feb. 22, 1765	Johannes Hoogteeling Geertruid Ploeg
	Laurens Conchlin Annatje Schurri	David July 1, 1765	
	Matthys Luister Barbara Holser	Johannes Mar. 25, 1765	Jan Luister Hilletje Snedeker
	Cornelius Brouwer Aaltje Aartsen	Adolf June 14, 1765	Izak Brouwer Jacomyntje Kwakkenbosch
Oct. 15	Samuel Pinkney Rachel Perdon	John May 4, 1765	Johannes Perdon Patience Odill
	Johannes la Roy Elizabeth van Cleek	Maria	Johannes Freer Maria van Cleek
Oct. 13	Peter Lassen Catharina Dolsen	Elizabeth Sep. 10, 1765	Johannes Dolsen Elizabeth Buys
	Arie Midlaar Margaretha Seyfer	Johannes June 19, 1765	Johannes Midlaar Mally Perdon
	Johannes van Steenberg Sara van Cleek	Barent Sep. 17, 1765	Baltus van Cleek Elizabeth de Graaf
Nov. 10	Constantyn Golneck Styntje Reyer	Martin Oct. 29, 1765	Cornelis Luister Susanna Brinkerhof
Dec. 8	Henrik Bell Catharina Simson	Abraham Sep. 26, 1765	Rudolf Zwartwoud Debora Wiltsee
1766 Jan. 12	Cornelis Tietsoort Maria Hegeman	Maria July 28, 1765	

*Original says "son of Johannes Monfort," etc.

The Reformed Dutch Church of New Hackensack

Date of Baptism	Parents	Name of Child and Date of Birth	Witnesses
	Nicolaas Tietsoort Elizabeth Treves	Johannes Oct. 8, 1765	
	Teunis Wiltsee Cornelia Bertele	Rudolphus Dec. 23, 1765	Rudolphus Zwartwoud Debora Wiltsee
Apr. 27	Cornelius van Keuren Elizabeth Westerveld	Benjaman Mar. 27	
May 18	Elias Nuwkerk Sara Launsbergen	Hester	
July 6	Nicolaas Meyer Elizabeth Limmerin	Hans Frederik	
Aug. 3	Doms. Isaäc Rysdyk Henrica Verwey	Henrica Alida July 30, 1766	Capt'n Jacobus Zwartwoud & Alida Brinkerhoff, mar. Gilbert Livingston & Catharina Crannel, mar. Elizabeth Crannel
	Johannes Rosekrantz Barbara Holst	Warren July 6, 1766	Antje Rosekrantz Frederik Rosekrantz
	Caspar Bel Betty Fontein	Hermannus	Hermannus Bel Marytje Poppeldorf
Aug. 2	Benjamin Filips Eipje Lasse	Benjamin	
	Jan Sanders Geertruy Lasse	Isaac	
	Willem Lasse Mally Storm	Catharina	

N. B. The parents of the 3 children are of the Lutheran faith.

Aug. 3	Jurrien Hofman Maria Miclef	William	Willem Edworth Anna Grawberger, mar.
	Joel du Boys Maria Hoogteyling	Sara	Benjamin du Boys Ariaantje Hoogteyling
Sep. 28	Nicolaas de Mares Semmy More	Antje July 30, 1766	Andries Heermans and his wife
	James Hiks Lydia Schurre	Maria Aug. 26, 1766	John Conchlin Maria Schurre, mar.
	Thomas Allin Hester Wiltsee	Johannes Aug. 14, 1766	Joris Brinkerhoff and his wife
Oct. 26	Philip Verplank Aafje Beekman	Geertruda	James Verplank Geertruy Verplank
	Benjamin Wee Betty Schut	Femmetje	
Nov. 26	Jan Perdon Annatje Lassen	Elizabeth Oct. 18, 1766	
	Jeremia du Boys Sara Hoogteyling	Jeremia Sep. 13, 1766	Jeremia du Boys Rachel Viele

Total baptised this year
    sons 11
    daughters 10
                21

1767 Jan. 25	Jan Müller Mary Leidt	Willem Nov. 28, 1766	Lodewyk Muller Lena Muller
	Gideon Townsend Louisje Montfoort	Gideon Dec. 28, 1766	Jan Juwel Jannetje Noordstrant, mar.

Baptismal Register

Date of Baptism	Parents	Name of Child and Date of Birth	Witnesses
Feb. 22	Pieter Willem Lassen Sara Buys	Lena Feb. 8	
	Wilhelmus Heermansse Antje Kniffin	Antje Jan. 12	Andries Heermanssen Rachel van Netten
	Paul Davidsen Mary Simson	Elizabeth Dec. 22	Hannes Roer Elizabeth la Roy
	Samuel Entene Rachel Kniffin	Elizabeth Sep. 17, 1766	
Apr. 19	"illegitimate daughter of" Martyn Bosch Marytje Storm	Geertruy	Pieter Emug Geertruy Coens
May 10	Cherrik van Keuren Maria Westerveld	Benjamin	Benjamin van Keuren Marytje van Keuren
	Jacobus Compten Jannetje Bollumer	Jacobus	
June 21	Johannes Lassen Sara Lassen	Maria	Willem Lassen Grietje Lassen
	David Duitscher Grietje Fontein	Abraham	
July 19	Isaac Wiltsee Catharina Zwartwoud	Jacobus June 27, 1767	James Hiks and his wife
	David Mecke Lena Storm	Maria	Goris Storm and his wife
	Laurens Hoff Tryntje Schurri	Johannes	Johannes Schurri Annatje Oudwater, mar.
Oct. 11	Johannes Steenbergen Saartje van Cleek	Jacobus	Johannes la Roy and his wife
	Aart Maston Rebecca Viele	Ariaantje	Cornelis Maston
Nov. 8	Cornelis Schot Annatje van Tessel	Maria	
Dec. 6	Cornelis Brouwer Alida Aarsen	Annatje	

Total baptised this year
sons   8
daughters   10
     18

Date of Baptism	Parents	Name of Child and Date of Birth	Witnesses
1768 Feb. 7	Baltus Viele Catharina Losee	Neeltje Dec. 27, 1767	Jan Losee Neeltje Losee
	Adam Deed Antje Rosenkrantz	Abraham Lent Dec. 13, 1767	Abraham Lent Antje Blom
Mar. 6	Willem Buys Elizabeth Schneider	Johannes Oct. 10, 1767	Johan Schneyder
	Jacob Becker Antonetta van Kleek	Baltus Jan. 10, 1768	Johannes la Roy & Elizabeth van Kleek, his wife
Apr. 3	Pieter Montfoort Anna Taren	Esther Feb. 22, 1768	Louisje Montfoort
	Pieter Hoff Saartje Schurri	Femmetje Mar. 18, 1768	
	Willem Lassen Marytje Storm	Elizabeth Jan. 14, 1768	Pieter Lassen and his wife
	Jan Juel Elizabeth Hilleken	Henricus Dec. 23	

The Reformed Dutch Church of New Hackensack

Date of Baptism	Parents	Name of Child and Date of Birth	Witnesses
	Laurens Conchlin Annatje Schurri	Henricus Mar. 4, 1768	
May 15	Francis Tsicoks or Gekocks Maria Wiltsee	Ezechiel Apr. 5, 1768	Ezekiel Pinckney & Nelly Wiltsee, his wife
	Elias Steenbergen Catharina Hoffman	Maria Apr. 12, 1768	Cherrik van Keuren & Maria Westerveld, his wife
June 5	Teunis Wiltsee Cornelia Bartley	Johannes Apr. 29, 1768	Johannes Wiltsee Cornelia Deeds
	Henrik Wiltsee Femmetje Reidt	Henricus Jan. 14, 1768	Kittey Reidt
July 3	Thomas Viele Eva Fishie	Jan Jan. 7, 1768	
July 31	Josua Duly Cornelia de Pue	Abraham Apr. 26, 1768	Pieter de Pue
Sep. 25	Mattheus van Keuren Annatje Green	Geertruda Aug. 29, 1768	William Gecocks Geertruy Lassen, mar.
Dec. 18	Jan Oostrum Lena Westerveld	Tiatje Nov. 20, 1768	Henrik Oostrum Tiatje Zwartwoud, mar.
	James Hiks Lydia Schurry	Elizabeth Nov. 10, 1769	Laurens Conchlin Annatje Schurry, mar.
1769 Jan. 8	Thomas Allen Hester Wiltsee	Henricus Oct. 17, 1768	Henrik Wiltsee Petronella de Boog
Feb. 5	"See following page."		
Mar. 6	Jesajas Reinderse Elizabeth Westerveld	Jacob Feb. 16, 1769	Thomas Ferdon & Alida Seyfer, his wife
	Adam Deeds Antje Rosenkrantz	Pieter Feb. 13, 1769	Pieter Deeds & Catharina Lent, his wife
Mar. 27	Jerry Jones Elizabeth Schurry	Lydia Feb. 24, 1769	
	Edward Schoonmaker Lydia Schepmoes twin sons	Antony Mar. 24, 1769 Edward Edmundus Mar. 24, 1769	Teunis van Bunschoten & Antje Slecht, his wife Joris Brinkerhoff & Ida Montfoort, his wife
Apr. 23	Carel Hoffman Elizabeth Seyfer	Carel Mar. 22, 1769	Jurriaan Hoffman Marytje van Cleef, mar.
	David Seyfer Ariaantje Hoogteyling	Willem Mar. 2, 1769	Willem Seyfer
eodem- dato	Laurens Hoff Cathrina Schurry	Femmetje	
May 14	Johannes Louw Aaltje Hoogland	Jacob Apr. 8, 1769	Jacobus Louw & Jenneke de Graaf, his wife
Feb. 5	"N. B. Forgotten on the foregoing page":		
	Pieter Lassen Catharina Dolfsen	Johannes Dec. 25, 1768	Nicolaas de Marees Semmy Moore
	Pieter Emugh Geertruy Coens	Geertruy Jan. 13, 1769	Johan Philip & Geertruy Lassen, his wife
July 3	Esajas Bartley Nelly Cammel	Henricus Apr. 14, 1769	Teunis Wiltsee and his wife
	Johannes Rosenkrantz Sara Schoonmaker	Maria May 24, 1769	Edward Schoonmaker Lydia Schepmoes, mar.
	Gideon Titsoort Grietje Bell	Willem May 30, 1769	Belly Titsoort and his wife
July 30	Isaac Wiltsee Cathrina Zwartwoud	Teunis July 19, 1769	Teunis Wiltsee and his wife

Baptismal Register

Date of Baptism	Parents	Name of Child and Date of Birth	Witnesses
Aug. 27	Johannes Steenbergen Sara van Kleek	Maria Aug. 18, 1769	Marytje van Keuren Isaac Lassen
	Johannes Top Grietje Emug	Henrik June 8, 1769	Henrik Top Cathrina Top
Sep. 23	David Duitscher Peggy Fontein	Pally Aug. 23, 1769	
	Wilhelmus Heermans Antje Kniffen	Wilhelmus	Henricus Heermans Rebecca Heermans
Oct. 24	Johannes Lassen Sara Lassen	Margriet Sep. 8, 1769	Simeon Lassen & Margriet Lassen, his wife
1770 Jan. 20	Johannes Cremer Catrina Flegelaar	Maria Dec. 2, 1769	Joost Bosch & Maria Demoet, his wife
	Johannes Dio Geertruis Cremer	Johannes Oct. 29, 1769	Martinus Overakker Grietje Cremer
	Frederik Rosenkrantz Femmetje Bell	Cathrina Dec. 29, 1769	

"N. B. Was forgotten to set down under the month November of the last year. The 18 day of November were baptized :" *

	Aart Maston Rebecca Viele	Meindert Oct. 10, 1769	Meindert Viele Rebecca Viele
eodem- dato	Cornelis Hegeman Phebe Ingerum	Maria Oct. 29, 1769	Joh. Hegeman Maria de Lange
"the 31 December of the same year, 1769 :"*	Jacob Titsoort Femmetje van Yvere	Dirkje Nov. 10, 1769	
1770 Mar. 18	Johannes la Roy Elizabeth van Kleeck	Baltus van Kleeck Feb. 4, 1770	Baltus van Kleeck Celetje Palmontier
	Pieter Hoff Sara Schurri	Johannes Schurry Feb. 5, 1770	Johannes Schurri & Annatje Oudewater, his wife
Apr. 15	Simeon Lasson Geertje van Keuren	Benjamin Mar. 10, 1770	Mattheus van Keuren Annatje van Keuren
	Philip Verplank Aafje Beekman	William Beekman Mar. 2, 1770	William Beekman
May 6	Elias Steenbergen Cathrina Hoffman	Michel Hoffman Apr. 1, 1770	Johannes Grauberger Hester Hoffman
	David Mecke Lena Storm	Carel Mar. 17, 1770	Carel Hoffman and his wife
July 15	Benjamin du Boys Catharina Peele	Petrus Peele Apr. 15, 1770	Ezekiel Peele Hilletje Peele
	Jacobus Zwartwoud Aaltje Brinckerhoff	Jacobus June 26, 1770	
	Jacob Bekker Antje van Kleek	Hannes June 27, 1770	Hannes Bekker and his wife
	Israël Lewis Catharina Losee	Rachel June 14, 1770	
Aug. 12	Pieter Viele Neeltje van Kleek	Barent July 10, 1770	Barent van Kleek Hesje Hoffman
	Louw Conchlin Annatje Schurry	Catharina July 14, 1770	

* These notes were written in English in the original.

The Reformed Dutch Church of New Hackensack

Date of Baptism	Parents	Name of Child and Date of Birth	Witnesses
Sep. 9	Thomas Farguson Elizabeth Dimant	Kesya Whitsunday, 1770	Edward Schoonmaker and his wife
Oct. 7	Marinus van Vlekkeren Helena van de Water	Jannetje Sep. 13, 1770	Benjamin van de Water Jannetje Simson
	Hannes Bosch, Jr. Helena Kidney	Maria Sep. 20, 1770	Henrik Bosch and his wife
	Adam Deeds Antje Rosenkrantz	Johannes Oct. 5, 1770	Hannes Rosekrans and his wife
	Pieter Lassen Cathrina Dolsen	Henricus Sep. 22, 1770	
Nov. 4	Izaak Burnett Alida Edworth	Elizabeth Oct. 13, 1770	Carel Hoffman and his wife
	Joel de Boys Maria Hooghteylingh	Maria Oct. 14, 1770	Bernardus Zwartwoud Neeltje Hoogteylingh
	Jacob Laan Annatje Conchlin	Jacob Oct. 16, 1770	John Conchlin and his wife
	Total of 26 children. 14 sons.		
1771 Jan. 6	Meindert Harris Marytje Jemens	Annatje Nov. 29, 1770	Annatje Conchlin Bayt Battison
Feb. 3	Pieter la Roy Rachel Maibe	David Dec. 15, 1770	David Flegelaar Geertje Oostrander
Mar. 30	David Seyfer Ariaantje Hooghteyling	Geertruid Mar. 9, 1771	Jan Hooghteyling Geertruy Hooghteyling
	James Hiks Lydia Jurry	Johannes Jurry Feb. 27, 1771	Pieter Oudewater and his wife
	Isaac de Milt Annatje Edword	Anna Margaretha Feb. 25, 1771	Willem Edword and his wife
Apr. 21	Jurriaan Hofman Maria McClave	Hester Mar. 7, 1771	Hannes Grauberger Hester Hofman
	Laurens Hoff Catrina Jurry	Anthony Mar. 22, 1771	
May 12	Teunis Wiltsee Cornelia Bartley	Petronella Apr. 20, 1771	
	Matthew Burnet Elizabeth Chickens	Maria Dorothea Feb. 29, 1771	Frederick Chickery and his wife
June 2	Jan Louw Brechje Meyer	Adolf Apr. 30, 1771	
	Jacob Bosch Dirkje Oostrum	Anna Maria May 9, 1771	Anna Maria Bosch Henrik Oostrum
	George Jewel Louisa Montfoort	Aaltje Mar. 14, 1771	Gysbert Schenk and his wife
Aug. 25	Edward Schoonma(ker) Lydia Schepmoes	Neeltje Aug. 10, 1771	Abraham Sleght and his wife
	Esajas Reinderse Elizabeth Westerveld	Ruben	
	Jerry Jones Elizabeth Jurry	Johannes July 6	
Sep. 22	Isaak Wiltsee Cathrina Zwartwoud	Adolf Zwartwoud Aug. 18, 1771	Adolf Zwartwoud and his wife
eodem dato	John Wiltsee Jane Lucky	James Aug. 18, 1771	
Nov. 15	Tserrik van Keuren Maria Westerveld	Celetje Oct. 17, 1771	Simeon Lassen Margriet van Keuren

Baptismal Register

Date of Baptism	Parents	Name of Child and Date of Birth	Witnesses
	Frederik Rosekrantz Femmetje Bell	Hannes Sep. 9, 1771	Johannes Rosekrants Sara Schoonmaker, mar.
	Jacob Bikker Antje van Kleek	Maria Oct. 24, 1771	Johannes Bekker Marytje Bekker
	Cornelis Titsoort Marytje Hegeman	Johannes Oct. 16, 1771	
	Benjamin van Keuren Nancy Saal Butcher	Robert Saal Sep. 5, 1771	Robert Saal and Maria, his wife
	Willem Lassen Maria Storm	Goris Sep. 18, 1771	Goris Storm and his wife
	Gideon Titsoort Grietje Bell	Henricus Oct. 27, 1771	Frederik Rosekrants and his wife
	Total for this year 24; 13 sons, 11 daughters.		
1772 Jan. 26	Francis Gekoks Maria Wiltsee	Samuel Dec. 24, 1771	David Gecoks and Grietje, his wife
	Nicolaas Brouwer Sara Drake	Sara Nov. 15, 1771	Thomas van Bremen and his wife
	Clemens Cornell Cornelia Deeds	James Nov. 20, 1771	Pieter Deeds, and James Heck and his wife
Mar. 22	Pieter Hoff Sara Schurry	Annatje Mar. 8, 1772	
	Thomas Muller Cathrina Teuschman	Annatje Jan. 9, 1772	Thomas van Bremen and his wife
	David Duitscher Peggy Fontaine	Antje Feb. 18, 1772	
	Thomas Jemens Sally Gregg	Meindert Feb. 23, 1772	Meindert Harris
Apr. 19	Henrik Maston Jacomyntje van de Bogert	Marretje Mar. 12, 1772	Willem Louw and his wife
	Elias de Lange Heyltje Burhans	Coenraad Mar. 4, 1772	Coenraad de Lange and his wife
May 17	Simeon Lassen Margriet van Keuren	Cathrina Apr. 13, 1772	Cathrina Buys Mattheus Buys
June 7	Barent van Kleek Tryntje Oudwater	Elizabeth May 1, 1772	Pieter Oudwater and his wife
June 4	Elias Steenbergen Maria Hoffman	Jacomina May 18, 1772	Elias Bunschoten Catelyntje Leids
July 5	John Connel Lucretia Reids	Isaak June 22, 1772	
Aug. 30	Wilhelmus Heermans Antje Kneffen	John July 12, 1772	Johannes Montfoort & Annatje Heermans, his wife
	Carl Hoffman Elizabeth Seyfer (twins)	Daniel, Aug. 15 & Annatje, Aug. 16, 1772	Daniel Hoffman & Maria Hoffman, his wife
	Jacobus Middag Lena Viele	Hester Aug. 9, 1772	Ahasuerus van Kleeck & Hester la Roy, his wife
	Andries Lasson Saartje Buys	Andries Aug. 6, 1772	
Oct. 25	Isaac Storm Elizabeth Losee	Abraham Oct. 1, 1772	
Nov. 29	Laurens Hoff Cathrina Schurry	Annatje Oct. 14, 1772	

The Reformed Dutch Church of New Hackensack

Date of Baptism	Parents	Name of Child and Date of Birth	Witnesses
1773			
Jan. 10	Isaac Lassen Marytje van Keuren	Matheus Oct. 17, 1772	Mattheus van Keuren and his wife
	Hugo van Cleek Maria Everitt	Jannetje Nov. 28, 1772	Ahasuerus van Cleek Jannetje van Cleek
Feb. 7	Johannes La Roy Elizabeth van Cleek	Johannes Jan. 5, 1773	Joel du Boys and his wife
	Joel du Boy Maria Hooghteyling	Joel Jan. 4, 1773	Johannes la Roy and his wife
	Petrus Peele Hilletje Middag	Joris Dec. 22, 1772	Joris Middag and his wife
	Frans la Roy Geertje Middag	Maria Oct. 5, 1772	Michel Pels and his wife
	Jacob Bosch Dirkje Oostrum	Henrik Jan. 26, 1773	
	Adam Deeds Antje Rosekrans	Antje Jan. 23, 1772	Jacobus Rosenkrans Sara Rosekrans
	Henrik Oostrum Phebe Pinckney	Rebecca Dec. 28, 1772	John Pinckney and his wife
	Abraham van Keuren Margriet Storm	Maria Nov. 27, 1772	Goris Storm and his wife
	Levi Quemby Nelly Wiltsee	Sara May 1, 1772	Samy Quemby and his wife
Apr. 4	Martinus Overakker Margriet Kramer	Michiel Feb. 6, 1773	Zacharias Kramer Anna Kramer
May 23	Martinus Bosch Dina Steenbergen	Mattheus May 6, 1773	Mattheus Buys and his wife
Apr. 4	Jan Louw Brechje Meyer	Saartje Dec. 25, 1772	
	Thomas Allon Hester Wiltsee	Willem Mar. 3, 1773	
May 2	Joseph Gonzales Margriet Duitscher	Maria Feb. 23, 1773	
	Willem Esch Elizabeth Dop	Maria Mar. 25, 1773	
	Willem Louw Sara Maston	Elizabeth Apr. 3, 1773	Barent Viele & Elizabeth Maston, his wife
	David Seyfer Ariaantje Hooghteyling	Nelly Apr. 13, 1773	Lodewyk Seyfer and his wife
	Bernardus Zwartwoud Neeltje Hoogteeling	Johannes Apr. 20, 1773	Johannes Zwartwoud and his wife
	Jacob Louw Jannetje de Graaf	Laurens Apr. 15, 1773	Hannes van Kleek Maria van Kleek
	Laurens Conchlin Annatje Jurry	Sara Mar. 27, 1773	
May 23	Clemens Cornes Cornelia Deeds	Pieter May 11, 1773	Pieter Deeds and his wife
	Isaac Burnet Alida Edworth	Johan Wilhelm Jan. 12, 1773	Willem Elsworth and his wife
	Martinus Bosch Dina Steenbergen	Mattheus	Mattheus Bosch and his wife
June 21	Meindert van de Bogert Tryntje Reinderse	Johannes May 25, 1773	Jacobus van den Bogert Annatje Gay

Baptismal Register

Date of Baptism	Parents	Name of Child and Date of Birth	Witnesses
	Jacob Palmontier Maria Palmontier	Damon Apr. 26, 1773	
	Johannes Lasson Clara Lasson	Cathrina May 15, 1773	Mattheus Buys Cathrina Lasson, his wife
	Benjamin van Keuren Annatje Butcher	Mattheus June 15, 1773	Mattheus van Keuren Celetje van Keuren
	James Morgen Phoebe Elsworth	Jannetje Aug. 9, 1772	Thomas van Bremen and his wife
	James Hiks Lydia Jurry	Robertson June 5, 1773	
July 18	Johannes de Milde Lena Emug	Philip June 11, 1773	Philip Emug and his wife
	Hannes Wiltsee Jane Luckey	Petronella June 19, 1773	Henrik Wiltsee and his wife
	Andries Oostrum Sara Louw	Johannes June 19, 1773	Johannes Louw and his wife
Aug. 15	Arie Middelaar Grietje Seyfer	Pieternella June 18, 1773	Carel Hoffman and his wife
	Josua Carman Jacoba van Kleek	Maria July 5, 1773	
	William Haskin Annatje Hegeman	Cathrina Apr. 17, 1773	
Oct. 3 by Dom. Livingston	David Dean Elizabeth Strickland	Elizabeth	
	Matthew Dimend Anne Mosure	Margaretha	
	Johs. Wiest Barbara Hoogteylingt	Johannes	
Oct. 10	Teunis Wiltsee Cornelia Bartley	Thomas Sep. 24, 1773	Thomas Hardin & Maria Blanck, his wife
	Jacob Bekker Antje van Kleek	Elizabeth Oct. 29, 1773	Pieter Viele & Nelly van Kleek, his wife
	Jan Maston Annatje Storm	Sara Aug. 23, 1773	Sara Storm Pieter Storm
	Jacob Lane Annatje Conchlin	Henrik Oct. 8, 1773	
Dec. 5	Johannes Louw Aaltje Hogeland	Abraham Nov. 7, 1773	
	Petrus Burhans Annatje Seyfer	Sara Nov. 14, 1773	Paulus Peele and his wife
1774 Jan. 23	Johannes Janssen Grietje Steenbergen	Johannes Nov. 29, 1773	Elias Steenbergen and his wife
Feb. 20	Arie van Bunschoten Margriet Hoffman	Jenneke Jan. 16, 1774	Johannes Bunschoten and his wife
Mar. 20	Izaak de Milde Annatje Edward	Elizabeth Feb. 1, 1774	Johannes de Milde and his wife
	John Farguson Rebecca Lawson	Elizabeth Feb. 26, 1774	
	Andries Oostrum Sara Seyfer	Johannes Feb. 6, 1774	Jan Oostrum and Helena
Apr. 17	Henrik van Vlekkeren Maria Sloth	Aaltje Mar. 16, 1774	

The Reformed Dutch Church of New Hackensack

Date of Baptism	Parents	Name of Child and Date of Birth	Witnesses
May 12	H. Bell Annatje Conchlin	Maria Apr. 13, 1774	John Conchlin and his wife
June 5	"See the following page"		
July 3	Joost Westerveld Maria van Kleeck	Cornelia June 18, 1774	Abraham Westerveld and his wife
	Adam Deeds Antje Rosenkrans	Henricus June 11, 1774	Jacobus Rosenkrans Cathrina Deeds
July 31	Elias Steenbergen Maria Hoffman	Elizabeth July 11, 1774	Carl Hoffman and his wife
	Cornelis Hegeman Phoebe Ingerum	Willem July 14, 1774	
June 5	Pieter Lasson Catharina Dolsen	Catharina May 9, 1774	
	Cornelis Brouwer Alida Aarssen	David Apr. 15, 1774	David Ackerman
	Jacob Coopman Maria la Roy	Johannes Mar. 6, 1774	
	Barent van Kleek Tryntje Oudewater twins	Beletje and Antoinetta May 12, 1774	Daniel Oudewater Helena Reynderse
Aug. 28	Lodewyk Seyfer Sara Tomkins	John Tomkins Aug. 16, 1774	Petrus Weaver Elizabeth Tomkins
	Jesajas Drake Antje Janssen	Willem Dec. 26, 1773	Richard Janssen and his wife
	Joseph Simson Elizabeth Dumond	Joseph June 28, 1774	
	Frederik Rosekrans Femmetje Bell	Henricus Aug. 15, 1774	Henrik Bell & Annatje Conchlin, his wife
Sep. 25	Daniel Uhl Jannetje Heyne	Helena Aug. 17, 1774	
	Willem Hogeland Rachel Couwenhoven	Willem Aug. 22, 1774	
Oct. 23	Simeon Lasson Margriet van Keuren	Annatje Oct. 2, 1774	Jan Forden and his wife
Dec. 18	Clemens Cornel Cornelia Deeds	Benjamin Dec. 14, 1774	Pieter Deeds and his wife
	Richard Lasson Sara Storm	Maria	William Lasson and his wife
1775 Jan. 15	John Cornel Cathrina Sardam	Sara Dec. 29, 1774	
	Henrik Wiltsee Margrietje Müller	Cornelia Dec. 23, 1774	Teunis Wiltsee and his wife
		John Churchwel Dec. 23, 1742	
		Hannah Churchwell, (wife of John) July 22, 1742	
	John Churchwel Hannah Churchwell	John May 26, 1769	
	John Churchwel Hannah Churchwell	Benjamin Dec. 4, 1770	
	John Churchwel Hannah Churchwell	Mary Sep. 28, 1772	

Baptismal Register

Date of Baptism	Parents	Name of Child and Date of Birth	Witnesses
	John Churchwel Hannah Churchwell	Samuel Sep. 9, 1774	
Feb. 12	Carel Hoffman Elizabeth Seyfer	Lodewyk	Lodewyk Seyfer and his wife
	Laurens Hoff Cathrina Shurry	Sara Jan. 9, 1775	
	Jacob Lahne Annatje Conchlin	John Dec. 31, 1774	
Mar. 12	Marten Overackker Margriet Cremer	Cathrina Jan. 30, 1775	
	Ezechiel Peelen Phoebe Thorn	Petrus Dec. 26, 1774	Elizabeth Peelen John Peelen
	Cherrik van Keuren Elizabeth Westerveld	Maria Mar. 3, 1775	
Apr. 9	Abraham van Keuren Margriet Storm	Sara Mar. 20, 1775	Sara Storm Richard Lasson
Ex illicito Coitu	Joseph Shammers Hester Hoffman	Joseph Shammers Feb. 25, 1775	Carel Hoffman and his wife
May 6	Henrik Viele Anna Waldon	Benjamin Apr. 5, 1775	Benjamin Viele Anna Viele
	Petrus Peele Hilletje Middag	Paulus Apr. 7, 1775	Petrus Burhans and his wife
	Johannes la Rue Elizabeth van Kleek	Levi Apr. 15, 1775	
May 28	David Seyfer Ariaantje Hoogteyling	Anna Apr. 13, 1775	Petrus Burhans and his wife
July 23	John Compton Sara Jewel	John	Richard Somes and his wife
	Wilhelmus Heermanse Anna Kniffen	Lewis June 17, 1775	Lewis Kniffen Thomas Muller
Aug. 20	Laurens Conchlin Annatje Jurry	Hester July 26, 1775	
	Gysbert Peele Phoebe Simson	Stephanus July 19, 1775	David Flugler Hilletje Peele
June 25	Izaak Burnet Alida Elsworth	Margaretha May 6, 1775	Matthias Cook Margaretha, his wife
	Elbert Montfoort Aaltje van Keuren	Maria May 28, 1775	
Sep. 17	Frans la Roy Geertje Middag	Petrus Aug. 25, 1775	Petrus la Roy & Rachel Mabey, his wife
Oct. 15	Louis du Boys Aleda van Kleek	Cathrina Sep. 21, 1775	Pieter Palmentier and his wife
	Daniel Oudewater Neeltje Harris	Petrus Sep. 27, 1775	Pieter Oudewater Beletje, his wife
	James Hicks Lydia Shurry	Rebecca Sep. 2, 1775	
	John Loosee Rebecca Harris	Joseph Sep. 17, 1775	Joseph Harris and his wife
Dec. 10	Joseph Heat Maria Oostrum	Maria Nov. 14, 1775	Jan Oostrum and his wife
	Joel du Boys Maria Hoogteyling	Cathrina Nov. 14, 1775	Wilhelmus Ploeg Cathrina Ploeg
	Petrus Burhans Annatje Seyfer	David Nov. 16, 1775	

The Reformed Dutch Church of New Hackensack

Date of Baptism	Parents	Name of Child and Date of Birth	Witnesses
	Andries Lasson Sara Buys	Pieter Dec. 2, 1775	Pieter Lasson and his wife
1776 Jan. 21	Isaac Wiltsee Cathrina Zwartwoud	Tiatje Oct. 11, 1775	Tiatje Zwartwoud Henrik Oostrum
	Adam Deeds Antje Rosekrans	Anna Cathrina Dec. 22, 1775	Pieter Deeds and his wife
	Henry Bell Annatje Conchlin	Cathrina Dec. 17, 1775	John Conchlin and his wife
	Richard Cook Lasson Saartje Storm	John Coock Dec. 4, 1775	Celetje Lasson
	William Hickbie Cathrina Verwey	Patty Sep. 3, 1775	
Mar. 17	Isaäc Norris Susanna Philips	Samuel Jan. 28, 1776	
	Pieter Hoff Cathrina Deeds	Laurens Feb. 9, 1776	
Ex illicito *Conceptu*	Nicolas Brouwer, Junr. Susanna van Bremen	Adolf Brouwer Feb. 20, 1776	
Apr. 14	Pieter van Bremen Lena Ackerman	Sarah Mar. 28, 1776	David Ackerman and his wife
Apr. 14	Barent P. van Cleeck Annatje du Boys	Levi Mar. 21, 1776	
	Gerrit Luyster Helena van de Voort	Cornelis Mar. 21, 1776	Cornelis Luyster and his wife
	Henricus Oostrum Phebe Pinckney	Henricus Mar. 5, 1776	Jan Oostrum and his wife
	Isaac Lasson Maria van Keuren	Sarah Mar. 21, 1776	
	Willem Lasson Maria Storm	Geertruy Nov. 14, 1776	
May 11	Jeremiah Johnes Elizabeth Shurry	Jeremiah Apr. 15, 1776	
	Jurriaan ter Wilgen Maria van Kleek	Antoinetta Mar. 27, 1776	Hugo ter Wilgen and his wife
	Elias de Lange Heyltje Burhans	Sarah Apr. 7, 1776	Henrik Pels and his wife
	William McFerson Martha Cromwel	Archibald Jan. 1, 1776	Pieter Oudwater and his wife
June 23	David Flegelaar Hilletje Peel	Susanna Feb. 22, 1776	Benjamin du Boys
July 21	Richard Somer Martha Jewel	Elizabeth June 24, 1776	
	Jacob Bekker Antje van Kleeck	Barent June 14, 1776	Barent van Kleeck & Cathrina Oudwater, his wife
	Daniel Shaw Bartheny Downey	Elizabeth Mar. 11, 1776	
	Jan Wiltsee Janny Luckey	Debora July 1, 1776	Adolf Zwartwoud and his wife
Aug. 18	Teunis van Bunschoten Elizabeth van der Burg	Jacomina July 18, 1776	Elias van Bunschoten and his wife
	Petrus Luyster Willemina Luyster	Cornelis July 22, 1776	

Baptismal Register

Date of Baptism	Parents	Name of Child and Date of Birth	Witnesses
Sep. 14	Dirck Luyster Engeltje Kouwenhoven	Aaltje Aug. 28, 1776	Petrus Luyster Sara Luyster
	Pieter Losee Sophia Smith	Jannetje May 31, 1776	Michiel Golnek and his sister
	Albert Hamelman Apollonia Montagne	Lena Aug. 13, 1776	
	Albert Montfoort Susanna Hoogland	Jannetje Aug. 23, 1776	
Oct. 13	William Haskins Anna Hegeman	John Aug. 3, 1776	
	William Rogers Cathrina Rouger	Hester Aug. 20, 1776	William ter Wilgen
	Samuel Steenbergen Annatje Zwartwoud	Maria July 28, 1776	
Dec. 8	Jacob Golnek Geertruid Hoogteyling	Christina Aug. 31, 1776	Constantin Golneck and his wife
	Joris Jewel Louisa Montfoort	Sara Nov. 7, 1776	
	John Churchwel Hanna Smith	Elizabeth Oct. 7, 1776	
	Levi Quimby Nelly Wiltsee	Izaak Sep. 29, 1776	
	Frederik Rosekrans Femmetje Bell	Sara Sep. 16, 1776	Petrus Rosekrans & Saartje, his wife
Dec. 26	Laurens Hoff Cathrina Jurry	Petrus Dec. 5, 1776	
Dec. 8	Ida van Yveren Maria Conchlin	Meindert Nov. 20, 1776	Burger van Yveren Femmetje, his wife
	Margriet Seyfer, his wife	Anna Oct. 24, 1776	Petrus Burhans and his wife
1777 Jan. 12	Andries van Yveren Johanna Pitt	Susanna Dec. 14, 1776	Meindert van Yveren
	Barent van Kleek Cathrina Oudwater	Maria Dec. 26, 1776	Jacob Bekker & Antonetta van Kleek, his wife
	Doms. Izaak Rysdyk, pastor at this place Henrica Verwey	Johanna Dec. 19, 1776	Aris van der Bilt and his wife
	Mattheus du Boys Frankje du Boys	Johannes Henricus Dec. 26, 1776	
	Petrus Peele Helletje Middag "See on Mar. 9, 1777."	Aart Feb. 12, 1776	Joris Middag Hester Middag
Feb. 9	Carl Hoffman Elizabeth Seyfer	Petrus Jan. 9, 1776*	
	Pieter Lasson Margriet Coock	Henrik Heermans Oct. 7, 1776	Sara Storm Richard Coock Lasson
	James Morgan Phoebe Elsworth	William Dec. 28, 1776	
Mar. 9	Petrus Peele Hilletje Middag	Aart Feb. 12, 1777	Joris Middag Hester Middag
Mar. 29	Rem Adriaanse Gerhardina Hoogland	Abraham Mar. 7, 1777	

* Date appears as 1776, probably meant to be 1777.

The Reformed Dutch Church of New Hackensack

Date of Baptism	Parents	Name of Child and Date of Birth	Witnesses
Apr. 27	Henrik Peele Hanna Waldon	Hilletje Mar. 13, 1777	Joris Middag and his wife
	Henrik Heermans Sara Noordstrant	Philippus Mar. 20, 1777	Sara Heermans Henricus Heermans
	Robert Palmer Hanna van Everen	Burnet Mar. 7, 1777	Daniel Oudwater and his wife
	Frans la Rou Sara Ellis	Elizabeth Mar. 7, 1777	Johannes la Roy Elizabeth van Kleek
	Jacob Lane Anna Conchlin	Laurens Apr. 5, 1777	Anna Surry
July 5	Dirk Hoogland Maria Madrass	Antje May 15, 1777	
Sep. 3	Meindert Reinderse Annatje Latson	Elizabeth June 28, 1777	Johannes Reinderse Anna Ott
	Henrik Maston Jacomina van de Bogert	Sara Aug. 2, 1777	William Low and his wife
	Barent Harris Jannetje Banneton	Gilbert	Joseph Harris and his wife
Oct.	James Davids Elizabeth Verwey	Susanna Sep. 23, 1777	Jarry Johnes and his wife
	Zacharias Flegelaar Jannetje Peele	Anna Sep. 22, 1777	William Lewis and his wife
	Daniel Oudwater Neeltje Harris	Anna Sep. 14, 1777	Joseph Harris and his wife
Aug. 31	Pieter van Bremen Lena Ackerman	Jannetje Aug. 18, 1777	Thomas van Bremen and his wife
	John Losee Rebecca Harris	Johannes Dec. 25, 1776	
	William Moth Letitia Losee	Ann	
Sep. 28	Bernardus Zwartwoud Neeltje Hoogteyling	Geertruy Sep. 16, 1777	Johannes Hoogteyling and his wife
	Cornelis Brouwer Alida Aarssen	Jannetje Dec. 31, 1776	
	Isaac Wiltsee Cathrina Zwartwoud	Gerhardus Aug. 31, 1777	Gerhardus Zwartwoud
Mar. 9	Petrus Peele Hilletje Middag	Aart Feb. 12, 1777	Joris Middag Hester Middag
Mar. 29	Rem Adriaanse Gerhardina Hoogland	Abraham Mar. 7, 1777	
Apr. 27	Henrik Peele Hanna Waldon	Hilletje Mar. 13, 1777	Joris Middag and his wife
	Henrik Heermans Sara Noordstrant	Philip Mar. 20, 1777	Sara Heermans Henricus Heermans
	Robert Palmer Hanna van Everen	Burnet Mar. 7, 1777	Daniel Oudwater and his wife
	Frans la Roy Sara Ellis	Elizabeth Mar. 7, 1777	Johannes la Roy Elizabeth van Cleek
	Jacob Lane Anna Conchlin	Laurens Apr. 5, 1777	Anna Shurry
May 31	Abraham Lazurley Jane de Lanoy	Sara Feb. 1, 1777	
	Hannes Low Alida Hoogland	Elizabeth Mar. 19, 1777	Willem Low Elizabeth Low

Baptismal Register

Date of Baptism	Parents	Name of Child and Date of Birth	Witnesses
	Moses Barber Rachel Losee	Laurens Feb. 23, 1777	
July 5	Dirk Hoogland Maria Madrass	Antje May 15, 1777	
Aug. 31	Pieter van Bremen Lena Ackerman	Jannetje Aug. 18, 1777	Thomas van Bremen and his wife
Sep. 3	Meindert Reinderse Anna Latson	Elizabeth June 28, 1777	Johannes Reinderse Anna Ott
	Henrik Maston Jacomina van de Bogert	Sara Aug. 2, 1777	Willem Louw and his wife
	Barent Harris Jane Banneton	Gilbert	Joseph Harris and his wife
Sep. 28	John Losee Rebecca Harris	Johannes Dec. 25, 1777	
	William Moth Letitia Losee	Ann	
	Bernardus Zwartwoud Neeltje Hoogteyling	Geertruy Sep. 16, 1777	Johannes Hoogteyling and his wife
	Cornelis Brouwer Alida Aarssen	Jannetje Dec. 31, 1776	
	Isaac Wiltsee Cathrina Zwartwoud	Gerhardus Aug. 31, 1777	Gerhardus Zwartwoud
Oct. 26	James Davids Elizabeth Verwey	Susanna Sep. 23, 1777	
	Zacharias Flegelaar Jannetje Peele	Anna Sep. 22, 1777	William Lewis and his wife
	Daniel Oudwater Neeltje Harris	Anna Sep. 14, 1777	Joseph Harris and his wife
Nov. 23	Adolf Brouwer Aaltje Holst	Jeremia Sep. 14, 1777	Jeremia Brouwer Elizabeth Johnes
	Ferdinand van Sickelen Elizabeth Brouwer (twins)	Maria & Cathrina Oct. 12, 1777	
	John P. Waldron Elizabeth Haight	Elizabeth Haight Sep. 19, 1777	Grove Band
	Francis Harris Engelina van de Water	Hannah Aug. 27, 1777	Pieter van de Water and his wife
	Izaak Burnet Alida Elsworth	Jannetje Feb. 6, 1777	
	Johannes la Roy Elizabeth van Kleek	Emilia Sep. 22, 1777	
	Adam Deeds Antje Rosekrantz	Jacobus Oct. 25, 1777	Jacobus Rosekrantz Sara Rosekrans
	Henry Bell Anna Conchlin	Anna	Laurens Conchlin and his wife
1778 Jan. 24	John Compton Sara Jewel	James Oct. 13, 1777	James Compton and his wife
	Pieter Lasson Maria Gecoks	Benjamin Dec. 30, 1777	
	James Hicks Lydia Schurry	Timothy Jan. 2, 1778	

The Reformed Dutch Church of New Hackensack

Date of Baptism	Parents	Name of Child and Date of Birth	Witnesses
	Clemens Cornel Cornelia Deeds	John Dec. 26, 1777	
	Ex illicito Johannes Schurry Gaunce *concubitu* Maria Lasson	Laurens	William Gekoks Geertruy Gekoks
	Adriaan Hegeman Cathrina Janssen	Maria Nov. 14, 1777	
	Nicolaas Janssen Elizabeth Water	Petrus Sep. 2, 1778	
Feb. 21	David Seyfer Ariaantje Hoogteyling (twins)	David & Johannes Hoogteyling Jan. 1, 1778	Johannes Hoogteyling, and his wife for the former, and Arie Middelaar for the latter.
	Isaak Morris Susanna Philips	Debora Nov. 29, 1777	
Apr. 19	Daniel Emugh Cathrina Diamond	Joseph Feb. 18, 1778	
	John Wiltsee Jane Lucky	Henrik Mar. 27, 1778	Henrik Wiltsee and his wife
	Henrik Wiltsee Margaretha Müller	Petrus Apr. 1, 1778	Petrus Rosekranz and his sister
	Petrus Lasson Cathrina Dolsen	Maria Mar. 26, 1778	
	Ezechiel Peele Phoebe Thorn	Joseph Jan. 11, 1778	Francis Hagemen and his wife
	Petrus Burhans Annatje Seyfer	Nelly Mar. 4, 1778	
	Joseph Schott Mary Gaunce	Izaäk Mar. 1, 1778	
	Jurriaan ter Willigen Maria van Cleeck	Barent Mar. 8, 1778	Barent van Cleeck Helena Palmontier, mar.
	Jacob Golneck Geertruy Hoogteyling	Jacob Mar. 10, 1778	Adam Deeds and his wife
June 14	Marinus van Vlekkeren Maria van de Water	Abraham Apr. 15, 1778	
	Isaak van Deusen Rachel Burgon	Isaak Oct. 26, 1776	
July 5	Jan Walron Elizabeth Oakes	Eva June 13, 1778	
July 19	Elbert Montfoort Susanna Hoogland	Henrik June 15, 1778	
Aug. 23	Jan Montfoort Anna Heermans	Henrik Aug. 2, 1778	
	William Haskins Anna Hegeman	Cathrina Aug. 2, 1778	
	Aart van der Bilt Anna Nagel	Pieter Aug. 4, 1778	
	Frans la Roy Geertje Middag	Bawtje Aug. 8, 1778	Joris Middag Elizabeth Peele, mar
Aug. 3	Pieter Hoff Cathrina Deeds "bap. by Ds. S. Freligh"	Catharina July 14, 1778	Pieter Deeds and Cornelia Deeds, wife of Clemens Cornel
Sep. 20	John van Sikkelen Catelina van Wyk	Maria Aug. 8, 1778	

Baptismal Register

Date of Baptism	Parents	Name of Child and Date of Birth	Witnesses
	Duncan Graham Sara du Boys	Mary Aug. 31, 1778	
	Albert Amerman Apollonia Montagne	Johannes July 19, 1778	
Sep. 27	Benjamin van Keuren Anna Butcher	Benjamin Sep. 8, 1778	
Nov. 26	Jacobus van de Water Rachel van Kleek	Aagie Sep. 25, 1778	
	Ida van Yveren Maria Conchlin	Elizabeth Oct. 10, 1778	Elizabeth Reinerse
Sep. 27	Steven Banker Cathrina Stevens	Maria Sep. 2, 1778	Gerardus Banker Maria Ogden
1779 Jan. 3	Samuel van der Voort Helena Oostrum	Jacobus Nov. 6, 1778	Jacob van der Voort & Metje Mulford, his wife
Jan. 17	Jan ter Heune Maria Hofman	Albert Oct. 11, 1778	Albert ter Heune and his wife
	Barent van Kleek Anna du Boys	Rachel Dec. 12, 1778	Jeremia du Boys Rachel Viele
	Francis Gecoks Mary Wiltse	James Oct. 26, 1778	
	John Dearin Mary Lasson	Mary Dec. 7, 1778	
	Benjamin Canz Alida van Amburgh	Benjamin Mar. 22, 1777	Pieter Hoff
Jan. 31	Abraham Wiltsee Celia Lucky	Jenny Jan. 7, 1779	
	James Dearen Geertruy Gecoks	Charles Jan. 9, 1779	
	Abraham Kip Hannah Hames	Maria Dec. 17, 1778	
Feb. 28	Levi Quimby Nelly Wiltsee	Catharine Jan. 26, 1779	
	Jacobus Westerveld Cathrina Ferdon	Anna Dec. 7, 1778	
	Dirk Hoogland Polly Metross	Peggy Dec. 17, 1778	
Mar. 14	Jacob Bekker Antonette van Cleeck	Johannes Feb. 4, 1779	Johannes Bekker and his wife
	Jacob Koopman Maria le Roy	Cathrine Dec. 17, 1779*	
	Pieter van Bremen Helena Ackerman	David Feb. 18, 1779	Sara Ackerman
Mar. 28	Isaac Sebring Cathrine van Bunschoten	Cathrine Jan. 19, 1779	Cornelis Sebring Margaretha Sebring
Feb. 7	Francis Hegeman Abigail Thorn	Elizabeth	
	James Davis Elizabeth Verwey	Cathrina May 13, 1779	
Mar. 5	Harmanus Jewel Elizabeth Hilleker	George Jan., 1777	George Jewel and his wife
	Harmanus Jewel Elizabeth Hilleker	Maria Oct. 11, 1778	George Jewel and his wife

* 1778.

The Reformed Dutch Church of New Hackensack

Date of Baptism	Parents	Name of Child and Date of Birth	Witnesses
	Henrik van Vlekkeren Maria Sloot	Cornelia Jan. 20, 1779	
Apr. 5	George Jewel Latetia Thorn	Nancy Mar. 4, 1779	
	Jacob Lahne Anna Conchlin	Christina Jan. 6, 1779	
May 2	William Stanton Mary Duytscher	John Mar. 6, 1779	
	Bernardus Zwartwoud Maria Brouwer	Robert	Bernardus Zwartwoud
May 16	Doms. Isaac Rysdyk Henrica Verwey	Petrus Apr. 21, 1779	Thomas Storm & Elizabeth Graham, his wife
May 31	Isaac van Deusen Rachel Burgon	Anna	
	Adolf Meyer Antje Hogeland	Aaltje	Jeremia Brouwer Antje Ask
June 27	Meindert Reynerse Annatje Latson	Anna May 3, 1779	Jacobus Latson Maria Edward
	Frederick Rosekraans Femmetje Bell	Frederick May 20, 1779	Frederick Rosekrans & Anna Moul, his wife
	William Heart Elizabeth Hoogteyling	Geertruy May 11, 1779	Johannes Hoogteyling and his wife
July 11	Henrik Peele Anna Waldon	Henrik June 23, 1779	Henrik Maston Jacomina van de Bogert
	Aart van de Bogert Cathrina Peele	Geertje Aug. 14, 1778	Simon Pels and his wife
Aug. 8	Laurens Hoff Cathrina Jurry	Jacob July 18, 1779	James Hicks and his wife
	Johannes la Roy Elizabeth van Kleeck	Barent June 14, 1779	
	Abraham Lent Margaretha Waldron	Abraham Brinkerhoff June 18, 1779	Abraham Lent and his wife
Aug. 23	Rem Adriaanse Gerhardina Hogeland	Willem July 31, 1779	
Sep. 23	John Churchill Hanna Smith	William Sep. 20, 1779	
Sep. 25	Barent van Kleeck Tryntje Oudewater	Susanna Aug. 31, 1779	
	Adolf Brouwer Aaltje Holst	Aaltje Aug. 26	
Nov. 7	Roelof Philips Cathrina van Bremen	Jan Oct., 1779	Thomas van Bremen and his wife
Dec. 25	Daniel Oudwater Neeltje Harris	Daniel	
1780 Jan. 23	Gideon du Boys Elizabeth Duitscher	Gideon Dec. 17, 1779	
	Ferdinand van Sickelen Elizabeth Brouwer	Jan Dec. 22, 1779	
	Wynes Manne Aaltje van der Burgh	Richard Dec. 12, 1779	
	Daniel Emugh Cathrina Schott	Maria Dec. 10, 1779	

Baptismal Register

Date of Baptism	Parents	Name of Child and Date of Birth	Witnesses
	Jacob Griffin Cathrina Hoffman	Carel Jan. 1, 1780	Carel Hoffman and his wife
Feb. 6	Francis Hegeman Abigail Thorn	Elizabeth	
	James Davis Elizabeth Verwey	Cathrina May 13, 1779	
Feb. 20	Jacob Golneck Geertruy Hoogteyling	Johannes Jan. 18, 1780	
Mar. 19	Albert Montfoort Aaltje van Keuren	Tjerrick Feb. 5, 1780	Tjerrick van Keuren and his wife
Apr. 9	James Douglas Mary Scudder	Isaac Scudder Jan. 1, 1780	Benjamin Douglas
	Jacob du Boys, junr. Femmetje Oostrum	Jacob Mar. 6, 1780	Jan Oostrum and his wife
Apr. 26	Jacob Hilleker Rachel Traves	James Oct. 13, 1779	
May 20	Albert ter Heun Maria Salover (twins)	Lucas & Barent Mar. 15, 1780	
June 3	Henrik Maston Jacomina van de Bogert	Anna Apr. 15, 1780	
	James Hicks Lydia Schurry	James May 2, 1780	
June 4	Jacob Brouwer Alida Aarssen	Hester Mar. 29, 1780	
	George Schroder Jane Brouwer	George Dec. 31, 1779	
	Thomas Müller Cathrina Colony	Jacob May 17, 1780	
June 25	Pieter Andr. Lasson Cathrina Dolfsen	Esther May 24, 1780	
	Jerry Johnes Elizabeth Jurry	Rachel May 19, 1780	
	Abijah Patterson Susannah Conchlin	Sara May 27, 1780	
	Pieter Hoff Cathrina Deets	Petrus June 2, 1780	
July 16	Henrik Wiltsee Margaretha Müller	Teunis June 24, 1780	
	Ezechiel Peele Phebe Thorn	Cathrina May 27, 1780	Benjamin du Boys and his wife
	Christoffel van Bommel Sara ter Wilgen	Antje May 8, 1780	Jeremia van Cleek Antje van Bommel, his wife
	Baltus van Cleek Elizabeth de Graaf	Cathrina June 8, 1780	Barent van Cleek and his wife
	William Philips Neeltje Heermans	Andries June 16, 1780	Andries Heermans and his wife
Aug. 6	Jacobus Lasson Maria Edwards	Willem June 30, 1780	Willem Lasson Elizabeth Bogert
	Ezechiel Pinckney Nelly Wiltsee	Ezechiel May 25, 1780	John Pinckney Maria Allen
	Casparus van Keuren Maria Oostrum * Text says S(on)	Aaltje* June 3, 1780	

The Reformed Dutch Church of New Hackensack

Date of Baptism	Parents	Name of Child and Date of Birth	Witnesses
Aug. 20	Peter Mesier Catherina Mesier	Abraham	
Sep. 16	John Cornell Cathrina Sardam	Margaretha Aug. 17, 1780	
	Benjamin van Keuren Nancy Butcher	Maria Aug. 19, 1780	
	Simeon la Roy Sara Low	Janneke July 18, 1780	Jan Bunschoten and his wife
	John Griffin Cornelia Hofman	Elizabeth	
	Jan McLeen* Lena van de Bogert *Niel written above Leen.	Meindert Aug. 3, 1780	Pieter van de Bogert Anna Davidsen
	Jan van de Voort Elizabeth Cornell	Thomas Cornell July 29, 1780	
Oct. 8	Petrus Peele Hilletje Middag	Sara Sep. 19, 1780	Jacob Turk and his wife
	Petrus Lasson Maria Gecocks	Margaretha	
	Abraham Lent, junr. Margaretha Waldrum	Antje Sep. 12, 1780	Petrus Waldrum Antje Waldrum
	Zacharias Clump Geertruis van Sickelen	Cornelis Oct. 2, 1780	
	Jacobus van de Water Rachel van Cleek	Peter	Peter van de Water and his wife
Oct. 28	Duncan Graham Sara du Boys	Alexander Oct. 4, 1780	
	Pieter Rosekrans Antje Westerveld	Abraham Sep. 22, 1780	Abraham Westerveld and his wife
	Chavis Underhill Maria van Bremen	Sara Aug. 20, 1780	Thomas van Bremen
Nov. 19	Meindert Viele Hanna Palmontier	Rochelle Oct. 9, 1780	Jan van Kleek Jannetje Viele, his wife
	Adolf Meyer Antje Hogeland	Cornelia Oct. 29, 1780	
	Henry Bell Annatje Conchlin	Elizabeth Oct. 15, 1780	
1781 Jan. 20	Abraham Wiltsee Celetje Lucky	Cathrina Nov. 24, 1780	
Feb. 11	Michel Weaver Margret Buys	Cathrina Dec. 3, 1780	
	Josua Bishop Esther La Roy	Levi Sep. 18, 1780	Cornelis Noordstrant Rebecca Storm
	Levi Quimby Nelly Wiltsee	Mary Dec. 22, 1780	
	William Lasson Mary Golneck	Andries Dec. 21, 1780	Pieter Lasson and his wife
	Samuel Lucky Rebecca Pinckney	Jane Nov. 11, 1780	
Mar. 26	Pieter Lasson Maria van Keuren	Henrik Dec. 10, 1780	
	Clemens Cornell Cornelia Deeds	Adam Deeds Feb. 4, 1781	Pieter Deeds and Antje Rosekrans, widow of Adam Deeds

Baptismal Register

Date of Baptism	Parents	Name of Child and Date of Birth	Witnesses
Mar. 4	James Davids Elizabeth Verwey	Cornelis Jan. 21, 1781	
	William Chatfield Elizabeth Reynders	Esajas Dec. 6, 1780	Andries Reinders Elizabeth la Roy
	Francis Jecocks Henry Wiltsee	Jane Feb. 8, 1781	Jan Wiltsee and his wife
Apr. 29	Henrik Ellis Margaretha Kip	Mary Apr. 16, 1780	
Apr. 29	Abraham Kip Hannah Hames	Jane Apr. 16, 1781	
	Jan ter Heune Maria Hoffman	Maria Mar. 20, 1781	
	Elias van Bunschoten, junr. Catelina Light	Mattheus Apr. 5, 1781	
	Jacob Meyer Cornelia Meyer	Mercy Apr. 5, 1781	
May 3	Francis Pels Cathrina van Cleek	Petrus Nov. 7, 1780	Hannes van Cleeck and his wife
May 20	Coenraad Oberhauser Maria Story	Johan Caspar Apr. 1, 1781	Caspar Gaunce Elizabeth Gaunce
July 29	Jan Heermansse Cathrina Griffin	Maria July 5, 1781	
	(Note in English says: "See the other page," where the entry is repeated).		
	Rem Adrianse Dina Hogeland	Jacob	
Apr. 15	Thomas Lewis Rachel van Bunschoten	Jacomina Oct. 26, 1780	Elias van Bunschoten and his wife
	Jan Dieren Maria Lasson	Jan Mar. 1, 1781	
May 3	Jan van Kleek Jane Viele	Rochelle Apr. 12, 1781	
	James Deeren Geertruy Jacokes	Rachel	
May 20	Pieter van Bremen Lena Ackerman	Pieter Apr. 19, 1781	
June 3	Petrus Burhans Anna Seyfer	Maria Apr. 24, 1781	
	Bernardus Zwartwoud, junr. Maria Brouwer	Cornelis Apr. 7, 1781	
	Gideon Rogers Rachel van Sylen	Johanna Apr. 18, 1781	Jannetje van Sylen Joseph Cane
June 3	Benjamin Bloom Jemima Thurston	Jacob Feb. 9, 1781	
July 8	Jan van Sickelen Catelina van Wyck	Theodorus June 18, 1781	
July 29	Jan Heermans Cathrina Griffin	Maria July 5, 1781	
	Rem Adriaanse Dina Hoogland	Jacob	
Aug. 19	Meindert Reinders Anna Latchen	Helena June 21, 1781	Jacobus Reinders Maria Camble
	Geerit Luyster Helena van de Voort	Susannah July 23, 1781	Dirk Luyster and his wife

The Reformed Dutch Church of New Hackensack

Date of Baptism	Parents	Name of Child and Date of Birth	Witnesses
Sep. 8	William Philips Alida van Bremen	William July 14, 1781	
	John Churchwell Hannah Smith	Rebecca Aug. 18, 1781	
	Barnard van Cleeck Anna du Boys	David Aug. 29	Joost Westerveld Maria, his wife
Sep. 30	Daniel Hoffman Maria Lyons	David Sep. 1, 1781	
	Meindert van de Bogert Anna Davisen	Meindert Apr. 19	
Sep. 30	Ferdinand van Sickelen Elizabeth Brouwer	Henricus Aug. 12, 1781	
	Samuel van der Voort Helena Oostrum	Johannes Sept. 2, 1781	
Oct. 24	Frederick Rosenkrans Femmetje Bell	Blandina Sep. 25, 1781	Jacobus Rosekrans and his wife
Oct. 24	Jacob Griffin Cathrina Hoffman	William Oct. 1, 1781	
	Tjerck van Keuren Elizabeth Westerveld	Jesajah Sep. 20, 1781	
Dec. 23	Andries Reinderse Elizabeth la Roy	Elizabeth Nov. 3, 1781	Hannes la Roy and his wife
Dec. 30	Ahazia du Vain Jane Collier	Maria Sep. 9, 1781	
Dec. 2	Mattheus van Keuren Hester Hoffman	Cherrick Nov. 7, 1781	
1782 Jan. 13	Robert Milliagen Rachel van de Water	John Dec. 23, 1781	Sarah van de Water
Feb. 24	Jan Rykman Maria Allen	Albert Zwartwoud Jan. 21, 1781	
	Daniel Emugh Cathrina Deinor	Geertruda Oct. 12, 1781	
	Michiel Golneks Cathrina Deeds	Cathrina Jan. 28, 1782	
	John Jay Elizabeth Bush	Cathrina Feb. 1, 1782	Aart van der Bilt
	Jan Lasson Anna van Sickelen	Cornelis Sep. 21, 1781	
Mar. 10	Adriaan Brinkerhoff Adriana van der Linden	Hester van der Linden Jan. 30, 1782	
	Ephraim Schouten Sarah la Due	Cathrina Jan. 15, 1782	Maria Schouten
Apr. 1	Barent van Cleek Elizabeth de Graaf	Barent Feb. 15, 1782	Barent de Graaf Antoinetta de Graaf
Apr. 20	Abyah Patterson Susannah Conchlin	Abraham Mar. 17, 1782	
	Isaac Lent Cornelia Lent	Antje Mar. 17, 1782	Abraham Lent and his wife
	The Rev. Isaac Rysdyk pastor at this place and Juffrow Henrica Verwey, his wife	Elizabeth Mar. 28, 1782	

Baptismal Register

Date of Baptism	Parents	Name of Child and Date of Birth	Witnesses
	Godfrey Wolven Nancy Maby	Willem Mar. 20, 1782	
Apr. 30	Caspar van Keuren Mary Oostrum	Jan Mar. 30, 1782	
Apr. 23	Jacob Golneck Geertje Hoogteyling	Geertje Mar. 1, 1782	
June 9	Cornelius van Sickle	(a son, record not completed)	
June 30	Alexander Elsworth Elizabeth Lasson	Rachel June 1, 1783	Hannes Waldrath Cathrina Lasson
Aug. 11	Hicky Bates Eva van Sickeler	Rachel May 29, 1782	
	Teunis Schutt Elizabeth Culver	Hannah June 27, 1782	
Sep. 1	William Stanton Maria Duitscher	Hannah Feb. 6, 1782	
Oct. 13	Peter Andries Lasson Cathrina Dolsen	James Sep. 15, 1782	
	Isaac Seebring Cathrina van Bunschoten	Jan Sep. 8, 1782	
	Jacobus van de Water Rachel van Cleek	Jan Sep. 8, 1782	
Nov. 3	Jacob Bekker Antje te Nette	Anna Aug. 18, 1782	
Sep. 23	Isaac Storm Abigail Graham	David July 29, 1782	
	Johannes la Roy Elizabeth van Cleek	Geertruy Aug. 24, 1782	
	Cornelis Noordstrant Sarah Remsen	Catelina Aug. 29, 1782	
	William Philips Neeltje Heerman	Cathrina Sep. 5, 1782	
	Jan Low Brechje Meyer	Brechje Dec. 14, 1782	Pietre Deeds Antje Deeds
Dec. 15	Jacob Heerman Cornelia Meyer	Eva Nov. 30, 1782	Eva Meyer
	Andries Heerman Sarah Montfoort	Adriana Nov. 19, 1782	
	Henrick Heerman Sarah Haight	Elizabeth Nov. 11, 1782	
	James Davis Elizabeth Verwey	James Sep. 8, 1782	
1783 Jan. 26	Pieter van Bremen Helena Ackerman	Thomas Dec. 6, 1782	
	Abraham Lent, junr. Margaretha Walrum	Elizabeth Dec. 22, 1782	Abraham Lent Elizabeth, widow of Abraham Brinckerhoff
Mar. 9	Jan Hoff Rebecca Storm	Jacob Jan. 28, 1783	
	James Hicks Lydia Schurry	Sarah Jan. 16, 1783	Laurens Hoff and his wife
	Jan ter Hune Mary Hoffman	Lena Feb. 14, 1783	
Apr. 20	Roelof Philips, junr. Cathrina van Bremen	Peter Mar. 19, 1783	

The Reformed Dutch Church of New Hackensack

Date of Baptism	Parents	Name of Child and Date of Birth	Witnesses
Feb. 16 Ex illicito Coitu	Harmanus van de Water* Elizabeth Sleght	Margaretha Oct. 10, 1783	Egbert du Mond Margrietje Elmendorff
	Thomas Geacocks Jemima Sherwood	James la Due Nov. 15, 1783	
May 24	Joost Westerveld Maria van Cleek	Abraham Apr. 24, 1783	
	Hannes Noordstrand Maria te Nette	Adriana Apr. 5, 1783	
	Jan Rykman Maria Allen	Abraham Apr. 21, 1783	
June 8	Jan Churchwell Hannah Smith	Emilie May 10, 1783	
	Clemens Cornell Cornelia Dates	Maria May 8, 1783	
	William Chatfield Elizabeth Reynders	David May 9, 1783	
	Alexander Elsworth Elizabeth Lasson "N. B. This belongs to 1782."	Rachel June 1, 1782	Hannes Waldrath Cathrina Lasson
July 13	John Deeren Mary Lasson	Margaretha June 24, 1783	
Aug. 3	Obadiah Cooper Maria van Bunschoten	Elias July 19, 1783	Antje van Bunschoten Elias van Bunschoten
	Stephen Laurens Mary Chatterton	Joseph May 20, 1783	
	Aris Middelaar Grietje Seyfer	Maria Apr. 8, 1783	Johannes Ferdon Nelly Hoffman
	Petrus Burhans Anna Seyfer	Willem June 30, 1783	Carel Hoffman and his wife
Aug. 21	James Deeren Geertruy Jacocks	James July 17, 1783	
	David Mackey Helena Storm	Goris Aug. 4, 1783	Goris Storm
	Goris Storm Annatje Rey	Jacob "4 years old at about Christmas time"	
Oct. 5	William McNeal Elizabeth Wiltsee	James July 27, 1783	
	Joseph Schutt Cathrina Fowler	Jan May 5, 1783	
Nov. 16	Robert Milgen Rachel van de Water	Pally Oct. 10, 1783	
Dec. 20	Francis Jacocks Maria Wiltsee	Elizabeth July 15, 1783	
May 4	Barent van Cleek Cathrina Oudwater	Jacoba Apr. 4, 1783	
	Abraham Sleght Ruth Rohe	Sarah Apr. 16, 1783	
	Aris Middelaar Grietje Seyfer	Lodewyk Jan. 12, 1783	
	Joseph Win Sarah Lasson	Nancy Mar. 10, 1783	Johannes Walrath Cathrina Lasson

*After the names is written "egt (elieden)" husband and wife, in spite of the fact that the child is called illegitimate.

Baptismal Register

Date of Baptism	Parents	Name of Child and Date of Birth	Witnesses
1784			
Jan. 11	Samuel Meyer Cathrina Frair	Cornelia Nov. 24, 1783	Cathrine Meyer
Feb. 1	Tunis van BunSchoten Elizabeth van der Burgh	Elias Dec. 27, 1783	
	Daniel Oudwater Neeltje Harris	Gitty Dec. 24, 1783	James Edmund & Getty, his wife
	Baltus Frair Jacoba van Cleek	Mary Dec. 4, 1783	John Frair and his wife
	Robert Wilson Cathrine Wiltsee	John Dec. 23, 1783	
Feb. 13	Daniel Emugh Cathrine Dimon	Phoebe Nov. 2, 1783	William Davis Phoebe Schott
Feb. 22	John Brouwer Elizabeth Gaunce	Mary Jan. 19, 1784	
	Ferdinand van Sickelen Elizabeth Brouwer	Ferdinand Jan. 11, 1784	
	Henry Wiltsee Margaret Muller	Mary Jan. 11, 1784	Peter Muller and Widow Müller
	John Deeds Elizabeth Lasson	Petrus Jan. 27, 1784	Peter Deed Cornelia Cornell
Mar. 14	Gysbert van de Bogert Jannetje Peele	Cathrine Feb. 18, 1784	Peter van de Bogert Cathrine van de Bogert
	Benjamin van Keuren Nancy Butcher	Anna Feb. 8, 1784	Matthew van Keuren and his wife
Apr. 4	Jacob Griffin Cathrine Hoffman	Richard Mar. 5, 1784	
	Baltus van Cleek Elizabeth de Graaff	John Mar. 1, 1784	
	Casparus van Keuren Mary Oostrum	Helena Jan. 28, 1784	
	Abyah Patterson Susannah Conchlin	Mary Feb. 21, 1784	
June 6	John Wiltsee Jannetje Luckey	Robert Luckey May 7, 1784	
July 18	John Rome Mary Dutcher	Neeltje June 24	
	John Hoff Rebecca Storm	Peter June 24	
	John Jay Elizabeth ter Bush	Joseph June 17, 1784	
July 17	Jarvis Underwood Mary van Bremen	Mary Feb. 16, 1784	
Aug. 8	John Lasson Anna van Sickelen	Matthew May 20, 1784	
	Matthew van Keuren Hannah Green	Thomas July 19, 1784	Thomas Jacoks Hannah van Bunschoten
	Jacob Golneck Geertje Hoogteylingh	Constantyn May 13, 1784	Constantyn Golneck and his wife
	John Hoogteylingh Hannah Hicks	Henricus June 27, 1784	
	Gilead Hunt Sarah Lasson	Simeon July 17, 1784	

The Reformed Dutch Church of New Hackensack

Date of Baptism	Parents	Name of Child and Date of Birth	Witnesses
Aug. 27	Meindert Veele Hannah Palmontere	Cornelis	
Aug. 29	Cornelis Brouwer Elizabeth Brisby	Robert Aug. 25, 1784	
Sep. 19	The Reverd. Isaac Rysdyk minister of this congregation Henrica Verwey	John Aug. 12, 1784	
	Jacob Bush Dirkje Oostrum	Jacob Nov. 21, 1783	
	Peter van Bremen Magdalena Ackerman	Sarah Aug. 30, 1784	Gelein Ackerman Sarah Ackerman, his wife
June 27	Isaac Conchlin Cateline van Bunschoten	Helena May 9, 1784	
	Willem Stoutenburgh, Junr. Elizabeth Conchlin	Willem Stoutenburgh, Junr. Mar. 8, 1784	
Oct. 30	John Bogardus Elizabeth Lasson	Cornelis July 27, 1784	Peter Andries Lasson
	William Broocks Sarah Aplle	Kniertje July 26, 1784	
	Jacobus Westerveld Henrica du Boys	Jacobus Westerveld July 6, 1784	Matthew du Boys and his wife
	Jacobus van de Water Rachel van Cleeck	Jacobus Sep. 11, 1784	Matthew du Boys and his wife
	John van Cleeck Jane Viele	Lawrens Sep. 30, 1784	
	John Rouger Elizabeth Duncan	Esther Aug. 19, 1784	
	Andries Reynders Elizabeth la Roy	Isajah Oct. 28, 1784	
	Michel Wever Margareth Buys	Matthew Sep. 20, 1784	
Nov. 21	James Lasson Mary Edworth	Peter Oct. 5, 1784	Peter Lasson and his wife
	Meindert Reinders Anna Lasson	Mary July 13, 1784	Joseph Gail and his wife
Dec. 26	William Philips Neeltje Heermans	Rachel Nov. 11, 1784	Andries Heermans and his wife
	Henry Lasson Mary van Keuren	Andries Nov. 6, 1784	
	Dominicus Montfoort Antonetta van Cleek	Jannetje Nov. 17, 1784	
1785 Jan. 26	William Meyer Elizabeth Wiltsee	William Oct. 26, 1784	
	John Miller Mary Cuiper	Elizabeth Dec. 30, 1784	Gideon Rogers and his wife
	Isaac Seebring Cathrine Van Bunschoten	Emilia Aug. 16, 1784	
	Lawrens Hoff Cathrine Shurry	Oliver Nov. 14, 1784	
	Jacob Hicks Sarah Steenbergh	John Nov. 16, 1784	
	William Hicks Anne de Graaf	Lydia Oct. 24, 1784	

Baptismal Register

Date of Baptism	Parents	Name of Child and Date of Birth	Witnesses
	George Jewel Letitia Montfoort	George July 29, 1784	
Jan. 30	Samuel Luckey Rebecca Pinckny	Robert Dec. 31, 1784	
Feb. 20	P. A. Lasson Cathrine Dolsen	Robert Jan. 15, 1785	
	Jacob Becker Antonetta van Cleek	Mary Dec. 22, 1784	
	Daniel Hoffman Mary Lions	Elizabeth Jan. 5, 1785	
	David Duitscher Lena Frair	Abraham Aug. 5, 1784	
	William Stanton Mary Dutcher	Jacomina Jan. 20, 1784	
	Michel Golnek Elizabeth Dates	Jan Reyerse	
	James Hicks Lydia Shurry	Rachel Dec. 27, 1784	
Mar. 14	William McCord Rachel Teerpenning	Jannetje Jan. 22, 1784	
	Bernhardus Zwartwoud Neeltje Hooghteyling	Bernhardus Feb. 17, 1785	
	John Johnson Elizabeth Ferdon	John Jan. 28, 1785	
	William McCollister Ellenor Wiltse	William Jan. 24, 1784	
	John Pinckney Elizabeth Pinckney	Ellenor Nov. 29, 1784	
Apr. 17	William Davis Phoebe Scott	Anna Nov. 1, 1784	
	William Philips Alida van Bremen	Henry Feb. 4, 1785	
	Adolf van de Water Phoebe Philips	Benjamin Mar. 20, 1785	
May 5	John Heermans Cathrine Griffin	Philip Apr. 18, 1785	
May 16	Jacobus Ackerman Sarah Conchlin	Gelein Mar. 22, 1785	Gelein Ackerman and his wife
	Matthew van Keuren Hester Hoffman	Mary Apr. 14, 1785	
	James McCradle Elizabeth Hoffman	James Apr. 24, 1785	
	Albert Westerveld Sally Merckel	Henrica Apr. 26, 1785	Joost Westerveld and his wife
June 5	Simeon Johnson Meyer Cornelia Thorn	Gilbert McPhoedrix Apr. 19, 1785	Gilbert Meyer Helena McCloud
	John Dates Elizabeth Lasson	Cathrine May 8, 1785	
	Simeon Frair Mary van Sickelen	Samuel Apr. 1, 1785	
	Obadiah Cooper Maria van Bunschoten	Mattheus May 11, 1785	Mattheus van Bunschote
	Simeon Johnson Meyer Cornelia Thorn	Margareth Hood	Coll. Gilbert Livingston, Junr. & Margareth, his wife

The Reformed Dutch Church of New Hackensack

Date of Baptism	Parents	Name of Child and Date of Birth	Witnesses
June 26	Cornelis Zwartwoud Sarah ter Bush	Meyndert May 30, 1785	
	John Churchwel Hannah Smith	Samuel Apr. 7, 1785	
July 18	Henry Bell Hannah Conchlin	Susannah May 26, 1785	
	Robert Milligan Rachel van de Water	Helena June 14, 1785	Peter van de Water and his wife
Aug. 7	Eliah van Bunschoten Annah van Keuren	Nelly Apr. 3, 1785	
	Peter Frair Cathrine van Bunschoten	Rachel July 11, 1785	
	Simeon Frair Lena Palmontere (twins)	Anna Maria & Deny June 7, 1785	
	Peter Storm Cathrine van de Voort	Margret July 7, 1785	
	Baltus Frair Jacoba van Cleek	Sarah June 22, 1785	
	William Coock Elizabeth Noxon	Matthias Jan. 28, 1785	
	Jacob du Boys Phoebe Oostrum	Andrew July 10, 1785	
Sep. 18	Aart Middag Lena van Vliet	Elizabeth Sep. 3, 1785	
	Peter Maston Cathrine Weldon	Aart July 28, 1785	
	Aart Middag Cathrine Bogert	Jacobus Middag Aug. 22, 1785	Jacobus Middag Antje Bogert
	Henry Wiltsee Mary Gecoks	Mary July 21, 1785	Mary Wiltsee
	Maas Oostrander Clara Monfoort	Anna Aug. 10, 1785	
	Gideon Rogers Rachel van Zuylen	William May 31, 1785	William Rogers and his wife
	Thomas Noxon Magdalene van Cleek	Simon Mar. 25, 1785	
	John Deerin Mary Lasson	Rachel Aug. 21, 1785	
	Thomas Warner Alida Fitchet	Rebeccah June 26, 1785	
	John Noordstrant Mary van Nette	Jacobus Aug. 6, 1785	
	Jacob Wiltsee Bartha Turner	Isaac July 30, 1785	
	Zacharias Klump Geertruy van Sickelen	Peter July 30, 1785	
Nov. 6	Rem Adriaanse Dina Hogeland	Elizabeth Oct. 5, 1785	
	John Emugh Lena Abel	John July 22, 1785	George Emügh and his wife
	George Emügh Mary Cline	Sarah July 3, 1785	

Baptismal Register

Date of Baptism	Parents	Name of Child and Date of Birth	Witnesses
	Isaac Lent Cornelia Lent	Metje Sep. 18, 1785	
	John Hegeman Sytje van der Bilt	Peter Oct. 2, 1785	
Nov. 20	Peter Palmontere Sarah Zwartwoud	Johanna Aug. 28, 1785	
	Elijah de Lange Heyltje Burhans	Lena Oct. 5, 1785	
	Aart Middag Le Roy Aafje Rome	Francis Sep. 9, 1785	
	Aris Rome Lydia Dutcher	John July 18	Cornelis Rome
	Christoffel van Bommel Sarah ter Willigen	Assuerus July 6, 1785	Assuerus van Cleek, Junr. Mary ter Willige
	Alexander Laughlin Mary Schneyder	James Mar. 5, 1785	
	Obadiah Wicks Elizabeth Miller	Lena May 30, 1785	
Dec. 26	Petrus Peele Hilletje Middag	Jannetje Nov. 30, 1785	
	John Heermans Sarah Haight	Andrew Nov. 30, 1785	
	Marten Hoffman Margareth Bayard	Henry Sep. 24, 1785	
Dec. 11	Peter van Bommel Cathrine van Cleek	Petrus van Cleek Nov. 2, 1785	
	Matthew Lasson Cornelia Hoffman	Simeon Oct. 19, 1785	Simeon Lasson Grietje van Tessel
	Abraham Oberhaüser Elizabeth Emugh	John Jurry July 3, 1785	John Hoffman and his wife
	John Hoffman Phrone Oberhauser	Elizabeth Oct. 10, 1785	Abraham Oberhaüser Elizabeth, his wife
Dec. 23	John Slecht Amy Dean	Mary June 4, 1785	
	Daniel Cannef Cornelia Amerman	Dirk Mar. 19, 1785	
1786 Jan. 13	Samuel Birdsall Mary Rapalje	Lydia Aug. 23, 1785	Henry Steenbergh Lydia Rapalje
	Samuel Meyers Cathrine Frair	Elias Dec. 4, 1785	Elias Frair and his wife
	William Chatfield Elizabeth Reynders	Hannah Nov. 3, 1785	
	Henry Kip Hester van der Burgh	Cathrine Aug. 26, 1785	
	Daniel Oudwater Neeltje Harris	Beljatte Oct. 6, 1785	
	Aaron Low Anna Fort	Rebecca Dec. 9, 1785	
	Thomas Louys Rachel van Bunschote	Leendert June 27, 1785	
	John Gay Mary Conchlin	Hannah June 18, 1785	

The Reformed Dutch Church of New Hackensack

Date of Baptism	Parents	Name of Child and Date of Birth	Witnesses
	John Haff Rebecca Storm	Sarah Nov. 20, 1785	
	William Light Lena Miller	Elizabeth Dec. 31, 1785	
	Simeon la Roy Sarah Low	Elizabeth Sep. 9, 1785	
	John Seebring Cathrine van Bunschoten	Abigail Oct. 29, 1785	
	Abraham Wiltsee Celetje Luckee	Isaac Dec. 16, 1785	
	Oostrander Cathrine van Valkenburgh	Jane Ann Aug. 15, 1785	Elmendorph Anna Croocke
Feb. 26	Teunis van Bunschoten Elizabeth van der Burgh	Sarah Jan. 8, 1786	
	Elias van Bunschoten Catelina Leidt	James Jan. 11, 1786	
	John Palmontere Mary Jurry	Adriana Oct. 11, 1785	Jacobus Palmontere Adriana Palmontere
	Albert Montfoort Aaltje van Keuren	Celetje Jan. 7, 1786	
	William King Elizabeth Downy	William Dec. 23, 1785	
	Benjamin Vermiljer Sarah Downy	Anna July 15, 1785	
	Benjamin Vermiljer Sarah Downy	George July 15, 1784	Isaac Downy Anna Downy
	John Verveelen Sarah Bloodgood	Mary Sep. 9, 1785	
	Peter van Cleek Alida Tellar	Luke Jan. 1, 1786	Luke Tellar Sarah Tellar
Apr. 9	John Jewl Cathrina Reynderse	Elizabeth Feb. 19, 1786	Cherrick van Keuren and his wife
	Casparus Westerveld Deborah Forth	Wyntje Mar. 8, 1786	
	John ter Heune Mary Hoffman	Jeremiah Mar. 4, 1786	
Apr. 23	Frederick Rosekrans Phoebe Bell	Antje Mar. 16, 1786	
May 14	John Challenor Gerretje Rome	Cornelis Mar. 24, 1786	
	Clemens Cornell Cornelia Dates	Margareth Apr. 9, 1786	
	Henry Peele Hannah Weldon	Elisha Apr. 8, 1786	Elisha Maston Elizabeth Haight
June 11	Samuel Lions Anna Losee	Elizabeth Apr. 18, 1786	
	Jacobus Westerveld Rebecca du Boys	Cornelis May 18, 1786	
	Casparus van Keuren Cathrina Oostrum	Celetje Jan. 8, 1786	
	Peter Lasson Mary Gacocks	Sarah Mar. 4, 1786	
	John Wiltsee Jane Luckee	Celetje May 20, 1786	

Baptismal Register

Date of Baptism	Parents	Name of Child and Date of Birth	Witnesses
	Andries Johnson Mary Lasson	William Dec. 23, 1786	
	Thomas Jacocks Mary Tobias	William Apr. 26, 1786	
July 1	Lawrens Haff Cathrine Jurry	Joseph June 3, 1786	
July 2	Francis la Roy Elizabeth van Cleeck	Stephen May 8, 1786	
	Peter Rosekrans Anna Westerveld	Cathrine May 15, 1786	
	John Westerveld Anna la Roy	Peter May 26, 1786	
July 23	Stephen Henrickson Elizabeth Pels	Henrik June 28, 1786	
	James Hicks Lydia Schurry	Cathrine June 20, 1786	
	Daniel Hoffman Mary Lions	Margareth June 26, 1786	
	Jacob Griffin Cathrine	Michael June 26, 1786	
	Jan Fan Sikle Catelina van Wyck	Elsje June 22, 1786	
Aug. 13	Peter Miller Sally Brisben	John Miller July 13, 1786	
	Johannes Pels Sally le Roy	Michiel July 8	
	Jan Lassen Anne van Sickeler	Femmetje July 8	
	Abraham van Nette Pally le Roy	Elizabeth July 8	
	John Carl Celetje Lasson	Mary July 8	
	Peter Weaver Lea Storm	Peter Jan. 1, 1786	
	Joseph Mott, Junr. Helena Palmontier	Jacobus van de Bogert June 11, 1786	
	Cornelis H. Bogert Maria Storm	Goris Storm May 4, 1786	
Sep. 3	John van Cleeck Jane Veele	Cornelis Aug. 9, 1786	
	William Hicks Anna de Graaf	Moses Aug. 8, 1786	Hester de Graaf Barent de Graaf
	Michael de Graaf Jane de Graaf	Abraham Aug. 6, 1786	
	John Pinckney Elizabeth Pinckney	Mary Aug. 9, 1786	
	William Meyer Elizabeth Wiltsee	John July 2, 1786	
	Peter du Pue Susanna Emmot	Elizabeth July 3, 1786	
Sep. 24	John Peele Nancy Doll	Mary Aug. 15, 1786	
Oct. 15	Peter Deyoo Elizabeth Frair	Sarah Sep. 20, 1786	Simeon Frair Mary Frair

The Reformed Dutch Church of New Hackensack

Date of Baptism	Parents	Name of Child and Date of Birth	Witnesses
Nov. 5	Adolf Meyer Antje Hogeland	Antje Sep. 27, 1786	
	Moses de Graaf Jannetje van de Water	Maria Frair Oct. 14, 1786	Jacobus van de Graaf and his wife
	Peter van Bremen Lena Ackerman	Cathrine Sep. 30, 1786	
Dec. 17	Hugo van Cleeck Adriana Palmontere	Ahasuerus Hugo Oct. 25, 1786	
	John Dates Elizabeth Lasson	Andrew Nov. 11, 1786	
	The Reverd. Isaack Rysdyk Henrica Verwey	Johanna Oct. 15, 1786	
Dec. 26	Henry Schoonmaker Jane Ackerman	Cornelia Dec. 1, 1786	
	Samuel Matthews Mary Compton	Mary Nov. 18, 1786	
	Cornelis Brewer Elizabeth Brisbey	Mary Dec. 7, 1786	
Dec. 21	Anthony Hoffman Elizabeth Snedeker	Anthony Nov. 23, 1786	Hannah Snedeker Jean Vemont & Sarah Snedeker, his wife
1787 Jan. 26	Nathan Frair Elizabeth van Bunschoten	Mary Dec. 16, 1786	
	Stephen van der Burgh Anne Daughty	Mary July 21, 1786	
	John Conchlin Cathrine Hegeman	Elizabeth Jan. 9, 1787	
	Peter Veele Gerretje Frair	Sarah Dec. 7	
	Meindert Reynerse Anna Matson	Meindert Oct. 25, 1786	
	William McCord Rachel Teerpenning	Johannes Dec. 12, 1786	Johannes Teerpenning Jannetje Frair
	Roger Roke Mary Light	Elias van Bunschoten Nov. 21, 1786	
	Nathaniel Banker Elizabeth Humphrey	David Nov. 16, 1786	
	John Meyer Susannah Busching	Abraham Nov. 15, 1786	
Feb. 18	Jacobus Ackerman Sarah Conchlin	Isaac Dec. 24, 1786	Isaac Conchlin and his wife
	Herman van Bunschoten Maria van Stoutenburgh	Jacobus Oct. 13, 1786	
	Jacob Wiltsee Berthia Turner	Penelope Jan. 25, 1787	
	Jacobus Reinderts Sarah Hunt	Sarah Sep. 13, 1786	Peter Hunt Hannah Frederick
	Henry Wiltsee Mary Geacocks	Isaac Nov. 7, 1786	
	Peter A. Lasson Cathrina Dolsen	Daniel Jan. 19, 1787	
	Henry Buys Cathr. Reinderse	Henricus Dec. 27, 1786	

Baptismal Register

Date of Baptism	Parents	Name of Child and Date of Birth	Witnesses
	Adolf van de Water Phebe Philips	Catharina Jan. 20, 1787	Cathrina Vervale Daniel Vervale
	Isaac Wood Hannah van Bunschoten	Mary Oct. 30, 1786	
	William Davis Phebe Scott	Mary Jan. 2, 1787	
	John Fisher Charity La Roy	John Sep. 5, 1786	
	Jacobus Oostrum Mary Lewis	Rachel Nov. 3, 1786	
	John Rapalje Anne de Lange	Sarah Nov. 19, 1786	
	John Weaver Margret Buys	Antonetta Nov. 9, 1786	
Mar. 6	Thomas Biaux Elizabeth van Cleeck	William Stuart Aug. 30, 1786	
	Peter Lansingh Sarah Biaux	Mary Oct. 15, 1786	
Mar. 11	Michael Golneck Elizabeth Dates	Adam Feb. 19, 1787	
	Henry Wiltsee Margareth Miller	Esther Feb. 10, 1787	Esther Wiltsee John Wiltsee
	Jacobus van de Water Rachel van Cleeck	Cathrina Feb. 4, 1787	
	Isaac Palmontere Sarah van Cleeck	Petrus Jan. 31, 1787	
Apr. 1	William Philips Cornelia Heermans	Anne Feb. 26, 1787	
	Henry Johnson Elizabeth Ferdon	Margaretha Feb. 8, 1787	
	Benjamin Geacocks Geertruy Ferdon	Mary Feb. 8, 1787	
	Alexander Laughter Mary Snyder	Elizabeth Feb. 9, 1787	
Apr. 15	Cornelis Zwartwoud Sarah ter Busch	Abraham Mar. 25, 1787	
	John Jay Elizabeth Bush	Henricus Mar. 15, 1787	
May 6	Barent van Cleeck Cathrine Oudwater	Sarah Mar. 28, 1787	
	Thomas Lewis Rachel van Bunschoten	Elias Apr. 10, 1787	
	John Hoffman Frony Oberhäuser	Mary Apr. 1, 1787	
May 27	James Latson Mary Edworth	Simon Mar. 19, 1787	Simon Pels, Junr. Margriet de Milt
	Obadiah Patterson Susannah Conchlin	David May 2, 1787	
	John Churchwell Hannah Smith	Hannah May 7, 1787	
	Thomas Oostrander Elizabeth Smith	James Mar. 25, 1787	
	Ezechiel Veele Ariaantje van Dine	Sytje Oct. 5, 1786	

The Reformed Dutch Church of New Hackensack

Date of Baptism	Parents	Name of Child and Date of Birth	Witnesses
	John Cornell Cathrina Suydam	Sytje May 11, 1787	
July 1	James Dearin Geertruy Geacocks	James	
	Gilead Hunt Celetje Lasson	Moses June 13, 1787	
	Francis La Roy Elizabeth van de Water	Sarah May 5, 1787	
July 3	William Barns Mary Brouwer (twins)	Mary & Susannah	
July 22	Andries Heermans, Junr. Sarah Noordstrand	Gerrit June 16, 1787	
	Henry Steenbergen Lydia Rapalje	Jacob June 9, 1787	Jacob Rapalje
	Obadiah Cooper Mary van Bunschoten	Teunis June 25, 1787	
	Robert Milligans Rachel van de Water	James June 10, 1787	
Aug. 12	Petrus Frair Cathrine van Bunschoten	John June 24, 1787	
	John Bogardus Elizabeth Lasson	Peter Mar. 11, 1787	Cathrine, widow of P. A. Lasson
	Andries Lasson Anna Brouwn	Cathrine July 1, 1787	
	John Haff Rebecca Storm	Elizabeth Apr. 26, 1787	
	Simeon Frair Pally van Sickeler	Sarah July 1, 1787	
	Levi van Cleeck Elizabeth Duly	Anna July 9, 1787	
Sep. 3	Elias Frair Mary van Cleeck	Lawrens Aug. 9, 1787	
	Jacobus Middag Sarah Middag	Zachariah Aug. 10, 1787	John Flegelaar Paulus Flegelaar
	Matth. Lasson Cornelia Hoffman	Carel Aug. 15, 1787	Carel Hoffman and his wife
Sep. 23	Zachariah Klump Geertruy van Sickeler	Zachariah Sep. 6, 1787	
	John Hegeman Sytje van der Bilt	Sytje Aug. 23, 1787	
	Egenas van Bunschoten Phoebe Maar	Mary Aug. 29, 1787	
	John Dearin Mary Lasson	Geertruy Sep. 1, 1787	
	James Hicks Lydia Schurry	Stephen Sep. 2, 1787	
Oct. 14	Herman Hoffman, Esqre. Cathrine Verplanck	Philip Verplanck Aug. 30, 1787	
	Aart Middag La Roy Aafje Rome	Johannes Rome Sep. 14, 1787	
	John Noordstrand Mary van Nette	Petrus Sep. 16, 1787	

Baptismal Register

Date of Baptism	Parents	Name of Child and Date of Birth	Witnesses
Oct. 29	Abraham Teller Margreth Waiman	Elizabeth Mar. 7, 1787	Solomon Goodale, & Elizabeth, his wife
	Abraham Teller Margreth Waiman	John Stoutenburgh Sep. 27, 1787	John L. Stoutenburgh Aletta Stoutenburgh, his wife
Nov. 4	Casparus Westerveld Deborah Fort	Rebecca Oct. 17, 1787	
	Benjamin Westerveld Deborah van Cleek	Anne Oct. 1. 1787	
	Daniel Verveele Cathrine van de Water	James Oct. 8, 1787	
Nov. 25	Hickey Bates Eve van Sicklen	Phebe Sep. 4	
	Gerardus Wiltsee Cathrine van Cleeck	Nela Oct. 15, 1787	
	Moses de Graaf Anne Mollin	Isaac Hegeman Sep. 10, 1787	
	William Light Lena Miller	Mary Oct. 16, 1787	
	Obadiah Weeks Elizabeth Miller	John Miller Sep. 10, 1787	
	Andrew Low Francina Forth	Rebeccah Sep. 26, 1787	
Dec. 16	John Reinderts Margret Steenbergen	Lena Oct. 21, 1787	
	William Philips Alida van Bremen	Deborah Oct. 12, 1787	
	Total 80 children, males females	39 41 — 80	

1788

Date of Baptism	Parents	Name of Child and Date of Birth	Witnesses
Jan. 6	James Luckey Mary Frair	Jane Nov. 20, 1787	
	Henry Lasson Mary van Keuren	Cathrine Aug. 15, 1787	
	Peter van der Burgh Elizabeth Messerol	Henry Dec. 15, 1787	
Jan. 27	Jonathan Jeacocks Sarah de Graaf	Anne Dec. 16, 1787	
	John Jewel Cathrine Reinderse	Henry Nov. 20, 1787	Henry Jewel Anne Jewel
	Henry Kip Hester van der Burgh	Sarah July 1, 1787	
	Elias van Bunschoten Anne van Keuren	Elizabeth June 15, 1787	
	Baltus Frair Jacoba Frair	John Oct. 18, 1787	
	Thomas Warner Alida Fetchet	Isaac Nov. 14, 1787	
	Lawrens van Cleeck Charity Warner (twins)	Jacobus & Elizabeth Oct. 12, 1787	
	Gilbert Thue Sarah Ott	John Dec. 10, 1787	

The Reformed Dutch Church of New Hackensack

Date of Baptism	Parents	Name of Child and Date of Birth	Witnesses
	Peter Weaver Lea Storm	Mary Nov. 17, 1787	
	William Stanton Mary Dutcher	Aagje Oct. 8, 1787	
	Peter van Cleek Alida Teller	Gabriel Dec. 2, 1787	Gabriel Ellis Cathrine Ellis
	John Brewer Elizabeth Gaunce	Elizabeth Nov. 17, 1787	
	Henry Schoonmaker Jane Ackerman	Lena Dec. 21, 1787	Peter van Bremen and his wife
Feb. 13	John Elsworth Sarah Rysdyk	Harriot July 23, 1786	Asuerus Elsworth Henriette Rysdyk
	John Elsworth Sarah Rysdyk	Susannah July 21, 1785	Mary, wid. Gillaspie
Mar. 9	John Palmontere Mary Jurry	Rachel Oct. 25, 1787	
	John Heermans Cathrine Griffin	John Jan. 28, 1788	
Feb. 17	Daniel Oudwater Cathrine Harris	Barent van Cleek Nov. 14, 1786	
	William Cooke Elizabeth Noxon	Olive Jan. 5, 1788	
	Gideon Rogers Rachel van Zuylen	John June 29, 1786	
	Peter Maston Cathrine Weldon	Jacobus Jan. 15, 1788	
Apr. 13	Eden van Everen Mary Conchlin	Laurens Nov. 5, 1787	Laurens Conchlin Anne Sherry, his wife
	Leendert van Brommelen Tiatje Oostrum	Elizabeth Nov. 6, 1787	
	Jacobus van Nette Lena Bush	Dirkje Feb. 26, 1788	Jacob Bush Dirkje Oostrum, his wife
May 4	John Wiltsee Jane Luckey	William Apr. 16, 1788	
May 17	Godfrey Wulven Nancy Maybe	William Apr. 8, 1788	
	Peter Dates Adriana Du Boys	Adam Apr. 29, 1788	
June 8	Andrew Reinderse Elizabeth la Roy	Aletta May 1, 1788	
	Jacob Griffin Cathr. Hoffman	John May 4, 1788	
July 20	Jacobus Westerveld Rebecca du Boys	Matthew June 15, 1788	
	Lucas Teller Sarah Snedeker	Abraham May 20, 1788	Abraham Teller Peggy Waheman, his wife
Mar. 9	John Palmontere Mary Jurry "was forgotten"	Rachel Oct. 25, 1787	
	John Heermans Cathrine Griffin	John Jan. 28, 1788	
June 29	William Stoutenburgh Elizabeth Conchlin	Henry Dec. 21, 1787	

Baptismal Register

Date of Baptism	Parents	Name of Child and Date of Birth	Witnesses
	Jacob Hicks Sarah Steenbergen	James Jan. 23, 1788	
Sep. 21	John Dates Elizabeth Lasson	Hannah Aug. 18, 1788	
	Albert Montfoort Aaltje van Keuren	Johanna Aug. 24, 1788	
	Peter Peele Hilletje Middag	Zachariah Aug. 11, 1788	
	Frederick Rosekrans Phebe Bell	Jacobus Aug. 26, 1788	
	Daniel Ward Amy Meyer	Abraham Aug. 10, 1788	
Sep. 21	Abraham van Nette Pally la Roy	David Aug. 18, 1788	
	(This entry has been crossed out)		
	William Meyer Elizabeth Wiltsee	David Aug. 18, 1788	
	Thomas W. Jakoks Mary Tobias	Ruth Mar. 2, 1788	
Oct. 12	John van Cleek Jane Veele	Aaltje Sep. 4, 1788	
	Henry Barns Anne Teerpenning	Henry Aug. 30, 1788	
	Henry van Sicklen Jane Dollas	Cornelis van Sicklen Sep. 15, 1788	
	Zachariah van Voorhees Nancy Springsteen (twins)	Christian Sep. 9, 1788 & Nancy Sep. 11, 1788	
	Henry Wiltsee Mary Jacocks	Cathrine Sep. 16, 1788	
Nov. 2	Gideon de Graaf Dina van Cleeck	Mary Sep. 17, 1788	
	Meindert Veele Johanna Palmontere	Mary Oct. 11, 1788	
	James van Cleeck Anne Veele	Rachel July 31, 1788	
	Michiel de Graaf Johanna de Graaf	Elizabeth Sep. 30, 1788	
	Moses de Graaf Jannetje van de Water	Jacobus Sep. 22, 1788	
	Hugo van Cleeck Adriana Palmontere	Petrus Oct. 4, 1788	
	Joseph Luckey Magdalena van Wagener	Margaretha Sep. 3, 1788	
	Adolf Meyer Antje Hogeland	Happy (a dau.) Aug. 18, 1788	
"Warwick Nov. 16"	Jacobus Jacobuz Cathrine de Marees	Gerrit Aug. 20, 1788	
	William Barns Mary Brouwer	Antony Gleen Aug. 30, 1788	
Nov. 22	Gideon du Boys Elizabeth Dutcher	Elizabeth Oct. 24, 1788	

The Reformed Dutch Church of New Hackensack

Date of Baptism	Parents	Name of Child and Date of Birth	Witnesses
	Bernardus Swartwoud Neeltje Hooghteyling	Henricus Oct. 23, 1788	
	Johannes Palmontere Sally la Roy	Seletje Oct. 24, 1788	
	Peter Bogert Anne van Cleek	Cathrina Nov. 1, 1788	Aart van de Bogert Cathrine, his wife
	Thomas Rogers Anne van Zeyl	Elizabeth Oct. 26, 1788	Elizabeth van Zeyl William Rogers
	Clemens Cornwell Cornelia Dates	Elizabeth Oct. 29, 1788	
Dec. 14	Lawrens Haff Cathrine Jurry	Cathrine Oct. 6, 1788	
	Peter de Joo Elizabeth Frair	Baltus Nov. 1, 1788	Baltus Frair Jacoba van Cleek
	Peter la Roy Jannetje Miserol	Jacob Sep. 18, 1788	
	Benjamin van de Water Elizabeth van Cleek	Mary Nov. 21, 1788	
	Johannes Hoogteyling Hannah Hicks	Lydia Nov. 1, 1788	
1789 Jan. 18	Francis Bogert Elizabeth Palmontere (twins)	Francis & Sarah June 7, 1788	
	Cornelis H. Bogert Rebecca Storm	Rebecca Nov. 24, 1788	
	Isaac Romein Sarah Frair	Helena Sep. 16, 1788	
Jan. 11	Peter Veele Gerritje Frair	Deborah Oct. 29, 1788	
	Samuel Meyer Cathrine Frair	Petrus Dec. 2, 1788	
	Andries Lasson Anne Brouwer	Mary Dec. 9, 1788	
	Ezechiel Veele Adriana van Dine	Philip (Vesick) Oct. 14, 1788	
	Samuel Matthew Mary Compton	Robert Dec. 21, 1788	
	Peter van Bramer Lena Ackerman	Johannes Dec. 19, 1788	
Feb. 15	Cornelius Swartwoud Sarah ter Bush	George Washington Dec. 20, 1788	
	Henry van Voorhees Hannah Flegelaar	Abraham Nov. 5, 1788	
	Aron Low Hannah Fort	Abraham Jan. 3, 1789	
Mar. 1	John Rosekrans Mary Hicks	Sarah Jan. 17, 1789	
	Francis van Tine Evah Luyster	Bartholomy Cowen Jan. 26, 1789	
	Adolf van de Water Phebe Philips	Henry Jan. 9, 1789	
Mar. 29	Jacobus Veele Cathrina Palmontere	Petrus Feb. 27, 1789	

Baptismal Register

Date of Baptism	Parents	Name of Child and Date of Birth	Witnesses
	James Dearin Geertruy Jacocks	William Feb. 27, 1789	
May 2	Peter Wyckoff Seytje van der Bilt	Wilhelmus Mar. 22, 1789	Femmetje Cornell
May 24	Henricus Schoonmaker Johannah Ackerman	Hannah Apr. 19, 1789	
May 31	Ferdinand van Sickelen Elizabeth Brouwer	Evah Feb. 16, 1789	
June 21	John P. Lasson Anne van Sickelen	William Mar. 23, 1789	
	Peter J. Lasson Amy Titus	Hannah May 23, 1789	
July 2	George Jewel Latitia Montfoort	John Aug. 2, 1789	
Aug. 16	John Haff Rebecca Storm	Hannah July 13, 1789	
	"and his wife" Geertruy van Keuren	Jonathan Brown Jan. 24, 1789	
	William Hicks Anne de Graaf	James July 26, 1789	
Sep. 13	Michael Wever Margaretha Buys	Elizabeth July 5, 1789	
Sep. 7	Joseph Luckey Magdalen van Wagener	Benjamin Aug. 14, 1789	
	Thomas Lewis Rachel van Bunschoten	Catelina July 5, 1789	
Sep. 27	Thomas Johnson Pally Hickbey	Lena Aug. 14, 1789	
	Aart Middag Lena van Vliet	Anne Aug. 3, 1789	
Nov. 1	John Luyster Cathrine van Aalst	Matthias Sep. 13, 1789	Matthias Luyster Anne van Bommel, his wife
	Jacob du Boys, Junr. Femmetje Oostrum	John Sep. 29, 1789	
	John Yates Geertruy Lasson	William Oct. 14, 1789	
	Michiel Gulneck Elizabeth Dates	Martin Oct. 11, 1789	
	William Filips Neeltje Heermans	Rebecca Aug. 26, 1789	
	John Elsworth Sarah Rysdyk	Mary Oct. 1, 1789	Mary Elsworth Henriette Rysdyk
Nov. 8	John Noordstrandt Mary van Nette	John Oct. 4, 1789	
	Jacob van der Burgh Cornelia Swartwoud	Nela Aug. 17, 1789	
Nov. 13	Simeon Le Roy Sarah le Roy	Getty Nov. 1, 1789	Elizabeth Reinders
	Peter van Cleek Alida Tellar	Mary Nov. 5, 1789	
Nov. 20	Aart Middag La Roy Aafje Rome	Gerritje Oct. 11, 1789	Gerritje Rome

The Reformed Dutch Church of New Hackensack

Date of Baptism	Parents	Name of Child and Date of Birth	Witnesses
	"The following items were omitted in the former transcription"		
May 10	Gerardus Wiltsee Cathrina van Cleeck	Teunis Apr. 25, 1787	
	Willem Lasson Mary Golneck	Willem July 26, 1787	
	John Forbus Martha van de Water	Mary Dec. 30, 1787	
Aug. 10	William Churchill Elizabeth Reynders	Jacob July 8, 1788	
	John Forguson Sarah van de Water	Samuel June 7, 1788	
	Peter Miller Sarah Brisby	Mary Mar. 17, 1788	
Aug. 24	Jacob Brinckerhoff Dinah van Wyck	Hannah June 29, 1788	
Aug. 31	Peter van Cleek Anna van Vliet	Sarah Aug. 8, 1783	
	Casparus van Keuren Mary Oostrum	Femmetje May 24, 1788	
	John Westerveld Anne la Roy	Antje Aug. 6, 1788	

BAPTISMAL REGISTER OF THE CONGREGATION AT HACKINSACK CONTINUED BY REVD. NICHS. VAN VRANKEN

Date of Baptism	Parents	Name of Child and Date of Birth	Witnesses
1791 Dec. 4	John Ellsworth Sarah Rysdick	Dorothy Sep. 7, 1791	Verdine Ellsworth Dorothy Ellsworth
" "	Henry Dymon Amy Matross	Isaac Scott Sep. 13, 1791	
" "	John Yates Gertruy	Simeon Oct. 3, 1791	
1792 Jan. 1	John A. Hagerman Sytye Van Der Belt	John Nov. 12, 1791	
" "	Michael Golneck Elizabeth Dietz	Styntye Nov. 2, 1791	
" "	William Chatfield Elizabeth Rynes	Reuben Nov. 4, 1791	
" "	Abraham Meyers Hannah Hoff	Sally July 6, 1791	
" "	John Dietz Mary Dubois	Jenny Oct. 7, 1791	
Jan. 29	John Rosevelt Mary Hicks	Lydia Jan. 2, 1792	
" "	Andrew Rynders Elizabeth Leroy	Maria Dec. 12, 1791	
" "	William Ferdon Hannah Westervelt	Elsje Dec. 17, 1791	
" "	John Rapalie Hannah Delaun	Rachel Nov. 10, 1791	
" "	Benjamin Jacocks Gertrude Ferdine	Hannah Dec. 23, 1791	
" "	Peter Depuy Susannah Nebbel	Nancy Oct. 6, 1791	

Baptismal Register

Date of Baptism	Parents	Name of Child and Date of Birth	Witnesses
Jan. 29	Peter Lawson Amy Titus	Peter Aug. 4, 1791	
" "	Peter Ferdon Peggy Tobias	Martinus Dec. 15, 1791	
" "	David Algee Mary Pinckney	John Nov. 22, 1791	
" "	William Abel Sarah Amy	Hendrick Apr. 26, 1790	
Feb. 26	Jacob Golneck Gertrude Hooghteeling	Martin Apr. 12, 1791	
" "	William Philips Nelly Heermans	Sally Feb. 5, 1792	Hendrick Heermans Sally (Heyet)
" "	Jacob Becker Antonetta Van Kleeck	Antonetta Jan. 15, 1792	
Apr. 15	Henry Schoonmaker Jane Ackerman	Maria Mar. 22, 1792	
" "	Jacob Griffin Catharine Hoffman	Maria Mar. 26, 1792	
" "	Thomas T. Jecocks Gitty Hays	Abm. Stoutenburgh Mar. 1, 1792	
" "	George Van Alst Caty Parson	Altye Jan. 17, 1792	
May 13	Zachariah Klump Gitty Van Sicklen	Catharine Apr. 15, 1792	
" "	John Hoff Rebekah Storm	Abraham May 6, 1792	
" "	Michael De Graff Jane De Graff	Lydia Mar. 30, 1792	
" "	Laurence Hoff Catharine Sherry	Laurence Apr. 16, 1792	
May 30	John Leyster Catharine Van Alst	John May 18, 1792	
June 24	William Philips Alida Van Breemer	Peter May 10, 1792	
" "	Cornelius Brewer Elizabeth Brisby	Sarah May 6, 1792	
" "	Peter A. Lawson Mary Jecocks	Wyntie May 26, 1792	
" "	John Brewer Elizabeth Gons	John May 24, 1792	
July 22	Gideon De Graff Dinah Van Kleeck	Elizabeth May 24, 1792	
Aug. 16	Thomas Wood Mary Churchwell	James May 23, 1792	
Aug. 19	Robert Todd Elizabeth Fer Valen	Oliver June 17, 1792	
" "	Henry Van Sickler Jane Dollis	Phebe July 19, 1792	
Oct. 21	Albert Montfoort, Junr. Altje Van Keure	Anna Sep. 12, 1792	
" "	Philip Van Derbilt Mary Jacobs	Catharine Aug. 9, 1792	
Nov. 18	Albert Westervelt Sally Markle	Abm. Oct. 19, 1792	

The Reformed Dutch Church of New Hackensack

Date of Baptism	Parents	Name of Child and Date of Birth	Witnesses
Nov. 18	Moses Vervalen Mary Heyett	Phebe Oct. 15, 1792	
" "	John Dearin Mary Lawson (twins)	James & Nancy Oct. 3, 1792	
" "	John Sherry Hicks Nancy Divine	Jane Aug. 27, 1792	
" "	Henry Hooghtaling Margaret Krankheit	Mary & Elsje Jan. 10, 1780 Matthias Apr. 28, 1782 Magdalen Sep. 13, 1783 Eve May 31, 1785 Susannah Aug. 4, 178(?)	
Dec. 16	Casparus Van Keure Maria Ostrum	Andw. July 1, 1792	
" "	Baltus Van Kleek Elizabeth DeGraff	Anna Oct. 28, 1792	
" "	Henry Jewel Elizabeth Van Kleek	Barent Sep. 28, 1792	
1793 Jan. 1	Peter Burgaw Mary Storm	Caty Dec. 10, 1792	
" "	Isaac Burgaw Anna Waldrom	Anna Nov. 24, 1792	
Jan. 15	James Thorn Jane Suydam	Phebe Jan. 7, 1793	Rynier Suydam
Mar. 10	Lewis Sniffin Jane Bogert	Elizabeth Jan. 9, 1793	
Apr. 21	Henry Wyckoff Sitea Van Der Bilt	Ares Feb.21, 1793	
June 2	John Deitz Elizabeth Lawson	Margaret Apr. 5, 1793	
June 16	Peter Van Bremen Magdalen Ackerman	William Apr. 22, 1793	
" "	Jacob Dubois Phebe Ostrum	Peter Mar. 17, 1793	
" "	John Jewel Catharine Rynders	Patty Aug. 12, 1792	
July 13	Adolphus Van De Water Phebe Phillips	Adolphus Apr. 20, 1793	
" "	Matthew P. Lawson Peggy Lawson	Polly May 10, 1793	
" "	John J. Lawson Lydia Miller	Sally Apr. 5, 1793	
Sep. 15	James Ackerman Sarah Conklin	Hannah July 30, 1793	
Oct. 15	Zachariah Klump Gertrude Van Sickler	Elizabeth Aug. 7, 1793	

Baptismal Register

Date of Baptism	Parents	Name of Child and Date of Birth	Witnesses
Oct. 15	Henry Philips Eunice Reeves	Abraham Feb. 15, 1791 Selah Reeves June 11, 1793	
" "	John M. Cook Elizabeth Sleght	Egbert Dumont Mar. 13, 1793	
Oct. 29	Nathan Leet Phebe Hoff	Catharine May 11, 1793	Laurence Hoff Catharine Shurry
1794 Jan. 1	John Hageman Sitea Van Der Bilt	Martha Nov. 25, 1793	
Jan. 26	John Rosecrants Mary Hicks	James Dec. 15, 1793	
" "	Warren Rosecrants Phebe Hoff	Sally Oct. 29, 1793	
" "	William P. Lawson Mary Yates	John Nov. 4, 1793	
" "	Benjamin Van De Water Elizabeth Van Kleeck	Elizabeth Dec. 25, 1793	
Feb. 23	Samuel Disbrow Anna Patterson	Abijah & Henry Sep. 11, 1793	
" "	John (S). Hicks Anna Divine	James Jan. 23, 1793	
Mar. 23	Peter Rosecrants Anna Westervelt	Sarah Jan. 29, 1794	
" "	James Dearin Gertrude Jecocks	Peter Feb. 21, 1794	
" "	Peter Van Derbergh Nelly Dutcher	Elizabeth Oct. 20, 1793	
" "	Peter Van Kleeck Anna Van Kleeck	Penelope Feb. 11, 1794	
" "	Abm. Dutcher Elizabeth Maxfield	David Sep. 24, 1793	
" "	James Yates Sarah Van Keure	William Mar. 10, 1794	
Apr. 21	Isaac Van Alst Styntie Gulneck	Constantine Gulneck Apr. 1, 1794	
" "	John Deitz Mary Dubois	Sarah Feb. 22, 1794	
" "	John Yates Gitty Lawson	Esther Mar. 15, 1794	
" "	Henry Diamond Amy Montross	Abm. Oct. 13, 1793	
" "	Betts Chatterdon Mary Valence	Joshua Apr. 14, 1791 John Pinckney Sep. 8, 1793	
May 18	Peter Burgaw Mary Storm	Anna Apr. 8, 1794	
" "	Abm. Fordon Nelly Cypher	Charles Apr. 15, 1794	

The Reformed Dutch Church of New Hackensack

Date of Baptism	Parents	Name of Child and Date of Birth	Witnesses
May 18	Samuel Meyer Catharine Fraer	Peter Mar. 24, 1794	
" "	Abm. Deitz Elizabeth Fowler	Caty Mar. 10, 1794	
" "	Elias Van Bunschoten Catalina Light	Jane May 2, 1794	
June 29	John Luyster, Junr. Catharine Van Alst	George May 17, 1794	
" "	Simon Lawson Sarah Ferdun	Rachel Jan. 20, 1794	
Aug. 3	Thomas Jeacocks Gitty Hays	Catharine July 22, 1794	
" "	Abm. Stoutenburgh, Decd. Catharine Jeacocks	Tobias Oct. 14, 1792	
Aug. 31	Thomas Wood Mary Churchill	John July 31, 1794	
Nov. 16	Abraham Hoogland Aletta Brewer	Martha Sep. 5, 1794	
" "	Thomas Jeacocks Mary Tobias	Gertrude Sep. 14, 1794	
Dec. 14	Michael De Graff Jane De Graff	Margaret Nov. 5, 1794	
" "	Isaac Burgaw Anna Waldron	Isaac Oct. 25, 1794	
Oct. 2	Peter Cornwell Elizabeth Baker	Sarah Sep. 9, 1794	
" "	Philip Van Der Bilt Mary Jacobs	Hannah Sep. 1, 1794	
Oct. 5	Charles Brouwer Elizabeth Hoffman	Francina Aug. 5, 1794	
Dec. 14	Casparus Van Keure Maria Ostrum	Elizabeth Oct. 23, 1794	
" "	Matthias Cook Rachel Swartwout	Altje Oct. 5, 1794	
" "	Henry Jewel Elizabeth Van Kleeck	Mary Oct. 5, 1794	
" "	Laurence Hoff Catharine Schurry	Maria Sep. 5, 1794	
" "	Sylvenus Pine Nelly Ter Bush	Eliza Sep. 23, 1794	
1795 Jan. 1	Matthew Lawson Nelly Hoffman	Matthew Oct. 17, 1794	
" "	Peter Lawson Mary Jeacock	James Oct. 28, 1794	
Jan. 18	Adolph Van Dewater Phebe Philips	Herman Oct. 27, 1794	
" "	Matthew P. Lawson Peggy Lawson	Peter July 16, 1794	
" "	Andrew Lawson Polly Clock	Andrew Oct. 31, 1794	
Jan. 20	Abm. Van Keure Petronella Wiltsie	Margaret Dec. 8, 1794	

Baptismal Register

Date of Baptism	Parents	Name of Child and Date of Birth	Witnesses
Feb. 15	Michael Hoffman Caty Van Sickler	Elizabeth Jan. 17, 1795	Charles Hoffman Elizabeth Cypher
" "	Albert Monfoort, Junr. Altje Van Keure	Cornelius Jan. 13, 1795	
" "	James Ackerman Sarah Conklin	Matthew Van Bunschooten Jan. 28, 1795	
" "	Michael Gulneck Elizabeth Deitz	Cornelia Jan. 25, 1795	
" "	Elias Dubois Hannah Hoff	Lawrence Nov. 28, 1794	
" "	Ezekiel Viele Adriana Van Dine	Mehitabel Jan. 13, 1795	
" "	William Letson Anna Dutcher	Jeremiah Jan. 18, 1795	
Apr. 5	John Dearin Mary Lawson	Simeon Mar. 16, 1795	
" "	John Lawson Anna Van Sickler	John Feb. 13, 1795	
" "	James Bogardus Lydia Jones	Maria Oct. 6, 1795	Elizh. Schurry
" "	William Phillips Alida V. Breemen	John Feb. 16, 1795	
May 25	Henry Schoonmaker Jane Ackerman	Jane Apr. 17, 1795	
June 20	Jacobus Bush Anatje Van Kleeck	Margaret Oct. 17, 1794	
July 1 *Illicito Concubito*	Douw Cornell Caty Jacobs	Richard Apr. 28, 1795	Henry Jacobs Hester V. Alst
July 26	James Middagh Sally Burhans	Peter July 4, 1795	
" "	Jacob Reynders Susan Flageler	Hetty Jan. 14, 1795	Andrew Reynders
" "	Stephen Monfoort Elizabeth Losee	Margaret July 5, 1795	
July 23	Peter P. Lawson Jane Van Breemen	Helena July 25, 1795	
Sep. 20	Jacob Griffin Catharine Hoffman	William Hoffman Aug. 18, 1795	
Nov. 1	Matthew V. Keure Rachel Hunt	William Sep. 16, 1795	
" "	John Taylor Jane Brower	James Oct. 2, 1795	
" "	Andrew Rynders Elizabeth Leroy	Caty Oct. 14, 1795	
" "	Joseph Pinckney Mary Dearin	Samuel Oct. 1, 1795	
" "	Lewis Sniffin Jane Bogart	Israel June 9, 1795	
Dec. 25	William Lawson Maria Gulneck	Christina Nov. 15, 1795	
" "	John Dates Elizabeth Lawson	Peter Oct. 7, 1795	

The Reformed Dutch Church of New Hackensack

Date of Baptism	Parents	Name of Child and Date of Birth	Witnesses
1796			
Jan. 10	Ares Van Derbilt Maria Losee	Ares Dec. 7, 1795	
Feb. 7	Peter Van De Burgh Nelly Dutcher	Amelia Dec. 16, 1795	
" "	Peter Oudtwater Mary Kennedy	Aletta Jan. 10, 1796	
" "	Cornelius Brewer Elizabeth Brisbon	Jacob Jan. 4, 1796	
" "	Paul Overly Elizabeth Payton	Maria Jan. 9, 1796	
" "	William Lawson Mary Yates	Maria Dec. 6, 1795	
Mar. 6	Zechariah Klump Gertrude Van Sickler	Rachel Jan. 29, 1796	
" "	Casper Gons Anna Shear	Casper Feb. 13, 1796	
	Thomas Wood Mary Churchwel	William Jan. 31, 1796	
Apr. 24	Henry Diamond Amy Montross	Mary Jan. 24, 1796	
" "	John Yates Gitty Lawson	Margaret Mar. 12, 1796	
" "	William Davis Phebe Scott	Elizabeth Jan. 5, 1795	
" "	John Rosecrans Mary Hicks	Rebekah Feb. 4, 1796	
May 16	Michael De Graaf Jane De Graff	Sarah Mar. 28, 1796	
June 12	John Hageman Sitea Van Der Bilt	Ares May 7, 1796	
" "	Dowe Cornell Garretye Van Voorhees	Catharine Apr. 30, 1796	
" "	Barent Steenbergh Phebe Ferdun	John Apr. 12, 1796	
" "	David Weeks Sarah Romeyn	Isaac Apr. 16, 1796	
June 20	Sylvenus Scofield Mary Griffin	Rhoda May 14, 1782	Jacob Griffin Catherine Hoffman
July 7	Abm. Dates Elizabeth Fowler	James Dec. 30, 1795	
July 10	John Medlar Caty Lawson	{ John Nov. 27, 1793 James Apr. 17, 1796	
" "	Cornelius Van Sickler Hannah Lawson	Sally Dec. 13, 1795	
Aug. 7	Matthew Lawson Eleanor Hoffman	Daniel June 30, 1796	
Sep. 4	Abm. Ferdun Nelly Cypher	Abm. Whitman July 19, 1796	
" "	Charles Brewer Elizabeth Hoffman	Lodowick Aug. 19, 1796	

Baptismal Register

Date of Baptism	Parents	Name of Child and Date of Birth	Witnesses
Sep. 4	Benjamin V. D. Water Elizabeth Van Kleeck	Catharine Aug. 18, 1796	
Oct. 9	Abm. Lawson Rachel Ferdon	William Aug. 24, 1796	
" "	Adolph Van De Water Phebe Phillips	Susannah Sep. 11, 1796	
" "	Peter Van Kleeck Anna Van Kleeck	Hannah Aug. 6, 1796	
" "	John Meyers, Deceased Mary McFadyen	Martha June 21, 1796	
Oct. 19	Joseph Jackson Sarah Griffen	Amelia Matilda July 22, 1796	
Nov. 14	James Ackerman Sarah Conklin	Catharine Oct. 19, 1796	
" "	Michael Hoffman Catharine Van Sickler	Charles Oct. 24, 1796	Charles Hoffman Elizabeth Cypher
1797 Feb. 4	Warren Rosecrants Phebe Hoff	Anna Jan. 14, 1797	
" "	William Traver Catharine Dates	Adam Thurston Jan. 16, 1797	
" "	Jeremiah Mead Mary Shear	Jesper Jan. 15, 1797	Jesper Gons Anna Shear
Apr. 23	Jacobus Middagh Sarah Middagh	John Mar. 27, 1797	
May 21	George Black Mary Griffen	Jane Mar. 6, 1795 Cornelia Mar. 24, 1797	
" "	Daniel Hoffman Francina Leroy	Anthony Apr. 16, 1797	
" "	Simon Lawson Sarah Ferdun	Samuel Ferdun Jan. 24, 1797	
" "	Andrew Lawson Mary Clock	Peter Clock Dec. 13, 1796	
July 2	John Rosekrans Mary Hicks (twins)	Anna Maria & Hannah Eliza June 9, 1797	
" "	Philip Van Der Bilt Mary Jacobs	Hetty June 12, 1797	
" "	Abijah Patterson, Decd. Susannah Conklin	Joanna	
" "	Joseph Pinckney Mary Dearin	Charlotte June 2, 1797	
" "	William Latson Anna Dutcher	Maria May 3, 1797	
" "	Andrew Low Francina Fort	Peter Dec. 3, 1796	
" "	Benjamin Churchil Mary Bloom	Mary Nov. 7, 1796	
" "	William Philips Aletta Van Breemen	Abraham May 10, 1797	
" "	Peter Dates Anna Gulneck, Deceased	John June 10, 1797	

The Reformed Dutch Church of New Hackensack

Date of Baptism	Parents	Name of Child and Date of Birth	Witnesses
July 2	Henry Jewel Elizabeth Van Kleeck	Martha May 16, 1797	Harme Jewel Elizabeth Hilleker
" "	Benjamin Jeacocks Gertrude Ferdon	Ezekiel June 6, 1797	
July 30	William Davis Phebe Scott	John Thomas Apr. 1, 1797	
" "	John S. Hicks Nancy Divine	Caty May 27, 1797	
Aug. 24	Abraham Hoogland Aletta Brower	William Brower July 3, 1797	Wm. Brower
" "	Peter Burgaw Mary Storm	Abm. June 24, 1797	
" "	Isaac Burgaw Anna Waldron	John Jan. 20, 1797	
Aug. 27	Thomas Jeacocks Gitty Hays	Maria Jan. 9, 1797	
Sep. 24	Adrian Covenhoven Barbarah Dubois	Peter Aug. 14, 1797	
" "	Aron Cole Esther De Graff	John June 16, 1797	
" "	Stephen Monfoort Elizabeth Losee	Anna Sep. 2, 1797	
" "	Casparus Van Keure Maria Ostrum	Jacobus Aug. 12, 1797	
" "	John Dates Elizabeth Lawson	Henry Aug. 14, 1797	
" "	Isaac Brown, not baptized Hilletje Pailey	Benjamin Pailey Jan. 25, 1797	Hannah Pailey
Dec. 10	Albert I. Monfoort Altje Van Keure	Jeremiah Oct. 22, 1797	
" "	Peter Lawson Jane Van Breemen	Catharine Oct. 29, 1797	
Oct. 29	James Dearin Gertrude Jeacocks	Thomas Sep. 21, 1797	
1798 Feb. 4	Peter Van Der Burgh Nelly Dutcher	Richard Dec. 17, 1797	
" "	George Jewel Maria Maxfield	Maria Dec. 14, 1797	
" "	John Taylor Jane Brower	Catharine Sep. 8, 1797	
" "	Matthew Van Keure Rachel Hunt	John Jan. 9, 1798	
Apr. 8	James Middag Sarah Burhans	Jesse Feb. 3, 1798	
" "	John Yates Gitty Lawson	Polly Feb. 25, 1798	
" "	Peter Oudtwater Mary Kennedy	Gitty Jan. 12, 1798	
" "	Paul Overlin Elizabeth Payton	Stephen Mar. 9, 1798	
Apr. 10	Henry Schoonmaker Jane Ackerman	Edward Mar. 26, 1798	

Baptismal Register

Date of Baptism	Parents	Name of Child and Date of Birth	Witnesses
Apr. 10	Jacob Brower Catharine Brower	Eliza Feb. 9, 1798	
Apr. 29	Isaac Everett Elizabeth Hageman	Benjamin Mar. 8, 1798	
" "	Peter Miller Sarah Brisby (twins)	Hendrick & Helena Jan. 23, 1798	
" "	William Lasson Mary Yates	Gideon Apr. 6, 1798	
" "	Michal Hoffman Caty Van Sickler	Maria Mar. 20, 1798	
May 20	Douw Cornell Garretye Van Voorhees	Eliza Mar. 14, 1798	
June 17	Caspar Gons Anna Shear	Elizabeth May 24, 1798	
" "	Bernard V. Steenbergh Phebe Perdun	Jacob Perdun May 7, 1798	
June 20	Peter Van Breemer Magdalen Ackerman	Magdalen Apr. 10, 1798	
July 2	Nazareth Brower Jane Brower	Cornelius Sep. 13, 1788 Betsy Jan. 23, 1792	
" "	James Yates Sarah Van Keuren (twins)	Rachel & Margaret May 11, 1798	
" "	Aaron Phillips Catharine Lawson	Hannah Apr. 17, 1798	
" "	John Medlar Catharine Lawson	William Feb. 9, 1798	
" "	John Compton Sarah Jewel	Charles Feb. 6, 1798	
" "	John Van Tassel Abigail Smyth	Martha Nov. 1, 1788 Mary July 25, 1792	
Aug. 19	John J. Dubois Phebe Stafford	Thomas June 10, 1798	Elizabeth Dubois
" "	Michael Gulneck Elizabeth Dates	Uriah July 2, 1798	
" "	John Van Der Bilt Jane Robison	Ares June 2, 1798	
Sep. 4	John Pinckney Deborah Acker	Isaac Dec. 17, 1797	
Sep. 16	Matthew Lawson Ellenor Hoffman	Maria Aug. 14, 1798	John Dearin Maria Lawson
" "	Henry Dimon Amy Montross	Jane May 18, 1798	
Oct. 21	Warren Rosecrants Phebe Hoff	Abraham Duryee Aug. 23, 1798	
" "	James Ackerman Sarah Conklin	Hetty Ann Sep. 25, 1798	

The Reformed Dutch Church of New Hackensack

Date of Baptism	Parents	Name of Child and Date of Birth	Witnesses
Oct. 21	John Churchil / Anna Luyster	Maria / July 17, 1798	
" "	Corns. Van Sicklen / Hannah Lawson	Ferdinand / June 26, 1798	
" "	William Lawson / Maria Gulneck	Stephen / Aug. 27, 1798	
" "	Martin Gulneck / Maria Van Kleeck	Peter / Aug. 1, 1798	
" "	Peter Low / Susannah V. Kleeck	Abraham / Sep. 6, 1798	
Dec. 23	Benjamin Kennedy / Sarah Losee	Abm. Losee / Nov. 19, 1798	

("The following being forgotten, was not inserted in its proper place.")

Date of Baptism	Parents	Name of Child and Date of Birth	Witnesses
1798 July 15	Jasper Cropsie / Magdalen Ackerman	Sarah / May 31, 1798	
1799 Feb. 3	Joshua Hall / Deborah Wiltsie	Jane / Jan. 3, 1799	John Wiltsie / Jane Luckey
" "	Ares V. Der Bilt / Maria Losee	George / Dec. 28, 1798	
Mar. 3	John Hageman / Sitea Van D Bilt	Gitty / Jan. 29, 1799	
" "	John Leroy / Hannah Westervelt	John / Jan. 9, 1799	
" "	Isaac Burgaw / Anna Waldron	Abm. / Jan. 27, 1799	
" "	William Davis / Phebe Scott	Henry Dimon / Jan. 25, 1799	
" "	John J. Hicks / Anna Divine	Timothy / Jan. 30, 1799	
" "	Benjamin Churchwell / Mary Bloom	Susannah / Jan. 24, 1799	
" "	Godfrey Wolfe / Nancy Maby	Teuntje / Jan. 3, 1799	
Apr. 21	John Cook / Elizabeth Slaght	Eliza Matilda / Jan. 1, 1799	
" "	Adolph V. D. Water / Phebe Phillips	Herman / Oct. 20, 1798	
May 12	Thomas Jeacocks / Gertruy Hays	Elizabeth / Dec. 20, 1798	
" "	Thomas Dearin / Esther Lossing	Benjamin / Sep. 26, 1798	
June 9	John Dates / Elizabeth Lossing	Elizabeth / May 7, 1799	
" "	Joseph Pinckney / Mary Dearin	Susan / Mar. 25, 1799	
June 12	John M. Luyster / Catharine Van Alst	Margaret Ann / May 24, 1799	
July 7	Peter Van Kleeck / Anna Van Kleeck	Peter / June 21, 1799	
" "	Paul Middagh / Catharine Masten	Jacomina / May 12, 1799	

Baptismal Register

Date of Baptism	Parents	Name of Child and Date of Birth	Witnesses
July 7	David Burhans Elizabeth Flageler, not Baptized	Sarah May 19, 1799	
" "	Matthew P. Lawson Margaret Lawson	Magdalena May 14, 1799	
" "	John Rosecrants Mary Hicks	John Menema May 28, 1799	
" "	Cornelius Brower Elizabeth Brisben	Elizabeth Jan. 12, 1799	
" "	Benjamin Cornel Elizabeth Jackson	Clemens Apr. 7, 1799	
Aug. 4	William Letson Anna Dutcher	Richard June 21, 1799	
Sep. 8	Reuben Meyer Catharine Van Voorhis	John May 2, 1799	
" "	Adolph Brower Letty Monfoort	Jane Aug. 1, 1799	
" "	John Churchill, Junr. Anna Luyster	Catharine Luyster Aug. 4, 1799	
" "	William B. Ver Plank Melinda Gordon	Mary Ann Catharine July 22, 1799	
Sep. 11	Henry Dodge, not baptized Sarah Rosecrants	Susan Maria Aug. 23, 1799	
Oct. 10	Ezekiel Viele Adriana Van Duyn	Ezekiel Aug. 31, 1799	
Oct. 13	Zechariah Klump Gertruy Van Sickler	Anna Aug. 30, 1799	
" "	Aaron Cole Esther De Graff	Catharine Aug. 9, 1799	
" "	Henry Schoonmaker Jane Ackerman	Henry Sep. 24, 1799	
" "	Simon Lawson, Junr. Sarah Ferdon	John Aug. 28, 1799	
" "	William Van Keure Margaret Lawson	James Sep. 11, 1799	
Nov. 10	George Jewel Mary Maxfield	Harme Sep. 7, 1799	
" "	William Phillips Alida Van Breemen	Caty Oct. 18, 1799	
" "	Benjamin Jeacocks Gertrude Ferdon	Caty Oct. 5, 1799	
Dec. 8	Benjamin V. D. Water Elizabeth Van Kleeck	Nelly Maxfield Nov. 25, 1799	
Dec. 29	John R. Todd Clarissa Cheesebrough	Robert Polaski Oct. 11, 1799	
1800 Jan. 18	George Black Mary Griffen	Henry Nov. 11, 1799	
" "	Daniel Hoffman Francina Leroy	John Dec. 22, 1799	
" "	John Taylor Jane Brower	Nazareth Sep. 12, 1799	
Feb. 23	Andrew Reynders Elizabeth Leroy	Amelia Caroline Jan. 11, 1800	

The Reformed Dutch Church of New Hackensack

Date of Baptism	Parents	Name of Child and Date of Birth	Witnesses
Feb. 23	Peter Van De Bogart Hannah Van Kleeck	Anna Nov. 18, 1799	
" "	John Du Bois Frances Stanford (twins)	Richard Woolsey & Ezekiel Stilwell Dec. 11, 1799	
" "	Jonathan Jeacocks Sarah De Graff	Sarah Jan. 20, 1800	
" "	Henry Jewel Elizabeth Van Kleeck	Caty Dec. 28, 1799	
Mar. 23	Peter Burgaw Mary Storm	Letty Catharine Jan. 19, 1800	
Apr. 20	Caspar Gons Anna Shear (twins)	Abm. & Israel Feb. 2, 1800	Israel Shear Anna Cramer
" "	Benjn. P. Lossing Rebekah O. Ferrel	Jane Feb. 3, 1800	Henry Schoonmaker Jane Ackerman
" "	Abm. A. Ferdon Gitty Lossing	Thomas Jeacocks Mar. 1, 1800	
May 18	Abm. Van Keure Nelly Wiltsie	John Apr. 26, 1800	John Wiltsie Jane Lucky
" "	Matthew V. Keure Rachel Hunt	Matthew Apr. 21, 1800	
" "	John Yates Gitty Lawson	Anna Mar. 22, 1800	
" "	James Ackerman Sarah Conklin	Tunis Apr. 21, 1800	
" "	Warren Rosecrants Phebe Hoff	Hannah Eliza Mar. 19, 1800	
June 15	Theodorus Vallo Elizabeth Jewel	Henry Apr. 17, 1800	
" "	Matthew Walker Euphemia Ogdon	Gideon Allen Apr. 7, 1800	
July 13	Aaron Low Amley Sabin	Cynthia Mar. 16, 1800	
" "	Benjamin Kennedy Sarah Losee	Hannah June 16, 1800	
Aug. 10	William Lawson Mary Yates	Margaret June 4, 1800	
" "	Aaron Phillips Catharine Lawson	Eliza Apr. 21, 1800	
Sep. 21	Derrick V Arsdalen Elizabeth Reynders	Maria Aug. 25, 1800	
" "	John H. Jewel Tryntye Reynders	Caty July 30, 1800	
" "	James Latsel Maria Edwards	Elizabeth June 3, 1800	John Dates Elizabeth Lassing
" "	Douw Cornell Garre Van Voorhis	John Aug. 13, 1800	
Oct. 23	John Nagel Elizabeth Reynolds	James Van Beuron Sep. 5, 1800	
" "	Peter Van Breemen Magdalen Ackerman	David Aug. 15, 1800	

Baptismal Register

Date of Baptism	Parents	Name of Child and Date of Birth	Witnesses
Oct. 26	Oliver Green, not baptized Jacomina Van Bunschooten	Henry Sep. 7, 1800	Tunis Van Bunschooten Elizabeth V. De Burgh
" "	Samuel Van Voorhis Sarah Cooper	Obadiah Sep. 1, 1800	
" "	Thomas Jeacocks Gertrude Hays	Jonathan Sep. 29, 1800	
Nov. 23	James Yates Sarah Van Keure	John Oct. 30, 1800	
" "	James G. Middagh Sarah Burhans	Eliza Oct. 4, 1800	
" "	Jacob Brouwer Catharine Brouwer	David Sep. 14, 1800	
1801 Jan. 4	John Cornel Phebe Pollock	Peter Oct. 10, 1800	Peter Cornel Elizabeth Becker
Feb. 1	John Shear Margaret Cornell	Anna Oct. 31, 1800	
" "	Isaac Everett Elizabeth Hageman	Esther Dec. 28, 1800	
" "	Henry Diamond Amy Montross	Gitty Dec. 15, 1800	
" "	Francis McKerrick Margaret Filkins	Caty Oct. 20, 1800	
Mar. 1	John Leroy Hannah Westervelt	Joseph Feb. 3, 1801	
" "	Myndert De Graff Penelope Van Kleeck	Stephen Jan. 24, 1801	
" "	John Churchwell Anna Luyster	Hetty Ann Jan. 10, 1801	
" "	John Monfoort Rachel Van Kleeck	Anna Maria Jan. 17, 1801	
Mar. 29	John Dates Elizabeth Lossing	Cornelia Jan. 21, 1801	
" "	John (S). Hicks Anna Divine	Hannah Feb. 10, 1801	
May 24	George Lossing Elizabeth Buck	Martin Dec. 7, 1800	
" "	James I. Middagh Sarah Middagh	Lena Apr. 13, 1801	
" "	Stephen Monfoort Elizabeth Losee	Francis Losee Mar. 30, 1801	
" "	Abraham Storm Mary Adriance	John Adriance Mar. 2, 1801	
May 24	John Tarepenny Hester Middagh	Rebeckah Apr. 17, 1801	
" "	Paul Flageler Catharine Paley	William Feb. 28, 1801	
" "	Simon Tarepenny Tine Van Bunschooten	Jane Feb. 12, 1801	
" "	Peter Van Breemen Polly Vail, not baptized	Catharine Feb. , 1801	
June 21	Abraham Philips, Junr. Elizabeth Brinckerhoff	Maria Apr. 14, 1801	

The Reformed Dutch Church of New Hackensack

Date of Baptism	Parents	Name of Child and Date of Birth	Witnesses
June 21	John Lucky Rachel Dearin	Charles Apr. 4, 1801	
" "	James Monger Margaret Divine	Christian Mar. 3, 1801	
" "	Andrew Lossing Mary Clock	Sarah Oct. 8, 1800	
" "	Joseph Harris Elizabeth Tarepenny	Joseph Feb. 5, 1801	
July 19	Philip Heermance Mary McBride	Sarah May 12, 1801	
" "	John H. DuBois Mary Cowenhoven	Catharine May 12, 1801	
Aug. 16	Paul Overly Elizabeth Payton	John July 4, 1801	
" "	Joseph Pinckney Mary Dearin	John Dearin Mar. 20, 1801	
Sep. 13	Thomas G. Willet Sarah Brett	Mary July 6, 1801	
" "	Isaac Burgaw Anna Waldron	Cornelia Ann Aug. 1, 1801	
Sep. 24	John Van Der Bilt Jane Robison	John Robison Aug. 9, 1801	
Oct. 8	William Hoffman Deborah Leroy	Peter Sep. 16, 1801	
" "	Edward Earle Sitea Van Duyn	John Sep. 26, 1800	
Oct. 11	John Rosecrants Mary Hicks	Mima Aug. 21, 1801	
" "	Abm. Ferdon Gitty Lossing	Caty Aug. 15, 1801	
" "	Cornelius Brower Elizabeth Brisben	Samuel Pinckney Aug. 9, 1801	
Nov. 8	Casper Gons Anna Shear	Samuel Oct. 14, 1801	
" "	Matthew Lossing Eleanor Hoffman	John Oct. 5, 1801	
" "	Willm. Van Keuren Margaret Lossing	Anna Maria Oct. 16, 1801	
" "	Nathaniel Smith Sally Patterson	Maria Eliza Sep. 27, 1801	
" "	Adolph Brower Letty Monfoort	Maria Oct. 16, 1801	
Dec. 6	Reuben Myer, not baptized Catharine Van Voorhis	Nancy Laurence Sep. 26, 1801	
" "	Abraham Wood, not baptized Catharine Jacobs	Hetty Aug. 24, 1801	
1802 Jan. 17	Thomas Spencer Mary Jewel	Elizabeth Sep. 20, 1801	
" "	Barnet Van Steenbergh Phebe Ferdon	Simon Dec. 16, 1801	
" "	Arie Cole Esther De Graff	Esther Nov. 17, 1801	

Baptismal Register

Date of Baptism	Parents	Name of Child and Date of Birth	Witnesses
Feb. 14	William Letsel Anna Dutcher	Charlotte Dec. 20, 1801	
" "	Godfrey Woolvin Nancy Mabie	Samuel Dec. 8, 1801	
" "	John Taylor Jane Brower	John Brower Oct. 25, 1801	
" "	Benjamin Lossing Rebekah Ferrel	Peter Lossing Oct. 28, 1801	
" "	Abraham Storm Eve Copeman	Abraham Dec. 12, 1801	
" "	Garret Van Duyn Maria Monfoort	Garret Monfoort Jan. 3, 1802	
" "	Peter Miller Sarah Brisben	Jane Nov. 26, 1801	
" "	Cornelius Brower Charlotte Green	Eliza Dec. 17, 1801	
Mar. 14	John Bishop Sarah Van Breemer	William Jan. 23, 1802	
Apr. 11	John Pelts Maria Monfoort	Suky Dec. 7, 1801	
" "	John Hageman Sitea Van Der Bilt	Anna Feb. 8, 1802	
" "	William Phillips Alida Van Breemen	Letty Feb. 7, 1802	
" "	Aurt Middagh Lena Van Vliet	John Feb. 25, 1802	
" "	David Burhans Elizabeth Flageler	Peter Feb. 10, 1802	
" "	John Yates Gitty Lossing	John Jan. 24, 1802	
" "	Francis McKerric Margaret Filkins	Amy Diamond Feb. 23, 1802	
June 6	Simon Lossing Sarah Ferdon	Abraham Mar. 2, 1802	
" "	William Traver Catharine Dates	Elias Feb. 12, 1800 Ann Eliza Jan. 12, 1802	
July 4	Daniel Tomkins Hester Odell	Walter Odell Feb. 12, 1802	James Odell Hester Cole
" "	William Stoutenburgh Elizabeth Concklin	Tunis May 9, 1802	
Aug. 1	William Lossing Mary Yates	Rachel June 24, 1802	
" "	William Ferdun Hannah Westervelt	Abraham Feb. 7, 1802	
" "	Abraham Van Keure Eleanor Wiltsie	Deborah July 2, 1802	
" "	Thomas Dean Esther Lossing	John June 12, 1802	
" "	Daniel Wright Mary Jeacocks	Sarah July 21, 1802	
Aug. 29	Derick Van nosdall Elizabeth Reynders	Margaret Aug. 3, 1802	

The Reformed Dutch Church of New Hackensack

Date of Baptism	Parents	Name of Child and Date of Birth	Witnesses
		"The two following items were omitted from their proper place."	
1802			
May 9	Abm. Van Horne Jemima V Bunschooten	James Feb. 8, 1802	
" "	Peter Van Kleeck Anna Van Kleeck	Deborah Mar. 16, 1802	
Sep. 23	Adolph Van De Water Phebe Phillips	John Aug. 7, 1800 Phebe June 30, 1802	
Sep. 26	Zachariah Klump Gitty Van Sickler	Samuel Aug. 19, 1802	
" "	Benjamin Kennedy Sarah Losee	Jane Aug. 8, 1802	
Oct. 24	Henry Du Bois Nelly Covenhovin	Adrian Sep. 18, 1802	
" "	George Black Mary Griffin	Maria May 27, 1802	
" "	Thomas T. Jeacocks Gertrude Hays	Rachel Aug. 16, 1802	
" "	Myndert V. De Bogert Hannah Forguson	Anna Maria Aug. 3, 1802	
" "	Warren Rosecrans Phebe Haff	Susannah Aug. 25, 1802	
Nov. 21	John Churchwell Anna Luyster	Jane May 17, 1802	
" "	John S. Hicks Anna Divine	William Oct. 14, 1802	
" "	Paul Middagh Catharine Maston	Henry Oct. 15, 1802	
" "	Henry Dutcher Mary Van Ieveren	Mary Ann Sep. 15, 1802	
1803			
Feb. 16	Douw Cornell Garretye V. Voorhis	Elias Jan. 13, 1803	
" "	Nazareth Brower Deborah Wiltsie	Harriet Feb. 4, 1803	
" "	Hall, deceased Deborah Wiltsie	Elisha July 12, 1795	Nazareth Brower
Feb. 27	Daniel Warren Elizabeth Hicks	John Robison Nov. 11, 1802	
" "	John Luckey Rachel Dearin	Thomas Pinckney Jan. 3, 1803	
Mar. 27	John Leroy Hannah Westervelt	Levi Feb. 21, 1803	
" "	John Monfoort Rachel Van Kleeck	Aletta Jan. 7, 1803	
" "	Henry Diamond Amy Montross	Joseph Jan. 27, 1803	
" "	John Nagel Elizabeth Reynolds	Barnet Feb. 4, 1803	
Apr. 4	Joseph Towne Elizabeth Merrit	Thomas Merrit July 14, 1792	

Baptismal Register

Date of Baptism	Parents	Name of Child and Date of Birth	Witnesses
Apr. 4	John Lossing Elizabeth Merrit	Anna, Dec. 26, 1796 Elizabeth, Dec. 25, 1798 Mary, Feb. 4, 1800 Hannah, July 12, 1801	
May 22	Peter Van De Bogert Hannah Van Kleeck	Aert Middagh Apr. 15, 1803	
" "	Daniel Hoffman Francina Leroy	Sally Apr. 12, 1803	
" "	John Cornwell Phebe Pollock	James Feb. 27, 1803	
" "	Matthew Van Keure Rachel Hunt	Susan Sep. 11, 1802	
" "	Aaron Phillips Catharine Lossing	Catharine Oct. 7, 1802	
" "	Moses Van Kleeck Jane Monfoort, Deceased	Monfoort Apr. 1, 1803	Dominicus Monfoort Anna Van Kleek, his wife
" "	James Yates Sarah Van Keuren	Polly Mar. 20, 1803	
" "	John Luyster Catharine Van Alst	Letty Maria Hulst Apr. 1, 1803	
" "	John Rosekrants Maria Hicks	Catharine Jan. 10, 1803	
" "	John Shear Margaret Cornell	Catharine Eliza Apr. 8, 1803	
May 25	Peter Cornwell Elizabeth Becker	Maria Eliza Feb. 3, 1803	
June 19	William Van Keure Margaret Lossing	Geertje Jeacocks May 10, 1803	
" "	James Ackerman Sarah Concklin	Jane Ann May 13, 1803	
July 17	Joseph Harris, Esqr. Elizabeth Tarepenny	Jane May 5, 1803	
" "	Peter P. Lossing Jane Van Breemen	Eliza June 17, 1803	
" "	Isaac Burgaw Anna Waldron	Andrew Crimshier May 29, 1803	
" "	Robt. Van Amburgh Freelove Du Bois	Jane Ann Apr. 5, 1803	
Aug. 23	Benjamin V. Keure Jacoba Van Kleeck	Benjamin July 12, 1803	
Sep. 11	Timothy Hicks Adriana Heermance	John Menema July 30, 1803	
" "	John Patterson Hannah Fowler	Anna Maria July 24, 1803	
" "	Benjamin Jeacocks Gertrude Ferdun	Robert Wiltsie Aug. 26, 1803	
" "	Andrew Losee Mary Clock	William Wilson Nov. 10, 1802	
" "	Abraham Lossing Rachel Ferdun	Mary July 23, 1803	

The Reformed Dutch Church of New Hackensack

Date of Baptism	Parents	Name of Child and Date of Birth	Witnesses
Oct. 9	Francis McKerric Margaret Filkins	Francis Sep. 11, 1803	
" "	Paul Overly Elizabeth Payton	Caty Aug. 17, 1803	
" "	John Low Eunice Palmer	Sally Ann July 24, 1803	
" "	Peter Haff Hannah Thrasher	Catharine Aug. 31, 1803	Catharine Haff
Nov. 3	John Bishop Sarah Van Breemen	Gabriel Sep. 9, 1803	
" "	William Hoffman Deborah Leroy	Peter Anthony Sep. 23, 1803	
Nov. 6	Thomas Willet Sarah Brett	James July 8, 1803	
1804 Jan. 1	William Todd Margaret Wiley, not baptized	Eliza Love Sep. 25, 1802	
" "	John H. Du Bois Mary Covinhoven	Barbara Ann Nov. 24, 1803	
Feb. 1	Henry Cramer Sarah Sherwood	Catharine May 9, 1799 Betsy Feb. 8, 1802	
Feb. 26	Zachariah Klump Gertruy Van Sickler	Harriot Feb. 4, 1804	
" "	George Middagh Elizabeth Bazeman	Aert Feb. 10, 1804	
" "	Daniel Warren Elizabeth Hicks	Lydia Dec. 16, 1803	
Apr. 19	Garret Borrome Sally Schoonmaker	Henry Mar. 18, 1804	Jane Ackerman
Apr. 22	William Letsel Anna Dutcher	Joseph Rogers Mar. 22, 1804	
Apr. 25	Samuel Bogardus Hannah Ackerman	John Ackerman Nov. 30, 1803	

BAPTISMAL REGISTER OF THE CONGREGATION OF NEW HACKENSACK DURING THE MINISTRY OF GEORGE BARKULO, V.D.M.

Date of Baptism	Parents	Name of Child and Date of Birth	Witnesses
1805 Dec. 1	Paul Middagh Catharine Maston	Thomas Casey	
Dec. 1	Robert Van Amber Freelove Du Bois	Jacob	
Dec. 15	Henry Jewel Elizabeth, his wife	Gitty Feb. 14, 1805	
" "	William H. Philipps Letty Van Bramer	Caroline May 11, 1805	
1806 Jan. 26	Joseph Harris Elizabeth, his wife	Eliza Nov. 18, 1805	
" "	Samuel Luckey, Junr. Mary Underhill	Mary Ann Oct. 11, 1805	
" "	Henry Dymon Amy Montross	Emeline May 16, 1805	

Baptismal Register

Date of Baptism	Parents	Name of Child and Date of Birth	Witnesses
Jan. 26	John Dearin Annatie Van Keuren	Anne Maria Dec. 1, 1805	
" "	John Lawson Elizabeth Merritt	Rachel Losee Aug. 19, 1805	
" "	Samuel Bogardus Hannah Ackerman	Francis Aug. 12, 1805	
Feb. 9	John Miller, not baptized Margaret Emans	Sarah Emans Sep. 6, 1805	
" "	Benjamin Van Keuren Jacoba V. Kleeck	Anne Maria Wiltsie Sep. 4, 1805	
" "	Nathaniel Smith Sarah Patterson	Patience Jan. 21, 1806	
Feb. 23	John Nagle Elizabeth Reynolds	George	
Mar. 31	Joseph Rogers Cornelia Waldron	Susan Ann Dec. 9, 1805	
Apr. 6	Casper Gonse Anne Shear	Henry Mar. 6, 1806	
" "	Jacobus Monfoort Ruth Van Voorhis	James Feb. 26, 1806	
Apr. 20	Reuben Meirs Catharine V. Voorhis	Abraham Dec. 6, 1805	
" "	John C. Shear Margaret Cornell	Israel Feb. 26, 1806	
May 4	John Cornwell Phebe Polluck	Hannah Eliza Mar. 19, 1806	
" "	William Lawson Mary Yates	James May 4, 1805	

These two were baptized by the Revd. Cornelius Brower.

June 1	John Luckey Rachel Dearin	Gitty Apr. 22, 1806	
" "	Joseph Pinckney Mary Dearin	Thomas Feb. 24, 1806	
" "	Timothy Hicks Adriantie Heermance	James May 13, 1805	
June 15	Peter Leroy Phebe Lawson	Anna Maria Apr. 22, 1806	
" "	Peter Waldron Edy Swartwout	Alletie Swartwout Apr. 13, 1806	
" "	Cornelius W. Brewer Elizabeth Green	Garrit Apr. 28, 1806	
July 13	William Lawson Anne Dutcher	Stephen V. Voorhis July 19, 1806	
July 30	Tcharick Monfoot Elizabeth Rynders	James V. Keuren Nov. 27, 1805	
Aug. 31	John Pells Maria Monfoort	Margaret Ann July 23, 1806	
Sep. 4	Nazareth Brewer Deborah Wiltsie	{ Henry Sep. 18, 1804 { William June 18, 1806	
" "	John Bishop, not baptized Sarah Van Bramer	Peter Oct. 24, 1805	

The Reformed Dutch Church of New Hackensack

Date of Baptism	Parents	Name of Child and Date of Birth	Witnesses
Sep. 4	Joshua Bishop, not baptized Rachel Dearin	Caty June 16, 1806	
" "	Derick Van Arstdalen Elizabeth Rynders	Sarah Apr. 3, 1804 Elizabeth May 11, 1806	
" "	Charles Brewer Elizabeth Hoffman	Catharine Ellenor Feb: 19, 1805	
" "	James C. Bogardus Mary Scutt	Cornelius Jan. 21, 1802 Sarah Ann Mar. 23, 1804 Amelia Apr. 19, 1806	
Sep. 28	Paul Overling Elizabeth "Batin or Patin"	Auly Apr. 9, 1806	
Oct. 12	Francis McCarrick Margaret Philkins	Eliza Sep. 6, 1806	
Dec. 21	Adrian Hageman Mary Hoffman	Jane Sep. 13, 1806	
" "	James Ackerman Sarah Concklin	Maria Nov. 7, 1806	
Dec. 22	Isaac Hansan, not baptized Anne Luyster	Catharine Nov. 21, 1806	
1807 Jan. 4	John T. Leroy Hannah Westervelt	Stephen Nov. 17, 1806	
Feb. 11	Gerrit Van Duyn Maria Monfoort	Oliver Nov. 17, 1806	
" "	Oliver Green Jemima Van Bunschoten	Sarah Dec. 30, 1806	
Apr. 5	Peter Wyckhoff Syta Van-derbilt	Syntie Maria Feb. 26, 1807	
" "	Peter P. Lawson Jane Van Bramer	Sarah Ann Feb. 20, 1807	
" "	Ares Van Derbilt Maria Losee	Philip Feb. 6, 1807	
Apr. 22	John Taylor Jane Brewer	Sarah Maria Nov. 19, 1806	
" "	Abraham Ferdun Gitty Lawson	John Jan. 22, 1807	
" "	John Wiltsie, Junr. Rebecca Gilliland	James Gilliland Dec. 4, 1806	
" "	Jacob Ferdun Sarah Lawson	Wyntie Sep. 13, 1806	
July 26	Peter Hageman Phebe Bogardus	Sytie Ann May 3, 1807	
Aug. 9	Bernard Velie Charlotte Shear	Israel Cromeline May 26, 1807	
" "	John Sypher Mary Cornwell	William Dec. 11, 1806	
Oct. 11	William Lawson Mary Yates	Charles Aug. 8, 1807	

Baptismal Register

Date of Baptism	Parents	Name of Child and Date of Birth	Witnesses
Oct. 11	Samuel Luckey, Junr. Mary Underhill	Robert Thompson Sep. 17, 1807	
" "	William Burhans Mary Smith	Henry Aug. 16, 1807	
Nov. 8	Peter A. Vandervoort Hannah V. Kleeck	Jeremiah V. Kleeck July 5, 1807	
" "	John H. June Catharine Rynders	John Rynders Mar. 9, 1807	
Dec. 6	John Bishop, not baptd. Sarah Van Bramer	Angeline Catharine Oct. 4, 1807	
1808 Jan. 17	David Tidd, not baptized Caty Luyster	Emeline Nov. 12, 1807	
" "	Henry Dubois Nelly Covenhoven	Barbary Dec. 4, 1807	
Feb. 28	John Millar, not baptized Margaret Emans	Letty June 3, 1807	
Mar. 2	Henry Jewel Elizabeth V. Kleeck	Eliza Ann Dec. 5, 1807	
" "	Joseph Rogers Cornelia Waldron	Alston Nov. 16, 1807	
" "	Adrian Hageman Maria Hoffman	John Jan. 29, 1808	
Mar. 7	Roeluf Van Voorhis Gashie Childs	Roeluf Augustus Sep. 13, 1807	
" "	William Conner Catharine Bogert	Eliza Apr. 19, 1805 / Anne Maria July 26, 1807	
" "	Tcharick Monfoort Elizabeth Rynders	Daniel Nov. 8, 1807	
" "	Martin Monfoort Catharine Dutcher, not baptized	Susannah Jan. 18, 1808	
Mar. 13	Simon Lawson Mary Miller	Sally Ellenor Dec. 18, 1807	
Mar. 27	Nazareth Brewer Deborah Wiltsie	Philip V. Cortlandt Mar. 7. 1808	
Apr. 24	Thomas T. Jacocks Gitty Hays	Helen Oct. 27, 1807	
May 29	Reuben Meirs, not baptized Catharine Van Voorhis	Phebe Jan. 13, 1808	
June 6	John Monfoort Rachel Van Kleeck	Jane Ann Mar. 25, 1808	
June 12	Thomas P. Lawson Eliza Lawson	Martha Mar. 28, 1808	
" "	John J. Leroy Hannah Westervelt	Mary Elizabeth Mar. 22, 1808	
" "	Silas Tidd, not baptzd. Mary Ostrander	Adelia Apr. 9, 1808	
July 24	John Pells Maria Monfoort	John June 23, 1808	
" "	Oliver Green Jemima Van Bunschoten	Mary June 4, 1808	

The Reformed Dutch Church of New Hackensack

Date of Baptism	Parents	Name of Child and Date of Birth	Witnesses
Aug. 7	Charles Griffin Mary Brewer	Cornelius Feb. 26, 1808	
" "	William Van Keuren Margaret Lawson	William Jacocks June 12, 1808	
" "	Peter Van Derbilt Mary Everitt	Mary Johannah May 20, 1808	
Aug. 21	Abraham Staats Hannah Davis	Phebe Ann Dec. 18, 1807	
" "	Richard Snedecor Phebe Jewel	Elizabeth June 29, 1808	
Sep. 18	John Sypher Mary Cornwell	James Henry Aug. 18, 1808	
" "	Matthew Lawson Sarah Lynderson	Mary Ann Aug. 18, 1808	
Oct. 16	Abraham T. Phillips Jane Phillips (twins)	James Henry & William Edward Aug. 27, 1808	
Oct. 30	Benjamin Shear Sytie Cornell	Catharine Ann Aug. 10, 1808	
" "	George Barkulo Hannah Seward	Seward Sep. 22, 1808	
" "	Joseph Pinckney, not baptized Mary Dearin	Joseph Augustus July 3, 1808	
Dec. 11	John Cornwell Phebe Pullock	Cornelia Ann Sep. 18, 1808	
Dec. 25	Theodorus Van Sicklen Phebe Bloom	Jemima Oct. 21, 1808	
" "	James Ackerman Sarah Concklin	Helen Oct. 24, 1808	
" "	William Lawson Anne Dutcher	Margaret Sep. 12, 1808	
1809 Feb. 19	Elias Van Bunschotin Syntie Veelie	John Dec. 5, 1808	
" "	Peter Hageman Phebe Bogardus	Mary Eliza Dec. 5, 1808	
" "	Jacob Weaver Jane Van Keuren	Michael Dec. 17, 1808	
" "	Joshua Bishop, not baptzd. Rachel Dearin	Caleb Nov. 19, 1808	
Feb. 23	Jacob A. Ferdun Sarah Lawson	Caty Maria Dec. 6, 1808	
" "	Aaron Philipps Catharine Lawson	Emeline Nov. 15, 1808	
" "	Benjamin B. Van Keuren Jacoba Van Kleeck	Catharine Oct. 5, 1808	
Feb. 23	Abraham Ferdun Gitty Lawson	Anthony Jan. 26, 1809	
" "	John Green Elizabeth Brewer	George Remer Jan. 25, 1809	
Mar. 5	Peter P. Lawson Jane Van Bramer	Julia Ann Feb. 5, 1809	

Baptismal Register

Date of Baptism	Parents	Name of Child and Date of Birth	Witnesses
Apr. 22	Abraham Dates Elizabeth Fowler	Hannah Mar. 30, 1798 Peter Oct. 27, 1800 Jane Ann Feb. 12, 1803 Sarah Mar. 2, 1805 Eliza Mar. 18, 1807	
Apr. 23	Casper Gonse Anne Shear	William Edwin	
July 30	Simon Lawson Mary Millar	Simon June 10, 1809	
Sep. 17	John Millar, not baptzd. Margaret Emans	Alfred May 30, 1809	
Nov. 19	Abraham Dates Elizabeth Fowler	Harriet Oct. 21, 1809	
Dec. 3	Thomas T. Jacocks Gertrude Hays	Jane Oct. 1, 1809	
" "	James Carter Wilhelmyntie Jacox	Gitty Maria Oct. 8, 1809	
Dec. 20	Garrit Van Duyn Maria Monfoort	John Jan. 30, 1809	
" "	Uriah Cornwell Phebe Thrasher, not baptized	Margaret Ann Feb. 5, 1808 Peter Luyster July 21, 1809	
1810 Jan. 4	John Monfoort Rachel Van Kleeck	Albert Oct. 7, 1809	
Jan. 25	Samuel Luckey, Junr. Mary Underhill	James Edgar Nov. 7, 1809	James Luckey Margaret Dearin
Jan. 30	Zachariah Medler Elizabeth Ferdun	Jane Oct. 7, 1805 Zachariah Aug. 20, 1807 Peter Sep. 18, 1809	
Feb. 25	Henry A. Monfoort Maria Philipps	Albert Nov. 9, 1809	
" "	Cornelius Klump Jane Luckey	John Luckey Oct. 14, 1809	
June 29	Nazareth Brewer Deborah Wiltsie	Sally Ann Apr. 4, 1810	
" "	Thomas P. Lawson Eliza Lawson	Peter Apr. 1, 1810	
" "	John Luckey Rachel Dearin, deceased	Rachel May 16, 1810	
" "	Charles Brewer Elizabeth Hoffman	Charles June 16, 1807 Michael June 15, 1810	

The Reformed Dutch Church of New Hackensack

Date of Baptism	Parents	Name of Child and Date of Birth	Witnesses
June 29	John Nagle Elizabeth Reynolds	Henry Apr. 28, 1810	
July 8	Peter Van Derbilt Mary Everitt	Benjamin Everitt	
July 22	Matthew Lawson Sarah Lynderson	Elizabeth Jane June 22, 1810	
Oct. 21	Joshua Bishop, not baptized Rachel Dearin	James Dearin Sep. 17, 1810	John Dearin
" "	William Lawson Mary Yates	Letty Ann Sep. 27, 1810	
" "	John Pells Maria Monfoort	Nelly Maria Aug. 13, 1810	
Dec. 27	John Sleght Alletie Swartwout	John Swartwout Oct. 22, 1810	
1811 Feb. 20	Reuben Meirs, not baptized Caty Van Voorhis	Warren Delancy Nov. 24, 1810	
1812 Jan. 12	Derick T. Brinkerhoff Margaret Schenck or Brett, deceased	Abraham, Oct. 6, 1798 George D., Feb. 3, 1801 Catharine, Feb. 21, 1803 Mary Ann, Oct. 13, 1805 William, Jan. 5, 1808 Margaret, Apr. 3, 1810	
" "	Derick T. Brinkerhoff Magdelen Monfoort	Helen Oct. 2, 1811	
Feb. 18	Cornelius Klump Jane Luckey	Samuel Dec. 27, 1811	
" "	Robert Van Amber Freelove Dubois	John Dubois June 13, 1811	
" "	William Van Keuren Margaret Lawson	Peter Apr. 11, 1811	
" "	Abraham Ferdun Gertrude Lawson	Robert Mar. 5, 1811	
" "	Henry Bogardus Gertrude Dearin	James Jan. 3, 1812	
" "	Henry Dymon Amy Montross	Clarinda, Nov. 14, 1807 Cromeline, Mar. 28, 1810	
" "	Jacob Weaver Jane Van Keuren	Abraham Feb. 7, 1810	
1811 July 7	Adonjah Palmer Mary Rynders	Phebe Jan. 28, 1811	
Oct. 13	Charick Monfort Elizebeth Rynders	Jane Sep. 5, 1810	

Baptismal Register

Date of Baptism	Parents	Name of Child and Date of Birth	Witnesses
Oct. 26	Samuel Luckey, Junr. Mary Underhill	Hellen Sep. 21, 1811	
" "	Peter P. Lawson Jane Vn. Bramer	Susan July 13, 1811	
Dec. 8	David Tidd Catherine Luyster	Peter Sep. 30, 1811	
" "	Abraham L. Dates Elizabeth Fowler	Henry Oct. 11, 1811	
Dec. 10	John C. Shear Margaret Cornell	John Cornell Oct. 12, 1811	
1812 Mar. 9	Richard Snedeker Phebe Jewell	Mar. 3, 1810	
July 18	John Cornwell Phebe Pollock	Robert June 30, 1811	

REGISTER OF BAPTISMS IN THE CONGREGATION OF NEW HACKENSACK
DURING THE MINISTRY OF THOMAS DE WITT
TO THE CHARGE OF WHICH HE WAS ORDAINED—NOV. 24, 1812.

Those marked * did not present their children.

1812 Nov. 26	Nazareth Brewer Deborah Wiltsie	George Clinton Mar. 17, 1812	
Dec. 6	William J. Dearin Jane Luckey	Gertrude July 17, 1812	
1813 Jan. 19	Oliver Green Jemima Vn. Bunschoten	Cornelia Apr. 26, 1812	
Jan. 19	John Van Der Bilt Jane Robinson*	Philip Beekman Sep. 7, 1809	
	Leonard Lewis Catherine Hoffman	Thomas May 24, 1812	
Jan. 29		Phebe Gomer, an adult Black, on confession of her faith	
Jan. 29		Betty Little, an adult black, on confession of her faith	
July 4	Henry DuBois Nelly Covenhoven	Sarah Ann Maria May 16, 1813	
July 4	Reuben Myers* Catherine Vn. Voorhis	Ellen Apr. 14, 1813	
Aug. 31	Robert Van Amburgh* Freelove Du Bois	Harriet Apr. 7, 1813	
Aug. 31	William Todd Margaret Wildey*	Esther July 13, 1813	
Nov. 7	Henry A. Monfoort Maria Phillips	Letty Maria Oct. 24	
Dec. 29	John Monfoort Rachel Van Kleeck	{ Barbara Eve Oct. 25, 1811 Celia Oct. 20, 1813	
Dec. 29	John A. Monfoort Jane Monfoort	Ellen Maria Sep. 2, 1813	
Dec. 29	Joseph Rogers Cornelia Waldron	Cornelia Nov. 16, 1813	

The Reformed Dutch Church of New Hackensack

Date of Baptism	Parents	Name of Child and Date of Birth	Witnesses
1814			
Jan. 2	John Pells Maria Monfoort	Sarah Eliza Nov. 1, 1813	
Jan. 7	Ares Vanderbelt Maria Losee	Peter Nov. 2, 1813	
Feb. 27	Abraham L. Dates Elizabeth Fowler	Maria Matilda Feb. 12, 1814	
May 20	Abraham A. Adriance Maria Bragaw	Anna Maria Mar. 13, 1814	
June 9	Samuel Luckey, Junr. Mary Underhill	Jane Mar. 28, 1814	
June 9	William J. Dearin Jane Luckey	Mary Ann Apr. 10, 1814	
June 19	Leonard T. Lewis Catherine Hoffman	Sarah Feb. 22, 1814	
July 21	Nazareth Brewer Deborah Wiltsie	Robert June 30, 1814	
Aug. 4	Adam Dates Rebecca Westervelt	Casparus Westervelt May 27, 1814	
Sep. 23		Catherine Dutcher, wife of Martin Monfoort, an adult, on confession of her faith	
Oct. 23	Martin Monfoort Catherine Dutcher	{ Hiram Mar. 21, 1810 Catherine Oct. 28, 1812	
Dec. 13	Richard Snediker Phoebe Jewell	{ Richard Mar. 31, 1812 Jane Ann Aug. 31, 1814	
Dec. 27	Cornelius Klump Jane Luckey	Peter June 18, 1814	
1815			
Jan. 27		James Dodge, an adult, on confession of his faith	
Jan. 27		Phoebe Platt, an adult, on confession of her faith	
Jan. 27	James Dodge Electa Seward	Catherine Nov. 14, 1814	
Mar. 12	Peter Dates, Deceased Jane Todd	Eliza Ann Jan. 20, 1815	
Mar. 26	John Cornwell Phoebe Pollock (twins)	Henry Benjamin & Sarah Maria Dec. 26, 1814	
June 18	Martin Monfoort Catherine Dutcher	Schenck May 30, 1815	
June 2		Helen Dodge, an adult, on confession of her faith Saul Gomaer } Blacks, on confession of their Susan, his wife } faith	
Aug. 13	William Hoogland Caroline Covenhoven	Nelly June 25, 1815	
(This entry is in a different handwriting and in lead pencil)			
Aug. 27	Saul Gomaer } Blacks Susan, his wife }	Jane Eliza Jan. 27, 1814	
Sep. 10	Reuben Myers* Catherine Van Voorhis	Egbert June 10, 1815	

76

Baptismal Register

Date of Baptism	Parents	Name of Child and Date of Birth	Witnesses
Sep. 24			Rebecca Vn. Nostrand, widow of Joseph Churchill, an adult, on confession of her faith
Oct. 5	Henry Diamond Amy Montross	Melinda May 11, 1813	
Oct. 22	Benjamin A. Sleght Caroline Ackerman	Edgar	
Nov. 10	William Churchill Cornelia Van Nostrand	John, Dec. 8, 1810 Caroline, Aug. 10, 1812 Sarah Ann, Nov. 5, 1814	
Nov. 10	Joseph Churchill (deceased) Rebecca Van Nostrand	Elizabeth, Dec. 22, 1810 Amelia, July 28, 1813	
Nov. 14	Adrian Hageman Maria Hoffman	Mary, Dec. 26, 1809 Daniel, Apr. 13, 1812 Adrian, June 17, 1814	
Nov. 16	Jack Potter Little* Blacks Susan, his wife	Stephen May 6, 1814	
Dec. 3	Henry A. Monfoort Maria Phillips	Jane Oct. 20, 1815	
Dec. 12	Robert Van Amburgh* Freelove Du Bois	Cornelia May 30, 1815	
Dec. 17	Jacob Phillips Elizabeth Berry	Mary Oct. 28, 1815	
1816			
Jan. 10	Jack Potter Little* Susan, his wife	Mary Eliza, Apr. 9, 1806 Rachel, Oct. 19, 1808 Sarah Helen, June 15, 1811	
Jan. 26	John C. Shear Margaret Cornell	Abraham Oct. 12, 1815	
May 25	Abraham L. Dates Elizabeth Fowler	John Jan. 10, 1816	
Aug. 11	Saul Gamaer blacks Susan	Phoebe Ann	
Aug. 21	Jack Potter Little* Susan, his wife	Richard	
Aug. 16	Nazareth Brewer Deborah Wiltse	James June 24	
Sep. 22	Matthew Luyster Jane Cornell	Edgar June 26, 1816	
Oct. 20	William J. Dearin Jane Luckey	Rachel	
Oct. 4			Phoebe Thrasher, wife of Uriah Cornwell
Oct. 4			Samuel Gomar, an adult black

The Reformed Dutch Church of New Hackensack

Date of Baptism	Parents	Name of Child and Date of Birth	Witnesses
Dec. 15	Abraham A. Adriance Maria Bragaw	Frances Henrietta Oct. 1, 1816	
1817 Jan. 26	Adrian Hageman Maria Hoffman	Cynthia Ann Dec. 12, 1816	
Jan. 31	William Churchill Cornelia Van Nostrand	Hannah Eliza Nov. 22, 1816	
June 1	Peter Vanderbilt Mary Everitt	Phoebe Elizabeth Mar. 16, 1817	
June 27	James Dodge Electa Seward	William Seward May 30, 1817	
June 27	John Cornwell Phoebe Pollock	Jacob Mar. 1, 1817	
June 29		Flora Sarah Gomair	Adult Blacks
June 19	Uriah Cornwell* Phoebe Thrasher	James Apr. 12, 1811 Huldah Apr. 23, 1813 Samuel Mar. 16, 1816	
July 4	Samuel Luckey, Jr. Mary Underhill	Sally Angeline Dec. 22, 1816	
July 4	Cornelius Klump Jane Luckey	Joanna Oct. 30, 1816	
Aug. 21	John D. Smith* Elizabeth Brewer	William Henry Sep. 10, 1809 Cornelius Brewer Dec. 21, 1812 Sarah Jane June 14, 1817	
1818 Feb. 13	James Sleght Eltsie De Riemer	Henry Augustus Nov. 17, 1817	
Mar. 6	Mathew Luyster Jane Cornell	John Henry Dec. 5, 1817	
May 13	Uriah Cornwell Phoebe Thrasher	Cornelius Jan. 18, 1818	
May 31	Martin Monfoort Catherine Dutcher	John Bergen Jan. 30, 1818	
May 31	Henry A. Monfoort Maria Phillips	John Angevine Apr. 6, 1818	
Aug. 23	Abraham L. Dates Elizabeth Fowler	Abraham	
Oct. 15	Sylvester Earle Dorothy Ackerman (Decd.)	Sophia Apr. 10, 1814 Sarah Aug. 4, 1815 Dorothy Maria Apr. 25, 1817	Sarah Ackerman
Oct. 15	Samuel Bogardus Hannah Ackerman	Samuel July 15, 1817	
1819 Jan. 24	Ezekiel Jewell Celia Van de Bogart	Jeremiah Van Kleeck Nov. 22, 1817	

Baptismal Register

Date of Baptism	Parents	Name of Child and Date of Birth	Witnesses
Feb. 7	Saul Gomar } Blacks Susan, his wife	Solomon Oct. 1, 1818	
Feb. 7	Jack Potter Little* Susan, his wife (Black)	Henrietta Orinda Oct. 9, 1818	
June 13	William Churchill Cornelia Van Nostrand	Catherine Feb. 6, 1819	
Aug. 27	Cornelius Westervelt Frances Tanner	James July 7, 1813 Charlotte Apr. 22, 1815 Levina May 2, 1817 Mary Jan. 9, 1819	
Aug. 27	William J. Dearin Jane Luckey	James Walter	
Sep. 5	Benjn. Van Arsdalen* Rebecca Van Nostrand	Havily July 22, 1819	
Sep. 19	Ezekiel Jewell Celia Van de Bogert	Mary Ann Aug. 16, 1819	
Oct. 17	Adrian Hageman Maria Hoffman	Caroline Aug. 29, 1819	
Nov. 12	Benjamin A. Sleght* Caroline Ackerman	Sarah Louisa Nov. 12, 1816 Franklin Feb. 5, 1818	

1820

Feb. 3	John Ganse Elizabeth Platt* (twins)	Thomas DeWitt Aug. 27, 1813 Bethiah Ward Dec. 23, 1815 Phoebe Platt & Ann Platt Dec. 7, 1817	
Feb. 6	James Dodge Electa Seward	Henry Dec. 28, 1819	
Feb. 20	John A. Monfoort Jane Monfoort	Oliver Perry· Oct. 18, 1819	
Feb.	Daniel Hoffman Martha Bethel	Olivia Louisa Aug. 16, 1819 (being their grand-child)	
May 28	Dr. Henry D. Sleght* Freelove Potter	Franklin Rush Oct. 27, 1813 Mehala Eliza Apr. 28, 1817	
Aug. 6	Martin Monfoort Catherine Dutcher	Mary Ann May 19, 1820	
Aug. 18	Cornelius Klump Jane Luckey	Almira June 16, 1820	
Oct. 28	John Budd Angelica Van Voorhes	Mary Ann May 18, 1815 Aletta June 24, 1818 Hannah Apr. 18, 1820	

The Reformed Dutch Church of New Hackensack

Date of Baptism	Parents	Name of Child and Date of Birth	Witnesses
Feb. 5	Ezekiel Jewell Celia Van de Bogert	Celia Eliza Dec. 30, 1820	
1821 Apr. 15	Cornelius Westervelt Frances Tanner	John Du Bois Feb. 12, 1821	
May 13	Jack Little* } Blacks Susan, his wife }	Samuel Dec. 9, 1820	
May 27	Peter Van der Bilt Mary Everitt	George Whitefield Dec. 23, 1820	
June 24	Henry C. Disbrow Elizabeth Losee*	{ George Edgar { Jan. 13, 1809 { Sarah Ann { Nov. 19, 1820	
June 24	John Cornwell Isabella Pollock	John Dates Nov. 2, 1820	
July 22	Adonijah Palmer Maria Reynders	Andrew Isaiah May 10, 1821	
Aug. 5	William J. Dearin Jane Luckey	Susan Adelia Apr. 7, 1821	
	William Churchill Cornelia Van Nostrand	Jane	
1822 Feb. 6	John R. Luckey Cornelia Bogardus	Susan Mar. 19, 1821	
Apr. 28	John Ganse Elizabeth Platt*	Hervey Doddridge	
June 23	Ezekiel Jewell Celia Vandebogart	Hannah Mar. 29, 1822	
June 9	James Dodge Electa Seward	Philander Seward May 17, 1822	
June 23	John Budd Angelica Van Voorhis	Thomas DeWitt Mar. 9, 1822	
July 4	Abraham Diamond Elizabeth Luckey	Emeline Dec. 4, 1821	
Aug. 13	Lewis Mosher*, not bapt. Mary Diamond	Hetty Ann Dec. 29, 1821	
Aug. 27	David Tidd* Catherine Luyster	Hetty Jane June 12, 1815	
Aug. 27	Michael T. Hyzer Cynthia Cornell	John Cornell Feb. 25, 1822	
Aug. 27	Adrian Hageman Maria Hoffman	Elizabeth July 2, 1822	
Nov. 2	Henry C. Disbrow Elizabeth Losee*	Avery L. Herrick	
Dec. 8	Monfoort Van Kleeck Elizabeth M. Dennison	Sarah Jane Sep. 12, 1822	
1823 Jan. 18	Benjamin A. Sleight* Caroline Ackerman	Ruth Amelia Aug. 20, 1822	
Jan. 18	John Ackerman* Maria Nelson	Isaac Oct. 22, 1822	
Feb. 5	Robert Van Amburgh* Freelove Du Bois	{ Adeline { Aug. 18, 1820 { Walter { May 15, 1822	

Baptismal Register

Date of Baptism	Parents	Name of Child and Date of Birth	Witnesses
Feb.	Oliver Todd Eliza Cornell	Robert	
Feb. 15	John A. Monfoort Jane Monfoort (twins)	Mary & Alida Jane Nov. 5, 1822	
Feb. 15	Cornelius Monfoort Sarah Overacker	Albert Sep. 29, 1822	
Sep. 1	Cornelius Westervelt Frances Tanner	Theron Aug. 3, 1823	
Sep. 22	Uriah Cornwell* Phoebe Thrasher	Hannah Elizabeth Mar. 18, 1823	
1824 Jan. 4	Ezekiel Jewell Celia Van de bogart	Cynthia Jane Nov. 9, 1823	
Feb. 29	Monfoort Van Kleeck* Elizabeth M. Dennison	Anna Maria Dec. 2, 1823	
May 23	John Budd Angelica Van Voorhis	Samuel Thorn Jan. 12, 1824	
May 30	William Churchill Cornelia Van Nostrand	Cornelius Oct. 30, 1823	
May 13	Matthew Luyster Jane Cornell	Maria Ann Feb. 16, 1824	
Sep. 20	Michael T. Hyzer Cynthia Cornell	Michael Thomas July 27, 1824	
Dec. 8	Peter Dearin Jane Van Amburgh	Antoinette July 5, 1824	
Oct. 23	Oliver Todd Eliza Cornell (twins)	Lafayette & Mary Elizabeth Feb. 19, 1824	
1825 Apr. 10	Adrian Hageman Maria Hoffman	James Aug. 22, 1824	
Apr. 15	Martin Monfoort Catherine Dutcher	Garret Stryker Mar. 23, 1823	
May 15	Lewis Mosher* Mary Diamond	Hannah	
May 22	Monfoort Van Kleeck* Elizabeth M. Dennison	Hannah Elizabeth Mar. 4, 1825	
June 19	Abraham F. Westervelt Hannah Lawson	Peter Fort Mar. 24, 1825	
June 12	Henry C. Disbrow Elizabeth Losee*	William Henry	
July 31	Ezekiel Jewell Celia Vandebogart	Henry Davis Mar. 5, 1825	
Aug. 4	Cornelius Klump Jane Luckey	Mary Jane Dec. 12, 1824	
Aug. 4	Cornelius Westervelt Frances Tanner	Rebecca Jane May 23, 1825	
Sep. 25	John A. Monfoort Jane Monfoort	Maria Aug. 7, 1825	
Dec. 10	Uriah Cornwell* Phoebe Thrasher	John I.	

The Reformed Dutch Church of New Hackensack

Date of Baptism	Parents	Name of Child and Date of Birth	Witnesses
1826			
Apr. 15	Oliver Todd Eliza Cornell	Caroline Aug. 13, 1825	
July 9	John Budd Angelica Van Voorhis	Catherine Mar. 9, 1826	

REGISTER OF BAPTISMS
during the Ministry of the Revd. M. W. Dwight

1826			
Dec 24	Monfort Van Cleek Eliza M. Dennison	Margaret Oct. 26, 1826	
Dec. 31	Abraham F. Westervelt Hannah Lawson	John Lawson June 21, 1826	
1827			
Jan. 21	Thos. I. Dering Marian Luckie	Gertrude Mar. 17, 1826	
Jan. 21	Matthew M. Lawson Ann Budd	James Alexander	
Apr. 14	Cornelius Westervelt Frances Tanner	Laura Ann	
Sep. 2	John A. Monfort Jane Monfort	Albert July 14, 1827	
Mar. 18	Philander Seward Susan Monfort	William Henry Nov. 30, 1826	
1828			
Oct. 16	John Gillespie Elizabeth Peebles	Garrit Peebles	
May 30	Monfort Vn. Cleek Eliza M. Denniston	Catharine Dwight	
Oct. 12	Abm. F. Westervelt Hannah Lawson	Elizabeth Merritt Apr. 1, 1828	
Oct. 12	John Viele Mary Lawson	Elizabeth Chatterton Oct. 27, 1827	
Nov.	Matthew M. Lawson Ann Budd	Esther Ann June 15, 1828	
1829			
Apr. 5	Philander Seward Susan Monfort	Philander George Nov. 10, 1828	
May 17	John Luyster Mary Yonni	John Yonni July 3, 1828	
May 31	Monfort Vn. Kleek Eliza M. Dennison	Eunice Apr. 11, 1829	
1830			
May 4	Schenck Ackerman Dorcas Jones	{ Mary Nov. 18, 1827 Martin Schenck Sep. 14, 1829 }	
	William Brewer Ann	(name of child and date of birth omitted)	
Nov. 5	Philander Seward Susan Monfort	Maurice Dwight Sep. 10, 1830	
1831			
Feb. 27	John U. Budd Angelica Vn. Voorhies	John Ten Broeck	

Baptismal Register

Date of Baptism	Parents	Name of Child and Date of Birth	Witnesses
Apr. 17	Monfort Vn. Kleeck Eliza Denniston	George Denniston Feb. 24, 1831	
1830 May 16	Cornelius Westervelt Frances Tanner	Allida Dec. 8, 1829	
1831 June 23	Thos. J. Dering Marian Lucky	Samuel Lucky Mar. 22, 1831	
July 3	Abraham Meyrs Elizabeth Cornell	Susan Jan. 9, 1821 Schenck Mar. 1, 1823 Ann July 16, 1825 Mercy Feb. 15, 1829	
Aug. 7	John Potter Rachel Little	(name of child and date of birth omitted)	
Aug. 7	John Little Susan	(name of child and date of birth omitted)	
Aug. 22	Stephen Thorn Mary Sleight	Sarah Elizabeth June 19, 1831	
1832 Jan. 27	Daniel Phillips Cynthia Palmer	John R. Hannah	
Sep. 16	Oliver Vn. Dyne Susan Smith	James Abraham July 13, 1828 Wm. Henry Dec. 18, 1832	

(As this baptism occurred Sep. 16, 1832, the birth date of Wm. Henry was probably Dec. 18, 1831).

1833			
Apr. 26	Robert Tanner Eliza F. Brewer	Marian Oct. 16, 1822 Cornelius B. May 16, 1824 Reuben R. May 28, 1827 Robert Sep. 3, 1829	
July 14	Monfort Van Kleek Elizabeth M. Denniston	James Van Keuren July 1, 1833	

REGISTER OF BAPTISMS
During the Ministry of the Revd. Cornelius Van Cleef
who was
Installed pastor of the Church of New Hackensack
December 17th, 1833
as successor to the Revd. Maurice W. Dwight
1833

1834 Feb. 9	Philander Seward Susan Monfort	Amelia Caroline June 25, 1833	

The Reformed Dutch Church of New Hackensack

Date of Baptism	Parents	Name of Child and Date of Birth	Witnesses
June 18	Schenk Ackerman Dorcas Jones	Jane May 14, 1833	
June 18	Benjamin A. Sleight Caroline Ackerman	Benjamin Sidney May 23, 1834	
1835			
Feb. 1	Abraham Meyers Elizabeth Cornell	Abraham	

The first child baptized in the new Church.

May 10	John U. Budd Angelica Van Voorhees	Angeline Nov. 29, 1834	
1836			
Feb. 12	Monfort Van Kleek Elizabeth M. Deniston	Harvey Dodridge Sep. 28, 1835	
June 3	Philander Seward Susan Monfort	James Adis Jan. 3, 1836	
June 5		Helen Jones, Adult	
1837			
Sep. 8	William B. Hoagland Susan Pelts	Sarah Amelia Nov. 1, 1836	
Sep. 8	Henry Ganse Caroline Dolson	Sarah Anna July 6, 1836	
Sep. 8	Thomas S. Dearin Mary Ann Luckey	Francis Feb. 21, 1837	
Sep. 10		Patty Farrington, wife of Henry Dimond	
Sep. 17	Stephen Thorn Mary Sleight	Samuel May 1, 1837	
Sep. 17	Benjamin H. Everitt Alletta M. Monfort	Helen Maria Apr. 9, 1837	
1838			
Jan. 12	Cornelius P. Ostrander Elizabeth Van Osdall	Margaret Ann Feb. 21, 1827 John Wiswall Sep. 13, 1829 Peter Mar. 5, 1832	
Jan. 12	Monfort Van Kleeck Elizabeth M. Denniston	Henrietta July 27, 1837	
1837			
Nov. 12	Henry D. Hayt	Peter Berry Oct. 8, 1835 Edward June 30, 1837	
1838			
Apr. 13	Henry Ganse Caroline Dolson	Amelia Oct. 23, 1837	
Apr. 13	Philander Seward Susan Monfort	Ogden Tallmadge Jan. 3, 1838	
Aug. 19		Judith Mills, Adult	
Dec. 7	Cornelius P. Ostrander Elizabeth Van Osdall	Mary Frances July 15, 1838	

Baptismal Register

Date of Baptism	Parents	Name of Child and Date of Birth	Witnesses
1839			
Apr. 19	James S. Monfort Barbara E. Hoagland	John Henry, Apr. 20, 1828 Stephen, Mar. 30, 1831 Cornelius Van Cleef, Nov. 2, 1838	
Apr. 19	Peter Van Keuren S. Angeline Luckey	Mary Luckey Sep. 1, 1838	
Dec. 27	John Monfort Maria G. Hutchins	Mary Jane Mar. 3, 1839	
1840			
Apr. 13	Monfort Van Kleek Elizabeth M. Denniston	Catharine Amelia Sep. 17, 1839	
Aug. 14	William B. Hoagland Susan Pelts	Abraham Oct. 10, 1839	
Aug. 14	Cornelius P. Ostrander Elizabeth Van Nosdall	James Cornell Apr. 8, 1840	
Dec. 24	Stephen S. Thorn Mary Sleight	Esther July 2, 1840	
Dec. 24	Benjamin Everitt Aletta M. Monfort	Marietta June 13, 1840	
1841			
Apr. 16	Henry Ganse Caroline Dolson	Henrietta Sep. 1, 1840	
Dec. 31	Henry D. Hayt	Susan July 4, 1841	
Dec. 31	Thomas S. Dearin Mary Ann Luckey	Thomas Seymour Aug. 22, 1841	
1842			
Jan. 2		Harvey D. Platt, Adult	
Apr. 15	Harvey D. Platt Phebe Carey	Mary Bethia, Jan. 12, 1836 Ebenezer Carey, Mar. 1, 1840	
Apr. 15	Phillip Van Der Bilt Phebe E. Van Der Bilt	John Platt Sep. 24, 1841	
Apr. 17		William Seward, Adult	
Apr. 17		Jane Phillips, Adult	
Apr. 17		Mrs. Ann E. Van Voorhees, Adult	
Aug. 26	Henry Ganse Caroline Dolson	Spencer Abeel Feb. 3, 1842	
Aug. 28		Jane A. Dubois, Wife of Emory Carpenter	
1843			
May 5	William B. Hoagland Susan Pelts	William Cornelius Van Cleef Sep. 27, 1842	
May 7		Helen Van Der Belt Lawson, Adult	
Sep. 8	Henry D. Hayt	Stephen May 12, 1843	
Sep. 8	James S. Monfort Barbara E. Hoagland	Washington Jones June 5, 1843	
Sep. 10		Belinda Van Amburgh, Adult	
Sep. 10		Harriet H. Potter, Adult	

The Reformed Dutch Church of New Hackensack

Date of Baptism	Parents	Name of Child and Date of Birth	Witnesses
1844			
Apr. 26	Benjamin Everitt Aletta M. Monfort	Henry Isaac Sep. 3, 1843	
Apr. 28			Letty Maria, wife of James Baxter
Aug. 30	Henry Ganse Caroline Dolson	Thomas DeWitt May 24, 1844	
Aug. 30	Phillip Van Der Bilt Phebe E. Van Der Bilt	Sarah Electa June 27, 1844	
Sep. 1			Sarah Jane Van Voorhis, Adult
1845			
Jan. 5			Mary Elizabeth Remsen, Adult
Aug. 29	Jacob V. B. Van Voorhees Ann Eliza Van Voorhees	Albina Sep. 17, 1839	
Aug. 31			Mary Angel, wife of Chauncy Knapp
1846			
Dec. 4	Henry Ganse Caroline Dolson	Jeremiah N. July 7, 1846	
Dec. 4	Phillip Van Der Belt Phebe Van Der Belt	Mary Sheafe July 12, 1846	
1847			
Mar. 12	Chauncy Knapp Mary A. Thorn	Marietta Sep. 2, 1846	
Mar. 14			Simeon Hitchcock, Adult
Apr. 12	Chauncy Knapp Mary A. Thorn	{ Sarah Ann T. July 24, 1839 Clarence C. Apr. 17, 1844	
1848			
Feb. 6			Mary Weeks, wife of Nathaniel Grant
Feb. 6			Jane Ann Monfort, Adult
Sep. 1	Henry Ganse Caroline Dolson	Caroline Elizabeth Mar. 23, 1848	
1849			
Apr. 1			John Jones, Adult
1850			
Mar. 10			Jane Thorn, wife of Teunis Ackerman
Mar. 10			Amelia Maria Potter, Adult
Mar. 10			Catharine Mary Potter, Adult
June 7	John C. Pudney Sarah E. Everitt	Elizabeth Everitt Sep. 5, 1849	
Aug. 30	C. Knapp Mary A. Thorn	Sidman Thorn Aug. 22, 1849	
Sep. 1			Henrietta Freelove Potter, Adult
1851			
Feb. 28	Henry D. Hayt Jane Berry	Charles Dennison May 20, 1850	
May 30	Henry Ganse Caroline Dolson	Clinton DeForrest Oct. 6, 1850	
June 1			Mary Marvin, Adult
Sep. 7			Mercy Van Amburgh, Adult
1852			
June 20			Julia Ann Jamieson (colored), Adult
Sep. 5			Susan Letitia Pells, Adult

Baptismal Register

Date of Baptism	Parents	Name of Child and Date of Birth	Witnesses
Sep. 3	Henry Ganse Caroline Dolson	Alson Sherwood Jan. 24, 1852	
1853 Sep. 2	William Baker Catharine E. Meddaugh	Annis Elizabeth Apr. 1, 1852	
Sep. 2	John Y. Bishop Mary E. Losee	Augusta Nov. 30, 1851	
1854 Sep. 3		Mary Louisa Seward, Adult	
Sep. 3		Mary Moore, wife of Chas. J. Howell, Jr.	
June 2	Harvey D. Platt Phebe Carey	Elizabeth Remsen Mar. 27, 1854	
Dec. 1	Alexander Bishop Jane Ann Couse	Emily Spencer Jan. 14, 1854	
Dec. 3		Catharine T. Grant, Adult	
1855 Sep. 7	John Y. Bishop Mary E. Losee	Mary Anna June 10, 1854	
Sep. 9		Mary Van Voorhis, Adult	
1856 Feb. 29	Charles J. Howell, Jr. Mary M. Dubois	Charles James Aug. 15, 1855	
Sep. 5	Alexander Bishop Jane Ann Couse	Anna Gertrude Aug. 22, 1855	
Sep. 5	Revd. Wm. A. Cornell Helen M. Wyckoff	William Augustus Aug. 11, 1855	
1857 May 31		Jane Eliza Thompson, Adult (coloured)	
Dec. 6		Henry Burroughs and his wife Alletta E. Bogardus, Adults	
1858 Apr. 11		Sarah Ann Seward, Adult	
May 23	John D. Westervelt Nelly Depuy	Cornelius July 4, 1857	
June 18	Alexander Bishop Jane Ann Couse	Ellen Shepherd Sep. 27, 1857	
June 18	John Jones Cynthia M. Needham	Henrietta Needham June 18, 1857	
June 20		Hellen Ann Rodgers, Adult	
Sep. 5		Mrs. Harriet Robinson, Adult	
Dec. 12		Samuel I. Robinson, Adult	
Dec. 12		Mrs. Delia D. Monfort, Adult	
Dec. 12		Mrs. Catharine Van Voorhis, Adult	
1859 Mar. 4	Charles J. Howell, Jun. Mary M. Dubois	Cornelius Dubois Aug. 7, 1858	
Mar. 4	Edgar Luyster Harriet Conover	Charles Edgar June 25, 1858	
Mar. 6		Sarah Johannah Ackerman, Adult	
" "		Louisa Catharine Hitchcock, Adult	
" "		Susan Mary Hopkins, Adult	

The Reformed Dutch Church of New Hackensack

Date of Baptism	Parents	Name of Child and Date of Birth	Witnesses
Mar. 6		Peter Gardner, Coloured, Adult	
June 5		Maria Jane Pells, Adult	
Sep. 4		Nelly, w. of J. V. B. Concklin, Adult	
Sep. 4		Elthea, w. of Henry Van Der Bilt, Adult	
Dec. 11		Mary Elizabeth, wife of William Van Amburgh, Adult	
1860			
Mar. 4		Susan Ann Monfort ⎫ Adults, Maria Louisa Monfort ⎭ Sisters	
Mar. 31	William Van Amburgh Mary Elizabeth Owen	Walter Ranson Dec. 6, 1855	
June 3		Belinda Concklin ⎫ Adults, Margaret E. Concklin ⎭ Sisters	
June 3		Mary E. Thompson, w. of Henry Smith. Coloured. Adult	
Aug. 31	John C. Pudney Sarah E. Everitt	John Ervin Oct. 11, 1859	
Aug. 31	John Monfort Martha J. Emmons	⎧ Sarah G. Teller ⎨ Aug. 10, 1856 ⎨ John Jacob ⎩ July 27, 1858	
Aug. 31	Rev. Wm. A. Cornell Hellen M. Wyckoff	Jacob Wyckoff Apr. 1, 1860	
Aug. 31	John D. Westervelt Nelly Depuy	Louis May 15, 1860	
Dec. 2		Catharine E. Monfort, Adult	
1861			
Mar. 1	Alexander Bishop Jane Ann Couse	Sophie Van Cleef Mar. 1, 1860	
Mar. 3		Mrs. Elizabeth Collins, Adult	
" "		Elizabeth M. Van Voorhis, Adult	
" "		Mary Jane Grant, Adult	
" "		Sarah Ann Grey, Adult	
May 31	John H. Luyster Gertrude K. Conover	Jennie Nov. 18, 1860	
June 2		Jane, w. of Alexander Bishop, Adult	
Aug. 30	William Baker Catharine E. Meddaugh	Mary Seward Mar. 24, 1861	
Dec. 1		William H. Dimond, Adult	
1862			
Mar. 24	J. (J.) Diddell Diana Storm	⎧ John Jackson ⎨ Aug. 27, 1854 ⎨ Jacob Storm ⎩ June 16, 1856	
May 30	Alexander Bishop Jane Ann Couse (twins)	Howard Alexander & Cornelius Van Cleef Jan. 25, 1862	
May 30	Charles J. Howell, Jun. Mary M. Dubois	Lydia Henchman Oct. 20, 186(1)	
Sep. 5	John D. Cornwell, Jun. Susan L. Pells	John James Jan. 4, 1862	

Baptismal Register

Date of Baptism	Parents	Name of Child and Date of Birth	Witnesses
1864			
June 3	John H. Luyster Gertrude K. Conover	Matthew Luyster July 21, 1863	
June 12		Jane Berry, w. of Henry D. Hayt, Adult	
July 26	Charles E. Hitchcock Sarah J. Ackerman	Irving May 28, 1864	
Sep. 2	John Jones Cynthia M. Needham	Joseph Jackson May 19, 1864	
1865			
Mar. 5		Chauncey Knapp, Adult Mrs. Eustacia Smith, Adult	
June 2	Alexander Bishop Jane Ann Couse	Sophie Van Cleef Feb. 12, 1865	
Sep. 3		Edward Flagler & his wife } Adults Charlotte Degroff	
Dec. 1	John H. Luyster Gertrude K. Conover	Warren Elisha May 24, 1865	
1866			
June 17		Mrs. Ruth Ann Schryver } & her son } Adults Edward H. Schryver }	
Aug. 31		George E. Salisbury, Adult	
Nov. 16	John D. Cornwell, Jun. Susan L. Pells	Jacob Ralph July 25, 1866	
Nov. 18		Mrs. Sarah M. Hicks, Adult	

REGISTER OF BAPTISMS DURING THE MINISTRY OF REV. HENRY WARD

Installed Pastor of The Reformed Church of New Hackensack, N. Y., July 2, 1867.

Date of Baptism	Parents	Name of Child and Date of Birth	Witnesses
1867			
Aug. 30	Leffert T. Bergen Mary C. Earle	Mary Dec. 15, 1866	
June 5	John H. Luyster Gertrude K. Conover	Hattie Conover Oct. 7, 1867	
	(Date of birth was probably 1866, or date of baptism was 1868)		
1868			
June 7		Catharine Belinda, w. of Stephen P. Monfort. Adult	
June 7		Mrs. Mary A. Vail, Adult	
Aug. 30	William Seward, Jr. Louisa M. Lockwood	William Apr. 11, 1868	
Aug. 30		Isaac D. Bostwick, Adult	
Dec. 4	Stephen P. Monfort Catharine B. Needham	James Henry, Jan. 29, 1858 Maria Needham, Jan. 5, 1860 Eleanor Kate, Oct. 16, 1862	
Dec. 4	Joseph P. Deyo Eliza Worden	Evelyn May May 2, 1860	
Dec. 6		William H. Tompkins, Adult	

The Reformed Dutch Church of New Hackensack

Date of Baptism	Parents	Name of Child and Date of Birth	Witnesses
1869			
Mar. 7		Mrs. Marianna Everett, Adult	
Mar. 7		Laura Vanderbilt, Adult	
Mar. 7		Annie Elizabeth Ostrander, Adult	
June 6		William L. Germond, Adult	
" "		Mrs. Jane Ann Van Dyne, Adult	
" "		Mrs. Maria Louisa Tompkins, Adult	
" "		Mrs. Helen E. Ackerman, Adult	
" "		Mrs. Mary C. Forshay, Adult	
" "		Deborah Ann Myers, Adult	
" "		Phebe Adelia Hawkes, Adult	
" "		Ann Augusta Townsend, Adult	
" "		Phebe Townsend, Adult	
" "		Irene Myers, Adult	
" "		Emma Jane Myers, Adult	
" "		Maria Louisa Robinson, Adult	
" "		Hannah Ellen Germond, Adult	
1870			
Mar. 4	Rev. Henry Ward / Caroline Davis	William Davis / June 16, 1869	
Mar. 4	William H. Tompkins / Maria Louisa Ackerman	Jacob Teller / Sep. 19, 1865	
Aug. 21	Edward Townsend / Sarah A. Seward	{ Kate Seward / Nov. 23, 1868 { Mary Louisa / Apr. 18, 1870	
1871			
Mar. 4	Daniel Werner / Margaret Fulmer	Sarah Remson / Oct. 14, 1870	
June 2	John H. Luyster / Gertrude K. Conover	John Dewitt / Sep. 24, 1870	
June 4		John R. Matthews, Adult	
June 4		James P. Organ, Adult	
June 4		Sarah Frances Ackerman, Adult	
Sep. 1	Charles E. Van Kleeck / Kate B. Rogers	Mary Eliza / Oct. 1, 1870	
Sep. 1	Isaac D. Bostwick (Dec'd) / Cornelia A. Bouton	Isaac Davis / Nov. 6, 1870	
Sep. 3		Saraettie Monfort, Adult	
Dec. 8	Samuel L. Dearin / Albina Van Voorhis	Ann Eliza / Feb. 15, 1871	
Dec. 10		Edgar Sedore, Adult	
1872			
Mar. 1	John R. Matthews / Anna S. Hunt	{ Emma Louisa / Mar. 22, 1861 { Mary Gertrude / Sep. 24, 1863	
Mar. 3		Charles Gage, Adult	
Mar. 3		Caroline Akin, Adult	

Baptismal Register

Date of Baptism	Parents	Name of Child and Date of Birth	Witnesses
Mar. 3		Abby Sedore, Adult	
June 2		Charles E. Van Kleeck, Adult	
" "		John A. Rogers, Adult	
" "		Ambrose D. Albertson, Adult	
" "		George Underhill, Adult	
" "		Charlotte A. Underhill, Adult	
" "		Mrs. Susan A. Phillips, Adult	
" "		Joseph Freeman, Adult	
" "		Jane Armstrong, Adult	
Aug. 30	George W. Phillips Susan A. Brinckerhoff	⎧ Susan A. ⎪ May 31, 1863 ⎨ George W. ⎪ Oct. 8, 1860 ⎪ Cynthia Louisa ⎩ Sep. 3, 1864	
Aug. 30	Philip Lauer Catharine Drieshmann	Eldora Oct. 25, 1871	
Sep. 22	William Seward, Jr. Louisa M. Lockwood	Edward Townsend Feb. 8, 1872	
1873 May 30	James C. Ackerman Sarah Frances Tompkins	Theodore J. Mar. 10, 1872	
May 30	Charles E. Hitchcock Sarah J. Ackerman	Austin Brundage July 30, 1872	
Aug. 29	Charles E. Van Kleeck Kate B. Rogers	Robert M. Sep. 28, 1872	
1874 Aug. 31	William Seward, Jr. Louisa M. Lockwood	George Schermerhorn Aug. 7, 1874	
Sep. 4	Rev. Henry Ward Caroline Davis	Henry Paige Feb. 13, 1874	
1875 June 6		Miriam Van Voorhis, Adult	
1876			
July 21	John Ed. McCord Alletta A. Yates	⎧ Sarah Maria ⎪ Feb. 15, 1867 ⎨ Edwin Yates ⎪ May 20, 1871 ⎪ John Erwin ⎩ Nov. 9, 1872	
Sep. 3		Ida Monfort, Adult	
1877 Sep. 13	Oliver S. Ackley Susan V. Cahoone	Grace Cahoone May 19, 1875	
Dec. 2		James C. Ackerman, Adult	
1878 June 2		Brundage Tompkins, Adult	
June 2		Elizabeth Van Wyck Tompkins, Adult	
Aug. 30	Rev. Henry Ward Caroline Davis	Alfred Wyckoff Mar. 28, 1878	

The Reformed Dutch Church of New Hackensack

Date of Baptism	Parents	Name of Child and Date of Birth	Witnesses
1879			
Feb. 28	Webster Wright Matilda Adams	Martha May Jan. 3, 1874	
Aug. 24	William Seward, Jr. Louisa M. Lockwood	Julia Lockwood Jan. 5, 1878	
1880			
May 30		Sarah Sylvester Seward, Adult	
" "		Sarah Sleight, Adult	
1881			
May 27	Henry Jones Harriet L. Conover	Ella Estella Aug. 30, 1880	
1882			
Sep. 1	James C. Ackerman Sarah F. Tompkins	Sarah Grace Dec. 7, 1881	
Sep. 1	Webster Wright Matilda Adams	Edith Warren Nov. 7, 1881	
1883			
June 1	Amos Brownell, (Dec'd) Emma L. Wooster	Aimee Wooster Apr. 30, 1882	
June 1	Rev. Henry Ward Caroline Davis	Herbert Emerson June 28, 1882	
1884			
Mar. 2		Catharine Phillips, Adult	
1886			
Mar. 7		Lulu DeGroot Hayt, Adult	
Mar. 7		Tunis Ackerman, Adult	
Sep. 2		Anthony Underhill, Adult	
1887			
May 27		Emilie B. Van Voorhis, Adult	

REGISTER OF BAPTISMS DURING THE MINISTRY OF REV. WM. A. DUMONT

Installed Pastor of the Reformed Church of New Hackensack, N. Y., Apr. 17, 1888.

1889			
Mar. 3		Mrs. Elizabeth Nostrand Pier, Adult	
" "		Minnie Pier, Adult	
" "		Clarence H. Pier, Adult	
" "		Wm. Edward Pier, Adult	
Mar. 18	Alexander Simons Lena Simons	John Smith July 29, 1888	
June 16	Wm. Alexander Dumont Martha Hay Dumont	Anna Gertrude Apr. 16, 1889	
June 16	Frederic Gresty Martha Gresty	Gertrude Mary Dec. 11, 1880 Frederic Hazelhurst Apr. 24, 1884	
1890			
Mar. 2		Allie A. Doughty, Adult	
June 1		Ida DeGroff, Adult	
June 1		Garetta Kate Seger, Adult	
Apr. 10		Elbert W. Van Tassell, Adult. Very ill. Elder J. B. Jones went with Pastor to his home.	

Baptismal Register

Date of Baptism	Parents	Name of Child and Date of Birth	Witnesses
July 13	Gerardus DeForest Underhill Lillie Stephenson Underhill	Walter DeForest July 28, 1889	
Sep. 7		Katie Theresa Vollmer, Adult	
" "		Mary Alice Mathews, Adult	
Dec. 10	Wellington White Sarah Cornelia White	Arthur Wellington Aug. 28, 1890	
Dec. 10	Wm. Van Dewater, deceased Helen Josephine Van Dewater	Albert Wellington Apr. 13, 1889	
July 13	William Sowdon Matilda R. Jones	William Kenneth Sep. 22, 1888	
1891 June 7		Catherine Thorn Akin, Adult	
" "		Mary Louise Shafer Seger, Adult	
" "		Priscilla Merritt Ackerman, Adult	
" "		Emma Marion Nostrand, Adult	
" "		Clinton Edward Stoutenburg, Adult	
Sep. 6		Theodore Christian, Adult	
" "		Washington Travis Christian, Adult	
" "		Anna Louisa Christian, Adult	
" "		Daisy Mary Christian, Adult	
" "		Stephen A. Bulmer, Adult	
" "		Augustus Earnest Bulmer, Adult	
" "		James William Bulmer, Adult	
" "		Irene D. Burroughs, Adult	
" "		Cora E. Warren, Adult	
" "		Jennie Carter Van Dyne, Adult	
" "		Edward J. Lawrence, Adult	
Sep. 4	Jacob Storm Diddell Clara Wooster	{ Harold Wooster Oct. 14, 1884 Joseph Jackson May 26, 1886	
Sep. 7	William Sowdon Matilda R. Jones	John Irving Oct. 12, 1890	
Sep. 14	Wm. Burton Madden Elizabeth Seward	Beatrice Lockwood Nov. 22, 1890	
Sep. 20	Eliphaz Delamater Anna Andrews	{ Mildred Jan. 7, 1889 Wilfred Schuyler Mar. 29, 1891	
Sep. 20	Wm. Alexander Dumont Martha Hay Dumont	Rachel White Feb. 5, 1891	
1892 June 5		Susie Emily Christian, Adult	
July 26		John M. Dorland, Adult	
" "		Phebe Jane Robinson, w. of Jno. M. Dorland, Adult	
" "		Jane Amelia Noxon, w. of Jno. H. Robinson	
Sep. 4		Hiram Brownell White, Adult	
" "		Clarence George White, Adult	

The Reformed Dutch Church of New Hackensack

Date of Baptism	Parents	Name of Child and Date of Birth	Witnesses
Sep. 4		Alfretta H. White, Adult	
Nov. 16	Peter S. MacKinlay Peter C. MacKinlay Mary L. Maholm	Mary Lee Maholm MacKinlay, Adult Marion Wilson Oct. 24, 1887	Gone to 2nd Pres. Ch., Germantown, Pa.
Dec. 4		Corris M. Dolson, Adult	
1893			
June 4		Edward Bloomfield Van Dyne, Adult	
" "		Samuel M. Ten Broeck, Adult	
" "		Catherine M. Ten Broeck, Adult	
" "		Lewis St. John Griffin, Adult	
" "		Delia F. Ward, Adult	
" "		Hester M. Morse, Adult	
" "		James Lewis Smith, Adult	
" "		James Young Luyster, Adult	
" "		Isaac Benjamin Horton, Adult	
" "		Theodore Anthony (Colored), Adult	
" "		Thomas E. Williams, Adult	
" "		Willis Van Voorhis, Adult	
" "		Herman C. Crozier, Adult	
" "		Frank Underhill, Adult	
" "		Wm. Germond, Adult	
June 2		Alfred P. Russell, Adult	"By immersion"
" "		Wm. G. Wright, Adult	
Sep. 3		Miss Inez Scofield, Adult	
1894			
Feb. 24	Robert S. Mathews Dora A. Cronkrite	Hazel Alice Jan. 18, 1890 Raymond Nov. 17, 1893	
July 29	William H. Knox Esther M. Holder	William Melbourne Sep. 9, 1893	
Sep. 9	William Sowdon Matilda R. Jones	Arthur Whitlock Nov. 1, 1893	
1895			
Mar. 3		Floyd Organ, Adult	
	Edgar A. Briggs	Mary A. Baptized in Pleasant Valley Pres. Ch. and dismissed to us with her parents.	
June 2		Charles J. Brower, Adult	
Sep. 1		Clarence D. Brower, Adult	
Dec. 1		Rachel Morris Doughty, Adult	
1896			
June 5		Jane Van De Bogert, Adult	
" "		Adah May Rogers, Adult	
" "		Nellie Scofield, Adult	
June 5	Mathew L. Van Wyck Minnie Monfort	DeWitt Apr. 23, 1891	
	Eliphaz Delemater Anna Andrews	Cornelia Jan. 27, 1895	

Baptismal Register

Date of Baptism	Parents	Name of Child and Date of Birth	Witnesses
June 5	Wm. A. Dumont Martha J. Hay	Martha Nevins Mar. 28, 1895	
June 5	Daniel Werner Christina Bennett	Cora May July 29, 1895	
1897 June 4	Jacob Storm Diddell Clara Wooster	Clara Wooster Apr. 8, 1896	
June 4		Emma J. Scofield, Adult	
" "		Theodore Winfield Christian, Adult. Died Jan. 27, 1922.	
" "		Louis Elbert Christian, Adult	
Aug. 15	William Scofield Emma J. Ferdon	Harriet Kissam Apr. 23, 1889	
Sep. 3	Elijah Rowe Anna L. Christian	Daniel Theodore Apr. 13, 1894 Ethel Grace Apr. 5	
Sep. 3	John R. East Mary Emma Westfall	Mary Catherine Mar. 3, 1897	
Dec. 5		Emma Lee, Adult	
1898 May 15		Howell W. Simpson	Sponsor: Thos. Bodden age 14 years. Very ill.
Sep. 2	Edward J. Lawrence Mary L. Sherwood	Sherwood E. Aug. 8, 1895	
Sep. 2	Edgar A. Briggs Mary Alice Mathews	Gertrude Mathews Sep. 18, 1897	
Sep. 2	Wm. A. Dumont Martha J. Hay	William Henry Oct. 18, 1897	
Dec. 2	Martin I. Hadden Emily Van Wagener	Gladys May June 25, 1898	
1899 Mar. 3		William Henry Augustus Lory, Adult	
" "		Grace Louise Lory, Adult	
" "		Mary Kesiah Lory, Adult	
Dec. 1	Clarence Van Tassell Ida Knapp	Wardell C. June 30, 1899	
Dec. 3		Julia Brinkerhoff Hauver, Adult	
" "		Florence A. Scofield	"
1900 Mar. 4		Charles Ten Broeck, Adult	
" "		Walter Livingston Ten Broeck, Adult	
" "		Emott Andrews Delemater, Adult	
" "		John Oscar Delemater, Adult	
" "		Wm. Henry Brower, Adult	
" "		Jane Augusta Brower, Adult	
" "		Caroline Hegeman Tanner, Adult	
" "		Mary Francis Tanner, Adult	
" "		Mary Johnston Cornwell, Adult	
" "		Helen Stockholm Cornwell, Adult	

The Reformed Dutch Church of New Hackensack

Date of Baptism	Parents	Name of Child and Date of Birth	Witnesses
Mar. 4		Wm. Monroe Scofield, Adult	
" "		Stella Moore Scofield, Adult	
" "		Chas. Wesley Hults, Adult	
" "		Elijah T. Rowe, Adult	
" "		Wm. Otto Stoutenburg, Adult	
(1901?, 1902?) Jan. 14		Maria Coapman Forman, Adult. Baptized in the home.	
		Maria Forman Leroy, Adult. Baptized in the home.	
1902 Mar. 23		Harold Waldo Delamater, Adult	
1903 Mar. 1		Harry Pells Scofield, Adult	
June 5	Wm. C. Fries Lona A. Vollmer	Vollmer Walter July 17, 1902	
June 7		Threse Clark Scruton, Adult	
Sep. 4	John J. Cornwell Mary Johnston	Elizabeth Johnston Sep. 30, 1902	
1904 June 2	Loyen Kilmer Susan Warner	Preston H. Mar. 11, 1894	
Sep. 2	Wm. H. Swezey Ida Monfort	John Albert May 30, 1902	
Sep. 2	Edgar A. Briggs Mary A. Mathews	Alice Emily Aug. 11, 1900	
Sep. 2	Andrew Termilliger Alice Smith	Edward	
Sep. 2		William Smith, Adult Nov. 11, 1891	
1905 Mar. 3		Lucy Hicks, Adult	
Mar. 5		Seward Baker Jackson, Adult	
1906 Jan. 7		Mildred Anna Robinson, Adult	
June 1		Norman Jones Scofield, Adult	
June 1	Elijah T. Rowe Anna L. Christian	{ Susan Ann Aug. 13, 1900 { John Herbert Nov. 20, 1902	
Nov. 29	Clarence Van Tassell Ida Knapp	George Edward Sep. 7, 1906	

MARRIAGE REGISTER
of the church of
NEW HACKENSACK
BEGINNING WITH THE YEAR 1765

Marriage Register

1765
Sep. 25 — Were married with a license by Dom. Fryenmoet, John Jewel, j. m. and Jannetje Monfoort, wid., both born and residing in Dutches County.

Marriage banns registered

1766
May 2 — Laurens Hoff, y. m., and Catharina Schurry, y. w.,* both b. and res. in N. Hakkensack. Married within the month after the third publication.

1767
Oct. 3 — Elias van Steenbergen, widr. of Rebecca Meeke, res. in Poughkeepsie, and Catharina Hoffman, y. w., b. at N. Haarlem and res. in N. Hakkensak. Mar. within the month after the third publication.
Sep. 19 — Jacob Becker, y. m. of Schoggarie, and Antje van Kleek, y. w., of N. Hakkensak, both res. there. Mar. Oct. 14, 1767.
Eodem dato — Pieter Hoff, y. m., and Sara Schurry, y. w., both b. and res. at N. Hakkensak. Mar. Oct. 13.

1768
Oct. 9 — Cornelis du Boys, y. m., b. at Poughkeepsie, and Catharina Buys, y. w., b. in Wecope, both res. in N. Hakkensak.

1769
Oct. 14 — Frederick Rosen-Krantz, y. m., b. in Viskil, and Femmetje Bell, y. w., b. in Oswego, both res. in N. Hakkens. Mar. within the month after the third publication.
Nov. 18 — Johannes Sleght, junr., y. m., b. in Kingston, and Amy Dean, y. w., b. in Westchester, both res. in N. Hakkensak. Mar. within the month after the third publication.

1770
Feb. 10 — Andries Oostrum, y. m., and Sara Seyfer, y. w., both b. and res. in Dutches Co. Mar. Mar. 15, 1770.
June 9 — Jacob Lane, y. m. of the Raretans, res. in Poughkeepsie, and Annatje Conchlin, y. w., b. and res. in Rumbouts Precinct. Mar. the 28th ditto.
Dec. 21 — Lodewyk Seyfer, y. m., of Poughkeepsie, and Sara Tonkins, y. w., of Westchester, both res. in Dutches Co. Mar. after the third publication.

1771
Mar. 16 — William Conchlin, y. m., b. and res. in Westchester Co., and Jannetje Brouwer, y. w., b. and res. in Rumbouts Prect. Mar. after the third publication.
Apr. 20* — Nicolaas Brouwer, y. m., b. in the Viskil, and Maria Burdsall, y. w., b. on Long Island, and res. in the Viskill.
May 4 — Obadia Patterson, y. m., of the Viskil, and Susanna Conchlin, y. w., of Charlotte Prect., both res. in N. Hakkensak. Certificate given June 3.
Petrus Peele, of Kingston, and Hilletje Middag, y. w., of Poghkeepsie, both res. in the Viskil. Mar. Nov. 15, after three proclamations of the banns.
Dec. 21 — Pieter Holst, y. m., and Antje Luister, y. w., the former b. in the Raretans and the latter in N. Hakkensak; both res. there.

1772
Apr. 18 — Richard Janssen, y. m., and Margrietje Steenbergen, y. w., both b. and res. in Pochkeepsie Prect.
N. B. The bride b. in Beekmans Prect.
" 24 — Martinus Bosch, y. m., at Pachqueick, and Blandina Steenbergen, y. w., b. in the Viskil, both res. in Pochkeepsie Prect. Certificate given June 10, 1772.
May 25 — Henricus Oostrum, y. m., of Rumbouts Prect., res. in N. Hakk, and Phoebe Pinckney, y. w., of Westchester Co., res. in Poghkeepsie Prect. Mar. June 11, 1772.
Aug. 6 — Laurens Kniepper, y. m., of Neuwied in Germany, and Cathrina Coens, y. w., b. in N. York, both res. in the Fishkill. Mar. after the third publication.
Oct. 31 — Petrus de Lange, y. m., b. and res. in Oswego, and Rachel Lewis, y. w., b. and res. in Poghkeepsie Prect. Mar. after the third publication.

1773
Jan. 16 — Steven Banker, y. m., of Viskil, and Rebecca Heermans, y. w., of Rheinbeek, both res. in New Hakkensak. Mar. after the third publication.
Abram Walden, y. m.' of the Nine Partners, Beekmans Prect., and Eva Dop, y. w., *ibid.*, both res. there. Mar. after the third publication.
Henrik Bell, y. m., of Oswego, and Annetje Conchlin, y. w., of Poghkeepsie, both res. in Beekmans Prect. Mar. after the third publication.

---

* The original record has J. D., or *Jonge Dochter*, literally, young daughter, meaning young, unmarried woman, maiden or spinster.
* This may be the date of marriage.

The Reformed Dutch Church of New Hackensack

Banns registered

Dec. 24   Henrik Wiltsee, y. m., of Rumbouts Prect., and Grietje Muller, y. w., b. in Poghkeepsie Prect., both res. in New Hakkensak. Mar. Jan. 23, 1774.

1774

          Andries Heermans, y. m., and Sara Noordstrant, y. w., both b. and res. in Rumbouts Prect. Mar. Jan. 9, after three proclamations.

Jan. 29   Dirk Luyster, b. on Long Island, and Engeltje Couwenhoven, y. w., b. at O. Hakkensak, both res. in Rumbouts Prect. Mar. after the third publication.

          Ida van Never, y. m., and Marytje Conchlin, y. w., both of Rumbouts Prect. Mar. Jan. 24, after three proclamations.

Mar. 26   William Mc. Clave, of Beekman Prect., and Maria Hoffman, y. w., b. and res. in Rumbouts Prect. Mar. after the third publication.

May 18   Albert Montfoort, y. m., b. on Long Island, and Aaltje van Keuren, y. w., b. in Pakeepsie Prect., both res. in N. Hakkensak. Mar. after the third publication.

July 31   Thomas Bruyn, of Pompton, and Annatje Hooghteylingh, of the Manor of Livingston. Mar. after the third publication.

          Charrick van Keuren and Elizabeth Westerveld, wid. of Isaak Reynderse. Mar. Sep. 22, with a license.

Oct. 29   Daniel Oudewater and Nelly Harris, both of the Fishkill.

          Benjamin Bloom and Jemimah Thuston, both of Rumbouts Prect. Mar. Nov. 20, after three proclamations.

          Pieter Hoff, widower of Sara Jurry, and Cathrina Deeds. Mar. Dec. 18, after three proclamations.

1775

May 13   Peter van Bremen, of Rumbouts Prect., and Lena Ackerman, of Poghkeepsie Prect. Mar. after the third publication.

July 3   John Crom, of Rochester, and Hester la Roy, of Rumbouts Prect. Mar. June 20, 1775.

          (a mistake for June 3, or else the date of marriage should be July 20, 1775)

" 15   Joseph Hiat of Westchester, and Maria Oostrum, of Rumbouts Prect. Mar. after the third publication.

1776

Jan. 20   Gideon Buys and Rachel Dearing, both of Poghkeepsie.

June 1   James Davidsz. and Elizabeth Verwey, both of N. Hakkensak. Mar. after the third publication.

Dec. 6   Izaäk Seebringh, of Long Island and res. in Viskil, and Cathrina van Bunschoten, b. and res. in New Hakkensak. Mar. after the third proclamation.

          (a marginal note says: "See y foll. page," where the entry is repeated).

          Zyn nog dat Jaar getrouwt (Were also married this year)

          This statement seems to apply to the entries of June 26 - Sep. 29, 1776, as well as to that of May 30, 1776. In other words, the dates seem to be those on which the marriages were celebrated, instead of those on which the banns were registered.

May 30   Hugo van Kleek, widower of Elizabeth Everitt, and Rachel Brinckerhoff.

June 26   James Davis and Elizabeth Verwey, both of N. Hakkensak.

          Henry Chase and Ruth Teed, both of the Viskil.

July 5   Paul Nelson and Hanna Churchill, both of Rumbouts Prect.

Aug. 8   Jan Tapper and Levina Nelson, both of Rumbouts Prect.

Sep. 14   Elias Frair and Maria van Cleeck, both of Poghkeepsie.

" 29   Laurens van Cleeck of Poghkeepsie, and Charity Warner, of Westchester Co., both in Poghkeepsie.

Dec. 6   Izaak Seebring, of Long Island and res. in the Viskil, and Cathrina van Bunschoten, of N. Hakkensak. Mar. after the third publication.

Eodem dato   George Livingston of Galloway in Schotland, and Fanny Maas of Poghkeepsie, both res. there.

Dec. 7   Barent Harris and Jane Farguson, both of Oswego.

          Daniel Emug of the Clove, and Cathrina Dyeman of Poghkeepsie. Mar. after the third publication.

1777

Jan. 13   Casparus Romein and Cathrina Cooper, wid. of John du Boys, both of Rumbouts Prect. Mar. after the third publication.

Eodem dato   Jacob Roode and Alida van Keuren, both of Poghkeepsie.

Feb. 21   Frederik Weissenfels, Lieut. Colonel of the regular troops of the United States of America, and Elizabeth Williams, wid. of Henry Bogert. Mar. the 26th ditto.

" 24   Laurens Lasson, junr., and Maria van Wagenen, both of the Wappans Kill. Mar. after the third publication.

Marriage Register

Banns
registered
Mar. 15 Gerrit Snedeker and Cathrina Farguson, both of Beekmans Prect. Mar. after the third publication.
" 29 John Griffin and Cornelia Hoffman, both of Rumbouts.
Apr. 5 Jacobus Lasson, b. in Rumbouts and res. in Poghkeepsie, and Maria Edward, b. and res. in Rumbouts.
John Griffin and Cornelia Hoffman, both of Dutches Co., Rumbouts Prect. Mar. Apr. 23, after the third proclamation.
Aug. 27 William Kily, b. in New Jersey, and Sara La Roy, b. in Rumbouts Prect., both res. in Rumbouts. Mar. after the third publication.
Eodem dato Louis Nadue, of Paris in France, and Jane Johnson, b. in Schotland, both res. in Poghkeepsie. Mar. after the third publication.
Sep. 6 Philip Cremer and Christina Oberhaüser, both b. and res. in Oswego, in Beekman's Prect. Mar. after the third publication.
" 26 Meindert Veele and Johanna Palmontier, both of and res. in Poghkeepsie. Mar. after the third publication.
Dec. 24 Abraham Wiltsee, b. in the Viskil, and Celetje Lucky, b. in Poghkeepsie Prect. and res. in New Hakkensak. Mar. after the third publication.
" 24 Henry Diamond of the Cloove, and Phoebe Perdon of Poghkeepsie Prect., both res. in Poghkeepsie Prect. Mar. after the third publication.
Eodem dato John Dieren and Maria Lasson, both of and res. in Poghkeepsie Prect. Mar. after the third publication.
1778
Feb. 7 Laurens Becker of Rheinbeek, and Maria de Graaf of Poghkeepsie. Mar. after the third publication.
" 15 Jacob Horsner and Maria Wiltsee, both b. and res. in Hoopwel. Mar. after the third publication.
" 27 Tilman Seabury and Cathrine Kip, both b. and res. in Poghkeepsie. Mar. after the third publication.
" 28 Thomas Beayaux and Elizabeth van Cleeck, both res. in Poghkeepsie. Mar. after the third publication.
Mar. 28 Caleb Bishop and Cathrine Philips, both of Rumbouts Prect. Mar. after the third publication.
Apr. 19 Samuel Johnson of Long Island, and Hanna Reyley of Ireland, both res. in Poghkeepsie. Mar.
Eodem dato Robert Lester of N. York, and Mary Wendel of N. York, both res. in Poghkeepsie. Mar. after the third publication.
May 12 Thomas Lester of New York, and Cathrina van Cleek, both res. in Poghkeepsie. Mar. after the third publication.
Jon ter Heun of Long Island, and Maria Hoffman, both res. in Rumbouts Prect. Mar. June 14, after lawful proclamation.
Simeon Lasson, widower, and Grietje van Tessel, both of Rumbouts Prect. Mar. July 5, after lawful proclamation.
John Adams and Mary Townsend. Mar. June 8, after lawful proclamation.
Aug. 7 Petrus Buys, widower of Hanna Hawl, and Antonetta Palmontier, wid. of Jacob Wever, both res. in Poghkeepsie Prect. Mar. after the third publication.
" 11 Petrus Viele, widower, and Gerritje Frair, both of and res. in Poghkeepsie Prect. Mar. by Dom. Freligh.
James Dearin and Geertruy Gecocks, both of and res. in Poghkeepsie Prect. Mar. Aug. 15, after lawful proclamation.
James Mc. Kenny of the Viskil, and Helena Schneyder of Poghkeepsie. Mar. Aug. 29.
John Philips and Elizabeth Canneff, both of Rumbouts Prect. Mar. Aug. 31, after lawful proclamation.
Nov. 21 Gilead Hunt of East-Chester County, and Selly Lasson, both res. in Poughkeepsie Prect. Mar. after the third publication.
" 22 Johannes Hilleker and Rachel Traves, both of Rumbouts Prect.
Dec. 19 Samuel Norris, b. and res. in the Nine Partners, and Abigail Hallick, b. in the Nine Partners and res. in Rynbeek. Mar. after the third publication.
Zie aan't einde van āo 1780.—See at the end of the year 1780. (It is not quite clear whether the entry of June 15, which was left out by mistake, belongs under 1778, or under 1779.)

1779
May 16 Johannes Rosel of Philips Manor, and Mary Stilwill of the Nine Partners, both res. in Rumbouts.
June 17 Isaac Churchwell and Hanna Philips, both of Rumbouts. Mar. after the third publication.

The Reformed Dutch Church of New Hackensack

Banns registered

" 26   Thomas Müller and Cathrina Conelly, both of Rumbouts Prect. Mar. after the third publication.
John Rapalje of "'t Sagertje," (literally: the Little Sawyer, meaning Saugerties), and Anna de Lange of the Nine Partners. Mar. after the third publication.

July 24   John Jay of Westchester Co., and Elizabeth Bush of the Viskil, both res. at New Hakkensak. Mar. after the third publication.

Aug. 20   Joshua Bishop and Hester la Roy, both of Rumbouts. Mar. after the third publication.

" 29   Ebenezer Dakins of Westchester, and Cathrina Müller of Rumbouts Prect. Mar. after the third publication.

Sep. 5   Jan Middelaar of Poughkeepsie Prect., and Matty van Tessel of Rumbouts. Mar. after the third publication.

" 11   Pieter Rosecrans of New Hakkensak, and Antje Westerveld of Old Hakkensak, both res. in Rumbouts Prect. Mar. after the third publication.

" 25   Goris Storm, widower, and Anna Ray, wid. of Johannes Ray, both res. in Poughkeepsie Prect. Mar. after the third publication.

Eodem dato   Henry van Cleeck, soldier of Coll. Cortland's regiment, and Anna Brouwer, both of Poughkeepsie Prect. Mar. after the third publication.

Eodem dato   William Philips and Cornelia Heermans, both of Rumbouts Prect. Mar. after the third publication.

Oct. 2   Henry Lasson and Elizabeth Crans (Craus?), both of the Clove. Mar. after the third publication.

Eodem dato   Jan Lasson of Pouchkeepsie Prect. and res. there, and Anna van Sickelen, of Long Island, and res. in Rumbouts Prect. Mar. after the third publication.

Eodem dato   Jeremia Mandigo, b. and res. in the Nine Partners, and Sara Elsworth of Newburg, res. in Rumbouts. Mar. after the third publication.

Nov. 21   Casparus van Keuren of Poughkeepsie Prect., and Maria Oostrum of New Hakkensack, both res. in New Hakkensak. Mar. after the third publication.

Eodem dato   Henry Johnson of Menissing, and Margaretha Ferdon of Poughkeepsie, both res. in Poughkeepsie Prect. Mar. after the third publication.

Dec. 4   Jan Heermans and Cathrina Griffin, both b. and res. in Rumbouts Prect. Mar. after the third publication.

" 5   Jarvis Underhill and Mary van Bremen, both of Rumbouts. Mar. after the third publication.

" 24   Henrik Lasson and Mary Lasson, wid., both of Poughkeepsie Prect. Mar. after the third publication.

1780
Jan. 15   Thomas Band and Penetta Steenbergen, both of Poughkeepsie Prect. Mar. after the third publication.

Eodem dato   Peter Bush of Rumbouts Prect., and Brechje Meyer of Haarlem, both res. in Rumbouts. Mar. after the third publication.

Eodem dato   Nathanaël Solmes and Lydia Durlin, both of Rumbouts. Mar. after the third publication.

Apr. 15   Jan van Cleeck and Jane Viele, both of Poughkeepsie Prect. Mar. after the third publication.
Jacob du Boys and Femmetje Oostrum. Mar. May 12. *Ex ipso gravidam.*

Eodem dato   Michael Wever of Oswego, and Margriet Buys of Egg harbour, both res. in Poughkeepsie. Mar. after the third publication.

Eodem dato   Gerrit Lansing and Anna Manne, both of Poughkeepsie. Mar. after the third publication.

May 12   Jeremia Clarck and Lydia Allen, both of Rumbouts Prect. Mar. after the third publication.

Eodem dato   Joseph Fowlar and Maria Lent, both of Rumbouts. Mar. after the third publication.

Eodem dato   George Schneider and Hannah Chandel, both of Poughkeepsie Prect. Mar. after the third publication.

June 4   Pieter van den Bogert of Poughkeepsie, and Anna Davis of Rumbouts. Mar. after the third publication.

" 11   Jacob Meyer of Haarlem, and Cornelia Meyer of N. Hakkensak. Mar. after the third publication.

Aug. 6   Samuel Kip of Rheinbeck, and Maria Middag of Marbletown, both res. in the Nine Partners. Mar. by Mr. Graham.

Sep. 4   John Lewis, b. in Rumbouts Prect., and Jane Davis, b. in New York, both res. in Poughkeepsie. Mar. after the third publication.

" 9   Stepen Calloo of the Nine partners, and Sara Drake, wid. Brouwer, of Rumbouts Prect., both res. in Rumbouts. Mar. after the third publication.

Marriage Register

Banns
registered
Oct. 15   Petrus Schoonhoven, b. in Hoopwel, and Cathrina Fitchard of Poughkeepsie. Mar. after the third publication.
Dec. 2   Nicolaas Fisher of New York, res. in Poughkeepsie, and Maria Müller, of Rumbouts Prect. Mar. after the third publication.
" 11   Daniel Smith and Sara Palmontier, both of and res. at Poughkeepsie. Mar. after the third publication.
" 16   Mattheus van Keuren and Hester Hoffman, both of Rumbouts Prect. Mar. after the third publication.
          Daniel Hoffman of Rumbouts, and Mary Lyons of Beeckmans Prect. Mar. after the third publication.
June 15   "Left out by mistake"
          Joseph Hegeman, b. on Long Island, and res. in the Nine partners, and Blandina Pels, b. and res. in Poghkeepsie.
1779 *Sie't begin van de Lyst in* ōo *1779*. (See the beginning of the list of the year 1779.)
Jan. 7   Obadiah Weecks of Long Island, and Elizabeth Müller of Pôkeepsie, both res. in Pôkeepsie Prect. Mar. after the third publication.
" 16   Georgius Reyder of Brunswick in Germany, and Jane Brouwer of New Hakkensak, both res. here. Mar. after the third publication.
" 23   Pieter Schryver of Straatsburg in Beekmans Prect., and Elizabeth Lasson, b. in Oswego, both res. in Oswego. Mar. after the third publication.
Feb. 14   William Davis of Rumbouts Prect., and Emy Crannel of Oswego, both res. in Rumb. Mar. after the third publication.
          James McCreedy of Rumb., and res. in Oswego, and Elizabeth Hoffman, b. and res. in Rumb. "Married after publishmt."
Mar. 3   Zacharias Clump and Geertje van Sickele, both of Rumbouts Prect. Mar. after the third publication.
          Roelof Philips and Cathrina van Bremen, both of Rumbouts. Mar. after the third publication.

1781
          James Montgomery and Jemima Tailor, both of New York. Mar. Jan. 1, without license or publication, *propter Gravitatem*.
Jan. 12   Theodorus Snedeker and Patty Betel, both of Poughkeepsie. Mar. after the third publication.
" 20   Peter du Puy of Cortlands Manor, and Susannah Emot of the Jerseys, both in New Hakkensak. Mar. after the third publication.
" 27   John Palmontier and Pally Jurrey, both of Poughkeepsie. Mar. after the third publication.
Feb. 3   Childs Justus of Long Island, and Maria McNeel, both of Rumbouts. Mar. after the third publication.
" 24   Andries Reynderse and Elizabeth laRoy, both of Rumbouts Prect. Mar. after the third publication.
Mar. 25   Hickey Bates of New York, and Eva van Sickelen of Long Island, both res. in Rumbouts Prect. Mar. after the third publication.
Apr. 8   Jacob Zwaart of The Hague in Holland, and Pally Russel of Poughkeepsie, both res. in Poughkeepsie. Mar. after the third publication.
" 14   Johannes Pels and Sara la Roy, both of and res. in Poughkeepsie Prect. Mar. after the third publication.
" 28   Michiel Golneck of Long Island, and Elizabeth Deeds, b. in New Hakkensak, both res. in N. Hakkensak. Mar. after the third publication.
          Alexander Gifford of Schotland, and Christina Cherrick of New York. Mar. after the third publication.
"Left out by mistake"
Jan. 27   Abraham Hogeland of N. Hakkensak, and Aaltje Brouwer of Long Island, both res. in N. Hakkensak. Mar. after the third publication.
Feb. 3   Isaac Lent of Cortlands Manor, and Cornelia Lent of N. Hakkensak. Mar. after the third publication.
Mar. 28   Jacobus L. van de Water of Rumbouts, and Amy Reiner of Poughkeepsie Prect., both res. in Hoopwel. Mar. after the third publication.
May 19   Baltus Frair and Jacoba van Cleek, both of Poughkeepsie. Mar. after the third publication.
July 28   John Brouwer and Elizabeth Gaunce, both of Pôkeepsie Prect. Mar. after the third publication.
Aug. 18   Teunis Schutt, b. in Fishkill, and Elizabeth Culver of Long Island, both res. in Rumbouts Prect. Mar. after the third publication.
Sep. 8   William Churchill and Elizabeth Coffin, both of Rumbouts. Mar. after the third publication.

The Reformed Dutch Church of New Hackensack

Banns registered

Sep. 22   Cornelis Noordstrant of Rumb. and Sara Remsen of Tappan. Married after 3 proclamations.
Oct. 25   Jan Ryckman of N. York, and Maria Allen of New Hakkensack, both res. in Dutches Co. Mar. after the third publication.
Johannes Rowe of Pokeepsie, and Maria Duitscher of the Viskil, both res. in New Hakkensack. "N. B. *Gebode gestuit.*" (Publication stopped).
Dec. 8   Jan Hoogteyling of Livingston Manor, and Hannah Hicks of Rumbouts Prect.
Dec. 14   Moses de Graaf and Jannetje van de Water, both of Rumbouts Prect. Mar. after the third publication.
Thomas Fr. Jacokes and Jemima Sherwood, both of Pôkeepsie Prect. Mar. Dec. 24.

1782
Apr. 27   Abraham Sleght, junr., of Kingston, and Ruth Rohe of the Viskil, both res. in Rumbouts Prect. Mar. after the third publication.
May 4   Pieter Wever and Lea Storm, both of Pokeepsie Prect. Mar. after the third publication.
" 13   James Culver of Long Island, res. in Charlotte Prect., and Adriana du Boys, b. and res. in Rumbouts Prect. Mar. after the third publication.
" 18   Gysbert van de Bogert, b. and res. in Beekmans Prect., and Jannetje Peele, wid. of Zacharias Flegelaar, b. in Kingston and res. in Rumbouts Prect. Mar. after the third publication.
July 5   Mattheus Wildy and Mary Bride. Mar. after the third publication.
Eodem dato   John Hoff, b. and res. in N. Hakkensak, and Rebecca Storm, b. in Pokeepsie Prect. and res. in Rumbouts. Mar. after the third publication.
Aug. 3   Wilhelmus T. Hooghteylingh of Ulster Co., and Rachel Johs. Hooghteyling of Dutches Co. Mar. after the third publication.
Eodem dato   Robert Fisk and Elizabeth Jones, both of Rumbouts Prect. Mar. after the third publication.
"   Joseph Schut of Dutches Co., and Cathrina Fowler of Ulster Co., both res. in Rumbouts Prect. Mar. after the third publication.
Sep. 10   Daniel Veal and Maria Hughson, both of Dutches Co. Mar. after the third publication.
Oct. 11   Israël Veal and Eleonora de Long, both of Beekmans Prect.
(It is uncertain whether this date represents the date of marriage or that of the registration of the banns).
Eodem dato   Isaac Wright and Levina Young, both of Rumbouts Prect. Mar. after the third publication.
"   Stephen Lawrence and Mary Chaterdon, both of Westchester Co. and res. in Pôkeepsie Prect. Mar. after the third publication.
Oct. 19   Jan Deeds and Elizabeth Lasson, both of Rumbouts Prect. Mar. after the third publication.
Nov. 25   Robert Wiltson of Rhode Island, and Cathrina Wiltsee of Rumbouts Prect. Mar. after the third publication.
(A note in different handwriting and ink, which is inserted above the names, says: "both of Westchester.")
" 30   Alexander Laughton and Mary Snyder, both of Pôkeepsie Prect. Mar. after the third publication.
Dec. 28   Isaac van Cleef of Long Island, and Anna Conchlin of Pôkeepsie, both res. in Rumbouts Prect. Mar. after the third publication.
June 23   Jan Hoff and Rebecca Storm, both of Rumbouts Prect. Mar. after the third publication.
" 30   Matthew Wildy of Hoopwel, and Mary Bryant of Philips pattern, both living in Hoopwel.

1783
June 21   Willem Davis and Phoebe Scott, both of Pôkeepsie Prect. Mar. after the third publication.
Aug. 31   Seth Johnes of Rhode Island, and Martha Johnson, wid. of Staten Island, both res. at New Hakkensak. Mar. after the third publication.
Sep. 13   John Jewel and Cathrina Reynders, both of Rumbouts Prect. Mar. after the third publication.
" 16   George Peeck and Hester Tapper, both of Pôkeepsie Prect. Mar. on certificate of consent.
" 21   Hendrik Hegeman of Reinbeek Prect., and Cathrina Griffin of Rumbout Prect. Mar. after the third publication.
Theodorus Adriaanse of the Viskil, and Cathrina van Hoek of New York. Mar. Sep. 25, on a certificate of consent of the parents.

Marriage Register

Banns
registered
Oct. 5   Cornelis Cornelissen Brouwer and Elizabeth Brisben, both of Pôkeepsie Prect. Mar. after the third publication.
Dec. 24   Albert Westerveld and Sarah Merckel, both of Rumbouts Prect. Mar. after the third publication.
Eodem dato   Maas Oostrander and Clara Monfoort, both of Rumbouts Prect. Mar. after the third publication.
  Jonathan Ogden Mosely of New Haven, and Gilly van Voorhees of the Viskil. Mar. Oct. 16, on a certificate of consent.

Beginning with 1784 marriages are entered in English

1784
Jan. 15   Married after lawful publishment, Albert Westervelt &
" 17   Entered William McCollister of Ulster County & Eleanore Wiltsee of Pokeepsie Prect. Married after lawfull publishment.
Mar. 13   Married John Clap of Rumbouts Prect. & Sarah Woolly of the Nine Partners.
" "   Married Frederick Dayton of Westchester & Hester de Grave of Pokeepsie Prect., Dutches County, after lawful publishmt.
" "   Entered Francis van de Bogert & Elizabeth Palmontere. Married the 13 of April, 1784.
" "   Entered William Hicks of New Hakkensak & Anna de Grave of Pokeepsie. Married after due publishment.
" 20   Married Henry Johnson of Menissing & Elizabeth Ferdon of Pokeepsie Prect., both living in Pokeepsie Prect.
" 7   Entered Jacobus Westerveld & Rebecca du Boys, both of Pokeepsie Prect. Married after lawful publishmt.
Aug. 19   Married Peter Maston & Cathrine Walden.
Sep. 4   Entered & married after lawful publishmt, John Swartwoud van de Bogert of Pokeepsie Prect. & Dina van de Bogert, both of Pokeepsie Prect.
" 12   Married Peter C. Bogardus & Metje van Tessel.
July 24   Entered Simeon Frair, Widower, & Lena Palmontere, widow. Married after lawful publishment.
Oct. 30   Married after lawful publishment, John Fisher of Pokeepsie and Charity la Roy.
Eodem dato   Isaac Noordstrant of Rumbouts & Pally Churchill, of the same place. Published but not married by me.
Dec. 8   Married Adolf van de Water & Phoebe Philips, both of Rumbouts Prect. After lawful Publishment.
" 11   Married Matthew Lasson & Rebecca Hoffman of Pokeepsie Prect., after lawful publishment.
Eodem dato   James Bunker & Mary Tippet, after lawful publishmt.
Entered same Day   Abraham Philips & Sarah Lawrens, both of Rumbouts. Married after lawful publishment.
Dec. 18   Entered Abraham Middag la Roy & Aafje Rome, both of Pokeepsie Prect. Married after lawful publishmt.

1785
Jan. 1   Entered Daniel Verveele & Cathrine van de Water, both of Rumbouts Prect. Married after lawful publishmt.
Eodem dato   Henry Wiltse & Mary Jacocks, both of Pokeepsie Prect. Married after lawful publishmt.
Feb. 19   Entered Joseph Mosher & Easter Jacocks, both of Dutches County; married after lawful publishment.
Eodem dato   Entered Gabriel Bishop & Sarah Every, both of Rumbouts. Married, after lawful publishment.
May 4   Married after lawful publishment, Thomas Jacocks & Mary Tobias, both of Pokeepsie Prect.
" 14   Entered John Westerveld & Anna la Roy, both of Pokeepsie Prect. Married after lawful publishment.
Aug. 14   Entered Andries Lasson & Anna Brouwer, both of Pokeepsie Prect.
Eodem dato   Peter Miller & Sarah Brisben, both of Pokeepsie Prect. Both married after lawful publishmt.
Sep. 23   Abraham Coon & Martha Every, both of New Hakkensak. Married after lawful publishmt.
  Samuel Goodrich of Middletown & Hannah Burche(r) of Old Hakkensak.
Oct. 20   Entered Ebenezer Staples & Mary Philips, both of Pokeepsie. Married after lawful publishmt.
Eod. dato   Gilbert Bloomer & Rachel Barton, both of Philips Prect.

The Reformed Dutch Church of New Hackensack

1786

Jan. 14 — Entered Henry Steenberg & Lydia Rappalje, both of Rumbouts Prect. Married after lawful publishmt.

Eodem dato — Peter Couwenhoven & Sarah van Sickelen, both of Rumbouts Precinct. Married after lawful publishment.

Feb. 26 — Entered Abraham van Nette of Rhinebeck & Pally la Roy of Rumbouts Prect. Married after publishmt.

" 28 — Abraham Hyat & Cathrine Leavens. Married after lawful publishmt.

Mar. 12 — Married upon a Certificate Isaac Wood & Hannah van Bunschoten of Pokeepsie Prect.

" 31 — Entered Benjamin Geacocks and Geertruy Ferdon, both of Pokeepsie Prect.

May 4 — Entered Peleg Spencer & Deborah Frost, both of Beekmans Prect. Married after lawful publishmt.

" 13 — Entered Robert Travis and Lena Lasson, both of Pokeepsie Prect. Married after lawful Publishmt.

" 31 — Entered George Coonley of Washington Prect. & Sarah Cramer of Beekman's Prect. Married after lawful publishmt.

June 17 — Entered Gerhardus Wiltsee of Rumbts. & Cathrina van Kleeck of Pokeepsie Prect. Married after lawful Publishmt.

" 24 — Entered Francis la Roy and Elizabeth van de Water; both of Rumbout Prect. Married after lawful Publishmt.

Oct. 11 — Entered Mattheus Buys & Sarah Palmontier, both of Pokeepsie Prect. Married Nov. 26.

Dec. 17 — Married upon Credit Moses de Graaf & Ann Murray, both of Pokeepsie Prect.

1787

Jan. 20 — Married upon Certificate Samuel Wa (ke or he) & Cathrine Pine, both of Beekman's Prect.

Entered James Wa (ke or he) & Rachel Dennis, both of Beekm. Prect. Married after lawful Publishmt.

Feb. 11 — Married Abraham LeQuier & Mary Seebring.

Apr. 30 — Entered Henry Barnes of Pokeepsie Prect. & Anna Teerpenning of Rumbts. Prect.

May 3 — Married on a Certificate, Stephen Seaman & Lydia De Lano of Poughkeepsie.

July 7 — Entered Aaron Cool & Hesther de Graaf, both of Poughkeepsie Prect.

Aug. 4 — Married John J. Lasson & Lydia Miller, upon Certific.

Oct. 14 — Married William Tahlman &

Aug. 1 — Married Jacobus van Nette of Albany County & Lena Busch of Rumb. Prect.

Jan. 1 — Married with Consent of the parents Michiel Schute & Cornelia Couwenhoven.

Feb. 11 — Married Abraham Le Quier & Mary Seebring.

Apr. 30 — Entered Henry Barns of Pokeepsie Prect. and Anna Teerpenning of Rumbouts. Lawfully published and married.

May 2 — Married at Rheinbeek Andrew Brosnahain (or Brosrahain) & Margret Rim, with Consent of all parties.

Dec. 8 — Entered John Ferguson & Sarah van de Water, both of Rumbouts Prect. Married after publishment.

" 16 — Married Gideon de Graaf & Dinah van Cleek, both of Poughkeepsie Prect.

" 24 — Married after publishmt. John Meyer from Lotharingen in Germany & Anna Wolff of Oswego.

Peter Wheeler & Mary Lasson, both of Poughkeepsie Prect.

1788

Jan. 30 — Married Andrew White & Rebecca Pooly. With Consent of parents.

Same day — James van Cleek & Anna Veele, with Consent of parents, of Poughkeepsie.

Feb. 2 — Married by lawful Publishment, Benjamin van de Water & Elizabeth van Cleek of Rumbouts precinct.

Mar. 10 — James Mills of New York & Mary Waddle of the Jerseys, both living in Poughkeepsie. Married upon Credit.

Apr. 6 — Entered Ahasuerus van Cleek, Junr. & Anne Roame, both of Rumbouts Prect. Married after publishment.

" " — Entered Simeon Frair & Hannah van Wagena, both of Poughkeepsie. Married after publishment.

" 27 — Entered Richard Griffen & Elizabeth Seebring, both of Rumbout Prect. Married after publishment.

May 15 — Married on Certificate, Hugh Montgomery & Mary Harpur of New York, both living in Fishkill.

Nov. 7 — Entered Thomas Johnson of New York & Pally Hickbey of Nine Partners, both living in Rumbouts Prect.

Dec. 13 — Entered William Lasson & Antje Dutcher, both of Rumbouts Prect. Married after Publishment.

" 14 — Married Nathan Concklin of Fishkill & Margareth Tonkins of Oswego.

Marriage Register

Feb. 20		Married Sylvester McDonald & Mary Kronchheid, both of the Nine Partners.
Mar. 3		Married Barent M. van Cleeck & Mary Ferdon, both of Poughkeepsie.
Same day		Married James Canneff & Elizabeth McBride, both of Rumbouts.
Aug. 20		Married Thomas Jacocks & Lydia de Graaf, both of Poughkeepsie Prect. After Publishment.
" 31		Married lawfully James Stevens & Aly Kennedy, widow van Amburgh.
Sep. 28		Married John Smith & Hipsey Cary, with Consent of parents.
Oct. 9		Lawfully married, Elias Steenbergen & Elizabeth Davis, both of Poughkeepsie Prect.
Nov. 2		Lawfully married, Jacob van der Burgh & Cornelia Swartwoud, both of Poughkeepsie.
July 10		Lawfully married, John Yates & Getty Lasson, both of Poughk. Prect.
1789		
Feb. 12		Lawfully married, George Holms of N. York & Cathrine Yurcks of Hopewell.
July 15		Lawfully married, John Fort & Susannah du Boys, both of Poughkeepsie Prect.
Sep. 7		Lawfully married, Johannes Veale & Cathrine Ferdon, widow Westerveld.
" 25		Married by Consent of parents, Samuel Pinckney & Sarah Brouwer, both of Poughkeepsie Prect.
Nov. 4		Married, John Westerveld & Anne Burhans, both of Poughkeepsie Prect.

MATRIMONIAL REGISTER

During the Ministry of George Barkulo — N. Hackensack

1805
Aug. 17   Daniel Van Voorhis to Margaret Haines.
Dec.. 4   Peter Pells to Mary Green.
"   7   Samuel Robinson to Sarah Furman.
"   12   John T. Griffin to Letitia Vermilie.
1806
Jan. 8   John Hoghlandt to Maria Waldron.
"   11   Peter Coolridge to Elizabeth Bownes.
"   27   Henry Waller to Melinda Gordon (Relict of William B. Verplanck).
Feb. 6   John Sypher to Mary Cornwell.
"   13   Henry Martin to Anne Mead.
"   16   Richard Travers to Phebe Banker.
"   22   Jacob Young to Elizabeth Lockwood.
Mar. 2   Henry Norris to Rhody Schofield.
"   "   James Given (or Gioen) to Susan Van Wyck.
"   15   James Weeks to Sarah Southard.
"   22   Daniel Giles to Phebe Baker.
Aug. 9   Ezekiel Ladoe to Sarah Bauker.
"   "   Ebenezer Sheerman to Mary Van Alst, formerly widow Mary Storm.
"   26   John Wiltsie to Winifred Rapalje.
"   30   Peter Hageman to Phebe Bogardus.
Sep. 7   James G. Middagh to Elizabeth Carman.
"   28   David Patterson to Clara Conklyn.
Oct. 11   Warren Giles to Phebe Palmer.
Dec. 4   Bartholomew Green to Deborah Dodge.
"   23   Stephen Geer to Ruth Codwise.
1807
Jan. 3   Jacob Hill to Amy Orange.
"   24   Revd. Cornelius D. Westbrook to Hannah V. Wyck.
"   29   Joseph Budd to Elenor Pinckney.
Feb. 21   Samuel Weid to Sarah Veal.
Mar. 24   Gilbert Green to Mary Patterson.
"   26   Stephen Monfoot to Alletie Adriance.
June 20   Richard Snedicor to Phebe Jewel.
"   27   Abraham Philipps to Jane Philipps.
"   29   Nathaniel Berry to Susan Clapp.
July 12   Jonathan Baker to Jane Van Vlecht.
Sep. 13   Benjamin Shear to Syntie Cornell.
"   16   Elias Van Bunschoten to Syntie Veelie.
"   26   Gerardus Vermilie to Charlotte Palmer.
Oct. 3   George Burris to Ann Collins.
"   10   Charles Westcot to Hannah Schofield.
"   12   Tompkins Ladoe to Mercy Gilbert.
"   24   William Harris to Nancy Secord.

The Reformed Dutch Church of New Hackensack

" 29 Duncan Graham to Ann Van Wyck.
Nov. 3 Solomon Smith to Elizabeth Coe.
" 14 William Beedle to Mary Van Voorhis.
Dec. 27 Thomas (slave of Matthew Mesier) to Margaret (slave of Jacobus Monfoort).
" 31 Jacob Adriance to Elizabeth Humphrey.
" " Henry Snyder to Elizabeth Hutchins.
1808
Feb. 14 John McFaddan to Martha Tompkins.
" 18 Daniel Sharp to Mary Esmond.
" 20 Benjamin De Lamater to Sarah Swartwout.
Mar. 3 Garrit Snedecor to Sarah Millar (widow of Jeremiah Millar, deceased).
" 27 Judith (slave of Peter Waldron) to William (slave of Cornelius R. Van Wyck).
Apr. 5 Peter P. Van Kleeck to Emily Lowe (widow of —— Lowe) her maiden name Savens.
" 7 Abraham Sleght, Junr. to Mercy Myer.
June 14 Martin Shar to Letitia Baldwin.
" 19 William Wiley to Catharine Bogardus.
" " King (a freeman) to Caty (slave of Joseph Jackson).
Aug. 27 William Pullock to Hannah Churchill.
Sep. 1 Lemuel Fuller to Mary Wilcox.
" 19 John Smith to Elizabeth Brower.
Nov. 2 John V. Hicks to Mary Esmond.
1809
June 3 Isaac Durling to Alletie Rynders.
Oct. 22 Peter Swaid to Gitty Allen.
Nov. 26 Caleb Nostrand to Hannah Valentine.
1810
Jan. 27 Abraham D. Van Wyck to Phebe Boerum.
Aug. 26 Israel Shear to Charity Pells, maiden name Angevine.
" " Joshua Underhill to Margaret Angevine.
Oct. 25 Andrew Lawson to Martha Jewel.
Nov. 3 Derick T. Brinkerhoff to Magdelen Southard, maiden name Monfoort.
Dec. 13 Frederick Strang to Catharine Hughson.
1811
Jan. 19 John Dorset to Nancy Wiley.
" " Richard C. Van Wyck to Elizabeth Thorne.
July 25 Jacob Covenhoven to Barbara Covenhoven.
1812
Jan. 15 Peter Philipps to Mary Bomp.
" 16 Isaac Byce to Mary Webb.

Marriages by the Rev. Thomas Dewitt

1813
Jan. 14 Ephraim Smith to Ann Gonse.
Jan. 16 Peter Roe to Cynthia Gage.
Mar. 18 Jacob Relf to Margaret Cornwell.
May 29 Peter Dates to Jane Todd.
Nov. 13 Benjamin A. Sleght to Caroline Ackerman.
1814
Jan. 5 James Dodge to Electa Seward.
Feb. 23 Nathaniel Bethel Snedeker to Margaret Monfoort.
Apr. 9 John Wolven to Hannah Wyckoff.
Apr. 16 George Black to Anna Patterson, widow of —— Disbrow.
June 2 Isaac I. Van Wyck to Amelia Matilda Jackson.
Aug. 27 Robert Sweet to Phoebe Schroeder.
1815
Mar. 8 Douw Velie to Hannah Van Der Bilt.
June 24 Aaron Hazen to Sally Tilyou.
Oct. 4 Joseph Miller to Nelly Dutcher.
Oct. 5 Charles Dutcher to Cynthia Low.
1816
July 31 Selah Budd to Mary Van Der Bilt.
Nov. 20 Joseph Budd to Freelove Townsend.
1817
Jan. 2 James Vail to Ann Monfoort.
Jan. 11 Gilbert Weeks to Jane Phillips.

Marriage Register

Feb. 6	Simson Dearin to Hetty Van der bilt.
Feb. 12	Peter J. Monfoort to Hetty Viele.
May 4	Ezekiel Jewell to Celia Van de Bogart.
Aug.	Zachariah I. Thompson to Phoebe Wyckoff.
Sep. 16	Morris Teller to Hannah Ackerman.
Sep. 23	Henry Disborough to Elizabeth Losee.
Oct. 20	James Parish to Mehilla Potter.
Nov. 12	Robert Luckey to Frances Nelson.

1818
Jan. 22	Daniel Platt to Phoebe Adriance.
Mar. 18	Abraham Myers to Elizabeth Cornell.
July 18	Benjamin Van Arsdalen to Rebecca Churchill.
Oct. 28	Abraham B. Stockholm to Eltsie D. Sleght.
Oct. 29	James Bennaway to Elizabeth Burnet.
Dec. 23	Mathew V. B. Ackerman to Helen Van Bramer.

1819
Jan. 14	George Vanderbilt to Helen Miller.
Jan. 26	Rev. Cornelius D. Westbrook of Fishkill to Sarah Beekman of Kingston.
Jan. 28	Nicholas Anthony to Phoebe Platt.
Feb. 11	Enos Jewell to Caroline Van Sickler.
Feb. 25	William B. Hoogland to Susan Pells.
May 13	Benjamin Pollock to Sarah Thurston.
Oct. 27	John Everitt to Jemima Southerd.

1820
Oct. 12	John D. Cornell to Phoebe Smith.
Oct. 31	Peter Hoffman to Rebecca Luckey.
Dec. 7	Robert Tanner to Eliza Brower.
Dec. 9	Anthony Thompson, living at Widow Teller's, Fishkill Lan to Phoebe James, living at James Dearin's—Blacks.
Dec. 23	to Phoebe Van Sickler.
Dec. 20	Benjamin Scofield to Phoebe Roe.

1821
Feb. 7	John Ackerman to Maria Nelson.
Mar. 14	Enos Mead to Catherine Hoffman.
Mar. 21	Abraham Diamond to Elizabeth Luckey.
Apr. 13	Cornelius Rynders to Teuntia Wolven.
Sep. 18	John Teller to Catherine Ackerman.
Nov. 7	Daniel A. Van Voorhis to Cornelia Nagel.
Nov. 13	Zebulon Phillips to Susan Maria Dodge.
Dec. 19	James Martin to Rebecca Klump.

1822
Jan. 24	Hervey E. Everitt to Letty M. H. Luyster.
July 3	John Middagh to Mary Warren.
Oct. 2	Isaac Burnet to Catherine Middagh.
Oct. 19	Stephen P. Shaw to Hannah Hicks.
Nov. 7	John Travis to Helen Middagh.

1823
Jan. 8	Abraham F. Westervelt to Hannah Lawson.
Mar. 2	Richard W. Southard to Susan Hallock.
Mar. 4	Peter Dearin to Jane Van Amburgh.
July 24	Benjamin Van Keuren to Jane Ann Hoffman.
Oct. 8	James Van Duyn to Catharine Hansen.
Oct. 16	Ezekiel Viele, Junr. to Eliza Green.
Oct. 23	William Brower to Ann Hulst.
Nov. 20	James Townsend to Ann Shear.
Dec. 28	Thaddeus Kirkham to Eliza Montross.

1824
Feb. 10	Nathan Westcott to Gertrude Luckey.
Mar. 3	Robert Gould to Mary Hecock, blacks.
Mar. 17	George W. Delavergne to Mary Yates.
Oct. 20	William Hicks to Maria Smith.
Nov. 17	Thomas J. Dearin to Mary Ann Luckey.
Nov. 20	Daniel H. Hosier to Catherine Eliza Shear.
Nov. 24	Francis Losee Monfoort to Maria Way.

1825
Mar. 9	Peter Delavergne to Ann Yates.
Oct. 5	Oliver Van Duyn to Susan Smith.

The Reformed Dutch Church of New Hackensack

Oct. 23 William Dutcher to Aletta Monfoort.
Oct. 27 John P. Dorland to Margaret Ann Pells.
1826
Jan. 18 Philander Seward to Susan Monfoort.
Feb. 23 Richard Grant to Maria Jewell.

REGISTER OF MARRIAGES
During the Ministry of Revd. M. W. Dwight

1827
Apr. 26 David Warner and Hannah Beaton.
May 31 John Luyster and Mary Yonni.
"   " John Potter Little and Rachel Potter Blacks.
"   "   and Gertrude Diamond.
Sep. 11 Charles B. Green and Mary Green.
Nov. 15 Gilbert Sherwood and Ann B. Platt.
1828
July 21 Simeon Gold and Mary Caldern (or Caldun). Blacks.
Oct. 8 Samuel Robinson and Harriet Phillips.
June 17 Samuel Yates and Elizabeth Monfort.
Oct. 23 James Downing and Mary Phillips.
Oct. 23 Nelson Grant and Rachel Cudgill Blacks.
Nov. 12 Peter Dates and Cynthia Ann Wyckoff.
Dec. 4 Jeremiah V. C. Monfort and Susan Patterson.
1829
Feb. 22 Seymour Lewis and Cornelia Van Wyck.
Mar. 18 Edwin De La Vergne and Antoinette Hewson.
Mar. 2 Jacob Van Bunschoten Concklin and Nelly Shute.
Oct. 8 Gerrit Brewer and Mary Robinson.
Oct. 8 Lawrence Myers and Jamima Weeks.
Dec. 30 William Smith and Sarah Marshall.
1830
Jan. 7 Francis Drake, a. 23, Mercht. and Rachel Lucky, a. 20, of Poughkeepsie.
        Wit.:
            Elias V. B. Concklin of Fishkill and Thomas Dering, Poughkeepsie.
Sep. 14 Abraham Casster (or Cassler) of Springfield and Nancy Shader of Fishkill.
Oct. 20 Abijah P. Robinson of Fishkill and Cynthia Jane Vn. Dyne of LaGrange.
Dec. 8 Abraham Smith and Ruth Jane Robinson of Fishkill.
Dec. 15 George B. Adriance and Sarah Thorn of Fishkill.
Dec. 22 Tunis Ackerman and Jane Thorn of LaGrange.
Dec. 23 Isaac Aiken of Green Bush and Hetty Ann Ackerman of LaGrange.
1831
May 19 Jeromus Vermilyea of LaGrange and Phebe Palmer of LaGrange.
May 26 Alexander Kudner of Fishkill and Hannah Monfort of LaGrange.
Sep. 13 Jeremiah D. Hughson of New York and Jane Mary Ann Drake of Fishkill.
Nov. 1 William Teller of Rhine Beck and Eliza Thorn of Fishkill.
Dec. 12 or 5 Jacob A. Robertson of New York and Hellen Ackerman of LaGrange.
Dec. 21 Joseph Brewer of Fishkill and Mary Farrington of Poughkeepsie.
Dec. 21 Samuel Luckey, Junr., of Poughkeepsie, and Deborah Brewer of Poughkeepsie.
·Dec. 22 Abraham Wynkoop of LaGrange and Jane Francis of Poughkeepsie, Blacks.
1832
Jan. 18 James Dates of Poughkeepsie and Hannah M. Vn. Dyne of LaGrange.
Apr. 9 William H. Dodge of New York and Catharine De La Vergne of LaGrange.
Apr. 18 Stephen Monfort of Fishkill and Phebe Bush of Fishkill.
Apr. 26 Albert Monfort of LaGrange and Margaret Monfort of LaGrange.
July 1 Charles Griffin of Poughkeepsie and Ellen Davis of Poughkeepsie.
Aug. 2 William D. Hunt of Poughkeepsie and Catharine Miller of Poughkeepsie.
Aug. 26 Lewis Rhodes of Poughkeepsie and Jane Burnet of Poughkeepsie.
Sep. 3 Anthony Purdy of Fishkill and Julia Heermance of Fishkill. Blacks.
Sep. 5 Timothy Hicks of Fishkill and Mary Compton of Fishkill.
Oct. 17 William Curtis of Fishkill and Maria Vn. Cleek of Fishkill.
Oct. 17 Barnet Burtis of Hilsdale and Mary Joan Vn. Der Bilt of LaGrange.
Oct. 20 Daniel Jackson of Fishkill and Harriet Lawrence of Fishkill.
Oct. 24 Zachariah Myers of Fishkill and   Jewell of Fishkill.
Oct. 30 Jacob Vn. Ambergh of Poughkeepsie and   Curtis of Poughkeepsie.
Dec. 6 Sylvester Potter of Fishkill and Sarah Ann Vermilyea of Fishkill.

Marriage Register

1833
Jan. 1 Charles Smith of Fishkill and Ann Maria Vn. Arsdale of Fishkill.
Feb. 7 James Henry Knapp of Fishkill and Leah Nelson of Fishkill.
Feb. 9 Joseph Rogers of Fishkill and Emilinda Mitchell of Fishkill.
Feb. 9 John Aikin of Fishkill and Elizabeth Weddles of Fishkill.

REGISTER OF MARRIAGES
During the Ministry of Revd. Cornelius Van Cleef

1834
Jan. 2 John Townsend, 2d, of LaGrange and Jemima Knapp of Fishkill.
Jan. 13 John W. Pierce of Kent, Putnam County, and Paulina Worden of Kent, Putnam County.
Feb. 2 William Cole of Fishkill and Priscilla Burnet of Fishkill.
Apr. 10 Benjamin Aikin of Greenbush, Rensselaer Co., and Maria Ackerman of LaGrange.
July 9 Thomas Warren of Fishkill and Jane Hasbrook of LaGrange. Coloured.
Aug. 3 Henrick B. Howe of Poughkeepsie and Almira Horton of Fishkill. Witness: Edward Howe of Poughkeepsie.
Aug. 19 William Shearer of Fishkill and Nancy Luke of Poughkeepsie. Witnesses: Edward Merritt and James Points of Fishkill.
Sep. 24 Joseph Barrett of Utica, N. York, and Mercy Miller of Poughkeepsie. Witness: John Miller, Poughkeepsie.
Sep. 30 Minard W. Velie of Poughkeepsie and Anna Eliza Brown of Peekskill.
Nov. 6 Robert Bowne of Fishkill and Letty Ann Secord of Fishkill.
Nov. 6 David Forman of Poughkeepsie and Gertrude Lawson of Poughkeepsie.
Dec. 3 William C. Voorhees of Fishkill and Sarah Earle of Fishkill.
Dec. 24 Isaac F. Tobias of Fishkill and Hannah E. Burnet of Fishkill. Witness: Garrett P. Burnet.
Dec. 25 Matthew Garragen of Fishkill and Caroline Foster of Fishkill. Witness: Aaron Foster.

1835
Jan. 12 Phillip B. Van Der Bilt of LaGrange and Mary E. Platt of Fishkill.
Feb. 4 Abram W. Stoutenburgh of Fishkill and Ann Smith of Fishkill.
Feb. 22 James Ruger of LaGrange and Juliann Dates of LaGrange. Witness: Peter Cornell.
Mar. 19 John D. Van Amburgh of Fishkill and Lucy Manning of Fishkill.
Apr. 14 Henry Ganse of Fishkill and Caroline Dolson of Fishkill.
Apr. 22 Milton Griffin of Poughkeepsie and Maria Bishop of Poughkeepsie.
Aug. 30 Henry Van Loon of Athens, Greene County, and Sarah Ann Morton of Athens, Greene County.
Sep. 2 Tunis Brinkerhoof of LaGrange and Susan Everitt of Poughkeepsie.
Sep. 10 Joseph E. Huson of Poughkeepsie and Helen Luckey of Poughkeepsie.
Sep. 30 James C. D. Brower of Fishkill and Rachel Ann Phillips of Fishkill.
Oct. 1 Arthur J. Dorland of Fishkill and Margaret Townsend of Fishkill.
Oct. 7 John Adriance of Fishkill and Jane Eliza Van Wyck of Fishkill.
Oct. 14 John Hicks of Fishkill and Eliza Hayes of Fishkill.
Oct. 24 Ira Bard of Poughkeepsie and Debby Ann Griffin of Poughkeepsie. Witness: Robert Dearin of Poughkeepsie.
Oct. 29 Heber Vanosdall of LaGrange and Adaline Vanosdall of Fishkill.
Nov. 18 Joseph A. Snook of Fishkill and Priscilla Dolson of Fishkill.
Nov. 26 Gilbert T. Budd of LaGrange and Harriet M. Pollock of LaGrange.
Dec. 16 Benjamin H. Everitt of Poughkeepsie and Alletta Maria Monfort of Fishkill.
Dec. 23 George Delavergne of Poughkeepsie and Joanna Klump of Poughkeepsie.

1836
Jan. 7 Peter Baisler of Fishkill and Mary Whitworth of Fishkill.
Jan. 7 William Brown of Fishkill and Mary Kenworthy of Fishkill.
Feb. 13 George Roberts of LaGrange and Susan Maria Secord of LaGrange. Witness: Peter Berry of LaGrange.
Feb. 24 Theodore Fowler, M.D., of Fishkill and Mary Ann Lounsberry of Fishkill.
Feb. 25 Egbert E. Noxon of LaGrange and Clarissa Patterson of Fishkill.
Mar. 23 Jacob Manning of Fishkill and Clarinda Van Kleek of Poughkeepsie.
May 15 Lawson (or Lanson) Purdy, Farmer, of LaGrange, and Sally Van Tine, Housekeeper, of Fishkill.
July 3 Sylvester M. Slater of LaGrange and Catharine M. Burritt of LaGrange.
Aug. 16 William Snow of Fishkill and Ann Warhurst of Fishkill.
Sep. 15 William Diddle of Fishkill and Sarah Monfort of Fishkill.
Oct. 12 John T. Monfort of LaGrange and Ann H. Tidd of LaGrange.

The Reformed Dutch Church of New Hackensack

Nov. 10   Henry Spencer of Beekman and Jemima Eliza Weeks of Fishkill.
Nov. 15   John Van Wie of Athens, Greene Co., and Mrs. Elizabeth M. Holmes of Athens, Greene Co.
Dec. 14   James Van Keuren of LaGrange and Mrs. Phoebe Boice of Fishkill.
Dec. 29   John Copeman of Poughkeepsie and Elizabeth A. Forman of Poughkeepsie.

1837
Feb. 2   Stephen W. Alger of LaGrange and Cornelia Ann Cornwell of Fishkill.
Mar. 9   Walter C. Copeman of Poughkeepsie and Susan Forman of Poughkeepsie.
Mar. 15   John Monfort of Fishkill and Maria G. Hutchins of Fishkill.
June 28   Jacob Hagadorn of Stanford and Margaret Nelson of Fishkill.
July 12   Peter Van Keuren of Poughkeepsie and Sally Angeline Luckey of Poughkeepsie.
Nov. 14   James E. Lewis of Poughkeepsie and Ellen Medel of Poughkeepsie.
Nov. 28   George W. Jones of Poughkeepsie and Jane Ann Morris of Poughkeepsie.
Dec. 27   Harvey Branson Van Duyn of LaGrange and Maria Matthews of Poughkeepsie.

1838
Jan. 17   Nathaniel Smith of Fishkill and Mrs. Eustacia Jones of Fishkill.
Feb. 28   James Baxter of Fishkill and Letty Maria Phillips of Fishkill.
Mar. 15   Jonathan L. Forman of Poughkeepsie and Maria Copeman of Poughkeepsie.
Mar. 21   Peter P. Monfort of Fishkill and Mrs. Elizabeth Stockholm of Fishkill.
Apr. 17   William G. Betts of New York City and Harriet Myers of Fishkill.
Sep. 25   Sidmon Thorn of Peru, Clinton Co., N. York, and Elizabeth Rowe of Fishkill.
Sep. 27   Andrew Bragaw of Poughkeepsie and Elizabeth Cromlish of Poughkeepsie.
Sep. 30   William Morrison of Fishkill and Melinda Pettit of Fishkill.
Dec. 20   Samuel H. Smith of Pleasant Valley and Jane Churchwell of Fishkill.

1839
Jan. 30   Albert Phillips of Fishkill and Maria Waldron of Fishkill.
Feb. 9   Seth Sherwood of Poughkeepsie and Susanna Rogers of Poughkeepsie.
Mar. 13   Benajmin Dearin of Poughkeepsie and Catharine Lawson of Poughkeepsie.
Sep. 3   Edward Lucas, calico printer, of Fishkill, and Mary Ann Baker, spinster, of Fishkill. Witness: William Lucas, farmer, and Wife, of Fishkill.
Sep. 12   Stephen Lucas of Fishkill and Mrs. Miriam Brower of Fishkill.

1840
Apr. 27   James Brower of Fishkill and Cordelia Dolson of Fishkill.
Jan. 16   John Robinson of LaGrange and Mrs. Phebe Cornwell of LaGrange.
Feb. 19   Walter Shrader of Fishkill and Almira Klump of Poughkeepsie.
Mar. 18   William Jones, blacksmith, of LaGrange, and Elmira Ann Potter of LaGrange.
Apr. 11   William Tomkins of Poughkeepsie and Elizabeth Weeks of Poughkeepsie.
Apr. 18   James Goodall, cloth winder, of Fishkill, and Agnes Harkison, spinster, of Poughkeepsie.
July 21   Jerome Van Voorhees of Fishkill and Catharine Meyers of Fishkill.
Oct. 21   Edward B. Van Dyne of LaGrange and Jane Ann Carter of LaGrange.
Nov. 5   Phillip B. Van Der Bilt of Fishkill and Phebe E. Van Der Bilt of LaGrange.
Nov. 11   Zophar I. Jones of Fishkill and Hannah Dates of Fishkill.

1841
Feb. 6   Allen Brown, farmer, of Poughkeepsie and Rachel Ann Cromwell, spinster, of Washington.
Mar. 2   Robert Lawson of Poughkeepsie and Hannah Budd of Poughkeepsie.
Apr. 29   Edgar Lawson of LaGrange and Hannah E. Van Nosdall of Fishkill.
Sep. 8   Adrian M. Cornell of LaGrange and Mellissa Dimond of Poughkeepsie.

1842
May 31   John C. Pudney of Fishkill and Sarah E. Everitt of Poughkeepsie.
Sep. 28   James S. Wiley of LaGrange and Deborah C. Pells of Poughkeepsie.
Oct. 6   William H. Rimph of Hyde Park and Susan Monfort of Fishkill.

1843
Feb. 15   Charles R. Tomkins, Blacksmith, of Fishkill and Gertrude Dates, Dress Maker, of Fishkill. Wit: Thomas Dates, Fishkill, and Sarah Churchill, Poughkeepsie.
Mar. 26   Simeon Roswell, farmer, of LaGrange and Mary Ann Jackson of Poughkeepsie. Wit: William Yates & Wife.
Sep. 12   William H. Dimond of Poughkeepsie and Maria Ann Luyster of Fishkill.

1844
July 2   Joseph Henry Jacocks of Fishkill and Clarinda Colden of LaGrange. Coloured.
Nov. 10   Noyes P. Record, chairmaker, of Poughkeepsie and Cornelia A. Dates, tailoress, of Poughkeepsie.
Nov. 20   Stephen I. Monfort of Fishkill and Caroline Meyers of Fishkill.

1845
Mar. 3   Abraham Bell, carpet weaver, of Poughkeepsie and Mrs. Jane Eliza Bloodgood of Poughkeepsie.

Marriage Register

May 22	Jeremiah Millard of Fishkill and Eliza Meyers of Fishkill.
Sep. 24	John Henry Yates of Fishkill and Jane Catharine Garner of Fishkill. Coloured.
Nov. 12	Peter D. Van Amburgh of Poughkeepsie and Amelia C. Rynders of LaGrange.
Dec. 3	Gilbert Thorn Turner of Poughkeepsie and Nancy E. Quick of Poughkeepsie.
Dec. 31	Monfort J. Van Kleeck of LaGrange and Margaret Ann Ostrander of LaGrange.

1846
Feb. 5	John M. Dubois of LaGrange and Mary Ann Van Duyn of LaGrange.
Feb. 12	John L. Potter of LaGrange and Jane E. Dearin of LaGrange.
Oct. 21	Obadiah Van Voorhis of Fishkill and Maria Haight of Fishkill.
Oct. 29	Darius Cabre of Fishkill and Ruth Ann Wright of Fishkill.
Nov. 25	James Y. Pollock of Fishkill and Mary Rhyne of Poughkeepsie.
Dec. 24	George Herley of Poughkeepsie, and Susanna Pendlebury of Pleasant Valley.

1847
Jan. 7	George Harris of Fishkill and Margaret Van Osdoll of Fishkill.
Feb. 3	John Phillip Dearin of LaGrange and Antonette Dearin of Poughkeepsie.
Feb. 25	John C. Dorsett of LaGrange and Catharine Brinckerhoff of Poughkeepsie.
Apr. 14	Nathaniel Codwise of LaGrange and Martha Wood of LaGrange.
July 28	John H. Dean of New York City and Harriet H. Potter of LaGrange.

1848
Jan. 18	William T. Meddaugh of LaGrange and Aletta M. Snedeker of Fishkill.
May 21	James Young of New York City and Hannah C. Potter of LaGrange.
May 24	Edwin R. Townsend of LaGrange and Jemima C. Van Der Belt of LaGrange.
Aug. 30	Samuel H. Mills of Poughkeepsie and Helen Van Der Belt Lawson of Poughkeepsie.
Sep. 21	John I. Phillips of Hughsonvill and Hannah Nelson of Matteawan.
Sep. 21	James H. Phillips of Franklindale and Doretta Van Osdoll of Fishkill.
Sep. 28	Schenck A. Meyers of Fishkill and Ann Bray of Newburgh.
Oct. 12	Edward Stephenson of Ansonia, Connecticut, and Sarah Burnett of LaGrange.
Oct. 16	William H. Compton of Springfield, Long Island, and Rebecca Hicks of Fishkill.
Nov. 8	George H. Everitt of Fishkill and Marianna Concklin of Fishkill.
Nov. 23	Gilbert Wood of Fishkill and Mary Phillips of Fishkill.
Dec. 3	Joseph F. Randolph of N. York City and Mary Ann Bishop of Po'keepsie.

1849
Mar. 7	John Jones of Fishkill and Cynthia M. Needam of Fishkill.
Dec. 5	Milford Cowl of Union Vale and Jane Wood of LaGrange.
Dec. 12	Benjamin H. Everitt of Pokeepsie and Mary Knapp of Fishkill.

1850
Feb. 21	Charles Robinson of Beekman and Anna Catharine Robinson of LaGrange.
May 22	Effingham Vanderburgh of Pokeepsie and Mary Yelverton of Pokeepsie.
Oct. 19	William Carr of LaGrange and Julia Shaw of LaGrange.
Nov. 27	Charles Dearin of Pokeepsie and Catharine Bishop of Pokeepsie.

1851
Jan. 1	John Y. Bishop of Pokeepsie and Mary E. Losee of Pokeepsie.
Jan. 15	Henry T. Jewell of LaGrange and Jane Ann Hitchcock of LaGrange.
Feb. 5	James S. Monfort of LaGrange and Sarah E. Yates of Fishkill.
Feb. 19	Eli Meyers of Fishkill and Jane Ann Monfort of Fishkill.
Mar. 12	Homer Wooden of Po'keepsie and Maria Jones of Po'keepsie.
June 1	Charles M. Marvin of Fishkill and Phebe H. De La Vergne of Fishkill.
Aug. 9	Charles Rogers of Po'keepsie and Belinda Williams of Po'keepsie.
Aug. 20	George M. Van Nort of N. York City and Mary Ackerman of Fishkill.
Nov. 26	John Williams of Fishkill and Sarah E. Brinckerhoff of Fishkill. Colour'd.

1852
Feb. 26	John D. Cornwell of Fishkill and Susan L. Pells of Fishkill.
Mar. 17	Menit Van Wert of New York City and Phebe Ackerman of Fishkill.
June 1	John B. Pells of Poughkeepsie and Mary W. Cabrey of Poughkeepsie.
June 17	Anthony Underhill, M.D., of Fishkill and Charlotte A. Marvin of Fishkill.
July 4	Alexander Bishop of Fishkill and Jane Ann of Fishkill.
July 5	David J. Shaw of Fishkill and Almina C. Jennings of Fishkill.
Sep. 11	Henry C. Croft of Middletown Point, N. J., and Harriet Ann Needham of Fishkill.

1853
Jan. 2	William Van Bogert of Peekskill and Jane Melissa Pollock of Fishkill.
Jan. 5	Hamilton N. Knapp of Fishkill and Aletta Jane Van Nostrand of Fishkill.
Mar. 9	James Edwin Sleight of LaGrange and Frances E. Titus of LaGrange.

1854
Apr. 12	Charles J. Howell, Jr., of Poughkeepsie and Mary M. Du Bois of Poughkeepsie.
Apr. 20	Levi Cass of West Troy and Catharine E. Pells of Poughkeepsie.

The Reformed Dutch Church of New Hackensack

June 15   P. George Seward of Fishkill and Sarah E. Marvin of Fishkill.
June 15   Maurice Dwight Seward of Fishkill and Mary Marvin of Fishkill.
Aug. 5   Joseph Tanner of LaGrange and Elizabeth McCleary of LaGrange.
Nov. 1   Theron Shaw and Margaret Ann Lockwood.

1855
Feb. 28   Thomas DeWitt Van Wyck of East Fishkill and Catharine Luyster of Fishkill.
July 11   John Hilliker of East Fishkill and Phebe E. Van Dyne of Poughkeepsie.
Sep. 6   Charles H. Crouse of Clinton and Malvina H. Sleght of Clinton.

1856
Jan. 16   Benjamin W. Brower of Fishkill and Eliza Barton of Fishkill.
Sep. 24   Edgar Luyster of Fishkill and Harriet Conover of Fishkill.
Nov. 27   Israel Griffen of Pleasant Valley and Jane M. Van Anden of Fishkill.
Nov. 11   Stephen P. Montfort of Fishkill and Catharine B. Needam of Fishkill.
Oct. 2   Edward Flagler of Lagrange and Helen M. Jones of Fishkill.

1857
Sep. 23   John Henry Luyster of Fishkill and Gertrude K. Conover of Fishkill.
Oct. 15   Francis B. Pye of New Haven, Ct. and Ruth Amelia Sleight of Fishkill.
Dec. 30   Martin S. Ackerman of Fishkill and Helen E. Van Bramer of East Fishkill.

1858
June 14   Richard W. Akin of New York City and Carrie L. Thorn of Fishkill.
June 27   Ervin Tyler Smith of New York City and Corneliaette Pudney of Poughkeepsie.
Aug. 29   James Dea(k)in of Lagrange and Julia Tracy of Lagrange.
Oct. 13   James Adis Seward of Fishkill and Mary Bethia Platt of Fishkill.
Dec. 1   Samuel Henry Smith of Fishkill and Mary Elisabeth Thompson of Fishkill. Coloured.

1859
Mar. 23   Joseph Van Voorhis of Fishkill and Amanda M. Haight of Fishkill.
Mar. 30   John Luyster, Jun., of Lagrange and Mary Ann Monfort of Fishkill.
July 10   David B. Worden of Patterson, Putnam Co., and Mary Jane Dingy of Sherman, Conn. Wit: Rachel Fairchild of Fishkill, N. Y.

1860
Jan. 1   Harvey E. Van Dyne of Poughkeepsie and Angelia Polhemus of Poughkeepsie.
Mar. 20   Benjamin Hopkins of Stormville, E. Fishkill, and Phebe F. Monfort of Stormville, E. Fishkill.
June 7   George Ackerman of Fishkill and Susan B. Brundige of Lagrange.
Sep. 5   Joseph G. Knapp of Fishkill or Iowa, and Mary L. Seward of Fishkill.
Oct. 3   Hon. Peter H. Silvester of Coxsackie, Greene Co., and Mrs. Sarah E. Seward of Fishkill, Dutchess Co.
Oct. 17   George J. Smith of Fishkill and Mary E. Ver Valin of Fishkill. Coloured.
Nov. 22   James Dearin of Poughkeepsie and Kate Dolson of Poughkeepsie.
Nov. 28   Charles W. Smith of Fishkill and Margaret E. Johnson of Fishkill. Coloured.

1861
Mar. 5   Nicholas Colden of Fishkill and Caroline Grey of Fishkill.
Apr. 24   William H. Peck of East Fishkill and Abigail White of Pawlings. Wit: Sophia Van Cleef.

1862
Mar. 4   Edgar D. Fletcher of Rochester, Minn., and Sarah Amelia Hoagland of Fishkill, N. Y.
May 17   James Spencer Van Cleef of Poughkeepsie and Harriet Mulford Howell of Sag Harbor, L. Island.
Sep. 18   Charles E. Hitchcock of Lagrange and Sarah J. Ackerman of Lagrange.
Dec. 27   Abram Smith of Fishkill and Mary Frances Coon of Fishkill. Coloured.

1863
Jan. 14   William H. Stoutenburgh of Fishkill and Anna M. Dolson of Poughkeepsie.
Dec. 22   Brundage Tompkins of Lagrange and Elizabeth V. W. Ackerman of Lagrange.

1864
Mar. 15   John C. Owen of East Fishkill and Mary C. Rynders of East Fishkill.
May 1   George E. Purdy of New Hamburgh and Ruth Van Nosdall of New Hamburgh.
July 29   James Kane of Fishkill and Ann Boylan of Fishkill.
Aug. 16   Peter Atkins of Fishkill and Mary F. Jacklin of Poughkeepsie. Coloured.
Sep. 14   John Cornwell of East Fishkill and Sarah Eliza Pells of Lagrange.
Oct. 6   John East of Lagrange and Sarah E. Van Der Bilt of Fishkill.
Oct. 26   William H. Tompkins of Lagrange and Maria L. Ackerman of Lagrange.

1865
Jan. 11   Isaac A. Atkins of Fishkill and Ann A. Bowlin of Poughkeepsie. Coloured.
Feb. 15   Samuel Luckey Dearin of Poughkeepsie and Albina Van Voorhis of Poughkeepsie.

Marriage Register

Mar. 23 James Frederick Hasbrook of Fishkill and Sarah E. Robinson of Fishkill. Coloured.
May 20 Isaac Williams of Fishkill and Clarinda C. Atkins of East Fishkill. Coloured.
June 11 Thomas Crilley of Wappingers Falls and Mary H. Sinsabaugh of New Hamburgh.
Sep. 13 Edgar Van Amburgh of Wappingers Falls and Gertrude Van Dine of Wappingers Falls.
Nov. 30 William D. Nelson of New York and Augusta Ladue of Fishkill.
Dec. 25 Alonzo W. Dolson of New York and Emma Disbrow of Wappingers Falls.
1866
Jan. 17 R. W. Gordon, Jun. of New York and Kate E. Monfort of Fishkill.
May 28 Samuel Ver Valin of Poughkeepsie and Susan A. Johnson of Poughkeepsie. Coloured.
July 4 Alonzo F. Tracy of Poughkeepsie and Mary E. Cromwell of Lagrange.
Oct. 3 George C. Wood of Fort Plain and Gezena A. Wagner of Fort Plain.
Nov. 17 Daniel Werner of Fishkill and Margaretha Vollmer of LaGrange.

REGISTER OF MARRIAGES
During the Ministry of Rev. Henry Ward

1867
Sep. 7 Edgar Sedore of Fishkill, N. Y. and Fanny Alton of Fishkill, N. Y.
Oct. 17 Edward Townsend of Cedar Falls, Iowa, and Sarah A. Seward of Fishkill, N. Y.
Nov. 13 John S. Forshay of Fishkill, N. Y. and Mary C. Hicks of Fishkill, N. Y.
1868
Mar. 25 Peter Myers of Fishkill, N. Y. and Elizabeth M. Van Voorhis of Fishkill, N. Y.
1869
Feb. 10 Richard M. Teller of Fishkill, N. Y. and Amelia I. Pudney of Fishkill, N. Y.
Mar. 24 William M. Stilwell of Poughkeepsie, N. Y. and Amelia M. Townsend, of Fishkill, N. Y.
Apr. 13 Obadiah P. Lawrence of Poughkeepsie and Sarah A. Dutcher of Fishkill, N. Y.
May 15 Alonzo G. Case of Poughkeepsie, N. Y. and Mary Frances McAvoy of Poughkeepsie, N. Y.
Sep. 5 Adolph Stigle of Fishkill, N. Y. and Rosa Younker of Fishkill, N. Y.
Nov. 17 Charles E. Van Kleeck of Fishkill, N. Y. and Kate B. Rogers of Fishkill, N. Y.
Dec. 25 James H. Riley of LaGrange, N. Y. and Sarah Jane Jaycox of LaGrange, N. Y. Colored.
1870
Feb. 3 Cornelius Jaycox of Fishkill, N. Y. and Mary Ida Demund of Fishkill, N. Y. Colored.
Aug. 10 Solomon Wright of East Fishkill and Mrs. Esther Harris of East Fishkill.
Aug. 17 Elvin B. Horton of East Fishkill and Emma Sedore of Fishkill.
Sep. 14 Isaac Terwilliger of Fishkill, N. Y. and Jane E. Baxter of Fishkill, N. Y.
Sep. 28 John James Gorman of Poughkeepsie, N. Y. and Mary E. Simpson of Poughkeepsie, N. Y.
Nov. 9 Edwin Barlow of LaGrange, N. Y. and Mrs. Anna C. Robinson of Fishkill, N. Y.
1871
Feb. 7 John Murphy of Poughkeepsie, N. Y. and Kate Reed of Poughkeepsie, N. Y.
Sep. 7 Peter Springsteen of Fishkill, N. Y. and Sarah Adkins of Fishkill, N. Y. Colored.
Nov. 30 Robert W. Dutcher of Fishkill, N. Y. and Susan M. Walters of Fishkill, N. Y.
Dec. 5 Henry Jones of Poughkeepsie, N. Y. and Irene Myers of East Fishkill, N. Y.
1872
Jan. 17 Myron B. Cornell of Poughkeepsie, N. Y. and Cornelia A. Dates of Poughkeepsie, N. Y.
Jan. 17 William H. Brower of LaGrange, N. Y. and Jane Augusta Tanner of LaGrange, N. Y.
Feb. 28 Jeremiah C. Brower of LaGrange, N. Y. and Mrs. Nelly Westervelt of Poughkeepsie, N. Y.
Feb. 28 George P. Vermilye of LaGrange, N. Y. and Henrietta Myers of Fishkill, N. Y.
June 19 Robert L. Lowe of Fishkill, N. Y. and Sarah J. Johnson of Fishkill, N. Y. Colored.
Aug. 1 Edward Smith of Fishkill, N. Y. and Mary E. Jennifer of Fishkill, N. Y. Colored.
Oct. 31 Nathaniel G. Hilliker of Fishkill, N. Y. andSarah E. Van Tassel of Fishkill, N. Y.
1873
Feb. 4 Augustus Smith of Fishkill, N. Y. and Agnes Coulter of Fishkill, N. Y.
Feb. 26 Casius M. C. Smith of LaGrange, N. Y. and Carrie A. Dorland of East Fishkill, N. Y.

The Reformed Dutch Church of New Hackensack

Oct. 16   Sanford Becker of Guilderland, N. Y. and Nettie Ogsbury of Guilderland, N. Y.
Nov. 20   Rev. William E. Davis of Manhasset, L. I. and Sener L. Valentine of Locust Valley, L. I.

1874
Feb. 11   Robert Wortman of Fishkill, N. Y. and Margaret Davis of Fishkill, N. Y.
Feb. 25   Harry H. Lane of Fishkill, N. Y. and Alida A. Martin of Fishkill, N. Y.
Mar. 11   Ebenezer C. Platt of Fishkill, N. Y. and Jennie Pells of Fishkill, N. Y.
Mar. 31   Nathaniel Hinckley of Patterson, N. Y. and Eliza Baker of Beekman, N. Y.
Apr. 11   John Riffenburg of LaGrange, N. Y. and Ida Clark of LaGrange, N. Y.

1875
Jan. 27   James W. Knapp of Poughkeepsie, N. Y. and Jennie M. Van Dyne of Poughkeepsie, N. Y.
Mar. 3   Austin T. Fink, M.D., of LaGrange, N. Y. and Elizabeth Everett Pudney of Poughkeepsie, N. Y.
Mar. 25   Jacob Linn of Wappingers Falls, N. Y. and Mary H. Lauer of LaGrange, N. Y.
Apr. 28   William Monroe Scofield of Fishkill, N. Y. and Emma J. Myers of East Fishkill, N. Y.
Nov. 9   William Smith of Wappingers Falls, N. Y. and Josephine Dutcher of Wappingers Falls, N. Y.
Nov. 18   Edward Dutcher of Fishkill, N. Y. and Tamar Horton of Fishkill, N. Y.
Dec. 29   Spencer Van Dyne of Poughkeepsie, N. Y. and Julia Norris of Hughsonville, N. Y.

1876
Mar. 23   Edward Rossell of Poughkeepsie, N. Y. and Annie Stevens of Poughkeepsie, N. Y.
June 7   Abram Van Valin of Poughkeepsie, N. Y. and Susan Trowbridge of Wappinger, N. Y.
July 2   William Babcock of Wappingers Falls, N. Y. and Gertrude Brundage of Wappingers Falls, N. Y.
July 3   Oscar F. Bigelow of Grafton, Mass. and Emma C. Smith of Poughkeepsie, N. Y.
Aug. 12   Joseph I. Doughty of Wappingers Falls, N. Y. and Mrs. Annie R. Scott of Wappinger, N. Y.
Sep. 6   I. T. Nichols Harcourt of Wappingers Falls, N. Y. and Annie E. Jaycox of Wappingers Falls, N. Y.
Oct. 18   Evan M. Johnson of Brooklyn, N. Y. and Mary S. Vanderbilt of New Hackensack, N. Y.
Oct. 25   John P. Monfort of Wappinger, N. Y. and Gertie Myers of Wappinger, N. Y.
Nov. 5   Jerry Lent of Stormville, N. Y. and Jennie B. Ashman of Chestnut Ridge, N. Y.

1877
Jan. 17   William Baker of New Hackensack, N. Y. and Mrs. Harriet A. Croft of New Hackensack, N. Y.
Mar. 6   Samuel I. Robinson of New Hackensack, N. Y. and Mrs. Letty A. Churchill of New Hackensack, N. Y.
Mar. 21   William H. Hunt of New Hackensack, N. Y. and Mary Elizabeth Donaldson of New Hackensack, N. Y.
Mar. 22   D. Wortman Rogers of Hopewell, N. Y. and Mary L. Van Nostrand of Hopewell, N. Y.
Apr. 2   Robert Monell of Poughkeepsie, N. Y. and Dora Avery of Cold Spring, N. Y.
Apr. 18   Henry Jones of New Hackensack, N. Y. and Mrs. Harriet Luyster of New Hackensack, N. Y.
June 28   Paul Vermilye of LaGrange, N. Y. and Libbie Van Vlack of East Fishkill, N. Y.
Aug. 4   Charles F. Tanner of Wappingers Falls, N. Y. and Eliza M. Baker of Wappingers Falls, N. Y.
Nov. 7   John J. Scofield of New Hackensack, N. Y. and Henrietta N. Jones of New Hackensack, N. Y.
Dec. 12   George Doyle of Barre Plains, Mass. and Susan A. Pearsall of Rochdale, N. Y.

1878
Apr. 4   Charles C. Andrews of LaGrange, N. Y. and Minnie May Vincent of LaGrange, N. Y.
May 7   John W. Rose of East Poughkeepsie, N. Y. and Emma F. Frear of East Poughkeepsie, N. Y.
May 19   George H. Norris of Hughsonville, N. Y. and Ida Dutcher of Wappingers Falls, N. Y.
July 10   John E. Millard of Poughkeepsie and Lina Donaldson of New Hackinsack.
July 31   James H. Barton of Wappingers Falls, N. Y. and Eva P. Traynor of Wappingers Falls, N. Y.
Dec. 18   Edgar F. Denee of Poughkeepsie, N. Y. and Alice C. Alexander of Poughkeepsie, N. Y.
Dec. 24   Cornelius Burnett of LaGrange, N. Y. and Mary A. Marginson of LaGrange, N. Y.

Marriage Register

1879

Jan. 23   S. P. Siver of Fishkill Landing, N. Y. and Mrs. Melissa Doty of Fishkill Landing, N. Y.
Jan. 29   John H. Adkins of Fishkill, N. Y. and Lena Brinkerhoff of Wappinger, N. Y.
Feb. 12   William B. Dusenbury of Poughkeepsie, N. Y. and Minnie I. McCord of LaGrange, N. Y.
Aug. 6   Henry G. Lee of Poughkeepsie, N. Y. and M. Jennie Martenette of Poughkeepsie, N. Y.
Sep. 24   Daniel Chatterton of Poughkeepsie, N. Y. and Jennie A. Smith of LaGrange, N. Y.
Nov. 26   James H. Marquet of Poughkeepsie, N. Y. and Margaret E. Winans of LaGrange, N. Y.
Nov. 27   Richard East of LaGrange, N. Y. and Jerlene Marquet of Poughkeepsie, N. Y.
Dec. 17   Walter C. Turner of Poughkeepsie, N. Y. and Anna M. Willsey of Wappinger, N. Y.
Dec. 23   William F. Knapp of East Fishkill, N. Y. and Mary C. Van Vlack of East Fishkill, N. Y.

1880

Jan. 3   John N. Riley of Fishkill Plains, N. Y. and Sarah J. D(e)mund of Fishkill Village, N. Y.
Jan. 18   George F. DeGraff of Poquonock, Conn. and Elizabeth Burnett of LaGrange, N. Y.
Feb. 29   Walter Shaw of LaGrange, N. Y. and Ada L. Miller of Barrytown, N. Y.
Mar. 4   George J. Brower of Brooklyn, N. Y. and Maggie E. Gibson of Wappingers Falls, N. Y.
Mar. 4   William E. Tibbs of Wappingers Falls, N. Y. and Ida McNear of Wappingers Falls, N. Y.
Mar. 24   Charles C. Van Voorhis of Brinkerhoffville, N. Y. and Jennie Matthews of Poughkeepsie, N. Y.
Mar. 24   Clinton V. R. Jaycox of Poughkeepsie, N. Y. and Anna E. Matthews of Poughkeepsie, N. Y.
Mar. 29   Walter Miller of Poughkeepsie, N. Y. and Jeannette Massie of Poughkeepsie, N. Y.
May 23   Hugh Quigley of Newark, N. J. and Annie Vail of Wappingers Falls, N. Y.
Aug. 15   Benjamin Knapp of Wappingers Falls, N. Y. and Annie Lee of Wappingers Falls, N. Y.
Sep. 15   Amos Brownell of LaGrange, N. Y. and Emma L. Wooster of LaGrange, N. Y.
Oct. 9   James B. Meddaugh of East Poughkeepsie, N. Y. and Nancy E. Wolven of East Poughkeepsie, N. Y.
Dec. 15   Charles J. Alley of LaGrange, N. Y. and Sarah L. Luyster of LaGrange, N. Y.

1881

Apr. 7   William T. Jewell of East Fishkill, N. Y. and Hattie Dorsett of East Fishkill, N. Y.
June 15   Eugene Ham of Verbank, N. Y. and Mary K. Sleight of LaGrange, N. Y.
Aug. 24   Cortland Secor of East Fishkill, N. Y. and Adelia Van Kleeck of LaGrange, N. Y.
Aug. 25   Herbert H. Holmes of New York City and Cora McCord of LaGrange, N. Y.
Oct. 15   Edward Downing of Poughkeepsie, N. Y. and Maria O'Neil of Poughkeepsie, N. Y.
Oct. 20   William H. Parkton of Patterson, N. Y. and Emma Schorn of Wappinger, N. Y.
Oct. 30   Carpenter Secor of Peekskill, N. Y. and Catharine Elizabeth Lauer of LaGrange, N. Y.
Dec. 7   James P. Beaton of Wappingers Falls, N. Y. and Mrs. Emma E. Pattison of New Hackensack, N. Y.
Dec. 28   George W. Meddaugh of LaGrange, N. Y. and Carrie M. Hadden of LaGrange, N. Y.

1882

Apr. 13   Galen D. Overocker of Poughkeepsie, N. Y. and Mary T. Landon of LaGrange, N. Y.
Apr. 27   William Underhill of Fishkill, N. Y. and Mary E. Griffin of Wappinger, N. Y.
June 11   William A. Jackson of Wappingers Falls, N. Y. and Georgia A. Wixson of New Hackensack, N. Y.
Aug. 23   Joseph Chase of New Hamburgh, N. Y. and Emma Brower of Wappingers Falls, N. Y.
June 15   James Brown of Wappingers Falls, N. Y. and Sarah Dutcher of Wappingers Falls, N. Y.
Sep. 19   Jacob S. Diddell of New Hackensack, N. Y. and Clara Wooster of LaGrange, N. Y.
Sep. 28   John H. Wood of New Hackensack, N. Y. and Miriam Van Voorhis of New Hackensack, N. Y.
Oct. 25   Eliphaz Delamater of LaGrange, N. Y. and Anna Andrews of LaGrange, N. Y.

The Reformed Dutch Church of New Hackensack

Oct. 25   John S. Myers of New Hamburgh, N. Y. and Minnie G. Drake of New Hamburgh, N. Y.
Dec. 6   Robert S. Matthews of Poughkeepsie, N. Y. and Dora A. Cronkrite of Matteawan, N. Y.
Dec. 21   Franklin P. Free of LaGrange, N. Y. and Katie A. Sleight of LaGrange, N. Y.

1883
Jan. 17   Elias T. Bryant of Beekman, N. Y. and Edith S. Chatterton of LaGrange, N. Y.
Mar. 21   James H. Velie of LaGrange, N. Y. and Katie Robinson of LaGrange, N. Y.
Apr. 18   Charles Plumb of Wappinger, N. Y. and Mrs. Mary C. Forshay of Wappinger, N. Y.
Oct. 17   Courtland M. Cummings of Wappinger, N. Y. and Agnes E. Johnson of Wappinger, N. Y.

1884
Jan. 1   James C. Germond of Milton Ferry, N. Y. and Katie F. Hoy of Wappingers Falls, N. Y.
Apr. 7   Charles V. East of LaGrange, N. Y. and Georgianna Belknap of Hopewell Junc., N. Y.
Apr. 9   Lewis B. Freeman of Clove Branch Junction, N. Y. and Mary Ida Brower of Clove Branch Junction, N. Y.
May 21   William H. Raymond of Poughkeepsie, N. Y. and Mary Winans of Titusville, N. Y.
Aug. 27   Hamilton King of Olivet, Mich. and Cora Lee Seward of Bloomington, Ill.
Oct. 28   George Cole Madden of Lansingburgh, N. Y. and Jestena B. Phillips of Wappingers Falls, N. Y.
Nov. 11   John J. Diddell of New Hackensack, N. Y. and Annie J. Wooster of LaGrange, N. Y.
Nov. 19   Meredith H. LeRoy of Poughkeepsie, N. Y. and Maria E. Forman of Poughkeepsie, N. Y.

1885
Feb. 1   Robert C. Macauley of Wappingers Falls, N. Y. and Minnie J. Brown of Wappingers Falls, N. Y.
Feb. 18   Lincoln A. Van Dewater of Crum Elbow, N. Y. and Augusta DeGroff of New Hackensack, N. Y.
Apr. 22   Charles A. Bishop of Poughkeepsie, N. Y. and Hattie Winans of Titusville, N. Y.
May 27   Lewis Shafer of LaGrange, N. Y. and Lizzie M. Smith of LaGrange, N. Y.
May 28   John Cahill of Fordham, N. Y. and Ida M. Ward of Clinton Point, N. Y.
Nov. 5   Elmer L. Pryor of Wappingers Falls, N. Y. and Cora I. Jaycox of Poughkeepsie, N. Y.
Nov. 22   Isaac McNear of Newburgh, N. Y. and Sarah Donahooe of Newburgh, N. Y.

1886
Jan. 3   Walter Hicks of Wappingers Falls, N. Y. and Effie G. Harris of Wappingers Falls, N. Y.
Feb. 10   William I. Scofield of Wappingers Falls, N. Y. and Emma J. Ferdon of Poughkeepsie, N. Y.
Feb. 17   Louis B. Briggs of LaGrange, N. Y. and Cora A. Lee of Arlington, N. Y.
Mar. 3   Nathanael Logan of Pleasant Valley, N. Y. and Annie C. Van Anden of Wappingers Falls, N. Y.
Mar. 23   Robert M. DeGarmo of Poughkeepsie, N. Y. and Sadie E. Stockholm of Hopewell, N. Y.
Sep. 5   Henry Bowden of Wappingers Falls, N. Y. and Delia E. Maroney of Wappingers Falls, N. Y.

1887
Feb. 2   Robert G. Temple of Wappingers Falls, N. Y. and Mary A. Delahanty of Wappingers Falls, N. Y.
Feb. 23   Maville J .Robinson of LaGrange, N. Y. and Minnie Allen of Arlington, N. Y.
June 29   John C. Kingman of Cedar Falls, Iowa, and Carrie A. Seward of New Hackensack, N. Y.
Oct. 5   John J. Cornwell, of New Hackensack, N. Y. and Mary M. Johnston of LaGrange, N. Y.
Oct. 19   William C. Shaw of Poughkeepsie, N. Y. and Lulu D. Haight of Poughkeepsie, N. Y.
Dec. 7   Coert A. Van Voorhis of New Hackensack, N. Y. and Mary S. Baker of New Hackensack, N. Y.

Marriage Register

REGISTER OF MARRIAGES
During the Ministry of Rev. Wm. A. Dumont

1888

Mar. 28 — James W. Moore of Low Point and Miss Mary E. Rogers of New Hackensack at house of bride's mother. Wit: Family and friends.

Dec. 12 — Fred J. Whitman of Wappingers Falls and Miss Hannah Rush of Wappingers Falls at Parsonage. Wit: Mrs. Annie Taylor, Miss Lena Smidell and Mrs. W. A. Dumont.

Dec. 19 — Peter M. Owen of Wappingers and Miss Mary E. Van Voorhis of Wappingers, at Parsonage. Wit: Mrs. Wm. Van Amburgh, Belinda Van Amburgh.

1889

Feb. 9 — John Eckler of Wappingers Falls and Miss Lottie Van Voorhis of Wappingers Falls, at Parsonage. Wit: Mrs. W. A. Dumont, Maggie McDonnell.

June 19 — Rich. C. Van Wyck, M.D. of Hopewell, N. Y. and Miss Lottie Underhill of New Hackensack, N. Y., at house of bride's parents. Wit: Family and friends. Ceremony performed by Rev. Denis Wortman, D.D.

July 4 — Charles D. Cole of Wappingers and Doretta Barton of Wappingers Falls, at Parsonage. Wit: Mrs. W. A. Dumont, Maggie McDonnell.

Nov. 20 — John Rooney of Poughkeepsie and Mrs. Sarah Dutcher Brown of Wappingers Falls, at Parsonage. Wit: Mrs. W. A. Dumont, Maggie McDonnell.

1890

Feb. 11 — Anton Wm. Walter of Sharon, Ct. and Annie M. Vollener of Noxon, at house of bride's parents. Wit: Family and friends.

June 18 — Chas. H. Hallock of N. Y. City and Miss Emma F. Hunt of Camelot, at house of bride's father, Camelot. Wit: Family & friends.

July 10 — Alexander King of New Hackensack and Willard Brown of Wappingers Falls. Colored. At house of Wm. H. Laurence. Wit: Wm. H. Laurence & Lillie Laurence.

Oct. 8 — Robert Johnston of N. Y. City and Sarah Silvester Seward of New Hackensack, at home of bride's father, New Hackensack. Wit: Family & friends.

Nov. 19 — Theron Williams of New Hackensack and Emily F. Owen of New Hackensack, at house of groom's father, Wappingers. Wit: Family & friends.

Dec. 30 — James Howard of Lagrange and Ella Ackerman of Noxon, at home of bride's father, Noxon, N. Y. Wit: Family & friends.

1891

Apr. 30 — Chas. Benjamin Robinson, colored, of New Hackensack and Josephine Mayers, white, of New Hackensack, at house of Wm. H. Laurence, colored. Wit: Wm. H. Laurence, Mrs. Wm. H. Laurence and others.

June 15 — Frederic W. Colden, colored, of New Hackensack and Stella Bowman, colored, of New Hackensack, at Parsonage. Wit: Robt. Johnston, Mrs. W. A. Dumont.

1892

Mar. 22 — John R. Phillips of New Hackensack and Kate Theresa Vollener of New Hackensack, at Parsonage. Wit: Mrs. W. A. Dumont, Annie Lauer.

June 18 — Harry McGuire Taylor of Poughkeepsie and Anna D. Howard of LaGrange, at house of bride's father, LaGrange, N. Y. Wit: Family and friends.

Aug. 31 — Verdine Van Vlack of Fishkill Plains and Josephine Conner of Fishkill Plains, at Parsonage. Wit: Martha J. Dumont, Hester A. Morse.

Oct. 19 — Edgar A. Briggs of Poughkeepsie and Mary Alice Matthews of Town of Poughkeepsie, at house of bride's brother, Oak Grove, N. Y. Wit: Family & friends.

Nov. 19 — John Fred Hoppe of East Poughkeepsie and Grace Maud Bassnett of East Poughkeepsie, at Parsonage. Wit: Kitty Lynch, Mrs. W. A. Dumont.

Nov. 30 — Henry N. Winchester of South Amenia and Frances Sleight of Titusville, at home of Misses Titus, Titusville, N. Y. Wit: Family and friends.

1893

June 11 — Patrick Laffin of Wappingers Falls and Margaret Reynolds of Wappingers Falls at Parsonage. Wit: Edwin DuBois, Lizzie Clark.

June 15 — Elijah T. Rowe of Wappingers Falls and Anna L. Christian of Noxon, N. Y., at home of bride's father near Noxon. Wit: Family and friends.

July 6 — Edward Murray of Poughkeepsie, N. Y. and Etta Woodin of Poughkeepsie, at Parsonage. Wit: Mr. & Mrs. Jno. Maby.

1894

July 3 — James Turner of Wappingers Falls and Adelaide Van Bogert of New Hackensack, at Parsonage. Wit: Arthur Van Bogert, Mrs. W. A. Dumont.

Dec. 12 — George W. Jones of Poughkeepsie and Addie S. Haines of Wappingers Falls, at home of bride's father, near Oak Grove. Wit: Family and friends.

The Reformed Dutch Church of New Hackensack

1895
Sep. 9 — Monroe Dickerson, colored, of Fishkill Village and Martha A. Yancie, colored, of Crooked Run, Va., at home of Abner Hasbrouck, colored, Mott's tenant house. Wit: Jno. P. Dickerson, Abner Hasbrouck.

1896
Mar. 18 — Fred Gustavus Paash of New Hackensack and Minnie Cora Rogers of Lagrangeville, at home of bride's mother, Lagrangeville, N. Y. Wit: Nat. F. Storm, Wife and family of Mr. Geddings.

1895
Dec. 12 — Jeremiah Hartenstine of Wappingers and Gertrude Lee of East Fishkill, at Parsonage. Wit: Martha J. Dumont, Louisa D. Ott.

1896
May 9 — William Gallagher of Wappingers Falls and Lillie M. Berkins of Wappingers Falls, at Parsonage. Wit: Martha J. Dumont, Mrs. Annie Smith.
July 20 — Wm. Henry Bolt of Stony Creek, Ct. and Fanny Helena Petherick of Poughkeepsie, at home of T. G. Bodden, South Road. Wit: Family and friends.
Aug. 22 — Fred Hart of Fishkill Plains and Ada G. Pitcher of Amenia, at Parsonage. Wit: Mrs. W. A. Dumont, Rose Sheehan.

1897
Feb. 18 — John S. Rockwell of Garrettsville, N. Y. and Emilie B. Van Voorhis of New Hackensack, at home of bride's father at Myers Cor. Wit: Family and friends. This marriage was performed by Rev. H. Ward of Closter, N. J.
Feb. 24 — Clarence Van Tassell of Wappingers and Ida Knapp of Myers Corners, at home of bride's father at Myers Cor. Wit: Family and friends.
June 23 — Myron Tracy Scudder of Albany, N. Y. and Martha Nevins Dumont of Far Hills, N. J., at home of bride's father at Far Hills, N. J. Wit: Family and friends.
Sep. 29 — Henry Burrell Turnbull of New York City and Almira Amelia Doughty of New Hackensack, at home of bride's father at New Hackensack, N. Y. Wit: Family and friends.
Sep. 29 — Remsen Rosell of Fishkill Plains, N. Y. and Mabel J. Terwilliger of Wappingers Falls, at Parsonage. Wit: Mrs. W. A. Dumont, Rose A. Sheehan.

1898
Mar. 12 — James Lewis Smith of Poughkeepsie and Minnie Maria Morris of Poughkeepsie, at home of P. Gray in Mr. Mott's tenant house. Wit: P. Gray, Sarah C. Gray.
Sep. 11 — Ralph H. Bailey of Wappingers and Mary E. Morse of Swarthoutville, at Parsonage. Wit: Martha H. Dumont, C. M. Holder.
Nov. 23 — Stiles P. Jones of Minneapolis, Minn. and Helen Louise MacKinlay of Manchester Bridge at home of bride's mother at Manchester Bridge. Wit: Family and friends.

1899
June 21 — Lewis B. Knapp of Fishkill-on-Hudson and Ida DeGroff of Wappingers at home of bride's parents near Wappingers Falls. Wit: Family and friends.
Aug. 2 — Charles T. Rogers of New Hackensack and Mary Louisa Robinson of New Hackensack, at Parsonage. Wit: C. M. Holder, Martha Dumont.
Aug. 10 — Jerse Bowman of Wappingers Falls and Hattie Jackson of New Hackensack, at Parsonage. Colored. Wit: Appie Clauson, Lizzie Bowman.
Sep. 27 — Isaac M. Forbes of Pittsburg, Pa. and Mary Louise Seger of New Hackensack, at home of bride's mother, New Hackensack. Wit: Family and friends.
Dec. 30 — George Faust of Poughkeepsie and Martha Albertson Disbrow of Poughkeepsie, at Parsonage. Wit: Thos. E. Phillips, Mrs. W. A. Dumont.

1900
June 27 — Fred D. Allendorf of New Hackensack and Ada L. Smith of Poughkeepsie, at home of bride's father, Poughkeepsie. Wit: Family and friends.
Sep. 12 — Edwin M. Scofield of Poughkeepsie and J. Josie Haight Williams of Noxon, at home of bride's parents, Noxon, N. Y. Wit: Family and friends.
Sep. 19 — William C. Fries of Pleasant Valley and Lona A. Vollmer of Noxon, at home of bride's parents, Noxon, N. Y. Wit: Family and friends.
Dec. 18 — William H. Swezey of Moore's Mills and Ida Monfort of Noxon, at home of bride's mother, Noxon, N. Y. Wit: Philip Lauer, Mrs. Philip Lauer, Family.

1901
Mar. 29 — John J. Brown of Wappingers Falls and Carrie G. Smith of Wappingers Falls, at home of Thos. Ireland, Camelot, N. Y. Wit: Thos. Ireland, Mrs. Thos. Ireland.
May 5 — Elijah Robinson of Fishkill Plains and Ada Graves of New Hackensack, at Parsonage. Colored. Wit: Dan'l Perry, Mrs. Dan'l Perry.
June 12 — Charles J. Brower of Poughkeepsie and Cora E. Warren of Noxon, N. Y., at home of bride's parents, Noxon, N. Y. Wit: John M. Bush, Mary S. Warren, Family.

Marriage Register

June 19	James H. Osterhout of New Hackensack and Jennie R. Hicks of New Hackensack, at home of bride's parents, New Hackensack. Wit: Eva M. Brower, Charles Hicks, Family.
Aug. 7	Titus I. Collins of Poughkeepsie and Martha M. Voight of Poughkeepsie, at home of bride's parents, Poughkeepsie. Wit: Anna Voigt, Wm. M. Baxter, Family.
Aug. 23	Judson Pollock of Poughkeepsie and Irene Burnett of Helena, Mon., at Parsonage. Wit: George Van Tine, Martha H. Dumont.
Nov. 28	Jacob R. Cornwell of New Hackensack and Susie E. Hoyt of Hughsonville, at home of bride, Hughsonville. Wit: Wm. B. Hoyt, Agnes Gillin and friends.
Dec. 12	Charles H. Lattin of Poughkeepsie and Sadie M. Hadden of Poughkeepsie, at Parsonage. Wit: Martha H. Dumont, Wm. H. Losee.

1902

Feb. 16	Augustus H. Townsend of Clove Branch and Mrs. Carrie Dayton McKee of Poughkeepsie, at Parsonage. Wit: Martha H. Dumont, Carrie Hicks.
May 12	Harry Rose of Arlington and Edith Rhodes of Poughkeepsie, at Parsonage. Wit: Martha H. Dumont, Isabella Phillips.
May 17	W. James Horton of Camelot and Barbara E. Simpson of Camelot, at Parsonage. Wit: Martha H. Dumont, Joseph Horton.
Aug. 28	Grant E. Smith of Poughkeepsie and Mary J. Anderson of Diddell, N. Y., at home of bride's father, Diddell, N. Y. Wit: Geo. Anderson, Margaret S. Anderson.
Nov. 2	Thomas H. Bell of Fishkill Plains and Eva M. Andrus of Fishkill Plains, at Parsonage. Wit: Martha H. Dumont, Anna Dumont.
Nov. 6	Jas. Wm. Steele of Cork, Ireland, and Mabel Lucy Barry of Cork, Ireland, at Brooklyn. Wit: Fred. G. Bolton, Isabella Singleton.
Nov. 16	Walter D. Heil of Matteawan and Edith M. Dolson of Matteawan, at Parsonage. Wit: Mrs. W. A. Dumont, Rachel W. Dumont.
Nov. 23	Harry C. Campbell of New Hackensack and Mary V. Tibbs of Nason, Va. Colored, at Parsonage. Wit: Carrie Pitcher, Martin Pitcher.
Nov. 24	Wm. H. A. Lory of Town of Poughkeepsie and Thora K. Larson of Poughkeepsie, at home of groom's parents, Town of Poughkeepsie. Wit: Grace E. Lory, Myron H. Briell.
Nov. 26	Wm. L. Prout of Fishkill Plains and Florence A. Scofield of Fishkill Plains, at home of bride's parents near Fishkill Plains. Wit: Blanche G. Vollmer, Edwin Irving.
Nov. 29	Frederic S. Van De Water of Rocky Point and Annie E. Frith of Noxon, at home of bride's parents near Noxon, N. Y. Wit: Harriet M. Frith, Mattie Van Dewater.
Dec. 9	John Tibbs of Nason, Va. and Carrie Pitcher of Nason, Va. Colored. At Parsonage. Wit: Mrs. W. A. Dumont, Mary T. Campbell.

1903

Jan. 30	Theodore Anthony of New Hackensack and Mary Robinson of Danbury, Ct., Colored. At house of Jno. Cornwell. Wit: Hiram Johnson, Martha Johnson.
Apr. 26	George A. Colden of New Hackensack and Belle E. Schoonmaker of Poughkeepsie. Colored. At Parsonage. Wit: Mrs. W. A. Dumont, Anna Dumont.
May 17	Charles Hicks of Fishkill Plains and Emma J. Jones of Poughkeepsie, at Parsonage. Wit: Mrs. W. A. Dumont, Anna Dumont.
Oct. 28	George L. Jaycox of Camelot and Altha C. Knapp of Oak Grove Dist. at home of bride's parents, Oak Grove. Wit: Geo. V, D. Knapp, Bertha M. Knapp.
Oct. 28	Clarence D. Brower of Schenectady and Catherine M. Ten Broeck of New Hackensack, at home of bride's mother at Myers Corner. Wit: Olive Brower Wood, Chas. G. Wood.
Nov. 6	Elias Clauson of Wappingers and Eliza Quick of Wappingers, at Parsonage. Wit: Mrs. W. A. Dumont, Anna Dumont.
Nov. 8	James E. Wolven of Poughkeepsie and Myrtle Rhodes of Poughkeepsie, at Parsonage. Wit: Mrs. W. A. Dumont, Rachel W. Dumont.
Dec. 8	William Ostrander of Stormville and Laura E. Hauver of Stormville, at Parsonage. Wit: Abram L. Robinson, Julia B. Robinson.

1904

June 28	Marshall K. Doughty of Poughkeepsie and Blanche G. Vollmer of Myers Corner, at home of bride's Grandfather, Myers Corner. Wit: Lucie C. Baker, Sherman Doughty.
Aug. 2	Archie M. Conner of Poughkeepsie and Lillian T. Hawley of Poughkeepsie, at Parsonage. Wit: Mrs. W. A. Dumont, Anna G. Dumont.
Aug. 14	Thos. Edward Horton of New Hamburg and Mary Ann Ervine of Wappingers Falls, at Parsonage. Wit: Mrs. John Convery, Mrs. W. A. Dumont.
Dec. 7	John James White of Town of Poughkeepsie and Laura Vignes Pitcher of Red Oaks, at home of bride's parents at Red Oaks Mill. Wit: Emily Pitcher, Martha Dumont.

The Reformed Dutch Church of New Hackensack

1905

Jan. 17 — Anton William Walter of Sharon, Ct., and Kate Elizabeth Vollmer of Noxon, N. Y., at home of bride's parents, Noxon, N. Y. Wit: Wm. C. Fries, Lona Fries.

Mar. 22 — Harry Arthur Campbell of Hilton, N. J. and Lottie May Jaycox of Poughkeepsie, at Parsonage. Wit: Mrs. W. A. Dumont, Rachel Dumont.

Mar. 26 — George W. Ganung of Poughkeepsie and Carrie A. Alexander of Poughkeepsie, at Parsonage. Wit: Mrs. W. A. Dumont, Anna G. Dumont.

Apr. 19 — Alexander Bishop, Jr., of New Hackensack and Hattie M. Frith of LaGrangeville, at home of bride's parents, LaGrangeville. Wit: Nellie S. Bishop, Esther J. Mercy.

May 28 — Floyd B. Hynds of Hyndsville and Mary K. Lory of Town of Poughkeepsie, at home of bride's parents, Town of Poughkeepsie. Wit: Grace L. Lory, Elmer J. Hynds.

July 3 — Albert Tower Ogden of Poughkeepsie and Agnes Edwards of New York City, at Parsonage. Wit: Mrs. W. A. Dumont, Anna G. Dumont.

Dec. 19 — Arthur Van Tassell of New Hackensack and Edna Mae Bagley of Poughkeepsie, at home of groom's parents, south of New Hackensack. Wit: Flora Van Tassell, J. Stewart Devons.

1906

Jan. 28 — James Mitchell Fraser of Wappingers Falls and May Ethel Lynn of Wappingers Falls, at Parsonage. Wit: Clara E. Hicks, William Hicks.

Nov. 10 — George Wilson Morgan of New York City and Helen Eloise Demuth of Oberlin, O., at Parsonage. Wit: J. A. Demuth, Wm. H. Morgan and friends.

Dec. 27 — Richard James Maloney of Poughkeepsie and Catherine Thorne Akin of New Hackensack, at New Hackensack Church. Wit: Wm. R. Maloney, Jr., Ella Heyer.

LIST OF MEMBERS AND COMMUNICANTS
of the church of
NEW HACKENSACK
1766—1906

Register of Members

A LIST OF THE MEMBERS AND COMMUNICANTS BELONGING TO THE CHURCH OF NEW HACKENSACK TAKEN UP 30 & 31 JULY, 1766.

1766		Andries Heermans
		Rachel Van Nette, his wife
		Thomas van Bremen
		Jane Oudwater, his wife
deceased		Jane Ferdon
		Clara, widow Heermans
deceased		John Rosekrans
		Sarah Schoonmaker, his wife
		Teunis Wiltsee. Elder
departed		Wilhelmus Heermans. Deacon
		Peter Dates
deceased		Cathrine Lent, his wife
departed		Anna Shurry, wife of Lawrens Conchlin
		Adolf Zwartwoud
		Deborah Wiltsee, his wife
deceased		Henry Bell
		Constyn Gulneck
		Christina Reyerse, his wife
deceased		Peter Oudwater
deceased		Beletje, his wife
deceased		John Shurry
deceased		Anna Oudwater, his wife
deceased		Philip Verplanck
deceased		Aafje Beekman, his wife
deceased		Abraham Lent
		Antje Bronckerhoff, his wife
		George Brinckerhoff
departed		Ida Montfoort, his wife
		Cornelius Luyster
deceased		Susanna Brinckerhoff, his wife
deceased		Mary Lewis, wife of Michiel Hoffman
deceased		Adriana Luyster, wife of Gerrit Noordstrant
deceased		John Lewis
Aug. 2		Received in the presence of the Elders:
		Matthias Luyster &
deceased		Barbara Holst, his Wife, &
		Cathrine Hoffman
Nov. 10		Received in the presence of the Elders:
deceased		Jacob Timmerman
1767		
Sep. 13		Received with a Certificate from Kingstown
deceased		Matthew I. du Boys &
		Cathrine du Boys, his wife
		Edward Schoonmaker &
deceased		Eltinge, his wife
deceased		Cornelis du Boys delivered his Attestation from Poughkeepsie to Communicate here.
1768		
July 20		Received in the presence of the Elders of Hoopwell and N. Hackensack:
		John Sleght, Junr.
1768		Received before the Elders, the following Persons:
		Henry Wiltsee
		Petronella de Boog, his wife
		Carel Hoffman
		Elizabeth Seyfer, his wife
departed		John Steenbergen
departed		Sarah van Keeck, his wife
departed		Isaac Wiltsee
		Cathrine Zwartwoud, his wife
deceased		Adam Dates
		Anna Rosekrans, his wife

The Reformed Dutch Church of New Hackensack

departed Laurens Conchlin
Cornelia Barthley, wife of Teunis Wiltsee
Jane Noordstrant, wife of John Jewel
Lydia Shurry, wife of James Hicks
deceased Sarah Shurry, wife of Peter Haff
Cathrine Shurry, wife of Lawrens Haff
Peter Luyster
Benjamin van Keuren
deceased Aaltje Luyster
deceased Sarah Luyster
Cornelia Dates
Hester Hoffman
Mary Hoffman

1769
Aug. 19 Came over to us from Long Ihland, with due Certificates
Aris van der Bilt and
deceased Anna Nagel, his wife
deceased Brechje Meyer, wife of John Low

1770
Jan. 21 Baptized and received in the Church
Samuel Dean and
Amy Dean, wife of John Sleght
At the same Day received, as members
Aris Middelaar &
Grietje Seyfer, his wife
deceased Cornelis Zwartwoud &
Catelina Spier, his wife
This year came over also from Long Iland
Abraham Westerveld &
Anna Bosveld, his wife.

1774
Oct. 22 Received from the Elders:
Matthew Buys
Albert Montfoort
Susanna Hogeland, his wife
Anna Butcher, wife of Benjamin van Keuren
John Müller

1776
Jan. 20 Received before the Elders:
John Wiltsee &
Jane Lucky, his wife
June 6 Received before the Elders:
Goris Storm &
deceased Peter Haff
Nov. 29 Received before the Kerkraad:
deceased Abraham Durrye, Junr.
deceased Peter A. Lasson
Cathrine Dolssen, his wife

N. B. During the war, from the last date until the 16 of July 1785, no members have been received.

1785
July 16 Received before the Elders:
Peter Rosekrans &
Anna Westerveld, his wife

1786
July 1 Received before the Elders:
Albert Montfoort, Junr.
Matthew van Keuren
Sarah du Boys, wife of Duncan Graham
Mary Bevoys, wife of Aris van der Bilt

1787
Jan. 6 Came in with a Certificate from New Palts
Ariana du Boys, widow of Solomon du Boys, and wife of Peter Dates

Register of Members

1782
Apr. 28   Received before the Elders:
          Frederick Rosekrans
          Abraham Sleght, Junr.
          Jacobus Sleght
          John Jay &
          Elizabeth ter Bush, his wife

1784
Aug. 28   Recd.
          Michiel Gulneck &
          Elizabeth Dates, his wife
          Phoebe Bell, wife of Frederick Rosekrans

1787   With Attest & are come in:
          From Long Island:
          John Hegeman &
          Seytje van der Bilt, his wife
          From Harlem:
          Benjamin van de Water & his wife

1788
May 2   Received before the Elders
          Cathrine Oudwater, wife of Barent van Cleeck &
          Aaltje van Keuren, wife of Albert Montfoort, Junr.
          With Attest from Flakebush is come over to us, as a member
          Seytje Hegeman
July 27   Have been unanimously chosen in Consistory for Elders:
          Aris van der Bilt & Theophilus Anthony
          Deacons: John Sleght & Peter Rosekrans.

1790
July 5   Received before the Elders
          Antje Speong, wife of Mathias Luyster
          Wilhelmina Luyster, wife of Peter Luyster
          Johannes Luyster, and Cathrine van Ahlst, his Wife
" 11   John Dates and Elizabeth Lassen, his Wife
          Received Aug. 5, Magdalena van de Water, wife of Peter van de Water.

A List of those who became members of the Congregation of New Hackinsack during the Ministry of Nichs. Van Vranken by Virtue of their Confession of Faith, viz:

1792
Aug. 16   Peter Wyckoff
          Cornelius Van Sickler, and
          Catharine Johnson, his Wife
          John Van Sickler
          John Hoff and Rebeckah Storm, his wife
          Martha Brower
          Thomas Wood, Baptized and received
          Femmetje Cornell
          Maria Amack, wife of John Hanse

1793
Nov. 7   Received before the Elders
          Elizabeth Wiltsie, Widow
          Jacob Griffin and
          Catharine Hoffman, his Wife
          Harme Jewel and
          Elizabeth Heliker, his Wife
          Robert Todd and
          Elizabeth Ver Vailen, his Wife
          Samuel Luckey
          William Hoffman and
          Deborah Leroy, his Wife
          John Cornell
          Martha Hageman, Wife of Archibald Divine, by Testimonials from New York
          William Lawson
          Mary Gulneck

The Reformed Dutch Church of New Hackensack

1794
Mary Churchel, Wife of Thomas Wood

1795
July 25 — Elizabeth Hoffman, Wife of Charles Brower

1796
July 7 — Warren Rosecrants and
Phebe Hoff, his Wife
Andrew Reynders and
Elizabeth Leroy, his Wife
Mary Dubois, Widow of John Dates
Magdalen Ackerman, Wife of Peter Van Breemer

1797
Aug. 24 — Aron Cole
Elizabeth Van Keure
Helena Hoffman, Wife of Matthew Lawson
Sarah Rosecrants, Wife of Henry Dodge

1798
Aug. 12 — Tunis Van Bunschooten and
Elizabeth Van De Burgh, his Wife
Nazareth Brower
Hannah Monfoort, Wife of James Van Keure
Rebeckah Pinckney, Wife of Samuel Luckey, Esqr.
Jane De Graff, Wife of Michael De Graff
Gertrude Ferdon, Wife of Benjamin F. Jeacocks
Mary Duncan, Wife of James Brisby

1799 — Received with Attestations from Long Island
Elizabeth Nagel, Wife of John Nagel and
Thomas, Negro Slave of John Nagel
At the same time before the Elders
Hester Cole, Wife of James Odel
Casper Gons and
Anna Shear, his Wife
Mary Newman, Wife of Thaddeus Raymond
Joseph Harris, Baptized and received by his Confession of faith

1800
Oct. 26 — Maria Ostrum, Wife of Peter Flageler and
Dinah Flageler, Widow of Joseph Golder were received by their Confession of faith

1801
Oct. 8 — James Monger, baptized and received
Anna Monfoort, Wife of John Cornell
John Lossing
Ares Van Der Bilt, Junr.
Jane Smyth, Wife of Henry Phillips
Maria Bogert, Widow
Peter Flageler
Margaret Abrams, Wife of Benjn. Cornel Baptized and Admitted

1802 — Isabella Pollock, Wife of John Cornnel was baptized and admitted

1803
Apr. 4 — Elizabeth Merrit, Wife of John Lossing was baptized and received as a Member
Hannah Lineson was Baptized and admitted
Nov. 6 — Deborah Wiltsie, Wife of Nazareth Brower
Sarah Lossing
Sitea Van Der Bilt, Wife of Peter Wyckoff
Catharine Conklin, Wife of Nichs. V. Vranken

CHURCH MEMBERS RECEIVED
During the Ministry of George Barkulo, N. Hackensack

1806
Aug. 7 — James Van Keuren, by Certificate from the reformed Dutch Church in the City of New York

Register of Members

1808
Mar. 24   Catharine Nagle, Daniel Hoffman, & Sarah Lynderson, wife of Matthew Lawson, all upon confession of their faith.—Sarah Lynderson was als baptized

1809
Apr. 20   Abraham Dates & Elizabeth Fowler, his wife (who was also baptized Joseph Talmage, all upon Confession of their Faith
Sep. 17   Silas Tidd, upon confession of his faith (he was also baptized
Nov. 10   Susannah Monfoort, wife of Albert Monfoort, upon confession of her faith

1812
July 18   Ann Dates

MEMBERS RECEIVED
During the Ministry of the Rev. Thomas DeWitt

1813
Jan. 29   Catelina Van Wyck, wife of John Van Sickler
Sarah Van Sickler, widow of Peter Cowenhoven
Phebe Gomaer ⎫ women of colour
Betty Little ⎭
   by confession of their faith
Jane Cornell, wife of Matthew Luyster
   by certificate from Dutch Church at Poughkeepsie
May 20   Hannah Tappen, wife of Samuel Luckey
Henry A. Monfoort &
Maria Philips, his wife
William Jewell
   on confession of their faith
Sep. 24   James Ackerman
Sarah Concklin, his wife
Stephen Monfoort
Maria Palmatier
Mary Luckey, Widow
Catherine Van Der Belt, wife of Abm. Patterson
Mary Everett, wife of Peter Vn Der Belt
Electa Seward, Died July 3, 1872—age 86
   on confession of their faith

1814
Jan. 28   Anne Storm, wife of Abraham Adriance
Catherine Van Alst, wife of John Luyster
   on confession of their faith
Dismis   Sarah Kennedy
   on certificate from the Presbyterian Church in Rutger Street, New York
May 20   decd. Abraham Adriance, on certificate from Reformed Dutch Church at Rhinebeck
Sep. 23   John Swartwout, Dismissed
John Beagle
   Vn Arsdalen, his wife
Catherine Dutcher, wife of Martin Monfoort, Died Feb. 28, 1878, aged 96

1815
Jan. 27   James Dodge, dismissed
Phoebe Platt, Decd.
Jacob Phillips
Elizabeth Berry, his wife
June 2   Mathew Luyster, Died June 29, '71, aged 82
Adrian Hageman, Died February 26, 1872, aged 90
Maria Hoffman, his wife
Helen Dodge
Sarah Hageman
Martha Hageman
Gertrude Lawson, wife of John Yates
Saul Gomar ⎫ Blacks ⎧ decd.
Susan, his wife ⎭   ⎩ dismis.
Sep. 22   Martin Monfoort
William Churchill
Cornelia Vn Nostrand, his wife, decd.
Rebecca Vn Nostrand, widow of Joseph Churchill
Amy Montross, wife of Henry Diamond

The Reformed Dutch Church of New Hackensack

	Mary Diamond
	Maria Reynders, wife of Adonijah Palmer
	Susan, wife of Jack Potter
1816	
Jan. 26	Jacob Van Bunschoten
	James Dearin
May	Susanna Tapper, wife of Ares Vanderbilt
	on certif. from Pres. church Rutger St. N. Y.
	Sal, wife of Jack Gardner (woman of colour)
	on confession
Sep. 27	Mary, wife of Abm. Montross
	Phoebe Thrasher, wife of U. Cornwell
	Samuel Gomaer, Black
1817	
Feb. 3	On certificate from Ref. Dutch Church at Greenwich (NY)
	James Jones &
	Sarah Sleight, his wife
June 12	Sarah Gomaer, Black
	Flora , Black, Deceased
Nov. 19	John Ganse
	Samuel Luckey, Jr.
	Mary Underhill, his wife
	Jane Luckey, wife of Corns. Klump
1818	
Mar. 5	Philip Nagel
	Jane Valentine, wife of Valentine
Aug. 2	Sylvester Earle, dismissed
Dec. 25	Ezekiel Jewell & Celia Van De Bogart, his wife
	Samuel Throop
	Caroline Ackerman, wife of Benj. A. Sleght
	Nancy Devine, wife of Sherry Hicks
1819	
Apr.	Cornelius Westervelt
	wife of Sam Gomaer, Black
Aug.	Frances Tanner, wife of Corns. Westervelt, also bap.
	Elizabeth Brinkerhoff, wife of Abm. H. Phillips.
1820	
Jan.	Peter Van Der Bilt
	Henry C. Disbrow
	Adonijah Palmer, also baptized
	John Cornell, dismis
	John T. Linson, dismis
	Derick Luyster, deceased
	Engeltje Covenhoven, his wife, dismissed
	Ruth, widow of John Robinson, also baptized
	Jane Robinson, wife of John Van der Bilt, also baptized
	Freelove Potter, wife of Dr. Henry D. Sleght, also baptized
	John A. Monfoort, Dead
	Jane Monfoort, his wife, Dead
	Maria Monfoort, widow of Theod. Monfoort
	Rachel, widow of Gideon Boice
	Jane Luckey, wife of Wm. J. Dearin
	Susan Monfoort, Dead
	Jemima Van Bunschoten, wife of O. Greer
	Jane Dadd, widow of Peter Dates
	Celia Monfoort, Dead, March 1873
	Hetty Ann Ackerman
	Catherine Ackerman, dismis, Dead
	Phoebe Smith, deceased
	Phoebe, a coloured woman living at Barnet E. Viele, also baptized
	on confession of their faith
	Helena Van Der Voort, wife of Garret Luyster
	on certificate from 2nd Ref. Dutch Church at Albany
May	John Budd, also baptized
	Isaiah Reynders

Register of Members

    John Boice, deceased
    Charles Dearin
    William Todd
    Margaret Wilde, his wife, also bap.
    Catherine Luyster, wife of D. Tidd
    Hannah Wyckoff, wife of John Wolven, dismissed
    Helen Miller, wife of Geo. Van der Bilt
    Eltsie Earle, dismissed
    Phoebe Budd
    Ann Thurston, also bapt.
    Hannah Lawson
    E(sther) Everitt, Dead. Died July 14, 1822
"A leaf containing register of members has been lost"
    Sarah Hicks
    Maria Nelson
    Anne Hanson
    John B. Luckey on con.
        Cornell, wife of John Myers, on c.

1822
    Ann Budd
    Ann Hulst, wife of Corns. W. Brower
    William Hicks

1823
    Ann Yates
    Eliz. Dennison, wife of Monf. Van Kleeck, on cert. from Bethlehem
    Maria Van Amburgh, Died Aug. 1888
    Cornelia, wife of John R. Luckey
    Mary Philips, on cer. from Rhinebeck
    Mary Lawson

1824
Sep.
    Francis Losee Monfoort
    Mary Monfoort, wife of N. B. Snediker
    Eliz. Platt, wife of John Ganse

1825
Oct.   Sarah, wife of Jesse Miller

1826
July 7   Henry Traver
    Elizabeth Cornell, wife of Abm. Myers
      on cert. from Poughkeepsie
    Eliza Cornell, wife of Oliver Todd

REGISTRY OF MEMBERS RECEIVED
During the Ministry of the Revd. M. W. Dwight

1828, Apr. 27 On Confession:	Catharine Patterson, Wife of John Robinson.	Dead
1829, Jan. 25 On Confession:	Maria Todd. Baptized.	Dismissed
By Certificate:	Elizabeth Hoffman, Wife of Isaac Everitt.	Dead
1829, Oct. 25 On Confession:	Mercy Myers. Baptized.	Dead
	Angelica Vn. Voorhies, Wife of John U. Budd.	Dead
1830, Apr. 23 On Confession:	Mary Sleight, Wife of Stephen Thorn.	Dead
	Dorcas Jones, Wife of Schenck Ackerman.	Dead
	Jane Jones.	Dead
	Betsey Cornwell.	Dead
1830, Aug. 25 On Confession:	Rachel Ann Southard. Baptized.	
	Susan Montfort.	Dead
	Mary Southard, Wife of Richard Southard.	
1830, Nov. 7 On Confession:	Susan Petty, Wife of Wm. Hoogland.	Dead
By Certificate:	Hester Todd.	Deceased
1831, Jan. 30 On Confession:	Mary Ann Luckey, Wife of Thos. Dearin.	Dead
1831, Apr. 22 On Confession:	James De La Vergne. Baptized.	Dismissed
	Wiley Todd.	Dead
	Mary Yonni, Wife of John Luyster.	Dead

131

The Reformed Dutch Church of New Hackensack

By Certificate:	Ann Sleght.	Dead
	Nelly Amelia Sleght.	Dead

1831, July 31 On Confession: Robert Van Amburgh. Entered the ministry.
    Elias V. B. Concklin.   Dead
    Patience Smith, Widow of Jno. Rich.   Dead
    Eliza Monfort.   Dismissed
    Mary Knapp. Baptized.   Dismissed
    Rachel Little, Wife of John Potter } Blacks
    Dinah Atkins

By Certificate: Prudence Robinson, Wife of Wm. Robinson.
    Dismissed to the West

1831, Nov. 5 On Confession: Jacob Van Amburgh.   Dismissed to the West
    Eliza Tanner, Widow of Robert Tanner.   Dead
    Sarah Riggs, Wife of   Dismissed

1832, Jan. 29 On Confession:
    Cynthia Palmer, Wife of Daniel Phillips. Baptized.
    Dismissed to Fishkill
    Mahala Eliza Sleght.   Dismissed
    Hagar Carman. A Black. Baptized.

By Certificate
    Martha Jones.   Died May 31, '88
    Jno. B. Jones.   Dismissed to Broome St., Dr. Brodhead, New York

1832, Apr. 29 On Confession
    Priscilla Merritt, Widow of Danl. Jones.   Dead
    Hannah Ackerman, Wife of Morris Teller.   Dead
    Sarah Ackerman.   Dead
    Letty Maria Monfort.   Dead

By Certificate
    Jefferson Cruger.   Dismissed to New York

1832, July 29 On Confession
    Jemima Southard, Widow of Jno. Everitt. Bapt.   Dismissed
    Susan Vn. Dyne, Wife of Oliver Vn. Dyne. Baptized.   Dismissed
    Gertrude Jewell.   Dismissed

1832, Oct. 28 On Confession
    Jane Wykoff.   Deceased
    Caroline Barclay, Wife of Andrew Low.   Dismissed

1833, Jan. 27 On Confession
    Sarah Maria Cornwell. Died June 10, 1902, aged 87 years

By Certificate
    Mary Ann Evertson, Wife of Jno. Given.   Dismissed

1833, Apr. 28 On Confession
    Jane Phillips, Wife of Abrm. Phillips.   Dead
    Freelove Dubois, Wife of Robert Vn. Ambergh.   Dead
    Eliza Hayes. Baptized.   Dismissed
    Hester Carman. Baptized.

By Certificate
    James M. Jones &   Dead
    Sarah Sleight, his Wife.   Dead
    Washington Cannady.   Dismissed

1838, Apr. 11 On Confession
    Benjamin H. Everitt.   Dismissed
    James S. Monfort.   Dead
    Barbara E. Hoagland, wife of J. S. Monfort.   Died Apr. 10, /91

1838, Apr. 13 On Confession
    Elizabeth Ann Todd.   Dead

By Certificate
    John B. Jones.   Died Feb. 4, 1896

1838 Aug. 11 On Confession
    Phillip B. Van Der Bilt. Suspended.   Dead
    Hannah Dates.   Dead
    Judith Mills. coloured.   Dismissed

Register of Members

1839, Apr. 16 By Certificate 　　Sarah Elizabeth Everitt.	Dead
1839, Apr. 19 By Certificate 　　John Leroy & 　　Getty Crapser, his wife.	Dismissed Dead
1839, Aug. 23 On Confession 　　Maria G. Hutchins, wife of John Monfort.	Dead
By Certificate 　　Letty Budd.	
1840, Apr. 17 On Confession 　　Schenck Ackerman. 　　Mrs. Mary Budd.	Dead Dead
By Certificate 　　Elizabeth Brinckerhoff, Wife of E. Flagler. 　　Gabriel Bishop and 　　Esther Yates, his Wife.	Dead Dead Dead
1840, Aug. 11 By Certificate 　　Mrs. Clarinda Gore.	Dead
1840, Dec. 24 On Confession 　　Phebe E., wife of Phillip Van Der Belt. 　　　　Dismissed to 1st Reformed, Poughkeepsie, May 31, /89	

REGISTER OF MEMBERS RECEIVED
During the Ministry of the Revd. Cornelius Van Cleef

1834, Feb. 2 On Confession 　　Catharine Tappan, widow of Peter Drake	Dismissed
1834, Apr. 27 On Confession 　　Maria Ackerman, wife of Benjamin Aikin	Dismissed
By Certificate 　　Sophia Somers Stillwell, wife of Revd. C. Van Cleef 　　Mary Brinckerhoff, wife of William Hutchings 　　Caroline Dolson	Dead Dead Dismissed
1834, Nov. 7 On Confession 　　Amelia Caroline Rynders	Dismissed
1835, Apr. 24 On Confession 　　Mary Yates, wife of George W. Delavergne	Dismissed
By Certificate 　　Elizabeth Phillips, wife of Henry D. Traver 　　Catharine E. Aikin, wife of Robert Thorn	Dismissed Dead
1836, Feb. 12 By Certificate 　　William Traver 　　Catharine Dates, Wife of William Traver	Dead Dead
1836, June 3 By Certificate 　　David Herd. Coloured	Dismissed
On Confession 　　Helen Jones	Dead
1836, Sep. 9 On Confession 　　Cornelia Way, Wife of Richard Van Voorhees	Dead
1836, Dec. 9 By Certificate 　　Margaret, wife of David Herd. Coloured	Dismissed
1837, May 5 By Certificate 　　Henry D. Hayt	Dismissed
1837, Sep. 8 On Confession 　　Cornelius P. Ostrander 　　Elizabeth Van Nosdall, his Wife 　　Sally Angeline Luckey, Wife of Peter Van Keuren 　　Patty Farrington, Wife of Henry Dimond	Dead Dead Dead

The Reformed Dutch Church of New Hackensack

1841, Apr. 13 On Confession
    Maria Van Nosdall, Wife of Henry Needham — Dead
    Lucy Gore, Wife of Daniel Bishop — Dismissed
    John Y. Bishop — Suspended

1841, Aug. 20 On Confession
    Alexander Bishop — Died Sep. 1914

1841, Dec. 31 On Confession
    Harvey D. Platt — Died Feb. 22, 1877
    Maria Eliza, Wife of Samuel Monfort — Dead
  By Certificate
    Phebe Carey, Wife of Harvey D. Platt — Dead

1842, Apr. 15 On Confession
    William Seward — Died Dec. 14/90
    Sarah E. Needham — Dismissed
    Jane Phillips
    Ann Eliza, wife of Jacob V. B. Van Voorhees — Died Sep. 21, 1869
  By Certificate
    Catharine Charlock, Wife of William Seward — Died Oct. 5, 1882
    Elizabeth Murray, Wife of Leonard J. Pells — Dismissed

1842, Aug. 26 On Confession
    Jane Ann Dubois, Wife of Emory Carpenter — Dismissed

1842, Dec. 28 By Certificate
    Jeremiah Platt & — Dead
    Phebe Everitt, his Wife — Dead
    Sarah Remsen, Wife of Dr. Remsen — Dead

1843, May 5 On Confession
    Helen Van Der Belt Lawson — Dismissed

1843, Sep. 8 On Confession
    Belinda Van Amburgh — Dismissed
    Harriet H. Potter — Dismissed

1844, Jan. 12 By Certificate
    Mrs. Sarah Hitchcock — Dead

1844, Apr. 26 On Confession
    Letty M. Phillips, Wife of James Baxter — Dead
  By Certificate
    Mrs. Mary Adriance — Dead

1844, Aug. 30 On Confession
    Mrs. Rachel Knapp — Dead
    Sarah Jane Van Voorhees — Dismissed
    Sarah Maria Meigs
  By Certificate
    Ann Van Amburgh — Died June 28/89

1844, Dec. 3 On Confession
    Mary E. Remsen — Died June 1, 1893
  By Certificate
    Mrs. Ann Delavergne — Dead

1845, Apr. 11 On Confession
    Mrs. Hannah Cope — Dead

1845, Aug. 29 On Confession
    Mary Angell, Wife of Chauncey Knapp — Dead

1846, Apr. 17 By Certificate
    Benjamin B. Coit, M.D. }
    Mrs. Cornelia A. Coit } — Both dismissed
    Obadiah C. Osborne }
    Mrs. Sarah Ann Osborne } — Both dismissed

1847, Mar. 12 On Confession
    Simeon Hitchcock — Died May 27, 1877

1847, June 4 On Confession
    Philander Seward — Dead

Register of Members

1847, Sep. 3 By Certificate	
Mrs. Catharine Pudney	Dismissed
Mrs. Eliza Brown	Dead
1848, Feb. 4 On Confession	
Mary Meeks, Wife of Nathl. Grant	Died Feb. 16, 1890
Jane Ann Monfort	Dismissed
1849, Mar. 30 On Confession	
John Jones	Died Mar. 13/91
Sarah Gertrude, Wife of J. V. B. Teller	Died May 7, 1899
1849, Nov. 30 On Confession	
Sarah L. Sleight	Died May 21/07
Sophia E. Sleight	Dismissed
Sophia Van Cleef	Dismissed
1850, Mar. 1 On Confession	
Jane Thorn, Wife of Tunis Ackerman	Died Apr. 8, 1884
Cynthia M. Needham, Wife of John Jones	
Dismissed Feb. 6, /96 to Pres. Ch. of New Hamburg, N. Y.	
Amelia M. Potter	Died Jan. 30, 1891
Catharine M. Potter	Dead
Maurice I. Seward	Dismissed
1850, June 7 By Certificate	
John C. Pudney &	Dead
Sarah E. Everitt, his Wife	Dead
1850, Aug. 30 On Confession	
Henrietta F. Potter	Dead
1850, Nov. 29 On Confession	
Martha J. Emmons, Wife of John Monfort	Dead
1851, May 30 On Confession	
Mary Marvin	Dismissed
1851, Sep. 5 On Confession	
Mercy Van Amburgh	Dismissed
1851, Dec. 5 By Certificate	
Mrs. Aletta Dorland	
1852, Mar. 5 By Certificate	
Susan Dorland (color'd)	Dismissed
1852, Jan. 13 On Confession	
Julia A. Jamieson	Dismissed
1852, Sep. 3 On Confession	
Hannah E. Cornwell	Dead
Susan L. Pells, wife of John Cornwell	Dead
By Certificate	
Mrs. Jane Robinson (color'd)	Dismissed
1852, Dec. 3 On Confession	
Henry Dates	Dead
1853, Mar. 4 On Confession	
Helen M. Everitt	Dismissed
1853, June 3 By Certificate	
Melinda Williams (color'd)	Dismissed
1853, Sep. 2 By Certificate	
William Baker &	Died Mar. 31, 1903
Catharine E., his Wife	Died Dec. 24, 1875
1854, June 2 By Certificate	
Elisha Conoyer }	Dismissed
Harriet, his wife }	
Mrs. Harriet Van Der Bilt	Dismissed Dead
1854, Sep. 1 On Confession	
Mrs. Cornelia Ann Alger	Dead
Mrs. Amanda Van Dyne	Dismissed

The Reformed Dutch Church of New Hackensack

    Mrs. Mary M. Howell   Dismissed
    Albina Van Voorhis   Dismissed
    Mary Louisa Seward   Dismissed
  By Certificate
    Charles J. Howell, Jr.   Dismissed

1854, Dec. 1 On Confession
    Catharine T. Grant   Died Apr. 5, 1905
    Gertrude K. Conover   Dismissed Apr. 25/95 to
                  Cong'l Ch., Po'keepsie, N. Y.
    Harriet Conover, wife of Henry Jones   Died Mar. 26, 1909

1855, Mar. 2 On Confession
    George Hardenburgh (Color'd)   Dismissed

1855, June 1 On Confession
    Ogden Seward   Dismissed

1855, Sep. 7 On Confession
    Mary Van Voorhis

1855, Nov. 30 On Confession
    Marietta Everitt   Died Aug. 7, 1902   Dismissed

1856, Sep. 5 By Certificate
    Mrs. Helen M. Cornell   Dismissed

1857, Feb. 27 On Confession
    Ellen Shepherd, wife of Rev. C. Van Cleef   Dismissed

1857, Mar. 29 On confession
    Jane Eliza Thompson (coloured)   Dismissed

1857, Dec. 4 On confession
    Henry Burroughs &   Died May 8, 1899
    his wife Alletta E. Bogardus   Died Sep. 1, 1900

1858, Apr. 9 On confession
    Sarah Ann Seward   Dismissed
    Jane Conover   Dismissed
    Henry D. Needham   Dead
  By certificate
    John D. Westervelt &   Dead
    his wife Nelly Depuy   Dismissed   Dead

1858, June 18 On confession
    John D. Cornwell, Jr.   Died Mar. 26, 1902
    Diana Storm, w. of J. J. Diddell   Died Dec. 2, 1896
    Maria Antoinette Hayt   Dismissed
    Esther Thorn   Dismissed
    Helen Ann Rogers   Died Dec. 11, 1888

1858, Sep. 3 On confession
    Harriet Phillips, w. of   Died Dec. 16, 1874
      Samuel I. Robinson, died Apr. 13, 1886.
    Jane Ackerman   Dead

1858, Dec. 10 On confession
    Samuel I. Robinson   Dead
    Delia D. Burroughs, w. of John D. Monfort   Dismissed
    Catharine Meyers, w. of Jerome Van Voorhis   Dead
  By certificate
    James W. Rogers &   Dead
    his wife Mary Be(s)ly Rogers   Died Nov. 27, 1888

1859, Mar. 4 On confession
    Anna M. Van Kleeck, w. of Schenck Monfort
    Mary Ann Monfort   Dismissed to Ref. Ch., Fishkill, Dec. 3, 1890
    Sarah Johanna Ackerman, mar. Hitchcock, Died Apr. 21, 1906
    Louisa C. Hitchcock   Died Nov. 11, 1895
    Susan Mary Hopkins   Dismissed to 1st Pres. Ch. of Poughkeepsie
      Feb. 13, 1904. Mar. Chas. Robinson.
    Peter Gardner. Colored.   Dead

Register of Members

1859, June 3	On confession W. C. Van Cleef Hoagland Maria Jane Pells	 Dead
1859, Sep. 2	On confession Nelly Shute, w. of J. V. B. Concklin. Elthea Purdy, w. of Henry Van Der Bilt By certificate Helen, w. of James P. Van Wagner	 Died Jan. 2, 1878 Dismissed Dismissed
1859, Dec. 2	On confession Mary E. Owen, w. of William Van Amburgh Mrs. Mahala Sampson, Coloured By certificate Dr. William A. Drinkwater & his w. Sarah E. Van Pelt Sarah, wid. of James Van Pelt Nicholas Sampson, Coloured	 Dead Dead Dead Dismissed, also Dismissed Dead
1860, Mar. 2	On confession Susan Ann Monfort Maria Louisa Monfort	 Dismissed } Sisters Dismissed
1860, June 1	On confession John Monfort Belinda Concklin Margaret E. Conklin Mary E. Thompson, Coloured w. of Henry Smith	 Dead Died Apr. 7, 1904 Died Aug. 2, 1907 Dismissed
1860, Nov. 30	On confession Catharine E. Monfort	 Dead
1861, Mar. 1	On confession Mrs. Elizabeth Collins Elizabeth M. Van Voorhis Mary Jane Grant Sarah Ann Gray, Coloured	 Dead Dismissed Suspended
1861, May 31	On confession Jane, w. of Alexander Bishop Sarah, w. of James Hicks By certificate Mrs. Sarah C. Winslow, w. of Leonard Winslow	 Died May 29, 1890 Dismissed Dismissed
1861, Nov. 29	On confession William H. Dimond & his wife, Maria Ann Luyster	 Dismissed Dead
1862, Feb. 28	By certificate David G(——) & Julia, his wife	 Dismissed Dismissed
1862, Dec. 5	On confession Sarah A. T. Knapp By certificate Mrs. Electa Dodge	 Dismissed Dead
1863, June 5	By certificate James R. Needham & his w., Anna DeWitt Phillips	 Dismissed Dismissed
1864, Mar. 4	By certificate Owen W. Angell & his w., Sarah E. Platt	 Dismissed "
1864, June 4	By certificate Mary E. Hayt w. of Harvey D. Platt	 Dismissed Dead
1864, June 5	On confession Jane Berry, w. of Henry D. Hayt,	 Dismissed

The Reformed Dutch Church of New Hackensack

1865, Mar. 3 On confession
    Chauncey Knapp   Dismissed
    Mrs. Eustacia Smith   Dead
   By certificate
    Mrs. Ta(——) Ostrander, w. of Peter Ostrander,   Dismissed

1865, June 2 By certificate
    Leffert T. Bergen &   Died Apr. 23, 1900
    his w., Mary C. Earle   Died Jan. 25, 1902
    Mrs. Abagail Dates, w. of Peter Dates,   Dead

1865, Sep. 1 On confession
    Edward Flagler &
    his w., Charlotte Degroff   Both dismissed

1865, Dec. 1 By certificate
    William St. John, &   Dead
    his w., Sophia & Dismissed to 1st Cong'l Ch., Ansonia, Conn.,
                        Dec. 12, 1905
    their son, Frank St. John   Dismissed Dead

1866, June 1 On confession
    Sylvester C. Cedore   Died Apr. 12, 1889
    Mrs. Ruth Ann Schryver   Dismissed
    Edward H. Schryver   Dismissed

1866, Aug. 31 On confession
    Joseph P. Deyo }   Dismissed
    Eliza Worden, his w. }   Dismissed
    George E. Salisbury   Dead

1866, Sep. 24 By certificate
    Jacob A. Schryver }
    Ann, his w. }   Dismissed

1866, Nov. 16 On confession
    Mrs. Sarah Matilda Hicks   Dead
   By certificate
    Ruth A. Birkins   Dead

During the Ministry of the Rev. H. Ward

1867, May 31 By certificate
    Catharine Ackerman, w. of John Teller   Dead

1868, Feb. 28 On confession
    Daniel Werner   Dismissed to RFD Church, Hyde Park, N. Y.
                        June 9, 1924
   By certificate
    William DeGroot   Died Feb. 16, 1887
    Maria Van Slyck, w. of D. H. Brown,   Dead

1868, June 5 On confession
    Catharine B. Needham, w. of Stephen P. Monfort,   Dismissed
    Mrs. Mary A. Vail   Dismissed
   By certificate
    Amanda M. Haight, w. of Joseph Van Voorhis   Dead

1868, Aug. 28 On confession
    Isaac D. Bostwick   Died Aug. 18, 1870
   By certificate
    Mrs. Nellie A. Bostwick   Dismissed
    Mrs. Susan Coe   Dead
    Allerton Trowbridge &   Dismissed
    Selina Trowbridge, his wife   Dismissed
    Susan Trowbridge   Dismissed
    Sarah Trowbridge   Dismissed

1868, Dec. 4 On confession
    William H. Tompkins   Dismissed Aug. 28, 1895

Register of Members

    By certificate
        John Delamater &   Died Apr. 27, 1891
        Sarah Terpening, his wife   Died Feb. 6, 1902
        Richard S. Van Wyck &   Dismissed
        Ann Augusta Scofield, his wife

1869, Mar. 5 On confession
        Mrs. Catharine E. Lauer   dead
        Mrs. Marianna Everett   dead
        Caroline Aurelia Trowbridge   Dismissed, Dead
        Annie Elizabeth Ostrander   Dismissed
        Elizabeth Everett Pudney, wife of Dr. A. T. Fink   Dismissed
                                                                        Died Dec. 1924
        Laura Vanderbilt (mar. Cantine)   Dismissed to First Ref. Ch. of
                                                                       Po'keepsie, May 31, 1889

1869, June 4 By certificate
        Joseph A. Platt &   Died Apr. 17, 1901
        Eliza A. Haviland, his wife   Died Feb. 21, 1897
        Parmelia Platt   Dead
        Joseph Simpson &   Dismissed
        Almira, his wife   dead
        Dr. Austin T. Fink   Dismissed Dead
        Mrs. Elizabeth Townsend   Dismissed
        Kate B. Rogers, mar. Chas. E. Van Kleeck   Dismissed to Pres. Ch.
                                                           of Wappingers Falls, Jan. 3, 1890
        Mary E. Rogers, mar. Jas. W. Moore   Dismissed to Pres. Ch.
                                                           of Wappingers Falls, N. Y.

    On confession
        Stephen P. Monfort   Dismissed
        John H. Luyster   Died June 6, 1887
        Edgar Luyster   Died Dec. 4, 1872
        William L. Germond   Suspended. Restored June 4, 1893. Died 1905
        Jane Ann, w. of Edward Van Dyne   Died July 1, 1888
        Maria Louisa Ackerman, w. of Wm. Tompkins   Died Mar. 24, 1901
        Helen E. Van Bramer, w. of Martin S. Ackerman,
                                                                              Died in 1897 in Buffalo
        Mary C. Hicks, w. of John S. Forshay,   Died Aug. 21, 1888
        Miss Annis Elizabeth Baker   Died Jan. 24, 1887
        Miss Deborah Ann Myers   Dismissed to Pres. Ch. of New
                                                           Hamburg, June 21, 1892
        Miss Sarah Gertrude Teller Monfort, sister of Mrs. S. P. Ten Brock,
                                                                              Died Jan. 1915
            "   Phebe A. Hawkes   Dismissed
            "   Ann Augusta Townsend   Dismissed, Dead
            "   Phebe Townsend   Dismissed
            "   Maria Louisa Robinson, mar. Edward Brower, Poughkeepsie
            "   Emily S. Bishop   Dead
            "   Hannah Ellen Germond   Dismissed. Dead
            "   Irene Myers   Dead
               Emma Jane Myers, mar. Monroe Scofield

1869, Sep. 10 On confession
        Philip Lauer   Died Dec. 21, 1904
        James Van Dyne &   Dead
        Catharine Van Dyne, his wife,   Dead

1870, Sep. 2 On confession
        Samuel Matthews   Died Nov. 18, 1888
    By certificate
        Gertrude Zimmer, w. of Samuel Matthews,   Died Dec. 6, 1890
        Isaac P. Smith   Dismissed

1870, Dec. 2 By certificate
        Sophia Manny, w. of J. M. Embury   Dismissed

1871, June 2 On confession
        John R. Matthews &   Dismissed Jan. 24, 1903 to M. E. Ch., Norwalk, Ct.
        Anna Statia Hunt, his wife   Dead
        Sarah Frances Tompkins, w. of James C. Ackerman Died Dec. 27, 1904
        James P. Organ   Died Feb. 21, 1923

The Reformed Dutch Church of New Hackensack

1871, Sep. 1 On confession
    Saraettie Monfort   Dismissed to Pres. Ch., Freedom Plains, Nov. 30, 1889

1871, Dec. 8 On confession
    Edgar Sedore &
    Fanny Alton, his wife

1872, Mar. 1 On confession
    Charles Gage   suspended
    Richard W. Akin &   Died Nov. 3, 1897
    Caroline Thorn, his wife   Died Apr. 7, 1881
    Mrs. Abby Sedore   Died July 29, 1888

1872, May 31 On confession
    Charles E. Van Kleeck   Dismissed to Pres. Ch. of Wappingers Falls, Jan. 3, 1890
    John A. Rogers   Died Feb. 28, 1923
    Ambrose D. Albertson   Dismissed
    John E. Pudney   Dismissed
    George W. Phillips &
    Susan A. Phillips, his wife
    Zopher I. Jones   Died Mar. 20, 1877
    George Underhill   Died
    De Witt Bergen   Dismissed
    Theodore E. Bergen   Died Oct. 28, 1877, aged 19
    Mrs. Charlotte A. Underhill   Died Nov. 5, 1905
    Henrietta N. Jones, mar. Jno. J. Scofield   Dismissed to M. E. Ch., Wappingers Falls, N. Y., Jan. 30, 1902
    Joseph Freeman, colored
    Jane Armstrong, colored   Died Apr. 25, 1896, at home of Rich. Akin

1872, Sep. 1 By certificate
    Mrs. Alletta A. McCord   Dismissed

1872, Dec. 6 By certificate
    Mrs. Nelly D. Brower   Died Dec. 18, 1874

1873, Aug. 31 By certificate
    Elizabeth M. Van Voorhis, w. of Peter Myers   Dismissed

1874, Mar. 1 By certificate
    John E. McCord   Died Apr. 20, 1882

1874, Sep. 4 By certificate
    Isaac Akin   Dead
    Arrabella Akin   Dismissed to the Christian Church of Machias, Feb. 8, 1894

1875, June 4 On confession
    Miriam Van Voorhis, mar. Jno. Wood, Poughkeepsie
    Minnie I. McCord, mar. Wm. Dusenbury   Dismissed to 2nd Methodist Episcopal Church of Po'keepsie, Feb. 21, 1891.

1876, June 2 By certificate
    James A. Seward   Died May 1, 1892
    Mrs. Mary B. Seward   Died Apr. 4, 1900
    On confession
    Charles A. Trowbridge   Dismissed
    Anna Vail McCord   Died Mar. 3, 1885
    Jennie Luyster   Dismissed Apr. 25, 1893 to Cong'l Ch. of Po'keepsie
          Died
    Clara Lauer
    Catharine Elizabeth Lauer
    Bertha Jane Lauer

1876, June 4 By certificate
    Alexander McElrath   Dismissed
    Mrs. Hannah McElrath   Dismissed

1876, Sep. 1 On confession
    Ida Monfort, mar. Wm. Swezey   (away)

1877, Mar. 2 By certificate
    Mrs. Harriet A. Baker   Died Nov. 25, 1915

Register of Members

1877, June 1 On confession
    Mrs. Margaret Werner   Died June 17, 1893

1877, Aug. 31 By certificate
    Mrs. Matilda Wright   Dismissed to the First Presbyterian Ch. of Plainfield, N. J., Feb. 8, 1894

1877, Dec. 2 On confession
    James C. Ackerman

1878, Mar. 1 On confession
    Mrs. Mary J. Francis   Died July 4, 1899

1878, June 2 On confession
    Brundage Tompkins &   Died Jan. 2, 1904
    Elizabeth Van Wyck Ackerman, his wife   Died Nov. 5 (?), 1914
    Sarah C. Fulmer, mar. Mr. Wellington White   (Poughkeepsie)

    By certificate
        Samuel B. Ackerman &   }Dismissed to Ref. Ch.,
        Delia Brinkerhoff, his wife }Hopewell, Mar. 17, 1890
        Phebe A. Hawkes   Dismissed to Ref., Fishkill, N. Y., Feb. 1, 1901
        Mrs. S. L. Van Benschoten   Dismissed
        Emma L. Wooster   Dismissed

1878, Aug. 30 By certificate
    Annie Josephine Wooster, mar. Jno. Diddell. Dismissed to Pres. Ch., Freedom Plains, N. Y., Apr. 6, 1900.
    Walter Underhill   }Dismissed Feb. 8, 1900 to 1st   Died
    Mrs. Adeline Underhill }Ref. Ch., Po'keepsie, N. Y.   Died
    Charles W. Underhill   (Poughkeepsie)
    Addie E. Underhill   Dismissed Feb. 8, 1900 to 1st Ref. Ch., Po'keepsie, N. Y.   Died
    Cornelius Miller   Died Mar. 3, 1889
    Mrs. Sarah Miller   Dismissed Nov. 25, 1891 to 2nd Reformed Ch., of Po'keepsie, N. Y.

1878, Nov. 28   Mrs. Letty Churchill, w. of Samuel I. Robinson   Dismissed to 1st Bapt., of Poughkeepsie

1879, May 30   Sarah C. Vermilyea, w. of Edward Hicks

1880, May 28 On confession
    Sarah Sleight   Dismissed
    Sarah S. Seward, mar. Robt. Johnston   Dismissed Dec. 3, 1891, to Ref. Ch. of Flushing, N. Y.
    Sarah A. Miller   Dismissed Nov. 25, 1891 to 2nd Ref. Ch., Po'keepsie, N. Y.

1880, Sep. 3 On confession
    Jacob Vollmer   Died 1916
    Mrs. Katie Vollmer   Dismissed to Church at Sharon, Conn., Feb. 26, 1918. Died at Sharon, Conn., Dec. 1924.

1880, Dec. 3 By certificate
    Mrs. Mary L. S. MacKinlay   Died Feb. 26, 1907
    Miss Helen L. MacKinlay   Dismissed Sep. 20, 1900 to Westminster Pres. Ch. of Minneapolis, Minn.

1881, May 27 On confession
    Caroline Davis, w. of Rev. Henry Ward   Dismissed
    By certificate
        Mrs. Amelia S. Pye   (Fishkill)   Died Mar. 1916

1881, Sep. 2 On confession
    Harriet L. McCord   Dismissed to Marble Collegiate Ch., N. Y. City, Apr. 27, 1892   Dead

    By certificate
        Mrs. Amelia C. Bostwick   Dismissed Apr. 22, 1889 to Washington St. M. E. Ch., Po'keepsie, N. Y.
        Sophia E .Sleight   (away)

The Reformed Dutch Church of New Hackensack

1882, Mar. 3 By certificate
    Francis Johnston   Died Mar. 11, 1889
    Mrs. Jane Johnston   Died May 21, 1890
    Miss Mary J. Johnston   Dismissed to Hyde Park Ref. Ch., East Orange, N. J., Nov. 27, 1909

1882, Sep. 1 On confession
    Miss Anna Gertrude Bishop   Dismissed to West 23d St. Pres. Ch., N. Y. City, Apr. 8, 1889

1882, Dec. 1 On confession
    Miss Sarah Remsen Werner

1883, Nov. 30 On confession
    Miss Sophie V. Bishop   Died July 14, 1891

1884, Mar. 2 On confession
    Catharine Phillips   Died Sep. 26, 1894
  By certificate
    Mrs. Isabella Collins   Dismissed to 1st Pres. Ch. of Wappingers Falls, June 25, 1889

1885, Mar. 1 On confession
    Miss Hattie T. Phillips   Dismissed to Pres. Ch. of Lansingburg, N. Y., Oct. 2, 1903.

1885, Dec. 4 On confession
    William D. Ward   Dismissed

1886, Mar. 5 On confession
    Lulu D. Haight   Dismissed
    Jacob T. Tompkins   (Myers Corners)
    Austin B. Hitchcock   (Myers Corners)
    Teunis Ackerman   Dismissed to 2nd Ref. Ch., Po'keepsie, Oct. 25, 1895
    Theodore J. Ackerman   Dismissed to the Reformed Church of Millbrook, N. Y., Apr. 1, 1924

1886, Sep. 3 On confession
    Dr. Anthony Underhill   Died Sep. 5, 1889
    Miss Mary Gertrude Matthews, mar. Ward Weyant. Dismissed Dec. 26, 1894, to Comforter (Dutch) Ref. Ch., N. Y. City

1887, Mar. 4 By certificate
    Dr. Charles E. Seger &   Died Dec. 10, 1896
    Agnes Schoonmaker, his wife   Dismissed Oct. 26, 1905 to 1st Cumberland Presbyterian Church, Pittsburg, Pa.   Died

1887, May 27 On confession
    Miss Emilie B. Van Voorhis   Dismissed to United Pres. Ch. of Garrettsville, N. Y., Oct. 7, 1897
  Rev. W. A. Dumont officiated at Consistory meeting (see minutes).

1888, Feb. 2 On confession
    Mary Bergen
  By certificate
    Cromeline Phillips   (away)   Died Feb. 11, 1897
    Warren Luyster   Dismissed to the Washington St. M. E. Ch. of Po'keepsie, Sep. 12, 1889.   Died 1926

During Ministry of Rev. W. A. Dumont there were received

1888, June 1 On confession
    Clara W. Bergen
  By certificate
    Mrs. Martha J. Dumont, from 18th St. M. E. Church of Brooklyn. Died
    Mrs. Maggie Van Dyne, w. of Alonzo Van Dyne, from Pres. Ch. of Wappingers Falls. (Oak Grove).   Died

1888, Sep. 2 On confession
    Mrs. Dora Mathews, w. of Robt. Mathews. Dismissed to Pres. Ch. of Salt Point, N. Y., Feb. 25, 1909

Register of Members

    Mrs. Martha Gresty, w. of Frederic Gresty   Dismissed to the Pres. Ch. of Wappingers Falls, N. Y., June 1, 1911.

1889, Mar. 3 By certificate
    MissSarah N. Jones from First Collegiate Reformed Church of Harlem, N. Y.   Died Aug. 8, 1894

On confession
    Mrs. Elizabeth Nostrand Pier, w. of Edward Pier. Joined Epis. Ch., Staatsburg, N. Y., Oct. 4, 1898. Died at Staatsburg, N. Y., Jan. 12, 1925.
    Miss Minnie Pier, mar. Hughes. Joined Epis. Ch., Staatsburg, Oct. 4, 1898. Died at Staatsburg, N. Y., Jan. 12, 1925.
    Clarence H. Pier. Joined Epis. Ch., Staatsburg, Oct. 4, 1898.
    Wm. Edward Pier. Dismissed to Hope Cong'l Ch., Springfield, Mass., June 8, 1893.
    Miss Nellie S. Bishop (Mrs. C. Van Voorhis)
    George F. Underhill. Dismissed to 2nd Ref. Ch., Poughkeepsie, Dec. 7, 1896.   Died
    Frank Müller   (away)

1889, June 2 On confession
    Miss Ella Ackerman. Dismissed Feb. 18, 1911 to Pres. Ch., Freedom Plains, N. Y. Mar. Jas. Howard.

1889, Sep. 1 On confession
    Miss Edith Vollmer. Dismissed to Ch., at Sharon, Conn., Feb. 26, 1918.
    Miss Katie E. Vollmer. Dismissed to Trinity M. E. Ch., Po'keepsie, July 30, 1900.

On re-confession
    Jans Peter E. Christiansen   (away)

1890, Mar. 2 By certificate
    Mrs. Hannah Maria Luyster, and   Died Mar. 14, 1894
    Mrs. Sarah L. Luyster, w. of Jas. Luyster. Both from the Presbyterian Church of Freedom Plains, N. Y.

On confession
    Allie A. Doughty. Dismissed to 2nd Ref. Ch., Po'keepsie, Oct. 1st, 1908. Mar. H. B, Turnbull,

1890, June 1 By certificate
    Chas. Dyson Luyster from Pres. Ch., Freedom Plains, N. Y. Dismissed to 3rd Pres. Ch. of Chicago, Ill   Died June 17, 1908.
    Mrs. Anna Delemater from M. E. Ch., LaGrangeville.

On confession
    Miss Ida DeGroff. Mar. Lewis Knapp.   (Beacon)
    Miss Armina Miller. Dismissed Nov. 25, 1891 to 2nd Reformed Ch. of Poughkeepsie
    Miss Gracie Agnes Seger. Dismissed to Cumberland Pres. Ch., Pittsburg, Pa., Oct. 19. 1904.
    Miss Garetta Kate Seger   (away)

1890, Sep. 7 On confession
    Miss Katie Theresa Vollmer. Dismissed to 4th Cong'l Ch., Hartford, Ct., Apr. 15, 1899. Mar. Jno. R. Phillips.
    Miss Mary Alice Mathews. Dismissed Feb. 15, 1893 to Pres. Ch., Pleasant Valley, N. Y.

1890, Dec. 7 By certificate
    Miss Phoebe Ann Vollmer from 1st Ref. Ch., Po'keepsie.

1891, Mar. 1 On confession
    Jacob Storm Diddell &
    Clara Wooster, his wife
    Ella Stella Jones. Dismissed to Washington St. M. E. Ch., Po'keepsie, Nov. 29, 1899.

1891, June 7 On confession
    Miss Catherine Thorn Akin   (Mrs. Maloney)
    Miss Augusta Anna Lauer   (Mrs. Charles Van Cot)
    Miss Mary Louise Shafer Seger. Dismissed to Cumberland Pres. Ch., Pittsburg, Pa., Oct. 19, 1904. Mar. Isaac M. Forbes.

The Reformed Dutch Church of New Hackensack

        Miss Priscilla Merritt Ackerman. Dismissed to Christ P. E. Ch., Po'keepsie, Mar. 19, 1903.
        Miss Emma Marion Nostrand. Joined Epis. Ch., Wapingers Falls, Apr., 1902.
        Miss Abbie Loni Vollmer. Dismissed to Millbrook Rfd. Ch., Apr. 26, 1917. Mar. Wm. C. Fries.
        Clinton Edward Stoutenburg   (away)

1891, Sep. 6 On confession
        Theodore Christian   Died Jan. 27, 1922.   (Father, Mrs. Elija Rowe)
        Washington Travis Christian   (away)
        Miss Anna Louisa Christian   Mar. Elijah Rowe
        Miss Daisy Mary Christian   (wife, George Baxter, away)
        Stephen A. Bulmer
        Augustus Earnest Bulmer   Dismissed Apr. 19, 1911 to Pres. Ch., Hughsonville, N. Y.
        James William Bulmer   (away)
        Miss Florence Eunice Bulmer   (away)
        Miss Irene De Vorois Burroughs   Mar. George Dingee. Dismissed May 19, 1906 to Pres. Ch., Wappingers Falls.
        Miss Sarah Matilda Warren.
        Miss Mary Susan Warren.   Died Aug. 20, 1905
        Miss Cora Eliza Warren.   Dismissed to 2nd Ref. Ch., Poughkeepsie, May 4, 1903.
        Justus Nelson Warren.   Died Feb. 28, 1898
        Edward J. Lawrence
        Miss Jennie Carter Van Dyne   Died Apr. 2, 1899

    By certificate
        Mrs. Mary L. Lawrence, w. of Edward J., from 1st Pres. Ch. of Pleasant Plains, N. Y.

1891, Dec. 6 By certificate
        Isaac Forbes, from Pres. Ch. of Wappingers Falls, N. Y. Died Apr. 5, 1900.
        Mrs. Isaac Forbes. Dismissed to Pres. Ch., New Hamburg, Feb. 23, 1904
        Miss Sarah M. Forbes, from West End Pres. Ch., N. Y. City. Dismissed to Pres. Ch., New Hamburg, Feb. 23, 1904.   Died

1892, Mar. 2 By certificate
        Robert Hutchinson   } From West End Pres. Ch., N. Y. City. Dismissed to Pres. Ch., New Hamburg, Feb. 23, 1904.
        Margaret J. Hutchinson
        Wm. J. Warren   Died May 30, 1905   } From M. E. Ch., LaGrangeville, N. Y.
        Elizabeth Warren   Died Mar. 28, 1921

1892, June 5 On Reconfession
        Martha J. Christian, w. of Theo. Christian   (away)

    On confession
        Susie Emily Christian   (away)

1892, Sep. 4 On confession
        Hiram Brownell White   Dismissed to Centenary M. E. Ch., Jersey City, N. J., Aug. 29, 1900
        Alfretta H. White   Dismissed to the Reformed Church of Poughkeepsie, Mar. 24, 1923
        Clarence George White   Dismissed to Metropolitan Temple (M. E.), New York City, Seventh Ave. & 14th St., Apr. 25, 1906

    On re-confession
        Mrs. Harriett Brownell White   Died Dec. 1920   (Mr. Brownell's)

1892, Dec. 4 On confession
        Peter Campbell MacKinlay   } Dismissed to 2nd Pres.
        Mary Lee (Maholm) MacKinlay, w. of above   Ch. of Germantown, Pa., Dec. 4, 1901
        Corris M. Dolson   (away)

1893, Mar. 5 On confession
        Henry Jones (Poughkeepsie)   Dead
        Eliphaz Delemater

Register of Members

1893, June 4 On confession
    Alexander H. Bishop (Myers Corner)
    Sarah Gracie Ackerman Mar. Geo. Stockholm. Dismissed to Christian Ch., Milan, N. Y., Dec. 28, 1910
    Alfred P. Russell Dismissed, Sep. 25, 1896, to Pres. Ch. of Matteawan, N. Y.
    William Germond (beyond Hu(m)istone) Died Mar., 1915.
    Wm. G. Wright Dismissed Dec. 1, 1900 to M. E. Ch., Jackson Corners, N. Y.
    John J. Scofield (Wappingers)
    Mrs. Caroline Dorland Smith   Died Feb. 8, 1911
    Elizabeth May Hayes   Died July, 1897
    Edward Bloomfield Van Dyne Dismissed to Meth. Epis. Ch., Wappingers, Dec. 3, 1907
    Samuel M. Ten Broeck Dismissed to 4th Pres. Ch., Spokane, Wash. Died before it was received, Jan. 1, 1907.
    Catherine M. Ten Broeck Dismissed to 2nd Glenville (Scotia) Ref. Ch., Apr. 9, 1907
    Lewis St. John Griffin (away) Dismissed Jan. 7, 1897 to Alexander Ave. Bapt. Ch., N. Y. City. (This last item has been crossed through and the note added "Letter returned").
    Delia F. Ward Joined Bapt. Ch. in Po'keepsie
    Hester M. Morse Dismissed to M. E. Ch., Poughquag, N. Y. Feb. 14, 1901
    Isaac M. Forbes Dismissed to Cumberland Pres. Ch., Pittsburg, Pa., Oct. 19, 1904
    James Lewis Smith (away)
    James Young Luyster
    Fred Gustavus Paash
    Isaac Benjamin Horton (Camelot)
    Theodore Anthony (colored)   Died 1904
    Thomas E. Williams   Died, buried May 21, 1899
    Willis Van Voorhis Hughsonville
    Herman C. Crozier Dismissed Nov. 23, 1895 to Pres. Ch., Hughsonville, N. Y.
    Frank Underhill   Died Mar. 26, 1926
    Mrs. Ellen Hayes   Died Apr. 1, 1908
    Mrs. Evaline Mackey   ·Died Jan. 3, or 4, 1898

  On re-confession
    John R. Phillips Dismissed to 4th Cong'l Ch. of Hartford, Ct., Apr. 15, 1899
    Mrs. Sarah Ann Sherwood   Died Mar. 4, 1906
    Ernest Hayes (away)
    Benjamin Chas. Robinson (colored) Elijah Rowe's house (away)

  By certificate
    Miss Emma Belle Houghtalin from Pres. Church of Freedom Plains, N. Y. (away)

1893, Sep. 3 On confession
    Inez Scofield Joined Pres. Ch., Hughsonville in 1906

  By certificate
    Mrs. Josephine Vollmer Van Dewater from the 1st Ref. Poughkeepsie, N. Y. Mar. Thos. Kasik

1893, Dec. 10 By certificate
    Chas. Palmer &   } From M. E. Church of Fishkill Village,
    Hattie L. Palmer, his wife } N. Y.

1894, Mar. 4 By certificate
    Walter S. Weeks &   } From 1st M. E. Church of Brooklyn, N. Y.
    Emma A. Weeks, his wife }

1894, Dec. 2 On re-confession
    Christina Bennett Werner, w. of Daniel Werner Dismissed June 9, to Reformed Church, Hyde Park, N. Y.

  By certificate
    Charles D. Luyster from Third Pres. Ch., Chicago, Ill. Killed by a fall June 17, 1908

The Reformed Dutch Church of New Hackensack

1895, Mar. 3 On confession
    Floyd Organ   (away)
  By certificate
    Edgar A. Briggs Died Dec. 4, 1909 ⎫
    Mary Alice Mathews Briggs, his wife ⎬ From Pres. Ch. of Pleasant
      died Mar. 13, 1923   Valley, N. Y.
    William E. Briggs (Arlington) ⎭

1895, June 2 On confession
    Charles J. Brower Dismissed to 2nd Ref. Ch., Poughkeepsie, May 4, 1903

1895, Sep. 1 On confession
    Clarence D. Brower Dismissed Apr. 9, 1907 to Second Glenville (Scotia) Ref. Ch., N. Y.

1895, Dec. 1 On confession
    Rachel Morris Doughty (16 Fairmount St., Arlington Poughkeepsie, N. Y.)

1896, June 7 By certificate
    Mathew L. Van Wyck from Ref. Ch., Hopewell, N. Y. Died May 6, 1902
    Minnie Monfort, his wife, from Pres. Ch. of Freedom Plains, N. Y. (Poughkeepsie)
  On confession
    Mrs. Janet Owens, w. of Jno. Owens.   Died Feb. 6, 1897
    Mrs. Jane Van De Bogert   Died July 30, 1907
    Adah May Rogers Dismissed to M. E. Ch., Bedford Station, N. Y., May 14, 1903.
    Nellie Scofield (away)

1896, Dec. 6 By certificate
    Philip Allandorf From Pres. Ch., Salt Point, N. Y. Died Sep. 17, 1907
    Fred Allandorf From Pres. Ch., Salt Point, N. Y. Dismissed to Pres. Ch. of Wappingers Falls, Sep. 4, 190(4)

1897, Mar. 7 On confession
    John Roach East
  By certificate
    Mrs. Julia A. B. Allendorf from Ref. Ch., Nassau, N. Y. Died Dec., 1922
    Richard Denney from M. E. Ch., North Highland, N. Y.

1897, June 6 On confession
    Mrs. Emma J. Scofield, w. of Wm. Scofield.   Died Jan. 26, 1901
    Theodore Winfield Christian Dismissed to M. E. Church, Fishkill, Apr. 28, 1915
    Louis Elbert Christian Dismissed to Calvary M. E. Ch., N. Y. City, Nov. 1, 1906
    Anna Gertrude Dumont
    Gertrude Mary Gresty Dismissed to Pres. Ch., New Hamburg, N. Y., Sep. 4, 1910

1897, Sep. 5 On re-confession
    Mary Emma Westfall, w. of John R. East

1897, Dec. 5 On confession
    Miss Emma Lee Dismissed June 20, 1906 to Zion Epis. Church of Wappingers Falls, N. Y.
  By certificate
    Mrs. Mabel Rosell, w. of Remsen Rosell from Meth. Epis. Ch. of Wappingers Falls. Dismissed to Meth. Epis. Church of Wappingers Falls, N. Y., May 17, 1911

1898, June 26 On confession
    David Alden Place (away)

1898, Dec. 4 On confession
    Rachel White Dumont (away)

1899, Mar. 12 By certificate
    Daniel Morrell Burroughs from Ref. Ch. of Newtown, Long Island. Died June 8, 190(1 or 7)

Register of Members

    Rachel Swenarton Burroughs, his wife from Ref. Ch. of Newtown, Long Island. Dismissed to Ref. Ch. of Flushing, N. Y., Apr. 8, 1903
    Joseph Morrell Burroughs, their son from Ref. Ch. of Newtown, Long Island. Dismisssed to Ref. Ch. of Flushing, N. Y., Apr. 8, 1903

On confession
    William Henry A. Lory (away)
    Grace Louise Lory Letter to Hedding M. E. Church, Poughkeepsie, N. Y., Dec. 28, 1923.
    Mary Kesiah Lory

1899, Sep. 3 On confession
    Clara Belle D. Stoutenburg Mar. Chas. Curtis

1899, Dec. 3 On confession
    Julia Brinkerhoff Hauver (away)
    Florance A. Scofield Mar. Wm. Prout
    Harold Wooster Diddell
    Joseph Jackson Diddell

1900, Mar. 4 On confession
    Maria Coapman Forman Examined & baptized in home, Jan. 14 Died Sep. 16, 1908
    Maria Forman Leroy Examined & baptized in home, Jan. 14
    Charles Ten Broeck
    Walter Livingston Ten Broeck Dismissed to Scocia Ref. Ch., June 2, 1908
    Emott Andrews Delemater   Died Sep. 6, 1900
    John Oscar Delemater   Died Feb., 1927
    Wm. Henry Brower   Died Jan. 15, 1918
    Jane Augusta Brower, his wife   Died Jan. 11, 1918
    Mrs. Caroline Hegeman Tanner
    Miss Mary Francis Tanner
    Mrs. Mary Johnson Cornwell (Wappingers)
    Helen Stockholm Cornwell Dismissed Aug. 21, 1922 by letter to Methodist Church of Pine Plains, N. Y.
    Wm. Monroe Scofield
    Stella Moore Scofield Mar. Winfield Christian. Dismissed to M. E. Church, Fishkill, Apr. 28, 1915
    Charles Wesley Hults (?)
    Elijah T. Rowe
    Wm. Otto Stoutenburg
    Wm. Kertlan Tanner   Died Nov. 19, 1902
    John James Cornwell Wappingers   Died
    Jacob Ralph Cornwell Dismissed to Pres. Ch., Hughsonville, N. Y., May 4, 1903
    Clarence Edward Rhyne Dismissed to M. E. Ch., LaGrangeville, Sep. 28, 1909
    Wesley Lee (2 S. White St., Poughkeepsie)
    Blanche Golder Vollmer Dismissed to Hedding M. E. Ch., Poughkeepsie, Sep. 16, 1905
    Myron H. Briell Dismissed to Pentecostal Ch. of the Nazarene, Poughkeepsie, Dec. 31, 1910

    On re-confession
        Joshua E. Lory (Red Mill)
        Maria C. Lory, his wife (died)
        Mrs. Jane A. Briell (Red Mills) Dismissed to Beacon, N. Y., May 11, 1915

1900, Sep. 2 By certificate
    Mrs. Ida Knapp Van Tassell from the Reformed Church, Fishkill, N. Y. Dismissed to Ref'd Church, Arlington, Nov. 29, 1914

1901, Dec. 1 By certificate
    Mr. Guy C. Blossom } From 1st Cong'l Ch. of Bellows Falls, Vt. Letter given to Trinitarian Congregational Church, Northfield, Mass., Jan. 14, 1922.
    Mrs. Guy C. Blossom }

1902, Mar. 30 On confession
    Harold Waldo Delamater
    Mildred Delamater

The Reformed Dutch Church of New Hackensack

   Wilfred Schuyler Delamater Transferred to the Reformed Church of Millbrook, N. Y., Oct. 26, 1922
   Grace May Whiten (away)

1902, Sep. 7 By certificate
   Cornelia Terwilliger, w. of Geo. D. Shirley from Reformed Church, New Paltz, N. Y.
   Mrs. Cynthia M. Jones from Pres. Church, New Hamburg, N. Y. Joined on confession in 1850.   Died Jan. 18, 1906

1903, Mar. 1 On confession
   Harry Pells Scofield (away)

1903, June 7 By certificate
   Mrs. Wm. Carroll from the 2nd Ref. Ch. of Poughkeepsie, N. Y. (Freedom Plains)
  On confession
   Threse Clark Scruton (?)

1903, Sep. 6 By certificate
   Mrs. Emma Lee Jackson from the Beekman Baptist Church Died Aug. 23, 1927.

1904, June 5 By certificate
   Carrie Pink Howell, w. of Walter Howell From Pres. Ch. of Pleasant Plains, N. Y.
  On confession
   Albert Wellington Van Dewater Transferred by letter to Emanuel Reformed Church, Poughkeepsie, Feb. 27, 1926

1904, Sep. 4 On confession
   Wm. Smith (?)

1905, Mar. 5 By certificate
   Orra Lee Jackson from Presbyterian Church, New Hamburg, N. Y.
   Altana Jackson from Presbyterian Church, New Hamburg, N. Y. Dismissed Oct. 25, 1914 to M. E. Church, Millbrook, N. Y.
   Frederick Allendorf } from Presbyterian Church, Wappingers
   Mrs. Frederick Allendorf } Falls, N. Y. Dismissed June 13, 1911 to Friends' Church, Poughkeepsie, N. Y.
  On confession
   Seward Baker Jackson (Hamilton)
   Lucy Hicks (colored) Dismissed Jan. 29, 1908, to

1905, June 4 On confession
   Martha Nevins Dumont
   Flora Van Tassell Dismissed Oct. 26, 1908, to First Pres. Ch., Poughkeepsie

1905, Sep. 17 By certificate
   Abram D. Van Wyck } From Reformed Church, Hopewell, N. Y.
   Miss Estelle J. Van Wyck }

1906, Jan. 7 On confession
   William Henry Dumont
   Mildred Anna Robinson

1906, June 3 On confession
   Norman Jones Scofield
   Daniel Theodore Rowe
   Ethel Grace Rowe

REGISTER OF OFFICERS
1765 — 1906
and
MINUTES OF THE CONSISTORY
of the church of
NEW HACKENSACK
1765 — 1856

ACTS AND RESOLVES OF THE ELDERS AND DEACONS
of the Dutch Reformed Church in New-Hakkensak.

The following Acts and Resolves are translated from the Dutch by me.
Issac Rysdyk.

A.D. 1765   A Copy of the Original Call of the Reverd. Isaac Rysdyk from Holland to serve this and the neighbouring Congregations, together with some Transactions, relative to his coming over and investment by the Reverd. J. C. Fryenmoet & are recorded in the Church book of Fishkill and in the loose papers, belonging to this Book, which, as there will be little occasion for, I have left in the Dutch.

1766   Acts of the Great Consistory of the 4 Congregations Pôkeepsie, Fishkill, N. Hakkensak and Hoopwel, held at N. Hakkensak 15 January 1766.
In this meeting an agreement was made between the respective Congregations relative to the Parsonage, wich the said Congregations were obliged to build for the Reverd Isaac Rysdyk, in which they agreed that the Congregation of Pôkeepsie should be excused from paying their proportion toward the building and maintaining of said parsonage, upon condition, that the Brethren of Pôkeepsie should pay to those of the Fishkill one half of the value of the parsonage house and lot in Pokeepsie, provided, the Kerkraad of Pokeepsie aforesd should agree thereto. See the Church resolves in the Church book of Fishkill.

Feb. 8   An election of one half of the Kerkraad was made for the ensuing two years, and were chosen unanimously, in the room of Capt. Cornelis Luyster, Teunis Wiltsee, as Elder, and in the room of the Deacon John Baptist Kip, Adolf Zwartwoud.

                                   Q. T.
                                       Isaac Rysdyk,
                                               minister.

Mar. 18   A meeting was held at New Hakkensak of the Kerkraad with those that had signed toward the building of a new Church, in which the following resolves were made.
1. That the steepel shall be set on one end of the Church, and that the measure of the Church shall be of 20 by 25 feet.
2. That the Trustees in Office shall continue, nam.
                 John Schurry
                 Peter Oudwater
                 Adolf Zwartwoud
                 Andrew Heermans
                 Abraham Lent
3. That the Trustees shall not be obliged to pay more than one half of the Subscription money, because the Condition is in the Head of the Subscription list that one half of that money Shall be paid at the beginning of the building of the Church, and another half when it shall be finished.
4. As to the right to the Seats shall be of value the Articles in the head of the Subscription list, only with this addition, that the Seats, which in case of death, Sale or exchange shall not be transferred within one year and six weeks, shall in such a Case return into the possession of the Trustees, or fall to the Church again.
5. Every Signer shall be obliged to pay the money he has signed on the day when it becomes due, but shall not deduct therefrom his wages, but whatsoever any one shall have earnt by riding or labour, for that he shall have right or preference, in proportion to his wages before Strangers to buy one or more Seats, besides his previous good right for what he has signed, and shall be allowed to bring in his wages for purchase money, provided always that no one shall have right to any seat, before the Value thereof shall be paid in full, except those to whom, for some reasons one or more seats might have been given gratis.
The rest of the articles are relative to the workmen and their wages,etc.
                                   Q. T.
                                   Isaac Rysdyk, Minr.

1767
Feb. 21   At a meeting of the Rev. Kerkraad it is unanimously resolved, that for the future a double set of Elders and Deacons shall be Chosen, as in the other combined Congregations, and that to this end, the present Kerkraad, with their own consent, shall continue one year longer, and an Elder & Deacon be chosen in addition to them. Upon which unanimously are elected.

The Reformed Dutch Church of New Hackensack

Elders	Deacons
Peter Oudwater	Wilhelmus Heermans
Teunis Wiltsee	Adolphus Zwartwoud
John Schurry	George Brinckerhoff
Thomas Van Bremen	Philip Verplank

At the same time were Chosen for Kirkmasters.
    Nicholas Brouwer &
    Lawrens Conchlin.
        Q. T.
            Isaac Rysdyk, Minr.

1768
Mar. 5 At a meeting of the Kerkraad was held the yearly election of Elders and Deacons and are unanimously chosen:
for Elders, in the room of Peter Oudwater & Teunis Wiltsee
    Cornelis Luyster & Adolph Zwartwoud
For Deacons, in the room of Wilhelmus Heermans & Adolf Zwartwoud
    Matthias Luyster & Edward Schoonmaker.
        Q. T.
            Isaac Rysdyk, Minr.

N. B. For Churchmaster was chosen, in the room of Nicholas Brouwer, Constantyn Gulneck.

May 16 The Church-Treasury was examined in the presence of the Kerkraad, and account given by Wilhelmus Heermans, by which it appeared after Deduction of necessary expenses, that there was yet in the Chest
    In ready money   £ 10 — 11 — 1
    In Notes:
    One Note of Teunis Wiltsee of   6 1 2
    One ditto of Peter Dates of   3
                      Sum total   19 — 12 — 3
To Peter Dates was paid out of the Chest for 4 months
    service, as Clercq £1—12—0   1 — 12 — 0
    remains in the Chest   18 —   — 3
                  Q. T.
                      Isaac Rysdyk, Minr.

June 1 Some Resolves, with respect to the Parsonage, taken by the 3 Congregations of Fishkill, N. Hackensak & Hopewell. See in the Dutch Record of this Date.

1769
Feb. 5 At a meeting of ye Kerkraad the yearly Election of Elders and Deacons was held and are unanimously chosen
For Elders, in the room of John Schurry and Thomas van Bremen, Mr. Philip Verplanck, Esqre, & George Brinckerhoff
For Deacons, in the room of said Philip Verplanck and George Brinckerhoff, Andrew Heermans & Matthew du Boys.
        Q. T.
            Isaac Rysdyk, Minr.

Apr. 24 A grand meeting of the 4 Congregations was held on account of a proposal from the Rev. Classis of Amsterdam, towards a reconciliation between the Coetus and Conferentie parties. See the Dutch record of this Date.

May 24 The Church acct. was made up in the presence of the Kerkraad, and acct. given by Messrs. Philip Verplanck and George Brinckerhoff, as follows.
    Found in the Treasury the money collected since ye last preceding acct. some necessary expences deducted to ye
    amt. of one pound 15/ & 6 pence in Cash   £ 7 — 17 — 1
    Ditto in Cash the remaining sum of last acct   18 —   3
                                       25 — 17 — 4
    Bro't over   £ 25 — 17 — 4
    A Note of Teunis Wiltsee of   7   2
    One ditto of John Montfoort   6   10
    One ditto of Peter Dates of 1 of June 1765, of   3
    A rect. of money lent by the Elders to Peter Dates for
        which they promised to repay the Chest.   1 — 12 —
    One ditto of money lent to the Elders   5 — 2
    In Cash   2 — 15 — 3¾

Register of Officers and Consistory Minutes

1769

May 24 In the above acct is a grand mistake, as the remaining Sum of last year was inadvertently Cast up with ye Notes, & money now found in the Chest.
The Church Treasury was examined in the presence of the Elders and Deacons and acct. made by Messrs. Philip Verpl. & George Brinckerhoff, as follows:

It appeared per acct. that the Collection in the Church since the last acct. amounts to	£ 9 — 12 — 7
Remainder of last yr. in Notes and Cash	18 — — 3
A rect. and promise of the Elders to restore to the Chest	1 — 12
	£ 29 — 4 — 10
Expence deducted	1 — 15 — 6
	£ 27 — 9 — 4
The Chest being examined, there was found In Notes	£ 16 — 10 — 2
A Rect. of the Elders of money advanced to Peter Dates	1 — 12
One ditto for Cash Lent to the Elders	5 — 2
In Cash	2 — 15 — 3
Several other articles	1 — 9 — 11
Sum total	£ 27 — 9 — 4

Q. T.
Isaac Rysdyk, Minr.

1770
Feb. 7 At a meeting of the Reverd. Kerkraad were unanimously elected for the 2 ensuing years:
Elders: Wilhelmus Heermans & Matthias Luyster
Deacons: Abraham Lent & Petrus Luyster.
Lawfully qualified on March the 18.
Q. T.
Isaac Rysdyk.

Mar. 26 The Church Treasury was examined in the presence of the Kerkraad, when it appeared after casting up the accts. of Rects. and expenditures that there remained in the Chest in Notes and money the sum of thirty three pound three shillings and eight pence. See the Dutch records of this date.
Q. T.
Isaac Rysdyk.

1771
Feb. 12 At a meeting of the Rev. Kerkenraad, one Half of the Session was unanimously chosen as follows:
Elders, John Shurry & Edward Schoonmaker
Deacons, Aris van der Bilt & Carel Hoffman.
The same were lawfully qualified.
Q. T.
Isaac Rysdyk.

May 13 The acct. of the Church Treasury was given by the Deacon Andries Heermans, when it appeared that there remained in the poor Chest the Sum of £ 37—14—5½.
Q. T.
Isaac Rysdyk.

Sep. 23 At a meeting of the Grand Kerkraad of the 4 Combined Congregations, and in Consequence of an invitation from the Dutch Church at New York, the minister Isaac Rysdyk & the Elder Richard Snedeker, were Committed to attend the universal meeting of all the Ministers of the Dutch Churches in the States of New York & New Yersey appointed to meet in New York on the 3d October & foll. to consult about means and ways of a reconciliation between the two parties of Coetus and Conference   instructions given accordingly. See the Dutch records of this date.
Accordingly articles of union and an Establishmt of Church-Governmt were drawn up and universally approved and adopted, and also by our Congregations on the 28 Octob following, in expectation of ye approbation of the right Revd Classis of Amsterdam.
Said articles of union etc are recorded in the Church-book of Fishkill, which are not transcribed in this book, because it is expected that they shall be translated and published in the English Language.

The Reformed Dutch Church of New Hackensack

1772
July 8   At a meeting of the Rev. Kerkenraad An account of the Church Treasury was made by the Deacons Abraham Lent and Petrus Luyster, when it was found that in the Chest remained the sum of £46 — 4 — 4.

1773
Feb. 6   At a meeting of the Revd Kerkraad were unanimously elected
       Elders: Abraham Westerveld & Mr. Philip Verplanck
       Deacons: John Rosekrans & John Montfoort.
                                           Q. T.
                                           Isaac Rysdyk.
The above Brethren were qualified April 4.

May 27   The acct. of the Church Treasury was made by the Deacon Aris van der Bilt, when it was found that in the Chest remained, in Notes and money the sum of £52 — 15 — 10.

1774
Mar. 20   At a meeting of the Revd. Kerkraad were chosen for the 2 ensuing years
Elders Carel Hoffman & Aris van der Bilt
Deacons Peter Dates & Benjamin van Keuren
                                         Q. T.
                                   Isaac Rysdyk.
The above Brethren were qualified, after ye usual proclamations. Some time after the Church Acct was made in my absence, when there remained in the Chest the sum of £60 — 10 — 5.

1775
Mar. 12   At a meeting of the R. Kerkraad were chosen
       Elders: Adolf Zwartwoud & Aris Middelaar
       Deacons: Albert Montfoort & Henry Wiltsee
                                     Q. T.
                               Is. Rysdyk.

Apr. 16   The Church Treasury was examined and found that there remained in the Chest the Sum of £69 — 16 — 7.

1776
Mar. 17   The New Kerkraad was chosen, as follows:
       Elders: Matthias Luyster and Lawrens Conchlin.
       Deacons: Joris Middag & Adam Dates.
                                 Q. T.
                            Is. Rysdyk.

Apr. 24   The Church Treasury was examined before the Kerkraad when it was found that there remained in the Chest, the sum of £63 — 12 — 1.

1777
June 8   At a meeting of the Reverd Kerkraad were chosen:
       Elders: John Shurry and Abraham Lent
       Deacons: John Churchwell & John Wiltsee.

Ditto 16   After Examination of the poor Chest, there remained this year in Chest, the Sum of £77 — 2 — 4.

1778
May 31   At a meeting of the Kerkraad, were elected
       Elders: Teunis Wiltsee & Peter I. Monfoort.
       Deacons: John du Boys & Peter Hoff.
qualified 19 July 1778.
                               Q. T.
                          Is. Rysdyk.

July 28   The poor Chest being examined & acct made, it appeared that there remained in the Chest the sum of £90 — 10 — 11.

1779
May 14   At a meeting of the Revd Kerkraad were chosen
       Elders: Teunis van Bunschoten & Aris van der Bilt
       Deacons: Abraham Durrye, junr & Peter A. Lasson.
       qualified on the 30 Ditto.

June 29   At the Church acct it appeared, that there remained in the Treasury the sum of £111 — 5 — 8.

1780
Apr. 3   At a meeting of the Revd Kerkraad the new Elders & Deacons were Chosen, as follows:

Register of Officers and Consistory Minutes

        Elders: Peter Dates and Johannes du Boys
        Deacons: Petrus Luyster & Albert Montfoort.
                          Q. T.
                          Isaac Rysdyk.

May 16   The Church acct. was made, when it appeared, that there remained in the Chest

In silver & Coppers	£ 2 — 19 — 8
In Notes	41 — 14 — 0
In paper money	10 — 2 — 0

There was so much less than last year, on account of the Depreciation of the paper Currency.

1786
Apr. 23   At a meeting of the Revd Kerkraad were unanimously elected:
        Elders: Dominicus Montfoort, and John Wiltsee
        Deacons: John Hegeman and Frederick Rosekrans.
                          Q. T.
                          Isaac Rysdyk.

1787
May 27   At a meeting of the Kerkraad were unanimously chosen
        Elders: John Montfoort and Petrus Luyster
        Deacons: Benjamin van Keuren & Albert Montfoort, junr.
                          Q. T.
                          Is. Rysdyk.

1788
July 27   At a meeting of the Kerkraad the annual Election of the Elders & Deacons was made, as follows:
        Elders: Aris van der Bilt & Theophilus Antony
        Deacons: John Sleght & Peter Rosekrans.
                          Q. T.
                          Isaac Rysdyk.

1789
May 29   At a meeting of ye kerkraad were unanimously elected
        Elders: John Churchwell & Elbert Montfoort
        Deacons: Thomas Oostrander & Clement Cornwell

June 17   A meeting of the kerkraad was held at the minister's house. Present, all. in which after prayer it was resolved as follows.

I. As it appeared necessary from the tenor of the Transport of the Church Land at this place, given in the year 1765 in Trust to Peter Oudwater & Cornelis Luyster Esqre, that two other Trustees should be Chosen on acct of the Decease of said Peter Oudwater, Messrs Aris van der Bilt, Elder & Elbert Montfoort, Deacon, were unanimously elected Trustees for the Church & Church Land in the room of said Peter Oudwater & Cornelis Luyster Esq.

II. An account was made of the minister's Salary which became due on the 1st of June 1788, by which it appeared that the minister had received in Cash & produce the sum of thirty four pound, fifteen shillings and four pence, so that of that year's salary remains due yet fifteen pound, four shillings & eight pence.

III. Resolved, that for the time to come, every-one of the members of the kerkraad, having had previous Notice of the Time appointed for holding the kerkraad and not appearing, shall be fined in the sum of four shillings and whosoever comes after the appointed hour, in the sum of two shillings. Lawful reasons, however shall excuse. Signed by all ye members: Isaac Rysdyk Presidt Theophilus Anthony, Peter Luyster, John Montfoort, Aris van der Bilt, Benjamin van Keuren, Elbert Montfoort, junr, Peter Rosekrans, John Sleght.

IV. Concluded by prayer.
                          Q. T.
                          Isaac Rysdyk, pres.

N. B. At the same meeting Mr. Theophilus Anthony was Chosen Deputy from this Congregation together with the Reverd Mr. Isaac Rysdyk, to attend the ordinary Classis of the middle District to be held at the New Paltz on the 1st Tuesday of July next, according to Adjournment, to whom Credentials are given.
                          Isaac Rysdyk, prest.

(The following items occupied a single page among blank pages of the book.)

1785
June 5   At a Meeting of the Revd. Kerkenraad were unanimously elected
        Elders: Ahasuerus van Cleek & Obadiah Cooper
        Deacons: Duncan Graham & Michiel Golneck.
Qualified at a convent. time.

The Reformed Dutch Church of New Hackensack

1786
Apr. 23   At a meeting of the Reverd. Kerkraad were unanimously elected.
          Elders: Dominicus Montfoort & John Wiltsee
          Deacons: John Hegeman & Frederick Rosekrans.
          Lawfully qualified.

1787
Apr. 15   At a meeting of the Reverd. Kerkraad were unanimously chosen:
          Elders: John Montfoort & Petrus Luyster.
          Deacons: Mr. Benjamin van Keuren and Albert Montfoort, Junr.

1788
May 13   At a meeting of the Reverd. Kerkraad were unanimously elected.
          Elders: Messrs. Theophilus Anthony & Aris van der Bilt.
          Deacons: John Sleght & Peter Rosekrans.

1789
May 29   At a meeting of the Reverd. Kerkraad were unanimously chosen:
          Elders: Messrs. John Churchwel & Elbert Montfoort
          Deacons: Thomas Oostrander & Clement Cornwell.

REGISTRY OF CHURCH-OFFICERS
IN THE CONGREGATION OF NEW HACKENSACK
(During the Ministry of George Barkulo, V.D.M.)

When said George Barkulo was called & took charge of the Congregation of New Hackensack (which was August 1st, 1805) the following persons constituted the Consistory of said Church or Congregation, Viz,

1805   Elders, Samuel Luckey, Esq., Ares Van der bilt, Teunis Van Bunschoten & Abraham Hoghlandt
          Deacons, John Luyster, Ares Van der bilt, Junr., Andrew Rynders & Peter Flagler

Jan. 1
1806   Elders— Casper Gonse & Clemens Cornwell were ordained in the places of Abraham Hoghlandt & Teunis Van Bunschoten
          Deacons—John Lawson & Harmah Jewel in the places of Aris Van der bilt, Junr., & Andrew Rynders

Jan. 18
1807   Elders— Albert T. Monfoort & William Seward were ordained in the places of Ares Van der bilt & Samuel Luckey, Esq.
          Deacons—James Van Keuren & John Van Sicklen, pro John Luyster & Peter Flagler.

Mar. 27
1808   Elders— Albert Monfoort & Dominicus Monfoort, pro Casper Gonse & Clemens Cornwell
          Deacons—Owing to the sickness of one of the deacons elect, they were not ordained till May 29, when Ares Van der bilt, Junr. & Peter Wyckhoff were ordained in the places of John Lawson & Harmah Jewel

Apr. 23
1809   Elders —Samuel Luckey, Esq. & John Hageman were ordained, pro William Seward & Albert Monfoort
          Deacons—Daniel Hoffman & John Lawson, pro James Van Keuren & John Van Sicklen

Feb. 14   Elders— Tunis Van Bunschoten   vice Domenicus Monfoort
1813   William Seward   Albert Monfoort
                  John Luyster   vice John A. Hageman, deceased
          Deacons—Abraham Dates   vice Ares Van Der Belt
                  James Van Keuren   Peter Wyckoff

Feb. 27   Elders— Ares Van Der Belt   vice Samuel Luckey
1814   John Luyster   reelected
          Deacons—Henry A. Monfoort   vice John Lawson
                  Stephen Monfoort   Daniel Hoffman

Feb. 12   Elders— Tunis Van Bunschoten   re-elected
1815   Casper Gonse   vice William Seward
          Deacons—James Ackerman   vice Abraham L. Dates
                  Joseph Tallmadge   vice James Van Keuren

Register of Officers and Consistory Minutes

Feb. 11 1816	Elders— Samuel Luckey Daniel Hoffman Deacons—James Dodge Mathew Luyster	vice vice	Ares Van der bilt John Luyster Henry A. Monfoort Stephen Monfoort
Feb. 23 1817	Elders— Jacob Van Bunschoten James Van Keuren Deacons—James Dearin Martin Monfoort	vice vice	Casper Gonse Tunis Van Bunschoten James Ackerman Joseph Tallmadge
Apr. 1818	Elders— Ares Van der Belt Stephen Monfoort Deacons—Adrian Hageman James Jones	vice vice	Saml Luckey Daniel Hoffman James Dodge Matthew Luyster
April 1819	Elders— William Seward Tunis Van Bunschoten Deacons—Samuel Luckey, Junr Henry A. Monfoort	vice vice	Jacob Van Bunschoten James Van Keuren James Dearin Martin Monfoort
April 1821	Elders— Jacob Van Bunschoten James Ackerman Deacons—Peter Van der bilt omitted in proper place	vice vice	William Seward Tunis Van Bunschoten Saml Luckey, Jr Henry A. Monfoor
April 1820	Elders— James Dearin Martin Monfoort Deacons—James Dodge John Ganse	vice vice	Ares Van der bilt Stephen Monfoort Adrian Hageman James Jones
April 1822	Elders— Samuel Luckey, Junr. Henry A. Monfoort Deacons—Philip Nagel Isaiah Reynders	vice vice	James Dearin Martin Monfoort James Jones Adrian Hageman
April 1823	Elders— Tunis Van Bunschoten John Ganse Deacons—John Van der Bilt Cornelius Westervelt	vice vice	James Ackerman Jacob Van Bunschoten Peter Van der Bilt re-elected
April 1824	Elders— Ares Van der bilt Daniel Hoffman Deacons—John A. Monfoort Matthew Luyster	vice vice	Samuel Luckey, Jr. Henry A. Monfoort Philip Nagel Isaiah Reynders
April 1825	Elders— Tunis Van Bunschoten Jacob Van Bunschoten Deacons—John Budd Charles Dearin	 vice vice	re-elected John Ganse John Van der Bilt Cornelius Westervelt

REGISTER OF CHURCH OFFICERS
During the Ministry of the Revd. M. W. Dwight.

1826, Jan. 5—	Elders John Luyster Cornelius Westervelt Deacons Isaiah Rynders Matthew Luyster	Vice Daniel Hoffman Ares Van Der Bilt Vice John A. Monfort Reelected
1827, Mar. 27—	Elders James Ackerman James Vn. Keuren Deacons George Vn. Der Bilt John U. Budd	Vice Jacob Vn. Bunschoten Teunis Vn. Bunschoten Vice Charles Dearin Reelected
1828, Feb. 4—	Elders James Dearin John Luyster Deacons Peter Vn. Der Bilt Henry Travers	Vice Cornels. Westervelt Reelected Vice Matthew Luyster James Vn. Keuren

The Reformed Dutch Church of New Hackensack

1829, Feb. 5—Elders
    Philip Nagel
    John Vn. Der Belt
  Deacons
    Isaiah Rynders
    Charles Dearin
Vice
  James Ackerman
  James Vn. Keuren
Vice
  John U. Budd
  George Vn. Der Bilt

1830, Feb. 1—Elders
    Peter Vn. Der Bilt
    Samuel Luckey
  Deacons
    John A. Monfort
    John U. Budd
Vice
  John Luyster
  James Dearin
Vice
  Peter Vn. Der Bilt
  Henry Traver

1831, Feb. 7—Elders
    Teunis Vn. Benschoten
    James Vn. Keuren
  Deacons
    Esaias Rynders
    Charles Dearin
Vice
  Phillip Nagel
  John Vn. Der Bilt

Reelected

1832, Feb. 6—Elders
    Peter Vn. Der Bilt
    Samuel Lucky
  Deacons
    John A. Monfort
    Henry Traver

Reelected

Vice
  Reelected
  John U. Budd

1833, Feb. 4—Elders
    Philip Nagel
    Jno. Vn. Der Bilt
  Deacons
    Esaias Rynders
    Charles Dering
Vice
  Tunis Vn. Bunschoten
  James Vn. Keuren

REGISTER OF CHURCH OFFICERS

During the Ministry of the Revd. Cornelius Van Cleef.

1834, Feb. 15—Elders
    Samuel Luckey
    Martin Monfort
  Deacons
    Henry D. Traver
    William Churchill
  Reelected
Vice Peter Van Der Bilt
  Reelected
Vice John A. Monfort

1835, Feb.   Elders
    Tunis Van Benschoten
    Matthew Luyster
  Deacons
    Isaiah Rynders
    George Van Der Bilt
Vice
  John Van Der Bilt
  Phillip Nagle

  reelected
Vice Charles Dearing

1836, Feb.   Elders
    Aries Van Der Bilt
    John A. Monfort
    Stephen Monfort for one year,
  Deacons
    John U. Budd
    William Todd
Vice
  Samuel Luckey
  Martin Monfort
Vice Tunis Van Benschoten, deceased
Vice
  Henry D. Traver
  William Churchill

1837, Feb.   Elders
    Matthew Luyster
    Peter Van Der Bilt
  Deacons
    George Van Der Bilt
    Henry D. Traver
  Reelected
Vice Stephen Monfort
  Reelected
Vice Isaiah Rynders

1838, Feb.   Elders
    Samuel Luckey
    John A. Monfort
Vice
  Ares Van Der Bilt
  reelected

Register of Officers and Consistory Minutes

	Deacons
	  Henry D. Hayt
	  James M. Jones
		Vice
		  John U. Budd
		  William Todd

1839, Feb.	Elders
	  John Van Der Bilt
	  Peter Van Der Bilt
	  Phillip Nagle for one year
	Deacons
	  Benjamin H. Everitt
	  Phillip Van Der Bilt
		Vice
		  Matthew Luyster
		  reelected
		Vice, Samuel Luckey
		Vice
		  George Van Der Bilt
		  Henry D. Traver

1840, Feb.	Elders
	  John A. Monfort
	  Phillip Nagle
	  James M. Jones for one year,
	Deacons
	  James S. Monfort
	  Henry D. Hayt
		
		Reelected
		Reelected
		Vice, Peter Van Der Bilt, decd.
		Vice
		  James M. Jones
		  Reelected

1841, Feb.	Elders
	  Schenck Ackerman
	  John Van Der Bilt
	Deacons
	  Benjamin H. Everitt
	  Phillip Van Der Bilt
		Vice
		  James M. Jones
		  Reelected
		
		  reelected
		  reelected

1842, Feb.	Elders
	  George Van Der Bilt
	  John A. Monfort
	Deacons
	  Henry D. Traver
	  James S. Monfort
		Vice
		  Phillip Nagle
		  Re-elected
		Vice
		  Henry D. Hayt
		  Re-elected

1843, Feb.	Elders
	  Jeremiah Platt
	  Schenck Ackerman
	Deacons
	  Harvey D. Platt
	  William Seward
		Vice
		  John Van Der Belt
		  Re-elected
		Vice
		  Benjamin H. Everitt
		  Phillip Van Der Belt

1844, Feb. 5	Elders
	  John A. Monfort
	  George Van Der Bilt
	Deacons
	  James S. Monfort
	  Henry D. Hayt
		
		Reelected
		reelected
		
		  reelected
		vice Henry D. Traver

1845, Feb. 3	Elders
	  Schenck Ackerman
	  Jeremiah Platt
	Deacons
	  Harvey D. Platt
	  William Seward
		
		reelected
		"
		
		reelected
		"

1846, Feb. 2	Elders
	  John A. Monfort
	  George Van Der Bilt
	Deacons
	  Henry D. Hayt
	  James S. Monfort
		
		reelected
		"
		
		reelected
		"

1847, Feb. 1	Elders
	  Schenck Ackerman
	  Jeremiah Platt
	Deacons
	  William Seward
	  Harvey D. Platt
		
		reelected
		"
		
		reelected
		"

1848, Feb. 7	Elders
	  John A. Monfort
	  Benjamin H. Everitt
		
		reelected
		vice George Van Der Bilt

The Reformed Dutch Church of New Hackensack

	Deacons	
	Henry D. Hayt	reelected
	John B. Jones	vice James S. Monfort
1849, Feb. 5	Elders	Vice
	Philander Seward	Jeremiah Platt
	James S. Monfort	Schenck Ackerman
	Deacons	Vice
	John Y. Bishop	William Seward
	Harvey D. Platt	reelected
1850, Feb. 4	Elders	Vice
	Matthew Luyster	John A. Monfort
	Benjamin H. Everitt	reelected
	Deacons	Vice
	Henry D. Traver	Henry D. Hayt
	John B. Jones	reelected
1851, Feb. 3	Elders	Vice
	William Seward	Philander Seward
	James S. Monfort	reelected
	Deacons	Vice
	Simeon Hitchcock	Harvey D. Platt
	John Y. Bishop	reelected
1852, Feb. 2	Elders	
	Matthew Luyster	reelected
	Benjamin H. Everitt	"
	Deacons	
	Henry D. Traver	reelected
	John B. Jones	"
1853, Feb. 7	Elders	
	James S. Monfort	reelected
	William Seward	"
	Deacons	
	Simeon Hitchcock	reelected
	John Jones	Vice John Y. Bishop
1854, Feb. 7	Elders	Vice
	John A. Monfort	Matthew Luyster
	George Van Der Bilt	Benjamin H. Everitt
	Deacons	Vice
	Harvey D. Platt	Henry D. Traver
	John B. Jones	reelected
1855, Feb. 5	Elders	
	James L. Monfort	reelected
	William Seward	"
	Deacons	
	Simeon Hitchcock	reelected
	John Jones	"
1856, Feb. 4	Elders	
	George Van Der Bilt	reelected
	Harvey D. Platt	Vice John A. Monfort
	Deacons	
	John B. Jones	reelected
	Charles J. Howell, Jr.	Vice Harvey D. Platt
1857, Feb. 2	Elders	
	James L. Monfort	reelected
	William Seward	"
	Deacons	
	Simeon Hitchcock	reelected
	John Jones	"
1858, Feb. 1	Elders	Vice
	Henry D. Hayt	George Van Der Bilt
	Harvey D. Platt	reelected
	Deacons	
	Charles J. Howell, Jun.	reelected
	William Baker	Vice—John B. Jones

Register of Officers and Consistory Minutes

1859, Feb. 7 Elders
    James L. Monfort   reelected
    William Seward   "
  Deacons   Vice
    Henry Burroughs   John Jones
    John D. Westervelt   Simeon Hitchcock

1860, Feb. 6 Elders
    Henry D. Hayt   reelected
    Harvey D. Platt   "
  Deacons
    Charles J. Howell, Jun.   reelected
    William Baker   "

1861, Feb. 4 Elders
    James L. Monfort   reelected
    William Seward   "
  Deacons
    Henry Burroughs   reelected
    Samuel I. Robinson   Vice—John D. Westervelt

1862, Feb. 3 Elders   Vice
    Henry D. Needham   Henry D. Hayt
    Harvey D. Platt   reelected
  Deacons   Vice
    John D. Cornwell, Jun.   Charles J. Howell, Jun.
    William Baker   reelected

1863, Feb. 2 Elders   Vice
    John Monfort   James L. Monfort
    William Seward   reelected
  Deacons   Vice
    William C. Van Cleef   Henry Burroughs
    Samuel I. Robinson   reelected

1864, Feb. 1 Elders
    Harvey D. Platt   reelected
    Henry D. Needham   "
  Deacons
    William Baker   reelected
    John D. Cornwell   "

1865, Feb. 6 Elders
    John Monfort   reelected
    William Seward   "
  Deacons
    Samuel I. Robinson   reelected
    John Jones   Vice—William C. V. C. Hoagland

1866, Feb. 5 Elders   Vice
    Leffert T. Bergen   Harvey D. Platt
    John B. Jones   Henry D. Needham
  Deacons
    William Baker   reelected

1867, Feb. 4 Elders
    John Monfort   reelected
    William Seward   "
  Deacons
    Samuel I. Robinson   reelected
    John Jones   "
    Joseph P. Deyo, to fill vacancy

LIST OF CHURCH OFFICERS
During the Ministry of Rev. Henry Ward.

1868, Feb. 3 Elders
    John B. Jones   Re-elected
    William St. John   Vice—L. T. Bergen
  Deacons
    William Baker   Re-elected
    Joseph P. Deyo   "

The Reformed Dutch Church of New Hackensack

1869, Feb. 1 Elders
    Wm. Seward — Re-elected
    John Monfort — " (died Sep. 6, 1869)
  Deacons
    Samuel I. Robinson — Re-elected
    John Jones — "

1870, Feb. 7 Elders
    John B. Jones — Re-elected
    William St. John — "
    Allerton M. Trowbridge — Vice—John Monfort, deceased
  Deacons — Vice
    Richard S. Van Wyck — William Baker
    Alexander Bishop — Joseph P. Deyo

1871, Feb. 10 Elders
    William Seward — Re-elected
    Allerton M. Trowbridge — "
  Deacons
    Samuel I. Robinson — Re-elected
    John Jones — "
    Joseph Simpson — vice—R. S. Van Wyck, resigned

1872, Feb. 5 Elders
    John B. Jones — Re-elected
    Samuel Matthews — vice—William St. John
  Deacons
    Joseph Simpson — Re-elected
    Alexander Bishop — "

1873, Feb. 3 Elders
    William Seward — Re-elected
    Allerton M. Trowbridge — "
  Deacons
    John Jones — Re-elected
    John H. Luyster — vice—Samuel I. Robinson

1874, Feb. 2 Elders
    John B. Jones — Re-elected
    Samuel Matthews — "
  Deacons
    Joseph Simpson — Re-elected
    Alexander Bishop — "

1875, Feb. 1 Elders
    William Seward — Re-elected
    Allerton M. Trowbridge — "
  Deacons
    John Jones — Re-elected
    John H. Luyster — "

1876, Feb. 7 Elders — Vice
    John B. Jones — Re-elected
    Samuel Matthews — "
  Deacons
    John R. Matthews — Joseph Simpson
    J. Edward McCord — Alexander Bishop

1877, Feb. 5 Elders
    William Seward — Re-elected
    Allerton M. Trowbridge — "
  Deacons
    John Jones — Re-elected
    John H. Luyster — "

1878, Feb. 4 Elders
    John B. Jones — Re-elected
    Samuel Matthews — "
  Deacons
    John R. Matthews — Re-elected
    James A. Seward — Vice—J. E. McCord

Register of Officers and Consistory Minutes

1879, Feb. 3   Elders
     William Seward   Re-elected
     John H. Luyster   Vice—A. M. Trowbridge
    Deacons
     James C. Ackerman   John H. Luyster
     John A. Rogers   John Jones

1880, Feb. 2   Elders
     John B. Jones   Re-elected
     Samuel Matthews   "
    Deacons
     James A. Seward   Re-elected
     John R. Matthews   "

1881, Feb. 7   Elders
     William Seward   Re-elected
     John H. Luyster   "
    Deacons
     James C. Ackerman   Re-elected
     John A. Rogers   "

1882, Feb. 13   Elders
     J. B. Jones   Re-elected
     Samuel Matthews   "
    Deacons
     John R. Matthews   Re-elected
     James A. Seward   "

1883, Feb. 19   Elders
     William Seward   Re-elected
     James A. Seward   Vice—J. H. Luyster
    Deacons
     James C. Ackerman   Re-elected
     John A. Rogers   "
     Wm. H. Tompkins   Vice—J. A. Seward, elected to Eldership

1884, Feb. 4   Elders
     John B. Jones   re-elected
     Samuel Matthews   "
    Deacons
     John R. Matthews   re-elected
     Jacob Vollmer   Vice—W. M. Tompkins

1885, Feb. 2   Elders
     William Seward   re-elected
     James A. Seward   "
    Deacons
     James C. Ackerman   re-elected
     Brundage Tompkins   Vice—John A. Rogers

1886, Feb. 1   Elders
     John B. Jones   Re-elected
     Samuel Matthews
    Deacons
     John R. Matthews   Re-elected
     Jacob Vollmer

1887, Feb. 7   Elders
     William Seward   Re-elected
     James A. Seward
    Deacons
     James C. Ackerman   Re-elected
     Brundage Tompkins

1888, Feb. 2   Elders
     J. B. Jones   Re-elected
     Samuel Matthews Died Nov. 18, 1888
    Deacons
     Jacob Vollmer   Re-elected
     Cromeline Phillips   Vice—John R. Matthews

The Reformed Dutch Church of New Hackensack

1889, Feb. 4 Elders
    William Seward, died Dec. 4 1890   Re-elected
    James A. Seward
    Jas. C. Ackerman to serve unexpired term of Sam'l Mathews, deceased
  Deacons   Vice
    John A. Rogers   Jas. C. Ackerman
    Wm. H. Tompkins   Brundage Tompkins

1890, Feb. 3 Elders
    John B. Jones   Re-elected
    Jas. C. Ackerman   "
  Deacons
    Jacob Vollmer   Re-elected
    Cromeline Phillips   "

1891, Apr. 6 Elders
    Jas. A. Seward (died May 1, 1892)   Re-elected
    Alexander Bishop   Vice—Wm. Seward, deceased
  Deacons
    John A. Rogers   Re-elected

1892, Apr. 4 Elders
    John B. Jones   Re-elected
    Jas. C. Ackerman   "
  Deacons
    Jacob Vollmer   Re-elected
    Crumeline Phillips   "
    Edward Lawrence for term of one year to fill vacancy

1893, Apr. 4 Elders
    Alexander Bishop   Re-elected
    Walter Underhill   Vice—Jas. A. Seward, deceased
  Deacons
    John A. Rogers   Re-elected
    Edward Lawrence   "

1894, Apr. 9 Elders
    John B. Jones (died Feb. 4, 1896)   Re-elected
    Jas. C. Ackerman   "
  Deacons   Vice
    Theodore Christian   Jacob Vollmer
    Jas. Y. Luyster   Crumeline Phillips

1895, Apr. 15 Elders
    Alexander Bishop   Re-elected
    Walter Underhill   "
  Deacons
    Edward Lawrence   Re-elected
    John Rogers   "

1896, Apr. 6 Elders
    James C. Ackerman   Re-elected
    Edgar A. Briggs   Vice—John B. Jones, deceased
    Wm. St. John   " Walter Underhill, resigned
  Deacons   Vice
    Robert Hutchinson   Theodore Christian
    Eliphaz Delemater   Jas. Y. Luyster

1897, Apr. 5 Elders
    Wm. St. John   Re-elected
    Theodore Christian   Vice—Alexander Bishop, resigned
  Deacons
    Edward Lawrence   Re-elected
    John Rogers   "

1898, Apr. 4 Elders
    James C. Ackerman   Re-elected
    Edgar A. Briggs   "
  Deacons
    Robert Hutchinson   "
    Eliphaz Delemater   "

Register of Officers and Consistory Minutes

1899, Apr. 3 Elders
    Theodore Christian   Re-elected
    Rob't. Hutchison   Vice—Wm. St. John, resigned
  Deacons
    Edward Lawrence   Re-elected
    Stephen Bulmer in place of John Rogers
    Mathew Van Wyck for one year to fill place of Rob't. Hutchison

1900, Apr. 10 Elders
    Edgar A. Briggs   Re-elected
    Ernest Hayes   Vice—Jas. C. Ackerman
  Deacons
    Eliphaz Delemater   Re-elected
    Mathew Van Wyck   "

1901, Apr. 8
    Theodore Christian   Re-elected
    Robert Hutchison   "
  Deacons
    Edward Lawrence   "
    Stephen Bulmer   "

1902, Apr. 7 Elders
    Edgar A. Briggs   Re-elected
    Ernest Hayes   "
  Deacons
    Eliphaz Delamater   "
    Guy C. Blossom in place of Mathew Van Wyck

1903, Apr. 6 Elders
    Theodore Christian   Re-elected
    Robert Hutchison   "
  Deacons
    Stephen Bulmer   "
    Monroe Scofield in place of Edward Lawrence

1904, Apr. 4 Elders
    Edgar A. Briggs   Re-elected
    Ernest Hayes   "
    Edward Lawrence for one year to fill unexpired term of R. Hutchison
  Deacons
    Eliphaz Delamater   Re-elected
    Guy C. Blossom

1905, Apr. 3 Elders
    Theodore Christian   Re-elected
    Edward Lawrence   "
  Deacons
    Stephen Bulmer   "
    Monroe Scofield   "

1906, Apr. 2 Elders
    Edgar A. Briggs   Re-elected
    Ernest Hayes   "
  Deacons
    Wm. Briggs in place of E. Delamater
    Abram D. Van Wyck in place of G. C. Blossom

MINUTES OF CONSISTORY
of the church of
NEW HACKENSACK
BEGINNING WITH THE YEAR 1789

Minutes of Consistory

1789
May 28 The Consistory met at the house of Mr. Theophilus Anthony and the following was resolved:

1

After prayer, the minister, presiding, having stated that the meeting of the Rev. Classis of the Middle District was to be held at Pôkeepsie, next Tuesday, the 2d of June, to which also from this congregation an elder should be sent as a delegate, Mr. Aris van der Bilt, elder, was chosen for that purpose, to whom credentials were handed.

2

The Rev. Consistory, having taken into consideration the condition of this church, have instructed the said elder to lay the present state of affairs of this church before the Rev. Classis; namely, that whereas the Rev. Mr. Rysdyk, their minister, owing to the non-payment of his salary by the churches of Fischkil and Hopewel, has found himself obliged to enter into an agreement with them, whereby, in exchange for the payment of the arrears of his salary and a sum of money in addition, he had to release them from their obligation toward him, so that the congregation of New Hakkensak, now standing alone and by themselves, are not able to raise a sufficient salary for the support of their minister. He is therefore to request the Rev. Classis, in the name of this Consistory, to take this matter into consideration and, if possible, to devise some means whereby this congregation may be enabled to support his Reverence and thereby to continue to enjoy the benefit of his services.

Q. T.*
Isaac Rysdyk, *Praeses*

1790
May 18 The meeting of the Consistory was held at the house of Domine Isaac Rysdyk P. M. Present:
Dom. Isaac Rysdyk, *Praeses*
Messrs. Aris van der Bilt ⎫
       Theophilus Antony ⎬ Elders
       Jan Churchwell ⎭
Messrs. Jan Sleght ⎫ Deacons
       Clement Cornwell ⎭

Art. I

Election of an elder to attend the Rev. Classis — After prayer, an election was held of an elder to go as a delegate from this congregation to the meeting of the Rev. Classis of Kingston, which is to be held on the first Tuesday in June next, at Poughkeepsie, and for this purpose was unanimously chosen Elder Aris van der Bilt, to whom credentials were given to take with him.

Art. II

Proposal to the Rev. Classis — The presiding minister informed the Bretheren that last year an elder on the part of this congregation made a proposal to the Rev. Classis regarding the inability of this congregation to raise a sufficient salary for the support of their minister, Domine Isaac Rysdyk, with the request that they might receive their Reverences' counsel and advice in the matter; whereupon the Rev. Classis resolved to submit this matter through their delegates to the Most Rev. Synod* for their deliberation and advice. The said delegates, however, for weighty reasons, have done nothing in the matter, but postponed action until the present year, so that it is necessary to bring this matter again to the attention of the Rev. Classis, namely, that Mr. Isaac Rysdyk has served this congregation as their pastor and minister faithfully and diligently for a period of more than 24 years; that they are not only satisfied with his useful services and his teaching and conduct, but, if it please the Lord, wish to continue to enjoy the same; that this congregation, however, being now alone and by themselves, and no longer combined with the two neighboring congregations of Viskil and Hopewell, owing to the dismissal of Dom. Rysdyk by those said congregations, find themselves unable to raise a sufficient salary for the support of his Reverence and his large family, and that they therefore humbly request this Reverend body to be pleased to take this matter into serious consideration and as far as possible to give them the benefit of their advice and assistance. [Resolved] that a copy of this article be furnished to the delegated elder, Mr. Aris van der Bilt.

---

* *Quod Testor*, which I certify, or attest.
* The original has *Hoog. E. Synode* (Hoog Eerwaarde Synode, literally: Highly Reverend Synod), which according to a resolution of the Synod of 1789, should be rendered as "The Most Reverend Synod." *Ecclesiastical Records of the State of New York*, 6: 4352.

The Reformed Dutch Church of New Hackensack

Art. III

A sexton appointed — The Consistory, taking into consideration the great necessity of keeping the church here, together with the church yard and the glebe, in proper order, have resolved as follows:

To all, whom it may Concern.

We, the Elders & Deacons of the Reformed Dutch Church in New Hackinsak, have authorised as we authorise by these presents Mr. Peter Dates, in the quality of the Sexton of said Church, to have and to hold the Care and oversight of said Church and Church-ground that no Harm be done to either of them. And also that no person or persons, not belonging to the Congregation of the Dutch Church in New Hakkinsak, that is, not paying towards the maintaining of the Minister of said Church, shall have a Right to bury their dead in the Church yard adjoining this Church, without paying the Sexton aforesd. the sum of eight shillings, however leaving it to the discretion of said Sexton to take a less sum from the Poor.

Strangers may not bury their dead in the Dutch church yard without paying 8 sh. to the grave digger.

Art. IV

Repairs of the church yard. — In order to put the church yard again into proper order, Deacon Clement Cornwell is appointed by the Rev. Consistory to employ a workman for that purpose, Elders Aris van der Bilt and Thephilus Antony promising each to guarantee the payment of one-half of the expense.

Art. VI*

House rent of the parsonage. — As to the house rent of the minister's leased dwelling for the year 1789, of which one-third must be paid by this congregation, it was resolved to repay the same partly out of the poor fund and partly by means of a collection to be taken up in and outside of the church. Whereupon the Rev. Consistory, after giving thanks to God, separated in love and peace.

Q. T.
Isaäc Rysdyk, *Praeses*

N.B. Same day, ye new Kerkraad was chosen unanimously, as follows:

Constyn Golneck
Duncan Graham } Elders,

Abraham Hogeland
Henry Schoonmaker } Deacons.

1790. July 16. At a meeting of the Consistory at the house of the minister, it was resolved, that the Charter, which is granted to the Dutch Congregations by the Assembly of the State of Newyork be adopted by the Elders and Deacons of this Congregation, in form, to which a meeting was appointed of the Consistory, to be held on the 13th of August ensuing.

Q. T.
Isaäc Rysdyk

TO ALL WHOM IT MAY CONCERN, WE, Nicholas Vn. Vranken, Minister, and John Monfort, Domenicus Monfort, John A. Hageman, Henry Schoonmaker, John Vn. Siclen, Peter Rosekrance, John Luyster, Junr., and Peter Wyckoff, Elders and Deacons of the Reformed Protestant Dutch Church established at Hackensack in the Town of Fishkill in Dutchess County and state of New York being duly elected agreeable to the rules and Usages of the Reformed Protestant Dutch Churches in the said state, DO CERTIFY, pursuent to the Act of the Legislator of the said state entitled An Act for making such Alterations in the act for incorporating religious societies as to render the same convenient to the Reformed Protestant Dutch Congregations, passed 7th March, 1788, that the name stile or title of us as Trustees of the said Church and Congregation thereof, and our successors forever as a body corperate by Virtue of the said Act, shall be known and distinguished by the Name of the Trustees of the Reform'd Protestant Dutch Church of New Hackensack. IN WITNESS whereof we have hereunto set our hands and Affixed our seals the Twenty-third day of september in the year of our Lord one thousand seven Hundred and Ninety three.

& sign'd
Nich's. Van Vrankin, V. D. M.

SIGNED AND SEALED
In the presence of
Harmah Jewell
Roeloff Schanck }

Elders { John Monfort
Domenicus Monfort
John Hageman
Henry Schoonmaker

*Thus in the original, Art. V being omitted.

Minutes of Consistory

a true Coppy by—
Sam'l Luckey, secty.

Deacons
- John Van Siclen
- Peter Rosekrans
- John Luyster, Junr.
- Peter Wyckoff

Dutchess County. Ss. Be it remembered that on the thirteenth day of October, in the year one thousand seven hundred and ninety three, personally appeared before me Zephaniah Platt, Esq., one of the Judges of the Court of Common Pleas, in and for said County, Harmah Jewell, one of the subscribing witnesses to the within Certificate who being duly sworn sayeth that he saw the Minister and the Elders and Deacons of the Reformed protestant Dutch Church within Mentioned whose names are specied in the within Certificate respectively sign, seal and execute the within Certificate as and for their Voluntary act and deed for the purposes therein, Declared, and I having examined the same and finding therein no material erasures or interlineations, do allow the same to be Recorded—an interlineation of the word Junior being first made before execution.

         Sign'd Zephaniah Platt.

Recorded on Book No. 1 of Church deeds or Certificates, pages 21, 22 and 23, this 20th day of November 1793.

         Sign'd Rob't. H. Livingston, Clerk.

This Certifies that a meeting of the Consistory of New Hackensack was held at the house of Mrs. Rysdike on the 24th Feby. 1795.

Elders
- Domenicus Monfort
- Peter Luyster
- Abm. Hogeland

Elders Present

Deacons
- John Van Siclen
- John Luyster

Deacons present

To provide a house for the widow Rysdike, Agreed upon the school house for that purpose but not finding the heads of the famoly at home to give them any notice, Apointed Abm. Hogeland & John Luyster as a Committee to go the Next day and warn them out on or before the first day of may, consequently it was done by these said Men with Abm. Myers and John Churchill as Witnesses.

Septr. 5th, 1795 this Certifies that at a Meeting of the Consistory of the of New Hackensack Held at the house of Matthias Luyster Certifying that Benjn. Vn. Keuren was chosen secretary in the room of Henry Schoonmaker and Peter Luyster Treasurer in the room of Domenicus Monfort. Certifying Likewise that the poor Chest is delivered in the Care of Samuel Luckey, Esqr., Containing £4—8—6 in Cash.

Elders present
 Peter Luyster

Deacons present
 Rob't Todd
 John Cornell
 Wm. Lawson
 Sam'l Luckey

Articles of Agreement made and concluded on this fourteenth day of March 1796 Between Samuel Luckey, Peter Luyster, John Cornell, Abraham Hogeland & Robert Todd, Consistory of protestant Dutch Church in Hackensack in the town of fishkill of the one part and Jeremiah Jones of the Town Aforesaid of the other part witnesseth that for and in Consideration of the Covenants herein after mentioned the said party of the second part doth promise and oblige himself by these presents to deliver peacable and quiet possession of all that house or tenement whereon the party of the second part now lives to the said party of the first part on or before the first day of may next—Ensueing the date hereof they the said party of the first part paying him the said party of the second part the full sum of ten pounds Current money of New-York on or before the first day of may next provided the said tenement is Delivered as aforesaid by the said party of the second part in witness whereof the parties to these presents have hereunto interchangably set their hands and seals the day & date above written.

         and sign'd by

Signed and Sealed
in presence of

Samuel Cooper
Jno. Robinson

Jeremiah Jones
Samuel Luckey
Peter Luyster
John Cornell
Abraham Hogeland
Robert Todd

       a Coppy

Messrs.
Samuel Luckey
Abraham Hogeland
John Cornell
Peter Luyster &
Robert Todd _____Gentlemen_____

New-Hackensack 16th Apl. 1796

The Reformed Dutch Church of New Hackensack

For Value Received please to pay to Samuel Cooper the within sum of Ten pounds and his receipt shall be in full Against your Humble Servant.

                        Sign'd   Jeremiah Jones

Received New Hackensack 16th Apl. 1796 Ten pounds Current money of New-York in full for and in behalf of Jeremiah Jones

        a Coppy   Sign'd   Samuel Cooper

April ye 16th 1796, at a Meeting of the Consistory of the Church of New Hackensack held at said Church to settle with Henry Schoonmaker on the Church book and find in favour of said Church the sum of 14/ against said Schoonmaker. Said day paid Jeremiah Jones ten pounds for possession of the school House £6—12—0 taken out of the poor Chest and £3—8—0 paid by Consistory.

Elders present

    Peter Luyster
    Benj'n Vn. Keuren

Deacons present

    John Cornell
    Samuel Luckey
    Robert Todd
    Wm. Lawson

Augt. ye 13th 1796 This Certifies that at a meeting of the Consistory of the Church of New Hackensack held at the house of Samuel Luckey, Esqr., that Aris Vn. Debelt was chosen treasurer in the Room of Peter Luyster, also that the poor Chest was delivered in the Care of Robert Todd Containing the sum of £1—19—9.

Elders present

    Benj'n Vn. Keuren
    John Willsie
    Aris Vn. Debelt
    Albert Monfort

Deacons present

    Robert Todd
    William Lawson
    William Huffman
    Jacob Griffin

Decr. ye 31st 1796 This Certifies that at a meeting of the Consistory of the Church of New Hackensack held at the house of Mrs. Hollett to make a just devision of the Rev. Vn. Vranken's service between the Dutch and English subscribers and find by the superscriptions that the 1/5 of the service is to be performed in the dutch Language & the remainder to be English.

Elders present

    Benj'n Vn. Keuren
    John Willsie
    Aris Vn. Debelt
    Albert Monfort

Deacons present

    Rob't Todd
    Wm. Lawson
    Wm. Huffman
    Jacob Griffin

July ye 10th 1797 this Certifies that at a Meeting of the Consistory of the Church of New Hackensack at said Church, that the poor Chest was Delivered in the hand William Huffman Containing the sum of £1—18—6

Elders present

    Aris Vn. Debelt
    Albert Monfort
    John Cornell
    Theophilus Anthony

Deacons present

    Robert Todd
    William Lawson
    William Huffman
    Clement Cornell

I Do hereby Certify that on the 18th day of September in the year of our 1797 Aris Vn. Debilt, Albert Monfort, Theophilus Anthoney, John Cornell, Clement Cornwell & William Huffman being a majorety of the trustees of the Reformed protestant Dutch Church of New Hackensack Exhibited to me on Oath an Inventory of All the estate both real and personal belonging to the said Church.

                            Sign'd   John Johnston

One of the Judges of the Court of Common pleas for the County of Dutchess.

1798, May ye 20th at a Meeting of the Consistory of the Church of New Hackensack held at said Church.
Elders and Deacons present: Rev'd. Nicholas Vn. Vranken, Presed't; Theophilus Anthoney, Aris Vn. Debelt, Albert Monfort & John Cornell, (Elders), Clement Cornwell, Andrew Rinders, William Huffman & Jacob Griffin, (Deacons)
the following persons were chosen Elders & Deacons (to wit)
Rob't Todd & Sam'l Luckey Elders in Room of Aris Vn. Debelt & Albert Monfort
Jno. Luyster & Aaron Cole Deacons in Room of Jacob Griffin & William Huffman.

1798, Augt. ye 22nd. Att a meeting of the Consistory of the Church of New Hackensack held at the house of the Widow Rysdyke

Minutes of Consistory

Elders present

Rev'd Nicholas Vn. Vranken, Pres'd.
Theophilus Anthoney
Robert Todd
John Cornell
Samuel Luckey

Deacons present

Clement Cornwell
Andrew Rinders

Resolved that the Consistory of the Church of New Hackensack do meet some day in the week after publication of the Administration of the Sacrament of the Lord's Supper to examin into the situation of the members of said Church. . . .
further, that Samuel Luckey is Chosen Secretary & treasurer in the Room of Aris Vn. Debelt, and on settlement of said Luckey Received of said Van Debelt—£0—6—4, further that the poor Chest is Delivered by William Huffman to Clement Cornwell Containing the sum of £1—18—11. further the Consistory being met Preparatory to the Administration of the Lord's Supper do feel themselves extremely Greaved on Account of the unhappy dispute which has for some time existed and yet Continues to exist between Messrs. Edward Schoonmaker and William Hoffman both Communing members of the Church as love and harmony are amongst the distinguishing characteristics of professing Christians and particularly enjoined by the Great King of Zion A Contrary conduct is highly Improper and is totaly Inconsistant with the fundamental principels and mild Institutions of that Kingdom which is Righteousness and peace and Joy in the Holy Gost and over which the prince of peace presides.

The Consistory considering themselves as Acountable to God for the pure Administration of the Sacrement of the Holy Supper and at the same time Consientious of the Great Impropriety of persons Communing together who stand at Irreconciliable Varience from each other find it their Indispensible duty to direct the aforesaid Edw'd Schoonmaker and Wm. Huffman to refrain for the present from the table of the Lord.

it would matter of great Joy if the above decision with regard to Edward Schoonmaker was not founded on Other motives than these already mentioned his having Lived and still Continues to Live Absent from his wife is a direct Violation of the word of God which expressly declares that whatever God hath joined together man shall not put assunder, it is offensive to the Church of Christ and such offences Ought to be Removed, the Consistory however not having minutely Investigated the cause of their seperation will be happy to learn that Mr. Schoonmaker is Intirely Innocent.

1799, Jany. 24th. A coppy of the above resolution transmitted to the said Edw'd Schoonmaker ————————————————————By Sam'l Luckey, secty. ————————

1799, July ye 7th. At a meeting of the Consistory of the Church of New Hackensack held at the house of the widow Rysindyke.
present the Rev'd. Nich's Vn. Vranken

Elders
{ John Cornell
  Robert Todd
  Sam'l Luckey
  Theophilus Anthoney }

Deacons
{ Clement Cornwell
  Andrew Rinders
  John Luyster
  Aaron Cole }

Resolved that the following persons be chosen for Elders & Deacons (to wit)

Albert Monfort & Charles Huffman } Elders in room of { John Cornell & Theophilus Anthoney

Tunis Vn. Bunschoten & Nazareth Brewer } Deacons in room of { Clement Cornwell & Andrew Rynders

The above Elders & Deacons to be Ordained ye 4th Augt. Ensueing.
recorded By Sam'l Luckey, Secty.

1799, July ye 11th. At a Meeting of the Consistory of the Church of New Hackensack held at the house of the widow Rysindyke
present the Rev'd Nich's Vn. Vranken, pres't.

Elders
{ Theophilus Anthoney
  Robert Todd
  John Cornell
  Sam'l Luckey }

Deacons
{ Clement Cornwell
  Andrew Rinders
  Aaron Cole }

The Consistory having Admonished Messrs. Edward Schoonmaker & William Huffman with Regard to the Unhappy difference existing between them and having Obtained an Acknowledgement from both as Annexious for a Reconciliation Accompanied with Confession of sincear sorrow together with a promise of mutual love & harmony—Therefore Resolved that they be again admitted into full Communion.

Sam. Luckey, secty.

The Reformed Dutch Church of New Hackensack

1799, Augt. ye 7th. At a meeting of the Consistory of the Church of New Hackensack held at the said Church
   present the Rev'd Nich's Vn. Vranken, pres't.

Charles Huffman Robert Todd Albert Monfort Sam'l Luckey } Elders		Nazareth Brewer Tunis Vn. Bunschoten } Deacons

Resolved that the poor Chest be delivered by Clement Cornwell to John Luyster, Junr., Containing the sum of £5—6—0
Resolved also that Robert Todd & Samuel Luckey with Henry Schoonmaker is Appointed a Committey to regulate the Church Books and settle with the said Schoonmaker on the Accounts with said Church.

                                                                        Sam'l Luckey, Secty.

1800, Feby ye 26th. At a meeting of the Consistory of the Church of New Hackensack held at the house of the Widow Risindyke
   present the Rev'd Nich's. Vn. Vranken, pres't

Elders { Robert Todd Charles Huffman Albert Monfort Sam'l Luckey }		Deacons { Nazareth Brewer John Luyster Tunis Vn. Bunschoten Aaron Cole

Resolved that from and after date John Luyster is to serve as Clerk and Sexton in the said Church to perform the following services (to wit) to read sit psalms, ring bell, bring water for baptizing and assist in opening and shutting the windows, etc., for which services he is to receive at the rate of ten dollars per year as Long as he shall be Continued in such services, farther that said Luyster is to receive out of the poor Chest the sum of ten dollars for past services and that an Order is to be Given to said Luyster for the same.

1800, July 13th. At a meeting of the Consistory of the Church of New Hackensack held at the house of the widow Rysendike

Elders present { Robert Todd Theophilus Anthoney Albert Monfort Sam'l Luckey }		Deacons present { Aaron Cole John Luyster Nazareth Brewer

The following persons was Chosen as Elders & Deacons (to wit)

Dominicus Monfort & Albert Monfort }	Elders in Room of	{ Robert Todd & Samuel Luckey
Joseph Harris & Casper Gonse }	Deacons in Room of	{ John Luyster & Aaron Cole

and that they be ordained ye 10th Augt. Ensueing.

1801, Feby ye 3rd. At a Meeting of the Consistory of the Reformed Dutch Church in New Hackensack held at the house of Samuel Cooper

Elders present { Albert H. Monfort Albert I. Monfort }	Deacons present	{ Nazareth Brewer Casper Gons Tunis Vn. Bunschoten Joseph Harris

Resolved that the poor Chest be Delivered by John Luyster to Casper Gons Containing the sum of £4—11—10
Also that an Order be given to John Luyster to receive from Casper Gons out of the poor Chest ten Dollars for services as Clerk, sexton, etc. to the 26th february 1801.
farther that 2 seats on No. 3 of Andris Haremans be transfered to John Monfort and from John Monfort to Albert H. Monfort
farther that 2 seats in No. 27 which is Confiscated of Lawrence Haff be transfered to Nazareth Brewer in stead of 2 seats he bot. of Edw'd Schoonmaker in No. 28 which had been sold by mistake to sd. Edward having been sold previously to Abm. Sleight & Mary Lenington. Done by Order of the Consistory.

                                                                     Sam'l Luckey, secty.

1801, Feby. ye 7th. I hereby Certify that on the 7th day of february in the Year 1801 Charles Huffman, Albert H. Monfort, Domenicus Monfort, Albert I. Monfort, Tunis Vn. Bunschoten & Nazareth Brewer being a Majority of the trustees of the Reformed protestant Dutch Church of New Hackensack exhibited to me on oath an Inventory of all the Estate both real and personal belonging to the said Church.
                    Sign'd Henry Livingston, one of the Judges of the Court of
                          Common Plees of the County of Dutchess.
                              Recorded by Sam. Luckey, secty.

Minutes of Consistory

1801, July ye 27th. At a Meeting of the Consistory of the Reformed prositant Dutch Church in New-Hackensack held at sd. Church

old Elders { Albert I. Monfort / Charles Huffman

Elders present { Domenicus Monfort / Albert H. Monfort / Henry Schoonmaker / John A. Hageman

old Deacon—Nazareth Brewer

Deacons present { Joseph Harris / Casper Gons

Resolved that Casper Gonse is to keep the poor Chest the Ensueing year farther that the Consistory met to settle but some of the Consistory being Absent they Could not settle
                                            Sam. Luckey, secty.

1801, Octbr. ye 17th. At a meeting of the Consistory of the reformed prostitant Dutch Church held at said Church

Elders present { Domenicus Monfort, Elbert H. Monfort / John A. Hageman & Henry Schoonmaker

William Lawson Deacon present

Resolved that the Consistory examin the Accounts and expenditures for meterials & Labour for repairing said Church and that the secretary enter the Accounts at Large on the Church book.

	L	S	D
Acct No. 1 Dominicus Monfort Materials	6—	7—	5
No. 2 John A. Hageman Do	3—	17—	6
No. 3 Monfort & Hageman for Labour	24—	13—	3
No. 4 Henry Schoonmaker materials	0—	8—	9
No. 5 Mrs. Rysendike for Cooking	1—	10—	0
	36—	16—	11

Different supper scription Lists

	£		
Domenicus Monfort	7—	16—	0
John A. Hagaman	5—	2—	4
Albert H. Monfort	6—	16—	0
William Lawson	1—	3—	7
Henry Schoonmaker	10—	6—	10
Due on Schoonmakers List	3—	14—	0
	34—	18—	9

                    Recorded by Sam'l Luckey, Secty.

1802, Augt. ye 1st. At a meeting of the Consistory of the reformed prostitant Dutch Church held at said Church
Resolved that the following persons be Chosen Elders & Deacons

Abraham Hogeland / Tunis Vn. Bunschoten } Elders in Room of { Domenicus Monfort / Albert H. Monfort

Aris Vn. Debelt, Junr. / & Andrew Rinders } Deacons in room of { Joseph Harris & / William Lawson

                    Recorded by Sam. Luckey, secty.

1802, Augt. ye 21st. at a meeting of the Consistory of the Reformed prostitant Dutch Church of New Hackensack held at the house of Adrian Covenhoven

old Elders { Domenicus Monfort / Albert H. Monfort

Elders present { Abraham Hogeland / John A. Hageman

Deacons present { Casper Gonse / Andrew Rinders / Aris Vn. Debilt, Junr.

Resolved that Casper Gons pay John Luyster out of the poor Chest ten Dollars due ye 26th Feby. 1802 for services as Clerk and sexton in said Church
farther that Casper Gons keep the poor Chest the Ensueing year Containing £9—15—0; farther resolved that Samuel Luckey is to Collect the money due for seats sold at Oction ye 26th Feby. 1800.
                                            Sam. Luckey, secty.

1802, Novm. ye 16th. At a meeting of the Consistory of the Reformed prostitant Dutch Church of New Hackensack held at the house of Peter Dates in the town of Fishkill

Elders present { John A. Hageman / Hen'y Schoonmaker / Abraham Hogeland / Tunis Vn. Bunschoten

Deacons present { Aris Vn. Debilt, Jun'r. / William Huffman / Andrew Rinders

The Reformed Dutch Church of New Hackensack

Resolved that Casper Gonse pay John A. Hageman five pounds fourteen shillings & 11 d. out of the poor Chest which will settle said Hageman's Account in full for expences laid out in Repairing said Church.

Sam. Luckey, secty.

1802,* Jany. 30. At a meeting of the Consistory of the Reformed prostitant Dutch of New Hackensack

Elders present: Domenicus Monfort, Albert Monfort, John A. Hageman, Henry Schoonmaker

Deacons present: Casper Gonse, Joseph Harris

Resolved that such of the Consistory as hold salorey lists present them for examination to enable the Elders to settle with the Revn'd Nich's Vn. Vranken for his Salorey for the year 1801..........

John A. Hageman recpt. dated 17th Decemr. 1801, sign'd N. V. Vranken	£ 14 — 5 — 0
Albert Monfort recpt. dated 9th Decbr. 1801, sign'd N. V. Vranken	10 — 14 — 6
Domenicus Monfort recept dated 1st Jany. 1802, sign'd N. V. Vranken	11 — 0 — 0
Cash remaining in the hand of Domenicus Monfort	1 — 7 — 0
Cash remaining in the hand of Henry Schoonmaker	7 — 14 — 0
Mr. John Hageman presented an Acc't for sixty bords @ 1/10	£ 5 — 10 — 0
Cartage 5/, freight 15/	1 — 0 — 0
	6 — 10 — 0

Recorded by Sam. Luckey, secty.

1803, Octbr. ye 23rd. At a meeting of the Consistory of the Reformed prostitant Dutch Church of New Hackensack held at said Church

Elders present: Aris Vn. Debelt, Abraham Hogeland, Tunis Vn. Bunschoten, Samuel Luckey

Deacons present: Andrew Rinders, Aris Vn. Debelt, Jun'r, John Luyster, Peter Flaglor

After settling with Casper Gonse on Account of poor money find a balance remaining in the poor Chest of £ 10—10—0 and said poor Chest with the Contents was Delivered by said Casper Gonse to John Luyster

Recorded by Sam. Luckey, sect'y.

1804, April ye 12th. At a meeting of the Consistory of the Reformed prostitant Dutch Church of New Hackensack held at the house of Peter Haff

Elders present: Abraham Hogeland, Tunis Vn. Bunschoten, Samuel Luckey

Deacons present: Aris Vn. Debelt, Jun'r, Andrew Rinders, Peter Flaglor

By Mutual Consent it is Agreedon that Peter Haff is to give possession to the said Consistory of the house and Lot Called the school house on or before the first day of may next Ensueing of which the said Peter was to have a Lease of for five years from the first day of may last, and that the said Consistory agree to pay or Cause to be paid unto the said Peter ten dollars on or before the first day of Novb'r. next for repairs done to said house more then his first years rent Amounted to.

Recorded by Order of Consistory   Sam. Luckey, sect'y.

1805, April ye 29th. The Consistories of the Reformed Dutch Churches of Hackensack & Hopewell met at the house of John Yates for the purpose of Prosecuting a Call upon Mr. George Barkuloe

Present
The Reverend Cornelius Brewer

Elders from New Hackensack
Aris Van der belt
Samuel Luckey
Tunis Vn. Bunschoten
Abraham Hogeland

Deacons from Do
John Luyster

Elders from Hopewell
Abraham Adriance
Cornelius Wiltsie
Cornelius R. Van Wick

Deacons from Do
Benjamin Waldren

The Consistories Opened with prayer.

After Conversation of some Length it was Resolved that Considering the preparatory steps made use of Agreeably to the Directions specified in the Constitution of the Reformed Dutch Churches and the particular Information from the persons Appointed to take the

* This date should be 1803 (?)

Minutes of Consistory

Opinion of the Congregation with respect to the Calling of Mr. George Barkulo a Candidate for the said Minestry it was Resolved that these Consistories will present a Call to the same and that the following shall be a Coppy for the same.

Record'd by Sam. Luckey, sect'y.

1805. At a Meeting of the Consistory of the Reformed Dutch Church of New Hackensack held at the house of John Yates the 6th day of May 1805 present at the Meeting

Elders { Tunis Vn. Bunschoten / Abraham Hogeland / Samuel Luckey

Deacons { John Luyster / Aris Vn. Debilt, Jun'r. / Andrew Rinders

Resolved that Samuel Luckey be paid out of the treasury the sum of Twenty Dollars for past servises as secretary and treasurer for said Consistory and for sundry Other servises by him performed — as witness our hands the day and year above written_____

Signed

Elders { Tunis Vn. Bunschoten / Abraham Hogeland / Sam. Luckey

Deacons { John Luyster / Andrew Rinders / Aris Vn. Debelt

Recorded by Sam. Luckey, sect'y.

1805 Copy of the Call presented to George Barkulo, by the United Congregations of New Hackensack & Hopewell_____

TO GEORGE BARKULO, Candidate for the sacred Ministry of the Gospel, We, Cornelius R. Vn. Wyck, Cornelius Wiltsie, Abraham Adriance, Richard H. Osbourn, Benjamin Waldron, Samuel Henderson & Isaac Secord, Elders and Deacons of the Reformed Dutch Church of Hopewell, and Aris Vn. Debelt, Samuel Luckey, Tunis Vn. Bunschoten, Abr'm hogelandt, John Luyster, Aris Vn. Debilt, Jun'r, Andrew Rinders & Peter Flagler, Elders & Deacons of the Reformed Dutch Church of New Hackensack

Wish Grace, Mercy & peace from God the Father and Jesus Christ our Lord_____

WHEREAS the Churches of Jesus Christ at Hopewell & New Hackensack are at present distitute the stated preaching of the Gospel of the word and the regular Administration of the Ordinances & are desirous of Obtaining the means of grace which God hath appointed for the salvation of sinners through Jesus Christ his son, And whereas the said Churches are well sattisfied of the piety, Gifts and Ministerial qualifications of you, George Barkulo, and have hope that your Labours in the gospel will be Attended with a blessing—Therefore we the said Elders & Deacons, have resolved to Call and we hereby in the fear of the Lord, Call you the said George Barkulo be our Teacher, to preach the word in truth & faithfulness, to Administer the sacraments Agreeably to the Institution of Jesus Christ, to maintain Christian Discipline, to edify the Congregations and the Youth by instructions and as a faithful servant of Jesus Christ to fulfill the whole work of the Gospel Ministry Agreably to the word of God, & According to the rules of our Reformed Dutch Churches established at the Last National Synod, held at dort, and ratified by the Ecclesiastical Judicatory, under which we stand, and to which you upon excepting this Call must with us remain subordinate—in fulfilling the Ordinary duties of your ministry, it is expressly stipulated, what besides preaching upon such texts of scripture as you may judge proper to select for our Instruction, you also explain a portion of the Hidelbergh Catechism, on the Lord's days, agreable to the Established order of the Reformed Dutch Church and that you farther Conform in rendering all that public service which is usual and has been the Constant practice of these Congregations—The particular services which will be required of you are these; that is to say;—You are to preach Alternately in the Church of at Hackensack and in the Church at Hopewell twice every Lord's day from the first of April, till the first of November, and once every Lord's day from the first day of November, till the first day of April, to Instruct the Youth by Catechetical Exercises at such stated times, as you & the Consistories may deem proper, you are to administer the sacrement of the Lord's supper twice a year at Least in each Congregation, visit the Congregations Annually and attend the sick when required.

To encourage you in the discharge of your important office we promise you in the name of these Congregations all proper attention, Love & obedience in the lord, & to free you from all worldly Cares and avocations, while you are dispensing spiritual blessings to us—we the said Elders & Deacons do promise for our selves and our Successors to pay you the sum of One hundred and fifty pounds Current Money of the state of New-York Yearly and every year as long as you continue to be minester of these Churches, and also thirty loads of firewood annually from the time of your commencing your service amongst us; that is to say; the one Equal half to be paid by the Elders & Deacons of the Congregation of Hopewell & Equal half to be paid by the Elders & Deacons of the Congregation of New Hackensack Likewise a personage to be procured within a year from this date, by the two Congregations as Nearly Central as may be with eight or ten Acres of Land, together with a Convenient dwelling house & other out houses for the accomodations of the same,

The Reformed Dutch Church of New Hackensack

for the performance of all which, as the said Elders & Deacons firmly in our Capacity as Consistories & also as trustees of the Temporalities aforesaid, bind ourselves and our successors firmly by these presents & in testimony of which have affixed hereunto our hands & the respective Seal of our Churches this twenty-ninth day of April one thousand eight Hundred & five.

Signed by the following Elders & Deacons of Hopewell (to wit)

Elders { Cornelius R. Vn. Wyck / Cornelius Wiltsie / Abraham Adriance   Deacon, Benjamin Waldron

Signed by the following Elders & Deacons of New Hackensack

Elders { Aris Vn. Debelt / Samuel Luckey / Tunis Vn. Bunschoten / Abreham Hogelandt   Deacon, John Luyster

Recorded by Sam. Luckey, sect'y.

1805, August the 1st, The aforesaid Call was excepted & Ministerial service Commenced by the said George Barkulo.

1805, Nov'r the 3rd. The said George Barkulo was Ordained in the Church at New Hackensack, Fishkill Town.

Present at the Ordination
The Reverend Cornelius Brower from poughkeepsie
the Rev'd Jacob Broadhead from Rhynbeck
the Rev'd Cornelius D. Westbrook from Fishkill

Record'd by Sam. Luckey, Secty.

1805 I do hereby certify that on the 30th day of May in the Year 1805 Aris Vn. Debelt, Samuel Luckey, Abraham Hogeland, Elders, and John Luyster & Aris Vn. Debelt, Jun'r, Deacons being a Majority of the trustees of the Reformed Dutch Church at Hackensack Exhibited to me on Oath an Inventory of all the estate both real and personal belonging to the said Church.

Signed, Robert Williams, one of the Judges of the Court of Common pleas for Dutchess County.

Record'd by Sam. Luckey, secty.

1805, Nov'r ye 8th. The Consistory of Dutch Reformed Church of New Hackensack met at the house of John Yates for the purpose of appointing a Committee to Correspond with a Commitee from the Dutch Reformed Church of Fishkill & Hopewell for the purpose of Devising way and means to dispose of Glebe Lands, parsonage House & Lot Belonging to the three said Churches.

Present

Elders { Aris Vn. Debelt / Abraham Hogeland / Samuel Luckey / Tunis Vn. Bunschoten   Deacons { Aris Vn. Debelt, Jun'r / Andrew Rinders

After Conversation of some length it was Resolved that Abraham Hogeland & Tunis Vn. Bunschoten were appointed to Conviene with a Committee from the said Churches of Fishkill & Hopewell to appoint a way and means for the sale of said Glebe Land & parsonage house & Lot above mentioned.

Sam. Luckey, sect'y.

1806, May the 13th. At a meeting of the Trustees of the Dutch Reformed Church of New Hackensack at the Dwelling house of John Yates in the Town of Fishkill.

Present

Elders { Clement Cornwell / Samuel Luckey / Casper Gonse   Deacons { Harmah Jewell / John Lawson / Aris Vn. Debelt, Jun'r / John Luyster

Resolved that a superscription be put in Circulation for the purpose of paying for the parsonage House & Lot which was purchased by the United Congregations of Hopewell and New Hackensack.

Sam. Luckey, sect'y.

1806, June the 16th. At a Meeting of the Trustees of the Reformed Dutch Church in New Hackensack, Held at the house of Rich'd Vn. Wyck in Fishkill Town.

Present

Elders { Aris Vn. Debelt / Sam. Luckey / Casper Gonse / Clement Cornwell   Deacons { Harmah Jewell / John Luyster / John Lawson

Minutes of Consistory

Resolved that Samuel Luckey be Appointed to lay out the Interes money Received from the Legacy Left to New Hackensack Church by the Last will and Testament of Peter Vn. Bunschoten Late of Fishkill Town, Decs'd.— as follows, to buy window Glass & puty & glaze the windows to purchace hooks and hang the window shuts & hang the bell over again, and what Money is Over to purchace Ceder singles and Cart them to said Church

Sam. Luckey, sect'y.

1806, Nov'r. the 26th. At a Meeting of the United Consistories of Hopewell & New Hackensack held at Mr. Staates New Hackensack

Article 1st

Consistory was opened with prayer by the Rev'd. Cornelius Brower

Article 2nd—Present at the Meeting

Members present		Elders of Hopewell		Deacons of Do.
Corn's R. Vn. Wick, Esqr.			Rich'd Osbourn	
Theodorus Adriance			John Storm	
Abraham Sleight				
Corn's Wiltsie				
Samuel Luckey, Esqre.		Elders of Hackensack	Harmah Jewell	Deacons of Do.
Aris Vn. Debelt			John Luyster	
Casper Gonse			John Lawson	
Clement Cornwell				

Rev'd Cornelius Brower — Rev'd Cornelius D. Westbrook
Tunis DuBois Advisory member

Article 3rd

Moderators Chosen } Rev'd Cornelius D. Westbrook, Presd't.
John Storms, Sect'y

Article 4th

Object of the Meeting Mr. Cornelius R. Vn. Wyck stated that the Object of the Meeting was the Investigate a Report Concerning their pasture the Rev'd George Barkulo which Charges him to have been Guilty of Intoxecation in the Vilage of Poughkeepsie on the 8th of October last, which was recognized by the Consistory as the Object of their meeting.

Article 5th

Cornelius R. Vn. Wyck & Samuel Luckey, Esqr. being deputed by said Consistory to wait Upon the Rev'd. George Barkulo at his Lodging Requesting his personal Attendance and received from him the following Observations in writing——

To the United Consistories of New Hackensack & Hopewell Assembled————
My Respected friends—
  The subject now under your Consideration has for some time laid heavily on my mind and greived my soul—not from any Consciousness of Guilt but it may prove a bar to my futer usefulness a cause of triumph to the enemies of Religion and a Reproach to the Interest of my Lord and Master I cannot but consider this affair Reather as my affliction then my sin—in the presence of that God whose I am & whome I would serve I can Acknowledge no Intended, Hence Can it Reasonably be supposed that in going to Attend one of the most solemn acts we are Called to witness, at a place where persons from every quarter of the county were expected to be Assembled, any one who had the Least sence of propriety or any Chareceter to suport could fall into so henious a sin—Nay though I trust my mind is feelingly alive to things of this kind I cannot Acknowledge guilt—should I Confess that a temperary derangement paroxism or something of this kind seized me perhaps this might not sattisfy the minds of all present—This however is the only source from which I can Unravel what is said to have followed, when Considering the numerous and peculiar Afflictions of my life I cannot but admire the wondrous Goodness of God that I have not long ere this been completely deranged—Reports Prejudicial to my caracter may be in circulation I think them unworthy of remarks, I shall only Notice that it said I seemed to be intoxecated before I Arrived at Poughkeepsie Mr. Westbrook saw me the Moment I Arrived there and must know my situation & I trust Mr. Suard is my friend and would not have left me had I been the situation Alluded to.

Sign'd George Barkulo.

Article 6th

We, the United Consistories of Hopewell and New Hackensack, having had Laid before us in writing from the Rev'd George Barkulo an Explanation of his Conduct & having Accurately Investigated the Reasons therein Assigned as well as Deliberately Investigated into his morrel deportment prier and subsequent to the Complaint entered to this board
  Resolved Unanimously, that we are fully sattisfied with the above Mentioned Explanation and that we consider him Honourably Acquited from Any Censure & that we Consider

The Reformed Dutch Church of New Hackensack

the disadvantagous Appearance of his conduct to have Arsen from an affliction to which According to his own account he is subject.
                             Sign'd Cornelius D. Westbrook, Presd't.
                             John Story,   sect'y.
                             Recorded by Sam. Luckey, sect'y.
Consistory Closed with prayer by the Rev'd. Corn's. D. Westbrook.

1806, Decbr. 27th, At a Meeting of the Consistory of the Reformed Dutch Church of New Hackensack held at the house of John Yates
                         present at the meeting

Elders { Aris Vn. Debelt / Sam'l Luckey / Clement Cornwell }   Deacons { John Luyster / Harmah Jewell }

Resolved that the following persons be Nominated for Elders and Deacons (to wit)

Elders { Albert I. Monfort in the place of Aris Vn. Debelt / William Sueard in the place of Samuel Luckey

Deacons { James Vn. Keuren in the place of John Luyster / John Vn. Sicklen in the place of Peter Flaglor
                                                        Sam. Luckey, sect'y.
The second sabeth after the above Eldrs & Deacons were Ordain'd.

1807, Jan'y. the 24th. At a meeting of the Consistory of the Reformed Dutch Church of New Hackensack held at the house of John Yates
                         Present at the meeting
Revn'd George Barkulo Opened Consistory with prayer

Elders { William Suard / Casper Gonse / Clement Cornwell }   Deacons { John Luyster / John Lawson }

1st. Resolved that Samuel Luckey be continued secretary and Treasurer and that he shall be Compensated for his services (to wit)

2nd. Resolved also that the poor Chest be put in the hands of James Vn. Keuren Containing the sum of £2—10—10 which sum Remained on settlement with John Luyster

3rd. Resolved farther that Samuel Luckey be Appointed to transcribe the Transferments & sales of the seats and also the Resolves of the Consistory in a New Church Book
Consistory Closed with prayer by the Rev'd George Barkulo.
                                             Sam. Luckey, sect'y.

1807, Aug't ye 1st. At a Meeting of the Trustees of the Reformed Dutch Church of New Hackensack held at the said Church.
                         Present at the meeting

Elders { Casper Gonse / Clement Cornwell / William Suard }   Deacons { Harmah Jewell / John Lawson / James Vn. Keuren / John Vn. Sicklen }

Resolved that Samuel Luckey is to furnish shingles, boards & Nails for to put a Ruff on the belconey and the south side of New Hackensack Church and William Suard is to furnish scafling poles, Employ Carpenters & also to Inspect the work.   by Order of the board.
                                             Sam'l. Luckey, sect'y.

1807, Nov'r. ye 24th. At a special meeting of the Consistories of the United Congregations of New Hackensack & Hopewell held at the House of Richard C. Vn. Wyck.
                       Present at the meeting

Elders from Hackensack { Casper Gonse / William Suard / Clement Cornwell / Albert I. Monfort }   Deacons from Do. { James Vn. Keuren / John Lawson / Harmah Jewell }

Elders from Hopewell { Abraham Shear / Theodorus Adriance / Abraham Sleight / Ram Adriance }   Deacons from Do. { Rich'd H. Osbourn / Jaromus Rapplege / John Storm }

Mr. Ram Adriance stated that the Object of this Meeting was to Investigate a Report Concerning their pasture the Rev'd George Barkulo which Charges him to have been guilty of Accasinal Intoxecation in the Town of Fishkill at the house of the said George Barkulo on the 4th of Nov'm Instant which was Recognized by the Consistories as the Object of their meeting.

We the United Consistories of Hopewell & New Hackensack having thoroughly Investigated the Charge Alleged against the Rev'd George Barkulo as well as Deliberately enquired his morral deportment prier & subsequent to the Complaint entered to this board, Resolved

Minutes of Consistory

Unanimously that we are fully sattisfied with the conduct of the said George Barkulo and that we Consider him Honourably acquited from any censure, and that we Consider the disadvantagous appearance of his Conduct to have Arisen from an affliction to which according to his own account he is subject.

Resolved unanimously that the proceedings of this meeting be read in the Churches of New Hackensack & Hopewell together with the following........

WHEREAS a report is now in circulation propopegated by some person or persons Respecting the Inconsistent Conduct of the Revr'd George Barkulo the Consistories of the United Congregations of the Reformed Dutch Churches of Hopewell & Hackensack being duly conveined for the express purpose of making strict Investigation into the same, previous notice having been given to his Accusers to appear before this board and to render sufficient testimony if any they can produce why the correcter of the said Barkulo should be thus Velified and after due Enquiry being made by us and nothing sattisfactory having been produced we are sattisfied that the said Report is unfounded and that the Deportment, walk and conversation of the Revr'd Barkulo is that of a CHRISTIAN and worthy shepard of his flock over which he has charge, and we trust that members of Religious and cevil societies will View the said Report with that Contempt which it justly merits.

Sign'd by order of the board   Abm. Sleight, presd't
John Storm, sect'y.

Ordered by the Consistory of Hackens Congregation that the above be read in Hackensack Church by Samuel Luckey. Consistory was Closed with prayer by the Revr'd George Barkulo.   Recorded by Sam'l Luckey, Sect'y.

1807, Decb'r. ye 2nd. At a meeting of the Consistory of the Reformed Dutch Church of New Hackensack held at the house of John Yates in fishkill Town
Present at the meeting

William Suard }
Clement Cornwell } Elders
Albert I. Monfort }
Casper Gons }

John Vn. Sicklen }
Harmah Jewell } Deacons
James Vn. Keuren }

Consistory met for the express purpose of sitling with Sam'l Luckey secretary & treasurer to the said Consistory, and after Accurately Investigating his Accounts, do find the said secretary & treasurer Indebted to said Congregation the sum of two pounds five shillings & 10 pence which sum of two pounds five shillings & 10 pence was paid to William Suard one of said Consistory——and——

Sign'd by the above Consistory (to wit)

Elders { William Suard
Clement Cornwell
Elbert I. Monfort
Casper Ganse }

Deacons { John Vn. Sicklen
Harmah Jewell
James Vn. Keuren }

Recorded by Sam'l Luckey, sect'y.

1808, Feb'y 20th. A Receipt taken from the Rev'd George Barkuloe in full for his Salory from the Congregation of New Hackensack Church up untill the first day of August one Thousand Eight hundred & seven $187—50/100   Sign'd George Barkulo
Record'd By Sam'l Luckey, sect'y.

Coppey of Certificate of the temperalleties of the Church

1808 June 30th I do hereby Certify that on the 30th day of June in the Year of our Lord 1808 William Suard, Elbert I. Monfort, Demenicus Montfort, Albert Monfort, John Vn. Siclen, Peter Wycoff, Aris Vn. Derbelt, Jun'r & James Vn. Keuren being the trustees of the Reformed Dutch Church of New-Hackensack exhibited to me on Oath an Inventory of all the Estate both Real and personal belonging to said Church.

John Johnston first Judge of the Court of
Recorded to order   Common pleas of the County of Dutchess
Sam'l Luckey, sect'y   Sign'd John Johnston

1808, May 31st At a Meeting of the Consistory of the Reformed Dutch Church of New Hackensack held at the house of John Yates in fishkill town.
Present at the Meeting
Revn'd George Barkulo, prs't.

Elders { Domenicus Monfort
William Suard
Albert Monfort }

Deacons { James Vn. Keuren
John Vn. Sicklen }

Consistory opened by prayer by G. B.

Mr. Clement Cornwell stated that the object of this meeting was to settle with the old Consistory &c

After examining the Acc'ts of Clement Cornwell find a balance in his hand of 9/2 which sum he p'd to Casper Gance & remain'd due on Cornwell's list from Jonath'n Dakin 6/4

The Reformed Dutch Church of New Hackensack

from Abm. States 8/. Also Resolved that Samuel Luckey Receive three pounds four shillings out of the treasury for transcribing Certain Records out of the old Church book into a new one.
Recorded by order of the board.
Sam'l Luckey, sect'y.

1809, July 11th. At a meeting of the United Consistories of Hopewell & New-Hackensak held at the house of Rich'd C. Vn. Wyck in fishkill town
Present the Revn'd George Barkuloe—Presd't

Elders from Hopewell { Theodorus Adriance, Abraham Sleight, Cornelius Wiltsie, Cornelius R. Vn. Wyck }   Deacons from do. { Richard Osbourn, Stephen Jackson }

Elders from New Hackensack { Domenicus Monfort, Samuel Luckey, John A. Hageman, Albert Monfort }   Deacons from do. { Daniel Huffman, Peter Wyckoff, John Lawson, Aris Vn. Derbelt }

Opened by prayer by the Revn'd George Barculo
Corn's R. Vn. Wyck Chosen President pro tem
& Samuel Luckey secretary
the Presedent stated that the object of this Meeting is to Investigate a Report in Circulation (to wit) that their Pasture George Barkuloe, not long since was Intoxicated, to which the said George Barkuloe Confessed he had been overtaken, and Requested to Continue his Labours among us for six months from the first of Aug't next to try if he Could Reconcile the Congregations and establish himself to his former standing, and that if he could not he would give up his Call—Which was agreed to by the Consistories and the said George Barkuloe—on Conditions that the said Consistories should assist him in Indeavouring to obtain a Reconciliation &c.

by order of the board
Corns. R. Vn. Wick, presd't pro-tem.
Sam'l Luckey, sect'y.

1810 Jan'y 24th the Consisories of the United Congregations of the Reformed Dutch Churches of New Hackensack & Hopewell met according to Agrement at the house of Rich'd C. Vn. Wyck in Fishkill town
Opened by prayer by the Revn'd G. Barkuloe

Elders from N. Hackensack { Samuel Luckey, Domenicus Monfort, John A. Hageman, Albert Monfort }   Deacons from do. { Aris Vn. Derbelt, Daniel Huffman, Peter Wycoff }

Elders from Hopewell { Cornelius Wiltsie, Theod's Adriance, Corn's R. Vn. Wyck }   Deacons from do. { Stephen Jackson, John Humphrey }

Cornelius R. Vn. Wyck Chosen sect'y
the object of the meeting was stated to be " to Assertain & determin Whether it would be most expedient that the Revn'd George Barkuloe should continue pasture of the United Congregations of New-Hackensack and Hopewell as heretofore or Whether the Connection which has subsisted between him and sd Congregations should be dissolved—this was Recognized to be the object of the meeting.
Different openions was entertain'd & advanc'd on that subject & as some of the members wished to Inform themselves more fully Concerning the disposition of the Congregations at large therefore—Resolved that this meeting stand adjourn'd till the first day of feb'y next to be holden at this place at 10 o'clock A. M.
Resolved that in the intervening time Each Elder belonging to the Congregations Accompanied by a Deacon, Visit his district or beat and essertain the mindes of the people therein Residing Relating to this subject.
Done in Consistory.
George Barkuloe, presd't.
sign'd Corn's. R. Vn. Wyck, sect'y.

1810 Feb'y 1st. the Joint Consistories of New-Hackensack and Hopewell met According to Adjournment
Opened as Usual by the Revn'd George Barkuloe

Elders from New Hackensack { Samuel Luckey, Domenicus Monfort, John A. Hageman, Albert Monfort }   Deacons from do. { Aris Vn. Derbelt, John Lawson, Peter Wycoff, Daniel Huffman }

Elders from Hopewell { Cornelius Wiltsie, Theod's Adriance, Corn's R. Vn. Wyck, Abm. Sleight }   Deacons from do. { Stephen Jackson, John Humphrey, Isaac Seacord }

Minutes of Consistory

The Minutes of the last meeting was read, and in pursuence of the last Resolution therein adopted, the Elders in their turn were Called to give such Information, as they had been able to Collect on the prosed subject.

After hearing from the Elders the opinion of the Congregations at large, it was found that a Majority of the Congregations thought that a seperation of the Connection between the said George Barkulo and the Congregations would be most Advisable and Beneficial for the prosperity of both parties—and as the Revn'd George Barkuloe stated that he was not prepared to give his proposels for a seperation therefore this Meeting stand Adjourn'd to the seventh day of feb'y Instant, at this place at 10 O'clock A. M.

George Barkuloe Pres't
sign'd Corn's. R. Vn. Wyck sect'y

1810 Wednesday 7th Feb'y Consistories met According to Adjournment
Opened by Prayer as Usual
Present the Revn't George Barkuloe

Elders from New Hackensack { Samuel Luckey / Domenicus Monfort / John A. Hageman / Albert Monfort }

Deacons from do. { Aris Vn. Derbelt / Peter Wycoff / Daniel Huffman }

Elders from Hopewell { Corn's. Wiltsie / Corn's R. Vn. Wyck / Thedr's Adriance / Abm. Sleight }

Deacons from do. { Stephen Jackson / John Humphrey / Isaac Seacord }

Abraham Sleight Chosen Pres't protem
& Corn's. R. Vn. Wyck sect'y

The Minutes of the former Meetings being Read, the preposels or prepositions of the Revn'd George Barkuloe up and Read in order and after Minute deleberation the preposels were Amended and Agreed to as follows—

The said Consistories Agree to pay the said George Barkuloe one hundred & twelve pounds ten shillings and twenty two loads of wood or an equevelent for the wood—and the Use of the personage as heretofore untill the first day of may 1811—and on the performance of which by the said Consistories, the said George Barkuloe Agree to give up his Call at the next meeting of the Clases of Poughkeepsie to be holden the 18th day of April next at Hopewell Church.

Abm. Sleight Pres't protem
Corn's R. Vn. Wyck sect'y

1810, Mc'h 13th At a Meeting of the United Consistories of New-Hackensack and Hopewell met by agreement at the house of Reubin Myers in the town of Fishkill
present
Revrn'd George Barkuloe

Elders from New Hackensack { Samuel Luckey / Domenicus Monfort / John A. Hageman }

Deacons from do. { Aris Vanderbilt / Peter Wycoff / Daniel Huffman / John Lawson }

Elders from Hopewell { Abraham Sleight / Corn's Wiltsie / Corn's R. Vn. Wyck }

Deacons from do. { John Humphrey / Isaac Secord }

The proceedings of the three former meetings were read and approved, Samuel Luckey, Esq'r. was Appointed as an Elder to attend Clases on wednesday the 18th of April at Hopewell Church. the Consistories as above have Adjourned to meet at Hopewell Church the 18th day of April next 1810 at 10 O'clock, A. M.

done in Consistory—George Barkuloe presd't
Sam'l Luckey sect'y

1810, Ap'l 7th
At a Meeting of the Consistory of the Reformed Dutch Church of New Hackensack held at the house of John Yates in the town of Fishkill

Elders present { Domenicus Monfort / Samuel Luckey / John A. Hageman / Albert Monfort }

Deacons present { Aris Vanderbelt / John Lawson / Peter Wycoff / Daniel Huffman }

Domenicus Monfort—Pres'd   Sam'l Luckey sect'y—

The object of the meeting was to examin our Receipts to find out how much we are in Arears with the Revn'd Barkuloe on salory
Setled with Domenicus Monfort on Salory List due 1st Aug't 1808, remains due $6.25
Setled with Albert Monfort and find he has p'd up
  William Suard not present
setled with Albert I. Monfort and find he has p'd up

The Reformed Dutch Church of New Hackensack

1809 setled with John A. Hageman on salory list due 1st Aug't 1809 p'd up recp't 49.50
setled with Albert Monfort on   do   do   p'd up as recp't 30.25
setled with Domen's Monfort the amont of list $43.50 p'd as recp't 30. 0
seled with Sam'l Luckey amount of his list $50.75 p'd as recp't 30. 0

amount of G. Barkuloe for 1808 is 187.50
rec'ts from G. Barkuloe to 1st Aug't 1808 amounts to $172.75
    balance due 14.75

amount of Salory up to 1st Aug't 1809 187.50
G. Barkulo recpts up to do   do 139.75
    balance due 47.75
    140.63

and the salory that will become due 1st may 1810 amounts to

which makes the whole sum due 1st may 1810 Amount to $203.13
And as there will be due 1st may 1810 to Mr. Barkuloe $203.13/100
Exclusive of wood it is to be setled by the Elders (in the following manner—
Samuel Luckey on list due 1st Aug't 1809 $20.75
Asses'd on list due 1st May 1810 40.66
    $61.41/100

Domenicus Monfort on List due 1st Aug't 1808 6.25
Asses'd on list due 1st Aug't 1809 13.50
Asses'd on list due 1st may 1810 40.66
    60.41

John A. Hageman on List due 1st may 1810 40.66
Albert Monfort on list due 1st may 1810 40.66
    $203.14

done in Consistory—Domenicus Monfort Pres'd
Sam'l Luckey, sect'y

1810, Ap'l 18th Agreable to Adjournment the United Consistories of New Hackensack and Hopewell met at the house Mr. Shear near the Church to Settle with the Revn'd George Barkuloe for his Salory up untill 1st may 1810 and to Receive from him his Call as pasture of s'd Congregations
Present at the Meeting the whole of Hackensack Consistory and the majorrity of Hopewell Consistory
When the said George Barkuloe by the Approbation of the Classes give up his Call and the above Consistories setled with him in full
The Consistory of New-Hackensack setled with him in the following manner
Samuel Luckey p'd on salory $61.40/100
and for arerages of wood 6.50
    $67.91

Domenicus Monfort p'd on Salory 60.41
John A. Hageman p'd on salory 40.66
Albert Monfort p'd on salory 40.66

and took recep't on salory & for wood to the same amount— $209.64

Annuel Report of the Church of New-Hackensack

Cences { Number of famolies — 105
Total of the Congregation not esertained
Members in communion pr. las report—
no previous report has been made

Communicants, Received } On Confession — 5
On Certificate — none
Dismissed — none
Suspended — none
Died — five
Total now in Communion — 51

Baptisms { Adults — 2
Infants — 21

Remarks embracing the internal state of Religion &c
    The state of this Congregation presents many things which are just Cause of regret and Humelation—Inniquity but two much abounds luke warmness, carelessness & Indifference in Matters of eternal moment prevail, & the ferver of love & spirit of devotion lan-

Minutes of Consistory

guish, neglect of famoly worship, want of attention to the Religeous instruction of Children & demastics, barreness & unfruitfulness under the means of Grace, worldly mindedness, & a want of Zeal in the cause of God are among the sins which prevail, & which make our harts sad We are not however warrented to mourn as those who have no hope there is still cause of gratitude & rejoyceing before the Lord, that he has not wholy forsaken us and written over us "Ichabod"—we have still reason to bless & praise God that here and there among us the cry is heard "what shall I do to be saved" and that of his Zion in this place it can still be said that this man and that man is born in her We have reason to bless and praise God, that still strengthens the things that remain, that he comforts the hearts of his people and enables them to press forward, towards the mark for the prize of the high Calling, which in Christ Jesus our Lord,

Sign'd George Barkulo V.D.M.

Dated 18th Ap'l 1810.

1810, Sept'm. 1st. At a Meeting of the Consistory of the Dutch Reformed Church of New-Hackensack held at the Church—Present at the Meeting

Elders { Domenicus Monfort / Samuel Luckey / Albert Monfort / John A. Hageman }   Deacons { Daniel Huffman / John Lawson }

Resolved that Samuel Luckey pay Casper Gonse out of the Money Arising from the Interest of the Legacy left by Peter Vn. Bunschoten Decs'd. which was Borrowed by William Suard last Year to Repair New-Hackensack Church.

Also that Domenicus Monfort & John A. Hageman are appointed Agents to buy metireals and hire work men, &c to shingle & paint the Remaind'r of the Church ruff &c.

Sam'l Luckey   sect'y

1810 Sept'r 27th The Consistory of the dutch Reformed Churchs of new Hackensack and Hopewell met at the house of Rich'd C. Vn. Wyck in fishkill town.

Present at the meeting

Elders from Hackensack { John A. Hageman / Samuel Luckey / Albert Monfort / Domenicus Monfort }   Deacons from do. { John Lawson / Aris Vn. Derbelt / Peter Wycoff / Daniel Huffman }

Elders from Hopewell { Theodorus Adriance / Cornelius Wiltsie / Cornelius R. Vn. Wyck }   Deacons from do. { Richard H. Osbourn / John Humphrey }

Corn's R. Vn. Wyck chosen presed't
Sam'l Luckey   sect'y

Samuel Luckey stated that the object of this meeting was to chuse a deligate to attend the next clases of Poughkeepsie, which is to be Holden in the town of Fishkill on the third Wednes day in octob'r next, and Cornelius R. Vn. Wyck was Chosen to attend s'd Clases and Rec'd his Crodentals.

done in Consistory
Corn's R. Vn. Wyck   presd't
Sam'l Luckey   sect'y

1811 Jan'y 22 at a meeting of the United Consistories of the Congregations of New-Hackensack & Hopewell at the house of Rich'd C. Vn. Wyck

Elders from Hackensack { Domenicus Monfort / Samuel Luckey / John A. Hageman / Albert Monfort }   Deacons from do. { Daniel Huffman / Peter Wycoff / Aris Van Derbelt / John Lawson }

Elders from Hopewell { Theodorus Adriance / Corn's Wiltse / Corn's R. Vn. Wyck / Ab'm. Sleight }   Deacons from do. { Stephen Jackson / John Humphrey }

Domenicus Monfort Chosen pres't & Stephen Jackson sect'y. Met for the purpose of taking some measures to make a call on the Revn'd John Walker or some other Minister to preach the Gosple to the said Congregations. Noted that the Revn'd John Walker be requested to preach again in each of the Churches & this meeting to Adjourn to ye 28th Inst. at this place at one o'clock P. M.—sign'd Domenicus Monfort Pres't

Stephen Jackson   sect'y

1811 Jan'y 28th Met persuent to Adjournment   Present at the Meeting

Elders from Hackensack { Domenicus Monfort / Samuel Luckey / John A. Hageman / Albert Monfort }   Deacons from do. { Daniel Huffman / Peter Wycoff / Aris Vn. Derbelt / John Lawson }

The Reformed Dutch Church of New Hackensack

Elders from Hopewell { Theodorus Adriance / Cornelius Wiltsie / Corn's R. Vn. Wyck / Ab'm. Sleight

Deacons from do. { John Humphrey / Stephen Jackson

Advisory Members from Hackensack { John Luyster, Albert I. Monfort, Andrew Rinders and James Vn. Keuren

Moved by Samuel Luckey & seconded Whether a superscription be put on foot for the Revn'd John Walker or Whether to send for the Revn'd Mr. Christy to preach for us first. the Resolution was Call'd and the state of the Votes as follows—

to put superscription on foot for Walker:
Domenicus Monfort
Samuel Luckey
John A. Hageman
Albert Monfort
Daniel Huffman
Peter Wycoff
Aris Vn. Derbelt
John Lawson
Theodorus Adriance
Corn's Wiltse
John Humphrey
Stephen Jackson

Voted to send for Mr. Christy:
Corn's R. Vn. Wyck
Ab'm. Sleight

Whereupon Resolved that a superscription be put on foot for the Revn'd John Walker & this Meeting Adjourn'd to 11th Feb'y next insueing at this place at ten o'clock A. M.

Domenicus Monfort—pres't
sign'd Stephen Jackson sect'y

1811 Feb'y 11th Met persuent to Adjournment. Present at the meeting

Elders from Hackensack { Domenicus Monfort / Samuel Luckey / John A. Hageman / Albert Monfort

Deacons from do. Daniel Huffman / Peter Wycoff / Aris Vn. Derbelt / John Lawson

Elders from Hopewell { Theodorus Adriance / Corn's Wiltse / Ab'm Sleight

Deacons from do. { John Humphrey / Stephen Jackson

Advisory Members from Hackensack { John Luyster, Tunis Vn. Bunschoten / William Suard, Casper Gonse, John Vn. Siclen

Advisory Members from Hopewell { Ram Adriance, John Storm / Tho's I. Storm

Moved and seconded to make a call on the Revn'd John Walker to be a stated menister for these United Congregations and to offer him the sum of three-Hundred & fifty Dollars Yearly and the Improvement of the personage—Each Congregation to have half of the service.

Also Agreed that the personage be transfered to John Storm and Tunis Vn. Bunschoten in trust—and this meeting Adjourn'd to the 19th Instn't at this place at one Oclock P. M.

Domenicus Monfort pres't
Sign'd Stephen Jackson sect'y

1811 Feb'y 19th Met pursuent to Adjournment. members present

Elders from Hackensack { Domenicus Monfort / Samuel Luckey / John A. Hageman / Albert Monfort

Deacons from do. { Daniel Huffman / Peter Wycoff / Aris Vn. Derbelt / John Lawson

Elders from Hopewell { Theodorus Adriance / Corn's Wiltse / Corn's R. Vn. Wyck

Deacons from do. { John Humphrey / Stephen Jackson

Moved and seconded that the Revn'd John Walker be Requested to preach in these two Congregations Alternatively untill the Classis meet.

Also Voted that Elder Samuel Luckey Represent the two Congregations at the next meeting of the Classes of Poughkeepsie which will be on the 17th Ap'l next Ensueing and this meetnig Adjourn'd to 17th Ap'l next at the house of John Yates in fishkill town at 9 oclock A. M.

N.B. Sam'l Luckey Requested to write the Call.

1811 April 17th persuent to Adjournment Consistories met with the Revn'd Corn's C. Cuyler—Members present at the meeting (to wit)

Minutes of Consistory

The Revn'd Corn's C. Cuyler V.D.M. Domenicus Monfort, Samuel Luckey, John A. Hageman, Albert Monfort, Theodorus Adriance, Cornelius Wiltse, Cornelius R. Vn. Wyck, Elders Daniel Huffman, Peter Wycoff, Aris Vn. Derbelt, John Lawson, John Humphrey and Stephen Jackson. The Meeting Opened by prayer by Revn'd C. C. Cuyler
 the Elder John A. Hageman was Chosen Presd't protem when the Consistory of New-Hackensack was Unanimous Agreed to make a call on the Revn'd John Walker and the Consistory of Hopewell Divided Resolved that the prosedings of this meeting be Laid befor the seperate meetings of the Consistory of New Hackensack and Hopewell

          Sign'd John A. Hageman pres't
 Closed with prayer.

1811 April 17th. At a seperate meeting of the Consistory of the Congregation of the Dutch Reformed Church of New Hackensack held at the house of John Yates. Present

Elders present { Domenicus Monfort, Samuel Luckey, John A. Hageman, Albert Monfort } Deacons present { Daniel Huffman, Peter Wycoff, John Lawson }

Whereas the United Consistories of New Hackensack and Hopewell at their joint meeting this day resolved to present a Call on the Candidate John Walker and to offer him the sum of three hundred and fifty dollars a Year and the Use and Improvement of the parsonage Resolved that we the Elders and Deacons of the Congregation of New Hackensack do hereby approve of the said Resolution Each Congregation to pay equal half of the salory and each to have half of the service as long as sd. Walker shall Continue our Joint Minister. Resolved that Elder John A. Hageman be Presedent pro tem and be hereby empowered and Instructed in our behalf to subscribe said Call and afix the seal of our Corperation in Conjunction with the Consistory of hopewell.

         sign'd John A. Hageman, pres't.
         Daniel Huffman, sect'y.

N.B. the above Call was moderated by the Revn'd Corns. C. Cuyler and Laid before the Classes by Elder Sam'l Luckey and Rejected on Acc't of Hopewell Consistory not being Agreed.

         Sam'l Luckey, sect'y.

Annuel Report of the Church of New-Hackensack

Cences: Number of famolies	105
Total of the Congregation not ecrtained	
Communicants: Members in Communion pr. las report	51
Received: On Confession	none
On Certificate	none
Dismissed by Certificate	3
Suspended	none
Died	none
Total in Communion	48
Baptisms: Adults	none
Infants	12

Dated 17th April 1811
Annual Report of the Church of New Hackensack continued

    Remarks embracing the Internal state of Religion, &c.
 The state of this Congregation presents many things which are just cause of mourning and Humelation the want of a stated Minister to preach the Gospel and administer the sacrements with sundry disappointments in endeavoring to Obtain one. In Consequence Innequity doth but too much abound in the Violation of the holy sabeth, lukewarmness, Carlessness & Indifference in matters of Eternal moment prevails, and the fervour of love and sperit of devotion in some measure languish Neglect of famoly worship, the want of Attention to the Religious Instruction of Children & demostices by Catechiseing in famolies & schools of tuetion—wordly mindedness & want of Zeal in the Cause of God are among the sins which prevail—for which we have Just reason to mourn,—We are not however warrented to mourn as those who have no hope, there is still cause to hope & Rejoice before the Lord, that he has not wholy forsaken us, We have still reason to bless and praise God, that there is still some among us that are zelious to promote the cause of religion in this place, that he still strengthens and Comforts the hearts of his people, and enables them to press forward to the mark of the prize and high Calling which is in Christ Jesus our Lord.
        sign'd Sam'l Luckey one of the Elders
Dated the 17th April 1811.

The Reformed Dutch Church of New Hackensack

1811, June 1st the Consistory of the Dutch Reformed Church of New-Hackensack met at the Church   Present at the meeting
          the Revn'd Corn's C. Cuylor

Elders { Samuel Luckey / Domenicus Monfort / Albert Monfort / John A. Hageman }   Deacons { Daniel Huffman / Aris Van Derbelt / John Lawson }

the Meeting was opened with prayer by the Revn'd C. C. Cuylor when Sam'l Luckey was chosen sect'y and Hannah Dubois wife of Barnet P. Van Kleeck and Susan Monfort wife of Albert Monfort was examined and ordered to be published to the Congregation and taken in full Communion—the meeting closed with prayer.
          sign'd Corn's. C. Cuylor Pres't P. M.
                   Sam'l Luckey   sect'y

1811, Aug't 5th At a meeting of the Consistory of the Reformed Dutch Church of New-Hackensack met at the Church, where a number of the Congregation by previous notice Attended to take into Consideration the expedency & propriety of making a call on the Revn'd Wilhelemus Elting to be their stated Menister in Conjunction with their sister Congregation of Hope well —Present Members at the meeting
          The Redn'd Eliphelet Price who preach'd a sermon by Request

Elders { Domenicus Monfort / John A. Hageman / Albert Monfort / Samuel Luckey }   Deacons { Aris Van Derbelt / Daniel Huffman / Peter Wycoff }

After sermon the object of the Meeting was taken up and discused when there was but one Openion on the subject all deemed it practicable Resolved that in order to take measures for the execution of this object the above Consistory agree to meet with the Consistory of Hopewell Congregation on monday the 12th Instant at one oclock P. M. at the house of John Robinsons in fishkill town to persue farther Measures on the subject.
          Closed by prayer by the Renv'd Eliphelet Price
                              Sign'd Sam Luckey—sect'y

1811 Aug't 12th. At a Meeting of the United Consistories of the Reformed Dutch Congregations of Hopewell and New-Hackensack at the house of John Robinson in the town of Fishkill — present at the meeting —

Elders from Hopewell { Corn's R. Vn. Wyck / Theod's Adriance / Ab'm Sleight / Corn's Wiltse }   Deacons from do. { Steph'n Jackson / Jno. Humphrey }

Elders from Hackensack { Domenicus Monfort / Samuel Luckey / John A. Hageman / Albert Monfort }   Deacons from do. { Peter Wycoff / Daniel Huffman / Aris Van Derbelt }

Corn's R. Vn. Wyck Chosen Chairman & Sam'l Luckey secretary
Mr. Corn's Wiltse reported that According to a previous notice the Consistories have met to take into Consideration the propriety of opening a superscription to make a call on the Revn'd Wilhelemus Elting to be their stated Menister,—after consulting at some length the members present Unanmously agree that a superscription be opened for the above purpose— Whereupon Resolved that these Consistories meet at this place on tuesday the 22nd Instant at 1 Oclock P. M. and that Corn's Wiltse Invite the Revn'd Corn's D. Westbrook to meet as Moderator and Sam'l Luckey is Requested to write said Call.
          Sign'd Corn's R. Van Wyck Pres't
                   Sam'l Luckey   sect'y

1811 Aug't 22nd According to agreement the United Consistories of Hopewell and New Hackensack met at the house of John Yates in Fishkill Town
          Present at the Meeting Revn'd C. C. Cuylor

Elders from Hopewell { Corn's R. Vn. Wyck / Theodorus Adriance / Abraham Sleight / Cornelius Wiltse }   Deacons from do { Stephen Jackson / John Humphrey / Rich'd H. Osbourn }

Elders from Hackensack { Domenicus Monfort / John A. Hageman / Samuel Luckey / Albert Monfort }   Deacons from do. { Peter Wycoff / John Lawson / Aris Vn. Derbelt / Daniel Huffman }

          Opened with prayer by the Revn'd C. C. Cuylor moderator
          aand Samuel Luckey Chosen secretary

Minutes of Consistory

the Revn'd Corn's C. Cuylor stated the object of this meeting was to make a Call on the Revn'd Wilhelemus Elting to be their stated Menister Each Congregation to Equel half of salory & Each to have Equl shear of the Service which was Unanimously Agreed to and Cornelius R. Vn. Wyck was Chosen to sign the Call in behalf of Hopewell & Samuel Luckey was Chosen to sign the Call in behalf of New-Hackensack—and Ab'm Sleight was appointed to present s'd Call to the said Wilhelemus Elting—and Corn's Wiltse was Chosen to attend the next Classes of poughkeepsie to be holden 3rd Wednesday in Octob'r next in Mr. Vaders Congregation— Also Corn's R. Vn. Wyck & Theodorus Adriance on behalf of Hopewell and Samuel Luckey and John A. Hageman on behalf of Hackensack was chosen a Committee to Arainge and book some former Resolves
    Closed by prayer by the Revn'd C. C. Cuylor, V.D.M.
                                      Sign'd Sam'l Luckey—Sect'y
N.B. Mr. Elting did not Except the Call—Amt of Call $600—use of personage & 15 loads wood

1811 Octob'r 22nd   At a Meeting of the Consistory of New-Hackensack Congregation at the of John Yates in Fishkill Town—Present at the meeting

Elders	Domenicus Monfort Albert Monfort Samuel Luckey John A. Hageman	Deacons	Peter Wycoff Aris Vn. Derbelt John Lawson Daniel Huffman

John a Hageman was Chosen Chearman and Samuel Luckey secretary
Resolved that Samuel Luckey and Aris Van Derbelt be a Committee to buy meterials, hire workmen &c to Repair paint &c the frunt of New Hackensack Church to be paid out of the money Arising from the Interest of the Money Left by Peter Vn. Bunschoten Decs'd
    done in Consistory   sign'd John A. Hageman Pres't
                                Sam'l Luckey   sect'y

1811 Octob'r 30th   at a meeting of the United Consistories of the Congregations of New-Hackensack and Hopewell at the house of John Robinson in the town of Fishkill Convened —members present at the meeting

Elders from Hackensack	Domenicus Monfort Samuel Luckey Albert Monfort John A. Hageman	Deacons from do.	John Lawson Daniel Huffman Aris Vn. Derbelt Peter Wycoff
Elders from Hopewell	Corn's Wiltse Theodorus Adriance Corn's R. Vn. Wyck	Deacons from do.	Rich'd Osbourn Isaac Seacord John Humphrey

Corn's R. Vn. Wyck was chosen Chearman and Samuel Luckey secretary
When Corn's R. Vn. Wyck stated that the object of this meeting was to chuse a Committee to wait on the Revn'd George Barkuloe to agree with him to give up the possession of the personage House and Lot for the Use of the Revn'd Wilhelemus Elting or any other Menister that we should obtain. Whereupon Cornelius Wiltse & Corn's R. Vn. Wyck chosen from Hopewell and Samuel Luckey & Aris Van Derbelt from New Hackensack and were Instructed to make the best bargain with the said G. Barkulo they Could According to their own Judgment.
                                    sign'd Corn's R. Vn. Wyck Pres't
    done in Consistory   Sam'l Luckey   sect'y

1811 Octob'r 30th   Coppy of Article of Agreemt &c
Article of Agreement made and Concluded on this thirtyeth day of Octob'r one thousand Eight Hundred and eleven Between George Barkulo of the town of Fishkill in the County of Dutchess and state of new-York of the first part and Cornelius R. Van Wyck, Cornelius Wiltse, Aris Van Derbelt and Samuel Luckey, a committee from the United Consistories of new-Hackensack and Hopewell Congregations of the second part, Agreeth as follows that the said party of the first part, Agree to leave the personage house and lot within three weeks notice if the said Congregations should obtain the Revn'd Wilhelemus Elting or any other Menister of a famoly to be their stated Menister, also that the said party of the first will Yeald up and Give possession of said house and personage on the first day of April next—on fulfilment of the above Article the parties of the second part Agree to free the party of the first part from paying any Rent for the time that the party of the first part shall have ocupied the said house and personage in Witness whereof the parties above mentioned have set their hands and afixed their seals the day and Year above mentioned

a true coppy from the original	George Barkulo - - - - -	0
	Corn's R. Vn. Wyck - - - - -	0
	Corn's Wiltse - - - - -	0
	Aris Van Derbelt - - - - -	0
Witness'd by Jacobus I. Swartwout	Sam'l Luckey - - - - -	0

                                      and sign'd

The Reformed Dutch Church of New Hackensack

1811 Decmb'r 17th at a Meeting of the United Consistories of the Dutch Reformed Congregations of Hopewell and New Hackensack Convenied at the house of the Widow Robinsons in the town of Fishkill

members present at the meeting

Elders from Hopewell { Corn's R. Vn. Wyck / Theodorus Adriance / Ab'm Sleight / Corn's Wiltse }   Deacons from do. { none

Elders from Hackensack { Sam'l Luckey / John A. Hageman / Domenicus Monfort }   Deacons from do. { John Lawson / Daniel Huffman / Aris Van Derbelt / Peter Wycoff

Cornelius R. Van Wyck chosen presedn't and Sam'l Luckey sect'y
Theodorus Adriance stated the object of the meeting Expediency of Circulating a superscription to make a call on the Revn'd Henry Polhamus to be our stated Menister after Consulting at some length on the subject, it was agreed that the superscription be postponed and Mr. Polhamus Invited to preach one more in each Church as many of the Congregations had not heard him. and Cornelius R. Van Wyck and Daniel Huffman be appointed a committee to draft a Letter and send it to the said Henry Polhamus on the subject—

sign'd   Corn's R. Vn. Wyck   Presd't
     done in Consistory   Sam'l Luckey   sect'y
N.B. the Letter was miscarried.

1812 Feb'y 29th At a Meeting of the United Consistories of the Congregations of Hopewell and New Hackensack at the house of the Widow Robinsons

members present at the meeting

Elders from Hopewell { Theodorus Adriance / Abraham Shear / John Storm }   Deacons from do. { Stephen Jackson / Thomas I. Storm / Jeromus Rapelye / Rich'd H. Osbourn

Elders from Hackensack { Samuel Luckey / Albert Monfort }   Deacons from do. { Peter Wycoff / John Lawson / Aris Van Derbelt

Samuel Luckey was chosen pres't and John Storm sect'y
Resolved Unanimously that Samuel Luckey and John Storm be a Committee to wait on the Revn'd Mr. Price in order to Assertain from him whether a Settlement in these two United Congregations in Conjunction with the Church at the point would meet his approbation, and report the Result as soon as Convenient.

     done in Consistory   sign'd   Sam'l Luckey   presd't
                                         John Storm   sect'y
N.B. Elder Domenicus Monfort appointed to attend next Clases

1812 Ap'r 9th At a meeting of the Consistory of the Reformed Dutch Congregation of New Hackensack at the house of John Yates in Fishkill town

members present at the meeting

Elders { John A. Hageman / Sam'l Luckey / Domenicus Monfort }   Deacons { John Lawson / Daniel Huffman / Aris Van Derbelt

Advisory Members William Suard and Casper Gonse
Samuel Luckey stated that the object of this meeting is to devise ways and means to procure money to pay off a Bond Given to Casper Gonse for money to repair the Church—remains due about one hundred and twenty Dollars.
Resolved that Domenicus Monfort and Samuel Luckey to be a Committee to borrow said sum of one hundred and twenty Dollars and pay off s'd Bond and that this Consistory promise to pay or Cause to be paid unto the said Monfort & Luckey Each one his equel shear of said sum if it should not be obtained otherwise to discharge the money borrowed

done in Consistory in presence of }   sign'd   Domenicus Monfort   pres't
Wm. Suard & Casper Gonse   Sam'l Luckey   sect'y

Annual Report of the Church of New Hackensack

Cences:
     Number of famolies one hundred & five
     Total of the Congregation not esertained

Communicants:
     Members in Communion pr. last report—   47
     Received: On Confession   two

Minutes of Consistory

On Certificate	none
suspended	none
Died	one
Total now in Communion	48
Dismissed by Certificate	one
Baptisms:	
Adults	none
Infants	sixteen

Dated 18th April 1812
Remarks Embraceing the Internal state of Religion—Bro't over—
The state of this Congregation presents many things for which we have just cause to mourn & Lement, the want of a stated Minister to preach the Gospel and Administer the Sacrements, with sundry disappointments in Endeavouring to Obtain one. In Consequence innequity doth but to much abound in the Violation of the Holy Sabeth, Lukewarmness, Carelessness & Indifference in matters of eternal moment prevails, and the fervour of Love & sperit of Devotion in some measure languish Neglect of famoly worship, the want of attention to the Relegious Instruction of Children and Domesticks in famolies and Schols of tuetion, and many other worldly mindedness prevails amongst us for for which Cause we have Reason to mourn. We are not however warrented to mourn as those who have no hope there is still cause of praise and rejoiceing before the Lord that he has not wholy forsaken us. We have still reason to bless and praise God that there is still cause of praise & rejoising before the Lord, that he has not wholy forsaken us. We have still reason to bless and praise God, that there is still some among that are religious and strive to premote the cause of Christ in this place and that the Lord still Comforts the hearts of his people and Enables them to press forward to the mark of the prise of the high calling which is in Christ Jesus our Lord
Dated New. Hackensack 18th Ap'l. 1812) sign'd Domenicus Monfort one of the Elders
record'd by Sam'l Luckey sect'y

1812 Ap'l 23rd at a Meeting of the United Consistories of Hopewell and New-Hackensack at the house of the Widow Robinsons on thursday
When John A. Hageman was chosen Chearman & John Storm Secretary
Present at the meeting

Elders from Hopewell	Theodorus Adriance Abraham Shear Abraham Sleight John Storm	Deacons from do.	Richard H. Osbourn Stephen Jackson Jeromus Rapleje Thomas I. Storm
Elders from N. Hackensack	Domenicus Monfort Samuel Luckey John A. Hageman	Deacons from do.	Daniel Huffman John Lawson

The Object of the meeting was stated by Mr. Huffman to take into Consideration the propriety of selling the personage belonging to the United Congregations of Hopewell and New-Hackensack
Resolved Unanimously that said Personage be advertised for sale and and possession to be given on the first of May 1813
Resolved Unanimously that said personage shall not be ocopied at present after Mr. Barkuloe's Removel
Resolved Unanimously that a Committee be appointed to wait on the Reverend Henry Polhemus to Asertain from him whether he would except a Call from the Congregations of Hopewell & New Hackensack and that John Storm be said Committee
sign'd John A. Hageman presd't
John Storm sect'y

1812 May 21st At a Meeting of the United Consistories of Hopewell & New-Hackensack at the house of John Yates for the purpose of making a call on the Revn'd Henry Polhamus of New Jersey, when the Revn'd C. C. Cuylor presided as Moderator and John Storm was chosen sect'y
Members Present—the Revn'd Corn's C. Cuyler

Elders from Hopewell	Abraham Shear Abraham Sleight John Storm	Deacons from do.	Thomas I. Storm Jeromus Rapleje
Elders from N. Hackensack	Domenicus Monfort John A. Hageman Samuel Luckey	Deacons from do.	Daniel Huffman John Lawson

Opened with prayer by the Revn'd C. C. Cuylor
When Abraham Sleight was chosen Presedent of the Consistory of Hopewell and Samuel Luckey Presedent of the Consistory of New Hackensack, whome respectively signed the

The Reformed Dutch Church of New Hackensack

Call in behalf of said Consistories—then Adjourned to meet on wednesday the 3rd day of June next at the house of the widow Robinson at one oclock P. M.

                                              Corn's C. Cuylor   moderator
                                              John Storm   Sect'y

1812 July 19th At a meeting of the Consistory of the Congregation of New-Hackensack at the Church Present at the Meeting
The Revn'd Corn's D. Westbrook   Opened with Prayer

Elders { Domenicus Monfort, Albert Monfort, John A. Hageman, Samuel Luckey }
Deacons { Daniel Huffman, Peter Wycoff, John Lawson }

The Object of the Meeting was to examine and Receive members in Communion Miss Ann Dates made open Confession of her faith and being found able to Give a Reason of the hope that was in her was Admitted to the Communion of the Church of Christ the meeting was closed with prayer
                done in Consistory)   By Corn's D. Westbrook pres'd protem
                                                                               Sam'l Luckey   sect'y

1812 Aug't 1st satturday At a meeting of the United Consistories New-Hackensack & Hopewell at the house of Widow Robinson when Samuel Luckey was chosen Chearman & John Storm sect'y
                                  present at the meeting

Elders from N. Hackensack { Samuel Luckey, Domenicus Monfort, Elbert Monfort, John A. Hageman }
Deacons { Peter Wycoff, Dan'l Huffman }

Elders from Hopewell { Theod's Adriance, Ab'm Shear, John Storm }
Deacon { Rich'd H. Osbourn }

The object of the meeting was stated by Samuel Luckey to take the Voice of the Consistories Respecting making a Call on Thomas Dewit a Candidate for the Menistry Resolved Unanimously that we put a subscription on foot Immediately for the above mentioned purpose Adjourned to meet again at this place on thursday the 13th Instant at 2 oclock P. M.
done in Consistory   sign'd { Sam'l Luckey Chearman, John Storm sect'y }

1812 Thursday 13th Aug't At a meeting agreeable to Adjournment when Samuel Luckey was again Chosen Presd't and John Storm sct'y. Members present

Elders from Hackensack { Samuel Luckey, Domenicus Monfort, Elbert Monfort, John A. Hageman }
Deacons from do. { Aris Vanderbelt, Daniel Huffman, John Lawson }

Elders from Hopewell { Theod's Adriance, John Storm, Abraham Sleight, Abraham Shear }
Deacons from do. { Stephen Jackson, Tho's I. Storm, Jeromus Rapleje, Rich'd H. Osbourn }

Resolved Unanimously that we make a call on the Revn'd Thomas Duwit, and that each Congregation raise the sum of three hundred & sixty Dollars making in the whole seven hundred & twenty Dls. and that we meet again at the house of the Widow Robinsons on the 14th Instant at one oclock P. M. to make said call & that the Revn'd Corn's D. Westbrook be Invited to preside as Moderator. Adjourned.
                done in Consistory   sign'd   Sam'l Luckey presd't
                                                                                   John Storm   Sect'y

1812 friday 14th Aug't According to Adjournment the Combined Consistories of New Hackensack & Hopewell met at the house of the Widow Robinsons in fishkill town
                                 Present at the meeting
                             the Revn'd Cornelius D. Westbrook

Elders from N. Hackensack { Samuel Luckey, Domenicus Monfort, Albert Monfort, John A. Hageman }
Deacons from do. { John Lawson, Peter Wycoff, Daniel Huffman, Aris Vanderbelt }

Elders from Hopewell { Theodorus Adriance, John Storm, Abraham Sleight, Abraham Shear }
Deacons from do. { Rich'd H. Osbourn, Tho's I. Storm, Jeromus Rapleje }

Minutes of Consistory

the meeting was Open'd with prayer by the Revn'd Corn's D. Westbrook. When the Elder Samuel Luckey was Appointed presed't protem
Whereas the United Consistories of New-Hackensack & Hopewell are well pleased with the piety & menisteriel talents & Acquirments of the Candidate Thomas Dewit therefore Resolved that we make out a call to the said Dewit and that we offer him in said call the Annual sum of seven hundred & twenty Dollars to be our Joint Menister. Resolved that this Joint Resolution be Laid before the Consistories of New-Hackensack & Hopewell in their seperate meetings for their seperate Approbation and execution Closed with prayer.
   done in Consistory   sign'd Sam'l Luckey pres'd Prot'm
Resolved that Daniel Huffman
lay s'd Call before s'd Tho's Dewit

1812 friday 14th Aug't At a meeting of the Consistory of New Hackensack held at the house of the widow Robinson in the town of fishkill
          present at the meeting

Elders { Domenicus Monfort / Albert Monfort / John A. Hageman / Samuel Luckey } Deacons { Aris Vanderbelt / John Lawson / Daniel Huffman / Peter Wycoff }

the Meeting was Opened with prayer & Samuel Luckey Chosen pres'd prot'm
Whereas the Combined Consistories of New Hackensack & Hopewell at their Joint meeting this day have Resolved to present a Call to the Candidate Thomas Dewit and to offer him in said call the sum of seven hundred & twenty Dollars therefore Resolved that we the Elders & Deacons of the Congregation of New Hackensack do heartily approve of said resolution and do in Consideration of one half of the pastoriel services promise to pay the Annuel sum of three hundred & sixty Dollars to said Dewit as long as he shall be our Joint Menister
Resolved that our presedent protem the Elder Samuel Luckey be hereby empowered & instructed in our name & behalf to subscribe said call and thereto to affix the seal of our Corperation in Conjunction with the Consistory of Hopewell Congregation
   Closed with prayer by the Revn'd Corn's D. Westbrook moderator
             sign'd Sam'l Luckey presd't protem
turn over to the Coppy of the Call
  To Thomas Dewitt Sac. Sanc. Min. Candidato Grace Mercy and Peace from God, our father, and Jesus Christ our Lord.
Whereas the Churches of Christ in the town of Fishkill known by the name of the combined congregations of New Hackensack & Hopewell are at present distitute of the stated preaching of the word, and the regular administration of the ordinances, and are desirous of obtaining the means of grace which God hath appointed for the salvation of sinners throug Jesus Christ his son, and
Whereas the said Churches are well sattisfied of the piety, Gifts and Munisterial qualifications of you Thomas Dewitt, and have a good hope that your labours in the Gospel will be attended with a blessing,—therefore, we the Elders, and Deacons of the combined Congregations of New Hackensack, and Hopewell have resolved to call, and we hereby solemnly and in the fear of the Lord do Call you the said Thomas Dewitt to be the pastor and teacher of our combined Congregations—to preach the word in truth, and faithfulness—to Administer the Holy sacraments agreably to the Institution of Christ—to Maintain Christian discipline—to edify the Congregations, and especially the youth by Catecheticas instruction and as a faithfull servant of Jesus Christ to fulfill the whole work of Gospel Menistry agreably to the word of God, and Constitution of our Reformed Dutch Church established in the National synod held at Dordrecht in 1618 and 1619 and explained by the Ecclesiastical Judicatory under which we stand, and to which you Accepting this call must with us Remain subordinate in fulfilling the ordenary duties of your ministry—it is expressly stipulated that besides preaching from such texts of scripture as You may Judge proper to select for our Instructions, You also explain a portion of the Heidelburgh Catechism in the Afternoon of those Lord's days of that section of the Year in which you shall preach two sermons each Lords day agreably to the established order of the Reformed Dutch Church, and that you further conform in Rendering all that publick service which is Usual, and has been in constant practice in our Congregations; the particular service which shall be required of you is to preach every Lord's day in the english Language, that is one sermon every Lord's day from the first of October to the first day of April—and two sermons from the first day of April to the first day of October on the Lord's day—to administer the Lord's supper at least four times every year—and to pay pastoriel visits to the members of said Congregations as often and at such times as shall by you and the Consistory be demed practicable and proper, all which service you shall perform in such a manner, and so devide between the said two Congregations as to give each as nearly as practicable the Moiety of the same in an Alternate succession.
To encourage you in the discharge of the duties of your Important office We in the name

The Reformed Dutch Church of New Hackensack

of the Churches which we represent all proper Attention, love, and obedience in the Lord, and to free you from worldly cares, and Avocations while you are speritual blessings to use. We the Elders and Deacons of the Combined Congregations of New-Hackensack and Hopewell do Jointly promise and Oblige our selves to pay unto you the said Thomas Dewit the sum of Seven hundred and twenty Dollars Yearly and every year so long as you shall continue our Minester in manner following that is to say we the Elders and Deacons of the Congregation of New Hackensack do promise & Oblige ourselves & our successors to pay unto you the sum of three Hundred & sixty dollars Yearly and every year —and We the Elders and Deacons of Congregation of Hopewell do promise and Oblige ourselves and our successors to pay unto You the sum of Three Hundred and sixty Dollars Yearly and every year.
Further more in order to Afford yo suitable time to Visit your friends and to give you all Necessary recreation and relaxation from Your Arduous labours we hereby give four free sabbaths,—For the faithful performance of all these stepulations, and of all the Christian duties we owe to our faithful pasture we bind ourselves and our successors firmly by these presents—The Lord incline Your heart to a cheerfull Accepance of this Call, and send you to us in the fulness of the blessing of the gospel of Christ—Done in joint meeting of the Consistories of New Hackensack & Hopewell, and also by the Consent of each Consistory seperately—In testamony whereof the Consistories of New-Hackensack & Hopewell have hereunto subscribed thro their Respective presedents and affixed the Respective seals of their Corperations this fourteenth day of August in the Year of our blessed Lord one thousand Eight hundred & twelve—1812.

Done in the presence and under the superentendance of Corn's D. Westbrook, V.D.M.
{ By order and in behalf of the Consistory of New Hackensack
Sam'l Luckey Pres't. X seal
By order and in behalf of the Consistory of Hopewell
Theodorus Adriance pres't X seal }

— A True Coppy —
The above Call Approv'd by the Classes of Poughkeepsie

1812 Dec'r 5th the Consistory of the Church of New Hackensack met at the house of John Yates   Present
the Revn'd Tho's Dewitt pasture

Elders { Samuel Luckey
John A. Hageman }   Deacons { Daniel Huffman
Peter Wycoff }

Opened with prayer.
Resolved that the next communion season be on the Last sabeth in January and that in the mean time the Congregation be Visited as far as is practicable.
After some conversation on the subject of Baptism it was Resolved that in as much as the General synod have not recognized the principel that no children but those one of whose parents at least is a member in full communion with the Church should be baptized, it would be Imprudent and unadvisable to act upon such Ground. Resolved that as baptism Includes the solomn profession of faith in a Covenant God on the part of the parents, all those who present their Children shall be interragated concerning their knowledge of the grounds of salvation—that the nature of the Baptismal vow which can only be made in faith, be explained—and that they be exorted to regard the pledge which they give thereby of seperating from sin—Obeying all the Commands of Christ and walking in felowship with the Church.
Resolved that all those who are fully Cremonal in their lives and Conversation be debared from offering their Children in baptism.
Resolved that this subject be considered more fully at another meeting of Consistory.
Resolved that Impressed with the importance of the exercise and feeling the Necessaty of endeavouring to raise members out of lukewarmness and to excite sinners to repentance—an attempt be made to Institute meetings for social prayer on sunday evening—that the Congregation be devided into two districts for the purpose one comprising the beat of Samuel Luckey & Albert Monfort and the other the beats of John A. Hageman & Domenicus Monfort further arrangements to be made by agreement.
Resolved that consistory adjourn to meet again at this place on Monday the 21st Ins't at one oclock P. M.
Closed with prayer   Attest Thomas Dewitt

1812 Dec'r 21st   According to Adjournm't Consistory met at the house of John Yates
Present Revn'd Thomas Dewitt

Elders { Domenicus Monfort
John A. Hageman
Samuel Luckey
Albert Monfort }   Deacons { Aris Vanderbelt
Peter Wycoff
John Lawson
Daniel Huffman }

Opened with prayer
The Resolutions respecting baptism passed at a preceeding meeting were Read in full meeting and Unanimously Adopted.

Minutes of Consistory

Resolved that catechising be commenced in the spring and that the Congregation be devided into three districts one on the eastern part of the Congregation one on the west side of Wappings Creek and one on the south.
Resolved that Domenicus Monfort together with Mr. Dewitt wait upon John Cornell and Clement Cornwell and admonish with Respect to their life and conversation.
    Closed with prayer.   Attest Thomas Dewitt

1813 Feb'y 14th the following persons were elected officers in the Church at New Hackensack (as follows)

Elders
- John Luyster in the room of John A. Hageman Deceased
- Tunis Vn. Bunschoten in the place of Domenicus Monfort
- William Suard on the place of Albert Monfort

Deacons
- Abraham L. Dates in place of Aris Vanderbelt
- James Vn. Keuren in place of Peter Wycoff

and the above persons were Ordained to their respective offices the Sabeth day following.

1813 feb'y 18th The Consistory (old and new members) met at the house of William Suard
present
Thomas Dewitt

Elders
- Samuel Luckey
- John Luyster
- Tunis Vn. Bunschoten
- William Suard

Deacons
- Daniel Huffman
- John Lawson
- Aris Vanderbelt
- Peter Wycoff
- James Vn. Keuren

The balance remaining in the poor Chest were $17. 15/100 and James Vn. Keuren was appointed to take Charge of the poor Chest and $16 5/100 of the poor money Appropriated to defraying the Ordenation expences, leaving a balance of $1 10/100 in s'd Chest. the house belonging to the Church was rented to Derick Luyster for one Year from the experation of the present lease for which he is to take Charge of the Church he is to open and close the door and windows build fires seasonably in said Church on days of worshop when the weather is Cold to Clean and sand the Church four times a Year and attend to they burying Ground.
Resolved that such persons who have for some time Absented themselves from the Lords supper be waited on by Mr Dewitt with the Elder of their Respective bounds, be requested to give their reasons and if these be Unsatisfactory that they be admonished
Resolved that the Lord's supper be Administered three times a Year (Viz) the last Sabeths in January, May & september and that the Consistory meet on the first tuesday of each of said Months.
    Closed with prayer   Attest Thomas Dewitt

May 21 1813 Consistory met at the Church   Present
the Revn'd Thomas Dewitt Pasture

Elders
- William Suard
- John Luyster
- Samuel Luckey
- Tunis Vn. Bunschoten

Deacons
- Daniel Huffman
- Abraham L. Dates
- James Vn. Keuren

The payment for the Personage was made the first may Instant and the quoto or shear for Hackensack being seven hundred and fifty Dollors was placed in the hand of Samuel Luckey treasurer who is Authorized to pay exesting debts and put the remainder at Interest as soon as Convenent.
    done in Consistory   Attest'd Thomas Duwitt

Sept'r 7th 1813 Consistory met at the Church   Present at the meeting
the Reverend Thomas Dewitt pasture

Elders
- William Suard
- Samuel Luckey

Deacons
- James Vn. Keuren
- Abraham L. Dates

Opened with prayer
Resolved that John Cornell be hereby suspended from the previledges of the Christian Church Untill he furnish evidences of repentence and reformation.
Resolved that the Elder John Luyster and decon James Vn. Keuren wait upon Harman Jewell & wife & Admonish them for Unchristian Conduct, & suspend them from Church previledges if they deem it expedient.
Closed with prayer.
    done in Consistory   Attested Tho's Duwitt
Sam'l Luckey   sect'y

The Reformed Dutch Church of New Hackensack

Statistical Return of the Congregation of New Hackensack Sept'r 1813

No. of famolies	105
total of Congre'n	680
in Comm'n last rep't	48
Recv'd on certific	9
since certifct	1
recv'd on conf's	9
suspend'd	1
disch'd	0
suspend'd	1
Recv'd on Certifi	1
total	55
Baptism Inf't	12
adults	2

The causis which tended for a time past to distract this Congregation and Consequently to Retard its spiritual growth have disappeared and we are happy to say there remembrance in a great measure lost—Good Understanding and harmony are Established—for the Continuence of them we desire to labour—the Ordinances ar well attended—a decent attention is throwout exhebited—as it Respects the state of living Religion among us we venture not to say much & in the adjassent parts—we may say within our bounds, the state of Morals and of Respect to Religion is Changed for the better—there is among us at present a number of enquiring souls—a few of our Members appear to be Revived and much engaged—in the midst of this we have Reason "to hang our harp upon the willows" and exercise Regret, altho not dispondency so as to discourage exertion, the lukewarm-warmness of many professors, the insensibility of heaven under the Constant droppings of the sanctuary—the neglect of Religious Instruction of Children—the profanation of the Lords day are among the subjects of our Regret and lamentation, & call for our labours—We desire to wait in prayer and hope upon Jesus Christ the Lord of the Vineyard.

Sign'd Thomas Duwitt
Sept'r 2nd 1813   pasture of the R. D. Church at N. Hackensack

1814 Octob'r 11th At a meeting of the Consistory at the Church according to Adjournment
Present at the Meeting

Elders { William Suard / Aris Van Derbelt / Tunis Vn. Bunschoten / John Luyster }   Deacons { Abraham L. Dates / James Vn. Keuren / Henry A. Monfort / Stephen Monfort }

Tunis Vn. Bunschoten chosen presedent & John Luyster sect'y protem
The object of the meeting was stated to settle the old Account with said Consistory & proceded to settl with the following persons

setled with Albert Monfort & all Acct's balenc'd & discharg'd
setled with Domenicus Monfort & found a balane due him of $7—53/100 which sum of $7—53/100 was paid to him by Samuel Luckey treasurer
setled with Aris Vanderbelt one of the Administrators of the estate of his Father Decs'd some of the papers not to be found Account on both sides Balenc'd and discharged
setled with William Suard & all Acct's setled & discharg'd
Adrian Hageman appeared to settle his Father's John A. Hageman's Acct's, but not having been able to find the old superscription lists that was in his father hand he was p'd by the Treasurer $9—36/100 for money advanced to pay Mr. Walkers board, suposed to be the balance due the s'd John A. Hageman Decs'd
setled with Samuel Luckey, as Secretary Treasurer &c and there remains in his hand as treasurer the sum of $54—77/00 after paying him up his salory to the above date

Recorded Sam'l Luckey sect'y

Statistical Report of the Dutch Reformed Church at New Hackensack Sept'r 1814

No. of Famolies	105
Total of Cong'n	680
In Com'n last report	55
Recv'd since on Conf'n	10
on Certf.	2
Disch'd	0
suspn'd	1
died	1
in Com'n	65
Baptisms, Inf'ts	13
adults	0

Remarks

Minutes of Consistory

The Congregation presents much the same Appearance as at the period of our last Report. We have witnessed no season of pecular revivel or Declension—A few have been added to the Church we trust of the Number such as shall be saved—Harmony and peace still prevail throughout, and attendance upon Ordenances is Undeminished—But a general indiference to the power and practice of Godliness is still prevelent—having reference not to morality but the life of Religion—part of the Congregation was Visited in the Cours of last spring with the prevelent Epidemic fever—to many famolies it was a period of Affliction—we had hoped to have discerned more abiding and general effects then we now discover—We trust however that the Lord will in due time pour upon our perched and baren fields the Early and latter rains of his Grace, that they may become well wattered and frutfull—We mourn not as those who have no hope.

Septemb'r 1st 1814

Signed Thomas Dewitt
Pasture of the Dutch Reformed
Church at New-Hackensack

Feb'y 15th 1814, the Consistory met pursuent to Appointment to Envestigate the conduct of Clement Cornwell a member in Communion with this Church
Present at the meeting

Rev'd Thomas Dewitt

Elders { William Suard / Samuel Luckey / Aris Vn. Derbelt / John Luyster

Deacons { James Vn. Keuren / Daniel Huffman

After a Consideration of the Report in circulation, and the testimony by which they were suported, it was Unamously Resolved that the charge of Intoxecation and of Imprudent and ungarded conversation with the world was substantiated——therefore——
Resolved that Clement Cornwell be, and he is hereby suspended from the previledges of Church Membership untill he furnish Evidences of Repentence and Reformation.

Sam'l Luckey sect'y

Statestical Report of the Congregation of New Hackensack septm'r 1815

No. of famolies	105
Total of Congre'n	700
In com'n pr last report	65
Received since on Certif't	0
on Conf'n	17
Dis Ch'd	2
suspend'd	0
died	2
Total in Commun'n	78
Baptismes, Adults	6
Infants	12

The number of members received during the last Year (as noticed in the Report) is seventeen, a Number larger then that Received in Any previous Year—Considerable portion are of the younger Class in life—Attention to external ordinances Continues undiminished—We have the sattisfaction of seeing our Members generally walking in Consistance with their profession, and have been freed from from any painfull Resort to discipline, amidst these gratifying Circumstances the state of our Congregation presents an aspect not much different from that at the period of our last Report, we still complain of the lukewarmness of many professors, and the want of much Visable power & blessing attending the Administration of Ordinances We have lately lost by death one of our praying fathers in Israel The small tokens of God's grace this day of small things & the state of sinners Accused Call for our faithfull & Enguaged labours We still Carry on partially our Catechetical exercises, but on Account of the dispersed state of the Congregation, not to the desired Extent

In behalf of the Consistory of New-Hackensack
september 5th 1815
sign'd Thomas Dewitt pastor
Recorded by Sam'l Luckey sect'y

At a meeting of Consistory held in the Church the 7th september 1815
Present

Revn'd Thomas Dewitt

Elders { Tunis V'n Bunschoten / John Luyster / Aris V'n Derbelt / Casper Gans

Deacons { Henry A. Monfort / James Ackerman / Samuel Luckey sect'y

It was Represented that a misunderstanding existed between Miss Rinders & James V'n Keuren two members of this Church which had proceded to Considerable lenth—it was

The Reformed Dutch Church of New Hackensack

Resolved that Mr. Dewitt with the Elder Mr. V'n Bunschoten wait upon them previous to the approaching Communion and endeavour to Effect an Amicable & spedy Reconseliation—Also Consistory setled with Tunis V'n Bunschoten & Henry A. Monfort superentendents to the work done on the Church at New Hackensack and found a balance due said Consistory of Eight cents which sum of 8Cts was paid into the treasury.

Septemb'r 13th 1815 The Consistory met in stated meeting at the Church
Present
Reven'd Thomas Dewitt

Elders { William Suard / Tunis V'n Bunschoten / Aris V'n Derbelt }   Deacons { Henry A. Monfort / Samuel Luckey sect'y }

The Case of Nazareth Brewer a non Communicating member for the space of six Years or Upwards was taken in Consideration
Resolved that a letter be addressed to Mr. Brewer Expressive of the Views of Consistory, and Acquaint him to meet with Consistory on Friday the 23 Instn't.
Recorded by Sam'l Luckey sect'y

sept'r 23rd according to Adjournment Consistory met
But Mr. Nazareth Brewer did not attend—therefore no business done.

1816 June 7th The trustees of the Church of New Hackensack met according to Agreement for the purpose Considering how they would lay out the money recv'd for Interest on the legacy left to said Church by Peter V'n Bunschoten Decs'd,
Present

Elders { Tunis V'n Bunschoten / Samuel Luckey / Caster Gons }   Deacons { James Dodge / Matthew Luyster }

Resolved that the Interest for the last Year (Viz) fifty two dol's & 50 Cents be laid out for Oil & paint to paint the inside of s'd Church and Samuel Luckey is Appointed to buy said oil and paint. done in Consistory   Sam'l Luckey sect'y

1816 March 14th Consistory met at the Church for the purpose of settling with James Ackerman Treasurer of the poor Chest

Elders present { Samuel Luckey / Daniel Huffman / Tunis V'n Bunschoten }   Deacons present { James Ackerman / Matthew Luyster }

After Examining sad poor Chest found remaining in Cast the sum of sixty two Dollars & forty three Cents When it was agreed the the s'd poor Chest is to remain in the hand of the s'd Ja's Ackerman
Sam'l Luckey sect'y

1816 May 6th Consistory met at the Church According to Appointment to Enquire into the state of the Congregation.
Present
Revn'd Thomas Dewitt

Elders { Samuel Luckey / Tunis V'n Bunschoten / Daniel Huffman }   Deacons present { James Ackerman / Matthew Luyster }

The Usual enquiries were made respecting the state of the Congregation. When it was Resolved that the cases of Clement Cornwell and John Cornell be referred to Classes at their next Session for advise with respect to their final Excommunication
Sam'l Luckey sect'y   Tho's Dewitt presnd't

1817 March 4th At a meeting of the Consistory of the Prodestent Dutch Church at New Hackensack held at the Church   Present
Revn'd Thomas Dewitt

Elders { Samuel Luckey / Daniel Huffman / Jacob V'n Bunschoten / Tunis V'n Bunschoten / Casper Gons }   Deacons { Matthew Luyster / James Dodge / James Dearen / Martin Monfort / James Ackerman }

It was Resolved that measure be taken respecting the seats forfeited by the death or removal of the former proprietors such seats as have been forfeited for the space of ten years and upwards shall be considered as for sale, and notice given accordingly—such as have been forfeited for a space of time less than ten Years shall be Allowed the prevelege of redemtion for six months from the of Notice from the Pulpit (Viz) 1
for transfering after 1 yr & 6 weeks after death or removel
The poor Chest was examined by the Deacons and there was found a balance of forty six Dollars & sixty Cents—James Dearin was appointed to the charge of the poor chest in the

Minutes of Consistory

place of James Ackerman—A settlement was made with Samuel Luckey as treasurer & secretary and on Audeting the Accounts found a balance in treasuary of Eight dollars & seventy one cents

N.B. the above notice was Given from the pulpit on the 16th same month

sign'd Thomas Dewitt presnd't
Sam'l Luckey sect'y

1817 June 6th At a meeting of the Consistory of the Reformed Dutch Church at New Hackensack held at said church   Present
Revn'd Thomas Dewitt

Elders { Tunis V'n Bunschoten
         Samuel Luckey

Deacons { James Dearin
          Marten Monfort
          Matthew Luyster

Resolved that Jacob V'n Bunschoten & James Dearin be a committee to purchase materiels, hire workmen & superintend the painting of the sealling &c of said Church

Sam'l Luckey sect'y

1818 June 5th Att a meeting of the consistory of the Reformed Dutch Church at New Hackensack held at s'd Church — Present —

Elders &c {
  Thomas Dewitt
  Jacob V'n Bunschoten
  James V'n Keuren
  Aris V'n Derbelt
  Samuel Luckey
  Stephen Monfort
}

Deacons &c {
  James Dearin
  Martain Monfort
  Matthew Luyster
  Adrian Hageman
  James Jones
}

Resolved that the Treasurer be Authorized to pay the difisiency on Mr. Dewitts salory for the year 1816 & 1817 amounting to $108 out of Moneyes in the treasury and $7 to Mr. Sharp for his servises as Chorister

sign'd Thomas Dewitt Presend't
Sam'l Luckey sect'y

1819 June 18 at a meeting of the Consistory of New Hackensack held at the Church —
Present —
Revn'd Thomas Dewitt

Elder
  Aris Van Derbelt
  Stephen Monfort
  William Suard

of old
Consistor
  Tunis V'n Bunschoten
  Jacob V'n Bunschoten
  James V'n Keuren
  Samuel Luckey, treasur'r

Deacons Adrian Hageman
         James Jones
         Henry A. Monfort
         Samuel Luckey, Jun'r

old deacon James Dearin

James Van Keuren paid the balance due on the Church bell
Resolved that the Interest on the legacy of Peter V'n Bunschoten be Appropriated to the Repairs of the roof and the painting of the south and west parts of the church and that william Suard & James Jones be a committee to attend to the same.

sign'd Tho's Dewitt Presedn't
Sam'l Luckey secretary

1819 septb'r 10th at a meeting of the consistory of New Hackensack Congregation at the Church — Present —
Revn'd Thomas Dewitt

Elders Tunis V'n Bunschoten
        William Suard
        Aris V'n Derbelt

Deacons James Jones
         Henry A. Monfort
         Samuel Luckey, Jun'r

A Settlement was made with Wm. Suard & Ja's Jones and their Vouchers for paint, Oil & work done on the church amounted to $60-72 and they had received $52.50 of the Interest on the legacy of Pet'r V'n Bunschoten and $8.22 paid to them out of the poor chest which is to be refunded from the Interest of next Year. a settlement was also made with Samuel Luckey their secretary & Treasurer and on examining the Accounts found a balance remaining in the treasury of sixteen dollars & seventy four Cents

Samuel Luckey, sect'y   sign'd Thomas Dewitt presed't

1820 Jan'y 25 The Consistory met at the Church — Present —
  revn'd Thomas Dewitt

Elders William Suard
       Aris Van Derbelt

Deacons Adrian Hageman
         James Jones
         Henry A. Monfort
         Samuel Luckey, Jun'r

The Reformed Dutch Church of New Hackensack

The Consistory Resolved to proceed to make preparations for the building of a small house Adjacent to the Church for the use of a person to take charge of the Church and for the Accomodation of the Consistory
it was Resolved that the dementions of the house be ten feet post with a box entry & a bed room house to be 25 feet by 18 and that Notice be given to Carpenters to send in their preposals for the carpenter work to Mr. Wm. Suard. And James Dearin & Martain Monfort were Nominated for Elders in the place of Aris Van Derbelt & Stephen Monfort & James Dodge & John Ganse were Nominated for Deacons in the place of Adrian Hageman & James Jones.

Closed with prayer
Sign'd Thomas Dewitt presn't

1820 may 30th The Consistory met at the Church — Present —

Elders
William Suard
Tunis V'n Bunschoten
James Dearin
Martain Monfort

Deacons
Henry A. Monfort
John Ganse
James Dodge

Resolved that Derick Luyster is Appointed sexton in the place of John Luyster for the Church at New-Hackensack to dig Graves, ring bell & Clean & take care of s'd Church &c Als that the legacy left by Peter V'n Bunschoten Decs'd shall be laid out this year for materiels to Repair the said Church, that Tunis V'n Bunschoten & James Dearin is Appointed to purchase the said materiels.

Sam'l Luckey sect'y

1820 Octob'r 31 At a meeting of the consistory of New Hackensack at the Church
present
Thomas Dewitt

Elders
Tunis V'n Bunschoten
William Suard
James Dearin
Martin Monfort

Deacons
Henry A. Monfort
John Gans

Resolved that nine dollars be paid out of the treasury on Account of Salory to Mr. Dewitt. Setled with their treasurer Sam'l Luckey Esq'r and found remaining in the treasury a balance of Sixty Cents.

Tho's Dewitt presd't

1821 March 8 At a meeting of the consistory of New Hackensack at the Church
— Present —

Elders
Thomas Dewitt
Marten Monfort
Jacob v'n Bunschoten
James Ackerman
Tunis V'n Bunschoten

Deacons
Peter Van Derbelt
Cornelius Westervelt
Hen'y A. Monfort
Samuel Luckey Jun'r
old James Dodge

The poor chest was Examined & there was found in it a balance of seventy six dollars ninety four cents—the chest was commited to the care of Decon Peter Van Derbelt—Messr's Jacob V'n Bunschoten & James Dearon were Appointed to Attend to the Repairs of the Church the Ensueing summer.

Tho's Dewitt Presd't

1822 sep't 2nd At a Meeting of the Consistory of Reformed prodestent Dutch Church at New Hackensack & met at the Church — Present —

Elders
James Ackerman
Henry A. Monfort
Samuel Luckey, Jun'r
Jacob V'n Bunschoten

Deacons
Philip Nagel
Isaiah Rinders
Cornelius Westervelt
Peter V'n Derbelt

old elder —James Dearin

The Object of the meeting was stated to settle with Samuel Luckey their secretary & Treasurer, After examining the Treasurer's book there was found a balance remaining in the treasury of three dollars & three cents which sum of three dollars & three cents was allowed to the said Treasurer for extra servises on a bond & Mortguage given by John Winans & one by Samuel Pinkney and the said Book ballenced
Also James Ackerman & Peter V'n Derbelt was chosen a committee to attend to the Repairing of the steple of Church the present season &c.

Sam'l Luckey sect'y

1823 feb'y 5th At a meeting of the Consistory of the Reformed Dutch Church at New-Hackensack met at s'd Church present at the Meeting

Minutes of Consistory

Revn'd Thomas Dewitt—president

Jacob V'n Bunschoten ⎫
James Ackerman ⎬ Elders
Samuel Luckey Jun'r ⎪
Henry A. Monfort ⎭

Peter V'n Derbelt ⎫
Cornelius Westervelt ⎬ Deacons
Josiah Rinders ⎪
Philip Nagel ⎭

the meeting was Opened with prayer by the president
The object of the meeting was to Elect new Church officers &c whereupon Tunis V'n Bunschoten & John Gans was Elected Elders in Roome of James Ackerman & Jacob V'n Bunschoten & John V'n Derbelt in Room of Peter V'n Derbelt & Cornelius Westervelt was realected Deacons
Resolved also that their secretary Samuel Luckey is hereby otherised to transfer seats grattis between Indevidiels if he can thereby regulate the pews better for the Accomedation of famolies
the meeting Closed with prayer by the presedn't —Tho's Dewitt—presdn't

N.B. the above Elders & Deacons were ordained ⎫
to their Respective offices on sabeth day ⎬ Sam'l Luckey sect'y
2nd March following ⎭

1823 March 4th At a meeting of the Consistory of the Reformed Dutch Church at New Hackensack—met at s'd Church, Present at the meeting
Revern'd Thomas Dewitt presedn't

Elders ⎧ Henry A. Monfort
⎨ Samuel Luckey Jun'r
⎪ Tunis V'n Bunschoten
⎩ John Ganse

Deacons ⎧ Cornelius Westervelt
⎨ John V'n Derbelt
⎪ Josiah Rinders
⎩ Philip Nagle

old Elders } Jacob V'n Bunschoten
James Ackerman

old Deacon { Peter V'n Derbelt

Consistory met for the purpose of setling with Peter V'n Derbelt treasurer of the poor chest and their was found Remaining in the poor chest one Hundred & six dollars, seventy two cts. & said poor chest was put in the hand of John V'n Derbelt one of the deacons— Also Tunis V'n Bunschoten & John V'n Derbelt was chosen a committee to lay out the money recv'd on the legasey of Peter V'n Bunschoten Decs'd in Repairs on the Church the Insueing season — sign'd — Thomas Dewitt Presd't

Sam'l Luckey sect'y

1823 March 21st At a meeting of the Minester and Elders of the Congregation of the Dutch reformed Church at New Hackensack by previous Notice from Jacob V'n Bunschoten —   Present at the meeting Revern'd Thomas Dewitt

Elders ⎧ Tunis V'n Bunschoten ⎫
⎨ Samuel Luckey Jun'r ⎬ the meeting was Opened by
⎪ Henry A. Monfort ⎪ prayer by the Revn'd Tho's
⎩ John Ganse ⎭ Dewitt Presedent of the meeting

The Object of the meeting was to receive from the s'd Jacob a donation to the said Congregation to the above named Minester & Elders a Deed in trust a Deed in trust for two Houses & lots in the Velage of Poughkeepsie formerly belonging to Samuel Pinkeny also one Vakent lot. Also Seven Hundred Dollars in Cash for the purpose of suporting the Gospel in the said Church—also for the said Minester and Elders to Execute a Decleration in trust to the said Jacob V'N Bunschoten—the above Writings was Executed and the money receved.
Resolved that their Treasurer Samuel Luckey shall have the above mentioned deed recorded on the County record and also to have the above mentioned houses & lots Ensured also the above mentioned seven hundred Dollas to be put in the Treasury & the said Treasurer is directed to put the said money out at Interest on suficient land security—Also the Tunis V'n Bunschoten & Henry A. Monfort was Chosen a Committee to examin the above Mentioned houses & see what Repairs is necesary & likewise to have the same done as they in their Judgment may deem Necessary—the meeting was closed with prayer by the
Reverend Thomas Dewitt presend't
recorded by Samuel Luckey sect'y

1823 Octob'r 20th at a meeting of the Consistory of the Reformed Dutch Church at New Hackensack met at the church present at the meeting,
Revrend Thomas Dewitt president

Elders ⎧ Tunis V'n Bunschoten
⎨ John Gans
⎩ Henry A. Monfort

Deacons { John V'n Derbelt
Philip Nagle

Meeting opened with prayer by the presedent
The Objeck of the meeting was to settle with their Samuel Luckey their secretary & Treasurer and after Examining the treasurer's books found a balance due Consistory of two

The Reformed Dutch Church of New Hackensack

dollars & seven Cents which sum was Allowed to s'd Secretary & Treasurer for Extra servises—meeting Closed with prayer by the presedent

            sign'd by Tho's Dewitt Presedent
            recorded by Sam'l Luckey Sect'y

1824 May 24th At a meeting of the Consistory of the Reformed dutch Church at New Hackensack met at the Church—present at the meeting
    reverend Thomas Dewitt president

Elders	Tunis V'n Bunschoten John Ganse Daniel Huffman Aris V'n Derbelt	Deacons	Matthew Luyster John A. Monfort Isaiah Rinders

  old Elder Samuel Luckey Jun'r   old Deacon Philip Nagle

Resolved that the Congregation be called together for the purpose of consulting them on the subject of Changing and repairing the Church

Resolved that Tunis V'n Bunschoten and Daniel Huffman be a Committee to Attend to the houses & lot in Poughkeepsie and make such repairs as they may deem Necessary and proper—Resolved that fifteen Dollars be allowed to the Clark and Treasurer for his Annuel Compensation.

  Closed with prayer   sign'd Thomas Dewitt, Presd't
              recorded by Sam'l Luckey sect'y

1824 Octob'r 11th At a Meeting of the Consistory of the Congregation of the Reformed Dutch Church at New Hackensack met for the purpose of settling with their Treasurer & Secretary &c present at the meeting

Elders	Tunis V'n Bunschoten Aris V'n Derbelt John Ganse Daniel Huffman	Deacons	John A. Monfort Cornl's Westervelt Matthew Luyster John V'n Derbelt

When Tunis V'n Bunschoten & John V'n Derbelt was chosen a Commitee to lay out the Interest of the Peter V'n Bunschoten fund for Repairs on the Church buildings.

Also Tunis V'n Bunschoten & Samuel Luckey be a Committee to attend to the Houses at Poughkeepsie

And after Examining the books of their Treasurer & Secretary they find a balance remaining in the treasury of four dollars & twenty-two Cents—

Closed with prayer by Elder John Ganse

            recorded by Samuel Luckey sect'y

1825 feb'y 25th At a meeting of the Consistory of the Reformed Dutch Church held at s'd Church — preasent at the meeting —
Revn'd Thomas Dewitt

Elders	Tunis V'n Bunschoten John Ganse Aris V'n Derbelt Daniel Huffman	Deacons	John V'n Derbelt Matthew Luyster John A. Monfort

                whose time was expired

The following persons were Chosen Officers for the following Year

  Elders   Tunis V'N Bunschoten reellected
        Jacob V'n Bunschoten in the place of John Gance
  Deacons   John Budd in the place of John V'n Derbelt
         Charls Dearin in the place of Cornelious Westervelt

Resolved that the Interes money of Peter V'n Bunschoten fund be appropriated to the repairing of the Church the insueing season

Resolved that Tunis V'n Bunschoten Daniel Huffman & John A. Monfort be a Committee to Attend the repairing s'd Church

            Attest Thomas Dewitt Presedent
            recorded Sam'l Luckey sect'y

N.B. the above officers Ordained the 27 day of March

1825 April 1st At a Meeting of the Consistory of the Reformed Dutch Church at New Hackensack at s'd Church — Present —
Revn'd Thomas Dewitt

Elders	Aris V'n Derbelt Tunis V'n Bunschoten Jacob V'n Bunschoten	Deacons	John A. Monfort Matthew Luyster John Budd Charles Dearin

  old Elder John Ganse   old deacons   Cornelius Westervelt
                               John V'n Derbelt

     Samuel Luckey treas'r

Minutes of Consistory

The poor chest was examined it was found to contain seventy four dollars & thirty two Cents & was committed to the care of Matthew Luyster
Resolved that the Committee appointed to attend the repairing the Church cause a Gutter to be made for the back side of the Church and and repair the frunt fence of the burying Ground
Resolved that Aris V'n Derbelt Matthew Luyster together with Esq'r Luckey be a committee to Visit the houses & lots belonging to this Church at Poughkeepsie and be Empowered to auhorize the building of a Barn at the lower house provided the Expence shall not exceed forty dollars in Case they shall deem it Expedient

Thomas Dewitt presedn't
Sam'l Luckey Sect'y

At a Meeting of the Consistory of the Reformed Dutch Church at New-Hackensack known in law the Trustees of the Reformed protestant Dutch Church at New Hackensack—held at the Church
Present Thomas DeWitt menister

Elders { Tunis V'n Bunschoten / Aris V'n Derbelt / Jacob V'n Bunschoten / Daniel Huffman

Deacons { Matthew Luyster / John A. Monfort / Charles Dearin / John Budd

Opened with prayer
A Communication was received from Hon. James Emott one of the Executors of the late Matthew V'n Bunschoten Deceased stateing that the Executors were prepared to pay the Legacy of fifteen hundred Dolars bequeathed to the Church at New Hackensack by Matthew V'n Bunschoten to Any person duly Authorised by a formal act of Consistory
Resolved that the Clerk and Treasurer of the Church Samuel Luckey Esq'r be hereby Authorised to receive the legacy Aforesaid and in the Name of the Consistor a receipt in full for the same
Resolved that the Clerk furnish a Certificate copy of the above resolution to the Executors of Mr. V'n Bunschoten
Resolved that the treasurer be Authroised to pay unto Mr. Potter $12.50/100 for his service as Corester for six months whenever it becomes due
Resolved that the Treasurer be Authorised to pay the Amount due to Clases minutes of Syned and Anueties
1825 May 24th   Signed   Thomas Dewitt Presedn't
                   Sam'l Luckey secretary

At a meeting of the Consistory of the Reformed Dutch Church at New Hackensack the 24 June — 1825 —
Present
Revn'd Thomas Dewitt

Elders { Tunis V'n Bunschoten / Jacob V'n Bunschoten / Aris V'n Derbelt / Daniel Huffman

Deacons { Charles Dearin / John A. Monfort / John Budd

Opened with prayer by S. S. Woodhull
The meeting was Called at the Request of the Committee appointed at the last session of General synod to Visit the Churches in the Classes of Poughkeepsie for the purpose of soliciting subscription for the Endowment of a third professorate—the Revn'd C. C. Cuylor, Dr. S. S. Woodhull & Mr. Abraham Van Nest appears as Members of the above Committee to Attend on the object of their commission after hearing the Committe
Mr. Jacob V'n Bunschoten one of the Elders subscribed fifteen hundred dollars and gave a check on the Middle Distrect bank for the same The Consistory Resolved to subscribe two Hundred and fifty Dollars and to pledge the Interest at 6 per Cent untill paid and although the Consistory do not feel at liberty to subscribe any more Yet they will extend the subscription Genneraly and pay the excess in the Amount of subscription
Closed with prayer by the revn'd C. C. Cuylor

Tho's Dewitt Pres't

Resolved also that their Treasurer Samuel Luckey is hereby authorised to loan out the fifteen hundred dollars the Legacy of the late Matthew V'n Bunschoten des'd to the s'd Church at six percent per Anum

Tho's Dewitt presedent
Sam'l Luckey sect'y

1826 Jan'y 19th At a meeting of the Prodestent Reformed Dutch Church at New Hackensack by appointment Consistory met at the Church and a number of Members — present at the Meeting

Elders { Aris V'n Derbelt / Jacob V'n Bunschoten / Tunis V'n Bunschoten

Deacons { Matthew Luyster / John Budd

with a Number of the Members

The Reformed Dutch Church of New Hackensack

Aris V'n Derbelt was chosen Presedent
it was stated that the Object of the Meeting is to take in Consideration the propriety or Impropriety of a seperation of the Congregations of Hopewell & New Hackensack Also to settle with their Samuel Luckey their Treasurer & secretary
After delebratry takeing in consideration the propriety or Impropriety of the said seperation Resolved Unanimously that it is at this time improper and Detrementel to the above Congregation of New Hackensack that a seperation should take place and have chosen Matthew Luyster & Abraham Montross a commitee to Attend on the Classis at Hopewell which is to Conviene on the thirty first Instant.
Also after Examining the books of the said Treasurer & secretary find a balence remaining in the treasury of One hundred & sixty four dollars & forty three cents which balance is Carried over on day book

        signed Aris V'n Derbelt presedent
        recorded by Sam'l Luckey secretary

At a meeting of the Consistory of the combined Congregations of New Hackensack and Hopewell conveined at the Church at New Hackensack February 13th 1826
Opened with Prayer by Rev'd C. D. Westbrook
      Present from New Hackensack

Elders { Daniel Huffman / Aris V'n Derbelt   Deacons { Matthew Luyster / John A. Monfort / Charles Dearin / John Budd

      from Hopewell

Elders { Henry Hulst / Coert Horten / Abraham R. Adriance   Deacons { John W. Brinkerhoff / John P. Luyster / Daniel Philips / Theodorus Storm

Revn'd C. D. Westbrook from the Neighbouring Congregation of Fishkill presided, and Matthew Luyster was Chosen Clerk
The Revn'd Thomas Dewitt laid before the Consistories the following resignation of his Call into their hands

  To the Consistories of the Reformed Dutches Churches of New Hackensack and Hopewell
  A Special Meeting of the Classis of Poughkeepsie was called to meet at Hopewell Jan'y 31 at which a memorial was presented from the Church at Hopewell requisting the Dessolution of the Combination existing between said Church and and the Church at New Hackensack a majority of the members which is Necessary to transact business of this Nature did not Appear the Members present advised that the proper mode of bringing the subject before Clases for Adjucation would be to resign my call into the of the Consistories In compliance with this Advice, I hereby Resign my call into the hands of the consistory from Originated praying that the Head of the Church would be preased to Grant his Gracious direction, and blessing for the promotion of his Glory and the prosperity of these our Churches, and that he would preserve to us the Unity of the sperit in the bonds of peace—   sign'd Thomas Duwitt
Feb'y 13th 1826

 Whereupon it was moved, and Seconded
That the resignation of our Pastor of his call into the hands of the Consistories for the purpose of referring the whole business to the Classis of Poughkeepsie at their Adjourned meeting at Poughkeepsie on the 14th Inst. be Accepted
 To which motion five of the members of the New Hackensack consistory present Voted in the Negative, and one declined Voting
 To which Motion seven of members of Hopewell Consistory being all the members present Voted in the Affertive
 It was also resolved that the elder Aris V'n Derbelt be Appointed a delegate from the combined Congregations of New Hackensack and Hopewell to the Clases of Poughkeepsie at their Adjourned meeting at Poughkeepsie on the 14th Inst.
The meeting was Closed with prayer by the Revn'd C. D. Westbrook
        sign'd Cornelius D. Westbrook
        Pres't pro tem
      and recorded Sam'l Luckey sect'y

 In Obedience to the Resolution of the Clases of Poughkeepsie passed at Poughkeepsie on the 14th of february at their Adjourned special Meeting transmited to you the following resolution
1st Resolved Unanimously that the resignation made by the Rev'd Thomas DeWitt of his Call and of his pastorate Charge over the combined Congregations of New Hackensack and Hopewell be Accepted and that the pastoral Connection between the Revn'd Thomas Dewitt and said combined Congregations be and is hereby dessolved

Minutes of Consistory

2nd Resolved Unanimously that the prayer of the congregation of Hopewell be Granted that the Connextion heretofore existing between the Congregations of New Hackensack and Hopewell be and is hereby dissolved
Poughkeepsie
Feb'y 14th—1826   sign'd Far'd H. Vanderveer
   To the Consistory of the Reformed   stated Clerk
   Dutch Church at Newhackensack

1826 March 14th At a meeting of the Consistory of the Reformed Dutch Church at New Hackensack by Adjournment convined at the Church
   Opened with prayer by Deacn Matthew Luyster
   Jacob V'n Bunschoten was chosen presedent pro tem
                  Present at the meeting

Elders { Jacob V'n Bunschoten / Tunes V'n Bunschoten / Daniel Huffman   Deacons { Matthew Luyster / Charles Dearin / John Budd / John A. Monfort

Matthew Luyster, Stated that the Object of the meeting was to take in Consideration the propriety of purchasing a personage for the Congregation of New Hackensack and other business that may accur.
Resolved that Matthew Luyster and James V'n Keuren is Appointed a Committee to look out for a suitable site for a Personage for the Congregation and report to the Consistory.
Resolved that Tunes V'n Bunschoten and Samuel Luckey Jun'r is Appointed a Committee to collect the rent of the houses in Poughkeepsie for the Present Year and to Rent s'd houses the Insueing Year
Resolved also that Samuel Luckey Jun'r is appointed an assistant to Samuel Luckey their present treasurer and secretary on Account of his indisposition of health
Resolved also that Tunis V'n Bunschoten is Appointed Delegate to attend the Classes of Poughkeepsie at their next meeting to be held on the last tuesday in April next.
   done in consistory   Jacob V'n Bunschoten was pres'd
        and   signd Sam'l Luckey secretary

1826 May 4th At a Meeting of the great Consistory of the Reformed Dutch Church met at the Church. The Object of the meeting was stated to take in consideration the choise of a suitable site for a Personage &c
                  Present at the meeting
Elders { Jacob V'n Bunschoten / Tunis V'n Bunschoten / Daniel Hoofman / Aris V'n Derbelt   Deacons { John Budd / Matthew Luyster   Advisery members / John Luyster / James V'n Keuren / James Dearin / James Ackerman / Samuel Luckey

Jacob V'n Bunschoten was Chosen Chearman pro tem
& Samuel Luckey secretary
Resolved that a Vote be taken whether we endeavour to purchase a site near the Church from Stephen Thorn or look for another. Voted Uananimously that we endeavour to purchace the house barn & lot on west side of the road opesit the Church and six Acres of Land East of the burying Ground, And that Tunis V'n Bunschoten James V'n Keuren & John Luyster be a commite to purchace the same, And report to the Consistory
Closed with prear by
deacon Matthew Luyster }   Recorded by Sam'l Luckey secretary

1826 may 23rd At a meeting of the Consistory of the Reformed protestant Dutch Church at New Hackensack by Appointment — Present —

Elders { Jacob V'n Bunschoten / Tunes V'n Bunschoten / Aris V'n Derbelt / Daniel Huffman   Deacons { John Budd / Charles Dearin / Matthew Luyster

The Meeting was opened with Prayer by Deacon Matthew Luyster
Mr. Jacob V'n Bunschoten Chosen chearman pro tem
Tunis V'n Bunschoten stated that the object of the meeting was to take in Consideration the propriety of repairing the personage house and lot, Agreed Unanimously that said house and lot be repaired as soon as Convenient
Resolved that Tunis V'n Bunschoten, John Luyster and James V'n Keuren be a commite to Purchase meteriels Imploy workmen and Overse that the said Repairs be done &c
                                   Recorded by Sam'l Luckey Secret'y

The Reformed Dutch Church of New Hackensack

1826 Sep'r 1st At a meeting of the Consistory of the Reformed protestent Dutch Church at New Hackensack, Met at the Church — Present —

Elders { Jacob V'n Bunschoten / Daniel Huffman / Tunis V'n Bunschoten }   Deacons { John Monfort / Charles Dearin / Matthew Luyster }

Jacob V'n Bunschoten was chosen to the chear and the meeting opened with prayer by Deacon Matthew Luyster Tunis V'n Bunschoten stated that object of the meeting is to take in consideration the propriety of making a call on some candidate as a stated Menister. After the subject in Consideration it was RESOLVED that a Call be posoned untill we hear some more of the Candedates for the Minestry Preach WHEREUPON Mr. Jacob V'n Bunschoten Varbely Authorised the consistory to Use the Interest of his Donation money to pay the different Candidates that should preach in the Church at New Hackensack Also to pay out of the said interest towards the salory of a Candedate if the said Consistory shall deem it proper to hire one to preach six months on triel.

Recorded by Sam'l Luckey sectr'y

1826 October 5th At a meeting of the consistory of the Reformed Duth Church at New Hackensack — Present —

Elders { Daniel Huffman / Jacob V'n Bunschoten / Tunis V'n Bunschoten / Aris V'n Derbelt }   Deacons { John Monfort / Matthew Luyster / Charles Dearin / John Budd }

Opened with prayer by Deacon Matthew Luyster
Mr. Jacob V'n Bunschoten was chosen presedent pro tem
Tunis V'n Bunschoten stated that the object of the meeting was to take in Consideration the propriety of calling a minester to be their stated pastor in said congregation Whereupon Resolved that a meeting be called of the congregation to attend at the Church on Monday the ninth Instant at two oclock in the afternoon to take in consideration of making a call on some devine or candidate for the ministry to be their stated pasture to preach the gospel Administer the sacraments &c. in the Reformed dutch Church at New Hackinsack to said Congregation Also who will be a proper person to present a call to according to the Voice of a majority of said Congregation Also that Elder Aris V'n Derbelt is to attend at the next Meeting of the Poughkeepsie Classes on tuesday the thirty first Instant in the Velige of Poughkeepsie

sign'd Jacob V'n Bunschoten pres'd protem
&   Sam'l Luckey   sect'y

1826 Octob'r 9th At a meeting of the Consistory and several of the members of the Reformed Dutch Church at New Hackensack met at the Church by Appointment — Present —

Elders { Aris V'n Derbelt / Tunes V'n Bunschoten / Jacob V'n Bunschoten }   Deacons { Matthew Luyster / John Monfort / with several of the members }

The meeting opened with prayer by Mr. John Luyster
Mr. Jacob V'n Bunschoten was chosen Presedent protem
The object of the Meeting was stated by Tunis V'n Bunschoten to make a choice of a Menister or a candidat for the Menistry to be their stated Menister to preach the Gospel to said Congregation in the said Church at New Hackensack—after due Deliberation and taking the Voice of the Consistory and Members present—
it was Resolved to circulate a superscription list to endeavour to rais money for salory to present a call to the Reverend M. W. Dwight to be their stated pasture &c.
Done in Consistory   Recorded by Sam'l Luckey sect'y

1826 Octob'r 17th At a meeting of the Consistory of the Reformed Dutch Church at New Hackensack—met at the Church by appointm't
Present

Elders { Jacob V'n Bunschoten / Tunis V'n Bunschoten / Aris Van Derbelt / Daniel Huffman }   Deacons { John Budd / Charles Dearin / John Monfort / Matthew Luyster }

Opened with Prayer by Mr. John Luyster
Mr. Jacob V'n Bunschoten was chosen presedent protemp'y
Mr. Tunis V'n Bunschoten stated that the Object of the meeting was to consult what sum should be Inserted in the call to be presented to the Revn'd Morace W. Dwight to be a stated Menister in the Congregation at New Hackensack—After due consideration on the subject it was
RESOLVED that the sum of 450 dollars with the Use of the personage house and land Yearly and every year be presented to the said Morace W. Dwight in said call as long as

Minutes of Consistory

he shall remain their Menister &c—Also that Elder Tunis V'n Bunschoten be appointed to present said call to the s'd Morace W. Dwight—
Also that Elder Tun V'n Bunschoten shall have his necessary expences paid out of the Treasury for going with said call—
done in Consistory
        Jacob V'n Bunschoten pres'd protemp'y
        recorded by Sam'l Luckey sect'y

1826 Octb'r 18th At a meeting of the Consistory of the Reformed Dutch Church at new Hackensack held at the Church by appointment
— Present —

Elders { Jacob V'n Bunschoten / Tunis V'n Bunschoten / Aris V'n Derbelt
Deacons { Matthew Luyster / John A. Monfort / John U. Budd

Jacob V'n Bunschoten was chosen Pres't protemp'y
Opened with prayer by the Revn'd Thomas Dewitt
A form of a Call upon the Revn'd Morace W. Dwight drafted in Pursuance of a Resolution of Consistory of Yeasterday was read
RESOLVED that the form be Approved and that the Presedn't protempore be Otherised to Sign the same and to Affix the seal of the Corporation—
The Call was then Executed and Moderated by the Revn'd Thomas Dewitt of Hopewell—
        Jacob V'n Bunschoten pres't protmpor
        Sam'l Luckey sect'y

1826 Dec'r 18th At a meeting of the Consistory of the Reformed Dutch Church at New Hackensack met at the Church by Appointm't — Present —
the Revn'd Morace W. Dwight —Presedent

Elders { Tunis V'n Bunschoten / Daniel Huffman / Aris V'n Derbelt
Deacons { John A. Monfort / Charles Dearin / Matthew Luyster

Opened with prayer by the Revn'd Morace W. Dwigh who stated that the object of the meeting was to take in Consideration the speritual state of the Church & make some regulations
1 Resolved that Bible classes be appointed at different places in the congregation (viz) at the school house near James Luckey's, 2d at the Church, 3rd at the school House near Peter V'n Derbelts
2 Resolved that Baptism be Administered as Resolved on the fifth day of Decemb'r one thousand eight hundred & twelve
Also that Communon in said Church be on the last sabeths in January last in April last in July & last in October
When John Luyster was elected Elder in place of Daniel Huffman and Cornelius Westervelt do. in place of Aris V'n Derbelt
Also Isaah Rinders elected deacon in place of John A. Monfort and Matthew Luyster was reelected Deacon—done in Consistory
Closed with prayer by Revn'd Morace W. Dwight who was presdn't
        Recorded by Sam'l Luckey secrt'y
N.B. also that the Interest on the M. V'n Bunschoten fund for the first Year be Appropriated to repairs of personage House

1827 Jan'y 22nd At a Meeting of the Consistory of the Reformed Dutch Church at New Hackensack met at the Church by Appointm't
Preasent, Revn'd Morace W. Dwight — Presedent —

Elders { John Luyster / Tunes V'n Bunschoten / Cornelius Westervelt
Deacons { Matthew Luyster / Isaiah Rinders / Charls Dearin

Opened with prayer by the presedent
Resolved that James Lewis Continews corester in said Church from the first day of Jan'y Instant at the Rate of twenty dollars per Year—Also that a man of a small famoly be got in house to be sexon in place of John Luckey on account of the said Luckey having too large a famoly—
Resolved that a superscription be put in sirculation to rais money to finish the personage house &c—
Resolved also that Matthew Luyster with Samuel Luckey J'r in the place of Tunis V'n Bunschoten to rent out the houses &c the Insueing Year & endeavour to collect the Rents &c
Also examining & editing the book of Samuel Luckey treasurer find a balance in favour of said treasurer of the sum of Nine Dollars & fifty six Cents—s'd balance on treasurers book—done in Consistory, the Revn'd Morace W. Dwight Presdn't.
Closed with prayer by the presdent—
        Recorded by Sam'l Luckey sect'y

The Reformed Dutch Church of New Hackensack

TO THE REVEREND MORACE W. DWIGHT—
Grace mercy and peace from God our Father, and Jesus Christ our Lord—
WHEREAS the Church of Jesus Christ at New Hackensack is at present destitute of the stated preaching of the of the word, and Regular administration of the ordinances, and is desirus of obtaining the means of Grace, which God has appointed for the salvation of sinners through Jesus Christ his son, and whereas the said Church is well sattisfied with the piety, Gifts and menisterial qualifications of you Morace W. Dwight, and hath good hope that your labours in the gospel will be attended with a blessing; Therefore we the Elders and Deacons of the Reformed Protestant dutch Church at New Hackensack has resolved to call, and do hereby call solemnly, and in the fear of the Lord You the said Morace W. Dwight to be our Pastor, and teacher to preach the word in truth and faithfulness, to administer the holy sacrements agreable to the Institution of Christ, to maintain Christian discipline, to edify the congregation, and Especially the youth by Catechatical instruction, and as a faithful servent of Jesus Christ to fulfill the whole work of the Gospel Ministry agreably to the word of God, and the excellent rules and Constitution of the Reformed Dutch Church estableshed in the last National Synot held in dordrecht, and Retefied, and explained by the Ecclesiastical Judicatory under which we stand, and to which you un on excepting this call, must with us remain subordenate—In fulfiling the Ordenary duties of Your menistry, it is Expressly stipulated that besides preaching upon such texts of scripture as you may think proper for our Instruction, You also explain a portion of the Hidleburgh Catechism on the Lords day agreable to the established order of the Reformed Dutch Church, and that you farther Conform in Rendering all that publick service which is usual, and has been in constant pratice in our congregation. The particulare service which will be required of you is to preach on every Lords day in the forenoon, and in the Afternoon as may by you and us deemed expedient; to Catechize the Youth, and to perform famoly Visitation as may be deemed by us Jointly expedient, and practicable, to Administer the sacrements and to attend to descipline Agreably to the Resolutions of Consistory.
To encourage yo in the performance of the duties of Your Important Office We promise you in the name of the Church all proper attention love and Obedience in the Lord; and to free you from worldly cares and Avocations while you are dispensing spiritual blessings unto us Wee the Elders and Deacons of the Reformed protestant Dutch Church at New Hackensack do promise and oblige ourselves to pay you Yearly and every Year the sum of four hundred and fifty dollars in Yearly payments together with the use of the Personage house and lot belonging to said Church as long as you Continue our minister.
For the faithful performance of all which We do herby bind our selves and our Successors by these presents;—The
The Lord encline your Hart to a Cheerful exceptance of this call, and send you to us in the fullness of the blessings of the Gospel of peace—
Done in Consistory and Subscribed in our behalf by the Presedent pro tempore of said Consistory, and sealed with the seal of the Corperation this eighteenth day of October in the Year of our Lord one thousand eight hundred and twenty six—Octob'r 18th 1826—
and signed Jacob V'n Bunschoten
Presedent pro tempore
Done and executed in the Meeting of the Consistory of New Hackensack Octob'r 18th 1826 in presence of Revn'd Thomas Dewitt
menister of the neighboring Church at Hopewell and moderated the Call

Approved and attested in Classes
Cornelius C. Cuylor sect'y

A. H. Kettle presedn't pro temp'r
Recorded by Sam'l Luckey sect'y
to the Consistory

The above named Morice W. Dwight was Installed pastor of the Reform'd protestant Duch Church at the 13th Demb'r 1826 at s'd Church
present—Revn'd Mr. Vandver, the rev'd Tho's Dewitt, the Revn'd Mr. Westbrook, the Revn'd C. C. Cuylor

1827 feb'y 20th At a meeting of the Consistory of the Reformed Dutch Church at New Hackensack by Appointm't — Present —

Elders
{ Tunis V'n Bunschoten
John Luyster
Cornelius Westervelt

Deacons
{ Isaah Rinders
John U. Budd
Charles Dearin
Matthew Luyster

Opened with prayer by Elder John Luyster
Tunis V'n Bunschoten was chosen presedent pro tem'r
Tunis V'n Bunschoten stated that the object of meeting was to take the selling of the Confisticated seats in in said Church
Resolved that the confisticated seats be offered for sale at oction on tuesday 27th March Insueing—sale to commence at 12 Oclock on that day when the conditions of sale will be

Minutes of Consistory

made known also that the above be published 3 sabeths previous from the pulpit also that notice be given as above that the seats whose former owners are dead or removed and their seats remains transferable to their Hiers &c be invited to call & have them transfered on that day

Resolved also that if Tunis V'n Bunschoten shall pay money in Advance on salory to the Revn'd Morace W. Dwight, the Consistory do promiss to Repay the same to him when the salory is Collected

Resolv'd also that Samuel Luckey Jun'r is to pay six percent Interest the Insueing year for the money loaned from the Consistory (Viz) up to the first day of May 1828 if he does not pay the principel in the spring

done in Consistory   Record'd by Sam'l Luckey sect'y

1827 March 27th At a meeting of the Consistory of the Reformed Dutch Church at New Hackensack—at at s'd Church by Appointm't

Present Elders: Jacob V'n Bunschoten, Tunis V'n Bunschoten, Cornelius Westervelt, John Luyster

Deacons: John U. Budd, Charles Dearin, Matthew Luyster, Isaiah Rinders

Opened with prayer by Deacon Matthew Luyster
and Jacob V'n Bunschoten chosen presedn't pro temp'r

The Object was stated by the presedent to sell the Confistocated acording to notice given,—and also to transact other business Concerning the temporaleties of the Church, and also to choose new Elders and Deacons—When—James Ackerman was chosen Elder in place of Jacob V'n Bunschoten and James V'n Keuren chosen Elder in place of Tunis V'n Bunschoten

George Van Derbelt chosen Deacon in place of Charles Dearin
and John U. Budd reelected Deacon
at which time a number of seats were sold
Done in Consistory   —Recorded by Sam'l Luckey sect'y

1827 may 4th At a meeting of the Consistory of the Reformed Dutch Church at New Hackensack, met by appointm't at the Church—

Present Elders: James Ackerman, James V'n Keuren, John Luyster, Cornelius Westervelt

Deacons: Isaiah Rinders, George V'n Derbelt, Matthew Luyster

Opened with prayer by Deacon Matthew Luyster
the Elder John Luyster chosen presedn't pro-tempor

the presedent stated that the Object of the meeting was to Receive the money that was collected in the treasury for seat sold in said Church on the 27th March last, and to transact other business that moigth Accrue. Resolved that James Ackerman and John Luyster be a commite to recceve the Interest money this Year on the legacy bequathed to said Church by Peter V'n Bunschoten Deceased and lay it out on meterials and work on repairs on the Church (Viz) to repair the front stoop and leading some leaks in the steaple &c
Done in Consistory   and Recorded by Samuel Luckey sect'y

1827 Sept'r 24th At a meeting of the Consistory of the Reformed Dutch Church at New Hackensack, met at the Church by Appointment
Present—the Revn'd Morace W. Dwight who presided as presedent

Elders: John Luyster, Cornelius Westervelt, James Ackerman, James V'n Keuren

Deacons: John U. Budd, Isaiah Rinders, Matthew Luyster

Opened with Prayer by the Revn'd Morace W. Dwight—as Presedn't—

it was stated by Elder John Luyster that the object of the meeting was to settle with Tunis V'n Bunschoten, John Luyster & James V'n Keuren a Commite Chosen to buy a Personage & repair the buildings on the same &c Also to settle with John Luyster & James Ackerman a commite chosen to repair frunt stoop, steple & build a wood house out of the Interest of Pt'r V'n Bunschoten fund,—After Examining the bills presented by the Commite V'n Bunschoten, Luyster & V'n Keuren found that they have expended $1892.81 (Viz) $1102.71 for the Glebe land & $790.10 for Repairing buildings &c and that there is due to said commite $40-42 more then the Money they had recv'd.—Also after setling with the said Luyster & Ackerman on the Interes of the Pt'r V'n Bunschoten fund found they had Expended $46-43½ & their Remained in their hands $6-6½ Resolved that the $6-6½ be laid out on repairing the stove pipes &c

done in consistory   Revn'd Morace W. Dwight Presendn't
Closed with prayer   Sam'l Luckey sect'y

The Reformed Dutch Church of New Hackensack

1828 feb'y 4th   At a Meeting of the Consistory of Reformed protestent Dutch Church at New Hackensack met at the Church by Appointment — Present — the revn'd Morace W. Dwight Presedent of the meeting

Elders { John Luyster
James V'n Keuren
Cornelius Westervelt }

Deacons { John U. Budd
Isaiah Rinders
Matthew Luyster }

Opened with Prayer by the Presedent

1st Resolved that the $1500 Dollars Loaned to Henry & moses Swift at seven per cent Annuealy shall be left with them three Year by their paying the Interest Puncktually at six p'r Cnt Annually from 2nd day of Jan'y 1828

2nd Resolved James V'n Keurent in the place of James Ackerman be a committe to purchace meterials and put Cutions in the pulpet & in the Minsers pew out of the Interest of Peter V'n Bunschoten fund &c

3rd Resolved that fifty Dollars per Year be added to the Revn'd Morace W. Dwight salory to commence from first day of Nov'r 1827

4th Resolved that James Dearin is Ellected Elder in place of Corn's Westervelt also that John Luyster is Reelected Elder
that Peter V'n Derbelt is elected deacon in place of Matthew Luyster and Henry D. Traver is elected Deacon in place of Isaiah Rinders
Also that examining & editing the books of Samuel Luckey their Treasurer find a balance in treasuray of two hundred and forty eight dollars and twenty five cents done in Consistory—s'd treasurer's book for balance $248-25 Whereof the Revrn'd Morace W. Dwight was Presedent
and Recorded by their Secretary Sam'l Luckey
Closed with prayer by the presedent

Sabeth day Feb'r 24th the following Elders & Deacons were Ordained to their office as above Elected on the fourth Instant
Elders—John Luyster & James Dearin)   (Deacons—Peter V'n Derbelt, Henry D. Traver

1828 Friday feb'r 29th   At a meeting of the Consistory of Reformed Protestant Dutch Church at New Hackensack met at the Church by Appointm't
Present at the meeting
Revn'd Morace W. Dwight Presedent

Elders { James Dearin
John Luyster
James V'n Keuren
James Ackerman }

Deacons { Isaiah Rinders
Peter V'n Derbelt }

Opened with Prayer by the Presedint
James V'n Keuren & Isaiah Rinders were Appointed to examine the state of the poor chest the Amount in the Chest was found to be thirty four Dollars & sixty four cents—the Accounts of Matthew keeper of the Poor chest were examined & found to be correct Consistory paid 25 Cts to Mr. Robinson and the poor Chest was commited to Peter V'n Derbeit —done in Consistory—

Recorded by Sam'l Luckey secretary

1828 may 14th   At a meeting of the Consistory of the Reform'd Dutch Church at New Hackensack met at the Church by Appointment — Present —
Revn'd Morace W. Dwight — Presedent
Elders—James Dearin & John Luyster)   Deacons—John U. Budd & Peter V'n Derbelt
Opened with prayer by the President—There not being a majority appearing there was not any Resolve made—When the treasurer Samuel Luckey was Informed that Clement and John Cornwell is to pay only 6 p'r cent interest on their respective Bonds
Sam'l Luckey sectr'y

1828 June 2nd   Att a meeting of the Consistory of the Reformed protestant Dutch Church at New Hackensack met at the s'd Church by Appointment —
Present Revn'd Morace W. Dwight — Presedent of s'd meeting

Elders { James V'n Keuren
James Ackerman
James Dearin }

Deacon { Peter V'n Derbelt }

Opened with prayer by the Presedent
Samuel Luckey Jun'r stated that the object of the meeting is to consult whether it would be advisable to sell the house & lot laying in pine s't of which Tho's Dewitt Sam'l Luckey Jun'r Tunis V'n Bunschoten Henry A. Monfort & John Gans hold the present deed in trust for the Consistory of said Church for the sum of fifteen hundred Dollars after due consideration RESOLVED Unanimously that said house & lot be sold at present on payments as follows five hundred dollars on the first day of may 1829 with personal securety at the option of the said Tho's Dewitt & Others as above mentioned and one thousand Dollars on

Minutes of Consistory

the first day of may 1833 secured by bond & Mortguage on s'd house & lot RESOLVED also that John Luyster & James V'n Keuren be a commite to have the pews in s'd Church painted also to have more orniment put on the pulpet & paint the barn & make a fence and gate in front of of the barn belonging to the personage—Closed with prayer by the Presedent
done in Consistory
Recorded by Sam'l Luckey sect'y

1828 Octob'r 16th At a Meeting of the Consistory of the Reformed protestent Dutch Church at New Hackensack met at the by Appointment
Present Revn'd Morace W. Dwight President

Elders { John Luyster / James Ackerman / James Dearin / James V'n Keuren } Deacons { George V'n Derbelt / John U. Budd / Peter V'n Derbelt }

Opened with Prayer by the President
The Presdent stated that the Object of the meeting was to Examin an Accuation in circulation against Sally Gardner of frequently being in the habit of Intemperance in the Use of speritous liquor
After Hearing and Weighing the testamony of the witnesses it was Unanimously RESOLVED that the said Sally Gardner be suspended from Communion in said congregation untill she shows her penetence for the crime proved agains her of Intemperence by the Use of speritues liquor. &c
Resolved also that Peter V'n Derbelt pay Angeline Luyster six Dollars out of the poor Chest also that said Peter pay Sinthe Wicof five Dolars out of poor Chest
Closed with prayer by the presedent
done in Consistory
Recorded by Sam'l Luckey sect'y

1829 feb'y 5th At a Meeting of the Consistory of the Reformed protestent Dutch Church at New Hackensack met at the Church by Appointm't Present
Revn'd Morace W. Dwight Presedent

Elders { John Luyster / James Ackerman / James V'n Keuren / James Dearin } Deacons { John U. Budd }

Opened with prayer by the President
The object of the meeting was stated to settle with Samuel Luckey their Treasurer and secretary after Examining & editting the treasurer's book find a balance in the treasury of fifty eight dollars & twenty six cents $58.26
Also to Elect two Elders & two Deacons in the place of those whose time is Expired—Elected Phillip Nagle in place of James Ackerman & John V'n Derbelt in place of James V'n Keuren Elders, and Charles Dearin in place of George V'n Derbelt & Isaiah Rinders in place of John U. Budd Deacons
the session Closed with prayer by the Presedent
recorded by Samuel Luckey secretary

1829 July 24th At a meeting of the Consistory Reformed Protestent Dutch Church at New Hackensack—met at the Church by Appointment — Present
Reven'd M. H. Dwight — Presedent

Elders { John Luyster / James Dearin / Phillip Nagle / John V'n Derbelt } Deacons { Peter V'n Derbelt / Isiah Rinders / Henry D. Traver }

The Presedent stated that the Object of the Meeting was to Enquire of the Consistory whether the walk & conversation of the Members in full Communion with s'd Congregation in their Respective beats was agreable to their profession as Christians—Nothing Accured—
Whereof Morace W. Dwight Presedent &
Sam'l Luckey Secretary

1829 sept 1st Att a Meeting of the Consistory of the Reformed Dutch Church at New Hackensack Mat at the Church by Appointm't — Preasent —
Revn'd M. W. Dwight — President —

Elders { John Luyster / John V'n Derbelt / James Dearin / Philip Nagle } Deacons { none attended }

Opened with prayer by the presed't M. W. Dwight

The Reformed Dutch Church of New Hackensack

Resolved that Sam'l Luckey Jun'r do close the Mortguage ag't Elias Taylor in Chancery, Also that said Sam'l do get the house above Mentioned Insured to the Amount of Eight hundred dolars, Resov'd Also that John V'n Derbelt & Philip Nagel be a commite to furnish meteriels to Repair the church steple with blinders Painting &c, Also that the treasurer deposin in their hands fifty two dl's & fifty Ct's which sum was paid to Johon V'n Derbels one of the commete for the same purpose by the Treasurer, Also that the Revn'd M. W. Dwight James Dearin & John Luyster be a commite to buy meteriels to paint the personage house repair fiences &c
Closed with prayer by the presedent

        Whereof M. W. Dwight was presedent and
        Sam'l Luckey secretary

1830 Feb'y 1st Consistory met for the Election of Officers — Presint
 M. W. Dwight Presedn't

Elders { John Luyster / John V'n Derbelt / Phillip Nagle / James Dearin   Deacons { Peter V'n Derbelt

Meeting was Opened with prayer by the Presedn't
 the following Officers wer then chosen
Peter V'n Derbelt in place of John Luyster
Elders Sam'l Luckey Jun'r in place of James Dearin
 Deacons { John U. Budd in place of Henry Traver
       John A. Monfort in place of Peter V'n Derbelt
 Closed with prayer by the Presedn't

        Revn'd M. W. Dwight Presedn't
        recorded by Sam'l Luckey sect'y

1830 feb'y 23rd At a meeting of the Consistory of the Reformed Dutch Church at New Hackensack met at s'd Church by appointm't — Present
Revn'd M. W. Dwight Presedint — Opened with prayer by the presedn't

Elders { John V'n Derbelt / Phillip Nagle / Samuel Luckey Jun'r / Peter V'n Derbelt   Deacons { Isaiah Rinders / John A. Monfort / Charles Dearin / John U. Budd

John V'n Derbelt stated that the object of the meeting was to settle with the Sam'l Luckey their treasurer & with Peter V'n Derbelt on the poor chest &c after examining the treasurrers Books find the treasury emty—also after examining the poor Chist find a balance in the poor Chest of forty three Dollars & sixty eight cents and the poor Chest was delivered over to John A. Monfort Containing the above sum of $43.68 — RESOLVED that the Revn'd M. W. Dwight Samuel Luckey Jun'r & Philip Nagle be a Commite to finish painting the personage house fiences &c which was not finished last fall also RESOLVED that John A. Monfort Give out of the poor Chest five dollars to Mrs. Hicks & five dollars to the widow Cornwell.

Closed with prayer by the presedn't   }   M. W. Dwight Presedn't
 done in Consistory   { Recorded by Sam'l Luckey sect'y

1830 tuesday Aug't 30th At a Meeting of the Consistory of the Reformed Dutch Church at New Hackensack met at the church by Appointment
Present Revn't M. W. Dwight Presedn't

Elders { John V'n Derbelt / Samuel Luckey Jun'r / Phillip Nagle / Peter V'n Derbelt   Deacons { Charls Dearin / John A. Monfort / John U. Budd / Isiah Rinders

Opened with prayer by the Presedent — who stated that the object of the meeting was to consult on the temporalities of the Church
Resolv'd that John V'n Derbelt & John A. Monfort be a Commite to lay out the Interest of the Peter V'n Bunschoten fund on the Church Resolv'd also that Peter V'n Derbelt & Isaiah Rynders be a commite to Get a well dug & stoned which John Robinson is to do for ten Dollars.

        Closed with Prayer by the Presedent
        Recorded by Sam'l Luckey sectr'y

1830 Nov'r 8th At a meeting of the Consistory of the Reformed Protestent Dutch Church at New Hackensack met at the Church by Appointm't
Present Revn'd W. M. Dwight Presedent

Minutes of Consistory

Elders { Samuel Luckey Jun'r / John V'n Derbelt / Peter V'n Derbelt / Phillip Nagle

Deacons { John U. Budd / Isaiah Rinders / John A. Monfort

Opened with prayer by the Presedent who stated that Object of the meeting was to contemplate on the temporaleties of the Church
RESOLVED that the Treasurer pay M. W. Dwight two dolars for well bucket well pole &c purchached by him
Resolved also that a New Bible be bought for the Use of the pulpet & that the treasurer pay fore the same

Closed with prayer by the Presedent
Recorded by Sam'l Luckey secretary

1831 Jan'y 27th At a meeting of the Consistory of the Reformed Protestent Dutch Church at New Hackensack met at the Church by Appointm't
Present Revn'd W. M. Dwight Presedent — Opened with prayer by the presed't

Elders { John V'n Derbelt / Peter V'n Derbelt / Philip Nagle / Samuel Luckey J'r

Deacons { John A. Monfort / John U. Budd / Esaias Rinders / Charles Dearin

It was stated that the object of the meeting was settle with Samuel Luckey their Treasurer and secretary After Examining the treasurer's Book find a balance in the treasury of thirteen dollars & Eighty seven Cents

Closed with prayer by the Presedent
Recorded by Sam'l Luckey Secretary

1831 Feb'y 7th At a meeting of the Consitory of the Reformed Protestant Dutch Church at New Hackensack met at the Church by Appointment present Revn'd M. W. Dwight presedent Opened with prayer by the presedent

Elders { John V'n Derbelt / Peter V'n Derbelt / Phillip Nagle

Deacons { John A. Monfort / Charles Dearin / John U. Budd / Esaias Rynders

It stated that the object of the meeting was to Elect new officers
The following officers were Chosen (Viz)

Elders { James V'n Keuren in place of John V'n Derbelt
        { Tunis V'n Bunschoten do Philip Nagle
Deacons { Charles Dearin reallected
        { Esaias Rynders do

Closed with Prayer by the Presedent
Recorded by Sam'l Luckey secretary

1831 M'ch 14th At a meeting of the Consistory of the Reformed Dutch Church at New Hackensack met at the Church by appointment present Reven'd Mores W. Dwight President Opened with Prayer by the Presdent

Elders { Tunis V'n Bunschoten / James V'n Keuren / Samuel Luckey Jun'r / Peter V'n Derbelt

Deacons { John A. Monfort / Esaias Rynders / John U. Budd

Resolved that James V'n Keuren & John A. Monfort are Appointed a Commite to superentend the Painting of the Church Resolved to Effect Insurance upon the Taylor house in pine Street

Closed with Prayer by the Presedent
Recorded by Sam'l Luckey Secreatry

1831 Octob'r 27th At a Meeting of the Consistory of the Church at New Hackensack met at the curch by appointment Members present

Elders { Tunis V'n Bunschoten / Sam'l Luckey Jun'r / James V'n Keuren / Peter V'n Derbelt

Deacons { Isaiah Rinders / John A. Monfort

Met to settle the Expence of buildin a wood house for the Revn'd M. W. Dwight when the building Commite (viz) Tunis V'n Bunschoten & James V'n Keuren brought in a bill of Expences to the Amount of $52.77 which was put in the treasury the Money to be Raised by superscription

Recorded by Sam'l Luckey Scttr'y

The Reformed Dutch Church of New Hackensack

1831 sept'r 1st Consistory met agreable to Call the Meeting was opened with prayer by the presedent — Members present M. W. Dwight pastre

Elders { Tunis V'n Bunschoten / James V'n Keuren / Peter V'n Derbelt

Deacons { John A. Monfort / John U. Budd / Isaiah Rinders / Charls Dearin

Resolved that the Wood house be built by superscription on the personage
Adjourned with prayer by the presedent
            Recorded by Sam'l Luckey sect'y

1831 Dec'r 15th Consistory met and was Opened with prayer by the presedent M. W. Dwigh

Elders { Tunis V'n Bunschoten / James V'n Keuren / Peter V'n Derbelt / Samuel Luckey Jun'r

Deacons { John A. Monfort

Agreed to recommend James De La Vergne to the Education Society, one hundred & ninety four Dl's & 75 Cents was brought in & paid over on account of Salory, Adjourned with prayer by the presedn't
            Recorded by Sam'l Luckey secretary

1832 Feb'y 6th Consistory met that the Church & was Opened with prayer by the prest't Members present — Morace W. Dwight presedent

Elders { Samuel Luckey Jun'r / James V'n Keuren / Peter V'n Derbelt

Deacons { John A. Monfort / John U. Budd

An Election of Officers then took place for the ensueing Year

Elders { Samuel Luckey Jun'r } Reelected
    { Peter V'n Derbelt Elders } do.
Deacons { John A. Monfort   reaalected
    { Henry Traver in place of John U. Budd

Resolved that Money be Appropriated from the poor Chest to pay the School Bill of the Widow Phebe Cornwell
Closed with prayer by the Presedent
            recorded by Sam'l Luckey secretary
   the above Ofisiers Ordained feb'y 26 Instnt

1832 Mc'h 6th the Consistory of the Reformed Protetent Dutch Church at New Hackensack met at Church by Appointm't present
the Revn'd M. W. Dwight Presedent — Opened with prayer by the pres't

Elders { Tunis V'n Bunschoten / Samuel Luckey Jun'r / Peter V'n Derbelt / James V'n Keuren

Deacons { John A. Monfort / Charls Dearin / Henry Traver / Isaah Rynders

1st Resolved to Enploy Sam'l Gomer to lay stone wall on the lower lot 2nd Also that five dollars Each be paid out of the poor Chest to Mrs. Wycoff & to Mrs. Phebe Cornwell 3 Resoved also that John A. Monfort Keep the poor Chest another Year

Closed with prayer by the presedn't { M. W. Dwight Presedn't / Sam'l Luckey sect'y

1832 June 1st At a Meeting of the Consistory of the Reformed Protestent Dutch Church at New Hackensack by Appoim't Members present —
   Presedn't Revn'd M. W. Dwight meeting Opened with prayer by the presedent

Elders { James V'n Keuren / Tunis V'n Bunschoten / Samuel Luckey Jun'r / Peter V'n Derbelt

Deacons { Eseiah Rinders

Presedent stated the Object of the meeting was to Settle with Eseiah Rinders as Ofosiating as Colester up to first may 1832 for which he is to be paid the sum of twenty five dollars as soon as it Can be collected Resolved also that the said Esisiah Rinders be paid at the rate of twenty five Dolars per Year from first of may 1832 as long as he remain Colester in the Church at New Hackensack Also that James V'n Keuren & Peter V'n Derbelt be a Commite to alter the pew No. 15 into short pews &c Closed with prayer by the presdent
         M. H. Dwight Presedent
         recorded by Sam'l Luckey sect'y

Minutes of Consistory

1832 Aug't 27th At a Meeting of the Consistory of the Reformed prostent Dutch Church at New Hackensack met at the Church by appoinment — present
the Revn'd Morace W. Dwight President

Elders { Tunis V'n Bunschoten / Samuel Luckey, Jun'r / James V'n Keuren / Peter V'n Derbels

Deacons { John A. Monfort / Charls Dearin / Isaiah Rinders / Henry D. Traver

Opened with prayer by the Presdent — Was to setle with Isaiah Rinders for past services as Correster and paid said Rinders 25 dollars and took rect't in full
Resolved that James V'n Keuren & Peter V'n Derbelt remain a Committe to make a new fienc on the west side of burying ground south of the Church and build Prevy to be paid out of the Interest on the Peter V'n Bunschoten fund —

Morace W. Dwight presedent
recorded by Sam'l Luckey Sect'y

1833 Jan'y 3rd Consistory met at the Church by Appointm't Opened with prayer by the Presdn't — present at the Meeting
Revn'd M. W. Dwight presedn't

Elders { Samuel Luckey Jun'r / James V'n Keuren / Peter V'n Derbelt

Deacons { Charls Dearin

Object of the meeting was to Settle up the Salory of the past Year the Collectors having made their reports the Amount due was paid in full & a recipt given — Closed with prayer by the Revn'd M. W. Dwight president

Rev'd M. W. Dwight was presedent
Recorded by Sam'l Luckey secretary

1833 feb'y 4th Consistory met at the Church by Appointment Opened with prayer by the presedent — Members present —
Revn'd Morice W. Dwight Presedent

Elders { Tunes V'n Bunschoten / James V'n Keuren / Peter V'n Derbelt / Samuel Luckey Jun'r

Deacons { John A. Monfort / Charls Dearin / Isaiah Rynders

Samuel Luckey Jun'r stated that the Object of the meeting was to Elect new Offisers and Settle with Samuel Luckey their treasurer & Secretary for the last Year — After Examing the said treasurers Book find a balance in the treasurey of nineteen Dollars and 30 Cents — RESOLVED that Phillip Nagle be elected Elder in place of Tuns V'n Bunschoten & John V'n Derbelt Elder be elected Elder in place of James V'n Keuren also that Charles Dearin & Iseaiah Rynders be Realected Deacons
Closed with prayer by the Presedent

Revn'd Morace W. Dwight Presedent
Recorded by Sam'l Luckey secretary

1833 M'ch 12 Consistory at the Church by Appointment, present
Revn'd M. W. Dwight president

Elders { John V'n Derbelt / Samuel Luckey Jun'r / Peter V'n Derbelt / Phillip Nagle

Deacons { Esaias Rynders / Henry D. Traver / John A. Monfort

Opened with prayer by the presedent
Consistory met to setle sundry Accounts with the treasurer which was setled to the Amount of twenty Dollars & sixty four Cents se treasurers Book same date
Closed with prayer by the Presedent

Revn'd Morace W. Dwight presdn't
Recorded by Sam'l Luckey sect'y

1833 Ap'l 26th Consistory of New Hackensack met pursuent to Notice and Opened with Prayer by the presedent — Present
The Reven'd Rev'd C. C. Cuyler presiding by Invitation

Elders { Sam'l Luckey Jun'r / Peter V'n Der Belt / John V'n Der Belt / Phillip Nagle

Deacons { John A. Monfort / Henry D. Traver

the Rev'd Morace W. Dwight stated that he had Received & Accepted a Call from the Reformed Dutch Church of Brooklyn Long Island Whereupon the following resolutions was passed RESOLVED that while we will make no opposition to the his Dismission on the

215

The Reformed Dutch Church of New Hackensack

other hand we will not take upon ourselves the Responsibility of Dismissing him & therefore refer the Whole Subject to the Descetion of the Classes of Poughkeepsie and will abide by their Desicion
Resolved that John V'n Derbelt be our Delegate to the next stated meeting of the Classes of Poughkeepsie to be held at Hopewell on the last tuesday of April Instent

Cornelius C. C. Cuyler Pres't pro Tem
Recorded from the minutes by Sam'l Luckey sect'y

1833 Sep't 1st At a Meeting of the Consistory and Several of the Members of the Reformed Dutch Church at New Hackensack Met at the Church by Appointment

Elders { Peter Van Debilt / Samuel Luckey / John Van Debilt / Phillip Nagel

Deacons { John A. Monfort / Henry D. Traver / Isaia Rinders / Charles Dearin

With Several of the Members
Samuel Luckey Chosen President protem
the Object of the Meeting Was Stated by Peter Van De Bilt to Make Choice of a Minister or Candidate for the Ministrey to be their Stated Minister to preach the Gospel to Said Congregation in the Said Church at New Hackensack — After due deliberation and takeing the Voice of the Consistory and Members present — It Was Unanimously Resolved to Circulate a Superscription List to indevour to Raise Money for Salary to present A Call to the Rev'd Cornelious Van Cleef to be their Stated pastor &c

Samuel Luckey Pres't protem
Done in Consistory S Luckey Sec't pro tem

1833 Sep't 23rd At a meeting of the Consitory of the Reformed Dutch Church at New Hackensack Met at the Church by appointment
Present Rev'd Charles Whitehead president pro tem by Invitation

Elders { Peter Van De Bilt / Samuel Luckey / John Van De Bilt / Phillip Nagel

Deacons { Henry D. Traver / John A. Monfort / Isaia Rinders

Opened With prayer by the President pro tem
The Object of the Meeting was Stated by John Van De Bilt to Consult What sum should be inserted in the Call to be presented to the Rev'd Cornelious Van Cleef to be a Stated Minister in the Congregation at New Hackensack
After a due Consideration on the subject it was Resolved unanimously that the Sum of Six hundred Dollars With the use of the personage house and Land yearly and Every year be presented to the said Rev'd Corlenious Van Cleef in Said Call as Long as he shall Remain their Minister & Also that the Elders Peter Van De Bilt and Samuel Luckey be appointed to present the Said Call to the Rev'd Cornelious Van Cleef — Also the above Elders shall have their nescesary Expences paid out of the treasury for going With Said Call

Charles Whitehead Pres't pro tem
Done in Consistory Samuel Luckey Sec't pro tem

1834 Feb'y 3rd At a meeting of the Consistory of the Reformed Dutch Church at New Hackensack Met at the Church by appointment
Present the Rev'd Cornelious Van Cleef President

Elders { Peter Van Der Bilt / Samuel Luckey / John Van Der Bilt / Phillip Nagel

Deacons { John A. Monfort / Henry D. Traver / Isaia Rinders / Charles Dearin

Opened with prayer by the president
the Object of the Meeting being Stated Was to Chose a New Sec't and Treasurer and to Settle up the Accounts of the Last year it being Voted that Samuel Luckey be Appointed Sec't and Treasurer in the place of Samuel Luckey Deseased
Closed with prayer by the President

Samuel Luckey Sec't

1834 Feb'y 10th At a meeting of the Consistory of the Reformed Dutch Church at New Hackensack Met at the Church by appointment
Present the Rev'd Cornelious Van Cleef president

Elders { Peter Van Der Bilt / Samuel Luckey / John Van Der Bilt / Phillip Nagel

Deacons { Henry D. Traver / Henry A. Monfort / Isaia Rinders

Minutes of Consistory

Opened With prayer by the president
the Object of the meeting being Stated Was that the Elders go through their Several beats of the Congregation and Know the minds of the pew holders and Congregation Respecting the Erection of a new and more Commodious House of Worship and Report accordingley Also to Chose two Elders and two deacons

Elders { Samuel Luckey Realected / Martin Monfort in the place of Peter Van Der Bilt
Deacons { Henry D. Traver Realected / William Churchel in the place of John A. Monfort

Adjourned to Meet again
Closed With prayer by the president

Samuel Luckey Sec't

1835 Feb'y 19th At a Meeting of the Consistory of the Reformed Dutch Church at New Hackensack Met at the Church by appointment
Present the Rev'd Cornelious Van Cleef President

Elders { John Van Der Bilt / Phillip Nagel / Samuel Luckey
Deacons { Henry D. Traver / Charles Dearin / William Churchill

Opened With prayer by the President
the Object of the Meeting was to Elect New Officers and to transact other business
Resolved that Tunis Van Bunschoten be Elected Elder in the place of Phillip Nagel and Matthew Luyster be Elected Elder in the place of John Van De Bilt and George Van De Bilt be Elected Deacon in the place of Charles Dearin and that Isaia Rinders be Realected Deacon
Closed with prayer By the president

Samuel Luckey Sec't

1835 March 17th at A Meeting of Consistory of the Reformed Dutch Church at New Hackensack Met at the Church by Appointment
present the Rev'd Cornelious Van Cleef President

Elders { Tunis Van Bunschoten / Matthew Luyster / Samuel Luckey
Deacons { Henry D. Traver / Isaia Rynders / William Churchel

Opened with prayer by the president
Resolved that the building Committee be requested to superintend the Erection of the fence around the New Church With discretionary power as to the fence railing &c.
Resolved that the sextons house be removed and placed in front of the Old Church
Resolved that Samuel Luckey and Henry D. Traver be a Committee to Superintend the Erection of this house
Closed with prayer by the president

Samuel Luckey Sec't

1835 April 13th at a Meeting of Consistory of the Reformed Dutch Church at New Hackensack met at the Church by Appointment
present the Rev'd Cornelious Van Cleef President

Elders { Tunis Van Bunschoten / Martin Monfort / Matthew Luyster / Samuel Luckey
Deacons { Isaia Ryders / Henry D. Traver / William Churchell

Opened With prayer by the President
Resolved that Mr. Bishop be Employed as the sexton for the year and that he Occupy the house as it now stands until Such time as the Consistory are prepared to Remove it
Resolved that Matthew Luyster and Tunis Van Bunschoten be a Committee to Call on Philander Seward to know if he had any resonable ground of Complaint Why the Sexton house Should not be removed in front of the Old Church
Closed with prayer by the President

Samuel Luckey Sec't

1835 May 5th At a Meeting of the Consistory of the Reformed dutch Church at New Hackensack Met at the Church by Appointment
Present the Rev'd Cornelious Van Cleef President

Elders { Tunis Van Bunschoten / Martin Monfort / Matthew Luyster / Samuel Luckey
Deacons { George Van De Bilt / Isaia Rynders / Henry D. Traver / William Churchwell

Opened with prayer by the president

The Reformed Dutch Church of New Hackensack

the Object of the Meeting Was to Settle the Accounts
The treasurers Account Was Examined and Was found to be Correct
The poor Chest Was examined and We also found it to have been Correctly Kept there being a ballance in it of Eighty four Dollars and Eighty four Cents
Resolved that Isaia Rynders Retain the poor Chest
Resolved that Aris Van De Bilt take pew No. 57 by paying one hundred & fifty Dollars for the same
Closed with prayer by the president

                                                              Samuel Luckey Sec't

1835 October 2nd At a Meeting of the Consistory of the Reformed dutch Church at New Hackensack Met at the Church by Appointmnt
Present the Rev'd Cornelious Van Cleef President

              Elders { Tunis Van Bunschoten / Martin Monfort / Matthew Luyster / Samuel Luckey   Deacon { Henry D. Traver

Opened With prayer by the President
Resolved that We take so mutch Money out of the poor Chest as can be spared to defray the Expences of removing and repairing the Sextons House
Closed With prayer by the president

                                                              Samuel Luckey sec't

1836 Feb'r 1st At a meeting of the Consistory of the Reformed dutch Church at New Hackensack Met at the Church by Appointment
Present the Rev'd Cornelious Van Cleef president

              Elders { Matthew Luyster / Martin Monfort / Samuel Luckey   Deacons { Henry D. Traver / William Churchwell

Opened with prayer by the President
The Object of the Meeting being stated Was to Settle with the Rev'd Cornelious Van Cleef and to Elect three Elders & two deacons

              Elders { John A. Monfort in the place of Martin Monfort / Aris Van Der Bilt in the place of Samuel Luckey / Stephen Monfort for one year in the place of Tunis Van Bunschoten Des'd
              Deacons { John U. Budd in the place of Henry D. Traver / William Todd in the place of William Churchwell

Closed with prayer by the President

                                                              Samuel Luckey sec't

1836 June 9th At a Meeting of the New and Old Consistory of the Reformed dutch Church of New Hackensack Met at the Church by Appointment
Present Aris Van Der Bilt President Protem

              Elders { Stephen Monfort / John A. Monfort / Aris Van Der Bilt / Matthew Luyster   Deacons { Isaia Rinders / William Todd
        Old E   Samuel Luckey   Old D   Henry D. Traver

Opened With prayer by the Elder Matthew Luyster
The Rev'd Cornelious Van Cleef Aded to Consistory and took his seat
The Object of the Meeting being stated Was to Settle up the Old Accounts and Examine the poor Chest Kept by Isaia Rynders and found all Correct and there Was forty nine dollars & ten Cents in poor Chest
Resolved that they pay Daniel Bishop Twenty two dollars out of poor Chest for Makeing fence &c
Resolved that they pay Matthew Luyster Twenty dollars and forty six Cents for Wood &c bought for the Church out of poor Chest
Resolved that they pay Jacob Dolson five dollars for Wood for the Church
Leaving a ballance in the poor Chest of One dollar and Sixty four Cents
Resolved that Isaia Rynders Keep the poor Chest
Closed With prayer by the President

                                                             Samuel Luckey Sec't

1837 Feb'r 25th at A Meeting of the Consistory of the Reformed dutch Church at New Hackensack Met at the Church by Appointment
Present the Rev'd Cornelious Van Cleef president

              Elders { Aris Van Der Bilt / Matthew Luyster / John A. Monfort   Deacons { Isaiah Rinders / George Van Der Bilt / William Todd

Minutes of Consistory

Opened With prayer by the president
The Object of the Meeting Was to Elect two Elders & two deacons

Elders { Peter Van Derbilt in the place of Stephen Monfort
         Matthew Luyster Realected
Deacons { Henry D. Traver in the place of Isaiah Rynders
          George Vanderbilt Realected

Closed With prayer by the President

                Samuel Luckey Sec't

1837 March 27th At a Meeting of the Consistory of the reformed dutch Church at New Hackensack Met by Appointment
Present the Rev'd Cornelious Van Cleef President

Elders { Matthew Luyster
         John A. Monfort
Deacons { Henry D. Traver
          William Todd

Opened With prayer by the President
the Object of the Meeting Was to Examin the poor Chest it was found to be correctley Kept and there Was a ballance in it of Twelve dollars and Eighty Six Cents and the poor Chest Delivered Over to Henry D. Traver
Adjourned With prayer by the president

                Samuel Luckey Sec't

1837 May 16th At a Meeting of the Consistory of the Reformed Dutch Church at New Hackensack Met at the Church by Appointment
Present the Rev'd Cornelious Van Cleef President

Elders { Matthew Luyster
         Peter Van Der Bilt
         John A. Monfort
Deacons { Henry D. Traver

Opened With prayer by the President
The Object of the Meeting Was to take in Consideration the propriety of haveing the Church and personage house Insured
Resolved that the Church be Ensured for $5000
Resolved that the personage house be Ensured for $750
Each of them in the Dutchess County Mutual Insurance Company
Closed With prayer by the president

                Samuel Luckey Sec't

1838 Feb'r 5th At a Meeting of the Consistory of the reformed dutch Church at New Hackensack Met by appointment
Present the Rev'd Cornelious Van Cleef President

Elders { Matthew Luyster
         Peter Van Der Bilt
         John A. Monfort
Deacons { George Van Der Bilt
          Henry D. Traver
          John U. Budd
          William Todd

Opened With prayer by the president
the object of the Meeting Was to Elect two New Elders and two New Deacons &c
Resolved that Samuel Luckey be Elected Elder in the place of Aris Van Der Bilt
Resolved that John A. Monfort be Realected Elder
Resolved that Henry D. Hayt be Elected Deacon in the place of John U. Budd
Resolved that James M. Jones be Elected Deacon in the place of William Todd
Closed &c

                Samuel Luckey Sec't

1838 April 11th at a Meeting of the Consistory of the Reformed dutch Church at New Hackensack Met by appointment
Present the Rev'd Cornelious Van Cleef President

Elders { Peter Van Der Bilt
         Matthew Luyster
         Samuel Luckey
Deacon { James M. Jones

Opened With prayer by the President
the Object of the Meeting being Stated
Resolved that We Repair the Barn and put an addition on the South End of it twelve feet Wide With new Sideing and New Shingles on the Whole and fix hovel &c
Resolved that a Superscription be Circulated in the Congregation to defray the expences &
Resolved that James M. Jones have power to agree With Daniel Bishop to do the Work
Closed with prayer by the President

                Samuel Luckey Sec't

The Reformed Dutch Church of New Hackensack

1838 June 28th at a Meeting of the Consistory of the Reformed dutch Church of New Hackensack Met by Appointment
Present the Rev'd Cornelious Van Cleef President

Elders	Matthew Luyster John A. Monfort Samuel Luckey Peter Van Derbilt	Deacons	Henry D. Traver James M. Jones

Opened with prayer by the President
the Object of the Meeting being Stated by the president
Resolved that We Settle up all the accounts With the paster also the books of the Secretary and treasurer and found the books all rite

1839 Feb'r 4th At a meeting of the Consistory of the Reformed dutch Church of New Hackensack pusuant to notice held at the Church
Present the Rev'd Cornelious Van Cleef President

Elders	Matthew Luyster Peter Van Derbilt John A. Monfort Samuel Luckey	Deacons	Henry D. Hait Henry D. Traver James M. Jones

Opened With prayer by the president
The object of the Meeting being Stated Was to Elect Three Elders and two Deacons and to Settle up all the Accounts of the past year
Resolved that John Vanderbilt be Elected Elder in the place of Matthew Luyster
Resolved that Peter Vanderbilt be Realected Elder
Resolved that Phillip Nagel be Elected Elder for one year in the place of Samuel Luckey
Resolved that Benjamin Everitt be elected Deacon in the place of George Van Der Bilt
Resolved the Phillip Van Der Bilt be elected Deacon in the place of Henry D. Traver
Closed with Prayer
C. Van Cleef, Pres't

March 18th 1839 At a meeting of the old and the new consistory of the Reformed Dutch Church of New Hackensack held in the Church pursuant to notice. The following persons were present. Rev. C. Van Cleef, President.

Elders—Matthew Luyster
    John A. Monfort
    John Van Der Bilt
Deacons—James M. Jones
    Henry D. Traver
    Phillip Van Der Bilt
Peter Van Der Bilt
Samuel Luckey
Phillip Nagle
Henry D. Hayt
Benjamin H. Everitt

opened with Prayer. The object of the meeting was stated to elect a New Treasurer & secretary to examine the poor chest & to elect one of the Deacons to take charge of the same.
Resolved That Henry D. Traver be Elected Treasurer & secretary.
Resolved—That Benjamin H. Everitt take charge of the poor chest. It was also
Resolved—That a new subscription list be circulated through the congregation to make up the deficiency of the Salary occasioned by deaths & removals.
It having been stated by the President that the Books & papers belonging to the Church has been kept with great care by the late Treasurer & his Father, It was
Resolved—That while we Cherish the Memory of Samuel Luckey Sen. who for many years was Treasurer & Secretary of the Consistory, we most cordially present our thanks to Samuel Luckey Jun'r for the Manner in which he has discharged these duties since the death of his Father.
Closed with Prayer, C. Van Cleef, Pres't

April 15th 1839. Consistory met according to notice. Opened with Prayer.
Present — C. Van Cleef, President.

Elders	Peter Van Der Bilt John A. Monfort John Van Der Bilt	Deacons	James M. Jones Benjamin Everitt Henry D. Hayt Phillip Van Der Bilt

Resolved That John Van Der Bilt be a delegate to attend the meeting of Classis on the last Tuesday of this month.
Resolved that the ground formerly occupied as the site of the old church & the yard in front of it be laid out in lots of 15 feet square & offered for sale at auction on the first Monday of May at 2 o'clock in the afternoon, also
Resolved—That the proceeds of the Sale be appropriated towards a new or more commodious Parsonage, also
Resolved—That Purchasers have six months credit.
consistory adjourned with Prayer, C. Van Cleef, Pres't.

Minutes of Consistory

1839 July 1st At a meeting of the consistory of the Reformed Dutch Church of New Hackensack held in the Church pursuant to notice, the following persons were present, Rev. C. Van Cleef president

Elders { John Vander Bilt / John A. Monfort / Philip Nagel / Peter Vander Bilt

Deacons { James M. Jones / Philip Vander Bilt

Opened with prayer the object was stated to take in Consideration the Situation of the Church
Resolved that it is necessary to paint the Church the ensuing fall and that Peter Vander Bilt and Philip Vander Bilt be a Committy to furnish paint and oil and superintend the same
Resolved that it is necessary to repair the Colums in front of the Church and John Vander Bilt and John Monfort be a commity to superintend the same
Resolved that a collection be taken up to aid the Colinization society
Consistory adjourned with prayr

C. Van Cleef President
H. D. Traver Sec't

Sep't 9th 1839 Consistory met opened with prayer
the following resolutions were passed, viz
Resolved That Phillip B. Van Der Bilt be authorized to have the Elders Decons & Pastors pews lined & cushioned
Resolved That the male Members of the congregation be requested to meet on Tuesday the 17th inst at 2 o clock P. M. to Consult with reference to a more Comodious Parsonage House

Closed with Prayr C. Van Cleef Pres't
H. D. Traver sec't

Oct 3d 1839 Consistory met & was opened with Prayr
Resolved That Mr. John Van Der Bilt attend the meeting of Classes as the Elder from this Church on the last Tuesday of this month at Glenham
The resolutions passed at the meeting of the male members of the congregation held the 17th of Sep't were then read — wherfore it was
Resolved That a Commitee be appointed to carry the resolutions into effect passed at meeting of the male members of the Congregation held the 17th ult to build a new Parsonage House
Resolved That the commitee consist of Stephen S. Thorn Philander Seward Schenck Aackerman John Van Der Bilt & Philip B. Van der Bilt with Benjamin Everitt Esq'r as their Chairman
Resolved That said Commitee be athorized to furnish the means for building
Resolved That said commitee have a discretionary power but one requested to Consult the Congregation

Closed with Prayr
C. Van Ceef Pres't
H. D. Traver Sect

Feb 3d 1840 Consistory regularly Covened & was opened with Prayr. This being the annual meeting for Election of officers the following persons were chosen Officers for the ensuing year

Elders
Mr. John A. Monfoort — reelected
Mr. Philip Nagele — do
Mr. James M. Jones in place of Peter Van Der Bilt for one year

Decons
Mr. James S. Monfoort in place of James M. Jones
Mr. Henry D. Hayt reelected
Resolved That Daniel Bishop be elected as Chorister & Sexton for one year from the 1st of May 1840 also
Resolved That Mr. Henry D. Hayt & Philip Van Der Bilt be a commitee to see that the Church is properly attended to

Closed with Prayr
C. Van Cleef Pres't
H. D. Traver Sect

March 2nd 1840 The Consistory met & was opened with Prayr. The Poor Chest was examined & was found to contain 20 Dollars wherfore it was
Resolved That 5 Dollars be given to Mrss Hicks It being understood that she was in need & that 15 Dollars be applied towards paying off the Church debt The pew No. 93 was sold to Mr. Abraham Sleight fo 60 Dollars & a certificate was ordered to be given to that effect

The Reformed Dutch Church of New Hackensack

Resolved That the building Commitee have liberty to use the stoves from the old Pasonage Hose for the new one now building if necessary
Closed with Prayr
C. Van Cleef Prest
H. D. Traver Sect

June 18th 1840 Consistory meet according to previous Notice given & was opened with Prayr
Resolved That a Colection be made on some suitable Sabbath to enable the consistory to pay the chorister
Resolved That Mr. Everitt pay $2.50 out of the Poor Chest for repairs of the Sextons Hose
Adjourned with Prayr
C. Van Cleef Prest.
H. D. Traver Sect.

June 27th 1840 Consistory met according to adjournment and was opend with prayr
Resolved That the old Parsonage House be offered for Sale whenever the new one shall be ready to be occupied
Resolved That the Building commitee be requested to sell the old Parsonage House at Public Auction at such time as they may think proper
Closed with Prayr
C. Van Cleef Prest
H. D. Traver Sect

August 11th 1840 Consistory met & was opened with Prayr
It was stated to consistory that Stephen S. Thorn Wished to purchase so much of the ground which was added to the old burial ground as lay between their family burial place & the fence on the north side Wherefore it was
Resolved that the consistory will sell to Stephen S. Thorn according to his request the ground in the burial ground between the fence and the ground now occupied upon the same Conditions & terms as the lots already sold also
Resolved That the same privilege be extended to Mr. Isaiah Rynders if requested
Closed with Prayr C. Van Cleef Pres't
H. D. Traver Sec't

Oct 31st 1840 Consistory met according to notice & was opened with Prayr
Resolved That Mr. Henry D. Hayt be appointed to attend to any business conected with the disposal of the lots in the burial ground.
Resolved that a new fence be made in front of the New Parsonage House & that John Van Der Bilt & James M. Jones be a commitee to attend to the same
Resolved That in collecting the Salary for the Pastor a paper be circulated to see what can be done in raising money for the Chorister
Closed with Prayr C. Van Cleef Pres't
H. D. Traver Sec't

Feb 1st 1841 The Consistory met & was opened with Prayr this being the annual meeting for the Election of Officers & other business the following persons were Chosen for the ensuing two years
Elders
Mr. Schenck Ackerman in place of James M. Jones
Mr. John Van Der Bilt reelected
Deacons
Mr. Benjamin H. Everitt reelected
Mr. Philip B. Van Der Bilt reelected
The Treasurers accounts was examined & were found to be correct
The Poor Chest was examined & found to contain the sum of $21.34 cents sixteen dollars 58/100 cents which was appropriated to incidental expences leaving a balance of four dollars 76/100 Cents
Resolved That Mr. Everitt retain the Poor Chest
Resolved that Daniel Bishop be continued as Chorister & sexton for one year from the 1st of May 1841
Resolved That in case an amicable arrangement can be made with the present occupants of Pew No. 65 it be either rented or sold at the apprisment as opportunity may offer.
Closed with Prayr
C. Van Cleef Pres't
H. D. Traver Sect

Feb 10th 1842
    Consistory met present Elders John Vander Bilt John A. Monfoort Scheck Aackerman Deacons H. D. Hayt James S. Monfort Phillip B. Van der Bilt Opend with prayr

Minutes of Consistory

This being the annual meeting for the election of officers the following persons were elected for the ensuing two years
    Elders George Van der Bilt in place of Philip Nagle
              John A. Monfoort reelected
    Decons H D Traver in place of H D Hayt
              James S. Monfoort reelected
the yearly settlement of accounts were then attended to after paying the salary of the Pastor Consistory adjourned with prayr
                                                C. Van Cleef Pres't
                                                Henry D. Traver Sec't

Feb 13th 1843 Consistory met and oppened with prayr by the president Rev C Va Cleef this being the annul Meeting for the Election of Officers the following persons were elected for the ensuing year
present   Elders   Deacons
            John Vanderbilt   Phillip Vanderbilt
            Scheck Ackerman   James Monfoort
                                            Bejamine Everitt
                                            Henry D. Traver
Resolved that Jeremiah Platt be elected Elder in place of John Van der Bilt whose term of office expires
Schenck Ackerman reelected
Deacons Harvy D Platt elected in place of Benjamin Everitt whose term of office expires
William Seward elected in place of Phillip Van der Bilt whose term Expires
Resolved that James S. Monfoort take Charge of the poor Chest the poor chest was examined & found to Contain Eleven dollars 59/100 cents the settlement of Accounts were attended to & the books Balanced
Resolved that Daniel Bishop be employed as corrister & Sexton for the ensuing year from the first of May next on the same Conditions as last year
                                    Closed with Prayr C. Van Cleef Pres't
                                                    H. D. Traver sec't

Feb 5th 1844
    Consistory of the reformed Dutch Church of New Hackensack met this being the annual Meeting
the meeting was opened with prayr present Cornelus Van Cleef President
Elders   Schenck Aackerman   Deacons
           John A. Monfoort   James S. Monfoort
           Jeremiah Platt   Henry D. Traver
                                            Wm. Seward
                                            Harvy D. Platt
The Settlement of accounts wer attended to the Books balanced & a receipt form the Pastor In full for salary for the past year was given
The Poor Chest was examined & found to Contain twenty four dollars 59/100 Cents
Resolved that Daniel Bishop be employed for ensuing year on the same terms as last year
Resolved that twelve dollars be taken from the poor Chest to pay a bill for repairing the sextons house
Resolved that twelve dollars be paid to Mr. Jones for the same purpose
Resolved That pew rent be applied to pay Interest on notes held by Mr. Platt & Patterson & Mrss Sherwood
Resolved That pew No. 11 be received from Scheck Ackerman
        Elders   Deacons
        George Van der bilt   James S. Monfort reelected
        John A. Monfoort
        Reelected
When on motion it was stated the Treasurer & Secretary should be employed without any remuneration for services therefore Resolved that Harvey D Platt be elected Treasurer & Secretary Closed with prayr
                                                   C. Van Cleef Pres't
                                                   H. D. Traver Sec't

August 15, 1843 The Consistory met and opened with Prayer Members all present The object of the Meeting was Stated by the Prest to be as follows. He having represented to Mr. Traver that their were reports concerning him touching a business transaction with Mr. Hervey B Van Dyne which reports were not only highly injurious to his Christian character but calculated from his Standing in the Church greatly to wound the cause of religion. Mr. Traver declared his inocence and wished a meeting of Consistory to be called that he might have an opportunity of making explanation to his Brethren

The Reformed Dutch Church of New Hackensack

The present meeting having been convened for that purpose Mr. Traver proceeded to give his explanations concerning the transaction with Mr. Van Dyne together with the reason why he compromised the offer as he did.

He answered questions and replied to objections put to Him by the Members of Consistory touching any reports they had heard The Note was produced and carefully examined and the Consistory after considering all the facts in the case within their knowledge and comparing them with the reports in circulation did unanimously acquit Mr. Traver of the charge fraud in this transaction. Whether he acted wisely in settling the affair as he did is a matter of individual opinion. It is to be hoped that the course Mr. Traver has pursued in coming before the Consistory in an open and friendly manure as well as their decision in his case may be satisfactory. If not the Constitution of our Church points out a remedy.

Resolved that the above record be publicly read at the close of the preparatory service.

H. D. Platt Clerk

Sep 26 1843 Consistory met all present Opened with Prayer.
This meeting was to try a complaint of Mr. Harvey B. Van Dyne against Mr. Henry D. Traver.
On the 15th of Sep. 1843 I called upon the Rev. C. Van Cleef The President of the Consistory of the Reformed Dutch Church of New Hackensack and formally entered a complaint against the said Traver
The Complaint is in the Words following viz
That the said Henry D. Traver altered a Note in his possession given to him by myself and Father in Law in the spring of 1842 which alteration consisted in the addition of four words viz "with interest from date" and which charge I shall endeavour to prove by the following witnesses, Messrs Robert Matthews Jeremiah C. Brower James Van Dyne and Edward B. Van Dyne

Harvey B. Van Dyne

The parties being present with their witnesses and being ready for trial Mr. Hervey D. Platt was chosen clerk pro. tem. The Rev. Mr. Johnson by consent of the parties was the counsel for the prosecution and the Rev. Mr. Mann for the defence. The witnesses were all put under oath and the testimony is as follows
    Prosecution
        Harvey B. Van Dyne
Note destitute of the words "with Interest from date" when He gave the Note. Mr. Matthews had the Note when He next saw it. Matthews drew the Note. Witness dated the Note. He dated it at Traver's House. Note given for $200.00 Note given for back Interest. Not anything said about Interest at the Time the Note was given In the House Van Dyne dated the Note. Mrs. Traver was in the room when witness dated the Note
Cross Ex No agreement between witness and Matthews about Interest Matthews objected to pay Interest on the Note, The words added were different than the general appearance of the Note. Witness says to the best of his belief that it is Traver's writing
    Robert Matthews
Drew the Note. Did not date it. Not any thing said about Interest at the time the witness drew the Note The words added were not in the witness writing. Said that Van Dyne said that the Note had not Interest on it. Witness made no provision to pay the Interest. Next saw it in the Hands of Vanick. Witness says that he thought that there had been some Liberty taken with the Note does not fix it on any one. Paid the Note and took it.
Cross Ex. Thinks that it would draw Interest. On opening the Note thought that Traver had added the words. Was not possitive first that their was any difference in the date or addition in the writing.
Had no design in leaving out Interest.
    Jeremiah C. Brower
Has seen the Note. Saw it in Van Dyne Hands. Thinks it was paid. Noticed the words. Thinks they differed from the Note or date. Did not intefier with the Note. Came in their proper place. The addition was the conversation when witness saw the Note. The addition in my opinion was not Van Dyne writing. Witness might be mistaken. Does not know that Traver made the addition. Van Dyne told Traver that their was something in the Note that He Van Dyne did not put in. Traver did not reply to Van Dyne's answer. Van Dyne did not say that Traver had done it. They were at Van Dyne's House. Was surprised that Traver did not answer Van Dyne. Thought that Traver was Guilty.
    James Van Dyne
Has seen Note. After it was paid. The first witness saw it H. Van Dyne had it. He noticed that addition. Cannot say who dated it. Thought it was Traver's. His impression strong that it was. Does not think it was H. Van Dyne. His knowledge of Traver's writing convinced witness. Dated and date differed material so much that it was Two Hand writing. Has had Traver's and Van Dynes Writing and compared them together. Thinks that the addition was in Travers writing

Minutes of Consistory

Cross Ex
Asked Van Dyne if He did not date the Note. Van Dyne asked witness if he did not see some other alteration. Said he did. Strong opinion that it was Travers writing. Only seen Traver write his name. Thinks that he would not have noticed the addition if his attention had not been called to it. Witness has not examined any of Traver's writing that he knew to be Travers.

Edward Van Dyne
Acquainted with H. Van Dyne's writing. Difference between date and dated. Saw it after it was paid. Had heard a report about the Note before witness saw the Note. Had not heard any agreement about Interest. Has seen Travers hand writing in the shape of receipts. Compared Traver's writing with the additional words in the Note. Thinks they were Traves.

Adam Traver
Was Home. Was in the House. Traver was for distroying the Note. Van Dyne said that he would fix it so that it would draw Interest Saw Van Dyne write the additional words. Saw Van Dyne write the date Sat near when Van Dyne wrote on the Note. First he heard of it was Two or three days since

Cross Ex
Positive that Traver did not write anything at the time. Did not know at the time what the Note was given for. Saw Van Dyne write it and read it after Van Dyne wrote it

Elias Traver
Has seen the Note. Yesterday was the first. Did not see any of Traver's writing. Examined the Note. Saw Two hand writing on it. Does not think that any was Traver's

Henry D. Hayt
Acquainted with Travers writing in some degree. Date and the additional words written by one person. Does not think the addition in Travers writing.

Morgan L. Traver
Acquainted with Brothers writing. Does not think their is any of his writing on the Note

Philander Seward
Not acquainted with Travers writing. Thinks their is a strong resemblance between date and the additional words

Leonard L. Pells
Has seen the Note. Does not see anything like Travers writing on the Note.

June 24, 1844 At a Meeting of the Consistory of the Reformed Dutch Church of New Hackensack according to notice held at the Church
Present Rev'd Cornelius Van Cleef Presedent

Elders	Deacons
Schenck Ackerman	James Monfort
Jeremiah Platt	Henry D. Hayt
George Van Derbelt	William Seward
John A. Monfort	Hervey D. Platt

Opened with Prayer. The object of the meeting was to examine and Settle the pecunay concerns of the Church. Which were done with general Sattisfaction.
Resolved . That Mr. Bishop bill be paid from the Poor Chest
Resolved That Mr. Traver be paid for his services as Tres. & Secetry
Consistory adjourned with Prayer

Rev'd C. Van Cleef Prest.
H. D. Platt Sect.

Feb 5, 1845 At a meeting of the Consistory of the Reformed Dutch Church of New Hackensack according to notice given held at the Church
Present Rev'd C. Van Cleef President

Elders	Deacons
Jeremiah Platt	James S. Monfort
Schenck Ackerman	Henry D. Hayt
John A. Monfort	William Seward
	Hervey D. Platt

Opened with Prayer
The object of the meeting was to elect officers for the ensuing Two Years and to attend to some pecunary business
Resolved That Mr. Bishop remain the coming Year the same as He has, on the condition that He thoroughly sweeps and dusts the Church once in four weeks, and that H. D. Platt notify Mr. Bishop to that effect
Resolved that at a sutable time a collection be made for two Sabbaths in the Church to obtain Money to erect a monument over the Grave of the Rev. Isaac Reysdyk formaly the Pastor of this Church

The Reformed Dutch Church of New Hackensack

The following persons were chosen for the ensuing Tow Years

Elders
Jeremiah Platt } reelected
Schenck Ackerman

Deacons
William Seward } reelected
Hervey D. Platt

Consistory closed with Prayer

Rev. C. Van Cleef Prest
H. D. Platt Scribe

March 31, 1845 At a Meeting of Consistory of the Reformed Dutch Church of New Hackensack according to notice held at the church.
Present Rev. C. Van Cleef President

Elders Schenck Ackerman
    Jeremiah Platt
    John A. Monfort
    George Van Derbelt

Deacons
    James S. Monfort
    William Seward
    H. D. Platt

Resolved   That stone wall on the East side of the Grave Yard should be staked and with chesnut Timber.
Messrs Ackerman & Monfort to get the Timber on the ground
Resolved that Jeremiah Platt be the Elder to go with Mr. Van Cleef to attend Classes at Glenham, which will be held on the third Tuesday of April at 10 0 A. M.
The Meeting was opened & closed by Prayer By the President

H. D. Platt Clerk

May 20, 1845 At a meeting of the Consistory of the Reformed Dutch Church of New Hackensack held at the Church pursuant to notice
The following persons were present

Rev. C. Van Cleef President

Elders
Schenck Ackerman   George Van Derbelt
Jeremiah Platt

Deacons
James S. Monfort   William Seward
Henry D. Hayt   Hervey D. Platt

Opened with Prayer
The object of the Meeting was to attend to the pecunary business of the Church which was done to the satisfaction of the Consistory But on looking forwards the prospect for meeting the debts of the Church was not as bright as it had been thefore
Resolved that on the 4 June the Congregation be called together to devise some plan that the Consistory may discharge the debt of the Congregation
All business being attended to the Meeting was closed with Prayer by the Rev. C. Van Cleef.

H. D. Platt Clerk

June 4 1845 Meeting at the Church according to Notice. Mr. John Luyster was called to the Chair and H. D. Platt Clerk
The meeting was opened with prayer by the Rev. C. Van Cleef who also stated the object of the meeting and requested the meeting to devise some plan that the Consistory might liquidate the debt of the Congregation.
Re'd   That Money should be raised by subscription to liquidate the debt of the Congregation
Res'd   The amount subscribed should be paid at the time of subscribing or at six or at nine months
Re'd   That the Committee to circulated the subscription be the Rev. C. Van Cleef & Jeremiah Platt
Res'd   That the subscription be drawn and circulated immediately
Res'd   That power be given to the committee to draw the Caption to the subscription
Res'd   That the Meeting adjourn with prayer

John Luyster Chairman   H. D. Platt, Clerk

Aug. 29, 1845
    Meeting at the Church according to notice. All of the Consistory present. Prayer by the Rev. Van Cleef who also stated that their are reports in circulation injuriously affecting the character & Standing of Mr. Phillip Nagle as Member of this Church
Res'd   Therefore that Mr. Nagle be requested to abstain from the Communion of the Lord's Supper until such time as the Consistory shall determine
Closed with prayer by the President.

H. D. Platt Clerk

1846 Jan 26
    Consistory met at the Church according to notice. The object was to rent the Pews for the coming Year & to pay Mr. Van Cleef part of His Salary which objects were accomplished

H. D. Platt

Minutes of Consistory

Feb 2, 1846
    Meeting of the Consistory at the Church accoding to Notice
Presant Rev. C. Van Cleef

Elders	John A. Monfort	Deacons	Henry D. Hayt
	Schenck Ackerman		James S. Monfort
	Jeremiah Platt		William Seward
			Hervey D. Platt

Opened and closed with Prayer by the Rev. C. Van Cleef
The object of the Meeting was to elect officers for the ensuing Two Years and to attend to the pecunary business of the Church which business was done to the satisfaction of all the Consistory
Resolved That the account of Jeremiah Platt of Pew rents and Plots sold in the Grave Yard be entered on the Church Book at full length
Re'd That Mr. Bishop remain the coming Year the same as he has the past and that H. D. Platt notify Bishop to that effect.
The following persons were reelected for the Two ensueing Years
    Elders John A. Monfort
                George Van Derbelt
    Deacons Henry S. Hayt
                 James S. Monfort
Consistory adjourned

                                              H. D. Platt Clerk

1846 April 15 The Consistory of the Reformed Dutch Church of New Hackensack met at the Church according to Notice present the Rev. C. Van Cleef
    Elders Schenck Ackerman
                Jeremiah Platt
                John A. Monfort
    Deacons William Seward
                 H. D. Platt

The Meeting opened with Prayer by the Rev. Mr. Van Cleef who also stated the object of the meeting was to hear Mr. Phillip Nagle respecting the crime alledged against Him
Whereas Mr. Phillip Nagle has been accused by the oath of Mrs. Harriet Lawson of being the Father of her illegitimate child and while the Consistory from the statements of Mr. Nagle believe him to be innocent yet under the peculiar circumstance of the case and for the good of the cause of religion, therefore
Resolved that until more light be shown upon the case the said Phillip Nagle be suspended from the Communion of the Church
The above preamble and resolution were unanimously adopted by the Consistory
The meeting closed with Prayer by the Rev. C. Van Cleef

                                              H. D. Platt Clerk

June 19, 1846
    The Consistory of the Reformed Dutch Church of New Hackensack met at the Church according to notice Present the Rev. C. Van Cleef
    Elders George Van Derbilt
      "   Jeremiah Platt
    Deacons H. D. Platt

The meeting opened with Prayer by the Rev. Van Cleef The cause of the meeting was to settle with Mr. Van Cleef and to pay some other small Bills which was done to the sattisfaction of all Meeting Closed with prayer by Mr. Van Cleef

                                              H. D. Platt Clerk

At a meeting of the Consistory of the reformed Dutch Church of New Hackensack at the Church present Rev. Van Cleef

Elders	S. Ackerman	Deacons	William Seward
"	George Van Derbelt		James S. Monfort
"	Jeremiah Platt		H. D. Platt
"	John A. Monfort		

Meeting opened with prayer The business before the Consistory were to appoint an elder to attend Classes which were to meet at New Hackensack the   Sep The Elder elected was John A. Monfort and to attend to fixing Posts and Railing about the Church Yard. Closed with prayer

                                              H. D. Platt Clerk

The Reformed Dutch Church of New Hackensack

Feb 1, 1847
    At a meeting of the Consistory of the Reformed Dutch Church of New Hackensack held in the Church pursuant to notice the following persons were present
Rev. C. Van Cleef President

Elders George Van Derbelt   Deacons James S. Monfort
          John A. Monfort   William Seward
          Jeremiah Platt   Hervey D. Platt

Opened with prayer by the President. The object of the meeting was to elect officers for the ensuing Two Years to examine accounts and to pay Mr. Van Cleef
Resolved That James S. Monfort and William Seward Bills be paid out of the Poor Chest
    In the Case of Daniel Bishop the following Preamble and resolutions were unanimously adopted.
    Whereas Mr. Daniel Bishop did of His own accord offer to the Consistory that he would lead the singing on the Sabbath for what they could collect for him from the Congregation provided He might remain in their House with the privilege of Sexton and
    Whereas He has without giving them timely notice and while they were in good faith making their annual appeal to the people in His behalf, broken His engagement not only by abandoning his post as chorister but by demanding from the Consistory that which they had never agreed to do and were not able to do if disposed either on account of the unwillingness of the people to contribute or His being in debt to so many and
    Whereas He might have resigned His office in an honourable manner
Therefore Resolved That this Consistory cannot but consider the contract of Mr. Bishop in violating an engagement of His own seeking not only dishonourable but as designed to make a false impression
Also Resolved That he be notified to vacate the premises he occupies at the end of thirty days also that His office as Sexton expires with this day.
    Resolved That the Clerk furnish Mr. Bishop with a Copy of the above preamble and resolutions. Dated Feb 1. 1847
The following persons were chosen officers for the ensuing Two Years

Elders   Schenck Ackerman   ⎫
             Jeremiah Platt   ⎬ relected
Deacons William Seward   ⎫
             Hervey D. Platt   ⎬ relected

The Meeting closed with prayer by the **President**

H. D. Platt Clerk

March 12, 1847
    At a Consistory Meeting after the preparatory Sermon at New Hackensack Church it was
    Resolved That Samuel Gomer be the Sexton of the Church the next Year commencing the first of April next and that He occupy the Sexton's House during that Time for special agreement see hereafter

H. D. Platt Clk

At a Consistory Meeting after Service April 11, 1847
Resolved that John A. Monfort be the Elder to accompany the Rev. C. Van Cleef to Hyde Park to attend Classes Ap 20.

H. D. Platt Clerk

May 21, 1847
    Consistory meeting at the Church according to appointment Opened with prayer by Mr. Van Cleef the President Present
Elders John A. Monfort, George Van Derbelt & J. Platt
Deacons William Seward and H. D. Platt
    The business before the Church was to settle with the Pastor and attend to the other pecunary business of the Church which was done to the satisfaction of the Consistory the meeting was closed by prayer

H. D. Platt Sect

Feb. 7, 1848.
    At a Meeting of the Consistory of the Reformed Dutch Church of New Hackensack held in the Church pursuant to notice the following persons were present
Rev. C. Van Cleef President

      Elders   John A. Monfort
                  Jeremiah Platt
                  George Van Derbelt
      Deacons James S. Monfort
                  William Seward
                  Henry D. Hoyt
                  Hervey D. Platt

Minutes of Consistory

Opened with prayer by the President the object of meeting was to elect Officers for ensueing Two Years examine accounts and to pay Mr. Van Cleef
Resolved That the following bills be paid out of the Poor Chest

    Mr. Van Cleef for Paint Oil &c $2.62
    Mr. William Seward repairing stoves "2.87
    " " " " Railing   "2.01
    Funeral expences S. Gomer   "9.00

The following persons were then elected for the ensuing Two Years. Elders John A. Monfort relected. Benjamin H. Evritt in the place of G. Van Derbelt Deacons Henry D. Hayt relected John B. Jones in the place of James S. Monfort. Mr. Van Cleef was called away and the Consistory Closed before the whole business was disposed of

                 H. D. Platt Sect

Feb. 16, 1848.
 Meeting of the Consistory at Mr. Van Cleef. Present Rev. C. Van Cleef Prs.
Elder Jeremiah Platt, Deacons William Seward H. D. Hoyt, H. D. Platt
Opened with Prayer by Mr. Van Cleef The Object of the Meeting was to elect Sexton for the Coming Year and to devise some plan to liquidate the Church debt and to build sheds around the Church Yard
Resolved that Peter Garner be the Sexton the coming Year commencing the first of Ap next and that He occupy the Sextons House during the time that He is Sexton, for special agreement see hereafter
The following preamble and resolution were adopted and ordered to be published, viz.
 That whereas individuals have at different times expressed to the Consistory a desire that an effort be made to build sheds around the Church and liquidate the remaining debt. Therefore Resolved That the Male members of the Congregation be requested to meet in the Church on Wednesday next at 1, O.Clock P. M. to consider the propriety of building sheds and liquidating the debt and if deemed practicable to devise ways and means to accomplish the same
Meeting Closed with prayer by the President

                 H. D. Platt Clk

 At a regular Meeting of the Male Members of the New Hackensack Congregation held on Wednesday March 1st 1848. Mr. Aris J. Vanderbelt was Chosen Chairman and John B. Jones Clerk
The object of the meeting was stated by Rev. C. Van Cleef
 When the Treasurer of the Church was called upon for his report
Resolved that we shall build sheds around the Church yard. The sheds to extend no farther west than the body of the Church
Resolved that debt on the Parsonage be paid first
Rs'd that a subscription be started in the Congregation for the purpose of liquidating the Parsonage debt and that it be started immediately
Resolved that another subscription be started immediately for the purpose of building sheds
Resolved that a commity of three be appointed to circulate the above subscription
    Messrs Edward Flagler
      Aris I. Van. Derbelt
      James S. Monfort be the Commity
Resolved that the money on the debt be paid on or before the first of May next
Resolved that the meeting adjourn
John B. Jones Clerk   Aries. I. Van Derbelt Chair
By order of the Consistory the above meeting was recorded
                 H. D. Platt Clerk

June 17. 1848. At meeting of the Consistory of New Hackensack Church. It was resolved that Jeremiah Platt be the Elder to accompany the Rev. C. Van Cleef to Hide Park to dismiss the Rev. A. Elmondorf
                 H. D. Platt Clrk
At meeting of Consistory of New Hackensack Church John A. Monfort was appointed Elder to attend Classes at Pokeepsie July 24
                 H. D. Platt C.

Sep 7, 1848. Matting of Consistory at the Church
Present Rev. C. Van Cleef Elder J. Platt
Deacons William Seward, Jones, and Platt
Prayer by the President.
Not much business was done as their was not a Quorum present.
Elder J. Platt was appointed to attend Classes at Pokeepsie on the 12th though Elder Evritt took His place
Closed with Prayer   H. D. Platt Clerk

The Reformed Dutch Church of New Hackensack

Sep 19. 1848
   Meeting of the Consistory of New Hackensack Church met according to appointment Present Rev. C. Van Cleef President
Elders Monfort Evritt and Platt
Deacons. Seward Jones & Platt
Meeting opened by Prayer by the President
The object of the Meeting was to examine the a/c and settle with Mr. Van Cleef The a/c of the Treasurer was examined and gave sattisfaction Elder Platts a/c was examined as far as it could as Matthew Luyster had not returned the list that had been in circulation for liquidating the debt on the Parsonage Mr. Van Cleef was settled in full for the past season
Mr. Jones in behalf of the Organ Society requested permission of the Consistory to put an organ in the Church It was unanimous resolved that leave be granted the Organ Society to put an organ in the Church Provided that the Congregation do not object and the Consistory incur no expence in connexion with it now or hereafter
Resolved that the Consistory take the voice of the Congregation when the Organ Society think proper.
Resolved that Secretary of the Consistory furnish Mr. Jones a Copy of the above resolutions for the benefit of the Organ Society
Meeting Closed with prayer by Rev. Van Cleef

H. D. Platt Clerk

Feb 5, 1849 At a Meeting of the Consistory of the Reformed Dutch Church at New Hackensack according to notice the following persons were present Rev. C. Van Cleef. Elders John A. Monfort Benjamin H. Evritt Deacons Henry D. Hayt Jones, Seward & Platt. The Meeting was opened with prayer by Rev. Van Cleef the meeting was called to elect Officers and to settled up the past Years business which could not be done on a/c of the Sickness of Elder Platt
the following persons were then elected for the ensuing Two Years Elders Philander Seward in the place of J. Platt, James S. Monfort in the place of Schenck Ackerman deceased, Deacons, John G. Bishop in the place of William Seward H. D. Platt relected.
The poor Chest on examination contained about Thirty dollars
Resolved. that Mrs. Rich have $10.00 Mrs. Monfort $5.00 Mrs. Hick, $5.00
Resolved that John B. Jones take charge of the Poor Chest
Resolved that Pete Garner be the Sexton the next Year commencing the first of Ap next having the privileges that He now has
Resolved That Seward & Jones be a commity to collect what was subscribed last season for liquidating the Parsonage debt and to get the ballance subscribed
Meeting Closed by prayer by the Presedent

H. D. Platt Clerk

March 22, 1849
   At a Meeting of the Consistory of the Reformed Dutch Church at New Hackensack according to notice the following persons were present Rev. C. Van Cleef Elders P. Seward, Evritt, J. S. Monfort Deacons, Hayt, Jones, Bishop, & Platt. The meeting was opened with prayer by the Presedent.
The object of the meeting was to devise some way to pay Mr. Pudny for Singing.
Resv'ed that the Consistory make an extra effort in their several districts to collect means for Mr. Pudney. Res'd that P. Seward examine the fence between the Parsonage & Mr. Thorn and have the power to get meterials and have the same repaired
Re'd That the meeting adjourn which was done with Prayer by Mr. Van Cleef

H. D. Platt Clerk

Ap 11, 1849.
   At a Meeting of the Consistory of the Reformed Dutch Church of New Hackensack according to notice. Persons present. Rev. C. Van Cleef Elders Seward, J. A. Monfort, J. S. Monfort, Deacons, Hayt, Jones, Bishop & Platt
Meeting was opened with prayer by the Presedent the object of the meeting was to attend to a petition for sheds that had been shown before them on Feb 5, 1849. Signed by a number of individuals, asking permission for the undersigned to erect sheds for their own accomodation on the east side of the Church Yard. And the Consistory not wishing to assume the responsibility, Resolved that a meeting of the Male Members of the Congregation be called in this place on Thursday next at 2 Oclock in the afternoon for the purpose of taking into consideration the above petition.
At a meeting of the Male Members of the Congregation held this 15th of Feb. 1849 for the purpose of taking in consideration the propriety of building sheds Philander Seward was chosen Chairman and Edward Flagler Secretary.
It was moved & seconded that a vote be taken of the Congregation wether we shall have

Minutes of Consistory

the priviledge of building sheds on the east end of the Yard as far as they are taken up which was put and carried unanimously.
Moved & seconded that a ground rent of Fifty Cts per Year shall be paid for each Shed which was carried
Moved & seconded As longe as the fifty cents per Year is paid so longe He has the priviledge of the ground which was carried
Moved & seconded that this annual ground rent shall be paid on or before the first Dec. each Year Which was carried.
Moved & seconded, that the fund arising from the above ground rent be appleing to paying the Tax on the Church property which was carried
Moved & Seconded that these sheds be built uniform which was carried
Moved & Seconded that a building Commity of Five be appointed which was carried
Resolved that Philander Seward Matthew Luyster, Mr. V. B. Ackerman J. V. B. Conklin and H. D. Hayt be that Commity
Moved & Seconded that this Meeting adjourn which was carried
                                                    Philander Seward, Chair
                                                    Edward Flagler Sect
Moved & Seconded that the Consistory adopt the above resolutions of the Congregation which was carried. Moved & Seconded that permission be granted to the building committee appointed by the Church Meeting for the purpose of building sheds on the East end of the Church Yard to build said Sheds leaving sufficient room on the South and North sides for the purpose of turning said corners
Resv'd That James S. Monfort be the Elder to accompany the Domine to attend Classes at Fishkill Landing on the 22d of this Month
Meeting Closed with prayer by Mr. Van Cleef
                                                    H. D. Platt Clerk

May 26, 1849.
At a meeting of the Consistory at the Church according to notice the following persons were present. Rev. C. Van Cleef Elders. Everitt, J. A. Monfort & J. S. Monfort Deacons Hayt, Jones, Bishop & Platt
The object of the Meeting was to attend to John C. Pudney as chorister which was done. John B. Jones was requested to pay Pudney out of the Poor Chest. Re'd that subscription be put in circulation to ascertain if their can means be obtained to pay Mr. Pudney for Singing in the Church
Re'd that Mr. Pudney be the Chorester the present Year should we succeed in raising the money necessary to pay Him which amount is Fifty dollars
Another object of the meeting was to settle with Jeremiah Platt as He was not able to attend on account of Sickness the first Monday in February. He was present made His statement and gave up all the papers relative to the Church
Re'd That the thanks of the Consistory be given Mr. Jeremiah Platt for His aid and liberality in conducting the financial concerns of the Church while a member of the Consistory
Re'd That the Clerk present Mr. Platt a Copy of the above resolution
Re'd that John B. Jones take charge of the Pew rents.
Re'd that Elder J. S. Monfort be paid from the Poor Chest the Classical expences
The Meeting Closed with prayer by the Presedent
                                                    H. D. Platt Clerk

Sep 3, 1849
At a meeting of the Consistory at New Hackensack Church according to notice the following persons were present Rev. Van Cleef James S. Monfort, Elder Hayt, Jones & Platt Deacons. The meeting was opened by prayer by the Presedent On their being but one elder present not much business was done James S. Monfort appointed as elder to go with the Domine to Glenham to attend the Classes on Sep 11. Jones & Platt were requested to examine the fence between Thorn & the Parsonage west of the Barn and get the materials and have the same repaired. Closed with Prayer by Rev. Van Cleef
                                                    H. D. Platt Clerk

No. 30, 1849
At Consistory meeting after the preparatory lecture. It was resolved that John C. Pudny should have the Church every Saturday evening during the winter to give instruction to the Choir and to all in the Congregation that wished to be instructed in Sacred Musick.
All of the Consistory present except P. Seward and all assenting to the above resolution.
                                                    H. D. Platt, Clerk

The Reformed Dutch Church of New Hackensack

Feb. 4, 1850
   Consistory met according to notice opened with prayer by the Presedent
Present Rev. C. Van Cleef Presedent

Elders { John A. Monfort
         James S. Monfort
         Benjamin H. Evritt

Deacons { J. B. Jones
          J. G. Bishop
          H. D. Hayt
          H. D. Platt

Re'd That the Pew that Abraham Myers purchased some time since but did not pay for it, return to the Church, but should Myers in a short time either pay the original amount or the annual rent He may occupy it
Resolved That subscription be put in circulation immediately to increase the Salary and also one to raise the Tax & the back salary for the past Year
Resolved that Mr. Van Cleef be paid Eight dollars out of the Poor Chest which amount is equivalent to His expences attending Synod the past Year
Resolved that if Stephen Hicks does not pay His Pew rent that John B. Jones rent it to some other Person
Resolved that Peter Gainer be the Sexton the coming Year on the same conditions and that He be requested to find seats in the Church for Strangers when they come when Church has commenced.
The Poor Chest was examined & contained about Twelve dollars Mrs. Maria Monfort had been helped to Five dollars but a short time before
The following Persons were chosen for the ensueing two Years. Elders Matthew Luyster in the place of John A. Monfort, Benjamin H. Evritt relected Deacons Henry D. Traver in the place of Henry D. Hayt, John B. Jones relected
Meeting closed by Prayer by the President

                                                                H. D. Platt Clerk

March 20, 1850
   At a consistory meeting at the Church accoring to notice. Opened by Prayer by the President. Present Rev. C. Van Cleef Elders Matthew Luyster B. C. Evritt. Deacons John G. Bishop John B. Jones H. D. Traver and H. D. Platt. The object of the meeting was to settle with the Pastor and devise means to meet the first of May. Matthew Luyster is furnish Four Hundred & Fifty Two dollars to pay Jeremiah Platts notes on the first day of May next
Re'd That John C. Pudny be paid out of funds in Hand should their be a deficiency when all is collected
Re'd That hereafter when Persons wish to bury in our Ground who do not pay to the support of the Church that they shall pay Three dollars. The Sexton to collect the same, and pay one dollar in the hands of the Treasurer for the benefit of the Church
Re'd That the fence on the Church & Parsonage ground be repaired this Spring and Elder Luyster agrees to furnish the money free of Interest provided they do not exceed Fifty dollars. The amount expended to be repaid one Year from next May
Re'd That H. D. Platt get and bring on the ground Fifty Chesnut fence railing to repair the fence on the Church property.
Re'd That Benjamin H. Evritt & H. D. Platt be a committee to put out the money that Philip B. Van Derbelt expects to pay to the Consistory on the first of May next
The Meeting adjourned Prayer by the Presedent

                                                                H. D. Platt Clerke

Ap 14, 1850
   At a Consistory Meeting at the Church after Service Elder Matthew Luyster was appointed to accompany the Domine to attend Classes at the Second Reformed Dutch Church at Pokeepsie on the third Tuesday of Ap

                                                                H. D. Platt Clerk

Ap 24, 1850
   Their was a Consistory Meeting appointed at the Church but their not being a quorum the business that was to have been done could not legally be done. Present Rev. C. Van Cleef Elders Luyster & Monfort Deacon H. D. Platt
The business was to make a note for Mr. Luyster and other arrangements for the first of May
The Clerks account was examined by Elder Monfort & pronounced correct On examination of accounts to was necessary to have Four Hundred & Eighty dollars with that that was in the Treasurers Hands to pay Jeremiah Platts Notes A note for the above named sum was given by the Consistory to Elder Luyster Signed by the President of Consistory & I have this day submitted the Note to Elder Evritt who acquises in what was done in relation to the above named Note

                                                                H. D. Platt Clk

Minutes of Consistory

At a Consistory Meeting held Aug. 30 at the the Church after the preparatory sermon Elder Matthew Luyster was appointed to go with the Pastor to attend Classes, who were to meet at Hopewell on third of Sep

H. D. Platt

Consistory Meeting at the Parsonage on the evening of the Ninth of Sep. Present Rev. C. Van Cleef Elders Luyster Monfort & Evritt. Deacons Jones, Traver & Platt Prayer by Rev. Van Cleef. The object of the Meeting was of a pecunary nature to devise ways & means to liquidate the Church debt, which would be Five Hundred dollars on the first of May next One Hundred dollars for painting & repairing the Parsonage Seventy five to repair the grave Yard fence Therefore Re'd that an effort be made to raise the sum of Seven Hundred dollars to enable the Consistory to accomplish the above named objects Re'd That Matthew Luyster & John B. Jones be a commity to circulate a subscription for the above named object. Meeting Closed with Prayer by the President

H. D. Platt Clk

1850 Feb 3.
Consistory met at the Parsonage according to appointment Present Rev. C. Van Cleef Elders Luyster Monfort & Evrett Deacons Jones, Traver, Bishop & Platt. Meeting opened with Prayer by the Presedent
It being the Annual Meeting to settle with the Pastor examine a/c and elect Officers for the ensueing Two Years, the Pecunary affairs of the Church for the Year past were in a better state than they had been for some Years in Settling with the Pastor there was only Seventy Cents short on subscription lists Therefore the Elders were not compelled to take the pew rents to pay the Pastor which enabled the Consistory to meet the current expences of the past Year. The Policy on the Parsonage expires in a short time, Elder Luyster appointed to attend to it.
Resolved that Jones pay the Pew rents to Elder Luyster the amount $77.20 The poor Chest Contained $25.69. Jones was requested to pay Elder Monfort $3. " for fixing the Church Chimney. Mrs. Monfort to have $5.00 and should the Pastor think proper she is to have $10.00. Mr. Van Cleef was requested to sell a part of a lot in the grave Yard to Jeremiah Millard for $12.50
Resolved that H. D. Hayt pay for His pew $12.25 If he occupies it
Res'd that John C. Pudny be continued Jones wait upon Him. Also that the present Sexton remain Jones notify Him that He keep the Church in better order than it has been the last Year. A request having been made by some of the Congregation that the Seven Hundred dollars that the Consistory wished to be raised for certain objects should be laid on the Pews owned & rented in the said Church so that it could be seen what the per cent would amount to and on Examination it will be about Eight cents on the dollar Re'd that the Consistory Call on the Congregation to ascertain if this is the most feasible way to raise the above named sum and if not to devise some way to rais it
The following persons were chosen Elders & Deacons for the Ensuing Two Years Elders William Seward in the Place of P. Seward whose time of service expires. James S. Monfort relected.
R'd that William Seward be the Clerk & Treasurer in place of H. D. Platt and that Platt hand to Him the Church Books Papers & Money
Deacons Simeon Hitchcock in the place of H. D. Platt whose time of Service expires John G. Bishop be relected.
H. D. Platt is requested to get for the Church one Hundred Chesnut fence railing at Beekman for 10c or 12c apiece there or 15c apice delivered here at the Church.
Moved that the Meeting adjourn Carried
Closed by Prayer by the Pastor

H. D. Platt clk

March 9th 1851 Consistory met at the Parsonag all the members being present and was opened with prayer by the President. The Elders having asertained the minds of the Pew holders reported that pews sufficient for paying off the debt make the necessary repairs would not be raised by taxing the pews wherefore it was
Resolved that another effort be immediately made to see what can be raised by voluntary subscription The Elders to report as soon as possible adjourned with Prayer
C. Van Cleef, Pres
Wm. Seward, Sec

March 25th 1851 Consistory met at the Church all the members being present (Except J. Bishop Deacon) and was opened with prayer by the President. Resolved that James S. Monfort be authorized to provide Paint and do the painting. And that James S. Monfort and William Seward authurised to procure the materials and put up the necessary fence
C. Van Cleef, Pres
Wm. Seward, Sec

The Reformed Dutch Church of New Hackensack

At a Consistory meeting after service April 13th 1851
Resolved Matthew Luyster be the Elder to accompany the Rev. C. Vancleef to Fishkill to attend Classis April 15th
Resolved that the deficiency be made up out of the Poor Chest to defray the expence of Classis

                              Wm. Seward, Sec

Aug 15th, 1851 Consistory met at the Church the members Present were Rev. C. Van Cleef President, Elders Matthew Luyster James S. Monfort William Seward, Deacons John B. Jones Henry D. Traver Simeon Hitchcock
and was opened with Prayer by the President
Resolved that the Balance due J. C. Pudney for Singing be paid out of Poor Chest %4.25 also one dollar for Minutes of Synod Resolved that the repairs of Bier be paid from Poor Chest. Matthew Luyster Elder Chosen to attend Classis at Fishkill Landing on the first Thursday in Sept and that J. S. Monfort and Wm. Seward be committee to fix railing in Church Yard

                           C. Van Cleef, Pres
                           Wm. Seward, Sec

Oct 10th Consistory met at the Church all the members being except Benjamin Everett, Elder, and John G. Bishop, Deacon and was opened with Prayer by the Pastor Resolved that James S. Monfort attend to enlargeing the burying ground and making stone fence and Wm. Seward attend to fixing Stoves and making Coal Box and that J. S. Monfort Procure Paint and paint the tower and balistrade of Church.
                     Closed with Prayer
                           C. Van Cleef, Pres
                           Wm. Seward, Sec

February 2d 1852 Consistory met at the Church according to appointment Present Rev C Vancleef Elders Everett Luyster Monfort, & Seward Deacons Traver Jones & Hitchcock Meeting opened with Prayer by the Presedent. Resolved that the balance of salery be paid out of Pew Rent $6.70 ($6.90 ?) And that the taxes be paid out of Pew rent $25.50
Resolved that John C. Pudney be continued corister and that H. D. Traver Wait on J. C. Pudney and notify him of his appointment, And that Peter S. Gardner be Sexton for the coming year
Resolved that Matthew Luyster & Benjamin Everett be reelected Elders and that John B. Jones and Henry D. Traver be reelected Deacons
                    Closed with prayer
                           William Seward, Sec

The following record contains the substance of what took place in reference to the case of Mr. Philip D. Van Der Belt
At the annual meeting of the consistory held on the 2d of February 1852 a free conversation was had respecting Mr. Philip B. Van Der Belt conduct in referance to selling liquor without licence and it was then thought that on the ground of common it was necessary to take the preparatory steps of Disiplin. On the 15th of the same month the Elders James S. Monfort and Benjamin H. Everett were appointed a committe to confer with Mr. Vander Belt in relation to the above matter. At a meeting of the Consistory held on the 2d of March the committee reported that they had discharged the duty assigned them and that the amount of what Mr. Van Der Belt said was the following. That he acknowledged that he was selling liquor without licence but he justified his conduct saying that his business was no more hurtful than farming and that if the Church was not satisfied with him he asked no odds of them or of any body else
Wherefore It was unanimously Resolved That the following Charge and Citation be served upon Mr. Van Der Belt—viz
Mr. Philip B. Van Der Belt
    Dear Sir
        Common   or general rumor charges you with selling liquor without licence also with selling it on the sabbath Therefore By order of the Consistory of the Reformed Dutch Church of New Hackensack you Mr. P. B. V. B. a member of said Church are hereby summoned to appear before said Consistory and answer to the Charge— herewith presented at the Church on the 4th of March at 7½ O Clock P. M.
Done in Consistory this   Signed C. Van Cleef—Pres
2d Day of March 1852   Wm. Seward Sec
After which consistory adjourned to meet in the Church on the 4th of March at 7½ P. M. Closed with Prayer by the President

March 4th 1852
    Consistory met according to adjournment and was opened with Prayer by the President all present except John Y. Bishop.

Minutes of Consistory

Mr. Van Der Belt not appearing sent to the Consistory a communication which was read—Wherefore it was unamously Resolved that Mr. Van Der Belt be cited to appear before the consistory the second time in the words following
Mr. Philip B. Van Der Belt
      Dear Sir
The Consistory acknowledge the receipt of your communication but they are nevertheless constrained to renew the Citation put in your hands yesterday and we do accordingly cite you to appear before us on the 11th of March at 7½ P. M. at the Church and we do earnestly hope that you will comply with this citation as it will be the last and by not so doing you will be liable to censure for contumacy—as for ourselves we have no choice in the matter, we are compelled to act according to the constitution of our Church. Consistory adjourned to meet in the Church, March 11th at 7½ P. M.
      Closed with Prayer
        C. Van Cleef Presedent

March 11th 1852 Consistory met according to adjournment and was opened with Prayer, members all preasant after wating a considerable time for Mr. Van Der Belt, he not appearing the Consistory after serious deliberation unanimously adopted the following Preamble and Resolution viz—That whereas Mr. Van Der Belt haveing been viseted by a committee and haveing been twice cited to appear before the Consistory and having in both instances refused to appear—
Therefore be it resolved That Mr. Philip B. Van Der Belt be and hereby is suspended from the Lords Supper on the ground of contumacy also resolved That the Clerk of Consistory furnish Mr. Van Der Belt with a copy of the above Preamble and Resolution. The Consistory having discharged what to them seemed an important duty Closed with Prayer
        C. Van Cleef, Pres
        Wm. Seward, Sec

August 19th 1852 Consistory met at the Church the Members present were Rev. C. Van Cleef President Elders M. Luyster, J. S. Mon Fort Wm. Seward Deacons J. B. Jones H. D. Traver S. Hitchcock.
Resolved that Matthew Luyster and J. B. Jones be Committee to enquire about painting the inside of the Church, and also resolved that James S. Mon Fort be the Elder to accompany the Rev. C. Van Cleef to Hyde Park to attend Classis on the first Tuesday in Sept
        C. Van Cleef, Pres
        Wm. Seward, Sec

Nov. 22d 1852 Consistory met at the Parsonage the Members present were Rev. C. Van Cleef Presedent Elders M. Luyster W Seward Deacons J. B. Jones H. D. Traver S. Hitchcock the Meeting was for the purpose of examining the accounts with regard to (Frescoing ?) the Church. The onley resolution passed was with regard to keeping the Church clean
Resolved that the sexton Sweep and dust the Church on the first week of evry month and thorowly dust it once in two weeks
        C. Van Cleef, Pres
        Wm. Seward, Sec

Feb 7th 1853 Consistory met at the Church according to appointment Present Rev. C. Van Cleef Elders Luyster, Everett, Monfort, Seward Deacons Traver Jones Hitchcock Meeting opened With Prayer by the Pres'd
Resolved that J. V. B. Vanvorhis May rent Pew No. 1. by paying $12.00 per anum and trim it himself as long as he wants it provided he will leave the trim in when he leaves it
Resolved that J. V. B. Teller may have Pew No. 98, on same conditions as J. V. B. Vanvorhis has his or he may have the priveolege of purchasing it by paying $200. Resolved that James S. Monfort and William Seward be reelected Elders and that Simeon Hitchcock be reelected Deacon an John Jones elected Deacon in the place of John Y. Bishop for the ensuing 2 years
Resolved that J. C. Pudney be corister for the comeing Year. Closed with Prayer
        C. Van Cleef, Pres
        Wm. Seward, Sec

Aug 25th 1853 Consistory met at the Church Present Rev. C. Van Cleef Elders Luyster Everett Monfort Seward Deacons J. B. Jones Meeting opened with Prayer by the Pastor the object of the meeting was to settle Accounts. After which the following resolution was passed
Whereas Mr. Philip Nagle by the force of circumstances rather than a belief that he was guilty was Suspended from the communion of the Church until such time as the Consistory should detirmin and as during this time as far as we know his conduct has been examplary

The Reformed Dutch Church of New Hackensack

Therefore Resolved that the Said Philip Nagle be and hereby restored to the Communion of the Church as formaly
Closed with Prayer   Wm. Seward Sec.

Feb 4th 1854
    Consistory met according to notice Opened with Prayer by the Presedent Present Rev. C. Van Cleef Presedent

Elders { Matthew Luyster / Benjamin H. Everett / William Seward   Deacons { J. B. Jones / H. D. Traver / S. Hitchcock

Resolved that W Seward and H D Traver be committee to attend to the loaning of money that is to be paid next spring
Resolved that Henry Lyon be sexton for the coming Year and that John C. Pudney be Corister. The following Preamble and Resolution was unamously adopted
That whereas the Classis of Poughkeepsie haveing requested the views of the Consistory as to the expediency of amending the style and title of Church Whereas be it
Resolved that in the opinion of the Consistory we deem highly inexpedient and are therefore decidedly opposed to any Change whatever in the stile and title of the Reformed Protestant Dutch Church in North America.
Resolved that Rev C. Van Cleef and W. Seward be committee to attend to repairs of fence around Sexton house and Parsonage
Resolved that John A. Monfort be Elder in place of Matthew Luyster and that George Van Derbelt in the place of B. H. Everett And that H. D. Platt be Deacon in place of H. D. Traver and that J. B. Jones be re elected for the ensuing two years.
    Closed with Prayer   W Seward Sec.

Oct 25th 1854
    Consistory met according to notice Opened with prayer by the President Present Rev. C. Van Cleef President

Elders { John A. Monfort / William Seward   Deacons { H. D. Platt / J. B. Jones / John Jones / S. Hitchcock

Resolved that the consistory purchase twelve of the new Psalm and Hymn Books eight of the small books for the Choir and four for Elders and Deacons of the large ones Resolved that the Books be paid for out of Poor Chest after examining accounts and such other business as come before them they adjourned
                                                            William Seward Sec.

Feb 5th 1855
    The annual Meeting of Consistory was held at the Parsonage. Opened with Prayer by the President. Present, Rev. C. Van Cleef President Elders John A. Monfort William Seward Deacons J. B. Jones H. D. Platt S. Hitchcock, J. Jones
Resolved that John C. Pudney be corister and that Henry Lyon be Sexton for the coming year Wm. Seward and James S. Monfort was reelected Elders, and Simeon Hitchcock John Jones was reelected Deacons for the ensuing two years. Closed with Prayer
                                                            William Seward Sec.
    At a regular meeting of the consistory of the Reformed Dutch Church of New Hackensack held April 3d 1855 the following members were present Rev C Van Cleef Elders John A. Monfort & William Seward Deacons Harvey D. Platt John B Jones Simeon Hitchcock and John Jones the following Preamble & Resolution were unanimously adopted —That wereas Edgar Luyster J. Jackson Diddle & John Luyster Sr have by a petition baring date March 7th 1855 requested of the Consistory the privolege of erecting Sheds on the east end of the Church yard according to resolutions passed at a meeting of the male members of the Congregation held Feb 15th 1849 & also by the Consistory in April 1849 recorded on our minutes the Substances is as follows viz that the privoleg of building Sheds on the east end of the Church yard be granted subject to a yearly ground rent of Fifty Cents for each Shed to be paid on or before the first of Dec. each year and the privolege of the ground rent continuing only as long as it is paid—also that the sheds be built uniform and sufficient room be left on the south and North ends for the purpose of turning the corners therefore—Be it resolved that the request of the Petitioners be granted provided als that said Petitioners and others who may erect sheds according to the above Specifications be required to paint uniformly the frunt of their Sheds which are in no case to occupy more space than nine feet by twenty four including the posts except by special permission also that if the rent of any Shed be not paid for two consecutive years said Shed shall be forfited to the Consistory It was further esolved that in order to prevent any misunderstanding in future as to either of the parties concerned the above Preamble and Resolution be recorded

Minutes of Consistory

in a special place in the book of minutes and that every person before building a Shed or Sheds be required to sign his name to the above which shall be considred in the light of a contract between the parties concerned and that evry applicant be furnished with a copy of the above Preamble and Resolution signed by the President and Clerk of Consistory
P.S. the lots are to be numbered beginning on south side of the east end of the Church yard by one two threes &c

                                      Rev C Van Cleef Pres.
                                      William Seward Sec.

	Lot No
J. Jackson Diddell	1
Edgar Luyster	2
John Y Luyster	3
Tunis Ackerman	4
Henry D. Hayt	5
Leonard C. Winslow	6
Cornelius Remsen	7
J. B. Jones	8
James H. Seward	9
Thomas J. Dearin	10
Jacob B. Teller	11
John Monfort	12
B. A. Sleight Est	13
Matthew B. Ackerman	14
	15
	16
	17
	18

April 1855 Received of J. J. Diddell one years ground rent for Shed 50/100
Feb 1856 do 50/100
May 1855 Received of Edgar Luyster 50/100
Jan 28th/58 Received of J. J. Diddell two years ground rent for shed 1.00

Sept 7th 1855 Consistory met at the Church Present Rev. C. Van Cleef President Elders George Van Derbelt James S Monfort William Seward Deacons H. D. Platt J. B. Jones S. Hitchcock the following resolution was passed. Resolved that the President of Consistory be and is hereby authurized to execute a satisfaction of the Mortgage of Harvy E. Everett to the Reformed Dutch Church of New Hackensack Recorded on the office of the Clerk of the County of Dutchess in liber 77 of Mortgage Page 392 and to sign his name and affix the Seal of said Church to the same
                                                    William Seward Sect.

Sept 10th 1855 Consistory met at the Church Present Rev C. Van Cleef President Elders John A Monfort George Vanderbelt William Seward James S. Monfort Deacons Simeon Hitchcock The following resolution was unanimiously adopted Resolved that Consistory take Bond & Mortgage on James S Monforts Farm for Six Hundred Dollars it being a part of legacy left Said Church by Peter Van Benscouton And also Resolved that the Coresters Salery be Collected at the Same time that the Ministers Salery is and Paid to Corister by the first of February of each year
                                                    William Seward Sect.

Feb 4th 1856 Consistory held their annual meeting at the Parsonage opened with Prayer by the President Present Rev C Van Cleef President

Elders	John A Monfort	Deacons
	James S Monfort	Harvy D Platt
	William Seward	John B Jones
		Simeon Hitchcock
		John Jones

Resolved that Mr. Dean have one Dollar Refunded that he paid for breaking ground in Grave Yard. Resolved that Mrs Monfort be Presented with ten Dollars from Poor Chest Resolved that James S Monfort and John B Jones and William Seward be a Commity to examin into the propriety of releasing Harrison Brown from Mortgage now held by the Church in connexion with twenty four acres of land now owned by Henry Van der Belt
Resolved that hereafter any person applying for the privelege of Buildin a Shed on the east end of the Church Yard shall be to build to build within Six months after he receives his title for the same or forfit his right to the ground
Resolved that the following officers be elected for the ensuing two years H. D. Platt in place of J. H. Monfort

The Reformed Dutch Church of New Hackensack

George Vander Belt reelected, Elders and Charles Howell in place of H. D. Platt John B. Jones reelected Deacons
and J. C. Pudney be Chorister the coming year. Closed with Prayer
William Seward Sect.

March 17th 1856 Consistory met at Parsonage meeting opened with Prayer
Present Rev C Van Cleef President

Elders H. D Platt
J S Monfort
Wm. Seward

Deacons J. B. Jones
S. Hitchcock
J. Jones
C. Howell

The Committy appointed to examine into the propriety of releasing Harrison Brown Mortgage Now held by Church. Said Mortgage was given to Church by Harvy E. Everett to secure the sum of one thousand Dollars since which time Everett sold house and lot to H. Brown it being a part of land conveyed to Church to secure the said one thousand Dollars The Commity reported favourably and it was unanimously Resolved that Brown be Released
Wm. Seward Sect.

Nov 10th 1856 Meeting of the Church according to notice for the purpose of increasing the salery of Rev C Van Cleef two hundred Dollar Aries J Vanderbelt was Called to the Chair and Wm H Hopkins Sect
The following resolution was adopted
Resolved that the undersigned agree to pay the sums set opposite our names for the purpose of raising $500 for the Salary of Rev C. Van Cleef to be paid to the Consistory This will be binding provided the full sum is raised and all subscription to other paper for this purpose cancelled
Aries J Vanderbelt Chair.
Wm. H. Hopkins Sect.

April 12th 1856 Consistory met at the Parsonage and was opened with Prayer Present Elders Monfort Seward and Platt Deacons Hitchcock Jones and Howell
It having been stated at a previous Meeting by the Pastor that if a room could be added to the Parsonage to be used as a Kitchen it would greatly promote his comfort convience and upon surveying premises it having been found practicable to build a suitable room Whereof it was unanously Resolved First that it is expedient to build a room in the rear of the Parsonage dwelling about Fifteen feet square including part of the Piazza Second that the expense of constructing Said room for the present defrayed by hireing the money the Consistory giving their Note for the same
Third that Messrs H. D. Platt and C. J. Howill be appointed a Committee with discretionary Power to carry into effect the above resolution by making a Contract with some suitable Person to have the work completed as soon as Convienient
Adjourned with Prayer
C. Van Cleef Presd.
W Seward Sect.

Feb 1st 1857

Consistory held their Anual meeting at the Church Opened with Prayer by the President Present Rev. C. Van Cleef Pres.

Elders
H. D. Platt
J. S. Monfort
W. Seward

Deacons
J. B. Jones
J Jones
S Hitchcock
C. J. Howell

The following Resolutions were unanimously adopted
Resolved that the Reasure of Poor Chest pay to Treas of Consistory out of Poor Chest Thurty Dollars. And thet Mrs Monfort be given Five Dollars Per Month for three months out of Poor Chest
Resolved that J C Pudney be Chorister for the coming year and that Henry Johnson be sexton for the ensuing year
Resolved that J. S. Monfort and W. Seward be reelected Elders and that S. Hitchcock and J Jones be reelected Dacons for the ensuing Two years.
Closed With Prayer
W. Seward Sect.

May 19th 1857 Consistory met at the Parsonage and was opened with Prayer by the President
Present Rev C Van Cleef

Elders
H D Platt
Wm. Seward

Deacons
C. J. Howell
S. Hitchcock

Minutes of Consistory

The following resolutions were unanimously adopted that the frunt and back room in the Parsonage be painted and that the frunt room be re Papered and that S. Hitchcock Superintend the work
and that the Railing in the Church yard be repaired and that W. Seward See to the repairing of it
    Closed with Prayer
                                                     Wm. Seward Sect.

Sept 8th 1857 Consistory met at the Church opened with Prayer by the President Members Present Rev C Van Cleef

    Elders   Deacons
    H D Platt   J. B. Jones
    J. S. Monfort   C. J. Howell
    Wm. Seward   S Hitchcock

On examining the roof of Church it was found in a bad condition and in order to repair it it was Resolved that the Balastrade be taken Down and thee nessesary repairs be made
Resolved that there be an effort made to rais one hundred and fifty Dollars for repairs on Church and Parsonage Insurance &c and a Committee be appointed for the purpose of visiting the Congregation in order to rais the said Sum of one Hundred and fifty Dollars and that C J Howell J. B. Jones and J. Jones be said Committee Closed With Prayer
                                                     W. Seward Sect.

Feb 1st 1858 Consistory met at the Church opened with Prayer by the President All the members present
Resolved that the south colum be repaired and the other three be painted as soon as possible and that the sexton House be repaired, Resolved that J. S Monfort be orthorised to attend to painting and repairing Colums and to repairing sexton House Resolved that a Commity be appointed to notify Henry Johnson to leave Secton House on the first of April next and that Simeon Hitchcock be said Committy. Resolved that James S. Monfort be Sexton for the comeing year Resolved that hereafter it shall be the duty of the Sexton to open the Church whenever there is to be sirvises build the fires when nessessary and keep the Church broom Clean and dusted and See that the stoves be taken down in the spring and put up in the fall also to saw and split the wood and put it under cover in the fall nessessary for the same and in consideration of the above he shall have the Sexton house and lot free of rent and the income from the grave yard
Resolved that J. C. Pudney be Chorister for the Comeing year
Resolved that H. D. Platt be paid ten Dollars out of Poor Chest fer Cash paid Rev James Bruster for two Sabbaths services and that Rev William Cornell be paid five Dollars out of the same funds for one sabbath When Rev C Van Cleef was absent
Resolved that balance due Rev C Van Cleef for salery be paid out of funds on hand
Resolved that a new book for record be purchased
Resolved that Henry D Hayt be Elder in the place of George Vanderbelt and that H D Platt be reelected and William Baker be Deacon in place of J. B. Jones and C J Howell be reelected Closed with Prayer
                                                     Wm Seward Sect.

At a meting of the Members of the Congregation of the Reformed Dutch of New Hackensack held this the 15 day of October 1858 at the Church to take into consideration the matter of building Sheds Henry D Hayt was appointed Chairman and John B Jones Secretary of said meeting
It was moved and carried that this meting adopt the resolution passed by the Consistory April 3d 1855 in reference to the building of Sheds
It was moved and carried that the doors be made to open on the inside of the Sheds
On motion it was carried that a building committee of three be appointed with power to erect Said Sheds on motion of J. J. Diddell
L. C. Winslow and J. B. Jones were appointed said Committee the meeting then adjourned
                                                     H. D. Hayt Chairman
                                                   J B Jones Sec.

Nov 1st 1858 Consistory met according to order
Present Rev C Van Cleef Elders H. D. Hayt J S Monfort H. D Platt Deacons C. J. Howell S. Hitchcock Opened with Prayer by the Presedent
Resolved that the Presedent and Clerk of Consistory are requested to sign their names to a certain paper presented by L. C. Winslow and also affix the Seal of the Church to the same.
Resolved that the Classical dues be taken out of Poor Chest, And also resolved Pollock have a ton of coal and that the same be Paid for out of Poor Chest Closed with Prayer
                                                     Wm. Seward Clerk

INDEX OF PEWS
of the church of
NEW HACKENSACK

Index of Pews

A statement or Index of the Number of Pews in the Reformed Dutch Church at New Hackensack also the No. of seats in each pew with the names of the Owners of seats, N.B. the letter S stands for Sold & the letter T for transfer in s'd Index.

Pew No. 1,
9 seats
purchasers'
names

1. Johanis Dubois, T. to Dominecus Monfort, T. to Monfort Vn. Kleeck
2. Do. —— Do.
3. Johanis Schurree, T. to Lawrance Haff
4. Do. —— Do. T. to Do. —— Do.
5. Redelphs Swartwout, T. to John Willsie
6. Do. —— Do. T. to Do. —— Do.
7. Mathias Luyster—T. to John Luyster
8. Gulian Ackerman, t. to Gulian Jas. Ackerman
9. Peter Deedts, T. to Abraham L. Dates

Pew No. 2,
29 seats
purchasers'
names

1. Peter Hay, S. to Isaac Hageman
2. Cornelius V. Wey, T. to Johanes Menaman, T. to John M. Rosekrans
3. Edward Schoonmaker, S. to Garrt V'n Bomell
4. Constine Golneck, T. to Peter Dates, Junr.
5. Do. —— Do. T. to Do. —— Do.
6. Henry Bell, T. to Henry Bell, S. to Abm. Sleight
7. John Conckling, T. to Lawrance Conklin, T. to Hen'y Conklin
8. Johanis Steenbergh, S. to John V'n Siclen, T. to his Widow Corlin
9. Stephen Thorn, T. to Sam'l Thorn, T. to Stephen S. Thorn
10. Corns. V. Wey, S. to Demenicus Monfort, T. to Garret V'n Dine
11. Johannes Bockhout, S. to Matthew V'n Bunshoten
12. Johannes Wiltsie, T. to Corn's Wiltsie
13. Johannes E. Scut, S. to John A. Hagaman, T. to Sitea Hageman
14. Peter Outwater, T. to Daniel Outwater, T. to Joseph Jackson
15. Do. —— Do. T. to Barnet B. V'n Kleeck, T. to Henry Jewell
16. Redolphus Swartwout T. to John Willsie
17. Ram Adriance, T. to Ab'm Adriance
18. Jacob Dubois, S. to Benj'n Everit, T. to Benjamin Everet
19. Do. —— Do. S. to Do. T. to Do —— Do.
20. John Haff, T. to Henry Dodge on Exchange, T. to James & Henry Dodge
21. Do. —— Do. T. to Do. —— Do. on Do. T. to Do.
22. Peter Haff, T. to Warren Rosekrans, T. to James Dodge
23. Do. —— Do. T. to Do. —— Do. T. to Do. —— Do.
24. John Cornell, T. to John C. Shear
25. Do. —— Do. T. to Do. —— Do.
26. Lawrance Haff, T. to Henry Dodge in Exchange, T. to James & Henry Dodge
27. Do. —— Do. T. to Do. —— Do. in Do. T. to Do.
28. Aurt Vandebelt, T. to Phillip V'n Dirbelt
29. Do. —— Do. T. to Aris V'n Derbelt

Pew No. 3
6 seats
purchasers'
names

1. Abraham Lent, T. to Abraham Lent
2. Do. —— Do. t. to Do. —— Do.
3. Andrias Heermans, T. to John Monfort, T. to Albert H. Monfort, T. to Henry A. Monfort
4. Do. —— Do. T. to Do. —— Do. T. to Do. —— Do.
5. Henry Haremans, T. to Sam'l. Cooper, T. to James Ackerman
6. Do. —— Do. T. to Do. —— Do.

Pew No. 4
6 seats
purchasers'
names

1. Peter Outwater, T. to Daniel Outwater, T. to Joseph Jackson, T. to Zephaniah Platt
2. Do. —— Do. T. to Do. —— Do. T. to Do. —— Do.
3. Isaac V. Noorstrant, T. to John Low, T. to Ab'm Duryea, T. to Phebe Duryea
4. Redolphs Swartwout, T. to John Willsie, T. to Zepheniah Platt
5. Peter H. Monfort, T. to son Henry Monfort, T. to Casper Ganse, T. to Zepheniah Platt
6. John Jewell, T. to Hannah Jewell, T. to son Henry Jewell

Pew No. 5
6 seats
purchasers'
names

1. Simon Bloom, T. to Ab'm Brinkerhoff, S. to Warren Dullensea, T. to Cornelius Remsen
2. Redolphus Swartwout, T. to Sarah Swartwout, T. to Ann Swartwout
3. Henry Bell, T. to Phebe Rosekrans, T. to Thos. Rosekrans, T. to Henry Dodge, T. to the Church in Exchange, S. to Warren Dullensea, T. to Corn's Remsen

The Reformed Dutch Church of New Hackensack

    4. Abraham Lent, T. to Catherine Bloom, S. to Warren Dullensea, T. to Cornelius Remsen
    5. Andris Haremans, s. to Warren Dullensea, T. to Cornelius Remsen
    6. Andris Haremans, S. to Warren Dullinsea, T. to Cornelius Remsen

Pew No. 6
6 seats purchasers' names
1. Peter Outwater, T. to Daniel Outwater, T. to Joseph Jackson, T. to his Executor, T. to Stephen S. Thorn
2. Do.   Do.   T. to Barnet B. Vn. Kleeck, T. to Andrew Rynders
3. Abraham Lent, T. to Abm. Lent, deceas'd, T. to Cornelius Klump
4. Do.   Do.   T. to Do.   Do. Deceas'd T. to Cornelius Klump.
5. Andrias Haremans, S. to John Pinkney, T. to Cornelius Klump
6. Do.   Do.   S. to John Pinkney, T. to Cornelius Klump

Pew No. 7
6 seats purchasers' names
1. Henry Haremans, S. to Sam'l. Cooper, T. to Joseph Jackson, T. to his Executor
2. Wilhelmus Heremans, T. to Claraw Monfort, S. to Abraham Adriance, 1818 given up, S. to Stephen S. Thorn
3. Tunis Wiltsie, T. to John Willsie, T. to Ab'm Duryea, T. to Phebe Duryea
4. William Edwards, T. to Anna Margaret Edwards, S. to Abraham Adrians, 1818 given up, S. to Stephen S. Thorn
5. Anna Edwards, T. to Anna Margaret Edwards, S. to Abraham Adrians, 1818 given up, S. to Stephen S. Thorn
6. Tjert V'n Keuren, T. to Albert I. Monfort, T. to his widow Lette Monfort

Pew No. 8
6 seats purchasers' names
1. Johanes Shuree, T. to Lawrance Haff, S. to James Ackerman
2. Johanes Shuree, S. to Henry Dodge, T. to the Church in Exchange, S. to James Ackerman
3. Teunis V'n Bunschoten, T. to Sarah Duryea, T. to Abm. Duryea, T. to Phebe Duryea
4. Teunis V'n Bunschoten, T. to Anna V'n Bunschoten, T. to Matthew V'n Bunschoten, T. to Sarah Ackerman
5. Do.   Do.   T. to Do.   Do.   T. to Do.   Do.   T. to Do.   Do.
6. Do.   Do.   T. to Do.   Do.   T. to Do.   Do.   T. to Moriah Palmeteer

Pew No. 9
6 seats purchasers' names
1. Nicholas Brower, S. to Peter Monfort, T. to Peter Monfort, T. to Joseph Jackson, T. to Executor
2. Nicholas Brower, S. to John A. Hageman, T. to Sitea Hageman
3. Johanis Shuree, T. to Peter Monfort, T. to Martin Monfort
4. Joris V. Noorstrant, S. to Thos. V'n Bramer, S. to Joseph Jackson, T. to Executor
5. Ardt. Middagh, T. to Joris Middaugh, T. to Ardt Middaugh, T. to John Diddell
6. Peter Outwater, T. to Daniel Outwater, T. to Joseph Jackson, T. to Executor

Pew No. 10
6 seats purchasers' names
1. Cornelius Luyster, T. to Patrus Luyster, T. to Corn's P. Luyster, T. to Isaac Everit
2. Do.   Do.   T. to   Do.   Do.   T. to   Do.   Do.   T. to Isaac Everet
3. Garrit Storm, S. to Aris V'n Debelt, T. to Peter V'n Derbelt
4. Joris Brinkerhoff, S. to Peter V'n Bunschoten, T. to Jacob V'n Bunschoten, T. to John A. Sleight
5. Bartholomew Crannel, S. to Reubin Tanner
6. Johannis Shuree, T. to Charles Huffman, T. to son Charles C. Huffman, S. to Isaac Evert

Pew No. 11
6 seats purchasers' names
1. Johannis Shurree, T. to Lawrance Haff, S. to Jacob Vn. Bunschoten, T. to Jacobus I. Swartwout, T. to Matthew Vn. B. Ackerman
2. Johannis Shurree, T. to Lawrance Haff, S. to Albert I. Monfort, T. to his widow Lette Monfort
3. Joris Brinkerhoff, T. to Isaac Adrians, S. to Matthew V. B. Ackerman
4. Mathias Luyster, T. to John Luyster
5. Do.   Do.   T. to Do.   Do.
6. John Haremans, T. to Phillip Harmans, T. to Wm. Suard, T. to Philander Suard, T. to Matthew V. B. Ackerman

Pew No. 12
6 seats purchasers' names
1. Jacobus Swartwout, T. to Jacobus I. Swartwout, T. to Mary Palmateer, T. to Jacob V. B. Concklin
2. Derick Brinkerhoff, S. to Matthew Vn. Bunschoten, T. to Jacob Vn. Bunschoten, T. to Jacob Vn. B. Teller
3. Same as No. 2

Index of Pews

    4. Redolphs Swartwout, T. to Jacobus R. Swarwout, T. to John A. Sleight, T. to Hannah Teller
    5. Joris Brinkerhoff, T. to Matthew V'n Bunschoten, T. to Jacob V'n Bunschoten, T. to Jacob V. B. Concklin
    6. Joris Brinkerhoff, T. to Jacob V'n Bunschoten, T. to Jacob V. B. Conklin

Pew No. 13
6 seats
purchasers'
names
1. Roeloff Schank, T. to Peter Ackerman
2. Luke Noorstrant, T. to Derick Brinkerhoff, Junr.
3. Henry Rosekrans, T. to John Rosekrans, T. to Moriah Rosekrans, wido
4. Peter Noorstrant, T. to Phillip Verplank, T. to Wm. Verplank, S. to Jas. Phillips
5. James Hicks, S. to Peter P. Lawson
6. John Churchell, T. to Wm. Churchell

Pew No. 14
6 seats
purchasers'
names
1. Gysbert Schanck, T. to Abm. Schank, T. to Sarah Ackerman, T. to Schank Ackerman
2. Do.   Do.   T. to Do.   Do.   T. to Do.   Do.   T. to Schank Ackerman
3. Isaac Brinkerhoff, T. to Derick Swartwout, S. to Nathan Baley, T. to John N. Baley
4. Isaac Brinkerhoff, T. to Isaac J. Swartwout
5. Lawrance Conckling, T. to Henry Conklin, T. to Robert Todd
6. Simon Bloom, T. to Ab'm Brinkerhoff, S. to James Dearin

Pew No. 15
25 seats
purchasers'
names
1. Baltus V. Kleeck
2. Johanis Rosekrans, T. to Anna Deeds, T. to Henry D. Traver
3. John Monfort, T. to Alb't H. Monfort, T. to Henry A. Monfort
4. Thomas V. Breemer, T. to Pt'r V'n Bramer, T. to Pt'r P. Lawson
5. John Ostrum
6. Ahazerus V. Kleeck
7. Henry Haremans, T. to Hen'y Schoonmaker, T. to his daughter Hellen Schoonmaker
8. Edward Schoonmaker, T. to Mary Rosekrans, T. to Anna Deeds, T. to Henry D. Traver

Disconued   9. James Hicks, Disannuled by making door in west end of the Church
Disconued   10. Do.   Do.   do.   do.   do.   do.
11. Peter Haff, T. to Ab'm Myers, T. to Sam'l Cooper, T. to Ja's Ackerman
12. Do.   Do.   T. to   Do.   Do.   T. to   Do.   Do.
13. Abraham Hogeland, T to Lette Hogeland, widow
14. Do.   Do.   T. to   do.   Do.   do.
15. Peter I. Monfort, T. to Stephen Monfort
16. Peter I. Monfort, T. to Peter Monfort
17. Frederick Rosekrans, T. to Thos. Rosekrans, T. to Heny. Dodge, T. to the Church in Exchange
18. Same as No. 17
19. Gulian Ackerman, T. to John Ackerman, T. to John Ackerman Bogardus
20. Gulian Ackerman, T. to Ja's Ackerman, son of John
21. John V'n Sicklen, one T. to Enes Jewell
22. John V'n Sicklen, one T. to Sarah Couenhoven

discon'd   23. Cornelius V'n Sicklen
discon'd   24. Do.   Do.
disanul'd   25. Johannis Dubois (disanuled by making door, wherefore there remains only 18 seats in the short pews

Pew No. 16
8 seats
purchasers'
names
1. Henry Rosekrans, T. to Ja's Rosekrans, S. to Peter V'n Derbelt
2. James Comton, T. to Mary Matthews, S. to Samuel Luckey
3. Joris Brinkerhoff, T. to Dan'l & Sarah Schanck, T. to Schanck Ackerman
4. Rodolphus Swartwout, T. to Charles Huffman, T. to son Charles C. Huffman, T. to Jane Monfort
5. Philip V'r Planck, T. to Catherine Verplank, S. to Peter V'n Derbelt
6. Philip V'r Planck, T. to Gartrude Verplank, S. to Samuel Luckey
7. Aurt Van Derbelt, T. to John V'n Derbelt
8. John Cornell, T. to daughter Margaret Shear

Pew No. 17
8 seats
purchasers'
names
1. Joris Brinkerhoff, T. to Dan'l Schank, T. to Sarah Ackerman, T. to Scank Ackerman
2. Joris Brinkerhoff, T. to Dan'l Schank, S. to Tunis V'n Bunschoten, T. to Abraham Sleight
3. Joris Brinkerhoff, T. to Isaac Adriance, S. to John Delevergn
4. Phebe Brown, T. to Antie Lent, T. to John A. Lent, S. to Tunis V'n Bunschoten, T. to Abraham Sleight

The Reformed Dutch Church of New Hackensack

    5. Minaster and famaly
    6. Minester and famoly
    7. Do.   Do.
    8. Do.   Do.

Pew No. 18
8 seats
purchasers'
names

1. Gysbert Schanck, T. to Ab'm Schanck, T. to Alleta Moriah Ackerman
2. Gysbert Schanck, T. to Ab'm Schanck, T. to John Ackerman, son of Peter
3. Isaac Brinkerhoff, T. to Sarah Brinkerhoff, T. to (L)itty Sleight
4. Baltus V. Kleeck, S. to Nathan Bayley, T. to John N. Bayley, T. to John Luckey, T. to Samuel Luckey, Jun'r
5. Lawrance Haff, S. to John Luckey, T. to Sam'l Luckey, Jun'r
6. Jacobus Swartwout
7. Derick Brinkerhoff, S. to Nathan Bayley, T. to Mary Bayley, T. to John Luckey, T. to Mary Luckey
8. Do.   Do.   S. to   Do.   Do.   T. to   Do.   Do.   T. to   Do.   Do. T. to do. do.

Pew No. 19
8 seats
purchasers'
names

1. Michael Huffman, T. to Daniel Huffman
2. John Heermans, T. to Sarah Hermans, T. to Philip Haremans, T. to Jeremiah B. V'n Kleeck, T. to his Wido Salee V'n Kleeck
3. Cornelius Luyster, T. to Petrus Luyster, T. to Ann Luyster, T. to Catharen V'n Dine
4. Do.   Do.   T. to   Do.   Do.   T. to   Do.   Do.   T. to Cathren V'n Dine
5. Jacobus Middagh, S. to Daniel Huffman
6. John Ostrom, T. to Nathan Bayley, T. to John N. Bayley, T. to Cornelius P. Luyster, T. to James V'n Dine
7. Cornelius Luyster, T. to daughter Catherine, T. to Cornelius P. Luyster, T. to James V'n Dine
8. Artd Middagh, T. to Hester Medaugh, T. to Aurt Medaugh, T. to Jeremiah V'n Kleeck, T. to his Wido Salee V'n Kleeck

Pew No. 20
8 seats
purchasers'
names

1. Matheus I. Dubois, T. to Rebeckah Westervelt
2. Peter Deeds, T. to Cornelia Cornwell, T. to her daughter, Elizabeth
3. Peter Deeds, T. to Catherine Haff, S. to Isaiah Rinders
4. Peter Deeds, T. to Abraham L. Dates
5. Johannis Rosekrans, T. to John Rosekrans, T. to Salle Monfort
6. Johannis Rosekrans, T. to John Rosekrans, T. to Moriah Monfort
7. Cornelius Dubois, S. to Elizabeth Todd
8. Constyn Gulnack, T. to Peter Dates, Jun'r, T. to his daughter, Eliza Ann

Pew No. 21
8 seats
purchasers'
names

1. Thomas V'n Bramer, T. to Peter V'n Bramer, T. to Helenah V'n Bramer
2. Magdeline Monfort, T. to Jacobus Monfort, T. to son Peter J. Monfort
3. Antie Terboss, Sold to Silvester Earl
4. Doratha Ackerman, T. to Doratha Ackerman, T. to Silvester Earl
5. Mariah Monfort, T. to Peter Monfort, T. to son Peter P. Monfort
6. Janitie Fort, T. to James Fort
7. Magdeline Monfort
8. Jacobus Monfort, T. to son, Elias Monfort

Pew No. 22
8 seats
purchasers'
names

1. Tunis Willsie, T. to John Willsie
2. Do.   Do.   T. to   Do.   Do.
3. John Hoghtaling
4. John Hoghtaling
5. Mariah Dubois, S. to Benj'n Everet, 2nd.
6. Mariah Dubois, S. to Benj'n Everit, T. to Benj'n Everit, 2nd.
7. Johanis Dubois
8. Do.   Do.

Pew No. 23
8 seats
purchasers'
names

1. Peter Outwater, T. to Barnet B. V'n Kleeck
2. Do.   Do.   T. to   Do.   Do.
3. Cornelius V'nKeuren, T. to Elizabeth V'n Keuren
4. Gulian Ackerman, T. to Ja's Ackerman
5. Do.   Do.   T. to   Do.   Do.
6. Peter I. Monfort, T. to Anne Cornell
7. Do.   Do.   T. to Susanah Monfort
8. Do.   Do.   T. to Mary Monfort

Index of Pews

Pew No. 24
8 seats
purchasers' names
1. Cornelius V. Wey, S. to Matthew Luyster
2. Do.   Do.   S. to Matthew Luyster
3. John Churchill, T. to son, William Churchill
4. Do.   Do.   T. to son,   do.   do.
5. Do.   Do.   T. to son,   do.   do.
6. David Sypher, S. to Matthew Luyster
7. Arie Medlar, S. to Matthew Luyster
8. Abraham Hogeland, T. to Lette Hogeland, widow

Pew No. 25
8 seats
purchasers' names
1. Kaarel Huffman, T. to his daughter, Elizabeth Brewer
2. Michael Golnack, S. to John Delevergn
3. Peter H. Monfort, T. to son, Henry Monfort, T. to Casper Ganse, T. to his son, Nicholas Ganse, Executor
4. Do.   Do.   T. to son, Stephen P. Monfort, T. to Casper Ganse, T. to his son, Nicholas Ganse, Executor
5. Do.   Do.   T. to son Stephen P. Monfort, T. to Casper Ganse, T. to his son Nicholis Gance Executor
6. John Jewell, s. to John Delevergn
7. Elias Newkerk, S. to Garit V'n Bomell, S. to John Delevergn
8. Henry Haremans, T. to Elbert Monfort, T. to Henry A. Monfort, T. to Casper Ganse, T. to his son, Nicholas Ganse, Executor

Pew No. 26
8 seats
purchasers' names
1. Lawrance Conklin, T. to Henry Conklin, T. to Rob't Todd, T. to Anne, wife of Christopher Jacocks
2. Lawrance Conklin, T. to Henry Conklin, T. to Tunis V'n Bunschoten
3. Isaac Willsie, S. to John Willsie, T. to Hannah V'n Keuren
4. Mathias Luyster, T. to John Luyster
5. Mathias Luyster, T. to Anne Hults, T. to son, Henry Hults, T. to Harvey E. Everitt, T. to Tunis V'n Bunschoten
6. Isaiah Rynders, S. to Demenicus Monfort, T. to Ann Monfort
7. John Conklin, Junr., S. to Saml. Luckey, T. to Moriah V'n Dine
8. Johanis V'n Steenbaragh, S. to Ab'm Hogeland, T. to Lette Hogelund, widow, S. to Tunis V'n Bunschoten

Pew No. 27
8 seats
purchasers' names
1. Jeremiah Jones, T. to John Yates
2. Redolphes Swartwout, T. to John Willsie, T. to Nazarth Brewer, T. to Obediah & Zakeriah Van Vorhes
3. Do. T. to D. Do. T. to Do.   Do.   T. to Obediah & Zakeririah Van Vorhis
4. Timothy Hicks, T. to Jacob Hicks, S. to John Delevergn
5. James Hicks, T. to daughter, Sarah Hicks
6. James Hicks, T. to John Rosekrans, T. to Moriah Rosekrans, wido
7. Johanis Shurey, T. to Lawrance Haff, T. to Nazareth Brewer, T. to Obediah & Zakeriah Van Voorhes
8. Do.   Do.   T. to   Do.   Do.   T. to   Do.   Do.   T. to Obediah & Zakerah Van Voorhis

Pew No. 28
8 seats
1. Bartholomew Crannell, S. to John A. Hageman, T. to Sitea Hageman
2. Do.   Do.   S. to Do.   Do.   T. to Do.   Do.
3. Nicholas Brower, S. to Corn's V'n Sicklen, S. to Sam'l Luckey, T. to Philander Suard
4. Do.   Do.   S. to Ab'm Sleight, S. to   Do.   Do.   T. to   Do.   Do.
5. Ahazerus V'n Kleeck, S. to Wm. Suard, T. to Philander Suard
6. Do.   Do.   S. to   Do.   Do.   T. to Philender Suard
7. Joris Medaugh, S. to Mary Lennington
8. John V'n Sicklen, T. to his widow, Corline

Pew No. 29
8 seats
purchasers' names
1. Andris Brastead, T. to Elizabeth Cooke, S. to Benjamin A. Sleight
2. Johones Shuree, T. to Matthius Dubois, T. to Cathrine Dubois, T. to John H. Dubois
3. Johones Shuree, T. to Matthius Dubois, T. to Cathrine Dubois, T. to Rebeckah Westervelt
4. Peter Outwater, T. to Daniel Outwater, T. to Joseph Jackson, T. to Sarah Jackson, widow
5. Do.   Do.   T. to   Do.   Do.   T. to   Do.   Do.   T. to Sarah Jackson, widow
6. Stephen Thorn, T. to Elizabeth Thorn, T. to Sam'l Thorn, T. to Stephen S. Thorn, T. to Corn's Westervelt
7. Phemetie Adriance, S. to Benjamin A. Sleight
8. Peter Harris, Esqr., T. to Henry Schoonmaker, T. to Corns. Westervelt

The Reformed Dutch Church of New Hackensack

A Statement or Index of the No. of pews in the Galory, also the No. of seats in each pew with the names of the Owners, etc. N. B. The letter S stands for sold and the letter T for Transfer

Pew No. 1	No entry
Pew No. 2	No entry
Pew No. 3	No entry
Pew No. 4, 8 seats purchasers' names	1. Jacobus Hannes 2. Cornelius Luyster 3. Do. Do. 4. Gilbert Levingston 5. Henry Willsie, T. to John Willsie 6. Tunis Willsie, T. to John Willsie 7. Nathaniel Hicks 8. Peter Outwater
Pew No. 5 6 seats purchasers' names	1. Johan Jost Snyder 2. Henry Bell 3. Redolphus Swartwout, T. to John Willsie 4. Joris Brinckerhoff 5. Peter Outwater, T. to Daniel Outwater 6. Do. Do. T. to Barnet B. Vn. Kleeck
Pew No. 6	No entry
Pew No. 7 6 seats	1. Matthew I. Dubois 2. Cornelius Dubois
Pew No. 8	No entry
Pew No. 9	No entry
Pew No. 10	No entry
Pew No. 11	No entry
Pew No. 12 8 seats	1. Charles Huffman 2. Elias Newkerk 3. David Sypher

1825, feb'y 25, Pew No. 2 in the Reformed Dutch Church at New Hackensack was Altered & made in short pews, Containing 3 seats each and was Numbered & balleted for and the names of the present Owners was put opiset said No. as followes &c

Pew No. 10 in No. 2	John Willsie Benjamin Everit do do

Pew No. 9 in No. 2	James Dodge, T. to John Everit
	  do do to John Everit
	  do do to John Everit

Pew No. 8 in No. 2	Isaac Hageman, S. to Benjamin Everit Garret V'n Bomell, S. to Benjamin Everit Abraham Sleight, S. to Benjamin Everit
Pew No. 7 in No. 2	Phillip V'n Derbelt, T. to Catherine Paterson Aris V'n Derbelt Consistory, an extra seat S. to Edger Luyster
Pew No. 6 in No. 2	Tunis V'n Bunschoten, T. to Harvey Everet Carline V'n Siclen, Widow Stephen S. Thorn
Pew No. 5 in No. 2	Garret V'n Dine, T. to his son Jas. V'n Dine Matthew V'n Bunschoten, Transferred to M. V. B. Ackerman Cornelius Wiltsey
Pew No. 4 in No. 2	Peter Dates, Jun'r, S. to John Luyster, Jun'r. do do do S. to do do John M. Rosekrans, to Moriah Rosecrans, his wido
Pew No. 3 in No. 2	Sitea Hagaman, wido Peter Monfort, S. to son Peter P. Monfort Henry Jewell
Pew No. 2 in No. 2	Abraham Adreans John C. Shear, T. to son John Shear do do T. to daughter Sarah Shear

Pew No. 1 in No. 2	James & Henry Dodge
	  do do do
	  do do do

Index of Pews

N.B. After the subdivision of pew No. 2 was Drawed for and Numbered in the book the workmen began to number on the wrong end and put on the numbers in consequence of which the figures had to be altered and reversed

1832 Aug't 15th, Pew No. 15 in the Reformed Dutch Church at New Hackensack was altered & and made in short pews Containing 3 seats each and was numbered and balleted for & the names of the present Owners was put opesit their Said No. respectively as follows &c

Pew No. 1   Henry D. Traver
in No. 15   Do.   Do.   Do.
            John Ackerman Bogardus

pew No. 2   Henry A. Monfort
in No. 15   Lette Hogeland
            Do.   Do.

pew No. 3   Stephen Monfort
in No. 15   Enes Jewel
            Sarah Covenhoven

pew No. 4   James Ackerman
in No. 15   Do.   Do.
            John Ackerman

pew No. 5   Baltis V'n Kleeck
in No. 15   John Ostrom
            Ahazerus V'n Kleeck

pew No. 6   Peter P. Lawson
in No. 15   Peter Monfort son of Pet'r I. do
            Hellen Schoonmaker

RECORD OF SALES AND TRANSFERS OF SEATS
in the Church of New Hackensack

No. 9   Aardt Middagh's seat in N. Hackingsack Church transferred to Joris Middagh, son of the aforesaid Aardt

No. 19   and is transferred to Hester Middagh, daughter of Joris Middagh; received for same 6/, Nov. 23, 1771.

No. 14   Isaac Brinckerhoff's seat in Do.— Do.—, transferred to Dirck Swartwout and Isaac Swartwout, sons of Jacobus Swartwout.

No. 18   and the woman's place to Widow Sarah Brinckerhoff; received for the same 9/, Nov. 23, 1771.

No. 24   Simon Bloom's seat in Do.— Do.—, transferred to Abraham Brinckerhoff; received
No. 5   Do. for the same 6/, Do.— Do.

No. 13   Petrus Noortstrant's seat &c transferred to Philip V. Planck; received for the same 3/, Nov. 23, 1771.

No. 4   Isaac V. Noortstrant's seat &c transferred to John Low; received for the same 3/, Nov. 23, 1771.

No. 5   Abraham Lent's seat &c transferred to Cathrina Bloom, widow; received &c 3/, Nov. 23, 1771.

No. 13   Luke Noortstrant's seat &c transferred to Dirck Brinckerhoff, Jun.; received 3/, Oct. 22, 1773.

No. 10   Joris Brinckerhoff's seat &c transferred to Peter V. Bunschooten; received 3/, Aug. 20, 17— (Page is torn here)

No. 12   Joris Brinkerhoff's seat &c transferred to Matheus and Jacob V. Bunschooten. Do. 6/, Do.

No. 19   John Heerman's seat &c transferred to Sarah Heerman; received 3/, Mar. 1, 1774.

No. 2
No. 4
No. 6   Peter Oudtwater's seats &c transferred to Daniel Oudtwater; received 15/,
No. 9   Sep. 22, 1778.
No. 5 gallery

No. 2
No. 4   Peter Oudtwater's seats &c transferred to Barent B. van Kleek; received
No. 6   15/, Sep. 22, 1778.
No. 5 gallery

The Reformed Dutch Church of New Hackensack

No. 13 ⎫
No. 11 ⎬ Seats of Philip V. Planck transferred to William Bt. Verplanck and the two lower ones to his daughters Catharine and Gertrude. Sept. 23, 1778.
No. 16 ⎭

No. 2   Seat of Cors. V. Wey transferred to Johs. Meynema; received 3/, Sep. 23, 1778.
No. 16 ⎫
No. 17 ⎬ Seats of Joris Brinkerhoff were transferred to Sarah Schenck and Daniel Schenck; received 9/, Sep. 23, 1778.
No. 17 ⎭

No. 11 ⎱ Seats of Joris Brinkerhoff were transferred to Isaac Adriance; received 6/, Sep. 23, 1778.
No. 17 ⎰

No. 1   Seat of Johannis Du Bois transferred to Dominicus Montfoort; received 3/, Sep. 30, 1778.
No. 7   Seat of Wilhelmus Heermanse transferred to Claraa Montfoort; received 3/, Sep. 30, 1778.
No. 11   Seat of John Heerman transferred to Philip Heerman; received 3/, Sep. 30, 1778.
No. 10   Seat of Johs. Schuree transferred to Karel Hoffman; received 3/, Sep. 30, 1778.
No. 16   Seat of Rudolphus H. Swartwout transferred to Karel Hoffman; received 3/, Sep. 30, 1778.
No. 2   Seat of John Conckling transferred to Laurens Conckling; received 3/, Sep. 30, 1778.
No. 17   Seat of Phebe Bloom transferred to Antie Lent; received 3/, Sep. 30, 1778.
No. 12   Seat of Rudolphus Swartwout transferred to Jacobus R. Swartwout; received 3/, Sep. 30, 1778.
No. 5   Seat of Rudolphus Swartwout transferred to Sarah Swarwout; received 3/, Sep. 30, 1778.
No. 8   Seat of Thunis V. Bunschoten transferred to Sarah Duryee; received 3/, Sep. 30, 1778.
No. 7   Seat of Willem Edwards transferred to Anna Margaritte Edwards; received 3/, Sep. 30, 1778.
No. 4   Seat of John Low transferred to Abrm. Duryee, Jun.; received for the same 3/, Sep. 30, 1778.
No. 27   Seat of Timothy Hicks transferred to Jacob Hicks; received 3/, Sep. 30, 1778.
No. 29   Seat of Andrias Breedstede transferred to Elisabeth Cooke; received 3/, Sep. 30, 1778.
No. 29   Seats of Peter Oudtwater transferred to Daniel Oudtwater; received 6/, Sep. 30, 1778.
No. 23   Seats of Peter Oudtwater transferred to Barnt B. van Kleek; received 6/, Sep. 30, 1778.
No. 29   Seats of Johs. Schuree transferred to Matheus DuBois; received 6/, Sep. 30, 1778.
No. 40   Seat of Johs. Schuree transferred to Kaarel Hoffman; received 3/, Sep. 30, 1778. (This entry crossed out in original).
No. 9   Seat of Johs. Schuree transferred to Peter J. Montfoort; received 3/, Sep. 30, 1778.
No. 16   Seat of Rudolphus Swartwout transferred to Karel Hoffman; received 3/, Sep. 30, 1778. (No. 16 crossed out in original).
No. 15   Seat of Edward Schoonmaker transferred to Mary Rosekranse; received 3/, Sep. 30, 1778.
No. 2   Seat of Henry Bell transferred to Henry Bell; received 3/, Sep. 30, 1778.
No. 5   Seat of Henry Bell transferred to Phebe Rosekranse; received 3/, Sep. 30, 1778.
No. 2   Seat of P. H. sold to Isaac Hegeman for 48/, and received Sep. 30, 1778.
No. 2   Seat of C. v. W. sold to Dominicus Montfoort for 48/, and received Sep. 30, 1778.
No. 2   Seat of E. S. sold to Gerret van Bommel for 49/, and received Sep. 30, 1778.
No. 2   Seat of H. B. sold to Abraham Sleght for 50/, and received Sep. 30, 1778.
No. 9   Seat of N. B. sold to Peter Monfoort for   , and received Sep. 30, 1778.
No. 9   Seat of N. B. sold to Thomas V. Bremen for 80/, and received Sep. 30, 1778.
No. 10   Seat of Garet Storm sold to Aardt V. D. Bilt for 82/, and received Sep. 30, 1778.
No. 25   Seat of E. N. sold to Gerret V. Bommel for 80/, and received Sep. 30, 1778.
No. 26   Seat of I. W. sold to John Wiltse for 91/, and received Sep. 30, 1778.
No. 26   Seat of J. R. sold to Dominicus Monfoort for 90/, and received Sep. 30, 1778.
No. 28   2 seats of   sold to Cors. V. Sickilen for 188/, and received Sep. 30, 1778.
No. 28   Seat of   sold to Mary Lennington for 96/, and received Sep. 30, 1778.
No. 28   Seat of   sold to Abrm. Sleght for 96/, and received Sep. 30, 1778.
No. 29   Seat of   sold to Isaac Hegeman for 98/, and received Sep. 30, 1778.
No. 18   Seat of   sold to Johanis DuBois for 62/, and received Sep. 30, 1778.
No. 4   Seat of   in the gallery sold to Johs. Wiltse for 32/, and received Sep. 30, 1778.

No. 1 2 seats ⎫
No. 8 1 seat ⎬ All belonging to Johannis Schurri, deceased, were transferred to Lawrence Hoff, Aug. 28, 1785.
No. 11 2 seats ⎪
No. 27 2 seats ⎭

Index of Pews

Seat of Rudolphus Zwartwout, H, to Johs. Wiltse: No. 1, 2; No. 2, 1; No. 4, 1; No. 8, 1; No. 27, 2; No. 5, 1 in gallery.
Seats of Tunis Wiltse to Johs. Wiltse: No. 7, 1; No. 22, 2; No. 4, 1. In Gy.and of Henry Wiltse, No. 4, 1 in gallery transferred at a convenient time. Received the sum of 3/ for each seat.

No. 8   Seats of Theunis V. Bunschoten in the New Hachingsack Church No. 8, were transferred to Antie van Bunschooten, his widow, at a convenient time.

No. 9   Seats of Daniel Oudtwater in the N. Hackensack Church:
Seat No. 9, and seat No. 29 transferred to Joseph Jackson
Seat No. 2 and all the remaining seats of Daniel Outwater were transferred to Joseph Jackson.

No. 10   Seats of Cornelius Luyster, No. 10 and No. 19, were transferred to his son Petrus
No. 19   and one to his daughter Catharina.
No. 9   Seat No. 9 of Peter Monfoort transferred to his son Peter.
No. 9   Seat No. 19 of Michiel Hoffman transferred to his son Daniel Hoffman.
No. 17   Seat of Daniel Schenck No. 17 transferred to his sister Sarah Ackerman.
N.B. Seats No. 3 and the seat of Clara Ostrander as also the seats of Wm. Heermans were transferred to Johanis Montfoort.

No. 15   March 6th 1794, one seat in No. 15, Transfer'd from Hendrick Heermans to Henry Schoonmaker
No. 5   One seat in No. 5 Transfered from Febee Rosekrans to Thomas Rosekrans May 3rd, 1794. Paid 8 Shillings
No. 15   Two Seats in No. 15 Transfered from Fredrick Rosekrans to Thomas Rosekrans May 3rd 1794. Paid 8 shill. for Each Seat
No. 15   One Seat in No. 15 Transfered from Mary Rosekrans to Ann Deeds, Daughter of Adam Deeds May 3rd 1794.   Paid 4 Shillings
No. 15   One Seat in No. 15 Transfered from Johanis Rosekrans to Ann Deeds, Widow of Adam Deeds, May 3rd, 1794.   Paid 8 Shillings
No. 20   Two Seats in No. 20 Transfered from Johanis Rosekrans to John Rosekrans May 3rd, 1794   Paid 16 Shillings
No. 13   One Seat in No. 13 Transfered from Henry Rosekrans to John Rosekrans May 3rd, 1794   Paid 8 Shillings
No. 23   One Seat in No. 23 Transfered from Peter I. Monfort to Anna Cornell May 19th, 1794   Paid 8 Shillings
No. 19   One Seat in No. 19 Transfered from John Ostrom to Nathan Baylie May 23rd 1794   Paid 8 Shillings
No. 15   One Seat in No. 15 which had been Confiscated is granted to John Ostrom the former Proprieter, by a Resolution of the Consistory May 23, 1794   Paid 8/
No. 23   One Seat in No. 23 Transfered from Peter I. Monfort to Susanah Monfort May 28th 1794   Rec'd 8/
No. 23   One Seat in No. 23 Transfer'd from Peter I. Monfort to Mary Monfort May 28th 1794   Rec'd 8/
No. 15   Two Seats in No. 15 Transfered from Peter I. Monfort to his sons Stephen and Peter Monfort May 28th, 1794   Rec'd 16/
No. 9   One Seat in No. 9 Transfered from Peter I. Monfort to his son Martin Monfort May 28th 1794   Rec'd 8/
No. 29   One Seat in No. 29 Transfered from Peter Harris to Henry Schoonmaker May 28th 1794
No. 15   Two Seats in No. 15 Transfered from Peter Haff to Abram Myer May 29th 1794   Rec'd 16/
No. 2   Two Seats in No. 2 Transfered from Peter Haff to Warren Rosekrans May 29th 1794   Rec'd 16/
No. 21   One Seat in No. 21 Transfered from Doritie Ackerman to Doritie Ackerman Sept. 13th, 1794   Rec'd 8/
One Seat No. 21 Transfered from Mariah Monfort to Peter Monfort Sept. 13th 1794   Rec'd 8/

No. 3   Two ⎫
No. 5   One ⎬ Transfered from Abram Lent, Senr. to Abram Lent Sept. 13th 1794
No. 6   Two ⎭   Rec'd. 5 Dolls.
No. 16   One Seat Transfered from Hendrick Rosekrans to James Rosekrans Sept. 13th 1794   Rec'd 8/
No. 2   One Seat ⎫
No. 26   Two " ⎬ Transfered from Lawrence Conklin to Henry Conklin, Sept. 13th 1794
No. 14   One " ⎭   Rec'd 4 Dolls.
No. 12   Two Seat of Derrick Brinkerhoff Sold at Vandue Purchased by Matthew Van Bun Schooten @ 48/   Paid £4:16:0
No. 18   2 Seats of Duirrick Brinckerhoff Sold to Nathan Bailey @ 43/   Paid 4— 6—0

The Reformed Dutch Church of New Hackensack

No. 14	1 Seat Derrick Swartwout Sold to Nathan Bayley	Paid 2— 3—0
No. 9	1 Seat of Nicholas Brower Sold to Edward Schoonmaker not paid, no sale	2— 6
No. 9	1 Seat of Nickolas Brower Sold to John A. Hageman	Paid 2— 6—0
No. 28	1 Seat of Nickolas Brower Sold to Edward Schoonmaker not paid for, no sale	2— 4—0
No. 28	1 Seat of Nickolas Brower Sold to Edward Schoonmaker and Given to Cornelia Schoonmaker not paid for, no sale	2— 4—0
No. 10	1 Seat of Bartholomy Crannell Sold to Ruben Tanner	Paid 2—13—0
No. 28	2 Seats of Bartholomy Crannell Sold to John A. Hegeman @ 45/	Paid 4—10—0
No. 26	1 Seat of Johannis Van Seanbeargh Sold to Abraham Holand	Paid 2— 1—0
No. 2	1 Seat of Johanes Van Steanbergh Sold to John Van Sicklon	Paid 1— 4—0
No. 2	1 Seat of Johanes Bookhout Sold to Mathew Van Bunschouten	Paid 1— 4—0
No. 2	1 Seat of Johanis E. Schut Sold to John A. Hageman	Paid 1— 0—0
No. 14	1 Seat of Henry Conklin Transfer'd to Robert Todd	Rec'd. 0— 4—0
No. 18	1 Seat of Baltus Van Kleak Sold to Nathen Bayley	Paid 2— 2—0
No. 9	1 Seat of Peter Monfort Transfered to Joseph Jackson	Rec'd 0— 4—0
No. 2	1 Seat of Joseph Jackson Transfered to Peter Monfort	Rec'd. 0— 4—0
No. 15	One Seat which had been Purchased at Vandue in Sept. 1778 and by Mistacke had not been put on Record by Domenicus Monfort, the Consistory Do Allow him his Seat Novr. 22nd 1794	
	Rec'd for Transferring three Seats from Tunis Van Bunschooten, Disceased, to Anne Van Bunschooten Transfer'd by Ralph Schenk Novm. 22nd 1794	Paid 0— 9—0
No. 19	one ⎫ Seats Transfered from Nathan Bailey, Deceased, to John	
No. 18	one ⎬ N. Bailey, February 15th 1796 Rec'd 4 Shill. for each	
No. 14	one ⎭ Seat	12/
	2 Seats in No. 18 Transfered from Nathan Bailey, Dec., to Mary Bailey February 15th 1796	Rec'd 8/

TRANSFERS OF SEATS

No. 9 23 Nov'r 1771	one seat of Aurt Middaugh Transfered to his son Aurt Middaugh	paid	0 3 0
No. 19 23 Nov'r 1771	one seat of Aurt Middaugh Transfered to Hester Middaugh daughter of Joris Middaugh	paid	— 3 0
No. 14 23 Nov'r 1771	One seat of Isaac Brinkerhoff Transfered to Derick Swartwout son of Jacobus Swartwout	paid	— 3 0
No. 14 23 Nov'r 1771	One seat of Isaac Brinkerhoff Transfered to Isaac Swartwout son of Jacobus Swartwout	paid	— 3 0
No. 18 23 Nov'r 1771	One set of Isaac Brinkerhoff Transfered to Widow Sarah Brinkerhoff	paid	— 3 0
No. 14 23 Nov'r 1771	One seat of Simon Bloom Transfered to Abraham Brinkerhoff	paid	— 3 0
No. 5 23 Nov'r 1771	One seat of Simon Bloom Transfered to Abraham Brinkerhoff	paid	— 3 0
No. 13 23 Nov'r 1771	One seat of Peter Norstront Transfered to Phillip Ver Plank	paid	— 3 —
No. 4 23 Nov'r 1771	One seat of Isaac V'n Noorstrant Transfered to John Low	paid	— 3 —
No. 5 Nov'r 23 1771	One seat of Abraham Lent Transfered to Catherine Bloom widow	paid	— 3 —
No. 13 Octob'r 22. 1773	One seat of Luke Noorstrant Transfered to Derick Brinkerhoff Jun'r	paid	— 3 —
No. 10 Aug't 20th 1775	One seat of Joris Brinkerhoff Transfered to Peter V'n Bunschotan	paid	— 3 —
No. 12 20th Aug't 1775	One seat of Joris Brinkerhoff Transfered to Matthew V'n Bunschoten	paid	— 3 —
No. 12 20th Aug't 1775	One seat of Joris Brinkerhoff Transfered to Jacob V'n Bunschoten	paid	— 3 —
No. 19 1st Mc'h 1774	One seat of John Heremans Transfered to Sarah Heermans	paid	— 3 —

Index of Pews

No. 2, 4, 6, 9, 22 sept'r 1778	four seats of Peter Outwater 1 in No. 2, 1 in No. 4, 1 in No. 6, & 1 in No. 9 Transfered to Danial Outwater	paid	— 12 —
No. 5 22 Sept'r 1778	One seat in Galory of Peter Outwater Transfered to Daniel Outwater	paid	— 3 —
No, 2, 4, 6 22 sept'r 1778	thre seats of Peter Outwater 1 in No. 2, 1 in No. 4 & 1 in No. 6 Transfered to Barnet B. V'n Kleeck	paid	— 9 —
No. 5 22 sept'r 1778	One seat in Galory of Peter Outwater Transfered to Barnet B. V'n Kleeck	paid	— 3 —
No. 13 23 sept'r 1778	One seat of Phillip Ver Planck Transfered to William B. Ver Planck	paid	— 3 —
No. 16 23 sept'r 1778	One seat of Phillip Ver Planck Transfered to his Daughter Catherine Ver Planck	paid	— 3 —
No. 16 23 sept'r 1778	One seat of Phillip Ver Planck Transfered to his Daughter Gatrude Ver Planck	paid	— 3 —
No. 2 23 sept'r 1778	One seat of Cornelius V'n Wey Transfered to Johones Menneman	paid	— 3 —
No. 16 23rd sept'r 1778	One seat of Joris Brinkerhoff Transfered to Daniel & Sarah Schanck	paid	— 3 —
No. 17 23 sept'r 1778	Two seats of Joris Brinkerhoff Transfered to Daniel & Sarah Schanck	paid	0 6 0
No. 11 23 sept'r 1778	One seat of Joris Brinkerhoff Transfered to Isaac Adriance	paid	— 3 —
No. 17 23 sept'r 1778	One seat of Joris Brinkerhoff Transfered to Isaac Adriance	paid	— 3 —
No. 1 30th sept'r 1778	One seat of Johannis Dubois Transfered to Demenicus Monfort	paid	— 3 —
No. 7 30th sept'r 1778	One seat of Willhelemus Heremans Transfered to Claraw Monfort	paid	— 3 —
No. 11 30th Sept'r 1778	One seat of John Heremans Transfered to Phillip Heremans	paid	— 3 —
No. 10 30 sept'r 1778	One seat of Johanis Shurrey Transfered to Charles Huffman	paid	— 3 —
No. 16 30 sept'r 1778	One seat of Redolphus H. Swartwout Transfered to Charles Huffman	paid	— 3 —
No. 2 30th sept'r 1778	One seat of John Concklin Transfered to Lawrance Concklin	paid	— 3 —
No. 17 30th sept'r 1778	One seat of Pheobe Bloom Transfered to Antie Lent	paid	— 3 —
No. 12 30 sept'r 1778	One seat of Redolphus Swartwout Transfered to Jacobus I. Swartwout	paid	— 3 —
No. 5 30th sept'r 1778	One seat of Redolphus Swartwout Transfered to Sarah Swartwout	paid	— 3 —
No. 8 30th sept'r 1778	One seat of Tunis V'n Bunschoten Transfered to Sarah Duryee	paid	— 3 —
No. 7 30th sept'r 1778	One seat of William Edwards Transfered to Anna Margaret Edwards	paid	— 3 —
No. 4 30th sept'r 1778	One seat of John Low Transfered to Abraham Duryee Jun'r	paid	— 3 —
No. 27 30th sept'r 1778	One seat of Timothy Hicks Transfered to Jacob Hicks	paid	— 3 —
No. 29 30th sept'r 1778	One seat of Andrias Breestede Transfered to Elezebeth Cooke	paid	— 3 —
No. 29 30th sept'r 1778	Two seats of Peter Outwater Transfered to Daniel Outwater	paid	— 6 —
No. 23 30th sept'r 1778	Two seats of Peter Outwater Transfered to Barnet B. V'n Kleeck	paid	— 6 —
No. 29 30th sept'r 1778	Two seats of Johanis Shuree Transfered to Matthew Dubois	paid	— 6 —
No. 10 30 sept'r 1778	One seat of Johanis Shuree Transfered to Charles Huffman	paid	— 3 —

The Reformed Dutch Church of New Hackensack

No.	Date	Description	Paid	Amount
No. 9	30th sept'r 1778	One seat of Johanis Shuree Transfered to Peter I. Monfort	paid	— 3 —
No. 16	30th sept'r 1778	One seat of Redolphus Swartwout Transfered to Charles Huffman	paid	— 3 —
No. 15	30th sept'r 1778	One seat of Edward Schoonmaker Transfered to Mary Rosekrance	paid	— 3 —
No. 2	30th sept'r 1778	One seat of Henry Bell Transfered to Henry Bell	paid	— 3 —
No. 5	30th sept'r 1778	One seat of Henry Bell Transfered to Phebe Rosekrans	paid	— 3 —
No. 2	30th Sept'r 1778	One seat of Peter Hay Sold as is suposed to Isaas Hagaman for	paid	2 8 —
No. 2	30th sept'r 1778	One seat of Cornelius V'n Wey sold as is suposed to Demenicus Monfort for	paid	2 8 —
No. 2	30th sep'r 1778	One seat of Edw'd Schonmaker sold to as supos'd Garret V'n Bomell for	paid	2 9 —
No. 2	30th sept'r 1778	One seat of Henry Bell Sold to as supos'd Abraham Sleight for	paid	2 10 —
No. 9	30th sept'r 1778	One seat of Nicholas Brower Sold to as supos'd Peter Monfort		
No. 9	30 sept'r 1778	One seat of Joris Noorstrant Sold to as supos'd Thomas V'n Bramer for	paid	4 0 --
No. 10	30th sept'r 1778	One seat of Garrit Storm Sold to supos'd Aardt V'n Debelt for	paid	4 2 —
No. 25	30 sept'r 1778	One seat of Elias Newkirk Sold to as supos'd Garrit V'n Bomell for	paid	4 0 —
No. 26	30th sept'r 1778	One seat of Isaac Willsie Sold to as supos'd John Willsie for	paid	4 11 —
No. 26	30th sept'r 1778	One seat of Isaac Rynders Sold to as supos'd Demenicus Monfort for	paid	4 10 —
No. 28	30th sept'r 1778	One seat of Nicholas Brower Sold to as supos'd Cornelius V'n Sicklen for	paid	4 8 —
No. 28	30th sept'r 1778	One seat of Joris Middaugh Sold to as supos'd Mary Lennington for	paid	4 6 —
No. 28	30th sept'r 1778	One seat of Nicholas Broer Sold to as supos'd Abraham Sleight for	paid	4 6 —
No. 29	30th sept'r 1778	One seat of Sold to Isaac Hageman for	paid	4 8 —
No. 18	30th sept'r 1778	One seat of Sold to Johanis Dubois for	paid	3 2 —
No. 4	30th sept'r 1778	One seat in Galory of Sold to Jahonis Wiltsie for	paid	1 12 —
No. 1	28th aug't 1785	Two seat of Johanis Shuree Transfered to Lawrance Haff		
No. 8	28th Aug't 1785	One seat of Johanis Shuree Transfered to Lawrance Haff		
No. 11	28th Aug't 1785	Two seats of Johanis Shuree Transfered to Lawrance Haff		
No. 27	28 Aug't 1785	Two seats of Johanis Shuree Transfered to Lawrance Haff		
No. 1		Two seats of Redolphus Swartwout Transf'd to John Willsie		3 x
No. 2		One seat of Redolphus Swartwout Transf'd to John Willsie		3 x
No. 4		One seat of Redolphus Swartwout Transf'd to John Willsie		3 x
No. 27		Two seats of Redolphus Swartwout Transf'd to John Willsie		3 x
No. 5 in Galory		one seat of Redolph's Swartwout Transf'd to John Willsie		3 x
No. 7		one seat of Tunis Willsie Transfered to John Willsie		3 x
No. 22		Two seats of Tunis Willsie Transfer'd to John Willsie		3 x
No. 4 in Galory		one seat of Tunis Willsie Transf'd to John Wiflsie		— 3 x
No. 4 in Galory		One seat of Henry Willsie Transf'd to John Willsie	p'd	0 3 —
No. 8		Three seats of Tunis V'n Bunschoten Transfered to Widow Antie V'n Bunschoten		

Index of Pews

No. 2	one 4 two 6 one 9 one & 29 two seats of Daniel Outwater Transfered to Joseph Jackson		
No. 10	two No. 19 two seats of Corn's Luyster Transfered to son Petrus Luyster		
No. 19	One seat of Corn's Luyster Transf'd to Daughter Catherine		
No. 9	One seat of Peter Monfort Transf'd to son Peter Monfort		
No. 19	One seat of Mich'l Huffman Transf'd to Dan'l Huffman		
No. 17	One seat of Daniel Huffman Transferred to Lanah Ackerman		
No. 31	all the seats of Claraw Ostrander and the seats of William Haremans Transfered to Johanis Monfort		
No. 15 6th Mc'h 1794	one seat of Henry Heermans Transfered to Henry Schoonmaker		
No. 5 3rd May 1794	One seat of Phebe Rosekrans Transfered to Thomas Rosekrans	paid	0 8 —
No. 15 3rd May 1794	Two seats of Frederick Rosekrans Transfered to Thomas Rosekrans	paid	— 16 —
No. 15 3rd May 1794	One seat of Mary Rosekrans Transfered to Ann Deeds daughter of Adam Deeds	paid	— 4 —
No. 15 3rd May 1794	One seat of Johanis Rosekrans Transfered to Ann Deeds Widow of Adam Deeds	paid	— 4 —
No. 20 3rd May 1794	Two seats of Johanis Rosekrans Transfered to John Rosekrans	paid	— 16 —
No. 13 3rd May 1794	One seat of Henry Rosekrans Transfered to John Rosekrans	paid	— 8 —
No. 23 19th May 1794	One seat of Peter I. Monfort Transfered to Anna Cornell	paid	— 8 —
No. 19 23rd May 1794	One seat of John Ostrom Transfered to Nathan Bayley	paid	— 8 —
No. 15 23rd May 1794	One seat of John Ostrom which had been Confisticated is granted to him again by the Consistory	p'd	— 8 —
No. 23 28th May 1794	One seat of Peter I. Monfort Transfered to Susanah Monfort	paid	— 8 —
No. 23 28th May 1794	One seat of Peter I. Monfort Transfered to Mary Monfort	paid	— 8 —
No. 15 28th May 1794	Two seats of Peter I. Monfort Transfered to sons Stephen & Peter Monfort	paid	— 16 —
No. 9 28th May 1794	One seat of Peter I. Monfort Transfered to son Martain Monfort	paid	— 8 —
No. 29 28th May 1794	One seat of Peter Harris Transfered to Henry Schoonmaker		
No. 15 29th May 1794	Two seats of Peter Haff Transfered to Abraham Myers	paid	— 16 —
No. 2 29th May 1794	Two seats of Peter Haff Transfered to Warren Rosekrans	paid	— 16 —
No. 21 13th sept'r 1794	One seat of Doratha Ackerman Transfered to Doratha Ackerman	paid	— 8 —
No. 21 13th sept'r 1794	One seat of Mariah Monfort Transfered to Peter Monfort	paid	— 8 —
No. 3 & 6 13th sept'r 1794	Two seats of Ab'm Lent in No. 5 & Two seats in No. 6 Transfered to Abraham Lent	paid	1 12 —
No. 16 13th sept'r 1794	One seat of Henry Rosekrans Transfered to James Rosekrans	paid	— 8 —
No. 2, 14 & 6	One seat in No. 2 one do. in No. 14 & two in No. 26 of Lawrance Concklin Transfered to Hen'y Concklin	paid	1 12 —
No. 12	Two seats of Derick Brinkerhoff sold to Matthew V'n Bunschoten @ 48/ Each	paid	4 16 —
No. 18	Two seats of Derick Brinkerhoff sold to Nathan Bailey @ 43/ each	paid	4 6 —
No. 14	One seat of Derick Swartwout sold to Nathan Bailey	paid	2 3 —
No. 9	One seat of Nicholas Brower sold to John A. Hageman	paid	2 6 —
No. 10	One seat of Bartholomy Crannell sold to Reubin Tanner	paid	2 13 —

The Reformed Dutch Church of New Hackensack

			L	S	D
No. 28	Two seats of Bartholomy Crannell sold to John A. Hageman @ 45/ each	paid	4	10	—
No. 26	One seat of Johanis V'n Steenbaragh sold to Abraham Hogeland	paid	2	1	—
			L	S	D
No. 2	One seat of Johanis Van Steenbergh sold to John V'n Sicklen	paid		1	4 —
No. 2	One seat of Johanis Bookhout sold to Matthew V'n Bunschoten	paid		1	4 —
No. 2	One seat of Johanis E. Scutt sold to John A. Hagaman	paid		1	0 —
No. 4	One seat of Henry Conklin Transfered to Robert Todd	paid			4 —
No. 18	One seat of Baltus V'n Kleeck sold to Nathan Bailey	paid		2	2 —
No. 9	One seat of Peter Monfort Transfered to Joseph Jackson	paid			4 —
No. 2	One seat of Joseph Jackson Transfered to Peter Monfort	paid			4 —
No. 15 22nd Nov'r 1794	One seat bo't in sept'r 1778 by Demenicus Monfort but not recorded the Consistory Allow him said seat				
No. 8 22 Nov'r 1794	Three seat of Tunis V'n Bunschoten Decs'd Transfer'd to Anne V'n Bunschoten widow	paid		—	9 —
No. 14, 18 & 19 15th feb'y 1796	One seat in No. 14 one in No. 18 & one in No. 19 of Nathan Bailey Transfered to John N. Bailey	paid		—	12 —
No. 18 15th feb'y 1796	two seat of Nathan Bailey Decs'd Transfered to Mary Bailey	paid			8 —
No. 2 8th Ap'l 1796	One seat of Henry Concklin Transfered to Cap't Tunis V'n Bunschoten	paid			4 —
No. 26	One seat of Henry Concklin Transfered to Robert Todd				
No. 26 8th Ap'l 1796	One seat of Henry Concklin Transfered to Tunis V'n Bunschoten	paid			4 —
No. 2 8th Ap'l 1796	One seat of Ram Adriance Transfered to Abraham Adriance	paid			4 —
No. 28 8th Ap'l 1796	Two seats of Ahazerus V'n Kleek Sold to William Suard @ 40/ each	paid	4	0	—
No. 26 8th Ap'l 1796	One seat of John Concklin Jun'r supos'd sold to Samuel Luckey for	paid	1	1	—
No. 9 8th Ap'l 1796	One seat of Sold to Henry Schoonmaker	paid	2	0	—
No. 7 8th Ap'l 1796	One seat supos'd of Henry Haremans sold to Samuel Cooper for	paid	1	19	—
No. 8 8th Ap'l 1796	One seat supos'd of Johanis Shuree sold to Henry Dodge for	paid	2	0	—
No. 3 8th Ap'l 1796	One seat of Henry Haremans Transfered to Phillip Haremans	paid			4 —
No. 23 8th Ap'l 1796	One seat of Cornelius V'n Keuren Transfered to Elizebeth V'n Keuren widow	paid			4 —
No. 9 6 feb'y 1797	One seat of Joris Middaugh Transfered to son Ardt Middaugh	paid			4 —
No. 25	One seat of Henry Haremans Transfered to Elbert H. Monfort	paid			4 —
No. 15	One seat of John Monfort Transfered to Elbert H. Monfort	paid			4 —
No. 15 11 feb'y 1799	One seat of Thomas V'n Bramer Transfered to Peter V'n Bramer	paid			4 —
No. 21 11 feb'y 1799	One seat of Thomas V'n Bramer Transfered to Peter V'n Bramer	paid			4 —
No. 14 26th feb'y 1800	Two seats of Gysbert Schank Transfered to Abraham Schank	paid			8 —
No. 18 26th feb'y 1800	Two seats of Gysbert Schank Transfered to Abraham Schank	paid			8 —
No. 2 26th feb'y 1800	One seat of Johanis Wiltsie Transfered to Cornelius Wiltsie	paid			8 —
No. 3 26th feb'y 1800	One seat of Henry Haremans Transfered to Sam'l Cooper which had been transf'd to Elbert H. Monfort by Mistake	paid			4 —

Index of Pews

Pew & Date	Description		L	S	D
No. 8 26th feb'y 1800	One seat of Sarah Durea Decs'd Transfered to Abraham	paid		4	—
No. 7 26th feb'y 1800	One seat of John Willsie Transfered to Abraham Durea	paid		4	—
No. 29 26th feb'y 1800	Two seats of Matthew Dubois Transfered to Catherine Dubois	had been paid			
No. 20 26th feb'y 1800	One seat of Matthew I. Dubois Transfered to Rebeckah Westervelt	which had been p'd			
No. 7 26th feb'y 1800	One seat of Matthew I. Dubois Transfered to John Henry DuBois	had been paid			
	the three seats above transf'd by order of Consistory				
No. 29 26th feb'y 1800	One seat of Stephen Thorn Transfered to Elizabeth Thorn widow	paid		4	—
No. 2 26th feb'y 1800	One seat of Stephen Thorn Transfered to Samuel Thorn	paid		4	—
No. 16 26th feb'y 1800	One seat of James Compton Des'd Transfered to daughter Mary Matthews	paid		8	
No. 11 26th feb'y 1800	One seat of Lawrance Haff Sold to Jacob V'n Bunschoten for	paid	1	10	—
No. 2 26th feb'y 1800	One seat of Jacob Dubois Sold to Benjamin Everit for	paid	1	14	—
No. 11 26th feb'y 1800	One seat of Lawrance Haff Sold to Albert I. Monfort for		1	10	—
No. 22 26th feb'y 1800	One seat of Moriah Dubois Sold to Benjamin Everit Jun'r for	paid	1	1	6
No. 22 26th feb'y 1800	One seat of Moriah Dubois Sold to Benjamin Everit for	paid	1	1	0
No. 15 27th May 1800	Two seats of Thomas Rosekrans Transfered to Henry Dodge	paid		8	—
No. 5 27th May 1800	One seat of Thomas Rosekrans Transfered to Henry Dodge	paid		4	—
No. 15 9th Aug't 1800	Two seats of Abraham Myers to Samuel Cooper	paid		8	—
No. 1 28th Jan'y 1801	One seat of Gulian Ackerman Decs'd Transfered to Gulian Ackerman son of Ja's Ackerman	paid		4	—
No. 15 28th Jan'y 1801	One seat of Gulian Ackerman Decs'd Transfered to his son John Ackerman	paid		4	—
No. 15 28th Jan'y 1801	One seat of Gulian Ackerman Decs'd Transfered to John Ackerman son of Ja's Ackerman	paid		4	—
No. 23 28th Jan'y 1801	Two seats of Gulian Ackerman Decs'd Transfered to his son James Ackerman	paid		8	—
No. 3 28th Jan'y 1801	Two seats of Andris Haremans Transfered to John Monfort which had been Neglected to Record				
No. 3 28th Jan'y 1801	Two seats of John Monfort Transfered to Albert Monfort			8	—
No. 27 28th Jan'y 1801	Two seats of Lawrance Haff Transfered to Nazareth Brewer, in rome of 2 bo't of Edw'd Schoonmaker in Mistake. done by order of Consistory	p'd		8	—
No. 10 19th July 1801	Two seats of Patrus Luyster Decs'd Transfered to Cornelius P. Luyster	paid		8	—
No. 19 19th July 1801	Two seats of Patrus Luyster Decs'd Transfered to Daughter Ann Luyster	paid		8	—
No. 2 20th feb'y 1802	Two seats of Constine Gulnack Transfered to Peter Dates Jun'r	paid		8	—
No. 21 20th feb'y 1802	One seat of Magdeline Monfort Transfered to Jacobus Monfort	paid		8	—
No. 11 2nd Sept'r 1802	One seat of Phillip Haremans Transfered to William Suard	paid		4	—

The Reformed Dutch Church of New Hackensack

			L	S	D
No. 20 6th May 1803	One seat of Peter Deeds Decs'd Transfered to Daughter Cornelia Cornwell	paid		4	—
No. 20 6th may 1803	One seat of Peter Deeds decs'd Transfered to Daughter Catherine Haff widow	paid		4	—
No. 3 16th may 1803	One seat of Samuel Cooper Transfered to James Ackerman	paid		4	—
No. 7 16th may 1803	One seat of Samuel Cooper Transfered to James Ackerman	paid		4	—
No. 15 16th may 1803	Two seats of Samuel Cooper Transfered to James Ackerman	paid		8	—
No. 1 12th July 1804	One seat of Matthias Luyster Transfered to John Luyster	paid		4	—
No. 2 12th July 1804	Two seats of Matthias Luyster decs'd Transfered to John Luyster	paid		8	—
No. 26 12th July 1804	One seat of Matthias Luyster Transfered to John Luyster	paid		4	—
No. 26 12th July 1804	One seat of Matthias Luyster Decs'd Transfered to Daughter Anne Huls	paid		4	—
No. 8 29th Ap'l 1805	Tree seats of Anna V'n Bunschoten decs'd Transfer'd to son Matthew V'n Bunschoten	paid		12	—
No. 27 5th June 1805	Two seats of John Willsie Transfered to Nazareth Brewer	paid		8	—
No. 13 24th Aug't 1807	One seat of Ralph Schank Decs'd Transfered to Peter Ackerman—by request of Jno. Ackerman	paid		4	—
No. 14 24th Aug't 1807	Two seats of Abraham Schank Transfered to Schank Ackerman, by request of Jno. Ackerman	paid		8	—
No. 18 24th Aug't 1807	One seat of Abraham Schank Transfered to Alletta Moriah Ackerman	paid		4	—
No. 18 24th Aug't 1807	One seat of Abraham Schank Transfered to John Ackerman son of Peter	paid		4	—
No. 4, 7, & 8 5th sept'r 1807	One seat in No. 4, one do. in No. 7 & one in No. 8 of Ab'm Durea Transfer'd to Phebe Durea widow	paid	1	4	—
No. 19 5th sept'r 1807	One seat of Catherine Luyster Transfered to Cornelius P. Luyster	paid		8	—
No. 29 5th sept'r 1807	One seat of Elizebeth Thorn Decs'd Transfered to son Samuel Thorn	paid		8	—
No. 13 5th sept'r 1807	One seat of John Churchell Decs'd Transfered to son William Churchell	paid		8	—
No. 17 5th sept'r 1807	One seat of Antie Lent Transfered to John A. Lent	paid		4	—
No. 7 5th sept'r 1807	One seat of Tjirk V'n Keuren Transfered to Albert I. Monfort	paid		8	—
No. 15 5th sept'r 1807	One seat of Peter V'n Bramer Decs'd Transfered to Peter P. Lawson	paid		8	—
No. 21 5th sept'r 1807	One seat of Peter V'n Bramer Decs'd Transfered to Helenah V'n Bramer widow	paid		8	—
No. 9 5th sept'r 1807	One seat of Thomas V'n Bramer sold to Joseph Jackson	paid	1	12	—
No. 13 5th sept'r 1807	One seat of James Hicks Decs'd sold to Peter P. Lawson	paid	1	4	—
No. 13 5th sept'r 1807	One seat of William B. V'r Plank Decs'd sold to James Phillips	paid	1	4	—
No. 4 5th sept'r 1807	One seat of John Jewell Decs'd Transfered to Harmah Jewell	paid		8	—
No. 28 5th sept'r 1807	One seat of Cornelius V'n Sicklen Decs'd Sold to Samuel Luckey for	paid	1	4	0
No. 28 5th sept'r 1807	One seat of Abraham Sleight Decs'd sold to Samuel Luckey for	paid	1	4	—

Index of Pews

			L	S	D
No. 10 2nd Mc'h 1809	One seat of Aris V'n Derbelt Decs'd Transfered to son Peter V'n Derbelt	paid		4	—
No. 16 2nd Mc'h 1809	One seat of Aris V'n Derbelt Decs'd Transfered to son John V'n Derbelt	paid		4	—
No. 2 2nd Mc'h 1809	One seat of Aris V'n Derbelt Decs'd Transfered to son Phillip V'n Derbelt	paid		4	—
No. 2 2nd Mc'h 1809	One seat of Aris V'n Derbelt Decs'd Transfered to son Aris V'n Derbelt	paid		4	—
No. 29 Dec'r 24th 1810	One seat of Catherine Dubois Decs'd Transfered to her son John H. Dubois	paid		4	—
No. 29 24 Dec'r	One seat of Catherine Dubois Decs'd Transfered to Her Daughter Rebekah Westervelt	paid		4	—
No. 4 14th Ap'l 1812	one seat of Peter H. Monfort Decs'd Transfered to his son Henry Monfort	Paid		4	—
No. 25 14th Ap'l 1812	one seat of Peter H. Monfort Decs'd Transfered to his son Henry Monfort	Paid		4	—
No. 25 14th Ap'l 1812	two seats of Peter H. Monfort Decs'd Transfered to his son Stephen P. Monfort	Paid		8	—
No. 19 14th Ap'l 1812	one seat of Sarah Hermans Decs'd Late wife of Jno. Meneman Transfered to Phillip Hermans her son	Paid		4	—
No. 6 24 may 1813	two seats of Andris Haremans Sold to John Pinkney for 5 dollars each	Paid	4	0	0
No. 18 sept'r 20 1813	two seats of Mary Bayley wife of Samuel Sackett Transfered to John Luckey	paid		8	0
No. 15 Nov'r 8th 1813	two seats of Abraham Hogeland Decs'd Transfered to to Lette Hogeland his widow	paid	0	8	0
No. 24 Nov'r 8th 1813	1 seat of Abraham Hogeland decs'd Transfered to Lette Hogeland widow of do.	paid	0	4	0
No. 26 Nov'r 8th 1813	one seat of Abraham Hogeland decs'd Transfered to Lette Hogeland widow of do.	paid	0	4	0
feb'y 28 1814 No. 18	one seat of John H. Bayley transferred to John Luckey the 28th day of february 1814	paid	0	4	0
No. 25 June 27 1814	one seat of Karrel Huffman Deceas'd Transfered to his daughter Elizabeth Brewer wife of Chl's Brewer	paid	0	4	0
1814 may 30th No. 27	one seat of Jeremiah Jones transferred to John Yates	p'd	0	4	0
No. 18 Sept'r 13	one seat of Lawrane Haff sold to John Luckey	Paid	2	0	0
No. 5 11th setb'r 1814	one seat of Sarah Swartwout Transfer'd to Ann Swartwout wife of Jacobus I. Swartwout	Paid	0	4	0
1815 June 14th No. 26	one seat of Lette Hogeland sold to Tunis V'n Bunschoten by her order for & the 17th she recv'd her money & p'd transfer	p'd	2	0	0
No. 2 28 dec'r	one seat one seat of John A. Hageman Transfer'd to his widow Sitea Hageman	rec'd	0	4	0
No. 9 28 Dec'r	one seat of do. do. do. Transfer'd to his widow Sitea Hageman	rec'd	0	4	0
No. 28 3rd sept'r 1816	two seats of do. do. do. Transfer'd to his widow Sitea Hageman	rec'd	0	8	0
No. 12	one seat of Jacobus Swartwout Transfered to Jacobus I. Swartwout	paid	0	4	0
No. 12 3 Sept'r 1816	one seat of Jacobus R. Swartwout Transfered to John A. Sleight	paid	0	4	0
No. 18 3 Sept'r 1816	one seat of Sarah Brinkerhoff Transfered to Letty Sleight	paid	0	4	0
No. 15 3 Sept'r 1816	one seat of Albert H. Monfort Transfered to Henry A. Monfort	paid	0	4	0
No. 25 3 Sept'r 1816	one of Albert H. Monfort Transfered to Henry A. Monfort	paid	0	4	0

The Reformed Dutch Church of New Hackensack

			L	S	D
No. 3 3 Sept'r 1816	two seat of Albert H. Monfort Transfered to Henry A. Monfort	paid	0	8	0
No. 1 3 sept'r 1816	one seat of Domenicus Monfort Transfered to Monfort V'n Kleeck	paid	0	4	0
No. 2 3 sept'r 1816	one seat of Domenicus Monfort Transfered to Garret Van Dine	paid	0	4	0
No. 26 3 sept'r 1816	one seat of Moneicus Monfort Transfered to Ann Monfort	paid	0	4	0
No. 26 3 sept'r 1816	one seat of John Willsie Transfered to Hannah V'n Keuren	paid	0	4	0
No. 26 3 sept'r 1816	one seat of Samuel Luckey Transfered to Moriah V'n Dine	paid	0	4	0
No. 4 3 sept'r 1816	one seat of Henry Monfort Transfered to Casper Gans	paid	0	4	0
No. 25 3 sept'r 1816	one seat of Henry Monfort Transfered to Casper Gans	paid	0	4	0
No. 26 4 Octb'r 1816	one seat of Ann Hults Transfered to her son Henry Hults	paid	0	4	0
No. 19 12th Octb'r	One seat of John N. Bailey Transfered to Cornelius P. Luyster	paid	0	4	0
No. 24 feb'y 6th 1817	two Seats of Cornelias V'n Wey one do. of David Sypher and one do. of Arie Medlord Sold to Matthew Luyster	paid	6	0	0
No. 10 Mc'h 4th 1817	one seat of Peter V'n Bunschoten Transfered to Jacob Bunschoten		0	4	0
No. 18 may 6th 1817	two seats of John Luckey Decs'd transfered to Samuel Luckey Juner	paid	0	8	0
No. 18 may 6th 1817	two seats of John Luckey Decs'd transfered to Marey Luckey widow	paid	0	8	0
No. 20 may 27th 1817	one seat of Peter Dates Jun'r Decs'd transfered to his daughter Eliza Ann	paid	0	8	0
No. 7 may 28 1817	one Seat of Albert I. Monfort Decas'd transfered to his widow Lette Monfort	paid	0	4	0
No. 29 July 14th 1817	one seat of Elizabeth Cooke sold to Benjamin A. Sleight	paid	2	0	0
No. 29 July 14th 1817	one seat of Phemetie Adriance decs'd sold to Benjamin A. Sleight	paid	2	0	0
No. 15 Aug't 20th 1817	one seat of Anna deeds Decs'd transfered to Anna Deeds	paid	0	8	0
No. 11 Aug't 26th 1817	one seat of Albert I. Monfort decs'd transfered to his widow Lette Monfort	paid	0	4	0
No. 2 Aug't 29th 1817	two seats of Warren Rosekrans transfered to James Dodge	paid	0	16	0
No. 15 Sept'r 2nd 1817	one seat of John Ackerman decs'd Transfered to John Ackerman Bogardus	paid	0	8	0
No. 1 sept'r 4th 1817	one seat of Peter Deeds dces'd transfered to Abraham L. Dates	paid	0	8	0
No. 20 sept'r 4th 1817	one seat of Peter Deeds decs'd transfered to Abraham L. Dates	paid	0	8	0
No. 10 sept'r 4th 1817	one seat of Charles Huffman decs'd transfered to son Charles C. Huffman	paid	0	8	0
No. 16 sept'r 4th 1817	one seat of Charles Huffman decs'd transfered to son Charles C. Huffman	paid	0	8	0
No. 21 Sept'r 4 1817	one seat of Antie Terbush sold to Silvester Earl	paid	2	0	0
No. 21 sept'r 4 1817	one seat of Dorethy Ackerman Transfer'd to Silvester Earl	paid	0	4	0
No. 14 sept'r 6th 1817	one seat of Abraham Brinkerhoff sold to James Dearin	paid	2	0	0

Index of Pews

			L	S	D
No. 24 sept'r 6 1817	three seats of John Churchell Transfered to son William Churchell	paid	1	4	0
No. 2 sept'r 6 1817	one seat of Johanes Meneman Transfered to John M. Rosekrans	paid	0	8	0
No. 4 sept'r 6 1817	one seat of Harmah Jewell Transfered to son Henry Jewell	paid		8	0
No. 27 sept'r 6 1817	one seat of James Hicks Transfered to daughter Sarah Hicks	paid	1	0	0
No. 27 sept'r 6 1817	one seat of James Hicks Transfered to John M. Rosekrans	paid	1	0	0
No. 2 sept'r 6 1817	of seat of Barnet B. V'n Kleeck transfered to Henry Jewell	paid		4	0
No. 5 sept'r 6 1817	one seat of Abraham Brinkerhoff sold to Warren Dullensea	paid	2	0	0
No. 5 sept'r 6 1817	two seats of Andris Haremans sold to Warren Dullensea @ $5.00 each	paid	4	0	0
No. 5 sept'r 8 1817	one seat of Catherine Bloom sold to Warren Dullensea	paid	2	0	0
No. 7 sept'r 6 1817	one seat of Claraw Monfort sold to Abraham Adrians		2	0	0
No. 7 sept'r 6 1817	two seats of Anna Margaret Edwards sold to Abraham Adrians $5.00 Each		4	0	0
Given up in 1818 he not having p'd for the same and going to move away					
No. 16 sept'r 6 1817	one seat of James Rosekrans sold to Peter V'n Derbelt	paid	2	0	0
No. 16 sept'r 6 1817	one seat of Catherine Ver Plank sold to Peter V'n Derbelt	paid	2	0	0
No. 19 sept'r 6 1817	one seat of Jacobus Middagh sold to Daniel Huffman	paid	2	0	0
No. 20 sept'r 6 1817	one seat of Cornelius Dubois sold to Elizabeth Todd	paid	2	0	0
No. 25 sept'r 6 1817	one seat of Michael Golnack sold to John Delevergn	paid	2	0	0
No. 25 sept'r 6 1817	one seat of John Jewell sold to John Delevergn	paid	2	0	0
No. 25 sept'r 6 1817	one seat of Garret V'n Bomell sold to John Delevergn	paid	2	0	0
No. 27 sept'r 6 1817	one seat of Jacob Hicks sold to John Delevergn	paid	2	0	0
No. 17 sept'r 6 1817	one seat of Isaac Adriance sold to John Delevergn	paid	2	0	0
No. 4 sept'r 6 1817	one seat of Casper Gons transferred to Zepheniah Platt	paid		4	0
No. 25 sept'r 6th 1817	one seat of Henry A. Monfort trasfered to Casper Gons	paid		4	0
No. 4 sept'r 6 1817	one seat of John Willsie transferred to Zephaniah Platt	paid		4	0
No. 6 sept'r 6 1817	one seat of Barnet B. V'n Kleeck transferred to Andrew Rynders	paid		4	0
No. 2 Octob'r 11th 1817	two seats of John Cornell transferred to John C. Shear	paid		8	0
No. 16 Octob'r 11th 1817	one seat of John Cornell transferred to daughter Margaret Shear	paid		4	0
No. 6 Dec'r 26th 1817	two seats of John Pinkney transfered to Cornelius Klump	paid		8	0

The Reformed Dutch Church of New Hackensack

			L	S	D
No. 2 Jan'y 1st 1818	four seats belonging to the Church transfered to Henry Dodge in Exchange for other seats			0	0
No. 5 Jan'y 1st 1818	1 seat of Henry Dodge transfered to the Church in Exchange			0	0
No. 8 Jan'y 1st 1818	one Seat of Henry Dodge transfered to the Church in Exchange			0	0
No. 15 Jan'y 1st 1818	two seats of Henry Dodge transfered to the Church in Exchange { and disanuled by making door			0	0
No. 8 Jan'y 1st 1818	2 Seats one of Lawrance Haff & one of the Church in Exchange with Henry Dodge Sold to James Ackerman	paid	4	0	0
No. 5 May 30th 1818	one Seat of s'd Church Sold to Warren Dullensea	paid	2	0	0
No. 2 Aug't 18 1818	2 seats of Benjamin Everit Deceas'd transfered to Benjamin Everet	paid		8	0
No. 22 Aug't 18 1818	1 seat of Benjamin Everit Deceas'd transfered to Benjamin Everit	paid		4	0
Jan'y 21 1819 No. 19	one seat of Phillip Haremans transfered to Daniel Huffman a mistake in Entring se below (this item has been crossed out)	paid		4	0
No. 19 Jan'y 21st 1819	one seat of Aurt Medaugh transfered to Daniel Huffman a mistake in entring se below (this item has been crossed out)	paid		4	0
No. 19 Jan'y 21 1819	one seat of Phillip Haremans transfered to Jeremiah B. Van Kleeck	paid		4	
No. 19 Jan'y 21 1819	one seat of Aurt Medaugh transfered to Jeremiah B. Van Kleeck	paid		4	
No. 29 Ap'l 14 1819	two seats of Joseph Jackson decs'd transfered to widow Sarah Jackson	paid		8	
No. 6 No. 7 No. 9 Ap'l 22 1819	one seat in No. 6, one seat in No. 7 & No. 9, 3 seats Transfered to Joseph I. Jackson Isaac I. V'n Wyck Executor to Joseph Jackson Decs'd & Catherine Jackson	paid	1	0	0
No. 25 July 1st 1819	two seats of Stephen P. Monfort Decs'd transfered to Casper Ganse	paid		8	0
No. 4 July 3 1819	two seats of Joseph Jackson Decs'd transfered to Zepheniah Platt			8	0
No. 16 Sept'r 22 1819	one seat of Charles C. Huffman Decs'd transfered to Jane Monfort wife of John A. Monfort	paid		4	0
No. 26 Aug't 5 1820	one seat of Robert Todd transfered to Anne Vandine Wife of Christopher Jacocks	paid		4	0
1821 No. 20 Jan'y 10	One seat of John Rosekrans transfered to Moriah Monfort	paid		4	0
No. 20 Jan'y 10	one seat of John Rosekrans transfered to Moriah Monfort	paid		4	0
1822, feb'y 7 No. 2	four seats of Henry Dodge decs'd transfered to his sons James & Henry	paid		16	0
1823 Aug't 20 No. 28	two seats of Wm. Seward decs'd transfered to son Philander Suard	paid		8	0
1823 Aug't 20 No. 11	one seat of Wm. Suard decs'd transfered to son Philander Suard	paid		4	0
1823 sept'r 3 No. 7 1823 sept'r 3	three seats belonging to the trustees Sold to Stephen S. Thorn @ £2—0—0 Each	paid	6	0	0
No. 2 1823 sept'r 3	one seat of Sam'l Thorn Decs'd transfered to son Stephen Thorn	paid		4	0
No. 2 1823 sept'r 27	one seat of Sam'l Thorn Decs'd transfered to son Stephen Thorn	paid		4	0
	one seat of John V'n Siclen Des'd transfered to his widow Corline	p'd		4	0

Index of Pews

Date / Pew	Description	Status	L	S	D
No. 28 Sept'r 27	one seat of John V'n Siklen Des'd transfered to his widow Corline	p'd		4	0
No. 15 1823 sept'r 27	one seat of John V'n Siclen Des'd transfered to Enes Jewell	p'd		4	0
No. 15 1823 Nov'r 11	one seat of John V'n Siclen Des'd transfered to Sarah Covenhoven	p'd		4	0
No. 21 1824 July 31	one seat of Janiti Fort transfered to her son James Fort	p'd		4	0
No. 20 1825 Ap'l 1	one seat in pew of Cornelea Cornwell to her daughter Elizabeth	p'd		4	0
No. 7 in No. 2 June 1825	1 seat in subdivision of No. 2 of Phillip V'n Derbelt transfered to Catherin				
No. 21 Octb'r 11th 1825	1 seat Transfered of Jacobus Monfort to his son Elias Monfort	paid	0	4	0
No. 21 Octb'r 11th 1825	one seat of Jacobus Monfort Decs'd Transfered to his son Peter J. Monfort	paid	0	4	0
Mc'h 27 1827 No. 8	2 seats of Matthew V'n Bunschoten decs'd trancefered to Sarah Ackerman by Varbel order of Jacob V'n Benschoten	X	0	16	0
Mc'h 27 1827 No. 8	1 seat of Matthew V'n Bunschoten decs'd transferred to Moriah Palmeteer by Varbel order of Jacob V'n Bunschoten	X	0	8	0
Mc'h 27 1827 No. 12	3 seats of Matthew V'n Bunschoten decs'd transferred to Jacob Jacob V'n Bunschoten by Varble order of said Jacob	p'd	0	12	0
Mc'h 27 1827 No. 15	2 seats of Anna Deeds decs'd T. to to Henry D. Traver	paid	0	8	0
Mc'h 27 1827 No. 12	3 seats of Matthew V'n Bunschoten decs'd transferred to Jacob V'n Bunschoten by Varbel order s'd Jacob mistake (this item has been crossed out)				
Mc'h 27 1827 No. 29	1 seat of Stephen S. Thorn Transfered to Cornelius Westervelt	paid	0	4	0
Mc'h 27 1827 No. 29	1 seat of (Stephen Thorn written in first, crossed out and "Henry Schoonmaker decs'd" written over it) Transfered to Cornelius Westervelt by Varbel order of his Daughter Hellen	X	0	4	0
March 27 1827 No. 15	1 seat of Henry Schoonmaker Transfered to his Daughter Hellen Schoonmaker	paid	0	4	0
March 27 1827 No. 5 in 2	1 seat of Matthew V'n Bunschoten Transfered to Jacob V'n Bunschoten by Varble order of said Jacob	paid	0	4	0
Mc'h 27 1827 No. 8 in No. 2	3 Seats (Viz) Isaac Hageman, Garret V'n Bomell & Abraham Sleight sold to Benjamin Everet	paid	8	16	0
Mc'h 27 1827 No. 20	1 seat of Catherine Haff sold to Isaiah Rinders	paid	0	18	0
Mc'h 27 1827 No. 29	4 Seats of Nazareth Brewer Decs'd Transfered to Obediah & Zakeriah Van Voorhes by his Executors	paid	1	12	0
No. 17 Mc'h 27	2 seats sold to Tunis V'n Bunschoten one of Daniel Schank & one of John A. Lent	p'd	4	1	0
May 4 No. 26	one seat of Henry Hults transfered to Harvey Everet	X	0	4	0
May 4 No. 4 in No. 2	two seats of Peter Dates Decs'd sold to John Luyster Jun'r 27th March 1827 for	paid	2	14	0
May 4 No. 7 in No. 2	one seat belonging to Consistory Sold to Edger Luyster 27th March 1827	p'd	1	0	0
May 8 No. pew 5	five seats of Warren Dullensea Transfered to to Cornelius Remson Bo't by John Ganse 29 June 1822	X	1	0	0
Octob'r 16 pew No. 9 in 2	3 seats in pew No. 9 in No. 2 Transfered from James Dodge to John Everet some time since	paid	0	12	0
No. 17 May 29	2 seats of Tunis V. Bunschoten Transfered to Abraham Sleight	paid	0	8	0

The Reformed Dutch Church of New Hackensack

Date / Pew	Description	Paid	£ s d
1830 feb'y 9th 2 seats No. 10	two seats of Cornelius P. Luyster Transfered to Isaac Everit	Paid	0 16 0
1830 No. 10 feb'y 9	one seat of Charles C. Huffman sold to Isaac Everet	paid	2 0 0
1830 sept'r 22 pew No. 10	one seat of Jacob V'n Bunschoten Transfer'd to John A. Sleight	p'd	0 4 0
1830 sept'r 22nd pew No. 11	one seat of Jacob V'n Bunschoten Transferred to Jacobus I. Swartwout	p'd	0 4 0
1830 sept'r 22nd pew No. 12	one seat of Jacobus I. Swartwout Transfer'd to Mary Palmateer	p'd	0 4 0
1830 sept'r 22nd pew No. 12	one seat of John A. Sleight Transfered to Hannah Teller	p'd	0 4 0
pew No. 21 Mc'h 22 1831	one seat of Peter Monfort Transfered to his son Peter P. Monfort	p'd	0 8 0
1831 Mc'h 22 pew No. 3 in No. 2	one seat of Peter Monfort in pew No. 3 in pew No. 2 Transfered to son Peter P. Monfort	p'd	0 8 0
1831 July 1 pew No. 28	2 seats of Samuel Luckey in pew No. 28 transfered to Philender Sewarard	p'd	0 8 0
1831 July 1st pew No. 16	one seat of Mary Matthews Sold to Samuel Luckey	p'd	2 0 0
1831 July 1st pew No. 16	one seat of Gatrude Ver Plank Sold to Samuel Luckey	p'd	2 0 0
1831 Sept'r 12	2 seats of Jacob V'n Bunschoten transfered to Jacob V. B. Teller	p'd	0 16 0
1831 sept'r 12	2 seats of Jacob V'n Bunschoten transfered to Jacob V. B. Concklin	p'd	0 16 0
1832 Aug't 27 No. 5 in 2	1 seat of Garret V'n Dine transfered to son James V'n Dine	p'd	0 4 0
No. 12	1 seat of Mary Palmateer transfered Jacob V. B. Concklin	p'd	0 4 0
No. 7	by cash for transfering on in pew No. 7 of the Executor of Joseph Jackson to Stephen S. thorn	p'd	0 4 0
No. 25	by cash for transfering 4 seats of Casper Gans to his son Nicholas one of the Executors	p'd	0 16 0
Sept 12	by cash for transfering one seat of Art Medaugh to John Diddell	p'd	0 4 0
No. 6 Nov'r 17	by cash for transfering two seats of Abraham Lent Deceas'd to Cornelius Klump		0 16 0
Nov'r 28 No. 26	by Cash for transfering one seat in in pew No. 26 from Harvey Everet to Tunis V'n Bunschoten	p'd	0 4 0
Nov'r 28 No. 6 in 2	by cash for transfering one seat of Tunis V'n Bunschoten to Harvey Everit		0 4 0
1833 feb'y 5 No. 2 in in 2	by Cash for transfering one seat in pew No. 2 in long pew No. 2 his son John Shear John C. Shear Dec'd	p'd	0 8 0
No. 19 feb'y 5	by cash for transfering one Seat of John C. Shear in pew No. 2 in pew No. 2 to his Daughter Sarah Shear	p'd	0 8 0
No. 19	by Cash for transfering 2 seats to James V'n Dine		0 8 0
feb'y 5 pew No. 13	by cash for transfering 2 seats to Catherine V'n Dine		0 8 0
feb'y 12	by Cash for transfering 1 seat in pew No. 13 of John Rosekrans to his widow Moriah Rosekrans	p'd	0 4 0
feb'y 12 pew No. 27	by cash for transfering 1 seat in pew No. 27 of John Rosekrans to his widow Moriah Rosekrance	p'd	0 4 0
Mc'h 12 pew No. 19	by cash for transfering 2 seats in pew No. 19 of Jeremiah V'n Kleeck to his Wido Salee V'n Kleeck		0 8 0
pew No. 11	by cash for one seat of Helinnah V'n Bramer sold to Matthew M. V. B. Ackerman		5 0 0
pew No. 5 in pew No. 2	by cash from Mathew M. Van Bunschoten Transfered to Matthew M. V. B. Ackerman		0 4 0

Index of Pews

pew No. 14 July 9	by cash from Achank Ackerman for transfering 2 seats to son Schank Ackerman	paid	0 16 0
pew No. 16 July 9th	by cash for Transfering one seat of Sarah Schank to son Schank Ackerman	paid	0 8 0
pew No. 17 July 9th	by cash for transfering one seat of Sarah Ackerman to her son Schank Ackerman	paid	0 8 0

**GIFTS FROM
PETER AND JACOB VAN BUNSCHOTEN**
TO THE CHURCH OF NEW HACKENSACK

Van Benschoten Gifts

WILL OF PETER VAN BUNSCHOTEN

In the Name of God, Amen, I Peter Van Bunschoten of the County of Dutchess in the town of Fishkill do this thirteenth day of July in the Year One thousand eight hundred and four make and publish this as my Last will and Testament
first, I Give and bequaith to the Hackensack Church situate in the said town of fishkill for ever the sum of seven hundred and fifty dollars for the purposes and on the terms and Conditions following (to wit) first that the Elders and Deacons or Other proper officers of said Church shall within a reasonable time after the receipt of said sum of seven hundred and fifty Dollars from my executors herein after mentioned place the same at Legal Interest secured by a bond and Mortguage and the Latter shall be on real property in the County aforesaid of suficient Value amply to secure the repayment of said Sum and the Annuel Interest thereon to Accrue—And that the said Elders and Deacons or such other officers as may for the time being legally act for said Church, may and are hereby empowered annually to expend the Interest of said sum in such repairs or Other Improvements to said Church as they may Judge Necessary and expedient—and also to Apply said Interest to the rebuilding annother Church or house of religious worship in the place where the present one is now standing in case the one now standing shall be destroyed by Accident or Otherwise But in no event shall the principal sum of seven hundred and fifty Dollars be Applied to any use or purpose whatsoever but is expressly Intended as a principel fund that Interest whereof is onely Intended to be applied to the repairing said Church or rebuilding another in manner as aforesaid—and in case it shall not be thought Necessary by the persons aforesaid at any one time to expend the Interest aforesaid or the whole of it in repairing and Improving said Church or rebuilding annother on the happening of the Contingincy aforesaid then I direct the persons aforesaid from time to time to put such Interest as may remain in their hands at use to some discreet person to be taken on bond in the County aforesaid and the said sum or sums so put out and secured shall also become a principel fund which also shall in no event be applied to any use or purpose whatsoever but is expressly Intended as a principel fund and the Interest thereof to be applied in the same manner as the Interest of the said sum of seven hundred and fifty dollars and in no other way and manner whatsoever And in case the money herein above mentioned and the Interest thereof shall not be applied or Used in the manner aforesaid by the persons aforesaid, I then give and bequaith the whole thereof to my residuary Legatees herein after named and to their heirs to be equally divided amongst them their heirs and Assigns and amongst the Latter by representation and not other wise.

a true coppy taken from the Original by

Sam'l Luckey sect'y

An Account of Receiving the Interest arising from the Legasy given and bequaithed to the Reformed Dutch Church of New Hackensack by the last will and testament of Peter V'n Bunschoten late of Fishkill town Decs'd ——— Dated the 13th day of July 1804 ———
Consistory of the Congregation of New-Hackensack

	By Samuel Luckey Cr	L	S	D
1806 June 3rd	By Cash Receiv'd from John Winans for one Year's Interest of the Legasey give to s'd Church by Peter V'n Bunschoten Late Deceas'd	21	0	0
1807 May 27th	By Cash Receiv'd from John Winans for one Year's Interest of the Legasey give to s'd Church by Peter V'n Bunschoten Late Deceas'd	21	0	0
1808 Ap'l 28	By Cash recv'd from John Winans for Interest	4	0	0
Septm'r 22	By Cash receiv'd from John Winans the remainder for one Years Interest of the Legasey give to said Church by Peter V'n Bunschoten Late Deceas'd	17	0	0
1809 sept'r 7th	By Cash Receiv'd from John Winans for one Years Interest of the Legasey give to s'd Church by Peter V'n Bunschoten of Fishkill Town Deceas'd	21	0	0
1810 Aug't 2nd	By Cash receiv'd from John Winans for one Years Interest of the Legasey give to s'd Church by Peter V'n Bunschoten of Fishkill town Deceas'd	21	0	0
1811 sept'r 19th	By Cash recv'd from John Winans for one Years Interest of the Legasy Give to s'd Church by Peter V'n Bunschoten of Late Fishkill town Deceas'd	21	0	0

The Reformed Dutch Church of New Hackensack

Date	Entry	£ s d
1812 Dec'r 11th	By Cash recv'd from John Winans for one Years Interest of the Legacy Give to s'd Church by Peter V'n Bunschoten late of Fishkill town Deceased	21 0 0
1813 Nov'r 22	By Cash recv'd from John Winans for one Years Interest of the Legacy Give to s'd Church by Peter V'n Bunschoten late of Fishkill town Deceased	21 0 0
1814 Aug't 2nd	By Cash Recv'd from John Winans for one Year's Interest of the legacy give to s'd Church by Peter V'n Bunschoten late of Fishkill town Decs'd	21 0 0
1815 June 7	By Cash recv'd from John Winans for one Years Interest of the legacy give to s'd Church by Peter V'n Bunschoten late of Fishkill town deceas'd—recv'd by the hand of Zadick Southwick	21 0 0
sept'r 19th	By Articles left when done repairing (to wit)	
	By nails returned £1—17—0	
	By Lath returned 2 0	
	By old nails sold 5 3	
	By 12½ bush'l lime sold 12 6	
	By 1 board sold 1 6	
	By loom lath & sand sold 10 0	
	By Cash from Wm. Suard 1 6	
	By 17 lb old nails sold 12 9	
	By Cash remaining in hand return'd in treasury 0 8	4 3 2
1816 May 28th	By Cash recv'd from John Winans by the hand of Zadick Southwick for one Years Interest of the legacy give to s'd Church by Peter V'n Bunschoten late of Fishkill town Deceased	21 0 0
	Amount Carried Over to page 2	235 3 2
1816 May 28th	By Amount bro't Over from page 1	235 3 2
1817 may 5	By Cash received from John Winans by the hand of Zadock Southwick for one Years Interest of the legacy give to said Church by Peter V'n Bunschotan late of Fishkill town Deceased	21 0 0
1818 Ap'l 27th	By Cash from Jacob V'n Bunschotan for oil sold after painting inside of the Church	2 0 0
may 29th	By Cash Recv'd from John Winans by the hand of Zadock Southwick for for one Years Interest of the legacy give to said Church by Peter V'n Bunschotan late of Fishkill town Deceased	21 0 0
1819 may 27	By Cash on bond & Mortguage given by John Winans & received by the hand of Ahab Arnold Esq'r for one year's Interest of the legacy given to said Church by Peter V'n Bunschoten late of Fishkill town Deceas'd	21 0 0
1820 June 12	By Cash on bond & Mortguage Given by John Winans & received by the hand of Ahab Arnold Esq'r for one Years Interest on the legasy Given to said Church by Peter V'n Bunschotan late of Fishkill town Deceased	21 0 0
1822 Aug't 31	By cash on bond & Mortguage given by John Winans & received from Rober Southwick & Co. for two Years Interest on the legasey given to s'd Church by Peter V'n Bunschoten late of Fishkill town Deceased	42 0 0
2 Octob'r 1823	By cash on bond & Mortguage given by John Winans & receiv'd from Rob't B. Southwick for one Year's Interest on the legasey given to the Church at New Hackensack by Peter V'n Bunschoten late of fishkill town Decs'd	21 0 0
1824 May 10	By cash on bon & Mortguage Given by John Winance & recv'd from Rob't B. Southwick & Co. for one Year's Interest on the legasey given to the Church at New Hackensack by Peter V'n Bunschoten late of Fishkill town Decs'd	21 0 0
1825 May 9	by cash from Rob't B. Southwick on bond & Mortguage of the Peter V'n Bunschoten fund for one Years Interest	21 0 0
1826 May 11	by cash from Rob't B. Southwick on bond & Mortguage of the Peter V'n Bunschoten fund for one Year's Interest	21 0 0
	Amount Carried to Page 4	£447 3 2

Van Benschoten Gifts

Date	Description			
1826 May 11	Amount Bro't from Page 2	447	3	2
1827 may 3rd	by cash from R. B. Southwick & Co. on bond & Mortguage of the Peter V'n Bunschoten fund for one Years Interest	21	0	0
1828 may 5th	by cash from R. B. Southwick & Co. on bond & Mortguage of the Peter V'n Bunschoten fund for one Year Interest	21	0	0
1829 Aug't 31	by cash from E. & S. Southwick for Interest on bond &c of Peter V'n Bunschotan for one Y'r up to 1st may last	21	0	0
1830 June 8	by cash from E. & S. Southwick for Interest on bond &c of Pet'r V'n Bunschoten fund for one Y'r Ints't up to 1st may 1830	21	0	0
1831 June 3rd	by cash from E. & S. Southwick for Interest on bond of the Peter V'n Bunschoten fund for one Y'rs Interest up to 1st may 1831	21	0	0
1832 Aug't 25th	by cash from E. & S. Southwick by hand of Samuel Luckey Jun'r on the Peter V'n Bunschoten fund for one Years Interest up to 1st may 1832	21	0	0
1833 May 25th	By cash from E. & S. Southwick by the hand of Samuel Luckey J'r on the Peter V'n Bunschoten fund for one years Interest	21	0	0
1834 July 3rd	By Cash from E. & S. Southwick Interest on this fund	21	0	0
1835 Octob'r 14th	By Cash from E. & W. Southwick Interest on this fund	21	0	0
1836 Octob'r 24th	by cash from E. & W. Southwick Interest on this fund	21	0	0
1838 March 13th	by Cash for, Interest on this fund up to May 1st 1837	21	0	0
June 16th	by Cash from Edward Southwick Interest on this fund	21	0	0

1839	Trustees of the R. D. Church at New Hackesack in account with Henry D. Traver treas & secretary			
June 22nd	to Cash paid Matthew Luyster for church debt Interest from P. V. B. fund in full	21	0	0
1840 June 15	to Cash paid Matthew Luyster interest in full	21	0	0
July 5th 1842	to Cash paid Matthew Luyster two years interest	42	0	0
				Cts
August 15th 1843	to Cash paid Jeremiah Platt for Mr. Luyster interest	$ 42	08	

An account of the Expenditure of the Interest arising from the Legacy Given and bequaithed to the Reformed Dutch Church of New Hackensack By the Last will and testament of Peter V'n Bunschoten Late of Fishkill Town Deceas'd ———— Dated the thirteenth day of July——— 1804———
Consistory of the Congregation of New Hackensack

		To Samuel Luckey Dr	L	S	D
1806 Aug't	1	to one Box window Glass	2	16	0
		to 5 lb. puttey @ 1/	0	5	0
		to ½ day going to Poughkeepsie for glass & puttey	0	4	0
	12th & 13th	to 2 half days Looking for Carpenter to work at Church	0	4	0
	20	to 1 day work helping Carpenter & blacksmith draw hooks &c	0	6	0
sept'r	9	to Cash p'd Abraham Staats for altering window hooks &c	1	12	0
	15	to Cash paid Isaac V'n Amburgh for hanging shuts Glazing windows &c	1	0	0
Octob'r	16	to one thousand shingles bo't at New-York	7	8	0
		to Cash p'd Samuel Bogardus for freight of do.	0	10	0
	20th	to Carting 1000 shingles from the Landing to the Church	0	16	0
1807 Mc'h	28	to 12 lb of 12 penny Nails @ 1/3	0	15	0
Ap'l	28	to 28 lb of 10 penny nails @ 1/3	1	15	0
		to 1 Jugg for Oil @ 3/6 & 2 Gall'n paint Oil @ 10/	1	3	6
		to 1 Cagg spanish Brown Wt. 28 lb @ 8 d	0	18	8
		to 1 Cagg white Lead Wt. 28 lb @ 1/6	2	2	0
		to going to Poughkeepsie for paint Oil nails &c	0	4	0
Aug't	24th	to Cash p'd for 36 boards for scaffolding &c @ 1/6	2	14	0
		to Riding s'd boards from Jno. Drakes to the Church	0	6	0

The Reformed Dutch Church of New Hackensack

27th	to 2000 Ceder shingles bo't at New-York @ £6-18-0	13 16 0
31st	to Cash p'd Francis Bogardus for freight of do.	1 0 0
sept'r 28	to 4 Gall'n 1 qt. Paint oil @ 10/ bo't at Holdins	2 2 6
	to a 2 gall'n Jugg @3/6 to 1 paint brush @ 5/ to one do. do at 4	0 12 6
	to 1 Cagg spanish Brown Wt. 56 lb @8d	1 17 4
	to Going to Poughkeepsie for paint Oil &c	0 4 0
Octob'r 21	to Cash p'd Isaac V'n Amburgh for Carpenter work at Church	2 16 0
	An Acc't of Expenditures on New Hackensack Church by William Suard on Acc't of the Legacy Left By Peter V'n Bunschoten Deceas'd (Viz)	
1807 Octb'r 22	to Cash p'd David Petterson for 5½ days work @ ?	2 4 0
23	to Cash p'd Moses Hunt for 9 days work @ 8/	3 12 0
	to s'd Suards own Charge	
	to ½ day 3/—to going to Rich'd V'n wyks for nails 4/	7 0
	to Cash p'd s'd V'n Wyck for nails	15 4
	to Going to Pudneys 2/ & Cash p'd for nails 6/	8
	to 133 shingles Dressed	1 2
	to Cash p'd for spirits for the workmen	18
	to some small nails	0 4
Date Jan'y 1808	to Cash p'd Adam D. Cornwill for board of workmen	2 12 4
	to Cash p'd Abraham Staats for board of do	7
1807 Dec'm 21	to Cash p'd John Van Amburgh for 8¼ day work @ 8/	3 6
1808 Jan'y 2	to Cash p'd Epheram Mills for 5¾ days work @ 8/	2 6
	Amount Carryed to page 2nd	65 5 6
1808 Octob'r 16	to Amount Bro't from page 1	65 5 6
	to 1000 Ceder shingles Bo't at New-York	6 8
	to Cash p'd Francis Bogardus for freight of do.	0 10
18th	to Carrying 1000 shingles from the landing to s'd Church	0 16 0
19	to 20 lb 8 penny nails @ 1/3	1 5 0
	to ½ day to poughkeepsie for s'd nails & Carrying them to the Church	0 4 0
Novemb'r 11	to Cash paid William Suard for money Advanced to pay Carpenters for work done at Hackensack Church	4 18 11
Decemb'r 31	to Cash p'd William Suard on order from the Trustees or Consistory seventeen Dollars and thirteen Cents to pay money that had been borowed and Expended on repairs of said Church of Hackensack	6 17 0
1809		
sept'r 25	to 2000 Ceder shingles bo't at New-York £6-0-0	12 0 0
	to Cash p'd Francis Bogardus for freight of do.	1 0 0
Octob'r	to Carrying 2000 Ceder shingles from the landing to the Church	1 12 0
1810 Octb'r 30	to Cash p'd Domenicus Monfort for shingleing & painting the North side roof of s'd Church as p'r bills & receipts	14 7 0
1811 Aug't 11	to ½ day over river Looking for seding at Millards	0 4 0
sept'r 5	to ½ day at Poughkeepsie looking for seding for Church	0 4 0
16	to 152 bo't at John Drakes Jun'r @ 1/4½ for the Church	10 8 0
	to riding 3 loads boards to the Church	1 4 0
17	to ½ day Looking for Carpenters & selling the old shingles &c	0 4 0
18	to 14 plank @ 2/6 & 18 boards @ 1/4 bo't of E. Shearman	2 19 0
	to riding s'd plank & boards to the Church	0 8 0
20	to 14 plank @ 2/3 & 18 boards @ 1/4 bo't of John Drake Jun'r	2 15 6
	to riding s'd boards to the Church	0 8 0
Octb'r 6	to 15 lb twelve penny nails @ 1/	0 15 0
	to 4 lb Eight penny nails at 1/	0 4 0
16	to 130 feet oak joice for windowes stoop &c @ 10/	0 13 0
	to 3 Gall'n paint oile @ 8/ bo't at Oliver Holdens	1 4 0
	to 1½ Caggs white Lead @ 42/ bo't of do.	3 3 0
	to bring paint olie & timber to the Church	0 8 0
	to 4 lb wrought nails @ 1/3	0 5 0
Nov'r 13	to 4lb ten penny Cut nails @ 1/	0 4 0
	to peice pine timber 11 by 9 & 24 feet long for Gutter by E. shearman	1 4 0

Van Benschoten Gifts

Date	Description	£ s d
	to riding s'd timber to the Church	0 8 0
	to riding stone for the stoop or platform	0 4 0
29	to Cleaning the Church of boards shavings &c	0 4 0
Dec'r 5	to taking off the old door hinges Lock &c and taking them to the black smiths	0 4 0
	to Cash p'd H. Dates for repairing hinges lock &c and making some nails	0 4 0
13	to a door lock & kee bo't at Drakes	0 8 0
	to 6 large spikes or bolts to fasten the Gutter	0 6 9
1812 June 10	to Cash p'd Peter Cooledge for work done to s'd Church	19 0 0
1813 June 6th	to ½ day over the river to Millards to buy boards siding &c	0 6 0
June 6	to 150 siding bo't of do. @ 1/3	9 7 6
	to 50 boards of do. at 1/4	3 6 8
July 5	to 8 plank bo't of D, & Bogardus & Co. @ 2/6	1 0 0
Aug't 19	to box Glass bo't of Oliver Holden 7 by 9	3 4 0
	to 4 lb Cutt nails @ 1/1 & 3 lb wrought 8 @ 1/6 & 3 lb wrought 10 1/4	0 12 10
		180 13 8
1813 Aug't 19	to Amount Bro't from page 2	180 13 8
	to ½ day to poughkeepsie to buy Glass putty nails &c	0 4 0
	to 6 lb putty bo't of O. Holden at same time @ 1/	6
	to riding 4 Loads siding boards plank &c to said Church	1 12 0
1814 Jan'y 4	to Cash p'd Wm. Suard for money advanced to Nathn'l Smith for work done on the Church in Octb'r Last	1 10 0
may 28th	to Cash p'd Wm. Suard to buy Paint Oil nails &c for the Church	12 0 0
June 24th	to Cash p'd Wm. Suard to pay Carpenters for repairing New Hackin Church &c	10 13 0
1815 June 27th	to Cash p'd Tunis V'n Bunschoten one of the Trustees for the Congregation of New Hackensack Church the money recv'd for Interest of the Donation of Peter V'n Bunschoten Decs'd to be Laid out for repairs on s'd Church	21 0 0
sept'r 19	to Cash p'd Henry A. Monfort one of the Trustees for the Congregation of New Hackensack Church to pay off the residue of the work & Materiels on repairs done on s'd Church	14 0 0
1816 Aug't 8th	to Cash p'd Joel West for Oil Paint &c for N. Hackensack Church as p'r bill	
	to 30½ Gall'n Linseed Oile @ 9/6	14 9 9
	to 4 Kegs white Lead Wt. 112 lb @ 1/2	6 10 8
	to 1 barrel for s'd oil	0 8 0
	to Cartage of do.	0 4 0
Octb'r 7	to Cash p'd Francis Bogardus for freight of do.	0 6 0
1817 Aug't 17	to Cash p'd Jacob V'n Bunschotan one of the trustees for Congregation of New-Hackensack Church on bills for expenc in repairs laid out on s'd Church	22 12 9
1818 June	to cash p'd Jacob V'n Bunschoten who was appointed to erect a new bell frame to the church £ 5-8-4 laid out previous & paid	15 11 8
1819 June 18	to cash p'd William Suard & James Jones a commitee chosen to paint the frunt & west end of N. Hackensack Church	21 0 0
1820 Octob'r 3	to cash p'd Tunis V'n Bunschotan & James Dearon a committee chosen to buy boards & nails to repair the east end of s'd Church	17 16 0
	to eight dollars p'd Sam'l Luckey Jun'r for money advanced out of the poor chest previously & laid as p'r bills	3 4 0
1822 sept'r 2nd	to cash p'd Jacob V'n Bunschoten & James Dearin a committee chosen p'd out of the Interest of the legasey left by Peter V'n Bunschoten late of Fishkill town Deces'd for money advanced by them to buy meterials and pay workmen on the church in the year 1821 as p'r bills on file in the treasury	20 11 11
1822 sept'r 2nd	to cash p'd James Akerman & Peter V'n Derbelt a Committee chosen to repair the steple of the church	24 12 0

The Reformed Dutch Church of New Hackensack

1823 Octb'r 20	to cash p'd Tunis V'n Bunschoten & John V'n Derbelt a Commitee chosen to paint the stiple of the church &c	21 0 0	
1824 may 24	to cash p'd John V'n Derbelt for money taken out of poor Chest last Year towards repairing the Church	5 15 0	
Octob'r 11	to cash p'd Tunis V'n Bunschoten and John Vanderbelt a commite chosen to repair the Church	15 5 0	
1825 May 23	to cash p'd Tunis V'n Bunschoten Daniel Huffman and John A. Monfort a committe chosen to paint the Inside of Church at New Hackensack	21 0 0	
June 11	to cash paid Tunis V'n Bunschoten one of above Committe to finish painting the above mentioned Church	8 0 0	
	Amount Carried to page 4	460 5 5	

1825 June 11	Amount Bro't from Page 3	460 5 5	
July	Tunis V'n Bunschoten, Daniel Huffman & John A. Monfort Commite to buy Meteriels & workmen to paint the inside of the Church—se bill $115.50		
1826 may 12	the £21-0-0 recv'd on Ints't p'd 11th on the Pt'r V'n Bunschoten p'd to the said Tunis, Daniel & John to replace the money they borrow'd to finish painting the Church Last Year &c		
1827 may 4	to cash p'd James Ackerman & John Luyster a commite Chosen to repair the Church steple Stoop &c	21 0 0	
1828 May 14	to cash p'd John Luyster & James V'n Keuren a Commifte chosen to cution the Pulpet carpet the steps, paint &c se bill	21 0 0	
1829 sept'r 1st	to cash to John V'n Derbelt & Phillip Nagel a Commite chosen to repair the steple of the Church with blinds round the belconey painting the same &c Expended se bill	21 0 0	
1830 Aug't 30	to cash to John V'n Derbelt & John A. Monfort a commite Chosen to buy Meteriel to repair the church &c	21 0 0	
1831 June 18	to cash p'd James V'n Keuren & John A. Monfort a commite to buy materiel to Paint the Church se bill	21 0 0	
1832 Aug't 27	to cash p'd James V'n Keuren & Peter V'n Derbelt a commite to lay out Interest of the Peter V'n Bunschoten Decs'd fund on the Church at New Hackensack	21 0 0	
1833 Nov'm 19	to Cash p'd Henry D. Traver & Isaia Rinders a committee to buy new stove pipe and drum out of the Interest of P. Van Bunschoten fund	8 6 10	
1834 Feb'r. 3rd	to Cash p'd for Bench in the pulpit	0 15 9	
	to Cash p'd for A New drum for the Church	4 2 6	
	to Cash p'd towards Meterials for to build a new Church	7 14 11	
Bo't Dec'r 23rd	to Cash p'd Schofield & Hall for 2 stoves bought for the New Church	8 0 0	
	toCash p'd T. W. Tallmadge for 2 stoves bought for the New Church	6 14 0	
1835	to Cash p'd B. Everit one of the Committee for the New Church	6 6 0	
1836 March 29th	to Cash p'd B. Everet one of the Committee for the New Church	21 0 0	
1837 May 16th	to Cash p'd to Matthew Luyster for Benjamin Everit to pay towards finishing the New Church	21 0 0	
1838 June 28th	to Cash paid to Matthew Luyster to pay towards Liqudating the debt on the New Church	21 00 00	

		Cr	
1839	Trustees in account with Henry D. Traver Sec & treasurer	L S D	
May 26	by cash of E. C. Southwick interest P. V. B. fund	21 0 0	
1840 June 6th	by Cash of E. C. Southwick interest P. V. B. fund	21 0 0	
July 3rd 1842	by Cash of E. C. Southwick interest P. V. B. fund	42 0 0	
		cts	
1843 August 12	by Cash of H. D. Varick interest on P. V. B. fund	$42 08	

Van Benschoten Gifts

AGREEMENT WITH JACOB VAN BUNSCHOTEN

TO ALL TO WHOM THESE PRESENTS SHALL COME Thomas Duwitt Tunis Van Bunschoten Samuel Luckey Junior, Henry A. Monfort & John Ganse all of the County of Dutchess and of the state of New York send Greeting, Whereas by Indenture bearing even date herewith and made between Jacob Van Bunschoten of the town of Fishkill in the said County of Dutchess of the first part and the said, Thomas Dewitt, Tunis Van Bunschoten, Samuel Luckey, Junior, Henry A. Monfort and John Ganse of the second part all the three following peices of Land situate in the Village of Poughkeepsie and which in a deed from Thomas P. Hopkins to the said Jacob Van Bunschoten bearing date the twenty sixth day of March in the year one thousand eight hundred and twenty two are described as follows (to wit): the first Begining at the south west corner of Lot No. 21 thence runing west along the north side of Pine street fifty feet to a stake thence Northerly along the east line of Lot No. 19 one hundred and fifty feet to a stake then easterly to the north west corner of Lot No. 21 fifty feet, thence along the west side of lot No. 21 one hundred and fifty feet to the place of beginning; The second peice, Begining at a stake drove in the ground at the south side of Montgomery and at the northwest corner of the premises here described and at the north east corner of John Majord lot and south eighty five degrees west, six chain twenty links and six inches to the north west corner of Joel Dubois lot thence south five degrees east one chain and fifty five links to land belonging to John Reade thence along the last mentioned land south eighty five degrees west one chain and six links, then north five degrees west one chain and fifty five links to the place of begining; The third Begining on the south side of Union street at a stone set in the Earth at the north east corner of this lot then running west along Union street sixty feet to a stone marked G. B. then running south along water street one hundred feet to a stone marked G. B. then east sixty feet to the corner of Joseph Harris and George B. Evertson's lots then north one hundred feet to the place of begining with the appurtenances, were remised, released and quit claimed to the said Thomas Duwitt Tunis Van Bunschoten Samuel Luckey Jun'r Henry A. Monfort and John Ganse as joint tenants and not as tenants in common, to have and to hold the same unto the said Thomas Duwitt, Tunis V'n Bunschoten, Samuel Luckey Jun'r, Henry A. Monfort and John Gans and the survivors and survivor of them and the heirs of such survivour and their and his assigns for ever, and whereas the said Jacob Van Bunschoten has this day also paid and delivered to the said Thomas Dewitt, Tunis Van Bunschoten, Samuel Luckey Jun'r, Henry A. Monfort and John Gance the sum of Seven Hundred Dollars— which said Conveyance and transfer of the said lots and property and the payment of the said sum of money were made and done upon the trusts and to the interest and purposes as is hereafter mentioned and declared

NOW THEREFORE KNOW YE that in consideration thereof the said Thomas Dewitt, Tunis Van Bunschoten Samuel Luckey Jun'r, Henry A. Monfort and John Ganse for themselves, their heirs executors and Administrators do hereby acknowledge testify declare and agree that the true Intent and meaning of the said conveyince and payment so made as aforesaid are and were upon the trusts and for the purposes following that is to say That they the said Thomas Dewitt, Tunis Van Bunschoten, Samuel Luckey Jun'r, Henry A. Monfort and John Ganse the survivors and survivor of them do and shall put and place the said sum of money so paid to them as aforesaid at Interest upon good and suficient security with the Interest thereof payable Yearly, and shall keep the same so put out at Interest untill the sale of the lands above described as is herein after mentioned and also untill such sale as aforesaid they do and shall lease and rent the said lots and premises for such terms and upon such rents as to them shall seem meet: and they shall from year to year and every Year while divine service shall be statedly performed in the Reformed protestant Dutch Church at New Hackensack in the town of Fishkill in Dutchess County, pay the aforesaid interest money and the rents and income of the said premises after deducting the costs and expences of this trust and they repairs and charges in relation to the said property to "The Trustees of the Reformed protestant Dutch Church of New Hackensack" to be applied by them to the suport and maintainance of the Gospel and ministry in the said Church and the congregation thereof But if at any time there shall not be any setled minister in the said Church or stated service therein the Interes of the said moneys and the said rents and income for the time of such Vakency shall Accumulate and become and be secured as principel, the Interest the Interest whereof to be paid and applied in manner aforesaid:— And also that they the said Thomas Dewitt, Tunis Van Bunschoten, Samuel Luckey Junior, Henry A. Monfort and John Ganse the survivors and survivor of them when they or he shall deem it of advantage to this trust do and may sell and dispose of all or any part of the said lands and premises aforesaid and so from time to time untill the whole are sold: and upon the sale of part or parts of the said premises the proceeds thereof as soon as conveniantly may be shall be put at Interest; and the Annual income thereof shall be paid and applied in the manner and for the purposes as is herein before stated:— And also that when all the said lands and premises shall be sold and disposed of and converted into

275

The Reformed Dutch Church of New Hackensack

money they the said Thomas Dewitt, Tunis Van Bunschoten, Samuel Luckey Junior, Henry A. Monfort and John Ganse the survivors or survivor of them or the heirs Executors and Administrators of such survivor do and shall pay over and deliver all the moneys herein before mentioned and the Income thereof in their hands and also the proceeds and produce of the said sales after deducting and retaining all charges and expences to the said Trustees of the Reformed Protestant Dutch Church of New Hackensack to be by them put out and placed at Interest on real security or in government stock and the Yearly Interest and income thereof to be by them applied to the suport and maintainence of the Gospel and ministry in the said Church and the Congregation thereof as aforesaid,

IN WITNESS whereof the said Thomas Dewitt, Tunis Van Bunschoten, Samuel Luckey Junior, Henry A. Monfort and John Ganse have hereunto set there hands and seals this twenty first day of March in the Year of our Lord one thousand eight hundred and twenty three.

Signed sealed and delivered }
   in the present of   }   signed by   Thomas Dewitt
                                                        Tunis Van Bunschoten
                                                        Samuel Luckey Jun'r
                                                        Henry A. Monfort
                                                        & John Ganse

Witness Samuel Luckey }
   and John Yates   }
a true coppey by Samuel Luckey Secretary

1823 Mc'h 21st Memorandum of the Donation Given by Jacob V'n Bunschoten of Fishkill Town, to the Trustees of the Reformed protestant Dutch Church at New Hackensaco as follows (Viz) one house and lot in pine street and one House & lot in Union street & one Vakent lot in Montgomery s't the above Houses & lots Valued at $2300.00 and at the same time the said doner Give to the said Trustees of the said Church & Congregation of the above Church in cash $700.00 at same time the said Jacob V'n Bunschoten Executed a deed in trust for the above mentioned houses & lots to the Revn'd Thomas Dewitt pastor and the Elders Tunis V'n Bunschoten, Samuel Luckey Jun'r, Henry A. Monfort & John Gance — After which the said houses & Lots was Rented out by their Agent Alexander Forbush se his account on file for Rents recv'd money paid out also for Interest Receved on said cash also fore repairs done on house in Union s't &c by Witing Adams and others se bills on file &c

1824 the Trustees of the Reformed Protestant Dutch at new Hackensack (Viz) Revn'd Thomas Dewitt pasture, and Elders Tunis V'n Bunschotem, Samuel Luckey Junior, Henry A. Monfort & John Ganse & succesor in office By Samuel Luckey their Treasurer exclusive of repairs done on the houses se Alexander Forbush's bill acct's &cc by cash on the above Donation recv'd   Cr.

Date	Description	D'ls	Cts
		700	00
1824 June 9th	By cash from Alexander Forbus their agent se his Acc't	81	9
1825 Jan'y 31	by Cash from s'd Alexander Forbush se his Acc't on file	124	32
May 4	by cash from Samuel Luckey Jun'r for Interest due	49	00
9	by cash from s'd Alexander Forbush se his Acc't on file	50	00
sept'r 11	by cash from s'd Forbush se his Acc't on file	1	16
1826 may 1	by cash from Samuel Luckey Jun'r for Interest due	42	00
July 4	by cash from s'd Forbush	93	00
sept'r 8	by cash from s'd Forbush	31	74
1827 feb'y 2	by cash from Alexan'r Fobus on rent	30	00
May 2	by from Samuel Luckey Jun'r $700.00 of principel and $39.67/100 for 11 months & 10 days Interest & bond Given up	739	67
14	by cash from James B. Frear on house in Union S't for rent the remainder lain in repairs &c (Viz) $73.17 se his bills on file	6	83
Aug't 4	by cash of Tunis V'n Bunschoten on rent of house in Union St. and a bill for repairs—Amounting to $1.50/100	18	50
sept'r 24	by cash by hand of Tunis V'n Bunschoten for rent on house in pine st. $21.62 & repairs by Jacob Palmer $8.38 se bill	30	00
nov'r 2	by cash recv'd of Tunes V'n Bunschoten on house in Union St.	10	0
1828 feb'y 4th	by cash of Tunis V'n Bunschoten recv'd on hous rent	46	21
1829 feb'y 9	by cash from Tunis V'n Bunschoten	4	45
"	by cash recv'd by Tunis V'n Bunschoten for rent repairs on the houses, taxes &c se bill, recpts &c on file	98	52
may 5	cash recv'd by the Consistory on the sale of the house in pine St	500	00
	cash recv'd by the Consistory on the sale of the house in Union St.	400	00

Van Benschoten Gifts

		Dol's	Cts
25	by cash from Tunis V'n Bunschoten for Ints't on house in pine St.	20	00
1830 Ap'l	by cash on Ints't by hand of Sam'l, Luckey Jun'r	35	00
29	by cash from Jas. Ackerman on Interest	54	00
may 4	by cash from Cleavland on Intes't	25	00
6	by cash from John Cornwell on Intrest, Creadited in Wrong Book p'd	33	00
	(This item has been crossed out)		
31	by cash from Cleavland on Ins't J. V. B. fund	60	00
Octb'r 8	by cash from Isaac Macay on Interest J. V. B. fund	38	00
	Amount Carried over	3321.	49

		$ Dls	Cts
1831 may 5th	By Amount Brought from 17th page	3321	49
6	by cash from James Ackerman on Interest on J. V'n Bunschoten fund	54	00
7	by cash from John Cornwell on Interest on J. V'n Bunschoten fund	33	00
sept'r 19	by cash from Sam'l Luckey Jun'r on Elias Taylor's Bond & mortguage for Interest	60	00
"	by cash which I had p'd for polesy on house in pine St.	10	00
Octb'r 1	by cash from Isaac Mackay on Interest due on the above fund	51	88
1832 Ap'l 27	by cash for rent on Vakent lot	3	75
May 5	by cash from James Ackerman for Interest on J. V'n Bunschoten fund	54	00
7	by cash from John Cornwell for Interest on J. V'n Bunschoten fund	33	
June 11	by Cash from Solomon V. Wheeler on Isaac Mackay bond for Intes't up to thiryeth Ap'l last on J. V'n Bunschoten fund	44	80
Aug't 25	By cash from Samuel Luckey Jun'r for Interest on Elias Taylor's bond & mortguage for Interest up to 1st of may 1832 on the Jacob V'n Bunschoten fund	60	00
1833 may 2'd	By cash from James Ackerman on bond paid up on the above fund	900	00
	by cash from James Ackerman on Interest	54	00
	by cash from Solomon V. Wheeler on Inst't	44	80
	by cash from E. H. Parmer on the J. V'n Bunschoten fund	60	00
	by Cash for Intst on the above fund	33	00
		4817	72

1834 May 2	by Cash from Christopher Jayes Mistake		
	(This item has been crossed out)		
6	by Cash from John Cornwell Interest on the Jacob Van Beunschoten	33	00
July	by Cash from E. H. Parmer on the J. Van Bunschoten fund Interest	60	00
Nov'm 28	by Cash from George V. Lumaree on the J. Van Bunschoten fund Int.	44	80
Decm'r 7	by Cash from George V. Lumaree on the J. Van Bunschoten fund. Interest	63	00
1835 May 4th	by Cash from George V. Lumaree principal of Thomas Hinton bond	900	00
	by Cash from George V. Lumaree Interest on the Jacob Van Bunschoten f'd	63	00
7th	by Cash from John Cornwell Interest on the J. V. Bunschoten fund	33	00
Sep't 5	by Cash from E. H. Parmer Interest on the Jacob Van Bunschoten fund	20	00
Decm'r 31	by Cash from E. H. Parmer Interest on this fund	10	00
Ap'l 25 1836	by Cash from E. H. Parmer Interest on this fund	25	00

The Reformed Dutch Church of New Hackensack

May 7th 1836	by Cash from John Cornwell Interest on this fund	33	00
"	by Cash from Peter Van Der Bilt principal	125	00
"	by Cash of Solomon V. Wheeler Interest on this fund	44	80
"	by Cash from James Van Keuren Interest on this fund	11	00
"	by Cash of Solomon V. Wheeler Interest on this fund	44	80
"	by Cash of Peter Van Derbilt Interest in full on this fund	6	88
1837	by Cash on the J. V. Bunschoten fund Interest for Last year uper house	65	00
Ap'l 20th	by Cash on the J. V. Bunschoten fund Interest on the uper house of Bates	70	00
May 1st	by Cash from Matthew Luyster Interest on the J. Van Bunschoten fund	45	60
8th	by Cash of John Cornwell Interest on the J. V. B. fund	33	00
Sept. 29th	by Cash of Solomon V. Wheeler Interest on the J. V. B. fund	44	80
1838 May 17th	by Cash of Solomon V. Wheeler on this fund	44	80
25th	by Cash from John A. Monfort of the Executors of James Van Keuren $200 principal and $24,81/100 Interest	224	81
		6875	01

	Trustees in account with H. DD. Traver sec & treasurer		
1839 April	by cash of Samuel Luckey 200 Principal $11.19/100 Interest on this fund	211	19
May 1st	by cash of M. Luyster 760. Dollars principle on J. V. B. fund	760	00
	by cash d. d. ten dollars interest on this fund	10	00
	by cash of Matthew Luyster forty dollars	40	00
		$ 1021	19

		$	cts
	The Consistory of the Reformed Dutch Church at New Hackensack to Henry D. Traver secretary and treasurer on the Jacob Van Benschoten fund bro't over	1021	19
1839 May 1	Recd of Matthew Luyster Interest in J. V. B. fund	35	60
May 20	by Cash of Henry D. Traver last year interest on this fund	50	00
	by Cash of Matthew Luyster interest Mistake (this item has been crossed out)		
May	by an assignment of Mortgage to the Consisto from H. D. Traver for one thousand dollars	1000	00
June 22nd	by Cash from John Cornwell interest on J. V. B. fund	33	00
July 17th	by Cash of S. V. Wheeler interest on this fund	44	80
1840 April 20	by cash of H. D. Traver interest on assignment of mortgage	50	00
May 1st	by cash of Cornelius ostrander interest on this fund	70	00
May 7th	by cash of Henry D. Traver Interest in full on this fund	20	00
May 7th	by Cash of John Cornwell Interes for one year in full	33	00
June 17th	by Cash of S. V. Wheeler Interest in full for one year	44	80
1841 May 1st	by Cash of H. D. Traver one thousand dollars principle and Loaned to Harvey Evritt on bond & mortgage	1000	00
May 3	by Cash of H. D. Traver interest in full for one year	70	00
May 5th	by Cash of C. Ostrander interest for one year	70	00
May 7th	by Cash of John Cornwell interest for one year	33	00
May 8th	by Cash of S. V. Wheeler interest in full for 1 year	44	80
1842 April 28th	by Cash of Cornelus Ostrander interest	70	00
May 8th	by Cash of Harvey E. Everitt interest	70	00
May 12th	by Cash of John Cornwell interest	33	00
July 16th	by Cash of S. V. Wheeler interest	44	80
July 20th	Received Harvey E. Everitt a mortgage for $1000		

1823 Mc'h 21st Memorandum of the donation given by Jacob V'n Bunschoten of Fishkill Town who give a deed in Trust to the Trustees of the Portestant Dutch Church at

Van Benschoten Gifts

new Hackensack as mention or C'r side (Viz) Valued $2300.00, also in cash $700.00 the rents & Interest expended as follows

The Trustees of the Reformed Protestant Dutch Church at New Hackensack (Viz) Rev'd Thomas Dewitt pasture and Elders Tunis V'n Bunschoten, Samuel Luckey Jun'r, Henry A. Monfort & John Gance & their sucsesors in office to Samuel Luckey their treasurer on the Jacob V'n Bunschoten fund D'r se their agent's Alexander Forbush Account on file   Dol's Cts

Date	Description	Dol's	Cts
April 16	to cash p'd Alexander Forbush for cash p'd for recording deed for Insurance & his fees on the same	$20	21
1824 June 18	to cash p'd Tunis V'n Bunschoten for repairs done on Vakent lot se his bill on file	13	12½
July 16	To cash p'd Revn'd Tho's Dewitt se recpt on file on salory	47	75
1825 feb'y	to cash p'd do. do. on Salory se recpt	124	00
may 10th	se Cyrus Berrey bill for repairs on house & lot in Union street $85.84 house & lot rented for $70.00		
1826 Mc'h 10th	to cash p'd Revn'd Tho's Dewitt Treasur'r for the Poughkeepsie Clasis	15	00
	to cash p'd Revn'd Tho's Dewitt on salory recpt	209	00
Ap'l 20	to cash p'd on the houses for Insurance &c	16	62
July 7	to cash p'd Revn'd Tho's Dewitt on salory recpt	93	00
Aug't 8	to cash p'd James Lewis as Corester recpt	13	00
sept'r 3	to cash p'd Revn'd Mr. Buckwell in addition to salory by the doners consent	2	00
12	to cash p'd Revn'd John Garritson by the doners Varbel order	5	00
Nov'r	to cash p'd Revn'd Mr. Morse by the Doners Varbel order	3	00
28	to cash p'd Tunis V'n Bunschoten for his expence to & from Waterford with Revn'd Morace W. Dwights call recpt	5	50
Dec'r 28	to cash p'd Jacob Boram Collector for County tax on houses & lots in the Velidge of Poughkeepsie recpt	6	75
1827 Jan'y 29	to cash p'd James Lewis as Correster in said Church recpt	12	00
feb'y 2	to cash p'd for a regester book for the revn'd Morace W. Dwight	2	00
Mc'h 30	to cash p'd for Insurence on houses & on houses &c	16	60
Mc'h 27	to cash p'd John Yates for dinners for the ministers at the Installation of the Revn'd Morice W. Dwight &c	3	62½
Ap'l 11	to cash p'd James Lewis in full as Correster for 3 months & 11 days recpt	5	50
may 4th	to cash p'd Tunis V'n Bunschoten one of the holders of the deed in trust by the Jacob V'n Bunschoten fund Given to Thomas Dewitt and other as above Named	700	00
"	to cash p'd Consistory on Salory to the Revn'd Morace W. Dwight	39	67
may 14	to cash in treasury in treasury $6.83 on rent Also $73.84 laid of for repairs, taxes & money p'd Cirus Berrey for repairs in 1825 over & above his rent which was $75.00 se said J. B. Frears bill on file		
Ap'l 28	to cash p's Revn'd Morace W. Dwight on salory by the hand of Deacon Mathew Luyster recpt	200	00
Aug't 22	to cash p'd revn'd Morace W. Dwight on salory by the hand of Elder John Luyster	54	00
	to Alexander Forbush commisions for collecting $6.00		
sept'r 24	to cash p'd Revn'd M. W. Dwight by hand of Treasurer $25.00	25	00
nov'r 22	to cash p'd Revn'd M. W. Dwight on salorey in full up to 1st nov'r 1827 by treasurer	171	00
	to cash p'd John Luyster to pay for wood brought for s'd M. W. Dwight	13	00
1828 Jan'y 15	to cash p'd Jacob Boram Collector for County tax on houses and lots in the Vilage of Poughkeepsie for 1827 recpt	3	96
April 26	to cash p'd to get the polesey Renenewed on the houses on the Velage of Poughkeepsie	16	62½
	to cash p'd Revn'd Morace Dwigight on salory	25	00
		1861	95½

The Reformed Dutch Church of New Hackensack

		Dol's	Cts
1828 Ap'l 5	Account Continued from page 17 Amo't bro't over	1861	95½
	To cash p'd Revn'd Morace W. Dwight on salory se recpt	100	00
may 14th	to cash p'd Revn'd Morice W. Dwight on Salory se recpt	100	00
July 25	to cash p'd Revn'd Morice W. Dwight on Salory se recpt	30	00
Dec'r 4	to cash p'd Revn'd Morace W. Dwight on Salory recpted	171	00
19	to cash p'd Revn'd Morace W. Dwight on Salory recpt'd	164	00
1829 feb'y 4th	to cash p'd Revn'd Morace W. Dwight of salary up to 1st Nov'r 1828 in full	10	00
	to cash p'd by Tunis V'N Bunschoten including taxes repairs done on the Houses in town of of Poughkeepsie se bill recpts &cc	102	97
Ap'l 16th	to Cash on salory to cash p'd Revn'd M. W. Dwight	30	00
may 5	to cash let on Bond out of money recv'd on sale of the house in Pine St $500.00 on the house in Union St $400.00 let to James Ackerman	900	00
22	to cash p'd Revn'd M. W. Dwight on Salory se recpt	60	00
1830 Ap'l 24	to cash p'd Revn'd M. W. Dwight on Salory recpt in full up to 1st Nov'r 1829	47	00
		3 576	92

June 2	to cash p'd Revn'd M. W. Dwight on Salory recpt	85	00
1831 Octb'r 8	to cash p'd Revn'd Morace W. Dwight on Salory recpt	70	00
1832 June 1st	to cash p'd Revn'd M. W. Dwight on Salory Recpt	98	0
Aug't 27	to cash p'd Revn'd M. W. Dwight se recpt	115	00
1833 may 3rd	to cash p'd Revn'd M. W. Dwight on Salory	160	00
2nd	to Cash loaned out to Thomas Hinton on Bond & Mortgage	900	00
Aug't 16th	to Cash p'd Rev'd M. W. Dwight on Sallary	20	00
Decm'r 6th	to Cash p'd Rev'd M. W. Dwight on Salary out of this fund	11	80
1834 May	to Cash p'd Rev'd C. Van Cleef on Salary out of J. Van Bunschoten fund	33	00
Aug't 1	to Cash p'd Rev'd C. Van Cleef out of J. Van Bunschoten on Sallary	167	80
1835 May 7th	to Cash p'd Rev'd C. Van Cleef out of this fund on Sallary $126	126	00
	Cash paid Rev'd C. Van Cleef out of this fund on Salary	74	80
June 1st	To Cash loaned to James Van Keuren 6 p'r Cent	200	00
"	To Cash Loaned to Peter Van Derbilt at 6 per Cent	125	00
1836 May 2nd	to Cash Loaned to Matthew Luyster at 6 per Cent	760	00
June 9th	to Cash p'd Rev'd C. Van Cleef on Sallary out of J. V. B. fund	50	00
	to Cash p'd Rev'd C. Van Cleef on Salary out of J. V. B. fund	115	48
Decm'r 15th	to Cash paid Rev'd C. Van Cleef on Salary out of J. V. B. fund	29	52
1837 April 5th	to Cash paid Rev'd C. Van Cleef on Salary out of J. V. B. fund	90	00
25th	to Cash p'd Rev'd C. Van Cleef on Salary out of J. V. B. fund	75	00
Sep't 30th	to Cash paid Rev'd C. Van Cleef on Salary out of J. V. B. fund	36	28
1838 May 25th	to Cash Loaned to Samuel Luckey at 6 per Cent	200	00
June 16th	to Cash paid Rev'd C. Van Cleef out of this fund	136	21
Decm'r 31st	To Cash paid Rev'd C. Van Cleef out of this fund	38	30
		7139	11
		6875	01
		264	10

Van Benschoten Gifts

		Dol's	Cts
1839 May 1st	Trustees in account with H. D. Traver Secretary & treasurer to cash loaned to Cornelius Ostrander on bond and mortgage nine hundred an Sixty dollars of J. V. B. fund	$960	00
	paid out forty dollars from Mr. Luyster	40	00
		$1000	00

	The Consistory of Reformed D. Church of New Hackensack to the reasurer & sect Dr. brot over	1000	00
1839 May 1st	to cash paid Rev. C. Van Cleef salary	$106	79
May 22	to Cash to Rev C Van Cleef salary	33	00
July 20th	to Cash to Rev C Van Cleef salary	44	80
1840 April 25th	to Cash paid Rev C Van Cleef	$120	00
May 5th	to Cash paid Rev C Van Cleef salary	20	00
	to Cash paid Rev C Van Cleef salary	33	00
	to Cash paid Rev C Van Cleef salary	44	80
1841 May 1st	to Cash to H. C. Everitt from H. D. Traver priciple	1000	00
May 3rd	to cash paid Rev C Van Cleef salary	70	00
May 5th	to cash paid Rev C Van Cleef salary	70	00
May 7th	to Cash paid Rev C Van Cleef salary	33	00
May 8th	to Cash to Rev C Van Cleef salary	44	80
1842 May 1st	to Cash to Rev C Van Cleef salary	70	00
8	to cash to Rev C Van Cleef salary	70	00
12	to cash to Rev C Van Cleef salary	33	00
July 20th	to cash to Rev C Van Cleef salary	44	80

	Trustees R. D. Church N Hackensack Dr		
1843 May 4th	Cash to Rev. C. Van Cleef for Salary from H. E. Everitt	70	00
May 4th	Cash to Rev C Van Cleef for Salary from C Ostrander	70	00
May 6th	To Cash to Rev C Van Cleef salary from J. Cornwell	33	00
	To Cash to Rev C Van Cleef salary from S V Wheeler	44	80
	Trustees Reformed Dutch Church N Hackensack Cr		
1843 May 1st	by Cash Harvey Everitt interest on J. Van Bunschoten fund	70	00
May 6	by Cash of Cornelus Ostrander on J Van Bunschoten fund	70	00
May 6	by Cash of S V Wheeler interest on J V B fund	44	80
May 8th	by Cash of John Cornwell interest on J V B fund	33	00

May 1, 1844, Matthew Luyster holds a note against the Reformed Dutch Church of New Hackensack which note grew out of the erection of the above named Church and also the making of the fence around the said Church.
The Interest on the Peter Van Bunschoten fund has been applied on the above named note in paying the Principal and a part of the principal
H. D. Platt Clerk

May 1, 1845. Interest from P. V Bunschoten fund paid to Mr. Luyster as Interest & part principal on His note
H. D. Platt

My 1, 1846. Interest from P. V. B. fund paid to M. Luyster
H. D. Platt Clerk

May 1, 1847 Interest from P. V. B. fund paid to Matthew Luyster as Interest and part Principal on His note
H. D. Platt

May 1, 1848 Interest from P. V. B. fund paid to Matthew Luyster
H. D. Platt

May 1, 1850. Interest from P. V. Bunschoten fund paid to Matthew Luyster as Interest a part principal
H. D. Platt

The Reformed Dutch Church of New Hackensack

Extract from the will of Matthew Van Bunschoten late of Fishkill deceased dated Aug't 26th 1818 To the trustees of the Reformed Dutch Church at Hackensack in the town of Fishkill by whatever name stile or title known and in thee Corperate Capacity the sum of fifteen hundred dollars to be placed out and the Interest only to be Used and Applied to and for the use and benefit of the Church in the support of the clergyman or otherwise and if such Interest is not at any time wanted then the the sum to become and remain principal to be put out at Interest as aforesaid and for the purposes aforesaid

       An extract & copy from the original
          made by Elexander Forbus
         and booked by Sam'l Luckey sect'y

se the extracts taken by said }
Alexander Forbus on file   }

SUNDRY ACCOUNTS

Sundry Accounts

SUNDRY ACCOUNTS

Trustees of the Reformed Dutch Church at New Hackensack to Samuel Luckey their treasurer —— Dr ——

Date	Description	Dls	Cent
1825 May 26	to cash Deposeted in hand of James Emott to be loaned out by Varble order of the Trustees	$1500	00
1827 feb'y 9th	to cash p'd Tunis V'n Bunschoten one of the commite to repair the Personage house out of Ints't on the above fund se recpt on file	105	00
1828	se settlement with Consistory 4th feb'y 1828 on my book to cash paid at sundry times to John Luyster & James V'n Keuren a Committee to repair Barn & Yard fence &c	105	00
1829	setlem't 5th feb'y 1829 se my book to cash paid at sundry times to John Luyster & James Dearin Commite to paint & Other repairs on personage house, settled with Consistory 23rd february 1830 se Church Book & my book also	90	00
1830	to cash p'd Samuel Luckey Jun'r one of the commite to fence front part of burying Yard also to purchace materiels setled with Consistory 27th Jan'y 1831—se my book as above	73	00
1831 June 21	to cash p'd Revn'd Morace W. Dwight on salory	97	00
1832 feb'y 22	to cash p'd Revn'd Morace W. Dwight on Salory	36	25
Ap'l 11th	to cash p'd Revn'd Morace W. Dwight out of the Ints't of the above fund up to 3rd feb'y last	63	75
		570	00
1833 feb'y 4	to cash p'd for Extra Expendures on the Church to James V'n Keuren & Peter V'n Derbelt Commitee	10	57
Ap'l 30th	to cash p'd the quester for Classicel Expence se recpt	9	00
1834 Jan'y 21	to Cash paid Rev'd C. Van Cleef out of this fund	90	00
Aug't 1st	to Cash paid Rev'd C. Van Cleef out of this fund	93	68
1835 May 5th	to Cash paid Rev'd C. Van Cleef out of this fund	54	00
31st	to Cash paid Rev'd C. Van Cleef out of this fund	36	00
1836 Ap'l 25th	to Cash paid Rev'd C. Van Cleef out of this fund	90	00
1837 Ap'l 5th	To Cash paid the Rev'd C. Van Cleef out of this fund	90	00
1838 May 7th	To Cash paid the Rev'd C. Van Cleef out of this fund	90	00
1839 May 1st	To Cash paid the Rev'd C. Van Cleef uot of this fund	72	00
1st	To Cash paid to Henry D. Traver 18 dol's for wood	18	00
		653	25
1st	To Cash paid C. Ostrander this fund one thousand five hundred Dollars priciple	1500	00
	Amount bro't over	$1500	00
1840 May 8th	to cash paid Rev C Vancleef Salary	85	00
	to cash paid Sec'y & treasurer for services	10	00
1841 Jan 9th	to cash paid Collector for taxes on parsonage & Church	10	00
May 6	to cash for secretary & treasurer to this date	10	00
May 7th	to cash to Rev. C. Van Cleef for salary	85	00
1842 Jan 12th	to cash paid Collector for taxes	10	00
May 10th	to cash paid Rev C Van Cleef for Salary	85	00
	to cash to sect & treasurer for services to this date	10	00
	to cash for insurance on house in water street	4	00
	to cash paid for recording mortguge of H. C. Everitt	1	65
	to cash paid tax on Church property	4	35
1843 May 6	to cash paid Rev C Van Cleef Salary	60	00
May 10th	to Cash to sect & treas for services to this date	10	00
August 15	to Cash to Rev C Van Cleef salary	25	00
Dec 30th	to Cash paid Collector tax on Church property	10	00

Trustees of the Reformed Dutch Church at New Hackensack by their Treasurer Samuel Luckey on Matthew Van Bunschoten fund   Cr.

Date	Description	Dol's	Cts
1825 May 26th	By Cash from James Emott one of the Executors and deposeted in his hand to be loaned out	1500	00

The Reformed Dutch Church of New Hackensack

1827 feb'y 2	By Cash from Moses & Henry Swift for Ints't on the Above	105	00	
1828 Jan'y 3rd	By cash from Moses & Henry Swift for Ints't as above	105	00	
1829 Jan'y 24	by cash from do. do. do. for Ints't at six in place of of seven per centum by agreement with Consistory	90	00	
1830 feb'y 3rd	by cash from Moses & Henry Swift for 1 Y'r Interst more	90	00	
1831 Jan'y 10th	by cash from Moses & Henry Swift for one Y'r Ints't more and p'd the principel at same time which was loaned out again 3rd february 1831 at six per sentum annually to Christopher Jacocks	90	00	
1832 feb'y 15	by cash from Christopher Jacocks for one Year Ints't more up to the third Instant	90	00	
		$ 570	00	
1834 Aug't 25				
January 4th	by Cash from Christopher Jaycocks for One years Interest	90	00	
May 2nd	by Cash from Christopher Jaycocks $1500 dollars the Matthew Van Bunschoten fund and Loaned it out Same time to Henry D. Traver at Six p'r Cent			
June	by Cash of Christopher Jaycocks in full for Interest to this date	113	25	
1835 May 2nd	by Cash of Henry D. Traver for one years Interest	90	00	
1836 Ap'l 25th	by Cash of Henry D. Traver for one years Interest	90	00	
1837 Ap'l 5th	by Cash of Henry D. Traver for one years Interest	90	00	
1838 May 7th	by Cash of Henry D. Traver for one years Interest	90	00	
1839 May 1st	by Cash of Henry D. Traver for one years Interest in full	90	00	
		653	25	
	By Cash rec'd May 1st 1839 of Henry D. Traver fifteen hundred Dollars in full being the M. V. Bunschoten fund and Loaned at the same time to Cornelus Ostrander	1500	00	
	Amount brot from (Cr.) page priciple	$ 1500	00	
1840 May 1st	by cash of Cornelus Ostrander one year Interest	105	00	
1841 May 6th	by cash of Cornelus Ostrander Interest	105	00	
1842 April 28th	by cash of Cornelius Ostrander interest	105	00	
1843 May 6th	by cash of Cornelius Ostrander interest Eighty dollars leaving twenty five dollars due	80	00	
August 15th	by cash of Cornelus Ostrander by the hands of John A. Monfort twenty five dollars interest	25	00	

The Trustees of the Reformed Dutch Church of New Hackensack in Account With Matthew Luyster   Cr.

The Trustees of the Reformed Dutch Church of New Hackensack in account with Matthew Luyster   Dr.,

		$	C't
1838 May 1st	then the trustees Received of Matthew Luyster Four Hundred dollars and gave their Note for the same	400	00
1839 Feb'r 4th	then the trustees Received of Matthew Luyster one hundred and twenty Nine 93/100 Dollars and gave their Note for the Same	129	93

ACCOUNTS OF THE POOR CHEST

Sept. 5th, 1795. This Certifies that at a meeting of the Consistory of the Church at New Hackensack held at the house of Matthew Luyster. Certifying that Benjamin Van Keuren was chose Secretary in the Room of Henry Schoonmaker and Peter Luyster treasurer in the room of Dominicus Montfort.
Certifying also that the poor Chest is Delivered in the care of Samuel Luckey, Esq.,
L S D
Containing 4—8—6 in Cash

Sundry Accounts

Copied— Elders present
   Peter Luyster

Deacons present
Robert Todd
John Cornell
William Lauson
Samuel Luckey

April 16th, 1796. At a meeting of the consistory of the Church at New Hackensack held at said Church to Settle with Mr. Henry Schoonmaker on the Church Book and find in favour of said Church the Sum of 14/ against said Schoonmaker.

                          L S
Said Day paid ten pounds to Jeremiah Jones for possession of the School House. 6—12.
           L S
taken out of the poor Chest and 3—8 paid by the Consistory.

Copied   Elders present
     Peter Luyster
     Benjamin Van Keuren

Deacons present
John Cornell
Samuel Luckey
Robert Todd
William Lauson

Aug. 15th, 1796. This certifies that at a meeting of the Consistory of the Church at New Hackensack held at the house of Samuel Luckey, Esq., That Aras Van Debilt was chose Treasurer in the room of Peter Luyster. Also that the poor Chest was de-
                        L S D
livered in the care of Robert Todd Containing the Sum of 1—19—9

Elders present
Benjamin Van Keuren
John Wilsie
Aras Van Debilt
Albert Montfort

Deacons present
Robert Todd
William Lauson
William Huffman
Jacob Griffen

Decemb. ye 31st, 1796. This Certifies that at a meeting of the Consistory of the Church at New Hackensack held at the house of Mr. Hollett to make a just Division of the Reverend Van Vranken's Service between the Dutch and English Subscribers, and find by the subscriptions that the ⅓ of his Service is to be performed in the Dutch Language, the remainder to be English.

Elders Present
Benjn. Van Keuren
John Willsie
Aras Van Debilt
Albert Montfort

Deacons Present
Robert Todd
William Lauson
William Huffman
Jacob Griffen

1797, February ye 6th. No. 9 One seat of Joris Middagh Transferred to his son Aardt Middagh,   Paid L-S-D
                                     0—4—0

July 10th, 1797. This Certifies that at a meeting of the Consistory of the Church of New Hackensack that they met at the Church that the Poor Chest was delivered in the Care of William Hoofman Containing the sum of £1—18—6.

Elders present
Ares Van Der Bilt
Elbert Monfoort
John Cornell
Chrisstuflis Anthony

Deacons present
Robert Todd
William Lauson
William Huffman
Cleamens Cornell

RECEIPTS FROM SALES AND TRANSFERS OF PEWS

1796
April 8th. Seats Transfered by Benjn. Van Keuren
In No. 2 One seat of Henry Concklin Transfered to Capt. Teunis Van Bunschoten. Paid 4/ for each seat.
" No. 26 One Seat of Henry Concklin Transfered to Robert Todd
" No. 26 One Seat of Henry Concklin Transfered to Teunis Van Bunschoten
June 25, No. 2 One Seat of Rem Adriance to Abraham Adriance
     The above Transfering paid to Abraham Hogeland

The Reformed Dutch Church of New Hackensack

			L S D
No. 28, Two Seats Sold to William Seward for	Paid	4—0—0
No. 26 One Seat sold to Samuel Luckey for	Paid	1-19—
No. 9 One Seat sold to Henry Schoonmaker for	Paid	2 0 0
No. 7 One Seat sold to Samuel Cooper for	Paid	1 19 0
No. 8 One Seat sold to Henry Dodge for		2 0 0
No. 3 One Seat of Henry Heermans Transfered to Philip Heermans	Paid	4 0
No. 23 One seat of Cornelius Van Keuren Deceased Transfered to Elizabeth Van Keuren paid to Henry Schoonmaker for transfering and is due from him to the church		8

L S D

Nov. 18 Gave Abraham Hoghland the sum of 6—17—6 being all the money I had received. for him to pay the Money he had taken up to pay the Parsonage

No. 25 One Seat of Hendrick Heermance Transferred to Elbert Moonfoor
No. 3 two Seats of Hendrick Heermance Transferred to Elbert Moonfoor
(this item is crossed out and the words "by mistake" written in margin.)
No. 15 one seat of John Monfort Transferred to Elbert Moonfoor, at 4/ per Seat £0—4—0
(the name Hendrick Heermance was originally written in this item and crossed out and the name John Monfort written over it) 0-16—0

1799 Febr. 11th, Seats Transfer'd by Sam'l Luckey
No. 15 one seat of Thomas Vn. Bramer, Deceasd., Transferred to Peter Vn. Bramer Recd. 0—4—0
No. 21 one seat of Thomas Vn. Bramer, Deceasd., transferred to Peter Vn. Bramer Recd 0—4—0
No. 14 two Seats of Gisbert Schank, Deceasd., transferred to Abm. Schank
No. 18 two Seats of   do   do   do   to Abm. Schank Feby. 26th, 1800 Recd. for transferring 0-16—0
No. 2 one seat transfer'd. from Jahonas Wiltse to Cors. Willse, Feby. 26th, 1800 Recd. for transfering 0—8—0
No. 3 one Seat of Henry Haramans Transfer'd to Sam'l Cooper which had been Transfer'd. to Albert H. Monfort by mistake in same page as above Rec'd. for transfering 4/ Feby. 26th, 1800 0—4—0
No. 8 one Seat of Sarah Derea transfered to Abm. Derea Feby. 26th, 1800 Rec'd. for T.
No. 7 one seat of John Wiltsie Transfer'd to Abm. Derea Feby. 26th, 1800 Rec'd. for T.
No. 29 two Seats transfer'd from Matthew I. Dubois to Catherine which by neglect ought to have been transferred shortly after his Death But was Neglected. Transfer'd Feby. 26th and paid for at first transfer
No. 20 one Seat transfer'd from Matthew I. Dubois to Rebecka(?) Westervelt which by Mistake had not been transfer'd shortly after his death Transfer'd Feby. 26th 1800
No. 7 in Gallery Transfer'd from Matthew I. Dubois to John Henry Dubois which by Mistake had not been transfer'd shortly after his Death. Transfer'd Feby 26th, 1800
No. 29 one Seat transfer'd from Stephen Thorn to Elizabeth Thorn Widow of sd. Stephen Deceas'd. Feby. 26th, 1800
No. 2 one Seat transfer'd from Stephen Thorn to Sam'l Thorn Feby. 26th, 1800. Rec'd. for transfering 2 seats, (viz) one to the Widow and one to Sam'l Thorn 0—8—0
No. 16 one Seat transfer'd from Jas. Comton, Deceas'd. to his daughter Mary Matthews, Feby. 26th, 1800   Rec'd. 0—8—0
No. 11 one Seat of Lawranc Haff sold to Jacob Vn. Bunschoten for 1-10—0
No. 2 two seats of Jacob Dubois sold to Benj'n Everit for 1-14—0
No. 11 one seat of Lawranc Haff sold to
No. 11 one seat of Lawranc Haff sold to Albert I. Monfort for 1-10—0
No. 22 one seat of Moria Dubois sold to Benjamin Everit, Junr. for 1—1—6
(the name Joseph Jackson was originally written in this item and crossed out and Benjamin Everit, Junr. written over it)
No. 22 one seat of Moria Dubois sold to Benjn. Everit for 1—1—0
No. 15 two Seats transferred from Thos. Rosekrans to Henry Doddg, May the 27th, 1800—Rec'd for transfering 0—8—0
No. 5 one Seat transfer'd from Thos. Rosekrans to Henry Dodge May 27th 1800—Rec'd for transferring 0—4—0

Sundry Accounts

No. 15	Two Seats transfer'd from Abraham Myers to Sam'l Cooper Augt. 9th, 1800		0—8—0
No. 1	one seat transfer'd from Gulian Ackerman, Deceas'd, to Gulian Ackerman, son of James Ackerman, Jany. 28th, 1801	Paid	0—4—0
No. 15	one seat transfer'd of Gulian Ackerman, Deceas'd, to his son, John Ackerman, Jany. 28th, 1801	Paid	0—4—0
No. 15	one seat transfer'd of Gulian Ackerman, Deceas'd, to John Ackerman, son of James Ackerman, Jany. 28th, 1801	paid	0—4—0
No. 23	two Seats transfer'd of Gulian Ackerman, Deceas'd, to his son James Ackerman, Jany. 28th, 1801	Paid	0—8—0
No. 3	two Seats transfer'd from Andris Haremans to John Monfort and from John Monfort to Albert H. Monfort which has been wrong Transfer'd heretofore done by order of the trustees by Sam'l Luckey, Secty. Chd. to Albert		0—8—0
No. 27	two seats which is confisticated by Lawrnc Haff, Transfer'd to Nazareth in Room of 2 seats which he Bought of Schoonmaker which had been sold to sd. Edw'd. in mistake, being sold previously to Mary Lennington and Abm. Sleight. sd. Nazreth with transfer Done by order of the trustees—Sam'l Luckey, secty.	Paid	0—8—0
	two Seats of Peter Luyster, Deceas'd, transfer'd to son Cornelius P. Luyster, July 19th, 1801	Rec'd.	0—8—0
19	to Seats of Peter Luyster, Deceas'd, transfer'd to his Daughter Ann Luyster, July 19th, 1801	Rec'd.	0—8—0
No. 2	two seats of Constantine Gulnack transfer'd to Peter Dates Junr., Feby. 20th, 1802.		0—8—0
No.	one seat of Constantine Gulnack transfer'd to Peter Daly, Junr., Feby. 20th, 1802	.	0—4—0
No. 21	1800, Feby. 20th, one seat of Magdelena Monfort, Deceas'd transfer'd to Jacobus Monfoort	paid	0—8—0
No. 11	Septm. 2nd, 1802, one seat transfer'd from Phillip Haremans to William Suard	paid	0—4—0
No. 20	one seat of Peter deeds, Deceas'd transferred to daughter Cornelia Cornwell, wife of Clement Cornwell the 6th May 1803	pd.	0—4—0
No. 20	one seat of Peter Deeds Deceas'd transfered to Daughter Catherene Haff, widow of Peter Haff, Dec'd. 6th May 1803	pd.	0—4—0

April 16th, 1796 Mr. Henry Schoonmaker reman In Debted to the Church in this book 14/
The Three Seats Sold to Edward Schoonmaker are not Settled for but remains Due against Said Edward Schoonmaker
(this item has been crossed through)

No. 3	One Seat of Samuel Cooper transfered to James Ackerman 16th May 1803	Paid	0—4—0
No. 7	one Seate of Samuel Cooper transfer'd to James Ackerman 16th May 1803	Paid	0—4—0
No. 15	two Seats of Sam'l Cooper transfered to Jas. Ackerman 16th May 1803 paid	Paid	0—8—0
No. 1	one seat of Mattheus Lyster, Deceas'd, transfered to son John Lyster, 12th July, 1804		0—4—0
No. 11	2 seats of Matthias Lyster, Deceas'd, transfer'd to son John Lyster, 12th July 1804		0—8—0
No. 26	one seat of Matthias Lyster, Deceas'd, transfer'd to son John Lyster, 12th July 1804		0—4—0
No. 26	one seat of Matthias Lyster, Deceas'd, transfer'd to Anne Huls, daughter of sd. Deceas'd, 12th July 1804		0—4—0
No. 8	3 seats of Anna Vn. Bunschoten, Deceas'd, transfer'd to son Matthew Vn. Bunschoten, Administrator, the 29th Apl. 1805	paid	0-12—0
No. 27	two seats of John Willsie Transfered to Nazareth Brewer the 5th day of June 1805		0—8—0
No. 13	1 Seat of Ralph Schank Transfered to Peter Ackerman 24th Augt. 1807 by request of John Ackerman	paid	4/
No. 14	2 seats of Abm. Schank transferred to Schank Ackerman 24th Augt. 1807 by request of John Ackerman	paid	4/
No. 18	1 seat of Abm. Schank Transfered to Alletta M. (mariah) Ackerman, 24th 1807 by request of John Ackerman	paid	4/
No. 18	1 seat of Abm. Schank Transfer'd to John Ackerman, son of Peter, 24th Augt. 1807, by request of Jno. Ackerman	paid	4/

The Reformed Dutch Church of New Hackensack

The following is a record kept of the sale of seats in the N. Hackingsack Church with the numbers of the pews and the seats in each pew and the names of those who chose the seats in each pew, etc.

Pew No. 1 Seats 9,	Names of Purchasers	Price
	1. Johannis Du Bois	£2
	2. Do	
	3. Johannis Schurree	
	4. Do	
	5. Rudolphus Swartwout H	
	6. Do	
	7. Mathias Luyster	
	8. Gulian Ackerman	
	9. Peter Deeds	
Do No. 2 Do 29,		2
	1. Peter Hay	
	2. Cornelius V Wey	
	3. Edward Schoonmaker	
	4. Constyn Golneck	
	5. Do	
	6. Henry Bell	
	7. John Conckling	
	8. Johannes Steenberg	
	9. Stephen Thorn	
	10. Cors. V. Wey	
	11. Johannes Boekhout	
	12. Johannes Wiltse	
	13. Johannes E. Schut	
	14. Peter Oudtwater	
	15. Do	
	16. Rudolphus Swartwout H	
	17. Ram Adriance	
	18. Jacob Du Bois	
	19. Do	
	20. John Haff	
	21. Do	
	22. Peter Haff	
	23. Do	
	24. John Cornell	
	25. Do	
	26. Lawrence Haff	
	27. Do	
	28. Aert Van der Billt	
	29. Do	
Do No. 3 Do 6.		2
	1. Abraham Lent	
	2. Do	
	3. Andrias Heermanse	
	4. Do	
	5. Henry Heermanse	
	6. Do	
Do No. 4, Do 6.		2
	1. Peter Outwater	
	2. Do	
	3. Isaac V. Noortstrant	
	4. Rudolphus Swartwout	
	5. Peter H. Monfoort	
	6. John Jewel	
Do No. 5, Do 6.		2 5
	1. Simon Bloom	
	2. Rudolphus Swartwout	
	3. Henry Bell	
	4. Abraham Lent	
	5. Andrias Heermanse	
	6. Do	

Sundry Accounts

Do No. 6 Do 6.	1. Peter Oudwater 2. Do 3. Abraham Lent 4. Do 5. Andrias Heermanse 6. Do	2 5
Do No. 7 Do 6.	1. Harry Heermanse 2. Wilhelmus Heermanse 3. Teunis Wiltse 4. Willem Edwards 5. Anna Edwards 6. Tjerk Van Keuren	L 2 5
Do No. 8 Do 6.	1. Johs. Shuree 2. Do 3. Theunis V. Bunschoten 4. Do 5. Do 6. Do	2 5
Do No. 9 Do 6.	1. Nicolas Brouwer 2. Do 3. Johannis Schuree 4. Joris V. Noortstrant 5. Aardt Middagh 6. Peter Oudwater	2 5
Do No. 10 Do 6.	1. Cornelius Luyster 2. Do 3. Gerrit Storm 4. Joris Brinckerhoff 5. Barthl. Crannel 6. Johannas Schuree	2 5
Do No. 11, Do 6.	1. Johannis Schuree 2. Do 3. Joris Brinckerhoff 4. Mathias Luyster 5. Do 6. John Heermanse	2 5
Do No. 12 Do 6.	1. Jacobus Swartwout 2. Dirck Brinckerhoff 3. Do 4. Rudolphus Swartwout 5. Joris Brinckerhoff 6. Do	2 5
Do No. 13 Do 6.	1. Roeloff Schanck 2. Luke Noortstrant 3. Henry Rosekrants 4. Peter Noortstrant 5. James Hicks 6. John Churchilll	2
Do No. 14 Do 6.	1. Gysbert Schenck 2. Do 3. Isaac Brinckerhoff 4. Do 5. Lawrence Konkling 6. Simon Bloom	2

The Reformed Dutch Church of New Hackensack

Do No. 15 Do 25.
1. Baltus V. Kleek
2. Johannis Rosekrans
3. John Monfoort
4. Thomas V. Breemen
5. John Ostrum
6. Ahazueras V. Kleek
7. Henry Heermanse
8. Edward Schoonmaker
9. James Hicks
10. Do
11. Peter Haff
12. Do
13. Abraham Hooghlandt
14. Do
15. Peter I. Monfort
16. Do
17. Fredrick Rosekrans
18. Do
19. Gulian Ackerman
20. Do
21. John Van Sickelen
22. Do
23. Cornelius Van Sickelen
24. Do
25. Johanis Du Bois

Do No. 16, Do 8.   2 5
1. Henry Rosekrants
2. James Compton
3. Joris Brinckerhoff
4. Rudolphus Swartwout
5. Philip Ver Planck
6. Do
7. Aert Van Der Bilt
8. John Cornell

Do No. 17 Do 8.   2 5
1. Joris Brinckerhoff
2. Do
3. Jufrouw Plaats
4. Phebe Bloom
5. Joris Brinckerhoff
6. Dom. Rysdyk
7. Do
8. Do

Do No. 18 Do 8.   2 5
1. Gysbert Schenck
2. Do
3. Isaac Brinckerhoff
4. Baltus V. Kleeck
5. Lawrence Haff
6. Jacobus Swartwout
7. Dirck Brinckerhoff
8. Do

Do No. 19 Do 8.   2 5
1. Michiel Hoffman
2. John Heermanse
3. Cornelius Luyster
4. Do
5. Jacobus Middagh
6. John Ostrum
7. Cornelius Luyster
8. Aardt Middag

Sundry Accounts

Do	No. 20	Do	8.	2

    1. Matheus T. Du Bois
    2. Peter Deeds
    3. Do
    4. Do
    5. Johanis Rosekrants
    6. Do
    7. Cornelius Dubois
    8. Constyn Golneck

Do   No. 21   Do   8.   2
    1. Thos. V. Breemen
    2. Magdelene Monfoort
    3. Antie Ter Boss
    4. Dorothea Ackerman
    5. Maria Monfoort
    6. Janetie Fort
    7. Magdalene Monfoort
    8. Jacobus Monfoort

Do   No. 22   Do   8.   L 2
    1. Tunis Wiltse
    2. Do
    3. John Hooghteeling
    4. Do
    5. Maria DuBois
    6. Do
    7. Johanis Du Bois
    8. Do

Do   No. 23   Do   8.   L 2
    1. Peter Oudtwater
    2. Do
    3. Cornelius Van Keuren
    4. Gulian Ackerman
    5. Do
    6. Peter I. Monfoort
    7. Do
    8. Do

Do   No. 24   Do   8.   L 2
    1. Cornelius V Wey
    2. Do
    3. John Churchill
    4. Do
    5. John Churchill
    6. David Sypher
    7. Aarie Medlar
    8. Abraham Hooghlandt

Do   No. 25   Do   8.   L 2
    1. Kaarel Hoffman
    2. Michiel Golneck
    3. Peter H. Monfort
    4. Do
    5. Do
    6. John Jewel
    7. Elias Nieuwkerk
    8. Henry Heermanse

Do   No. 26   Do   8.   L 2   5
    1. Lawrence Konkling
    2. Do
    3. Isaac Wiltse
    4. Mathias Luyster
    5. Do
    6. Isaiah Rynerse
    7. John Conkling, Jur.
    8. Johannes Steenberg

The Reformed Dutch Church of New Hackensack

Do No. 27 Do 8.   L2 5
        1. Jeremiah Jones
        2. Rudolphus Swartwout
        3. Do
        4. Timothy Hicks
        5. James Hicks
        6. Do
        7. Johannis Schuree
        8. Do

Do No. 28 Do 8.   L2 5
        1. Barthl. Crannell
        2. Do
        3. Nicolas Brouwer
        4. Do
        5. Ahazueros V. Kleek
        6. Do
        7. Joris Middagh
        8. John Van Sickelen

Do No. 29 Do 8.   2 5
        1. Andrias Bredstede
        2. Johs. Schuree
        3. Do
        4. Peter Oudtwater
        5. Do
        6. Stephen Thorn
        7. Phemetie Adriance
        8. Peter Harris, Esqr.

The following are gallery seats. Done in Nieuw Hackingsack, May 4, 1767
Pew No. 1 Seats 8.   Names of Purchasers   Price
        1.   L1 5
        2.
        3.
        4.
        5.
        6.
        7.
        8.

Do No. 2 Do. 8.   L1 5
        1.
        2.
        3.
        4.
        5.
        6.
        7.
        8.

Do No. 3 Do 8.   L1 5
        1.
        2.
        3.
        4.
        5.
        6.
        7.
        8.

Do No. 3 Do 8.   L1 5
        1. Jacobus Hannes
        2. Cors. Luyster
        3. Do
        4. Gilbert Livingston
        5. Henry Wiltse   to John Willsie
        6. Teunis Wiltse to John Willsie
        7. Nath. Hicks
        8. Peter Outwater

Sundry Accounts

Do No. 5 Do 6.　　　　　　　　　　　　　　　　　　　　　　　L 1 5
    1. Johan Jost Snyder
    2. Henry Bell
    3. Rudolphus H. Swartwout to John Willsie
    4. Joris Brinckerhoff
    5. Peter Oudtwater
    6. Do

Do No. 6 Do 6.　　　　　　　　　　　　　　　　　　　　　　　L 1 5
    1.
    2.
    3.
    4.
    5.
    6.

Do No. 7 Do 6.　　　　　　　　　　　　　　　　　　　　　　　L 1 5
    1. Matheus I. Du Bois
    2. Cornelius Du Bois
    3.
    4.
    5.
    6.

Do No. 8 Do 6.　　　　　　　　　　　　　　　　　　　　　　　L 1 5
    1.
    2.
    3.
    4.
    5.
    6.

Do No. 9 Do 8.　　　　　　　　　　　　　　　　　　　　　　　L 1 5
    1.
    2.
    3.
    4.
    5.
    6.
    7.
    8.

Do No. 10 Do 8.　　　　　　　　　　　　　　　　　　　　　　　L 1 5
    1.
    2.
    3.
    4.
    5.
    6.
    7.
    8.

Do No. 11 Do 8.　　　　　　　　　　　　　　　　　　　　　　　L 1 5
    1.
    2.
    3.
    4.
    5.
    6.
    7.
    8.

Do No. 12 Do 8.　　　　　　　　　　　　　　　　　　　　　　　L 1 5
    1. Kaarel Hoffman
    2. Elias Nieuwkerk
    3. David Sypher
    4.
    5.
    6.
    7.
    8.

INDEX

INDEX TO NAMES WHICH APPEAR IN
BAPTISMAL AND MARRIAGE REGISTERS
1757-1906

Index to Names Appearing in Baptismal and Marriage Registers

A

Aarsen, Alida, 13, 20, 24, 25, 29
Aartsen, Aaltje, 11
Abel, Hendrick, 51
  Lena, 38
  William, 51
Acker, Deborah, 59
Ackerman, (*See also Akkerman*)
  Caroline, 77, 79, 80, 84, 108
  Catharine, 57, 109
  David, 20, 22
  Dorothy, 78
  Elizabeth V. W., 114
  Ella, 119
  Gelein, 36, 37
  George, 114
  Hannah, 52, 68, 69, 78, 109
  Helen, 72
  Hellen, 110
  Helen E., 90
  Helena, 27, 33
  Hetty Ann, 59, 110
  Isaac, 42, 80
  Jacobus, 37, 42
  James, 52, 55, 57, 59, 62, 67, 70, 72
  James C., 91, 92
  Jane, 42, 46, 51, 55, 58, 61, 62, 68, 84
  Jane Ann, 67
  Johannah, 49
  John, 80, 109
  Lena, 22, 24, 25, 31, 42, 48, 100
  Magdalen, 52, 59, 60, 62
  Magdalena, 36
  Maria, 70, 111
  Maria L., 114
  Maria Louisa, 90
  Martin S., 114
  Martin Schenck, 82
  Mary, 82, 113
  Mathew V. B., 109
  Matthew Van Bunschooten, 55
  Phebe, 113
  Priscilla Merritt, 93
  Sara, 27
  Sarah, 36, 78
  Sarah Frances, 90
  Sarah Grace, 92
  Sarah J., 89, 91, 114
  Sarah Johannah, 87
  Schenck, 82, 84
  Theodore J., 91
  Teunis, 86
  Tunis, 62, 92, 110
Ackley, Grace Cahoone, 91
  Oliver S., 91
Adams, John, 101
  Matilda, 92
Adkins, John H., 117
  Sarah, 115
Adriaanse, Abraham, 8, 23, 24
  Catalina, 8
  Elizabeth, 38
  Joris, 8
  Rem, 23, 24, 28, 38
  Theodorus, 104
  Willem, 28
Adriance, Abraham A., 76, 78
  Alletie, 107
  Anna Maria, 76
  Frances Henrietta, 78
  George B., 110
  Jacob, 31, 108
  John, 111
  Mary, 63
  Phoebe, 109
  Rem, 31
Aiken, Isaac, 110
Aikin, Benjamin, 111
  John, 111
Akin, Caroline, 90
  Catherine Thorn, 93
  Catherine Thorne, 122
  Richard W., 114
Akkerman, Antje, 7
  Gelein, 7, 8
  Jacobus, 8
Albertson, Ambrose D., 91
Alexander, Alice C., 116
  Carrie A., 122
Algee, David, 51
  John, 51
Alger, Stephen W., 112
Allen, (*See also Allin, Allon, Ellen*)
  Gitty, 108
  Henricus, 14
  Lydia, 102
  Maria, 29, 32, 34, 104
  Minnie, 118
  Thomas, 14
Allendorf, Fred D., 120
Alley, Charles J., 117
Allin, Elizabeth, 7
  Hanna, 7
  Johannes, 12
  John, 7
  Maria, 8
  Thomas, 7, 8, 12
Allon, Thomas, 18
  Willem, 18
Alton, Fanny, 115
Amerman, (*See also Hamelman*)
  Albert, 27
  Cornelia, 39
  Johannes, 27
Amy, Sarah, 51
Anderson, Geo., 121
  Margaret S., 121
  Mary J., 121
Andrews, Anna, 93, 94, 117
  Charles C., 116
Andrus, Eva M., 121
Angevine, Charity, 108
  Margaret, 108
Anthony, Nicholas, 109
  Theodore, 94, 121
Aplle, Sarah, 36
Armstrong, Jane, 91
Ashman, Jennie B., 116
Ask, Antje, 28
Asse, Alida, 10
  Maria, 10
  Matth., 10
Atkins, Clarinda C., 115
  Isaac A., 114
  Peter, 114
Avery, Dora, 116

B

Babcock, William, 116
Bagley, Edna Mae, 122
Bailey, Ralph H., 120
Baisler, Peter, 111
Baker, Annis Elizabeth, 87
  Cornelia, 7
  Eliza, 116
  Eliza M., 116
  Elizabeth, 54
  Jonathan, 107
  Lucie C., 121
  Mary Ann, 112
  Mary S., 118
  Mary Seward, 88
  Phebe, 107
  William, 87, 88, 116
Baldwin, Letitia, 108
Band, Grove, 25
  Thomas, 102
Banker, David, 42
  Gerardus, 27
  Maria, 27
  Nathaniel, 42
  Phebe, 107
  Steven, 27, 99
Banneton, Jane, 25
  Jannetje, 24
Banta, David, 7
Barber, Laurens, 25
  Moses, 25

Bard, Ira, 111
Barkulo, George, 72
  Seward, 72
Barlow, Edwin, 115
Barnes, Henry, 106
Barns, Antony Gleen, 47
  Henry, 47, 106
  Mary, 44
  Susannah, 44
  William, 44, 47
Barrett, Joseph, 111
Barry, Mabel Lucy, 121
Bartley, (See also Bertele, Bortley)
  Cornelia, 14, 16, 19
  Esajas, 14
  Henricus, 14
Barton, Doretta, 119
  Eliza, 114
  James H., 116
  Rachel, 105
Bassnett, Grace Maude, 119
Bates, Hickey, 45, 103
Bates, Hicky, 33
  Phebe, 45
  Rachel, 33
Battison, Bayt, 16
Bauker, Sarah, 107
Baxter, James, 86, 112
  Jane E., 115
  Letty Maria, 86
  Wm. M., 121
Bayard, Margareth, 39
Bazeman, Elizabeth, 68
Beaton, Hannah, 110
  James P., 117
Beayaux, (See also Biaux)
  Thomas, 101
Becker, (See also Bekker, Bikker)
  Antonetta, 51
  Baltus, 13
  Elizabeth, 63, 67
  Jacob, 13, 37, 51, 99
  Laurens, 101
  Mary, 37
  Sanford, 116
Beedle, William, 108
Beekman, Aafje, 12, 15
  Sarah, 109
  William, 15
Bekker, Anna, 33
  Barent, 22
  Elizabeth, 19
  Hannes, 15
  Jacob, 15, 19, 22, 23, 27, 33
  Johannes, 17, 27
  Marytje, 17
Bel, Anna, 8
  Caspar, 12
  Henrik, 8, 9
  Hermannus, 9, 12
  Margaretha, 11
  Petrus, 11
  William, 11
Belknap, Georgianna, 118
Bell, Abraham, 11, 112

Anna, 25
Cathrina, 22
Elizabeth, 30
Femmetje, 15, 17, 20, 23, 28, 32, 99
Grietje, 14, 17
H., 20
Henrik, 11, 20, 99
Henry, 2, 25, 30, 38
Maria, 20
Phebe, 47
Phoebe, 40
Susannah, 38
Thomas H., 121
Bennaway, James, 109
Bennett, Christina, 95
Bergen, Leffert T., 89
  Mary, 89
Berkins, Lillie M., 120
Berrit, Wyntje, 8
Berry, Elizabeth, 77
  Jane, 86, 89
  Nathaniel, 107
  Peter, 111
Bertele, (See also Bartley, Bortley)
  Cornelia, 10, 12
  Elizabeth, 10
Betel, Patty, 103
Bethel, Martha, 79
Betts, William G., 112
Biaux, Sarah, 43
  Thomas, 43
  William Stuart, 43
Bigelow, Oscar F., 116
Bikker, Jacob, 17
  Maria, 17
Birdsall, (See also Burdsall)
  Lydia, 39
  Samuel, 39
Bishop, Alexander, 87, 88, 89, 113
  Alexander, Jr., 122
  Angeline Catharine, 71
  Anna Gertrude, 87
  Augusta, 87
  Caleb, 72, 101
  Charles A., 118
  Catharine, 113
  Caty, 70
  Cornelius Van Cleef, 88
  Ellen Shepherd, 87
  Emily Spencer, 87
  Gabriel, 68, 105
  Howard Alexander, 88
  James Dearin, 74
  John, 65, 68, 69, 71
  John Y., 87, 113
  Joshua, 70, 72, 74, 102
  Josua, 30
  Levi, 30
  Maria, 111
  Mary Ann, 113
  Mary Anna, 87
  Nellie S., 122
  Peter, 69
  Sophie Van Cleef, 88, 89

William, 65
Black, Cornelia, 57
  George, 57, 61, 66, 108
  Henry, 61
  Jane, 57
  Maria, 66
Blanck, Maria, 19
Blom, Antje, 13
Bloodgood, Jane Eliza, 112
  Sarah, 40
Bloom, Benjamin, 31, 100
  Jacob, 31
  Mary, 57, 60
  Phebe, 72
Bloomer, Gilbert, 105
Bodden, T. G., 120
  Thomas, 95
Boerum, Phebe, 108
Bogaard, Aaltje, 7
Bogardus, Alletta E., 87
  Amelia, 70
  Catharine, 108
  Cornelia, 80
  Cornelis, 36
  Cornelius, 70
  Francis, 69
  Henry, 74
  James, 55, 74
  James C., 70
  Jan, 9
  John, 36, 44
  John Ackerman, 68
  Maria, 55
  Peter, 44
  Peter C., 105
  Phebe, 70, 72, 107
  Samuel, 68, 69, 78
  Sara, 9
  Sarah Ann, 70
Bogart, Jane, 55
Bogert, Antje, 38
  Catharine, 71
  Cathrina, 48
  Cathrine, 38
  Cornelis H., 41, 48
  Elizabeth, 29
  Francis, 48
  Goris Storm, 41
  Henry, 100
  Jane, 52
  Peter, 48
  Rebecca, 48
  Sarah, 48
Boice, Phoebe, 112
Bollumer, Jannetje, 13
Bolt, Wm. Henry, 120
Bolton, Fred G., 121
Bomp, Mary, 108
Boomman, Margaretha, 10
Borhans, Heyltje, 11
Borrome, Garret, 68
  Henry, 68
Bortley, (See also Bartley, Bertele)
  Cornelia, 7
Bosch, Anna Maria, 16
  Geertruy, 13
  Hannes, Jr., 16

Index

Henrik, 16, 18
Jacob, 16, 18
Joost, 15
Maria, 16
Martinus, 18, 99
Martyn, 13
Mattheus, 18
Bostwick, Isaac D., 89, 90
  Isaac Davis, 90
Bouton, Cornelia A., 90
Bowden, Henry, 118
Bowlin, Ann A., 114
Bowman, Jerse, 120
  Lizzie, 120
  Stella, 119
Bowne, Robert, 111
Bownes, Elizabeth, 107
Boylan, Ann, 114
Bragaw, Andrew, 112
  Maria, 76, 78
Bray, Ann, 113
Brett, Margaret, 74
  Sarah, 64, 68
Brevoort, Elizabeth, 7
Brewer, ——, 82
  Aletta, 54
  Ann, 82
  Catharine Ellenor, 70
  Charles, 56, 70, 73
  Cornelis, 42
  Cornelius, 51, 56
  Cornelius W., 69
  Deborah, 110
  Eliza F., 83
  Elizabeth, 46, 72, 78
  Garrit, 69
  George Clinton, 75
  Gerrit, 110
  Henry, 69
  Jacob, 56
  James, 77
  Jane, 70
  John, 46, 51
  Joseph, 110
  Lodowick, 56
  Mary, 42, 72
  Michael, 73
  Nazareth, 69, 71, 73, 75, 76, 77
  Philip V. Cortlandt, 71
  Robert, 76
  Sally Ann, 73
  Sarah, 51
  William, 69, 82
Bride, Mary, 104
Briell, Myron H., 121
Briggs, Alice Emily, 96
  Edgar A., 94, 95, 96, 119
  Gertrude Mathews, 95
  Louis B., 118
  Mary A., 94
Brincherhof, Marytje, 7
Brinckerhoff, Aaltje, 15
  Abraham, 33
  Catharine, 113
  Elizabeth, 33, 63
  Hannah, 50
  Jacob, 50

Rachel, 100
Sarah E., 113
Susan A., 91
Brinkerhof, Antje, 8
  Catharina, 7
  Dirk, 8
  Elizabeth, 8
  Femmetje, 8
  Johnes, 8
  Susanna, 11
Brinkerhoff, Aaltje, 9, 10
  Abraham, 74
  Adriaan, 32
  Alida, 12
  Catharine, 74
  Derick T., 74, 108
  George D., 74
  Helen, 74
  Hester van de Linden, 32
  John, 7
  Joris, 12, 14
  Lena, 117
  Margaret, 74
  Mary Ann, 74
  Rachel, 7
  Susanna, 8
  Tunis, 111
  William, 74
Brisben, Elizabeth, 61, 64, 105
  Sally, 41
  Sarah, 65, 105
Brisbey, Elizabeth, 42
Brisbon, Elizabeth, 56
Brisby, Elizabeth, 36, 51
  Sarah, 50, 59
Broocks, Kniertje, 36
  William, 36
Brosnahain (or Brosrahain), Andrew, 106
Brouwer, Aaltje, 28, 103
  Adolf, 11, 22, 25, 28
  Anna, 102, 105
  Annatje, 13
  Anne, 48
  Catharine, 63
  Charles, 54
  Cornelia, 20
  Cornelis, 13, 24, 25, 36
  Cornelis Cornelissen, 105
  Cornelius, 11
  David, 20, 63
  Elizabeth, 25, 28, 32, 35, 49
  Francina, 54
  Hester, 29
  Izak, 11
  Jacob, 10, 29, 63
  Jane, 29, 103
  Jannetje, 24, 25, 99
  Jeremia, 25, 28
  John, 35, 103
  Maria, 28, 31
  Mary, 35, 44, 47
  Nicholaas, 7, 9, 17, 99
  Nicholas, Junr., 22
  Robert, 36
  Sara, 17, 102

Sarah, 107
Brouwn, Anna, 44
Brower, (See also Brewer, Brouwer)
  Adolph, 61, 64
  Aletta, 58
  Benjamin W., 114
  Betsy, 59
  Catharine, 59
  Charles J., 94, 120
  Clarence D., 94, 121
  Cornelius, 59, 61, 64, 65
  Eliza, 59, 65, 109
  Elizabeth, 61, 108
  Emma, 117
  Eva M., 121
  George J., 117
  Harriet, 66
  Jacob, 59
  James, 112
  James C. D., 111
  Jane, 55, 58, 59, 61, 65
  Jane Augusta, 95
  Jeremiah C., 115
  Maria, 64
  Mary Ida, 118
  Miriam, 112
  Nazareth, 59, 66
  Samuel Pinckney, 64
  William, 58, 109
  William H., 115
  Wm. Henry, 95
Brown, Allen, 112
  Anna Eliza, 111
  Benjamin Pailey, 58
  Isaac, 58
  James, 117
  John J., 120
  Minnie J., 118
  Sarah Dutcher, 119
  Willard, 119
  William, 111
Brownell, Aimee Wooster, 92
  Amos, 92, 117
Brundage, Gertrude, 116
Brundige, Susan B., 114
Bruyn, Thomas, 100
Bryant, Elias T., 118
  Mary, 104
Buck, Elizabeth, 63
Budd, Aletta, 79
  Angeline, 84
  Ann, 82
  Catherine, 82
  Gilbert T., 111
  Hannah, 79, 112
  John, 79, 80, 81, 82
  John Ten Broeck, 82
  John U., 82, 84
  Joseph, 107, 108
  Mary Ann, 79
  Samuel Thorn, 81
  Selah, 108
  Thomas DeWitt, 80
Bulmer, Augustus Earnest, 93
  James William, 93

Stephen A., 93
Bunker, James, 105
Bunschoten, Elias, 17
  Jan, 30
  Johannes, 19
Burche(r), Hannah, 105
Burdsall, Maria, 99
Burgaw, Abm., 58, 60
  Anna, 52, 53
  Andrew Crimshier, 67
  Caty, 52
  Cornelia Ann, 64
  Isaac, 52, 54, 58, 60, 64, 67
  John, 58
  Letty Catharine, 62
  Peter, 52, 53, 58, 62
Burgon, Rachel, 26, 28
Burhans, Anne, 107
  David, 21, 61, 65
  Henry, 71
  Heytje, 17, 22, 39
  Maria, 31
  Nelly, 26
  Peter, 65
  Petrus, 19, 21, 23, 26, 31, 34
  Sally, 55
  Sara, 19

Sarah, 58, 61, 63
Willem, 34
William, 71
Burnet, Elizabeth, 109
  Garrett P., 111
  Hannah E., 111
  Isaac, 18, 109
  Izaak, 21, 25
  Jane, 110
  Jannetje, 25
  Johan Wilhelm, 18
  Margaretha, 21
  Maria Dorothea, 16
  Matthew, 16
  Priscilla, 111
Burnett, Cornelius, 116
  Elizabeth, 16, 117
  Irene, 121
  Izaak, 16
  Sarah, 113
Burris, George, 107
Burritt, Catharine M., 111
Burroughs, Henry, 87
  Irene D., 93
Burtis, Barnet, 110
Busch, Lena, 106
Buschling, Susannah, 42
Bush, (*See also* Busch, ter Bush)

Elizabeth, 32, 43, 102
Jacob, 36, 46
Jacobus, 55
John M., 120
Lena, 46
Margaret, 55
Peter, 102
Phoebe, 110
Butcher, Anna, 27
  Annatje, 19
  Nancy, 30, 35
  Nancy Saal, 17
Buys, Catharina, 99
  Cathrina, 17
  Elizabeth, 11
  Gideon, 100
  Henricus, 42
  Henry, 42
  Johannes, 13
  Margareth, 36
  Margaretha, 49
  Margret, 30, 43
  Margriet, 102
  Mattheus, 17, 18, 19, 106
  Petrus, 101
  Saartje, 17
  Sara, 13, 22
  Willem, 13
Byce, Isaac, 108

C

Cabre, Darius, 113
Cabrey, Mary W., 113
Cahill, John, 118
Cahoone, Susan V., 91
Caldern (or Caldun), Mary, 110
Calloo, Stephen, 102
Camble, Maria, 31
Cammel, Nelly, 14
Campbell, Harry Arthur, 122
  Harry C., 121
  Mary T., 121
Cane, Joseph, 31
Cannef, Daniel, 39
  Dirk, 39
Canneff, Elizabeth, 101
  James, 107
Canz, Benjamin, 27
Carey, Phebe, 85, 87
Carl, John, 41
  Mary, 41
Carman, Elizabeth, 107
  Josua, 19
  Maria, 19
Carpenter, Emory, 85
Carr, William, 113
Carter, Gitty Maria, 73
  James, 73
  Jane Ann, 112
Cary, Hipsey, 107
Case, Alonzo G., 115
Cass, Levi, 113
Casster (or Cassler), Abraham, 110

Challenor, Cornelis, 40
  John, 40
Chandel, Hannah, 102
Chatfield, David, 34
  Esajas, 31
  Hannah, 39
  Reuben, 50
  William, 31, 34, 39, 50
Chaterdon, Mary, 104
Chatterdon, Betts, 53
  John Pinckney, 53
  Joshua, 53
  Daniel, 117
  Edith S., 118
  Mary, 34
Chase, Henry, 100
  Joseph, 117
Cheesebrough, Clarissa, 61
Cherrick, Christina, 103
Chickens, Elizabeth, 16
Chickery, Frederick, 16
Childs, Gashie, 71
Christian, Anna L., 95, 96, 119
  Anna Louisa, 93
  Daisy Mary, 93
  Louis Elbert, 95
  Susie Emily, 93
  Theodore, 93
  Theodore Winfield, 95
  Washington Travis, 93
  William Travis, 93
Churchil, Benjamin, 57
  John, 60
  Maria, 60

Churchill, Amelia, 77
  Caroline, 77
  Catharine Luyster, 61
  Catherine, 79
  Cornelius, 81
  Elizabeth, 77
  Hanna, 100
  Hannah, 108
  Hannah Eliza, 78
  Jacob, 50
  Jane, 80
  John, 28, 77
  John, Jr., 61
  Joseph, 77
  Letty A., 116
  Mary, 54
  Pally, 105
  Rebecca, 109
  Sarah, 112
  Sarah Ann, 77
  William, 28, 50, 77, 78, 79, 80, 81, 103
Churchwel, Benjamin, 20
  Elizabeth, 23
  Hannah, 20, 21
  John, 20, 21, 23, 38
  Mary, 20, 56, 57
  Samuel, 21, 38
Churchwell, Benjamin, 60
  Emilie, 34
  Hannah, 43
  Hetty Ann, 63
  Isaac, 101
  Jan, 34
  Jane, 66, 112

Index

John, 32, 43, 63, 66
Mary, 51
Rebecca, 32
Susannah, 60
Clap, John, 105
Clapp, Susan, 107
Clarck, Jeremia, 102
Clark, Ida, 116
   Lizzie, 119
Clauson, Appie, 120
   Elias, 121
Cline, Mary, 38
Clock, Mary, 57, 64, 67
   Polly, 54
Clump, Cornelis, 30
   Zacharias, 30, 103
Codwise, Nathaniel, 113
   Ruth, 107
Coe, Elizabeth, 108
Coens, Cathrina, 99
   Geertruy, 13, 14
Coffin, Elizabeth, 103
Colden, Clarinda, 112
   Frederic W., 119
   George A., 121
   Nicholas, 114
Cole, Aaron, 61
   Aron, 58
   Arie, 64
   Catharine, 61
   Charles D., 119
   Esther, 64
   Hester, 65
   John, 58
   William, 111
Collier, Jane, 32
Collins, Ann, 107
   Elizabeth, 88
   Titus, I., 121
Colony, Cathrina, 29
Compten, Jacobus, 13
Compton, Charles, 59
   James, 25
   John, 21, 25, 59
   Mary, 42, 48, 110
   William H., 113
Conchlin, Anna, 24, 25, 28, 104
   Annatje, 16, 19, 20, 21, 22, 30
   Annetje, 99
   Antje, 10
   Catharine, 15
   David, 11
   Elizabeth, 36, 42, 46
   Hannah, 38
   Helena, 36
   Henricus, 14
   Hester, 11, 21
   Isaac, 36, 42
   Izak, 10
   Johannes, 9, 11
   John, 12, 16, 20, 22, 42
   Laurens, 7, 9, 11, 14, 18, 21, 25, 46
   Louw, 15
   Maria, 23, 27
   Mary, 39, 46

Marytje, 100
Mattheus, 9
Sara, 11, 18
Sarah, 37, 42
Susanna, 99
Susannah, 29, 32, 35, 43
William, 99
Conchling, Abraham, 7
   Laurens, 7
   Susanna, 7
Concklin, Belinda, 88
   Elizabeth, 65
   Elias V. B., 110
   J. V. B., 88
   Jacob Van Bunschoten, 110
   Margaret E., 88
   Marianna, 113
   Nathan, 106
   Nelly, 88
   Sarah, 67, 70, 72
Conelly, Cathrina, 102
Conklin, Sarah, 52, 55, 57, 59, 62
   Susannah, 57
Conklyn, Clara, 107
Connel, Isaak, 17
   John, 17
Conner, Anne Maria, 71
   Archie M., 121
   Eliza, 71
   Josephine, 119
   William, 71
Conover, Gertrude K., 88, 89, 90, 114
   Harriet, 87, 114
   Harriet L., 92
Convery, Mrs. John, 121
Coock, Margriet, 23
   Matthias, 38
   William, 38
Cook, Altje, 54
   Egbert Dumont, 53
   Eliza Matilda, 60
   John, 60
   John M., 53
   Margaretha, 21
   Matthias, 21, 54
Cooke, Olive, 46
   William, 46
Cool, Aaron, 106
   Meindert, 7
Coolridge, Peter, 107
Coon, Abraham, 105
   Mary Frances, 114
Coonley, George, 106
Coopman, (See also Koopman)
   Jacob, 20
   Johannes, 20
Cooper, Cathrina, 100
   Elias, 34
   Mattheus, 37
   Obadiah, 34, 37, 44
   Sarah, 63
   Teunis, 44
Copeman, Eve, 65
   John, 112

Maria, 112
Walter C., 112
Cornel, Benjamin, 20, 61
   Clemens, 20, 26, 34, 61
   Jane, 77
   John, 20, 26, 63
   Peter, 63
   Sara, 20
Cornell, Adam Deeds, 30
   Adrian M., 112
   Catharine, 56
   Clemens, 17, 30, 40
   Cornelia, 35
   Cynthia, 80, 81
   Douw, 55, 59, 62, 66
   Dowe, 56
   Elias, 66
   Eliza, 59, 81, 82
   Elizabeth, 30, 83, 84, 109
   Femmetje, 49
   Jacob Wyckoff, 88
   James, 17
   Jane, 78, 81
   John, 30, 44, 62
   John D., 109
   Margaret, 63, 67, 69, 75, 77
   Margareth, 40
   Margaretha, 30
   Maria, 34
   Myron B., 115
   Peter, 111
   Richard, 55
   Syntie, 107
   Sytie, 72
   Sytje, 44
   William A., 87, 88
   William Augustus, 87
Cornes, Clemens, 18
   Pieter, 18
Cornwell, Clemens, 48
   Cornelia Ann, 72, 112
   Cornelius, 78
   Elizabeth, 48
   Elizabeth Johnston, 96
   Hannah Eliza, 69
   Hannah Elizabeth, 81
   Helen Stockholm, 95
   Henry Benjamin, 76
   Huldah, 78
   Jacob, 78
   Jacob R., 121
   Jacob Ralph, 89
   James, 67, 78
   John, 67, 69, 72, 75, 76, 78, 80, 114
   John D., 113
   John D., Jun., 88, 89
   John Dates, 80
   John I., 81
   John J., 96, 118
   John James, 88
   Jno., 121
   Maria Eliza, 67
   Margaret, 108
   Margaret Ann, 73
   Mary, 70, 72, 107
   Mary Johnston, 95

Peter, 54, 67
Peter Luyster, 73
Phebe, 112
Robert, 75
Samuel, 78
Sarah, 54
Sarah Maria, 76
Uriah, 73, 77, 78, 81
Coulter, Agnes, 115
Couse, Jane Ann, 87, 88, 89, 113
Couwenhoven, (See also Kouwenhoven)
Cornelia, 106
Engeltje, 100
Peter, 106
Rachel, 20
Covenhoven, Adrian, 58
Barbara, 108
Caroline, 76
Jacob, 108
Nelly, 66, 71, 75
Peter, 58

Covinhoven, Mary, 68
Cowenhoven, Mary, 64
Cowl, Milford, 113
Cramer, Anna, 62
Betsey, 68
Catharine, 68
Henry, 68
Sarah, 106
Crannel, Catharina, 12
Elizabeth, 12
Emy, 103
Crans, Elizabeth, 102
Craus, Elizabeth, 102
Cremer, (See also Krymer)
Geertrius, 15
Grietje, 15
Johannes, 15
Maria, 15
Margriet, 21
Philip, 101
Crilley, Thomas, 115
Croft, Harriet A., 116
Henry C., 113

Crom, John, 100
Cromlish, Elizabeth, 112
Cromwel, Martha, 22
Cromwell, Mary E., 115
Rachel Ann, 112
Cronkrite, Dora A., 94, 118
Croocke, Anna, 40
Cropsie, Jasper, 60
Sarah, 60
Crouse, Charles H., 114
Crozier, Herman C., 94
Cudgill, Rachel, 110
Cuiper, Mary, 36
Culver, Elizabeth, 33, 103
James, 104
Cummings, Courtland M., 118
Curtis, ——, 110
William, 110
Cypher, See also Cuiper, Seyfer, Sypher)
Elizabeth, 55, 57
Nelly, 53, 56

D

Dakins, Ebenezer, 102
Dates, (See also Deed, Deeds, Deets, Deits, Deitz, Dietz)
Abraham, 56, 73, 78
Abraham L., 75, 76, 77, 78
Adam, 46, 76
Andrew, 42
Casparus Westervelt, 76
Catharine, 57, 65
Cathrine, 37
Cornelia, 34, 40, 48, 63
Cornelia A., 112, 115
Eliza, 73
Eliza Ann, 76
Elizabeth, 37, 43, 49, 59, 60
Gertrude, 112
Hannah, 47, 73, 112
Harriet, 73
Henry, 58, 75
James, 56, 110
Jane Ann, 73
John, 37, 42, 47, 55, 57, 58, 60, 62, 63, 77
Juliann, 111
Maria Matilda, 76
Peter, 46, 55, 57, 73, 76, 108, 110
Sarah, 73
Thomas, 112
Daughty, Anne, 42
Davids, Cornelis, 31
James, 24, 25, 31
John, 8
Richard, 8
Susanna, 24, 25
Davidsen, Anna, 30
Elizabeth, 13
Paul, 13
Davidsz., James, 100
Davis, Anna, 37, 102

Caroline, 90, 91, 92
Cathrina, 27, 29
Elizabeth, 56, 107
Ellen, 110
Hannah, 72
Henry Dimon, 60
James, 27, 29, 33, 100
Jane, 102
John Thomas, 58
Margaret, 116
Mary, 43
Willem, 104
William, 35, 37, 43, 56, 58, 60, 103
William E., 116
Davisen, Anna, 32
Dayton, Frederick, 105
Dea(k)in, James, 114
Dean, Amy, 39, 99
David, 19
Elizabeth, 19
John, 65
John H., 113
Thomas, 65
Dearen, Charles, 27
James, 27
Dearin, (See also Deeren, Deerin, Dering, Dieren)
Ann Eliza, 90
Anne Marie, 69
Antoinette, 81
Antonette, 113
Benjamin, 60, 112
Charles, 113
Francis, 84
Geertruy, 44
Gertrude, 74, 75
James, 44, 49, 52, 53, 58, 101, 109, 114
James Walter, 79
Jane E., 113

John, 27, 44, 52, 55, 59, 69, 74
John Phillip, 113
Margaret, 73
Mary, 27, 55, 57, 60, 64, 69, 72
Mary Ann, 76
Nancy, 52
Peter, 53, 81, 109
Rachel, 64, 66, 69, 70, 72, 73, 74, 77
Robert, 111
Samuel L., 90
Samuel Luckey, 114
Simeon, 55
Simson, 109
Susan Adelia, 80
Thomas, 58, 60
Thomas J., 109
Thomas S., 84, 85
Thomas Seymour, 85
William, 49
William J., 75, 76, 77, 79, 80
Dearing, Rachel, 100
de Boog, Petronella, 14
de Boys, Elias, 8
Jacob, 8
Jenneke, 8
Jeremia, 8
Joel, 8, 16
Johannes, 8
Maria, 16
Rachel, 8
Sara, 8
Deed, Abraham Lent, 13
Adam, 13
Peter, 35
Deeds, Adam, 14, 16, 18, 20, 22, 25, 26, 30
Anna Cathrina, 22
Antje, 33

Index

Cathrina, 20, 22, 26, 32, 100
Cornelia, 14, 17, 18, 20, 26, 30
Elizabeth, 9, 103
Henricus, 20
Jacobus, 25
Jan, 104
Johannes, 16
John, 35
Petrus, 35
Pieter, 9, 10, 14, 17, 18, 20, 22, 26, 30, 33
Deeren, James, 31, 34
  John, 34
  Margaretha, 34
  Rachel, 31
Deerin, John, 38
  Rachel, 38
Deets, Cathrina, 29
  Johannes, 9
  Pieter, 9
DeGarmo, Robert M., 118
de Graaf, (See also Graaf, van de Graaf)
  Abraham, 41
  Anna, 41
  Anne, 36, 49
  Antoinetta, 32
  Barent, 32, 41
  Elizabeth, 11, 29, 32, 47
  Gideon, 47, 106
  Hester, 7, 41
  Hesther, 106
  Isaac Hegeman, 45
  Jacobus, 47
  Jane, 47
  Jannetje, 18
  Jenneke, 14
  Johanna, 47
  Lydia, 107
  Maria Frair, 42
  Mary, 47
  Michael, 41, 56
  Michiel, 47
  Moses, 42, 45, 47, 104, 106
  Sarah, 45, 56
De Graaff, Elizabeth, 35
De Graff, Elizabeth, 51, 52
  Esther, 58, 61, 64
  George F., 117
  Gideon, 51
  Jane, 51, 54, 56
  Lydia, 51
  Margaret, 54
  Maria, 101
  Michael, 51, 54
  Myndert, 63
  Sarah, 62
  Stephen, 63
de Grave, Anna, 105
  Hester, 105
DeGroff, Augusta, 118
  Charlotte, 89
  Ida, 92, 120
Deinor, Cathrina, 32
Deits, Margaret, 52
Deitz, Abm., 54

Caty, 54
Elizabeth, 55
John, 52, 53
Sarah, 53
de Joo, Baltus, 48
  Peter, 48
Delahanty, Mary A., 118
De Lamater, Benjamin, 108
  Eliphaz, 93, 117
  Harold Waldo, 95
  Mildred, 93
  Wilfred Schuyler, 93
de Lange, Anna, 102
  Anne, 43
  Coenraad, 17
  Elias, 17, 22
  Elijah, 39
  Lena, 39
  Maria, 15
  Petrus, 99
  Sarah, 22
De Lano, Lydia, 106
de Lanoy, Jane, 24
Delaun, Hannah, 50
De La Vergne, Delavergne, Catharine, 110
  Edwin, 110
  George, 111
  George, W., 109
  Peter, 109
  Phebe H., 113
Delemater, Cornelia, 94
  Eliphaz, 94
  Emott Andrews, 95
  John Oscar, 95
de Long, Eleonora, 104
de Marees, Cathrine, 47
  Nicholaas, 14
de Mares, Antje, 12
  Nicholaas, 12
de Milde, Elizabeth, 19
  Izaak, 19
  Johannes, 19
  Philip, 19
de Milt, Anna Margaretha, 16
  Isaac, 16
  Margriet, 43
Demoet, Maria, 15
Demund, Mary Ida, 115
D(e)mund, Sarah J., 117
Demuth, Helen Eloise, 122
  J. A., 122
Denee, Edgar F., 116
Deniston, Elizabeth M., 84
Dennis, Rachel, 106
Dennison, Eliza M., 82
  Elizabeth M., 80, 81
Denniston, Eliza, 83
  Eliza M., 82
  Elizabeth M., 83, 84, 85
de Pue, Cornelia, 14
  Peter, 41
  Pieter, 14
Depuy, Nancy, 50
  Nelly, 87, 88
  Peter, 50
De Riemer, Eltsie, 78

Dering, Gertrude, 82
  Samuel Lucky, 83
  Thomas, 110
  Thomas J., 83
  Thos. I., 82
Devons, J. Stewart, 122
de Wit, Endero, 8
  Johannes, 8
Deyo, (See also de Joo, Dio)
  Evelyn May, 89
  Joseph P., 89
Deyoo, Peter, 41
  Sarah, 41
Diamond, (See also Dimant, Dimend, Dimon, Dimond)
  Abraham, 53, 80, 109
  Cathrina, 26
  Emeline, 80
  Gertrude, 110
  Gitty, 63
  Henry, 53, 56, 63, 66, 77, 101
  Joseph, 66
  Mary, 56, 80, 81
  Melinda, 77
Dickerson, Jno. P., 120
  Monroe, 120
Diddell, Clara Wooster, 95
  Harold Wooster, 93
  J. (J.), 88
  Jacob S., 117
  Jacob Storm, 88, 93, 95
  John J., 118
  John Jackson, 88
  Joseph Jackson, 93
  William, 111
Diderik, Daniel, 7
Dieren, Jan, 31
  John, 101
Dietz, Elizabeth, 50
  Jenny, 50
  John, 50
Dimant, Elizabeth, 16
Dimend, Margaretha, 19
  Matthew, 19
Dimon, Cathrine, 35
  Henry, 59
  Jane, 59
Dimond, Henry, 84
  Mellissa, 112
  William H., 88, 112
Dingy, Mary Jane, 114
Dio, Johannes, 15
  Marytje, 7
Disborough, Henry, 109
Disbrow, ——, 108
  Abijah, 53
  Anna, 108
  Avery L. Herrick, 80
  Emma, 115
  George Edgar, 80
  Henry, 53
  Henry C., 80, 81
  Martha Albertson, 120
  Samuel, 53
  Sarah Ann, 80

William Henry, 81
Divine, Anna, 53, 60, 63, 66
  Margaret, 64
  Nancy, 52, 58
Dodge, Catherine, 76
  Deborah, 107
  Helen, 76
  Henry, 61, 79
  James, 76, 78, 79, 80, 108
  Philander Seward, 80
  Susan Maria, 61, 109
  William H., 110
  William Seward, 78
Dolfsen, Catharina, 14
  Cathrina, 29
Doll, Nancy, 41
Dollas, Jane, 47
Dollis, Jane, 51
Dolsen, (See also Dolfsen)
  Catharina, 11, 20
  Cathrina, 16, 26, 33, 42
  Cathrine, 37
  Johannes, 11
Dolson, Alonzo W., 115
  Anna M., 114
  Caroline, 84, 85, 86, 87, 111
  Cordelia, 112
  Corris M., 94
  Edith M., 121
  Kate, 114
  Priscilla, 111
Donahooe, Sarah, 118
Donaldson, Lina, 116
  Mary Elizabeth, 116
Donnly, Izak, 11
  Sara, 11
Dop, Elizabeth, 11, 18
  Eva, 99
  Pieter, 10
Dorland, Arthur J., 111
  Carrie A., 115
  John M., 93
  John P., 110
Dorset, John, 108
Dorsett, Hattie, 117
  John C., 113
Doty, Melissa, 117
Doughty, Allie A., 92
  Almira Amelia, 120
  Joseph I., 116
  Marshall K., 121
  Rachel Morris, 94
  Sherman, 121
Douglas, Benjamin, 29
  Isaac Scudder, 29
  James, 29
Downey, Bartheny, 22
Dowing, Edward, 117
  James, 110
Downy, Anna, 40
  Elizabeth, 40
  Isaac, 40
  Sarah, 40
Doyle, George, 116
Drake, Francis, 110
  Jane Mary Ann, 110
  Jesajas, 20

Minnie G., 118
Sara, 17, 102
Willem, 20
Drieshmann, Catharine, 91
DuBois, (See also de Boys)
  Adrian, 66
  Barbara Ann, 68
  Barbarah, 58
  Barbary, 71
  Catharine, 64
  Edwin, 119
  Elias, 55
  Elizabeth, 59
  Ezekiel Stilwell, 62
  Freelove, 67, 68, 74, 75, 77, 80
  Henry, 66, 71, 75
  Jacob, 52
  Jane A., 85
  John, 62
  John H., 64, 68
  John J., 59
  John M., 113
  Lawrence, 55
  Mary, 50, 53
  Mary M., 87, 88, 113
  Peter, 52
  Richard Woolsey, 62
  Sarah Ann Maria, 75
  Thomas, 59
du Boy, Joel, 18
du Boys, Adriana, 46, 104
  Andrew, 38
  Anna, 27, 32
  Annatje, 22
  Benjamin, 12, 15, 22, 29
  Cathrina, 21
  Clara, 9
  Cornelis, 99
  Elizabeth, 47
  Frankje, 23
  Geertruid, 11
  Gideon, 10, 28, 47
  Henrica, 36
  Jacob, 29, 38, 102
  Jacob, Junr., 29, 49
  Jeremia, 11, 12, 27
  Jeremias, 9
  Joel, 11, 12, 18, 21
  Johannes, 9
  Johannes Henricus, 23
  John, 49, 100
  Louis, 21
  Marytje, 9
  Mattheus, 23
  Matthew, 36
  Petrus Peele, 15
  Rachel, 11
  Rebecca, 40, 46, 105
  Sara, 9, 10, 12, 27, 30
  Susannah, 107
  Tanneke, 9
  Thomas, 9
Duitscher, Abraham, 13, 37
  Antje, 17
  David, 13, 15, 17, 37
  Elizabeth, 28
  Margriet, 18

Maria, 33, 104
Pally, 15
Duitser, Annatje, 7
  David, 8
  Jacomyntje, 8
  Margriet, 9
  Margrietje, 9
  Maria, 9
  Wilhelmus, 7
Duly, Abraham, 14
  Elizabeth, 44
  Josua, 14
Dumon, Margrietje, 8
du Mond, Egbert, 34
  Elizabeth, 20
Dumont, Anna, 121
  Anna G., 121, 122
  Anna Gertrude, 92
  Martha, 121
  Martha H., 120, 121
  Martha Hay, 92, 93
  Martha J., 119, 120
  Martha Nevins, 95, 120
  Rachel, 122
  Rachel W., 121
  Rachel White, 93
  Mrs. W. A., 119, 122
  Wm. A., 95
  Wm. Alexander, 92, 93
  William Henry, 95
Duncan, Elizabeth, 36
du Pue, Elizabeth, 41
du Puy, Peter, 103
Durlin, Lydia, 102
Durling, Isaac, 108
Dusenbury, William B., 117
Dutcher, (See also Duitscher, Duitser)
  Abm., 53
  Anna, 55, 57, 61, 65, 68
  Anne, 69, 72
  Antje, 106
  Catharine, 71
  Catherine, 76, 78, 79, 81
  Charles, 108
  David, 53
  Edward, 116
  Elizabeth, 47
  Henry, 66
  Ida, 116
  Josephine, 116
  Lydia, 39
  Mary, 35, 37, 46
  Mary Ann, 66
  Nelly, 53, 56, 58, 108
  Robert W., 115
  Sarah, 117
  Sarah A., 115
  William, 110
du Vain, Ahazia, 32
  Maria, 32
Duytscher, Mary, 28
Dyeman, Cathrina, 100
Dymon, Clarinda, 74
  Cromeline, 74
  Emeline, 68
  Henry, 50, 68, 74
  Isaac Scott, 50

Index

E

Earle, Dorothy Maria, 78
  Edward, 64
  John, 64
  Mary C., 89
  Sarah, 78, 111
  Sophia, 78
  Sylvester, 78
East, Charles V., 118
  John, 114
  John R., 95
  Mary Catherine, 95
  Richard, 117
Eckler, John, 119
Edmund, Getty, 35
  James, 35
Edward, Annatje, 19
  Maria, 28, 101
Edwards, Agnes, 122
  Maria, 29, 62
Edword, Annatje, 16
  Willem, 16
Edworth, Alida, 16, 18
  Mary, 36, 43
  Willem, 12
Ellen, Rachel, 10
  Thomas, 10
Ellis, Cathrine, 46
  Gabriel, 46
  Henrik, 31
  Mary, 31
  Sara, 24

Ellsworth, Asuerus, 46
  Dorothy, 50
  John, 50
  Verdine, 50
Elmendorff, Margrietje, 34
Elmendorph, ——, 40
Elsworth, Alexander, 33, 34
  Alida, 21, 25
  Harriot, 46
  John, 46, 49
  Mary, 49
  Phoebe, 19, 23
  Rachel, 33, 34
  Sara, 102
  Susannah, 46
  Willem, 18
Emans, Margaret, 69, 71, 73
Emmons, Martha J., 88
Emmot, (*See also Nebbel*)
  Susanna, 41
Emot, Susannah, 103
Emug, Daniel, 100
  Grietje, 15
  Lena, 19
  Philip, 19
  Pieter, 13
Emugh, Daniel, 26, 28, 32, 35
  Elizabeth, 39
  Geertruda, 32
  Geertruy, 14
  George, 38

John, 38
  Joseph, 26
  Maria, 28
  Phoebe, 35
  Pieter, 14
  Sarah, 38
Entene, Elizabeth, 13
  Samuel, 13
Ervine, Mary Ann, 121
Esch, Maria, 18
  Willem, 18
Esmond, Mary, 108
Everett, Benjamin, 59
  Esther, 63
  Isaac, 59, 63
  Marianna, 90
Everitt, Benjamin, 85, 86
  Benjamin H., 84, 111, 113
  Elizabeth, 100
  George H., 113
  Helen Maria, 84
  Henry Isaac, 86
  Hervey E., 109
  John, 109
  Maria, 18
  Marietta, 85
  Mary, 72, 74, 78, 80
  Sarah E., 86, 88, 112
  Susan, 111
Every, Martha, 105
  Sarah, 105

F

Fairchild, Rachel, 114
Fan Sikle, Elsje, 41
  Jan, 41
Farguson, (*See also Forguson*)
  Cathrina, 101
  Elizabeth, 19
  Jane, 100
  John, 19
  Keysa, 16
  Thomas, 16
Farrington, Mary, 110
  Patty, 84
Faust, George, 120
Ferdine, Gertrude, 50
Ferdon, (*See also Perdon*)
  Abm., 64
  Abm. A., 62
  Cathrina, 27
  Cathrine, 107
  Caty, 64
  Elizabeth, 37, 43, 105
  Elsje, 50
  Emma J., 95, 118
  Geertruy, 43, 106
  Gertrude, 58, 61
  Thomas Jeacocks, 62
  Johannes, 34
  Margaretha, 102
  Martinus, 51
  Mary, 107

Peter, 51
  Phebe, 64
  Sarah, 61, 65
  Thomas, 14
  William, 50
Ferdun, Abm., 56
  Abm. Whitman, 56
  Abraham, 65, 70, 72, 74
  Anthony, 72
  Caty Maria, 72
  Elizabeth, 73
  Gertrude, 67
  Jacob, 70
  Jacob A., 72
  John, 70
  Phebe, 56
  Rachel, 57, 67
  Robert, 74
  Sarah, 54, 57
  William, 65
  Wyntie, 70
Ferrel, Rebekah, 65
  Rebekah O, 62
Fer Valen, Elizabeth, 51
Fetchet, Alida, 45
Filips, Benjamin, 12
  Rebecca, 49
  William, 49
Filkins, (*See also Philkins*)
  Margaret, 63, 65, 68
Fink, Austin T., 116

Fisher, John, 43, 105
  Nicholaas, 103
Fishie, Eva, 14
Fish, Robert, 104
Fitchard, Cathrina, 103
Fitchet, (*See also Fetchet*)
  Alida, 38
Flagelaar, Zacharias, 25
Flageler, Elizabeth, 61, 65
  Paul, 63
  Susan, 55
  William, 63
Flagler, (*See also Vlegelaar*)
  Edward, 89, 114
Flegelaar, Anna, 24, 25
  Catrina, 15
Flegelaar, David, 16, 22
  Hannah, 48
  John, 44
  Paulus, 44
  Susanna, 22
  Zacharias, 24, 104
Flugler, David, 21
Fletcher, Edgar D., 114
Fontaine, Peggy, 17
Fontein, Betty, 12
  Grietje, 13
  Peggy, 15
Forbes, Isaac M., 120

The Reformed Dutch Church of New Hackensack

Forbus, John, 50
  Mary, 50
Forden, Jan, 20
Fordon, Abm., 53
  Charles, 53
Forguson, (*See also Farguson*)
  Hannah, 66
  John, 50, 106
  Samuel, 50
Forman, David, 111
  Elizabeth A., 112
  Jonathan L., 112
  Maria Coapman, 96
  Maria E., 118
  Susan, 112
Forshay, John S., 115
  Mary C., 90, 118
Forth, Deborah, 40
  Francina, 45
Fort, Anna, 39
  Deborah, 45
  Francina, 57
  Hannah, 48
  John, 107
Foster, Aaron, 111
  Caroline, 111

Fowlar, Joseph, 102
Fowler, Cathrina, 34, 104
  Elizabeth, 54, 56, 73, 75, 76, 77, 78
  Hannah, 67
  Theodore, 111
Fraer, Catharine, 54
Frair, Anna Maria, 38
  Baltus, 35, 38, 45, 48, 103
  Cathrina, 35
  Cathrine, 39, 48
  Deny, 38
  Elias, 39, 44, 100
  Elizabeth, 41, 48
  Gerretje, 42
  Gerritje, 48, 101
  Jacoba, 45
  Jannetje, 42
  John, 35, 44, 45
  Lawrens, 44
  Lena, 37
  Mary, 35, 41, 42, 45
  Nathan, 42
  Peter, 38
  Petrus, 44
  Rachel, 38
  Samuel, 37

Sarah, 38, 44, 48
Simeon, 37, 38, 41, 44, 105, 106
Francis, Jane, 110
Fraser, James Mitchell, 122
Frear, Emma F., 116
Frederick, Hannah, 42
Free, Franklin P., 118
Freelich, Hiskia du Boys, 9
  Willem, 9
Freeman, Joseph, 91
  Lewis B., 118
Freer, Blandina, 8, 10
  Egje, 8
  Jannetje, 7, 8
  Johannes, 11
  Simson, 9
Fries, Lona, 122
  Vollmer Walter, 96
  William C., 96, 120, 122
Frith, Annie E., 121
  Harriet M., 121, 122
Frost, Deborah, 106
Fuller, Lemuel, 108
Fulmer, Margaret, 90
Furman, Sarah, 107

G

Gacocks, (*See also Geacocks, Jacocks, Tsicoks*)
  Mary, 40
Gage, Charles, 90
  Cynthia, 108
Gail, Joseph, 36
Gallagher, William, 120
Gamaer, Phoebe Ann, 77
  Saul, 77
  Susan, 77
Ganse, (*See also Gaunce, Gons, Gonse*)
  Alson Sherwood, 87
  Amelia, 84
  Ann Platt, 79
  Bethiah Ward, 79
  Caroline Elizabeth, 86
  Clinton DeForrest, 86
  Henrietta, 85
  Henry, 84, 85, 86, 87, 111
  Hervey Doddridge, 80
  Jeremiah N., 86
  John, 79, 80
  Phoebe Platt, 79
  Sarah Anna, 84
  Spencer Abeel, 85
  Thomas DeWitt, 79, 86
Ganung, George W., 122
Gardner, Peter, 88
Garner, Jane Catharine, 113
Garragen, Matthew, 111
Gaunce, Caspar, 31
  Elizabeth, 31, 35, 46, 103
  Johannes Schurry, 26
  Laurens, 26
  Mary, 26

Gay, Annatje, 18
  Hannah, 39
  John, 39
Geacocks, (*See also various spellings following Jacocks, Tsicoks*)
  Benjamin, 43, 106
  Geertruy, 44
  James la Due, 34
  Mary, 42, 43
  Thomas, 34
Gecocks, David, 17
  Geertruy, 101
  Maria, 30
  William, 14
Gecoks, Francis, 27
  Geertruy, 27
  Grietje, 17
  James, 27
  Maria, 25
  Mary, 38
Geer, Stephen, 107
Gekocks, Ezechiel, 14
  Francis, 14
Gekoks, Francis, 17
  Geertruy, 26
  Samuel, 17
  William, 26
Germond, Hannah Ellen, 90
  James C., 118
  Wm., 94
  William L., 90
Gibson, Maggie E., 117
Gifford, Alexander, 103
Gilbert, Mercy, 107
Giles, Daniel, 107
  Warren, 107

Gillaspie, Mary, 46
Gillespie, Garrit Peebles, 82
  John, 82
Gilliland, Rebecca, 70
Gillin, Agnes, 121
Given (or Gioen), James, 107
Gold, Simeon, 110
Golneck, (*See also Gulneck*)
  Adam, 43
  Constantyn, 11, 35
  Geertje, 33
  Jacob, 26, 29, 33, 35, 51
  Johannes, 29
  Mary, 30, 50
  Martin, 11, 51
  Michael, 43, 50
  Michiel, 103
  Styntje, 50
Golnek, Christina, 23
  Constantin, 23
  Jacob, 23
  Jan Reyerse, 37
  Michel, 37
  Michiel, 23
Golneks, Cathrina, 32
  Michiel, 32
Gomaer, (*See also Gamaer*)
  Jane Eliza, 76
  Saul, 76
  Susan, 76
Gomair, Sarah, 78
Gomar, Samuel, 77
  Solomon, 79
  Saul, 79
  Susan, 79
Gomer, Phebe, 75

Index

Gons, Abm., 62
  Caspar, 59, 62
  Casper, 56, 64
  Elizabeth, 51, 59
  Israel, 62
  Jesper, 57
  Samuel, 64
Gonse, Ann, 108
  Casper, 69, 73
  Henry, 69
  William Edwin, 73
Gonzales, Emanuel, 9
  Jacobus, 8, 9
  Joseph, 9, 18
  Maria, 18
Goodale, Elizabeth, 45
  Solomon, 45
Goodall, James, 112
Goodrich, Samuel, 105
Gordon, Melinda, 61, 107
  R. W., Jun., 115
Gorman, John James, 115
Gould, Robert, 109
Graaf, Johannes, 10
  Johannes Pouwels, 10
Graham, Abigail, 33
  Alexander, 30
  Duncan, 27, 30, 108
  Elizabeth, 28
  Mary, 27
Grant, Catharine T., 87
  Mary Jane, 88
  Nathaniel, 86

Nelson, 110
  Richard, 110
Grauberger, Hannes, 16
  Johannes, 15
  Pieter, 10
Graves, Ada, 120
Grawberger, Anna, 12
Gray, P., 120
  Sarah C., 120
Green, Annatje, 14
  Bartholomew, 107
  Charles B., 110
  Charlotte, 65
  Cornelia, 75
  Eliza, 109
  Elizabeth, 69
  Gilbert, 107
  Hannah, 35
  Henry, 63
  John, 72
  Mary, 71, 107, 110
  Oliver, 63, 70, 71, 75
  George Remer, 72
  Richard, 7
  Sarah, 70
Gregg, Sally, 17
Gresty, Frederic, 92
  Frederic Hazelhurst, 92
  Gertrude Mary, 92
  Martha, 92
Grey, Caroline, 114
  Sarah Ann, 88
Griffen, Israel, 114

Mary, 57, 61
  Richard, 106
  Sarah, 57
Griffin, Carel, 29
  Cathrina, 31, 102, 104
  Gathrine, 37, 46
  Charles, 72, 110
  Cornelius, 72
  Debby Ann, 111
  Elizabeth, 30
  Jacob, 29, 32, 35, 41, 46, 51, 55, 56
  John, 30, 46, 101
  John T., 107
  Lewis St. John, 94
  Maria, 51
  Mary, 56, 66
  Mary E., 117
  Michael, 41
  Milton, 111
  Richard, 35
  William, 32
  William Hoffman, 55
Gulneck, (*See also Golneck*)
  Anna, 57
  Cornelia, 55
  Maria, 55, 60
  Martin, 49, 60
  Michael, 55, 59
  Michiel, 49
  Peter, 60
  Styntie, 53
  Uriah, 59

H

Hadden, Carrie M., 117
  Gladys May, 95
  Martin I., 95
  Sadie M., 121
Haff, (*See also Hoff*)
  Catharine, 68
  Cathrine, 48
  Elizabeth, 44
  Hannah, 49
  John, 40, 44, 49
  Joseph, 41
  Lawrens, 41, 48
  Peter, 68
  Phebe, 66
  Sarah, 40
Hagadorn, Jacob, 112
Hageman, (*See also Hegeman*)
  Adrian, 70, 71, 77, 78, 79, 80, 81
  Anna, 65
  Ares, 56
  Caroline, 79
  Cynthia Ann, 78
  Daniel, 77
  Elizabeth, 59, 63, 80
  Francis, 26
  Gitty, 60
  James, 81
  Jane, 70
  John, 53, 56, 60, 65, 71

Martha, 53
  Mary, 77
  Mary Eliza, 72
  Peter, 70, 72, 107
  Sytie Ann, 70
Hagerman, John, 50
  John A., 50
Haight, Amanda M., 114
  Elizabeth, 25, 40
  Lulu D., 118
  Maria, 113
  Sarah, 33, 39
Haines, Addie S., 119
  Margaret, 107
Hall, ——, 66
  Elisha, 66
  Jane, 66
  Joshua, 60
Hallick, Abigail, 101
Hallock, Chas. H., 119
  Susan, 109
Ham, Eugene, 117
Hamelman, (*See also Amerman*)
  Albert, 23
  Lena, 23
Hames, Hannah, 27, 31
Hansan, Catharine, 70
  Isaac, 70
Hansen, Catharine, 109
Harcourt, I. T. Nichols, 116

Hardin, Thomas, 19
Harkison, Agnes, 112
Harpur, Mary, 106
Harris, Annatje, 16
  Barent, 24, 25, 100
  Cathrine, 46
  Effie G., 118
  Eliza, 68
  Elizabeth, 68
  Esther, 115
  Francis, 25
  George, 113
  Gilbert, 24, 25
  Hannah, 25
  Jane, 67
  Joseph, 21, 24, 25, 64, 67, 68
  Meindert, 16, 17
  Neeltje, 21, 24, 25, 28, 35, 39
  Nelly, 100
  Pieter, 10
  Rebecca, 21, 24, 25
  Sara, 10
  William, 107
Hart, (*See also Heart*)
  Fred, 120
Hartenstine, Jeremiah, 120
Hasbrook, James Frederick, 115
  Jane, 111

Hasbrouck, Abner, 120
Haskin, Cathrina, 19
  William, 19
Haskins, Cathrina, 26
  John, 23
  William, 23, 26
Hauver, Laura E., 121
  Julia Brinkerhoff, 95
Hawkes, Phebe Adelia, 90
Hawl, Hanna, 101
Hawley, Lillian T., 121
Hay, Martha J., 95
Hays, Eliza, 111
  Gertrude, 63, 66, 73
  Gertruy, 60
  Gitty, 51, 54, 58, 71
Hayt, Charles Dennison, 86
  Edward, 84
  Henry D., 84, 85, 86, 89
  Lulu DeGroot, 92
  Peter Berry, 84
  Stephen, 85
  Susan, 85
Hazen, Aaron, 108
Heart, Geertruy, 28
  William, 28
Heat, Joseph, 21
  Maria, 21
Heck, James, 17
Hecock, Mary, 109
Heerman, Adriana, 33
  Andries, 33
  Elizabeth, 33
  Eva, 33
  Henrik, 33
  Jacob, 33
  Neeltje, 33
Heermance, Adriana, 67
  Adriantie, 69
  Julia, 110
  Philip, 64
  Sarah, 64
Heermans, Andrew, 39
  Andries, 12, 29, 36, 100
  Andries, Junr., 44
  Anna, 26
  Annatje, 11, 17
  Antje, 8
  Claratje, 7, 11
  Cornelia, 43, 102
  Gerrit, 44
  Hannatje, 8
  Hendrick, 51
  Henricus, 8, 11, 15, 24
  Henrik, 24
  Israel, 9
  Jan, 31, 102
  John, 17, 37, 39, 46
  Neeltje, 29, 36, 49
  Nelly, 51
  Philip, 7, 24, 37
  Philippus, 24
  Rebecca, 15, 99
  Sara, 24
  Wilhelmus, 8, 9, 15, 17
Heermanse, Lewis, 21
  Wilhelmus, 21
Heermansse, Antje, 13

Jan, 31
Maria, 31
Wilhelmus, 13
Heermanssen, Andries, 13
Hegeman, Adriaan, 26
  Anna, 23, 26
  Annatje, 19
  Cathrine, 42
  Cornelis, 15, 20
  Elizabeth, 27, 29
  Francis, 27, 29
  Hendrik, 104
  Joh., 15
  John, 39, 44
  Joseph, 103
  Maria, 11, 15, 26
  Marytje, 17
  Peter, 39
  Sytje, 44
  Willem, 20
Heil, Walter D., 121
Hendrickson, Stephen, 41
Henrikson, Henrik, 41
Herley, George, 113
Hewson, Antoinette, 110
Heyer, Ella, 122
Heyet, (See also Hiat, Hyat)
  Sally, 51
Heyett, Mary, 52
Heyne, Jannetje, 20
Hiat, Joseph, 100
Hickbey, Pally, 49, 106
Hickbie, (See also Hikbi)
  Patty, 22
  William, 22
Hicks, (See also Hikkes, Hiks)
  Carrie, 121
  Cathrine, 41
  Caty, 58
  Charles, 121
  Clara E., 122
  Elizabeth, 66, 68
  Gilbert, 10
  Hannah, 35, 48, 63, 104, 109
  Jacob, 36, 47
  James, 21, 25, 28, 29, 33, 37, 41, 44, 47, 49, 53, 69
  Jane, 52
  Jennie R., 121
  John, 36, 111
  John J., 60
  John Menema, 67
  John S., 53, 58, 63, 66
  John Sherry, 52
  John V., 108
  Lucy, 96
  Lydia, 36
  Maria, 67
  Mary, 48, 50, 53, 56, 57, 61, 64
  Mary C., 115
  Moses, 41
  Rachel, 37
  Rebecca, 21, 113

Sarah, 33
Sarah M., 89
Stephen, 44
Timothy, 25, 60, 67, 69, 110
Walter, 118
William, 36, 41, 49, 66, 105, 109, 122
Hikbi, Willem, 10
Hikkes, Johannes, 10
  Timotheus, 10
  Elizabeth, 14
Hiks, Johannes Jurry, 16
  James, 12, 13, 14, 16, 19
  Maria, 12
  Robertson, 19
Hill, Jacob, 107
Hilleken, Elizabeth, 13
Hilleker, Elizabeth, 27, 58
  Jacob, 29
  James, 29
  Johannes, 101
Hilliker, John, 114
  Nathaniel G., 115
Hinckley, Nathaniel, 116
Hiskok, Elsje, 10
  Willem, 10
Hitchcock, Austin Brundage, 91
  Charles E., 89, 91, 114
  Irving, 89
  Jane Ann, 113
  Louisa Catharine, 87
  Simeon, 86
Hoagland, (See also Hogeland, Hoogland)
  Abraham, 85
  Barbara E., 85
  Sarah Amelia, 84, 114
  William B., 84, 85
  William Cornelius VanCleef, 85
Hoff, (See also Haff)
  Abraham, 51
  Annatje, 17
  Anthony, 16
  Cathrina, 26
  Femmetje, 13, 14
  Hannah, 50, 55
  Jacob, 28, 33
  Jan, 33, 104
  Johannes, 13
  Johannes Schurry, 15
  John, 35, 51, 104
  Laurence, 53, 54
  Laurens, 13, 14, 16, 17, 21, 22, 23, 28, 33, 99
  Lawrens, 36
  Maria, 54
  Oliver, 36
  Peter, 35
  Petrus, 23, 29
  Pieter, 13, 15, 17, 22, 26, 27, 29, 99, 100
  Phebe, 23, 57, 59, 62
  Sara, 21
Hoffman, Annatje, 17
  Anthony, 42, 57

Index

Carel, 14, 15, 16, 19, 21, 29, 34, 44
Carl, 17, 20, 23
Catharina, 14, 99
Catharine, 51, 55
Catherine, 56, 75, 76, 109
Cathr, 46
Cathrina, 15, 29, 32
Cathrine, 35
Charles, 55, 57
Cornelia, 39, 44, 101
Daniel, 7, 17, 32, 37, 41, 57, 61, 67, 79, 103
David, 32
Eleanor, 56, 64
Elizabeth, 37, 39, 54, 55, 56, 70, 73, 103
Ellenor, 59
Henry, 39
Herman, 44
Hesje, 15
Hester, 15, 21, 32, 37, 103
Jane Ann, 109
John, 39, 43, 61
Jurriaan, 14
Lodewyk, 21
Margareth, 41
Margriet, 19
Maria, 17, 20, 31, 59, 71, 77, 78, 79, 80, 81, 100, 101
Marten, 39
Mary, 33, 40, 43, 70
Michael, 55, 57
Michal, 59
Michel, 7, 11
Nelly, 34, 54
Nicolaas, 8
Olivia Louisa, 79
Peter, 64
Peter Anthony, 68
Petrus, 23
Philip Verplanck, 44
Rebecca, 105
Robert, 109
Sally, 67
William, 12, 64, 68
Hofman, Cornelia, 30
Hester, 16
Johannes, 11
Juriaan, 16
Jurrien, 12
Maria, 27
Hogeland (*See also Hoagland, Hoogland*)
Aaltje, 19
Abraham, 103
Antje, 28, 30, 42, 47
Dina, 31, 38
Gerhardina, 28
Willem, 9, 20
Hoghlandt, John, 107
Holder, C. M., 120
Esther M., 94
Holmes, Elizabeth M., 112
Herbert H., 117
Holms, George, 107
Holser, Barbara, 11
Holst, Aaltje, 25, 28
Barbara, 12
Pieter, 99
Hooghtaling, Elsje, 52
Eve, 52
Henry, 52
Magdalen, 52
Mary, 52
Matthias, 52
Susannah, 52
Hoogteeling, Gertrude, 51
Hooghteyling, Ariaantje, 16
Geertruy, 16
Neeltje, 37, 48
Rachel Johs., 104
Hooghteylingh, Annatje, 100
Maria, 16
Neeltje, 16
Wilhelmus T., 104
Hoogland, (*See also Hoagland, Hogeland*)
Aaltje, 10, 14
Abraham, 54, 58
Alida, 24
Antje, 24, 25
Dirk, 24, 25, 27
Engeltje, 9
Gerhardina, 23, 24, 28
Martha, 54
Nelly, 76
Peggy, 27
Susanna, 23, 26
Willem, 10
William, 76
William B., 109
William Brower, 58
Hoogteeling, Johannes, 9, 11
Maria, 11
Neeltje, 18
Rachel, 9
Sara, 11
Wilhelmus, 10
Hoogteling, Johannes, 10
Hoogteyling, Ariaantje, 14, 18, 21, 26
Elizabeth, 28
Geertje, 33
Geertruid, 23
Geertruy, 26, 29
Jan, 16, 104
Johannes, 24, 25, 26, 28, 48
Lydia, 48
Maria, 12, 18, 21
Neeltje, 24, 25
Sara, 12
Hoogteylingh, Geertje, 35
Henricus, 35
John, 35
Hoogteylingt, Barbara, 19
Hopkins, Benjamin, 114
Susan Mary, 87
Hoppe, John Fred, 119
Horsner, Jacob, 101
Horton, Almira, 111
Elvin B., 115
Isaac Benjamin, 94
Joseph, 121
Tamar, 116
Thos. Edward, 121
W. James, 121
Hosier, Daniel H., 109
Howard, Anna D., 119
James, 119
Howe, Edward, 111
Henrick B., 111
Howell, Charles J., Jr., 87, 88, 113
Charles James, 87
Cornelius Dubois, 87
Harriet Mulford, 114
Lydia Henchman, 88
Hoy, Katie F., 118
Hoyt, Susie E., 121
William B., 121
Hughson, (*See also Hewson, Huson*)
Catharine, 108
Jeremiah D., 110
Maria, 104
Hulst, Ann, 109
Hults, Chas. Wesley, 96
Humphrey, Elizabeth, 42, 108
Hunt, Anna S., 90
Emma F., 119
Gilead, 35, 44, 101
Moses, 44
Peter, 42
Rachel, 55, 58, 62, 67
Sarah, 42
Simeon, 35
William D., 110
William H., 116
Huson, Joseph E., 111
Hutchins, Elizabeth, 108
Maria G., 85, 112
Hyat, Abraham, 106
Hynds, Elmer J., 122
Floyd B., 122
Hyzer, John Cornell, 80
Michael T., 80, 81
Michael Thomas, 81

I

Ingerum, Phebe, 15
Phoebe, 20

Ireland, Thos., 120

Irving, Edwin, 121

J

Jacklin, Mary F., 114
Jackson, Amelia Matilda, 57, 108
  Daniel, 110
  Elizabeth, 61
  Hattie, 120
  Joseph, 57, 108
  Mary Ann, 112
  Seward Baker, 96
  William A., 117
Jacobs, Catharine, 64
  Caty, 55
  Francis, 8
  Henry, 55
  Mary, 51, 54, 57
Jacobuz, Gerrit, 47
Jacobus, 47
Jacocks, (*See also various spellings following Gacocks, Tsicoks*)
  Benjamin, 50
  Easter, 105
  Elizabeth, 34
  Francis, 34
  Geertruy, 34, 49
  Hannah, 50
  Helen, 71
  Jane, 73
  Joseph Henry, 112
  Mary, 47, 105
  Thomas, 41, 105, 107
  Thomas T., 71, 73
  William, 41
Jacokes, Geertruy, 31
  Thomas Fr., 104
Jacoks, Thomas, 35
Jacox, Wilhelmyntie, 73
Jakoks, Ruth, 47
  Thomas W., 47
James, Phoebe, 109
Jamieson, Julia Ann, 86
Janssen, Antje, 20
  Cathrina, 26
  Johannes, 19
  Nicolaas, 26
  Petrus, 26
  Richard, 20, 99
Jay, John, 32, 35, 43, 102
  Cathrina, 32
  Henricus, 43
  Joseph, 35
Jaycox, Annie E., 116
  Clinton V. R., 117
  Cora I., 118
  Cornelius, 115
  George L., 121
  Lottie May, 122
  Sarah Jane, 115
Jeacock, Mary, 54
Jeacocks, Anne, 45
  Benjamin, 58, 61, 67
  Catharine, 54
  Caty, 61
  Elizabeth, 60
  Ezekiel, 58

Gertrude, 54, 58
Jonathan, 45, 62, 63
Maria, 58
Mary, 65
Rachel, 66
Robert Wiltsie, 67
Sarah, 62
Thomas, 54, 58, 60, 63
Thomas T., 66
Jecocks, Abm. Stoutenburgh, 51
  Francis, 31
  Gertrude, 53
  Jane, 31
  Mary, 51
  Thomas T., 51
Jemens, Marytje, 16
  Meindert, 17
  Thomas, 17
Jennifer, Mary E., 115
Jennings, Almina C., 113
Jewel, (*See also Juel, Juwel*)
  Aaltje, 16
  Anne, 45
  Barent, 52
  Caty, 62
  Eliza Ann, 71
  Elizabeth, 62, 68
  George, 16, 27, 28, 37, 49, 58, 61
  Gitty, 68
  Harmanus, 27
  Harme, 58, 61
  Henry, 45, 52, 54, 58, 62, 68, 71
  John, 45, 49, 52, 99, 104
  John H., 62
  Joris, 23
  Maria, 27, 58
  Martha, 22, 58, 108
  Mary, 54, 64
  Nancy, 28
  Patty, 52
  Phebe, 72, 107
  Sara, 21, 23, 25
  Sarah, 59
Jewell, ——, 110
  Celia Eliza, 80
  Cynthia Jane, 81
  Enos, 109
  Ezekiel, 78, 79, 80, 81, 109
  Hannah, 80
  Henry Davis, 81
  Henry T., 113
  Jeremiah Van Kleeck, 78
  Maria, 110
  Mary Ann, 79
  Phebe, 75
  Phoebe, 76
  William T., 117
Jewl, Elizabeth, 40
  John, 40
Johnes, Elizabeth, 25
Jarry, 24

Jeremiah, 22
Jerry, 29
Rachel, 29
Seth, 104
Johnson, Agnes E., 118
  Andries, 41
  Evan M., 116
  Henry, 43, 102, 105
  Hiram, 121
  Jane, 101
  John, 37
  Lena, 49
  Margaret E., 114
  Margaretha, 43
  Martha, 104, 121
  Samuel, 101
  Sarah J., 115
  Susan A., 115
  Thomas, 49, 106
  William, 41
Johnston, Mary, 96
  Mary M., 118
  Robert, 119
Jones, (*See also Johnes*)
  Dorcas, 82, 84
  Elizabeth, 104
  Ella Estella, 92
  Emma J., 121
  Eustacia, 112
  George W,. 112, 119
  Helen, 84
  Helen M., 114
  Henrietta N., 116
  Henrietta Needham, 87
  Henry, 92, 115, 116
  Jeremias, 9
  Jerry, 14, 16
  Johannes, 16
  John, 86, 87, 89, 113
  Joseph Jackson, 89
  Lydia, 14, 55
  Maria, 113
  Matilda R., 93, 94
  Stiles P., 120
  Thomas, 9
  William, 112
  Zophar I., 112
Jorksen, (*See also Jurrigsen*)
  Catharina, 7
  Johannes, 7
  Willem, 7
Jurrey, Pally, 103
Jurrigsen, Johannes, 7
Jurry, (*See also Schurry, Sherry*)
  Annatje, 18, 21
  Cathrina, 23, 28
  Cathrine, 41, 48
  Catrina, 16
  Elizabeth, 16, 29
  Lydia, 16, 19
  Mary, 40, 46

Index

Sara, 100
Juel, Henricus, 13
  Jan, 13

June, John H., 71
  John Rynders, 71
  Justus, Childs, 103

Juwel, Engeltje, 8
  Jan, 12
  John, 8

K

Kane, James, 114
Keizerryk, Bastiaan, 7
Kennedy, Abm. Losee, 60
  Aly, 107
  Benjamin, 60, 62, 66
  Hannah, 62
  Jane, 66
  Mary, 56, 58
Kenworthy, Mary, 111
Kick, Jacomyntje, 8
Kidney, Helena, 16
  Johanna, 8
Kigerer, Doretje, 10
Kilmer, Loyen, 96
  Preston H., 96
Kily, William, 101
King, Alexander, 119
  Hamilton, 118
  William, 40
Kingman, John C., 118
Kip, Abraham, 27, 31
  Cathrine, 39, 101
  Henry, 39, 45
  Jane, 31
  Margaretha, 31
  Maria, 27
  Samuel, 102
  Sarah, 45
Kirkham, Thaddeus, 109
Klump, Almira, 79, 112
  Anna, 61
  Catharine, 51

Cornelius, 73, 74, 76, 78, 79, 81
  Elizabeth, 52
  Harriot, 68
  Joanna, 78, 111
  John Luckey, 73
  Mary Jane, 81
  Peter, 38, 76
  Rachel, 56
  Rebecca, 109
  Samuel, 66, 74
  Zachariah, 44, 51, 52, 56, 66, 68
  Zacharias, 38
  Zechariah, 61
Knapp, Altha C., 121
  Benjamin, 117
  Bertha M., 121
  Chauncey, 89
  Chauncy, 86
  Clarence C., 86
  George V. D., 121
  Hamilton N., 113
  Ida, 95. 96, 120
  James Henry, 111
  James W., 116
  Jemima, 111
  Joseph G., 114
  Lewis B., 120
  Marietta, 86
  Mary, 113
  Mary Angel. 86

Sarah Ann T., 86
  Sidman Thorn, 86
  William F., 117
Kneffen, Antje, 17
Knickebakker, Johannes, 8
Kniepper, Laurens, 99
Kniffen, Anna. 21
  Antje, 13, 15
  Lewis, 21
  Rachel, 13
Knox, William H., 94
  William Melbourne, 94
Koopman, (*See also Coopman*)
  Cathrine, 27
  Jacob. 27
Kosse Jacomyntje, 9
Kouwenhoven, Engeltje, 23
Kramer, Anna, 18
  Margriet, 18
  Zacharias, 18
Krankheid, Francyntje, 7
Krankheit, Margaret, 52
Kronchheid, Mary, 107
Krymer, (*See also Cremer*)
  Geertruy, 10
  Johannes, 10
  Lena, 10
Kudner, Alexander, 110
Kwakkenbosch, Jacomyntje, 11

L

Laan, Jacob, 16
Ladoe, Ezekiel, 107
  Tompkins, 107
Ladue, Augusta, 115
la Due, Sarah, 32
Laffin, Patrick, 119
Lahne, Christina, 28
  Jacob, 21, 28
  John, 21
Landon, Mary T., 117
Lane, (*See also Laan, Lahne*)
  Harry H., 116
  Henrik, 19
  Jacob, 19, 24, 99
  Laurens, 24
Lansing, Gerrit, 102
Lansingh, Mary, 43
  Peter, 43
la Roy, (*See also la Rue, la Rou, Le Roy*)
  Aart Middag, 9, 44, 49
  Abraham Middag, 105
  Anna, 41, 105
  Anne, 50

Baltus van Kleeck, 15
  Barent, 28
  Bawtje, 26
  Charity, 43, 105
  David, 16
  Elizabeth, 7, 10, 13, 31, 32, 36, 40, 46, 103
  Emilia, 25
  Esther, 30
  Francis, 41, 44, 106
  Frans, 8, 9, 18, 21, 26
  Geertruy, 33
  Gerritje, 49
  Hannes, 32
  Hester, 17, 100, 102
  Jacob, 48
  Jan, 10
  Janneke, 30
  Johannes, 11, 13, 15, 18, 24, 25, 28, 33
  Johannes Rome, 44
  Maria, 11, 18, 20
  Michel, 8
  Pally, 47, 106
  Peter, 48

Petrus, 21
Pieter, 16
Sally, 48
Sara, 8, 101, 103
Sarah, 44
Simeon, 8, 30, 40
Simon, 10
Stephen, 41
la Rou, Elizabeth, 24
  Frans, 24
Larson, Thora K., 121
la Rue, Johannes, 21
Levi, 21
Lasse, Catharina, 12
  Eipje, 12
  Geertruy, 12
  Willem, 12
Lassen, (*See also Lansing, Lasse, Lassing, Lasson, Lauson, Lawson, Lossing*)
  Annatje, 12
  Cathrina, 17
  Elizabeth, 11, 13
  Femmetje, 41

Geertruy, 14
Goris, 17
Grietje, 13
Henricus, 16
Isaac, 15, 18
Johannes, 13, 14, 15
Lena, 13
Margriet, 15
Maria, 13
Matheus, 18
Peter, 11
Pieter, 13, 14, 16
Pieter Willem, 13
Sara, 13, 15
Simeon, 15, 16, 17
Willem, 13, 17
Lassing, Elizabeth, 62
Lasson, Andries, 17, 22, 30, 36, 44, 48, 105
Anna, 36
Annatje, 20
Benjamin, 15, 25
Carel, 44
Catharina, 20
Cathrina, 19, 33, 34
Cathrine, 44, 45
Celetje, 22, 41, 44
Clara, 19
Cornelis, 32
Daniel, 42
Elizabeth, 33, 34, 35, 36, 37, 42, 44, 47, 103, 104
Esther, 29
Geertruy, 22, 49
Getty, 107
Gideon, 59
Hannah, 49
Henrik, 30, 102
Henrik Heermans, 23
Henry, 36, 45, 102
Isaac, 22
Jacobus, 29, 101
James, 33, 36
Jan, 32, 41, 102
Johannes, 19
John, 35
John Coock, 22
John J., 106
John P., 49
Laurens, 100
Lena, 106
Margaretha, 30
Maria, 20, 26, 31, 101
Mary, 27, 34, 38, 41, 44, 48, 102, 106
Matth, 44
Matthew, 35, 39, 105
P. A., 37, 44
Peter, 36, 40
Peter A., 42
Peter Andries, 36
Peter J., 49
Petrus, 26, 30
Pieter, 20, 22, 23, 25, 30
Pieter Andr., 29
Pieter Andries, 33
Richard, 20, 21
Richard Cook, 22

Richard Coock, 23
Robert, 37
Sara, 22
Sarah, 34, 35, 40
Selly, 101
Simeon, 15, 20, 39, 101
Willem, 22, 29, 50
William, 20, 30, 49, 59, 106
Latchen, Anna, 31
Latsel, Elizabeth, 62
James, 62
Latson, Anna, 25
Annatje, 24, 28
Jacobus, 28
James, 43
Maria, 57
Simon, 43
William, 57
Lattin, Charles H., 121
Lauer, Annie, 119
Catharine Elizabeth, 117
Eldora, 91
Mary H., 116
Philip, 91, 120
Laughlin, Alexander, 39
James, 39
Laughter, Alexander, 43
Elizabeth, 43
Laughton, Alexander, 104
Launsbergen, Sara, 12
Laurence, Lillie, 119
Wm. H., 119
Laurens, Joseph, 34
Stephen, 34
Lauson, Purdy, 111
Lawrence, Edward J., 93, 95
Harriet, 110
Obadiah P., 115
Sherwood E., 95
Stephen, 104
Lawrens, Sarah, 105
Lawson, Abm., 57
Andrew, 54, 57, 108
Catharine, 58, 59, 62, 72, 112
Caty, 56
Charles, 70
Christina, 55
Daniel, 56
Edgar, 112
Eliza, 71, 73
Elizabeth, 52, 55, 58
Elizabeth Jane, 74
Esther Ann, 82
Gertrude, 74, 111
Gitty, 53, 56, 58, 62, 70, 72
Hannah, 56, 60, 61, 82, 109
Helen Van Der Belt, 85, 113
Helena, 55
James, 54, 69
James Alexander, 82
John, 53, 55, 61, 69
John J., 52
Julia Ann, 72
Letty Ann, 74
Magdalena, 61
Margaret, 61, 62, 72, 74

Maria, 56, 59
Martha, 71
Mary, 52, 55, 82
Mary Ann, 72
Matthew, 54, 56, 59, 72, 74, 82
Matthew P., 52, 61
Peggy, 52, 54
Peter, 51, 54, 58, 73
Peter A., 51
Peter Clock, 57
Peter P., 55, 70, 72, 75
Phebe, 69
Polly, 52
Purdy, 111
Rachel, 54
Rachel Losee, 69
Rebecca, 19
Robert, 112
Sally, 52
Sally Ellenor, 71
Samuel Ferdun, 57
Sarah, 70, 72
Sarah Ann, 70
Simon, 54, 57, 71, 73
Simon, Junr., 61
Stephen, 60
Susan, 75
Thomas P., 71, 73
William, 55, 56, 57, 60, 62, 69, 70, 72, 74
William P., 53
Wyntie, 51
Lazurley, Abraham, 24
Sara, 24
Leavens, Cathrine, 106
Lee, Annie, 117
Cora A., 118
Emma, 95
Gertrude, 120
Henry G., 117
Leet, Catharine, 53
Nathan, 53
Leids, Catelyntje, 17
Leidt, (*See also Light*)
Catelina, 40
Mary, 12
Lek, Catrina, 10
Lengden, Elizabeth, 8, 9
Nelly, 9
Thomas, 9
Lent, Abraham, 7, 13, 28, 32, 33
Abraham, Junr., 30, 33
Abraham Brinkerhoff, 28
Antje, 30, 32
Catharina, 9, 14
Catrina, 9, 10
Cornelia, 32, 39, 103
Elizabeth, 9, 33
Isaac, 7, 32, 39, 103
Izaac, 7
Jerry, 116
Johannes, 9
Maria, 102
Metje, 39
LeQuier, Abraham, 106

Index

LeRoy, Leroy, (See also LaRoy)
Aart Middag, 39
Anna Maria, 69
Deborah, 64, 68
Elizabeth, 50, 55, 61
Francina, 57, 61, 67
Francis, 39
Getty, 49
Jonn, 60, 63, 66
John J., 71
John T., 70
Joseph, 63
Levi, 66
Maria, 27
Maria Forman, 96
Mary Elizabeth, 71
Meredith H., 118
Pally, 41
Peter, 69
Sally, 41
Sarah, 49
Simeon, 49
Stephen, 70
Lester, Robert, 101
Thomas, 101
Letsel, Charlotte, 65
Joseph Rogers, 68
William, 68
Letson, Jeremiah, 55
Richard, 61
William, 55, 61, 65
Lewis, (See also Louis, Louys)
———, 108
Catelina, 49
Elias, 43
Israel, 15
Jacomina, 31
James E., 112
John, 102
Leonard, 75
Leonard T., 76
Maria, 11
Mary, 43
Rachel, 15, 99
Sarah, 76
Seymour, 110
Thomas, 8, 31, 43, 49, 75
William, 24, 25
Leyster, John, 51
Libston, (See also Livingston)
Catharina, 8, 9
Jacobus, 8
Judith, 8
Light, (See also Leidt)
Catalina, 54
Catelina, 31
Elizabeth, 40
May, 42, 45
William, 40, 45
Limmerin, Elizabeth, 12
Linn, Jacob, 116
Lions, Elizabeth, 40
Mary, 37, 41
Samuel, 40
Little, Betty, 75

Henrietta Orinda, 79
Jack, 80
Jack Potter, 77, 79
John, 83
John Potter, 110
Mary Eliza, 77
Rachel, 77, 83
Richard, 77
Samuel, 80
Sarah Helen, 77
Stephen, 77
Susan, 77, 79, 80, 83
Livingston, (See also Libston)
George, 100
Gilbert, 12
Gilbert, Junr., 37
Margareth, 37
Lockwood, Elizabeth, 107
Louisa M., 89, 91, 92
Margaret Ann, 114
Logan, Nathanael, 118
Loosee, John, 21
Joseph, 21
Lory, Grace E., 121
Grace L., 122
Grace Louise, 95
Mary K., 122
Mary Kesiah, 95
Wm. H. A., 121
William Henry Augustus, 95
Los, Bastiaan, 7
Daniel, 7
Magdalene, 7
Losee, Andrew, 67
Anna, 40
Catharina, 13, 15
Elizabeth, 17, 58, 63, 80, 81, 109
Jan, 13
Jannetje, 9, 23
Johannes, 24, 25
John, 24, 25
Letitia, 24, 25
Maria, 56, 60, 70, 76
Mary E., 87, 113
Neeltje, 13
Pieter, 23
Rachel, 25
Sarah, 60, 62, 66
Wm. H., 121
William Wilson, 67
Lossing, Abraham, 65, 67
Andrew, 64
Anna, 67
Benjamin, 65
Benjn. P., 62
Catharine, 67
Eliza, 67
Elizabeth, 60, 63, 67
Esther, 60, 65
George, 63
Gitty, 62, 64, 65
Hannah, 67
Jane, 62
John, 64, 67
Margaret, 64, 67

Martin, 63
Mary, 67
Matthew, 64
Peter, 65
Peter P., 67
Rachel, 65
Sarah, 64
Simon, 65
William, 65
Louis, Frances, 8
Izaac, 7
Marytje, 7
Richard, 7
Lounsberri, Sara, 10
Lounsberry, (See also Launsbergen)
Mary Ann, 111
Louw, Abraham, 19
Adolf, 16
Elizabeth, 18
Jacob, 14, 18
Jacobus, 14
Jan, 16, 18
Johannes, 10, 14, 19
Laurens, 18
Saartje, 18
Sara, 19
Willem, 10, 17, 18, 25
Louys, Leendert, 39
Thomas, 39
Low, Aaron, 39, 62
Abraham, 48, 60
Andrew, 45, 57
Aron, 48
Brechje, 33
Cynthia, 62, 108
Elizabeth, 24
Hannes, 24
Jan, 33
John, 68
Peter, 57, 60
Rebecca, 39, 45
Sally Ann, 68
Sara, 30
Sarah, 40
Willem, 24
William, 24
Lowe, Emily, 108
Robert L., 115
Lucas, Edward, 112
Stephen, 112
William, 112
Luckee, Celetje, 40
Jane, 40
Luckey, Benjamin, 49
Elizabeth, 80, 109
Gertrude, 109
Gitty, 69
Helen, 111
Hellen, 75
James, 45, 73
James Edgar, 73
Jane, 19, 45, 46, 60, 62, 73, 74, 75, 76, 77, 78, 79, 80, 81
Jannetje, 35
Janny, 22
John, 66, 69, 73

315

John R., 80
Joseph, 47, 49
Margaretha, 47
Mary Ann, 68, 84, 85, 109
Rachel, 73
Rebecca, 109
Robert, 37, 109
Robert Thompson, 71
S. Angeline, 85
Sally Angeline, 78, 112
Samuel, 37
Samuel, Junr., 68, 71, 73, 75, 76, 78, 110
Susan, 80
Thomas Pinckney, 66
Luckie, Marian, 82
Lucky, Celetje, 30; 101
 Celia, 27
 Charles, 64
 Jane, 16, 26, 30
 John, 64
 Marian, 83
 Rachel, 110
 Samuel, 30
Ludlow, Mary, 8
Luister, Antje, 99
 Ariaantje, 8

Arriaantje, 7
Cornelis, 8, 9, 11
Jan, 11
Johannes, 11
Matthys, 11
Neeltje, 10
Sara, 7
Luke, Nancy, 111
Luyster, Aaltje, 23
 Anna, 60, 61, 63, 66
 Anne, 7
 Catharine, 75, 114
 Catherine, 80
 Caty, 70
 Charles Edgar, 87
 Cornelis, 22
 Dirck, 23
 Dirk, 31, 100
 Edgar, 77, 87, 114
 Evah, 48
 George, 54
 Gerrit, 22, 31
 Harriet, 116
 Hattie Conover, 89
 James Young, 94
 Jennie, 88
 John, 49, 67, 82, 110

John, Junr., 54, 114
John Dewitt, 90
John H., 88, 89, 90
John Henry, 78, 114
John M., 60
John Yonni, 82
Letty M. H., 109
Letty Maria Hulst, 67
Margaret Ann, 60
Maria Ann, 81, 112
Mathew, 78
Matthew, 77, 81, 89
Matthias, 49
Petrus, 22, 23
Sara, 23
Sarah L., 117
Susannah, 31
Warren Elisha, 89
Willemina, 22
Lynderson, Sarah, 72, 74
Lynch, Kitty, 119
Lynn, May Ethel, 122
Lyons, (*See also Lions*)
 Maria, 32
 Mary, 103

M

McAvoy, Mary Frances, 115
McBride, Elizabeth, 107
 Mary, 64
McCarrick, (*See also McKerric*)
 Eliza, 70
 Francis, 70
McClave, (*See also Miclef, Van Cleef*)
 Maria, 16
 William, 100
McCleary, Elizabeth, 114
McCloud, Helena, 37
McCollister, William, 37, 105
McCord, Cora, 117
 Edwin Yates, 91
 Jannetje, 37
 Johannes, 42
 John Ed., 91
 John Erwin, 91
 Minnie I., 117
 Sarah Maria, 91
 William, 37, 42
McCradle, James, 37
McCreedy, James, 103
McDonald, Sylvester, 107
McDonnell, Maggie, 119
McFaddan, John, 108
McFadyen, Mary, 57
McFerson, Archibald, 22
 William, 22
McKee, Carrie Dayton, 121
McKenny, James, 101
McKerric, Amy Diamond, 65
 Francis, 65, 68

McKerrick, Caty, 63
 Francis, 63
McLeen, Jan, 30
 Meindert, 30
McNeal, James, 34
 William, 34
McNear, Ida, 117
 Isaac, 118
McNeel, Maria, 103
McNiel, Jan, 30
 Meindert, 30
Maar, Phoebe, 44
Maas, Fanny, 100
Mabey, (*See also Maibe, Maybe*)
 Rachel, 21
Mabie, Nancy, 65
Maby, Jno., 119
 Nancy, 33, 60
Macauley, Robert C., 118
Mackey, (*See also Mecke*)
 David, 34
 Goris, 34
MacKinlay, Helen Louise, 120
 Marion Wilson, 94
 Mary L. Maholm, 94
 Peter S., 94
Madden, Beatrice Lockwood, 93
 George Cole, 118
 Wm. Burton, 93
Madrass, (*See also Metross*)
 Maria, 24, 25
Maholm, Mary Lee, 94
Maibe, Rachel, 16

Maloney, Richard James, 122
 Wm. R., Jr., 122
Mandigo, Jeremia, 102
Manne, Anna, 102
 Richard, 28
 Wynes, 28
Manning, Jacob, 111
 Lucy, 111
Marginson, Mary A., 116
Markle, Sally, 51
Maroney, Delia E., 118
Marquet, James H., 117
 Jerlene, 117
Marshall, Sarah, 110
Martenette, M. Jennie, 117
Martense, Susanna, 7
Martin, Alida A., 116
 Henry, 107
 James, 109
Marvin, Charles M., 113
 Charlotte A., 113
 Mary, 86, 114
 Sarah E., 114
Massie, Jeanette, 117
Masten, Catharine, 60
 Henrik, 8
 Sara, 8
 Sophia, 8
Maston, Aart, 13, 15, 38
 Anna, 29, 42
 Ariaantje, 13
 Catharine, 66, 68
 Cornelis, 13
 Elisha, 40
 Elizabeth, 18
 Henrik, 17, 24, 25, 28, 29

Index

Jacobus, 46
Jan, 19
Marretje, 17
Meindert, 15
  Peter, 38, 46, 105
  Sara, 18, 19, 24, 25
Mathews, Hazel Alice, 94
  Mary A., 96
  Mary Alice, 93, 95
  Raymond, 94
  Robert S., 94
Matthew, Robert, 48
  Samuel, 48
Matthews, Anna E., 117
  Emma Louisa, 90
  Jennie, 117
  John R., 90
  Maria, 112
  Mary, 42
  Mary Alice, 119
  Mary Gertrude, 90
  Robert S., 118
  Samuel, 42
Matross, Amy, 50
Maxfield, Elizabeth, 53
  Maria, 58
  Mary, 61
Maybe, (*See also Mabey*)
  Nancy, 46
Mayers, Josephine, 119
Mead, Anne, 107
  Enos, 109
  Jeremiah, 57
  Jesper, 57
Mecke, (*See also Mackey*)
  Carel, 15
  David, 13, 15
  Maria, 13
Meddaugh, Catharine E., 87, 88
  George W., 117
  James B., 117
  William T., 113
Medel, Ellen, 112
Medlar, (*See also Middelaar*)
  James, 56
  John, 56, 59
  William, 59
Medler, Jane, 73
  Peter, 73
  Zachariah, 73
Meeke, Rebecca, 99
Meirs, Abraham, 69
  Phebe, 71
  Reuben, 69, 71, 74
  Warren Delancey, 74
Merckel, Sally, 37
  Sarah, 105
Mercy, Esther J., 122
Merrit, Elizabeth, 66, 67
Merritt, Edward, 111
  Elizabeth, 69
Mesier, Abraham, 30
  Catherina, 30
  Matthew, 108
  Peter, 30
Messerol, Elizabeth, 45

Metross, (*See also Madrass*)
  Polly, 27
Meyer, Aaltje, 28
  Abraham, 42
  Adolf, 28, 30, 42, 47
  Amy, 47
  Antje, 42
  Brechje, 16, 18, 33, 102
  Cathrine, 35
  Cornelia, 7, 30, 31, 33, 35, 102
  Cornelia Hood, 37
  David, 47
  Eva, 33
  Gilbert, 37
  Gilbert McPhoedrix, 37
  Hans Frederik, 12
  Happy, 47
  Jacob, 31, 102
  Johannes, 7
  John, 41, 42, 61, 106
  Mercy, 31
  Nicolaas, 12
  Peter, 54
  Petrus, 48
  Reuben, 61
  Samuel, 35, 48, 54
  Simeon Johnson, 37
  William, 36, 41, 47
Meyers, (*See also Meirs*)
  Abraham, 50, 84
  Caroline, 112
  Catharine, 112
  Eli, 113
  Elias, 39
  Eliza, 113
  John, 57
  Martha, 57
  Salley, 50
  Samuel, 39
Meyrs, Abraham, 83
  Ann, 83
  Mercy, 83
  Schenck, 83
  Susan, 83
Micki, (*See also Meeke*)
  Rebecca, 10
Miclef, (*See also McClave*)
  Maria, 12
Middag, Aart, 38, 49
  Anne, 49
  Elizabeth, 38
  Geertje, 8, 9, 18, 21, 26
  Helletje, 23
  Hester, 17, 23, 24
  Hilletje, 18, 21, 24, 30, 39, 47, 99
  Jacobus, 9, 17, 38, 44
  Jacobus Middag, 38
  James, 58
  Jesse, 58
  Joris, 18, 23, 24, 26
  Maria, 102
  Sarah, 44
  Zachariah, 44
Middagh, Aert, 68
  Aurt, 65

  Catherine, 109
  Eliza, 63
  George, 68
  Helen, 109
  Henry, 66
  Hester, 63
  Jacobus, 57
  Jacomina, 60
  James, 55
  James G., 63, 107
  James I., 63
  John, 57, 65, 109
  Lena, 63
  Paul, 60, 66, 68
  Peter, 55
  Sarah, 57, 63
  Thomas Casey, 68
Middelaar, (*See also Medlar*)
  Arie, 19, 26
  Aris, 34
  Jan, 102
  Lodewyk, 34
  Maria, 34
  Pieternella, 19
Midlaar, Arie, 11
  Johannes, 11
Milgen, Pally, 34
  Robert, 34
Millar, Alfred, 73
  Jeremiah, 108
  John, 71, 73
  Letty, 71
  Mary, 73
  Sarah, 108
Millard, Jeremiah, 113
  John E., 116
Miller, Ada L., 117
  Catharine, 110
  Elizabeth, 36, 39, 45
  Helen, 109
  Helena, 59
  Hendrick, 59
  Jane, 65
  John, 36, 69, 111
  John Miller, 41
  Joseph, 108
  Lena, 40, 45
  Lydia, 52, 106
  Margareth, 43
  Mary, 50, 71
  Mercy, 111
  Peter, 41, 50, 59, 65, 105
  Sarah Emans, 69
  Walter, 117
Milliagen, John, 32
  Robert, 32
Milligan, (*See also Milgen*)
  Helena, 38
  Robert, 38
Milligans, James, 44
  Robert, 44
Mills, James, 106
  Judith, 84
  Samuel H., 113
Miserol, Jannetje, 48
Mitchell, Emilinda, 111
Mollin, Anne, 45

317

Monell, Robert, 116
Monfoort, Albert, 73, 81
  Albert J., 58
  Aletta, 66, 110
  Alida Jane, 81
  Ann, 108
  Anna, 58
  Anna Maria, 63
  Barbara Eve, 75
  Catherine, 76
  Celia, 75
  Clara, 38, 105
  Cornelius, 81
  Daniel, 71
  Dominicus, 67
  Ellen Maria, 75
  Francis Losee, 63
  Garret Stryker, 81
  Henry A., 73, 75, 77, 78
  Hiram, 76
  Jacobus, 69, 108
  James, 69
  Jane, 67, 75, 77, 79, 81
  Jane Ann, 71
  Jannetje, 99
  Jeremiah, 58
  John, 63, 66, 71, 73
  John A., 75, 79, 81
  John Angevine, 78
  John Bergen, 78
  Letty, 61, 64
  Magdalen, 74
  Magdelen, 108
  Margaret, 55, 108
  Maria, 65, 69, 70, 71, 73, 74, 76, 81
  Mary, 81
  Mary Ann, 79
  Martin, 71, 76, 78, 79, 81
  Oliver Perry, 79
  Peter J., 109
  Schenck, 76
  Stephen, 55, 58, 63
  Susan, 110
  Susannah, 71
  Tcharick, 71
Monfoot, James V. Keuren, 69
  Stephen, 107
  Tcharick, 69
Monfort, Albert, 82, 110
  Aletta, 85, 86
  Alletta M., 84
  Alletta Maria, 111
  Catharine Belinda, 89
  Catharine E., 88
  Charick, 74
  Cornelius Van Cleef, 85
  Delia D., 87
  Eleanor Kate, 89
  Elizabeth, 110
  Hannah, 110
  Ida, 91, 96, 120
  James Henry, 89
  James S., 85, 113
  Jane, 74, 82
  Jane Ann, 86, 113
  Jeremiah V. C., 110
  John, 85, 88, 112
  John A., 82
  John Henry, 85
  John Jacob, 88
  John P., 116
  John T., 111
  Kate E., 115
  Margaret, 110
  Maria Louisa, 88
  Maria Needham, 89
  Mary Ann, 114
  Mary Jane, 85
  Minnie, 94
  Peter P., 112
  Phebe F., 114
  Saraettie, 90
  Sarah, 111
    Sarah G. Teller, 88
  Stephen, 85, 110
  Stephen I., 112
  Stephen P., 89, 114
  Susan, 82, 83, 84, 112
  Susan Ann, 88
  Washington Jones, 85
Monger, Christian, 64
  James, 64
Montagne, Apollonia, 23, 27
Montfoort, Albert, 23, 29, 40, 47, 100
  Albert, Junr., 51, 55
  Anna, 51
  Antje, 7
  Celetje, 40
  Claratje, 11
  Cornelius, 55
  Dominicus, 36
  Elbert, 21, 26
  Esther, 13
  Francis Losee, 109
  Hendrik, 10
  Henrik, 26
  Ida, 14
  Jan, 26
  Jannetje, 23, 36
  Johanna, 47
  Johannes, 11, 17
  Latitia, 49
  Letitia, 37
  Louisa, 16, 23
  Louisje, 12, 13
  Maria, 21
  Pieter, 7, 10, 13
  Sarah, 33
  Tjerrick, 29
Montgomery, Hugh, 106
  James, 103
Montross, (See also Matross)
  Amy, 53, 56, 59, 63, 66, 68, 74, 77
  Eliza, 109
Moore, James W., 119
More, Semmy, 12, 14
Morgan, George Wilson, 122
  James, 23
  William, 23
Wm. H., 122
Morgen, James, 19
  Jannetje, 19
Morris, Debora, 26
  Ezebia, 10
  Isaak, 26
  Jane Ann, 112
  Minnie Maria, 120
Morrison, William, 112
Morse, Hester A., 119
  Hester M., 94
  Mary E., 120
  Sarah Ann, 111
Mosely, Jonathan Ogden, 105
Mosher, Hannah, 81
  Hetty Ann, 80
  Joseph, 105
  Lewis, 80, 81
Mosure, Anne, 19
Moth, Ann, 24, 25
  William, 24, 25
Mott, Jacobus van de Bogert, 41
  Joseph, Junr., 41
Moul, Anna, 28
Mulford, Metje, 27
Muller, Annatje, 17
  Cathrina, 102
  Elizabeth, 103
  Grietje, 100
  Jacob, 29
  Jan, 12
  Lena, 12
  Lodewyk, 12
  Margaret, 35
  Margaretha, 26, 29
  Margrietje, 20
  Maria, 103
  Peter, 35
  Thomas, 17, 21, 29, 102
  Willem, 12
Murphy, John, 115
Murray, Ann, 106
  Edward, 119
Myer, Mercy, 108
  Nancy Laurence, 64
  Reuben, 64
Myers, (See also Meirs, Meyers)
  Abraham, 109
  Deborah Ann, 90
  Egbert, 76
  Ellen, 75
  Emma J., 116
  Emma Jane, 90
  Gertie, 116
  Harriet, 112
  Henrietta, 115
  Irene, 90, 115
  John S., 118
  Lawrence, 110
  Peter, 115
  Reuben, 75, 76
  Schenck A., 113
  Zachariah, 110

Index

N

Nadue, Louis, 101
Nagel, Anna, 26
  Barnet, 66
  Cornelia, 109
  George, 69
  Henry, 74
  James Van Beuron, 62
  John, 62, 66, 69, 74
Nebbel, (See also Emmot)
  Susannah, 50
Needham, Catharine B., 89, 114
  Cynthia M., 87, 89, 113
  Harriet Ann, 113
Nelson, Frances, 109
  Hannah, 113
  Leah, 111
  Levina, 100
  Maria, 80, 109

Margaret, 112
Paul, 100
William D., 115
Nieuwkerk, (See also Nuwkerk)
  Elias, 10
  Sara, 10
Noordstrand, Adriana, 34
  Hannes, 34
  John, 44
  Petrus, 44
  Sarah, 44
Noordstrandt, John, 49
Noordstrant, Catelina, 33
  Cornelies, 8
  Cornelis, 30, 33, 104
  Gerrit, 7, 8
  Isaac, 105
  Jacobus, 38

Jannetje, 10, 12
Johannes, 7
John, 38
Sara, 24, 100
Norris, George H., 116
  Henry, 107
  Isaac, 22
  Julia, 116
  Samuel, 22, 101
Nostrand, Caleb, 108
  Emma Marion, 93
Noxon, Egbert E., 111
  Elizabeth, 38, 46
  Jane Amelia, 93
  Simon, 38
  Thomas, 38
Nuwkerk, Elias, 12
  Hester, 12

O

Oakes, Elizabeth, 26
Oberhaüser, Abraham, 39
  Christina, 101
  Coenraad, 31
  Elizabeth, 39
  Frony, 43
  Johan Caspar, 31
  John Jurry, 39
  Phrone, 39
Odell, (See also Oodel)
  Hester, 65
  James, 65
Odill, Patience, 11
Ogden, Albert Tower, 122
  Maria, 27
Ogdon, Euphemia, 62
Ogsbury, Nettie, 116
O'Neil, Maria, 117
Oodel, Hester, 9
Oosterhoud, Sara, 11
Oostrander, ——, 40
  Anna, 38
  Geertje, 16
  James, 43
  Jane Ann, 40
  Maas, 38, 105
  Thomas, 43
Oostrum, Andries, 19, 99
  Cathrina, 40
  Dirkje, 16, 18, 36, 46
  Helena, 27, 32
  Henricus, 22, 99
  Henrik, 14, 16, 18, 22
  Femmetje, 10, 29, 49, 102
  Jacobus, 43

Jan, 8, 9, 10, 14, 19, 21, 22, 29
Johannes, 8, 19
Maria, 21, 29, 100, 102
Mary, 33, 35, 50
Phoebe, 38
Rachel, 43
Rebecca, 18
Tiatje, 14, 46
Ott, Anna, 24, 25
  Louisa D., 120
  Sarah, 45
Orange, Amy, 107
Organ, James P., 90
  Floyd, 94
Osterhout, James H., 121
Ostrander, Annie Elizabeth, 90
  Cornelius P., 84, 85
  James Cornell, 85
  John Wiswall, 84
  Margaret Ann, 84, 113
  Mary, 71
  Mary Frances, 84
  Peter, 84
  William, 121
Ostrum, Maria, 52, 54, 58
  Phebe, 52
Oudewater, Annatje, 15
  Daniel, 20, 21, 100
  Petrus, 21
  Pieter, 16, 21
  Tryntje, 20, 28
Oudtwater, Aletta, 56
  Gitty, 58

Peter, 56, 58
Oudwater, Anna, 24, 25
  Annatje, 9, 13
  Barent van Cleek, 46
  Beleltje, 11
  Beletje, 21
  Beljatte, 39
  Cathrina, 22, 23, 34
  Cathrine, 43
  Daniel, 24, 25, 28, 35, 39, 46
  Francis, 10
  Gitty, 35
  Jannetje, 7, 9
  Pieter, 10, 11, 17, 22
  Thomas, 10
  Tryntje, 17
Overacker, Sarah, 81
Overakker, Cathrina, 21
  Marten, 21
  Martinus, 15, 18
  Michiel, 18
Overlin, Paul, 58
  Stephen, 58
Overling, Auly, 70
  Paul, 70
Overly, Caty, 68
  John, 64
  Maria, 56
  Paul, 56, 64, 68
Overocker, Galen D., 117
Owen, Emily F., 119
  John C., 114
  Mary Elizabeth, 88
  Peter M., 119

P

Paash, Fred Gustavus, 120
Pailey, (See also Peele)
  Hannah, 58
  Hilletje, 58

Paley, Catharine, 63
Palmentier, Dama, 10
  Jacobus, 8
  Johannes, 10

Pieter, 8, 21
Willem, 10
Palmer, Adonijah, 80
  Adonjah, 74

Andrew Isaiah, 80
Burnet, 24
Charlotte, 107
Cynthia, 83
Eunice, 68
Phebe, 74, 107, 110
Robert, 24
Palmontere, Adriana, 40, 42
　Adriane, 47
　Cathrina, 48
　Elizabeth, 48, 105
　Hannah, 36
　Isaac, 43
　Jacobus, 40
　Johanna, 39, 47
　Johannes, 48
　John, 40, 46
　Lena, 38, 105
　Peter, 39
　Petrus, 43
　Rachel, 46
　Seletje, 48
Palmontier, Antonetta, 101
　Celetje, 15
　Damon, 19
　Hanna, 30
　Helena, 26, 41
　Jacob, 19
　Johanna, 101
　John, 103
　Maria, 19
　Sara, 103
　Sarah, 106
Parish, James, 109
Parkton, William H., 117
Parson, Caty, 51
Patin, Elizabeth, 70
Patterson, (See also Battison)
　Abijah, 29, 57
　Abraham, 32
　Abyah, 32, 35
　Anna, 53, 108
　Anna Maria, 67
　Clarissa, 111
　David, 43, 107
　Joanna, 57
　John, 67
　Mary, 35, 107
　Obadia, 99
　Obadiah, 43
　Sally, 64
　Sara, 29, 69
　Susan, 110
Pattison, Emma E., 117
Payton, (See also Patin)
　Elizabeth, 56, 58, 64, 68
Pearsall, Susan A., 116
Peck, William H., 114
Peebles, Elizabeth, 82
Peeck, George, 104
Peel, Hilletje, 22
Peele, (See also Pailey)
　Aart, 23, 24
　Catharina, 15
　Cathrina, 28, 29
　Elisha, 40
　Elizabeth, 26

Ezechiel, 26, 29
Ezekiel, 15
Gysbert, 21
Henrik, 24, 28
Henry, 40
Hilletje, 15, 21, 24
Jannetje, 24, 25, 35, 39, 104
John, 41
Joris, 18
Joseph, 26
Mary, 41
Paulus, 11, 19, 21
Peter, 47
Petrus, 18, 21, 23, 24, 30, 39, 99
Sara, 30
Stephanus, 21
Zachariah, 47
Peelen, Elizabeth, 21
　Ezechiel, 21
　John, 21
　Petrus, 21
Pells, Catharine E., 113
　Charity, 108
　Deborah C., 112
　Jennie, 116
　John, 69, 71, 74, 76
　John B., 113
　Margaret Ann, 69, 110
　Maria Jane, 88
　Nelly Maria, 74
　Peter, 107
　Sarah Eliza, 76, 114
　Susan, 109
　Susan L., 88, 89, 113
　Susan Letitia, 86
Pels, Blandina, 103
　Elizabeth, 41
　Francis, 31
　Henrik, 22
　Johannes, 41, 103
　Michel, 18
　Michiel, 41
　Petrus, 31
　Simon, 28
　Simon, Junr., 43
Pelts, John, 65
　Suky, 65
　Susan, 84, 85
Pendlebury, Susanna, 113
Perdon, Elizabeth, 12
　Jan, 12
　Johannes, 11
　Mally, 11
　Phoebe, 101
　Rachel, 11
Perdun, Phebe, 59
Perry, Dan'l, 120
Petherick, Fanny Helena, 120
Pettit, Melinda, 112
Philip, Johan, 14
Philipps, Aaron, 72
　Abraham, 107
　Caroline, 68
　Emeline, 72
　Jane, 107

Maria, 73
Peter, 108
William H., 68
Philips, Abraham, 53, 57, 105
　Andries, 29
　Anne, 43
　Cathrina, 33
　Cathrine, 101
　Deborah, 45
　Hanna, 101
　Henry, 37, 53
　Jan, 28
　John, 101
　Mary, 105
　Peter, 33, 51
　Phebe, 43, 48, 54
　Phoebe, 37, 105
　Rachel, 36
　Roelof, 28, 103
　Roelof, Junr., 33
　Sally, 51
　Selah Reeves, 53
　Susanna, 22, 26
　William, 29, 32, 33, 36, 37, 43, 45, 51, 57, 61, 102
Philkins, Margaret, 70
Phillips, Aaron, 59, 62, 67
　Abraham, Junr., 63
　Abraham T., 72
　Albert, 112
　Catharine, 67, 92
　Caty, 61
　Cynthia Louisa, 91
　Daniel, 83
　Eliza, 61
　George W., 91
　Hannah, 59, 83
　Harriet, 110
　Isabella, 121
　Jacob, 77
　James H., 113
　James Henry, 72
　Jane, 72, 85, 108
　Jestena B., 118
　John, 55
　John I., 113
　John R., 83, 119
　Letty, 65
　Letty Maria, 112
　Maria, 63, 77, 78
　Mary, 77, 110, 113
　Phebe, 52, 57, 60, 66
　Rachel Ann, 111
　Susan A., 91
　Thos. E., 120
　William, 55, 65
　William Edward, 72
　Zebulon, 109
Pier, Clarence H., 92
　Elizabeth Nostrand, 92
　Minnie, 92
　Wm. Edward, 92
Pierce, John W., 111
Pinckney, Charlotte, 57
　Elenor, 107
　Elizabeth, 37, 41
　Ellenor, 37

Index

Ezechiel, 14, 29
Isaac, 59
John, 18, 29, 37, 41, 59
John Dearin, 64
Joseph, 55, 57, 60, 64, 69, 72
Joseph Augustus, 72
Mary, 41, 51
Phebe, 18, 22
Phoebe, 99
Rebecca, 30
Samuel, 55, 107
Susan, 60
Thomas, 69
Pinckny, Rebecca, 37
Pinkney, Ezechiel, 11
John, 11
Samuel, 11
Pine, Cathrine, 106
Eliza, 54
Sylvenus, 54
Pitcher, Ada G., 120
Carrie, 121
Emily, 121
Laura Vignes, 121
Martin, 121
Pitt, Johanna, 23

Platt, Ann B., 110
Daniel, 109
Ebenezer C., 116
Ebenezer Carey, 85
Elizabeth, 79, 80
Elizabeth Remsen, 87
Harvey D., 85, 87
Mary Bethia, 85, 114
Mary E., 111
Phoebe, 76, 109
Ploeg, Cathrina, 21
Geertruid, 10, 11
Gertruid, 9
Wilhelmus, 21
Plumb, Charles, 118
Points, James, 111
Polhemus, Angelia, 114
Pollock, (See also Pullock)
Benjamin, 109
Harriet M., 111
Isabella, 80
James Y., 113
Jane Melissa, 113
Judson, 121
Phebe, 63, 67, 75
Phoebe, 76, 78
Polluck, Phebe, 69

Pooly, Rebecca, 106
Poppeldorf, Marytje, 12
Potter, Amelia Maria, 86
Catharine Mary, 86
Elmira Ann, 112
Freelove, 79
Hannah C., 113
Harriet H., 85, 113
Henrietta Freelove, 86
John, 83
John L., 113
Mehilla, 109
Rachel, 110
Sylvester, 110
Prout, Wm. L., 121
Pryor, Elmer L., 118
Pudney, Amelia I., 115
Corneliaette, 114
Elizabeth Everett, 116
Elizabeth Everitt, 86
John C., 86, 88, 112
John Ervin, 88
Pullock, Phebe, 72
William, 108
Purdy, Anthony, 110
George E., 114
Pye, Francis B., 114

Q

Quemby, Levi, 18
Samy, 18
Sara, 18
Quick, Eliza, 121

Nancy E., 113
Quigley, Hugh, 117
Quimby, Catharine, 27
Izaak, 23

Levi, 23, 27, 30
Mary, 30

R

Randolph, Joseph F., 113
Rapalie, John, 50
Rachel, 50
Rapalje, Jacob, 44
John, 43, 102
Lydia, 39, 44
Mary, 39
Sarah, 43
Winifred, 107
Rappalje, Lydia, 106
Ray, Anna, 102
Johannes, 102
Raymond, William H., 118
Record, Noyes P., 112
Reed, Kate, 115
Reeves, Eunice, 53
Reids, Lucretia, 17
Reidt, Femmetje, 14
Kittey, 14
Reinders, ——, 10
Andries, 9, 31
Elizabeth, 49
Helena, 31
Jacobus, 31
Jesajas, 9
Johannes, 10
Mary, 36
Meindert, 31, 36
Tryntje, 10
Reinderse, Aletta, 46

Andrew, 46
Andries, 32
Cathr., 42
Cathrine, 45
Elizabeth, 24, 25, 32
Esajas, 16
Jacob, 14
Jesajas, 14
Johannes, 24, 25
Meindert, 24, 25
Ruben, 16
Tryntje, 18
Reinderts, Jacobus, 42
John, 45
Lena, 45
Sarah, 42
Reiner, Amy, 103
Reinerse, Elizabeth, 27
Relf, Jacob, 108
Remsen, Mary Elizabeth, 86
Sara, 104
Sarah, 33
Rey, Annatje, 34
Reyder, Georgius, 103
Reyer, Styntje, 11
Reyley, Hanna, 101
Reynders, Amelia Caroline, 61
Andrew, 55, 61
Andries, 36

Cathrina, 104
Elizabeth, 31, 34, 39, 50, 62, 65
Hetty, 55
Isajah, 36
Jacob, 55
Maria, 80
Tryntye, 62
Reynderse, Andries, 103
Cathrina, 40
Helena, 20
Isaak, 100
Reynerse, Anna, 28
Meindert, 28, 42
Reynolds, Elizabeth, 62, 66, 69, 74
Margaret, 119
Rhodes, Edith, 121
Lewis, 110
Myrtle, 121
Rhyne, Mary, 113
Riffenburg, John, 116
Riley, James H., 115
John N., 117
Rim, Margaret, 106
Rimph, William H., 112
Roame, Anne, 106
Roberts, George, 111
Robertson, Jacob A., 110
Robinson, Abijah P., 110

Abram L., 121
Anna C., 115
Anna Catharine, 113
Charles, 113
Chas. Benjamin, 119
Elijah, 120
Harriet, 87
Jane, 75
John, 112
Jno. H., 93
Julia B., 121
Katie, 118
Maria Louisa, 90
Mary, 110, 121
Mary Louisa, 120
Maville J., 118
Mildred Anna, 96
Phebe Jane, 93
Ruth Jane, 110
Samuel, 107, 110
Samuel I., 87, 116
Sarah E., 115
Robison, Jane, 59, 64
Rockwell, John S., 120
Rodgers, Hellen Ann, 87
Roe, Peter, 108
 Phoebe, 109
Roer, Hannes, 13
Rogers, Adah May, 94
 Alston, 71
 Charles, 113
 Charles T., 120
 Cornelia, 75
 D. Wortman, 116
 Elizabeth, 48
 Gideon, 31, 36, 38, 46
 Hester, 23
 Johanna, 31
 John, 46
 John A., 91
 Joseph, 69, 71, 75, 111
 Kate B., 90, 91, 115
 Mary E., 119
 Minnie Cora, 120
 Susan Ann, 69
 Susanna, 112
 Thomas, 48
 William, 23, 38, 48
Rohe, (See also Roke)
 Ruth, 34, 104
Roke, Elias van Bunschoten, 42
 Roger, 42
Rome, (See also Roame)
 Aafje, 39, 44, 49, 105
 Aris, 39
 Cornelis, 39
 Gerretje, 40, 49
 John, 35, 39
 Neeltje, 35
Romein, Ariaantje, 8

Casparus, 100
Helena, 48
Isaac, 48
Romeyn, Sarah, 56
Roode, Jacob, 100
Rooney, John, 119
Rose, Harry, 121
 John W., 116
Rosecrans, John, 56
 Pieter, 102
 Rebekah, 56
 Susannah, 66
 Warren, 66
Rosecrants, Abraham Duryee, 59
 Anna, 57
 Hannah Eliza, 62
 James, 53
 John, 53, 61, 64
 John Menema, 61
 Mima, 64
 Peter, 53
 Sally, 53
 Sarah, 53, 61
 Warren, 53, 57, 59, 62
Rosekraans, Frederick, 28
Rosekrans, Abraham, 30
 Antje, 18, 22, 30, 40
 Anna Maria, 57
 Cathrine, 41
 Frederick, 40, 47
 Frederik, 20, 23
 Hannah Eliza, 57
 Henricus, 20
 Jacobus, 32, 47
 John, 48, 57
 Peter, 41
 Petrus, 23
 Pieter, 30
 Saartje, 23
 Sara, 18, 23, 25
 Sarah, 48
Rosekrants, Catharine, 67
 Frederik, 17
 Johannes, 17
 John, 67
Rosekrantz, Antje, 12, 25
 Frederik, 12, 17
 Hannes, 17
 Jacobus, 25
 Johannes, 12
 Warren, 12
Rosekranz, Petrus, 26
Rosel, Johannes, 101
Rosell, Remsen, 120
Rosenkrans, Antje, 20
 Blandina, 32
 Frederick, 32
 Jacobus, 18, 20
Rosenkrantz, Antje, 13, 14, 16

S

Saal, Maria, 17
 Robert, 17
Sabin, Amley, 62
Salisbury, George E., 89

Salover, Maria, 29
Sanders, Isaac, 12
 Jan, 12
Sardam, Cathrina, 20, 30

Cathrina, 15
Frederick, 99
Frederik, 15
Hannes, 16
Johannes, 14
Maria, 14
Rosevelt, John, 50
 Lydia, 50
Rossell, Edward, 116
Roswell, Simeon, 112
Rouger, Cathrina, 23
 Esther, 36
 Johannes, 10
 John, 36
 Moses, 10
 Philippus, 10
 Willem, 8
Row, Martha, 8
 Mercy, 7
Rowe, (See also Roe, Rohe, Row)
 Daniel Theodore, 95
 Elijah, 95
 Elijah T., 96, 119
 Elizabeth, 112
 Ethel Grace, 95
 Johannes, 104
 John Herbert, 96
 Susan Ann, 96
Ruger, James, 111
Rush, Hannah, 119
Russel, Pally, 103
Russell, Alfred P., 94
Rutsen, Cornelia, 9
 Johannes, 9
Ryckman, Jan, 104
Rykman, Abraham, 34
 Albert Zwartwoud, 32
 Jan, 32, 34
Rynders, Alletie, 108
 Amelia C., 113
 Andrew, 50, 55
 Catharine, 52, 71
 Caty, 55
 Cornelius, 109
 Elizabeth, 69, 70, 71, 74
 Maria, 50
 Mary, 74
 Mary C., 114
Rynes, Elizabeth, 50
Rysdick, Sarah, 50
Rysdyk, Elizabeth, 32
 Henrica Alida, 12
 Henriette, 46, 49
 Isaac, 12, 28, 32, 36, 42
 Izaak, 23
 Johanna, 23, 42
 John, 36
 Petrus, 28
 Sarah, 46, 49

Savens, Emily, 108
Schenck, Gysbert, 16
 Margaret, 74
Schepmoes, Lydia, 14, 16

Index

Schneider, Baltus, 10
  George, 102
  Elizabeth, 10, 13
  Jacob, 10
  Magdelena, 10
Schneyder, Helena, 101
  Johan, 13
  Mary, 39
Schofield, Hannah, 107
  Rhody, 107
Schoonhoven, Jones, 9
  Leena, 9
  Petrus, 103
Schoonmaker, Antony, 14
  Belle, 121
  Cornelia, 42
  Edward, 14, 16, 58
  Edward Emundus, 14
  Hannah, 49
  Henricus, 49
  Henry, 42, 46, 51, 55, 58, 61, 62
  Jane, 55
  Lena, 46
  Maria, 51
  Neeltje, 16
  Sally, 68
  Sara, 14, 17
Schorn, Emma, 117
Schot, Cornelis, 13
  Maria, 13
Schott, Cathrina, 28
  Izaak, 26
  Joseph, 26
  Phoebe, 35
Schouten, Annatje, 7
  Cathrina, 32
  Ephraim, 32
  Mally, 7
  Maria, 9, 32
  Simon, 7
Schroder, George, 29
Schroeder, Phoebe, 108
Schryver, Edward H., 89
  Pieter, 103
  Ruth Ann, 89
Schurre, Lydia, 12
  Maria, 12
Schurri, Annatje, 11, 14
  Johannes, 13, 15
  Saartje, 13
  Sara, 15
  Tryntje, 13
Schurrig, Annatje, 7, 9
  Catrina, 9
  Elizabeth, 9
  Johan, 8
  Johannes, 7, 9
  Maria, 9, 11
  Rachel, 10
Schurry, (*See also Jurry, Sherry, Shurry, Surry*)
  Annatje, 14, 15
  Catharina, 99
  Catharine, 54
  Cathrina, 14, 17
  Elizabeth, 14, 55

Lydia, 14, 25, 29, 33, 41, 44
Sara, 17, 99
Schut, Betty, 12
  Joseph, 104
Schute, Michiel, 106
Schutt, Hannah, 33
  Jan, 34
  Joseph, 34
  Teunis, 33, 103
Scofield, Benjamin, 109
  Edwin M., 120
  Emma J., 95
  Florence A., 95, 121
  Harriet Kissam, 95
  Harry Pells, 96
  Inez, 94
  John J., 116
  Nellie, 94
  Norman Jones, 96
  Rhoda, 56
  Stella Moore, 96
  Sylvenus, 56
  William, 95
  William I., 118
  William Monroe, 96, 116
Scott, (*See also Schot, Schut, Scutt*)
  Annie R., 116
  Phebe, 43, 56, 58, 60
  Phoebe, 37, 104
Scruton, Threse Clark, 96
Scudder, Mary, 29
  Myron Tracy, 120
Scutt, Mary, 70
Seabury, Tilman, 101
Seaman, Stephen, 106
Sebring, (*See also Seebring*)
  Cathrine, 27
  Cornelis, 27
  Isaac, 27
  Margaretha, 27
Secor, Carpenter, 117
  Cortland, 117
Secord, Letty Ann, 111
  Nancy, 107
  Susan Maria, 111
Sedore, Abby, 91
  Edgar, 90, 115
  Emma, 115
See, Catharina, 7
Seebring, Abigail, 40
  Elizabeth, 106
  Emilia, 36
  Isaac, 33, 36
  Izaak, 100
  Jan, 33
  John, 40
  Mary, 106
Seebringh, Izaak, 100
Seger, Garetta Kate, 92
  Mary Louise, 120
  Mary Louise Shafer, 93
Seward, Amelia Caroline, 83
  Carrie A., 118
  Cora Lee, 118
  Edward Townsend, 91

Electa, 76, 78, 79, 80, 108
Elizabeth, 93
George Schermerhorn, 91
Hannah, 72
James Adis, 84, 114
Julia Lockwood, 92
Mary L., 114
Mary Louisa, 87
Maurice Dwight, 82, 114
Ogden Tallmadge, 84
P. George, 114
Philander, 82, 83, 84, 110
Philander George, 82
Sarah A., 90, 115
Sarah Ann, 87
Sarah E., 114
Sarah Silvester, 119
Sarah Sylvester, 92
William, 85, 89
William, Jr., 89, 91, 92
William Henry, 82
Seyfer, (*See also Cuiper, Cypher, Sypher*)
  Alida, 14
  Anna, 21, 31, 34
  Annatje, 19, 21, 26
  David, 14, 16, 18, 21, 26
  Elizabeth, 14, 17, 21, 23
  Geertruid, 16
  Grietje, 19, 34
  Johannes Hoogteyling, 26
  John Tomkins, 20
  Lodewyk, 18, 20, 21, 99
  Margaretha, 11
  Margriet, 23
  Nelly, 18
  Sara, 19, 99
  Willem, 14
Shader, Nancy, 110
Shafer, Lewis, 118
Shammers, Joseph, 21
Shar, Martin, 108
Sharp, Daniel, 108
Shaw, Daniel, 22
  David J., 113
  Elizabeth, 22
  Julia, 113
  Stephen P., 109
  Theron, 114
  Walter, 117
  William C., 118
Shear, (*See also Shar*)
  Abraham, 77
  Ann, 109
  Anna, 56, 57, 59, 62, 63, 64
  Anne, 69, 73
  Benjamin, 72, 107
  Catharine Ann, 72
  Catharine Eliza, 67
  Catherine Eliza, 109
  Charlotte, 70
  Israel, 62, 69, 108
  John, 63, 67
  John C., 69, 75, 77
  John Cornell, 75
  Mary, 57
Shearer, William, 111
Sheehan, Rose, 120

The Reformed Dutch Church of New Hackensack

Rose A., 120
Sheerman, Ebenezer, 107
Sherry, Anne, 46
  Catharine, 51
Sherwood, Gilbert, 110
  Jamima, 34
  Jemima, 104
  Mary L., 95
  Sarah, 68
  Seth, 112
Shrader, Walter, 112
Shurry, (*See also Jurry, Schurry, Sherry, Surry*)
  Anna, 24
  Catharine, 53
  Cathrina, 21
  Cathrine, 36
  Elizabeth, 22
  Lydia, 21, 37
Shute, Nelly, 110
Silvester, Peter H., 114
Simons, Alexander, 92
  John Smith, 92
  Lena, 92
Simpson, Barbara E., 121
  Howell W., 95
  Mary E., 115
Simson, Catharina, 11
  Catrina, 8, 9
  Jannetje, 16
  Joseph, 60
  Mary, 13
  Phoebe, 21
Singleton, Isabella, 121
Sinsabaugh, Mary H., 115
Siver, S. P., 117
Slaght, Elizabeth, 60
Slater, Sylvester M., 111
Slecht, Antje, 10, 14
  John, 39
  Mary, 39
Sleght, (*See also Slaght*)
  Abraham, 16, 34
  Abraham, Junr., 104, 108
  Benjamin A., 77, 79, 108
  Edgar, 77
  Elizabeth, 34, 53
  Eltsie D., 109
  Franklin, 79
  Franklin Rush, 79
  Henry Augustus, 78
  Henry D., 79
  James, 78
  Johannes, Junr., 99
  John, 74
  John Swartwout, 74
  Malvina H., 114
  Mehala Eliza, 79
  Sarah, 34
  Sarah Louisa, 79
Sleight, Benjamin A., 80, 84
  Benjamin Sidney, 84
  Frances, 119
  James Edwin, 113
  Katie A., 118
  Mary, 83, 84, 85
  Mary K., 117

Ruth Amelia, 80, 114
Sarah, 92
Sloot, Maria, 28
Sloth, Maria, 19
Smidell, Lena, 119
Smith, Abraham, 110
  Abram, 114
  Ada L., 120
  Alice, 96
  Ann, 111
  Annie, 120
  Augustus, 115
  Carrie G., 120
  Cassius M. C., 115
  Charles, 111
  Charles W., 114
  Cornelius Brewer, 78
  Daniel, 103
  Edward, 115
  Elizabeth, 43
  Emma C., 116
  Ephraim, 108
  Ervin Tyler, 114
  Eustacia, 89
  George J., 114
  Grant E., 121
  Hanna, 23, 28
  Hannah, 32, 34, 38, 43
  Henry, 88
  James Lewis, 94, 120
  Jennie A., 117
  John, 107, 108
  John D., 78
  Lizzie M., 118
  Maria, 109
  Maria Eliza, 64
  Mary, 71
  Nathaniel, 64, 69, 112
  Patience, 69
  Phoebe, 100
  Samuel H., 112
  Samuel Henry, 114
  Sarah Jane, 78
  Solomon, 108
  Sophia, 22
  Susan, 83, 109
  William, 96, 110, 116
  William Henry, 78
Smyth, Abigail, 59
Snedecor, Elizabeth, 72
  Garrit, 108
  Richard, 72
Snedeker, Aletta M., 113
  Elizabeth, 42
  Gerrit, 101
  Hannah, 42
  Hilletje, 11
  Nathaniel Bethel, 108
  Richard, 75
  Sarah, 42, 46
  Theodorus, 103
Snedicor, Richard, 107
Snediker, Jane Ann, 76
  Richard, 76
Sniffens, Antje, 9
  Israel, 9
Sniffin, Elizabeth, 52
  Israel, 55

Lewis, 52, 55
Snook, Joseph A., 111
Snow, William, 111
Snyder, Henry, 108
  Mary, 43, 104
Solmes, Nathanael, 102
Somer, Elizabeth, 22
  Richard, 22
Somes, Richard, 21
Southard, Magdelen, 108
  Richard W., 109
  Susan, 107
Southerd, Jemima, 109
Sowdon, Arthur Whitlock, 94
  John Irving, 93
  William, 93, 94
  William Kenneth, 93
Spencer, Elizabeth, 64
  Henry, 112
  Peleg, 107
  Thomas, 64
Springsteen, Nancy, 47
  Peter, 115
Staats, Abraham, 72
  Phebe Ann, 72
Stafford, Phebe, 59
Stanford, Frances, 62
Stanton, Aagje, 46
  Hannah, 33
  Jacomina, 37
  John, 28
  William, 28, 33, 37, 46
Staples, Ebenezer, 105
Steele, Jas. Wm., 121
Steenberg, (*See also van Steenberg*)
  Antje, 10
  Blandina, 10
  Elias, 10, 11
  Elizabeth, 10
  Henry, 106
  Jacobus, 9, 10, 11
  Johannes, 10
  Tobias, 10
Steenbergen, (*See also van Steenbergen*)
  Annatje, 7
  Blandina, 99
  Dina, 18
  Elias, 14, 15, 17, 19, 20, 107
  Elizabeth, 20
  Grietje, 19
  Henry, 44
  Jacob, 44
  Jacobus, 7, 13
  Jacomina, 17
  Johannes, 13, 15
  Margret, 45
  Margrietje, 99
  Maria, 14, 15, 23
  Michel Hoffman, 15
  Penetta, 102
  Samuel, 23
  Sarah, 47
Steenbergh, Barent, 56
  Henry, 39

Index

John, 56
Sarah, 36
Stephenson, Edward, 113
Stevens, Annie, 116
   Cathrina, 27
   James, 107
Stigle, Adolph, 115
Stilwell, William M., 115
Stilwill, Mary, 101
Stockholm, Abraham B., 109
   Elizabeth, 112
   Sadie E., 118
Stokholm, Neeltje, 10
Storm, Abraham, 17, 63, 65
   Annatje, 19
   David, 33
   Diana, 88
   Goris, 13, 17, 18, 34, 102
   Helena, 34
   Isaac, 17, 33
   Jacob, 34
   John Adriance, 63
   Lea, 41, 46, 104
   Lena, 13, 15
   Mally, 12
   Margret, 38
   Margriet, 18, 21
   Maria, 17, 22, 41
   Mary, 52, 53, 58, 62, 107
   Marytje, 13
   Nat. F., 120
   Peter, 38
   Pieter, 19
   Rebecca, 30, 33, 35, 40, 44, 48, 49, 104
   Rebekah, 51
   Saartje, 22
   Sara, 19, 20, 21, 23
   Thomas, 28
Story, Maria, 31
Stoutenburg, Clinton Edward, 93
   Wm. Otto, 96
Stoutenburgh, (*See also van Stoutenburgh*)
   Abm., 54
   Abram W., 111
   Aletta, 45
   Henry, 46
   John L., 45
   Tobias, 54
   Tunis, 65
   Willem, Junr., 36
   William, 46, 65
   William H., 114
Strang, Frederick, 108
Strickland, Elizabeth, 19
Striklin, Fransyntje, 7
   Jonathan, 7
Surry, Anna, 24
Suydam, Cathrina, 44
   Jane, 52
   Rynier, 52
Swaid, Peter, 108
Swartwoud, (*See also Zwartwoud*)
   Bernardus, 48
   Cornelia, 49, 107
   Cornelis, 48
   George Washington, 48
   Henricus, 48
Swartwout, Alletie, 74
   Edy, 69
   Rachel, 54
   Sarah, 108
Sweet, Robert, 108
Swezey, John Albert, 96
   William H., 96, 120
Sypher, (*See also Cuiper, Cypher, Seyfer*)
   James Henry, 72
   John, 70, 72, 107
   William, 70

T

Tahlman, William, 106
Tailor, Jemima, 103
Tanner, Caroline Hageman, 95
   Charles F., 116
   Cornelius B., 83
   Frances, 79, 80, 81, 82, 83
   Jane Augusta, 115
   Joseph, 114
   Marian, 83
   Mary Francis, 95
   Reuben R., 83
   Robert, 83, 109
Tappan, Elizabeth, 11
   Teunis, 11
Tapper, Hester, 104
   Jan, 100
Taren, Anna, 13
   Jacobus, 8
   Johannes Rutsen, 9
   Jonathan, 8, 9
   Nancy, 10
Tarepenny, (*See also Teerpenning*)
   Elizabeth, 64, 67
   Jane, 63
   John, 63
   Rebeckah, 63
   Simon, 63
Taylor, (*See also Tailor*)
   Annie, 119
   Catharine, 58
   Harry McGuire, 119
   James, 55
   John, 55, 58, 61, 65, 70
   John Brower, 65
   Nazareth, 61
   Sarah Maria, 70
Teed, Ruth, 100
Teerpenning, (*See also Tarepenny*)
   Anna, 106
   Anne, 47
   Johannes, 42
   Rachel, 37, 42
Tellar, Alida, 40, 49
   Luke, 40
   Sarah, 40
Teller, Abraham, 45, 46
   Alida, 46
   Elizabeth, 45
   Izaac, 9
   John, 109
   John Stoutenburgh, 45
   Lucas, 46
   Morris, 109
   Richard M., 115
   William, 110
Temple, Robert G., 118
Ten Broeck, Catherine M., 94, 121
   Charles, 95
   Samuel M., 94
   Walter Livingston, 95
ten Broek, Sara, 7
te Nette, (*See also van Nette*)
   Antje, 33
   Maria, 34
ter Bosch, Maria, 7
ter Busch, Sarah, 43
ter Bush, (*See also Bush*)
   Elizabeth, 35
   Nelly, 54
   Sarah, 38, 48
ter Heun, Albert, 29
   Barent, 29
   Jon, 101
   Lucas, 29
ter Heune, Albert, 27
   Jan, 27, 31
   Jeremiah, 40
   John, 40
   Maria, 31
ter Hune, Jan, 33
   Lena, 33
ter Wilgen, Ahasuerus, 8
   Antoinetta, 22
   Hugo, 22
   Juriaan, 8, 22
   Sara, 29
   William, 23
ter Willige, Mary, 39
ter Willgen, Barent, 26
   Jurriaan, 26
   Sarah, 39
Terwilliger, Andrew, 96
   Edward, 96
   Isaac, 115
   Mabel J., 120
Teuschman, Cathrina, 17
Thompson, Anthony, 109
   Jane Eliza, 87
   Mary E., 88
   Mary Elizabeth, 114
   Zachariah I., 109
Thorn, (*See also Taren*)
   Abigail, 27, 29

Carrie L., 114
Cornelia, 37
Eliza, 110
Esther, 85
James, 52
Jane, 86, 110
Latetia, 28
Mary A., 86
Phebe, 29, 52
Phoebe, 21, 26
Samuel, 84
Sarah, 110
Sarah Elizabeth, 83
Sidmon, 112
Stephen, 83, 84
Stephen S., 85
Thorne, Elizabeth, 108
Thrasher, Hannah, 68
  Phebe, 73
  Phoebe, 77, 78, 81
Thue, Gilbert, 45
  John, 45
Thurston, Jemima, 31
  Sarah, 109
Thuston, Jemimah, 100
Tibbs, John, 121
  Mary V., 121
  William E., 117
Tidd, Adelia, 71
  Ann H., 111
  David, 71, 75, 80
  Emeline, 71
  Hetty Jane, 80
  Peter, 75
  Silas, 71
Tietsoort, Catharina, 11
  Cornelis, 11
  Gideon, 11
  Johannes, 12
  Maria, 11
  Nicolaas, 12
  Sara, 11
Tilyou, Sally, 108
Tippet, Mary, 105

Titsoor, (*See also Tiet-soort*)
  Belly, 14
  Cornelis, 17
  Dirkje, 15
  Gideon, 14, 17
  Henricus, 17
  Jacob, 15
  Johannes, 17
  Willem, 14
Titus, Amy, 49, 51
  Frances E., 113
Tobias, Isaac F., 111
  Mary, 41, 47, 54, 105
  Peggy, 51
Todd, Caroline, 82
  Eliza Love, 68
  Esther, 75
  Jane, 76, 108
  John R., 61
  Lafayette, 81
  Mary Elizabeth, 81
  Oliver, 51, 81, 82
  Robert, 51, 81
  Robert Polaski, 61
  William, 68, 75
Tomkins, Charles R., 112
  Daniel, 65
  Elizabeth, 20
  Sara, 20
  Walter Odell, 65
  William, 112
Tompkins, Brundage, 91, 114
  Elizabeth Van Wyck, 91
  Jacob Teller, 90
  Martha, 108
  Sarah F., 92
  Sarah Frances, 91
  William H., 89, 90, 114
Tonkins, Margareth, 106
  Sara, 99
Top, Cathrina, 15
  Henrik, 15

Johannes, 15
Towne, Joseph, 66
  Thomas Merrit, 66
Townsend, Amelia M., 115
  Ann Augusta, 90
  Augustus H., 121
  Edward, 90, 115
  Edwin R., 113
  Freelove, 108
  Gideon, 12
  James, 109
  John, 2d, 111
  Kate Seward, 90
  Margaret, 111
  Mary, 101
  Mary Louisa, 90
  Phebe, 90
Tracy, Alonzo F., 115
  Julia, 114
Traver, Adam Thurston, 57
  Ann Eliza, 65
  Elias, 65
  William, 57, 65
Travers, (*See also Treves*)
  Engeltje, 7
  Richard, 107
Traves, Rachel, 29, 101
Travis, John, 109
  Robert, 106
Traynor, Eva P., 116
Treves, Elizabeth, 12
  Engeltje, 7
Trowbridge, Susan, 116
Tsicoks, Ezechiel, 14
  Francis, 14
Turk, Jacob, 30
Turnbull, Henry Burrell, 120
Turner, Bartha, 38
  Berthia, 42
  Gilbert Thorn, 113
  James, 119
  Walter C., 117

U

Uhl, Daniel, 20
  Helena, 20
Underhill, Anthony, 92, 113
  Charlotte A., 91
  Chavis, 30
  Frank, 94

George, 91
Gerardus DeForest, 93
Jarvis, 102
Joshua, 108
Lillie Stephenson, 93
Lottie, 119

Mary, 68, 71, 73, 75, 76, 78
Sara, 30
Walter DeForest, 93
William, 117
Underwood, Jarvis, 35
  Mary, 35

V

Vail, Annie, 117
  James, 108
  Mary A., 89
  Polly, 63
Valence, Mary, 53
Valentine, Hannah, 108
  Sener L., 116
Vallo, Henry, 62
  Theodorus, 62
Van Aalst, Cathrine, 49
Van Alst, Altye, 51

Catharine, 51, 54, 60, 67
Constantine Gulneck, 53
George, 51
Hester, 55
Isaac, 53
Mary, 107
Van Amber, Jacob, 68
  John Dubois, 74
  Robert, 68, 74
Vn. Ambergh, Jacob, 110
Van Amburgh, Adeline, 80

Alida, 27
Aly, 107
Belinda, 85, 119
Cornelia, 77
Edgar, 115
Harriet, 75
Jane, 81, 109
Jane Ann, 67
John D., 111
Mercy, 86
Peter D., 113

Index

Robt., 67
Robert, 75, 77, 80
Walter, 80
Walter Ransom, 88
William, 88
Mrs. William, 119
Van Anden, Annie C., 118
Jane M., 114
Vn. Arsdale, Ann Maria, 111
V., Vn. & Van Arsdalen, Benjn., 79
Benjamin, 109
Derrick, 62
Havily, 79
Maria, 62
Van Arstdalen, Derick, 70
Elizabeth, 70
Sarah, 70
van Binneschuiten, Catelyntje, 10
Teunis, 10
Van Bogert, Adelaide, 119
Arthur, 119
William, 113
Van Bommel, Anne, 49
Antje, 8, 29
Assuerus, 39
Christoffel, 29, 39
Peter, 39
Petrus van Cleek, 39
van Bramer, Vn. Bramer, Helen, 109
Helen E., 114
Jane, 70, 72, 75
Johannes, 48
Letty, 68
Peter, 48
Sarah, 69, 71
Van Breeman, Jane, 55
Aletta, 57
Alida, 55, 61, 65
Catharine, 63
David, 62
Jane, 58, 67
Peter, 62, 63
Sarah, 68
Van Breemer, Alida, 51
Magdalen, 59
Peter, 59
Sarah, 65
van Bremen, Alida, 32, 37, 45
Catharina, 9
Cathrina, 28, 33, 103
Cathrine, 42
David, 27
Jannetje, 24, 25
Maria, 30
Mary, 35, 102
Peter, 36, 42, 46, 52, 100
Pieter, 22, 24, 25, 27, 31, 33
Sarah, 22, 36
Susanna, 22
Thomas, 7, 9, 17, 19, 24, 25, 28, 30, 33
William, 52

van Brommelen, Elizabeth, 46
Leendert, 46
V. Bunschooten, Jacomina, 63
Jemima, 66
Tine, 63
Tunis, 63
van Bunschote, Mattheus, 37
Rachel, 39
van Bunschoten, Van Bun Schoten, Vn. Bunschoten, (*See also Bunschoten*)
Antje, 34
Aris, 19
Cateline, 36
Catharina, 8, 9
Cathrina, 33, 100
Cathrine, 27, 36, 38, 40, 44
Egenas, 44
Eliah, 38
Elias, 9, 22, 31, 34, 35, 40, 45, 54, 107
Elizabeth, 42, 45
Hannah, 35, 43, 106
Herman, 42
Jacob, 8
Jacobus, 42
Jacomina, 22
Jacomyn (tje), 9
James, 40
Jane, 54
Jemima, 70, 71, 75
Jenneke, 19
Maria, 8, 34, 37
Mary, 44
Mattheus, 31
Nelly, 38
Rachel, 31, 43, 49
Sarah, 40
Teunis, 14, 22, 40
Tunis, 35
Van Bunschotin, Elias, 72
John, 72
van Cleeck, Ahasuerus Hugo, 42
Anna, 44
Antonette, 27
Barent, 26, 43
Barent M., 107
Barent P., 22
Barnard, 32
Cathrine, 50
Cathrine, 45
Cornelis, 41
David, 32
Dina, 47
Elizabeth, 41, 43, 45, 101
Hannes, 31
Henry, 102
Hugo, 42, 47
Jacobus, 45
James, 47
Jan, 102
John, 36, 41
Laurens, 100

Lawrens, 36, 45
Levi, 22, 44
Maria, 26, 100
Mary, 44
Petrus, 47
Rachel, 36, 43, 47
Sarah, 43
van Cleef, Isaac, 104
James Spencer, 114
Marytje, 14
Sophia, 114
van Cleek, Vn. Cleek, (*See also van Kleeck*)
Aaltje, 47
Ahasuerus, 8, 18
Ahasuerus, Junr., 106
Anne, 48
Antonetta, 37
Antonette, 36
Assuerus, Junr., 39
Baltus, 11, 29, 35
Barent, 7, 29, 32, 34
Blandina, 9, 10, 11
Catharine Dwight, 82
Cathrina, 29, 31, 101
Cathrine, 39
Deborah, 45
Dinah, 106
Elizabeth, 10, 11, 18, 33, 48, 106
Gabriel, 46
Hugo, 18
Jacoba, 7, 34, 35, 38, 48, 103
James, 106
Jannetje, 18
Jeremia, 29
John, 35, 47
Leendert, 7
Luke, 40
Magdalene, 38
Margaret, 82
Maria, 11, 34, 110
Mary, 8, 49
Monfort, 82
Peter, 40, 46, 49, 50
Pieter, 7
Rachel, 30, 33
Saartje, 13
Sara, 7, 8, 9, 10, 11
Sarah, 50
Tryntje, 7
Van D Bilt, Sitea, 60
van de Bogard, Catharina, 8
Van De Bogart, Vandebogart,
Anna, 62
Celia, 78, 80, 81, 109
Peter, 62
van de Bogert, (*See also Bogert, van Bogert, van den Bogert*)
Aart, 28, 48
Aert Middagh, 67
Anna Maria, 66
Cathrine, 35, 48
Celia, 79, 80
Dina, 105

327

The Reformed Dutch Church of New Hackensack

Francis, 105
Geertje, 28
Gysbert, 35, 104
Jacomyntje, 17
Jacomina, 24, 25, 28, 29
Jane, 94
Johannes, 18
John Swartwoud, 105
Lena, 30
Meindert, 18, 32
Myndert, 66
Peter, 35, 67
Pieter, 30
van de Burg, Susanna, 8
V. de Burgh, van de Burgh, Van De Burgh, (*See also van der Burgh*)
Amelia, 56
Elizabeth, 63
Peter, 56
van de Gaaf, Jacobus, 42
van den Bogaard, Cornelis, 7
Jacobus, 8
Neela, 7
van de Graaf, Jacobus, 42
Pieter, 102
Van Der Belt, Vanderbelt,
Ares, 76
Jemima C., 113
Peter, 76
Phebe, 86
Phillip, 86
Mary Sheafe, 86
Sytye, 50
V. der Bilt, van der Bilt, Van Der Bilt, Van-Derbilt, Vanderbilt,
Aart, 26, 32
Ares, 56, 59, 60, 70
Aris, 23
Benjamin Everitt, 74
Catharine, 51
Elthea, 88
George, 60, 109
George Whitefield, 80
Hannah, 54, 108
Henry, 88
Hetty, 57, 109
John, 59, 64, 75
John Platt, 85
John Robison, 64
Laura, 90
Mary, 108
Mary Joan, 110
Mary Johannah, 72
Mary S., 116
Peter, 72, 74, 78, 80
Phebe E., 85, 86, 112
Phoebe Elizabeth, 78
Philip, 51, 54, 57, 70
Philip Beekman, 75
Phillip, 85, 86
Phillip B., 111, 112
Pieter, 26
Sarah E., 114
Sarah Electa, 86
Seytje, 49

Sitea, 52, 53, 56, 65
Syta, 70
Sytje, 39, 44
Van Derbergh, Elizabeth, 53
Peter, 53
van der Burg, Elizabeth, 22
van der Burgh, Vanderburgh,
Alida, 28
Effingham, 113
Elizabeth, 35, 40
Henry, 45
Hester, 39, 45
Jacob, 49, 107
Mary, 42
Nela, 49
Peter, 45, 58
Richard, 58
Stephen, 42
van der Linden, Adriana, 32
van de Ryp, Antje, 10
van Deusen, Anna, 28
Isaac, 28
Isaak, 26
V. D. Water, van de Water, Van Dewater, Vanderwater,
Aagie, 27
Adolf, 37, 43, 48, 105
Adolph, 54, 57, 60, 66
Adolphus, 52
Albert Wellington, 93
Benjamin, 16, 37, 48, 53, 57, 61, 106
Catharina, 43
Catharine, 57
Cathrina, 43
Cathrine, 45, 105
Elizabeth, 44, 53, 106
Engelina, 25
Engeltje, 9
Frederic S., 121
Harmanus, 34
Helen Josephine, 93
Helena, 16
Henry, 48
Herman, 54, 60
Jacobus, 27, 30, 33, 36, 43
Jacobus L., 103
Jan, 33
Jannetje, 42, 47, 104
John, 66
Lavinus, 9
Lincoln A., 118
Margaretha, 34
Maria, 26
Martha, 50
Mary, 48
Mattie, 121
Nelly Maxfield, 61
Peter, 30, 38
Phebe, 66
Pieter, 25
Rachel, 32, 34, 38, 44
Sarah, 32, 50, 106
Susannah, 57
Wm., 93

van der Voort, Vandervoort,
Jacob, 27
Jacobus, 27
Jeremiah V. Kleeck, 71
Johannes, 32
Peter A., 71
Samuel, 27, 32
van de Voort, Cathrine, 38
Helena, 22, 31
Jan, 30
Thomas Cornell, 30
van Dine, Adriana, 48, 55
Ariaantje, 43
Gertrude, 115
Van Duyn, Adriana, 61
Garret, 65
Garret Monfoort, 65
Garrit, 73
Gerrit, 70
Harvey Branson, 112
James, 109
John, 73
Mary Ann, 113
Oliver, 70, 109
Sitea, 64
Van Dyne, Vn. Dyne,
Cynthia Jane, 110
Edward B., 112
Edward Bloomfield, 94
Hannah M., 110
Harvey E., 114
James Abraham, 83
Jane Ann, 90
Jennie Carter, 93
Jennie M., 116
Oliver, 83
Phebe E., 114
Spencer, 116
Wm. Henry, 83
van Everen, (*See also Van Ieveren, van Never, van Yvere*)
Eden, 46
Hanna, 24
Laurens, 46
van Every, Burger, 11
Femmetje, 11
Rachel, 11
van Hoek, Cathrina, 104
Van Horne, Abm., 66
James, 66
Van Ieveren, Mary, 66
Van Keure, Abm., 54, 62
Abraham, 65
Altje, 51, 55, 58
Andw., 52
Benjamin, 67
Casparus, 52, 54, 58
Deborah, 65
Elizabeth, 54
Geertje Jeacocks, 67
Jacobus, 58
James, 61
John, 58, 62
Margaret, 54
Matthew, 55, 58, 62, 67
Sarah, 53, 63

Index

Susan, 67
William, 55, 61, 67
van Keuren, Van Keuren,
  Aaltje, 7, 21, 29, 40, 47, 100
  Abraham, 18, 21
  Alida, 100
  Anna, 35
  Anna Maria, 64
  Annah, 38
  Annatje, 15, 69
  Anne, 45
  Anne Maria Wiltsie, 69
  Benjamin, 12, 17, 19, 27, 30, 35, 69, 109
  Benjamin B., 72
  Caspar, 33
  Casparus, 29, 35, 40, 50, 102
  Catharine, 72
  Celetje, 16, 19, 40
  Charrick, 100
  Cherrick, 13, 14, 21, 32, 40
  Cornelis, 7, 8
  Cornelius, 12
  Derk, 8
  Elizabeth, 8
  Femmetje, 50
  Geertje, 15
  Geertruy, 49
  Geertruda, 14
  Helena, 35
  James, 112
  Jan, 33
  Jane, 72, 74
  Jesajah, 32
  Margriet, 16, 17, 20
  Maria, 8, 18, 21, 22, 30
  Mary, 36, 37, 45
  Mary Luckey, 85
  Marytje, 13, 15, 18
  Mattheus, 14, 15, 18, 19, 32, 103
  Matthew, 35, 37
  Peter, 74, 85, 112
  Robert Saal, 17
  Sara, 21, 59, 67
  Thomas, 35
  Tjerck, 32
  Tjerrick, 29
  Tserrik, 16
  William, 64, 72, 74
  William Jacocks, 72
V. Kleeck, van Kleeck, Vn. Kleeck, (*See also van Cleeck*)
  Adelia, 117
  Ahasuerus, 17
  Anatje, 55
  Anna, 53, 57, 60, 66, 67
  Anna Maria, 81
  Antje, 22
  Antonetta, 51
  Baltus, 15
  Barent, 22, 28
  Cathrina, 106
  Charles E., 90, 91, 115
  Deborah, 66

Dinah, 51
Elizabeth, 13, 15, 24, 28, 53, 54, 57, 58, 61, 62, 71
George Denniston, 83
Hannah, 57, 62, 67, 71
Hannah Elizabeth, 81
Henrietta, 84
Jacoba, 67, 69, 72
Maria, 20, 60
Mary Eliza, 90
Monfoort, 67, 80, 81
Monfort, 83, 84
Monfort J., 113
Moses, 67
Penelope, 53, 63
Peter, 53, 57, 60, 66
Peter P., 108
Rachel, 63, 66, 71, 73
Robert M., 91
Sarah Jane, 80
Susanna, 28
Susannah, 60
Van Kleek, Aleda, 21
  Anna, 52
  Antje, 15, 17, 19, 99
  Antoinetta, 20
  Antonetta, 13, 23
  Baltus, 52
  Barent, 15, 17, 20, 23, 27
  Beletje, 20
  Catherine Amelia, 85
  Clarinda, 111
  Elizabeth, 17, 21, 25, 52
  Eunice, 82
  Hannes, 18
  Harvey Dodridge, 84
  Hugo, 100
  Jacoba, 19
  James Van Keuren, 83
  Jan, 30, 31
  Maria, 18, 22, 23
  Monfort, 82, 83, 84, 85
  Neeltje, 15
  Nelly, 19
  Rachel, 27
  Rochelle, 31
  Sara, 15
Van Loon, Henry, 111
van Nette, (*See also te-Nette*)
  Abraham, 41, 47, 106
  David, 47
  Dirkje, 46
  Elizabeth, 41
  Jacobus, 46, 106
  Mary, 38, 44, 49
van Netten, Rachel, 13
van Never, (*See also van Everen*)
  Ida, 100
Van Nort, George M., 113
Van Nosdall, (*See also Van Osdall*)
  Derick, 65
  Elizabeth, 85
  Hannah E., 112
  Margaret, 65

Ruth, 114
Van Nostrand, Aletta Jane, 113
  Cornelia, 77, 78, 79, 80, 81
  Mary L., 116
  Rebecca, 77, 79
Van Osdall, Vanosdall, (*See also Van Nosdall*)
  Adaline, 111
  Elizabeth, 84
  Heber, 111
Van Osdoll, Doretta, 113
  Margaret, 113
van Schurrvan, Pietje, 7
van Sickele, Geertje, 103
van Sickelen, (*See also Fan Sikle*)
  Anna, 32, 35, 102
  Anne, 49
  Cathrina, 25
  Eva, 103
  Evah, 49
  Ferdinand, 25, 28, 32, 35, 49
  Geertruis, 30
  Geertruy, 38
  Henricus, 32
  Jan, 28, 31
  Maria, 25
  Mary, 37
  Sarah, 106
  Theodorus, 31
van Sickeler, Anne, 41
  Eva, 32
  Geertruy, 44
  Pally, 44
van Sickle, ——, 33
  Cornelius, 33
Van Sicklen, Corns., 60
  Eve, 45
  Ferdinand, 60
  Gitty, 51
  Henry, 47
  Jemima, 72
  Theodorus, 72
Van Sickler, Anna, 55
  Caroline, 109
  Catharine, 57
  Caty, 55, 59
  Cornelius, 56
  Gertrude, 52, 56
  Gertruy, 61, 68
  Gitty, 66
  Henry, 51
  Phebe, 51
  Phoebe, 109
  Sally, 56
van Sickley, Cornelis, 47
van Sikkelen, John, 26
  Maria, 26
v. Stambergen, Johanes, 7
  Michiel v. Cleek, 7
van Steenberg, (*See also Steenberg*)
  Barent, 11
  Grietje, 9
  Jacobus, 9

Johannes, 9, 10, 11
Sara, 10
van Steenbergen, (See also Steenbergen)
  Elias, 99
  Johannes, 8
Van Steenbergh, Barnet, 64
  Bernard, 59
  Jacob Perdun, 59
  Simon, 64
van Stoutenburgh, Maria, 42
van Sylen, (See also van Zeyl, van Zuylen)
  Jannetje, 31
  Rachel, 31
Van Tassel, John, 59
  Martha, 59
  Mary, 59
  Sarah E., 115
Van Tassell, Arthur, 122
  Clarence, 95, 96, 120
  Elbert W., 92
  Flora, 122
  George Edward, 96
  Wardell C., 95
van Tessel, Annatje, 13
  Grietje, 39, 101
  Matty, 102
  Metje, 105
van Texel, Dirk, 7
  Maria, 7
van Tine, Bartholomy Cowen, 48
  Francis, 48
  George, 121
  Sally, 111
van Tyn, Mally, 10
Van Valin, (See also Ver Valen)
  Abram, 116
van Valkenburgh, Cathrine, 40
Van Vlack, Libbie, 116
  Mary C., 117
  Verdine, 119
Van Vlecht, Jane, 107
van Vlekkeren, Aaltje, 19
  Abraham, 26
  Cornelia, 28
  Henrik, 19, 28
  Jannetje, 16
  Marinus, 16, 26
van Vliet, Anna, 50
  Lena, 38, 49, 65
  Petrus, 9
Van Voorhees, (See also Voorhees)
  Abraham, 48
  Albina, 86
  Angelica, 84
  Ann E., 85
  Ann Eliza, 86
  Christian, 47
  Garretje, 56, 59
  Gilly, 105
  Henry, 48
  Izak, 10

Jacob V. B., 86
Jerome, 112
Nancy, 47
Steven, 10
Zachariah, 47
Van Voorhes, Angelica, 79
Vn. Voorhies, Angelica, 82
V. Voorhis, Van Voorhis, Vn. Voorhis,
  Albina, 90, 114
  Angelica, 80, 81, 82
  Catharine, 61, 64, 69, 71, 87
  Catherine, 75, 76
  Caty, 74
  Charles C., 117
  Coert A., 118
  Daniel, 107
  Daniel A., 109
  Elizabeth M., 88, 115
  Emilie B., 92, 120
  Garre, 62
  Garretye, 66
  Joseph, 114
  Lottie, 119
  Mary, 87, 108
  Mary E., 119
  Miriam, 91, 117
  Obadiah, 63, 113
  Roeluf, 71
  Roeluf Augustus, 71
  Ruth, 69
  Samuel, 63
  Sarah Jane, 86
  Stephen, 69
  Willis, 94
van Wagena, Hannah, 106
van Wagenen, Maria, 100
van Wagener, Emily, 95
  Magdalen, 49
  Magdalena, 47
Van Wert, Menit, 113
Van Wie, John, 112
Van Wyck, Abraham D., 108
  Ann, 108
  Catelina, 31, 41
  Cornelia, 110
  Cornelius R., 108
  DeWitt, 94
  Dinah, 50
  Hannah, 107
  Isaac I., 108
  Jane Eliza, 111
  Mathew L., 94
  Richard C., 108, 119
  Susan, 107
  Thomas DeWitt, 114
van Wyk, Catelina, 26
  Feben, 8
  Sara, 8
van Wyke, Cathrina, 10
van Yvere, Femmetje, 15
  Meindert, 10
  Sara, 10
van Yveren, Andries, 23
  Berger, 9
  Burger, 8, 23

Elizabeth, 27
Femmetje, 23
Ida, 23, 27
Maria, 9
Meindert, 23
Susanna, 23
Willem, 9
van Zeyl, Anne, 48
  Elizabeth, 48
van Zuylen, (See also van Sylen)
  Rachel, 38, 46
Veal, Daniel, 104
  Israel, 104
  Sarah, 107
Veale, Johannes, 107
Veele, Anna, 106
  Anne, 47
  Cornelis, 36
  Deborah, 48
  Ezechiel, 43, 48
  Jacobus, 48
  Jane, 41, 47
  Meindert, 36, 47, 101
  Mary, 47
  Peter, 42, 48
  Petrus, 48
  Philip (Vesick), 48
  Sarah, 42
  Syntie, 72
  Syntje, 43
Veelie, Syntie, 107
Velie, (See also Veal, Viele)
  Douw, 108
  Israel Cromeline, 70
  James H., 118
Vemont, Jean, 42
Vermilie, Gerardus, 107
  Letitia, 107
Vermiljer, Anna, 40
  Benjamin, 9, 40
  George, 40
  Jannetje, 11
  Johannes, 9
  Sarah, 8, 9
Vermilye, George P., 115
  Paul, 116
Vermilyea, Jeromus, 110
  Sarah Ann, 110
Verplanck, Cathrine, 44
  William B., 107
Ver Plank, Verplank,
  Geertruda, 12
  Geertruy, 12
  James, 12
  Mary Ann Catharine, 61
  Philip, 12, 15
  William B., 61
  William Beekman, 15
Vervale, Cathrina, 43
  Daniel, 43
Vervalen, Moses, 52
  Phebe, 52
Ver Valin, (See also Fer Valen, Van Valin)
  Mary E., 114
  Samuel, 115

Index

Verveele, Daniel, 45, 105
  James, 45
Verveelen, Abraham, 7
  Mary, 40
  John, 40
  Petrus, 7
Verweelen, Johanna, 7
  Moses, 7
Verwey, Cathrina, 22
  Elizabeth, 24, 25, 27, 29, 31, 33, 100
  Henrica, 12, 23, 28, 32, 36, 42
Viele, (See also Veal, Velie)
  Anna, 21
  Baltus, 13
  Barent, 15, 18

Benjamin, 21
Bernard, 70
Elizabeth Chatterton, 82
Ezekiel, 55, 61
Ezekiel, Junr., 109
Henrik, 21
Hetty, 109
Jan, 14
Jane, 31, 36, 102
Jannetje, 30
John, 82
Lena, 9, 17
Mehitabel, 55
Meindert, 15, 30
Minard W., 111
Neeltje, 13
Petrus, 101
Pieter, 15, 19

Rachel, 8, 9, 12, 27
Rebecca, 13, 15
Rochelle, 30
Thomas, 14
Vincent, Minnie May, 116
Vlegelaar, Catrina, 10
Voight, Anna, 121
  Martha M., 121
Vollener, Annie M., 119
  Kate Theresa, 119
Vollmer, Blanche G., 121
  Kate Elizabeth, 122
  Katie Theresa, 93
  Lona A., 96, 120
  Margaretha, 115
Voorhees, William C., 111

W

Waddle, Mary, 106
Wagner, Gezena A., 115
Wahe, James, 106
  Samuel, 106
Waheman, Peggy, 46
Waiman, Margreth, 45
Wake, (See Wahe)
Walden, Abram, 99
  Cathrine, 105
Waldon, (See also Waldrom, Waldron, Waldrum, Walron, Walrum, Weldon)
  Anna, 21, 28
  Hanna, 24
Waldrath, (See also Walrath)
  Hannes, 33, 34
Waldrom, Anna, 52
Waldron, Alletie Swartwout, 69
  Anna, 54, 58, 60, 64, 67
  Cornelia, 69, 71, 75
  Elizabeth Haight, 25
  John P., 25
  Margaretha, 28
  Maria, 107, 112
  Peter, 69, 108
Waldrum, Antje, 30
  Margaretha, 30
  Petrus, 30
Walker, Gideon Allen, 62
  Matthew, 62
Waller, Henry, 107
Walrath, (See also Waldrath)
  Johannes, 34
Walron, Eva, 26
  Jan, 26
Walrum, Margaretha, 33
Walter, Anton Wm., 119
  Anton William, 122
Walters, Susan M., 115
Ward, Abraham, 47
  Alfred Wyckoff, 91
  Daniel, 47, 68

Delia F., 94
H., 120
Henry, 90, 91, 92
  Henry Paige, 91
  Herbert Emerson, 92
  Ida M., 118
  William Davis, 90
Warhurst, Ann, 111
Warner, Charity, 45, 100
  David, 110
  Isaac, 45
  Rebeccah, 38
  Susan, 96
  Thomas, 38, 45
Warren, Cora E., 93, 120
  Daniel, 66
  John Robison, 66
  Lydia, 68
  Mary, 109
  Mary S., 120
  Thomas, 111
Water, Elizabeth, 26
Way, Maria, 109
Weaver, (See also Wever)
  Abraham, 74
  Antonetta, 43
  Cathrina, 30
  Jacob, 72, 74
  John, 43
  Mary, 46
  Michael, 72
  Michel, 30
  Peter, 41, 46
  Petrus, 20
Webb, Mary, 108
Weddles, Elizabeth, 111
Wee, Benjamin, 12
  Femmetje, 12
Weecks, Obadiah, 103
Weeks, (See also Wicks)
  David, 56
  Elizabeth, 112
  Gilbert, 108
  Isaac, 56
  James, 107
  Jamima, 110

Jemima Eliza, 112
John Miller, 45
Mary, 86
Obadiah, 45
Weid, Samuel, 107
Weissenfels, Frederik, 100
Weldon, Cathrine, 38, 46
  Hannah, 40
Wendel, Mary, 101
Werner, Cora May, 95
  Daniel, 90, 95, 115
  Sarah Remsen, 90
Westbroek, Sara, 9
Westbrook, Cornelius D., 107, 109
Westcot, Charles, 107
Westcott, Nathan, 109
Westfall, Mary Emma, 95
Westerveld, Abraham, 20, 30, 34
  Albert, 37, 105
  Anna, 27, 41
  Annatje, 7, 8
  Anne, 45
  Antje, 30, 50, 102
  Benjamin, 45
  Casparus, 7, 40, 45
  Cathrine, 107
  Cornelia, 20
  Cornelis, 8, 40
  Dirk, 8
  Elizabeth, 7, 9, 10, 12, 14, 16, 21, 32, 100
  Femmetje, 8, 9
  Henrica, 37
  Jacobus, 27, 36, 40, 46, 105
  John, 41, 50, 105, 107
  Joost, 20, 32, 34, 37
  Lena, 8, 9, 10, 14
  Maria, 13, 14, 16, 32
  Matthew, 46
  Peter, 41
  Rebecca, 45
  Roelof, 8
  Wyntje, 40
Westervelt, Abm. 51

The Reformed Dutch Church of New Hackensack

Abraham F., 81, 82, 109
Albert, 51, 105
Allida, 83
Anna, 53
Charlotte, 79
Cornelius, 79, 80, 81, 82, 83, 87
Elizabeth Merritt, 82
Hannah, 50, 60, 63, 65, 66, 70, 71
James, 79
John D., 87, 88
John DuBois, 80
John Lawson, 82
Laura Ann, 82
Levina, 79
Louis, 88
Mary, 79
Nelly, 115
Theron, 81
Peter Fort, 81
Rebecca, 76
Rebecca Jane, 81
Wever, Elizabeth, 49
Jacob, 101
Matthew, 36
Michael, 49, 102
Michel, 36
Pieter, 104
Wheeler, Peter, 106
White, Abigail, 114
White, Alfretta H., 94
Andrew, 106
Arthur Wellington, 93
Clarence George, 93
Hiram Brownell, 93
John James, 121
Sarah Cornelia, 93
Wellington, 93
Whitman, Fred J., 119
Whitworth, Mary, 111
Wicks, (*See also Weecks*)
Lena, 39
Obadiah, 39
Wiest, Johs., 19
Johannes, 19
Wilcox, Mary, 108
Wildey, Margaret, 75
Wildy, Mattheus, 104
Matthew, 104
Wiley, James S., 112
Margaret, 68
Nancy, 108
William, 108
Willet, James, 68
Mary, 64
Thomas, 68
Thomas G., 64
Williams, Belinda, 113
Elizabeth, 100
Isaac, 115
John, 113
J. Josie Haight, 120
Theron, 119
Thomas E., 94
Willsey, Anna M., 117
Wilson, John, 35
Robert, 35

Wiltse, Deborah, 77
Ellenor, 37
Henry, 105
Hester, 7
Izaak, 9
Johannes, 9
Mary, 27
Wiltsee, Abraham, 27, 30, 40, 101
Adolf Zwatwoud, 16
Cathrina, 30, 104
Cathrine, 35, 47
Catrina, 10
Celetje, 40
Cornelia, 20
Debora, 11, 12, 22
Eleanore, 105
Elizabeth, 10, 34, 36, 41, 47
Esther, 43
Gerardus, 45, 50
Gerhardus, 24, 25, 106
Hannes, 19
Henricus, 11, 14
Henrik, 14, 19, 20, 26, 29, 100
Henry, 31, 35, 38, 42, 43, 47
Hester, 8, 10, 12, 14, 18
Isaac, 13, 14, 22, 24, 25, 38, 40, 42
Isaak, 16
Izak, 10, 11
Jacob, 38, 42
Jacobus, 13
James, 16
Jan, 22, 31
Jenny, 27
Johannes, 10, 14
John, 16, 26, 35, 40, 43, 46
Maria, 14, 17, 34
Mary, 35, 38, 101
Nela, 45
Nelletje, 11
Nelly, 14, 18, 23, 27, 29, 30
Penelope, 42
Petronella, 16, 19
Robert Luckey, 35
Rudolphus, 12
Teunis, 10, 12, 14, 16, 19, 20, 29, 50
Tiatje, 22
William, 46
Wiltsie, Deborah, 60, 66, 69, 71, 73, 75, 76
Eleanor, 65
James Gilliland, 70
John, 60, 62, 107
John, Junr., 70
Nelly, 62
Petronella, 54
Petrus, 26
Wiltson, Robert, 104
Wiltzee, Catharina, 7
Izaac, 7
Teunis, 7
Win, Joseph, 34
Nancy, 34

Winans, Hattie, 118
Margaret E., 117
Mary, 118
Winchester, Henry N., 119
Wixson, Georgia A., 117
Wolfe, Godfrey, 60
Teuntje, 60
Wolff, Anna, 106
Wolven, (*See also Wolfe, Woolvin, Wulven*)
Godfrey, 33
James E., 121
John, 108
Nancy E., 117
Teuntia, 109
Willem, 33
Wood, Abraham, 64
Chas. G., 121
George C., 115
Gilbert, 113
Hetty, 64
Isaac, 43, 106
James, 51
Jane, 113
John, 54
John H., 117
Martha, 113
Mary, 43
Wood, Olive Brower, 121
Thomas, 51, 54, 56
William, 56
Wooden, Homer, 113
Woodin, Etta, 119
Woolvin, Godfrey, 65
Samuel, 65
Woolly, Sarah, 105
Wooster, Annie J., 118
Clara, 93, 95, 117
Emma L., 92, 117
Worden, David B., 114
Eliza, 89
Paulina, 111
Wortman, Denis, 119
Robert, 116
Wright, Daniel, 65
Edith Warren, 92
Isaac, 104
Martha May, 92
Ruth Ann, 113
Sarah, 65
Solomon, 115
Webster, 92
Wm. G., 94
Wulven, Godfrey, 46
William, 46
Wyckhoff, Peter, 70
Syntie Maria, 70
Wyckoff, Ares, 52
Cynthia Ann, 110
Wyckoff, Hannah, 108
Helen M., 87
Hellen M., 88
Henry, 52
Peter, 49
Phoebe, 109
Wilhelmus, 49
Wykhof, Geertje, 8
Wynkoop, Abraham, 110

Index

Y

Yancie, Martha A., 120
Yates, Alletta A., 91
  Ann, 109
  Anna, 62
  Esther, 53
  Geertruy, 50
  James, 53, 59, 63, 67
  John, 49, 50, 53, 56, 58, 62, 63, 65, 107
  John Henry, 113
  Margaret, 56, 59
  Mary, 53, 56, 59, 62, 65, 69, 70, 74, 109
  Polly, 58, 67
  Rachel, 59
  Samuel, 110
  Sarah E., 113
  Simeon, 50
  William, 49, 53, 112
Yelverton, Mary, 113
Yonni, Mary, 82, 110
Young, Jacob, 107
  James, 113
  Levina, 104
Younker, Rosa, 115
Yurcks, Cathrine, 107

Z

Zwaart, Jacob, 103
Zwartwoud, (*See also Swartwoud*)
  Abraham, 43
  Adolf, 16, 22
  Annatje, 23
  Bernardus, 16, 18, 24, 25, 28, 37
  Bernardus, Junr., 31
  Betje, 7
  Catharina, 7, 9, 11, 13
  Cathrina, 14, 16, 22, 24, 25
  Catrina, 10
  Cornelis, 7, 31, 38, 43
  Elizabeth, 7
  Geertruy, 24, 25
  Gerhardus, 24, 25
  Jacobus, 12, 15
  Johannes, 7, 18
  Meyndert, 38
  Robert, 28
  Rudolf, 11
  Rudolphus, 12
  Sarah, 39
  Tiatje, 14, 22

www.ingramcontent.com/pod-product-compliance
Lightning Source LLC
Chambersburg PA
CBHW050333230426
43663CB00010B/1838